D0593994

THE

ANTI-FEDERALISTS

THE

ANTI-FEDERALISTS:
SELECTED WRITINGS AND SPEECHES

SELECTED AND EDITED, WITH AN INTRODUCTION
AND HEADNOTES, BY

BRUCE FROHNEN

WITH A FOREWORD BY JOSEPH SOBRAN

Since 1947
REGNERY
PUBLISHING, INC.
An Eagle Publishing Company • Washington, DC

Library of Congress Cataloging-in-Publication Data

Published in the United States by
Regnery Publishing, Inc.
An Eagle Publishing Company
One Massachusetts Avenue, NW
Washington, DC 20001

Distributed to the trade by
National Book Network
4720-A Boston Way
Lanham, MD 20706

Printed on acid-free paper.
Manufactured in the United States of America

10 9 8 7 6 5 4 3 2

Books are available in quantity for promotional or premium use. Write to Director of Special Sales, Regnery Publishing, Inc., One Massachusetts Avenue, NW, Washington, DC 20001, for information on discounts and terms or call (202) 216-0600.

CONTENTS

FOREWORD

The debate over the ratification of the Constitution ranks high among the political controversies of recorded history. It is almost unimaginable that such a debate—so serious, literate, and philosophical—should occur in the United States at the end of the twentieth century. But it could and did happen in 1787.

Most Americans today only dimly remember hearing of that debate. If they know anything about it, they know only the side presented by "Publius"—the collective pen name of Alexander Hamilton, James Madison, and John Jay—in *The Federalist*. Only a few specialists are familiar with the Anti-Federalist arguments of Cato, Brutus, Centinel, the Federal Farmer, Patrick Henry, John De Witt, and others. As usually happens, the losing side has been assumed to be wrong and has fallen into neglect. To most moderns, there seems to have been nothing to debate. The ratification of the Constitution is presented to them as an unambiguous triumph of Progress over Reaction.

This is a pity, because the issues in the ratification debate are of permanent interest, and it is by no means obvious that the right side won. If the debaters could return today, Publius might ruefully admit that the apprehensions of Cato et al. have proved only too well founded.

What were those apprehensions? They are framed in a language of politics that has grown unfamiliar to us; we no longer understand our own political ancestors. They spoke constantly of such dangers as "usurpations" of power, "invasions" of the people's rights, and "consolidated" government. We need to understand exactly what they meant by such now-unfamiliar words.

In principle, both sides agreed that these things were evils. But Publius and other Federalists argued that the Constitution, in its exquisite design, would prevent their occurrence. The powers of the national government would be "few and defined," while those remaining with the states would be "numerous and indefinite." Thus Madison, in *The Federalist* No. 45. Besides, the people would always be vigilant against usurpations of any powers not "granted" or "delegated" to the national government in the Constitution itself. Hamilton, the most ardent champion of a stronger central government, even argued (in No. 28) that state militias would be able to control such usurpations; in other words, he envisioned civil war as a remedy for abuses of power! Such rebellion against the "general" government would merely be an exercise of "that original right of self-defense, which is paramount to all positive forms of government"—a right Americans had recently invoked against English rule. (This view of the militias underlies the widely misunderstood Second Amendment, which was designed to prevent the national government from obtaining a monopoly of weaponry. Today, of course, it is absurd to imagine the state militias opposing the military might of the national government.)

Hamilton also contended that a Bill of Rights was unnecessary, since the national government would have only those "few and defined" powers delegated to it. The principle of the Constitution was that *any power not authorized was forbidden.* To claim or exercise an unauthorized power was what all sides understood as usurpation. This being so, Hamilton argued (No. 84), a Bill of Rights would be not only superfluous, but confusing, by implying an opposite presumption: namely, that the national government could do anything it was not expressly forbidden to do. Here, at least, he had a point: today it is generally assumed that the "federal government" (itself a misnomer for what has become a central government of boundless power) violates the Constitution only when it transgresses against a few specific "preferred freedoms"—of speech, press, and so forth—expressly mentioned in the Bill of Rights.

But the Bill of Rights is not merely a list of particulars. The Ninth and Tenth Amendments, framed to meet Anti-Federalist objections, tell us how to construe to whole Constitution. The Ninth says: "The enumeration in the Constitution of certain rights shall not be construed to deny or disparage others retained by the people." The Tenth says: "The powers not delegated to the United States [i.e., the national government] by the Constitution, nor prohibited by it to the states, are reserved to the states respectively, or to the people."

Taken together, these clauses mean that the Constitution is not meant as a complete list of the people's rights, but does afford a complete list of the national government's powers. This reflects the consensus of Americans in 1787 (remembering 1776) that rights are given by our Creator, while the powers of government are given—"delegated"—by the consent of the people. An exhaustive list of rights is impracticable; but an exhaustive list of the government's powers, as "we the people" chose to endow them, is precisely what the Constitution was represented to be.

The question, of course, was whether the national government could actually be confined to its enumerated powers. And here is where the Anti-Federalists, often ridiculed by their opponents, have been vindicated by history. For the national government has far surpassed the darkest predictions of the Constitution's most pessimistic opponents. Today we live under a form of government that both sides in the ratification debate would have immediately recognized, and condemned, as "consolidated"—that is, totally centralized, with virtually absolute sovereignty.

Today the national government itself arbitrarily decides what the Constitution means. It claims a monopoly of interpreting the very document that was intended to restrain it. As Jefferson warned in the Kentucky Resolutions of 1798, it has become the sole and final judge of the extent of its own powers. And it has used this prerogative to enlarge those powers to monstrous dimensions.

Like many great changes, this one is almost too large to be noticed. Few Americans discern that the "federal" government long ago ceased to be truly federal. We have become accustomed to its usurpations of countless powers never delegated to it. The U.S. Supreme Court almost never finds Congress's usurpations unconstitutional. Instead, the Court habitually declares "unconstitutional" *those very powers that were to be reserved to the states and the people.* Thus we are suddenly informed that the states have been violating the Constitution throughout their existence by maintaining unequal legislative districts (though in essence, the U.S. Senate does the same thing) or by restricting abortion. And the state legislatures have no means of defense or redress against the federal courts. So much for our fabled "checks and balances."

The federal judiciary, in other words, has become an agent of centralization, denying the right of self-government to the states. In this the national government has abandoned the philosophy of the generation that ratified the Constitution, and has adopted the predominant vices of twentieth-century politics, in which consolidated government—whether labelled Fascist, Communist, "liberal," or "democratic"—is regarded as a positive good. Few people fully grasp the profundity of this revolution, which has alienated us from our own forebears; fewer still are outraged by it. Even to mention the Ninth and Tenth Amendments is to invite puzzled stares. These clauses have proved sadly ineffectual in preventing the lawless acquisition of power.

Publius might reply that the tyranny of the national government stems from the abuse of the Constitution, especially by ill-advised amendments conferring vast new powers (such as income taxation) on that government. Without a doubt, the plain meaning of the Constitution has been ignored and distorted. But after all, Publius assured his readers that such abuses would be virtually impossible, because of the design of the Constitution itself, whose careful distribution of powers would prevent any level or branch of government from achieving a monopoly of power. The simple fact is that the Constitution has failed in its proclaimed purpose. The states and the people, rendered defenseless, now retain only such rights and powers as the national government chooses to allow them.

Publius could not fairly answer that all this was unforeseeable. The authors collected in this volume bear witness that it was foreseen—in principle, if not in extent. Only a madman could have imagined how far, under the Constitution, the national government would eventually go. (Who ever dreamed that it would one day regulate smoking?) But many sane men understood that it might go much further than the Federalists admitted.

Hamilton himself was one of those who immediately set to work expanding the national government's power beyond the narrow limits specified in the text of the Constitution; in arguing for the creation of a national bank, he appealed to the "necessary and proper" clause whose vague latitude had alarmed the Anti-Federalists. Yet even Hamilton would surely be shocked at how far such loose construction has been taken in our time, in, for instance, the use of the "interstate commerce clause" to nullify the basic structure of the Constitution.

The Anti-Federalists have never enjoyed the prestige of the Federalists who prevailed. But their prescient forebodings still deserve a hearing from anyone who understands that history often makes wrong turns, and that history's "losers" may still have much to tell us. It is not too late for us to learn from them.

JOSEPH SOBRAN

INTRODUCTION

Many of the writings and speeches in this volume are of the first rank in terms of rhetorical skill, analytical depth, and insight into abiding issues of American politics. But few Americans have read them. *The Federalist,* a collection of essays written to encourage ratification of the Constitution, has been consistently available in print since the early days of the republic. Essays written by "Anti-Federalists," however, have been available sporadically at best until well into this century.

This situation is understandable for the simple reason that the Anti-Federalists did not produce under a single title and pen name a collection equal in quality and depth to *The Federalist,* an unquestioned classic of political science. While many of the writings included here, for example all the essays written under the pen names of Brutus and Impartial Examiner, are of abiding significance, others, such as those of Cato and Centinel, are of more uneven quality, containing first-rate essays alongside writings important only as commentary on events of the time. Moreover, posterity is rarely as kind to the losers as to the winners of important conflicts. The Anti-Federalists "lost" the battle over ratification, and having failed to prevent adoption of the Constitution, they suffered predictable consequences. Their arguments against a strengthened central government were labeled wrong, and the assumptions regarding human nature and ordered liberty at the root of these arguments were dismissed as irrelevant.

To make matters worse, the fact that the Federalists won ratification of the Constitution soon gave way to the mistaken view that there had been no serious battle over ratification to begin with. Thus, not only Anti-Federalist arguments, but also many of the Federalist positions, along with the very nature of the Articles of Confederation under which Americans lived until the Constitution's adoption, have been shrouded in obscurity. For its own sake and for the light it throws on issues of agreement and disagreement during the founding era, an understanding of Anti-Federalist thought is, therefore, important.

Since the 1960s scholars have shown increased interest in Anti-Federalist thought principally out of a desire to find an underground political vision opposed to the individualism and commercialism they find so dominant and abhorrent in contemporary society. This anachronistic project rests on the assumption that Federalists and Anti-Federalists held fundamentally differing views, with Federalists espousing a commercial republic dominated by aristocratic elites and Anti-Federalists defending an agrarian democracy of strong communities in which individual rights were freely subordinated to the popularly determined, political common good. Unfortunately, this interpretation misconstrues the thought of nearly everyone involved in the American founding era and turns the Anti-Federalists into an exotic species of plant that flowered only briefly and fitfully in the unfriendly American soil.

On the contrary, Anti-Federalist thought was distinctly American. It addressed the common—and persistent—American concern to protect local life from the corrupting influence of centralized governments and political appointees who would enforce their wills on local communities. Anti-Federalists were relatively successful, winning significant concessions from Federalists, most importantly a Bill of Rights aimed at protecting state and individual prerogatives and limiting the scope and power of the federal government. But Anti-Federalists won these concessions only by articulating American conceptions of what men need to lead good lives in common.

Anti-Federalists and Federalists valued a way of life lived and idealized for centuries in Britain, the mother country, and in

America. Anti-Federalists opposed adoption of the Constitution, but they did not oppose it out of a desire to establish or protect some strange communal utopia. Rather, they believed the Constitution would undermine and eventually destroy the concrete institutions, beliefs, and practices they, and the Federalists, held as a sacred inheritance. As we face the consequences of the twentieth century's fascination with centralized bureaucratic programs, it would perhaps serve us well to re-examine the thought of those who first warned against granting excessive power to the American national government.

In this introduction I begin by outlining the way of life valued by both Anti-Federalists and Federalists. This fundamentally local existence has often been characterized as agrarian and democratic. It was both. But American agrarianism, *pace* most interpreters of the founding period, arose less from any principled objection to commerce than from an insistence on localism and a refusal to value wealth and power over freedom and virtue. Similarly, American democratism arose less from any ideological commitment to direct popular rule than from an insistence on equality before the law and a distrust of political elites. The local life valued by all Americans was, in other words, principally characterized by its commitment to well ordered liberty, a liberty shaped and constrained by law and custom and religion-based virtue or good character.

Next I outline the terms of the debate over how best to protect Americans' commonly valued way of life. This outline requires, first, a discussion of the disorders afflicting the United States in 1787 as they were differently characterized by Anti-Federalists and Federalists. Second, it requires discussion of the central question at issue in the ratification debates: to what extent was greater centralization of political power necessary to address America's disorders? Anti-Federalists recognized the problems presented by trade barriers between states, massive public debt, inflation, and tax revolts like the infamous Shays' Rebellion, which almost brought about the overthrow of the government in Massachusetts. But Anti-Federalists rejected

Federalist assertions that these problems demanded a central government invested with the power to act directly on the people—for example, taxing them individually rather than through requisitions on the states. Anti-Federalists feared that such a central government would destroy the states' ability to protect the rights and interests of communities and individuals. These loyal, Anti-Federal citizens raised centuries-old issues involving sovereignty and representation in arguing for more modest reforms to the Articles of Confederation.

Finally, I will address the specific concessions won by the Anti-Federalists. The Bill of Rights is seen today as a manifesto of radical individualism. But it was made a part of the Constitution, less to defend the abstract rights of community-less individuals from all possible constraints than to protect traditional, common law rights and, as important, the historical prerogatives of the states from federal interference.

In the end, the ratification debates were an argument among men who were dedicated to a common heritage, and who were as often close friends as political rivals. The compound republic that resulted from their conflict was a creature of compromise and accommodation; their government was an attempt to harmonize local autonomy with national sovereignty. The cataclysmic Civil War may have brought this compromise to an end. That fate may even have been inevitable given the fragility of human nature and public order. But the decades of well-ordered liberty Anti-Federalists helped secure make their thought worthy of consideration, particularly in an era of ever-increasing centralization and ever-shrinking freedom.

COMMON ASSUMPTIONS

Anti-Federalists emphasized concerns that had been common to Americans since the founding of the colonies and had been at issue in the War for Independence. American colonists had participated in a small way in the Glorious Revolution of 1688, in which an English king had lost his throne for seeking to undermine traditional principles and institutions in England, and Americans had declared independence because they believed the British government irretrievably hostile to their inherited British principles and institutions.

Both the American and the Glorious revolutions were seen by their respective protagonists as returns (or revolvings back) to a way of life that God had intended for man and that tradition had confirmed and protected for centuries. That way of life, begun in Britain and brought to America, was lived principally in local communities dominated by family, church, and various local associations. To the extent it was a part of daily life, politics was largely local—played out at the town meeting, in the neighborhood assembly, and on the jury. Because members of a local communities shared the same basic interests and characters, and because men of substance generally had the right to speak for their interests and combine with their fellows to protect them, local governments were not greatly feared.

In addition, this life was, in American eyes, fundamentally free. The average man was not oppressed by a local lord demanding allegiance and personal labor. This average citizen was not liable to be visited at any moment by a tax collector with the power to bankrupt him. He could not be pressed into service in the armed forces or on the road crew. He seldom saw any government official save his local, elected leaders. Perhaps most important, he owned his own land or could look forward to owning it after a few years of service. Communities as a matter of course enforced public standards of morality, but he could simply pick up and leave, if those standards became too onerous or, as likely, if he found that the particular religious denomination dominant in his community did not live up to his own principles.

Americans had significant independence and freedom: but were members of communities that had purpose. Even when this purpose, as on the frontier, was little more than mere survival, a distinctly religious character pervaded the community.

True, there was no specific national theology in America beyond a vague and inclusive Protestant Christianity. Nevertheless, American communities demanded particular modes of behavior and even dress, in accordance with their common religious vision. In fact, towns habitually taxed residents to support the locally dominant church and expected citizens to abide by particular, religiously-based moral rules in their public and private lives.

Early American communities, therefore, can usefully be characterized as democracies of custom. The people (meaning all men of independent means) ruled themselves concerning virtually every aspect of their daily lives—without resorting to the machinery of politics. In the days before bureaucrats invested with executive and legislative powers had been charged with managing the people's lives, most men came in contact with government only in time of war or through some legal dispute. And when they did have dealings with the government, prescriptive rules guided the encounter.

For example, the centuries-long tradition of common law rights and responsibilities had been developed in Britain and had been imported in vigorous form by the American colonists. The common law was the essence of Anglo-American freedom, because it protected individuals from rulers who might seek to hold and even punish them without trial, who might seek forced confessions, or who might resort to show trials in which hand-picked judges provided the desired verdict.

The common law dictated adherence to set, customary procedures, one of the most prominent being trials in the hands of juries of "the vicinage" or immediate surrounding area. Americans considered these juries vital to free government, because only those who knew the characters and circumstances involved in a particular case could decide that case fairly and in a way upholding public virtue and order. Far from seeking jurors who knew nothing of the parties involved in a lawsuit or criminal trial, Americans sought only jurors who knew the background and habits of those being judged. Only men with such knowledge could render a proper verdict. The vast majority of cases involving ordinary people were decided by local citizens, who saw it as their duty and their interest to uphold customary law and, in the light of given circumstances, apply it equally to all. Of course citizen jurors did not make all decisions regarding guilt and innocence. Some cases were appealed to a higher, judge-only court. And even at the trial level there was great respect for the instructions given by judges. But judges themselves were constrained by common law and an abiding respect for custom and tradition.

Neither judges nor juries in early America sought to make law. They sought to apply fairly the moral norms embodied in existing law and custom. Moreover, even in using these customary legal rules, juries did not seek to "do justice" without reference to other, higher authorities. In addition to statutes, precedents, and the possibility of appeals, juries were constrained by the long held custom of deference to religious authority. While "the voice of the people is the voice of God" was a common political statement during this era, the people were not deemed, on their own, capable of constructing a moral life. Law and custom rested on religious foundations. After all, were not the Ten Commandments, handed down from God, the basis of all proper human laws? In addition, the common law had been heavily influenced by religious canon law. Finally, individuals and communities were deeply influenced by religion and religious leaders.

Indeed, the integral role of religion in public life during the founding period is too often overlooked. Even elections were held to religious standards; election day sermons reminded the people that only virtuous rulers could obey the will of God and thereby keep the community virtuous, safe, and free. Political leaders were duty-bound to uphold God's law, in part by holding the people to their obligations and to standards of active virtue. Fulfilling one's duties to God, providing for one's family, giving aid to one's neighbors, dealing fairly with others in business, and doing one's public duty in the militia or other community institution—all these acts made one a good man. And only communities in which the majority of citizens were good men could be free, because only in such communities could public order and private needs be seen to without resort to tyrannical laws and administrators.

Tyranny, to the American mind, generally came well armed. Americans carried on the centuries-old English hostility toward government-paid, standing armies. Standing armies were in fact a relatively new invention—or a re-invention of an institution from the ancient world; and the English people had maintained their freedoms against royal usurpations largely because they had kept their kings from building powerful permanent armies. At the end of the seventeenth century, a time when the French king could command well over 100,000 armed men, the English drove James II from his throne in part because he employed some 40,000 soldiers.

The American alternative to the standing army was the militia. In the militia, an institution most strongly championed by Anti-Federalists, men learned habits of independence and good order as they learned to love yet more the country that now trusted them to bear arms in its defense. Militia were a bulwark against tyranny because they were made up of free, independent, armed men deeply attached to their local communities and their home units. Militia also rendered unnecessary the corrupt government-paid troops needed to enforce order in less virtuous countries.

On its own, however, not even the militia could keep rulers in line. Anti-Federalists and Federalists agreed on one fundamental aspect of human nature: self-love. They recognized a tendency in all men to put their respective private interests above those of others and above the common good. How to combat this proclivity was an important question for both Anti-Federalists and Federalists.

Anti-Federalists argued that rulers must stand for frequent elections, rotate in and out of office, and remain geographically close to the people. Otherwise, rulers would lose touch with the people, cease identifying their own interests with those of their constituents, and begin subverting freedom and the common good for their private ends. The Constitution's separation of powers, the Anti-Federalists argued, were not sufficiently complete to prevent rulers from forming among themselves alliances opposed to the public good. The Constitution's checking and balancing of one ruler's self-interest against the others was mere wishful thinking. As Patrick Henry, perhaps the most famous Anti-Federalist, pointed out at length during his 9 June 1788 address to the Virginia ratifying convention, checks on power could be of no avail unless they accounted for self-love. Checks merely written into the Constitution would be useless, because only virtuous political officers would abide by them.

Both Anti-Federalists and Federalists constructed political theories on the recognition that virtue was necessary but limited, and limited by geography in particular. But Federalists insisted that the people would retain sufficient virtue to pick representatives with character good enough that the Constitution's checks and balances would keep these representatives honest and public-interested. Anti-Federalists discounted the Constitution's methods for maintaining virtue in public officers. But the Anti-Federalists believed in the virtue of the people themselves. Provided they continued to be raised in local communities in which self-rule and mutual accommodation taught them proper habits, Americans would retain the character needed for well-ordered liberty. Unfortunately, they argued, the new Constitution would destroy these necessary communities by crowding out their role in the people's daily lives, subverting juries, and taking for the national government the tax monies needed for even modest local government.

UNCOMMON TROUBLES

Anti-Federalists and Federalists had a common vision of the good life. Where they differed was in their respective views concerning the Constitution's capacity to undermine that life or to

preserve it in the face of present and future troubles. This disagreement was in some ways technical. Both sides engaged in
long, detailed discussions of particular aspects of constitution-
making, from the proper length of congressional terms to the
probable effects of federal bankruptcy laws.

However, the issues at stake in the ratification debates were
important. True, Anti-Federalists and Federalists were not
deadly enemies engaged in warfare over the nature of God, man
and society; true, they were neighbors arguing over changes proposed to the form of what was, and would remain, a republican
government of mixed and limited powers that left significant
authority to states and localities. Nonetheless, the argument cen-
tered around the fundamental question of whether it is possible to
maintain both local liberty and a strong central government, and
in that kind of debate, technical details and practical facts matter.

The debate gained urgency because times were hard. Personal bankruptcies were common, public debts were enormous,
and rebellion had broken out in Massachusetts over high taxes.
What is more, a number of state governments were floating
schemes to pay off their debts with devalued currency, and
states were becoming increasingly hostile to one another as
interstate tariffs increased and legal commerce fell off.

But Anti-Federalists saw no cause for alarm. They tended to
characterize the troubles as a natural, passing consequence of the
long war with Britain. A favorite passage from the Bible was
that section from First Kings in which it is noted that "Judah
and Israel dwelt safely, every man under his vine and under his
fig tree." Popular in American public discourse since before the
War for Independence, this passage had long evoked visions of
pastoral simplicity and happiness. Anti-Federalists like Patrick
Henry used it to assert that times were not as bad as the Federalists claimed. Indeed, Anti-Federalists sensed conspiracy in
Federalist calls for quick action. Why such haste, if not to dupe
the people into signing away their liberties?

Because they viewed America's social and economic condition
as manageable and likely to improve over time, Anti-Federalists

did not share the Federalists' conviction that only a significantly strengthened federal government could take the actions needed to protect currency, contracts, and property from unruly mobs and state legislatures. Anti-Federalists rarely agreed that it was necessary or wise to allow the federal government to act directly on the people by, for example, passing laws and setting up courts to enforce those laws. Such a federal government would be a sovereign state rather than a mere creature of an agreement among sovereign states. So Anti-Federalists proposed only minor changes to the Articles of Confederation. For example, many Anti-Federalists proposed granting Congress an additional modicum of power to enforce its monetary requisitions on the states but opposed granting the power to tax individuals. The Anti-Federalists were willing to increase the powers of the central government. But they were not willing to create a new sovereign they believed would dominate and eventually destroy the states.

SOVEREIGNTY

It is not wrong to view the Anti-Federalists as conservative in the sense that they objected to the Constitution as too radically changing customary political forms and as thus endangering Americans' traditional way of life. Several Anti-Federalists accused Federalists and their supporters of failing to show proper respect for traditions going back through the War for Independence to the British Glorious Revolution of 1688.

The Anglo-American "revolutionary" tradition was based in significant measure on suspicion of centralized political power. In London or any American capital, central governments were viewed as dangerous. Individuals could not protect their interests in central governments. Representation might help, but representatives might seek to promote one community or interest at the expense of others. The Glorious Revolution was produced by fear of James II's army, his attempts to rule without

Parliamentary check, and his desire to destroy local charters granting significant autonomy to counties and municipalities. James and his defenders had argued that the king's powers were not subject to limitations from Parliament or local charters, because he was a sovereign. There could be only one seat of power, and that power could not be limited by other institutions. During the 1760s and 1770s, the British found themselves in the awkward position of echoing James II in arguing that there could be only one sovereign, Parliament, which could do as it willed with and in America. Such assertions made clear to Americans that their 150–year-old traditions of local autonomy were in peril. War and independence were the results.

In opposing adoption of the Constitution, many Anti-Federalists returned to arguments used during the debate over independence. For example, they repeated the distinction between internal and external taxation at issue during the Stamp Act crisis. American colonists had conceded Britain's right to regulate America's trade with other nations, but they would not concede to Britain the right to tax the colonists by imposing and collecting duties on goods sold within the American colonies.

According to the colonists, external taxation concerned matters of empire, of the relations between America and the mother country or between the empire as a whole and foreign nations. Matters of empire were within the province of British government. But to tax American colonists directly was to act as their sovereign in internal affairs—as their direct, proper government. Because the colonists were not and could not be represented properly in far off Britain, they could not possibly consent to such taxes. And because they could not consent to the taxes, the taxes could not be just.

Anti-Federalists believed conditions in their new republic closely paralleled those of the British empire. The central government had the right to see to issues relating to the states only in those areas where the states had to act as one—principally in dealing with foreign powers. For the central government to tax Americans directly, let alone legislate for them and enforce laws through its own courts, would be to endanger the autonomy and freedom of states, communities, and individuals. Such power would lift the central government to the status of a sovereign, which could oppress some for the benefit of others.

Federalists claimed, however, that the Constitution did not set up a wholly centralized government. By delegating only limited powers to the center, the Constitution, they asserted, provided for a compound sovereignty; it ceded limited authority to the federal government, leaving the bulk of political power with the states. Moreover, they argued, by separating powers among the legislative, executive, and judicial branches, the Constitution had provided barriers to rulers sufficient to force them to stay within the bounds of their authority. It was toward refuting these claims that most of the Anti-Federalist arguments were directed.

Anti-Federalists pointed out the dangers many Constitutional provisions posed to state rights and prerogatives. For example, the Constitution granted the federal government the power to tax the people directly. Anti-Federalists, as we have heard, argued in response that the central government would use this power to oppress the people, taxing them so heavily that, first, the people's freedom would disappear and, second, the states and localities would have nothing left to tax. This latter effect would leave states and localities dependent on grants from the center for survival. The Anti-Federalists also argued that the Constitution granted the federal government power to pass laws and to enforce these laws through its own system of courts. Judges in the employ of the central government would work to extend their own jurisdiction, finding ever more issues within the purview of federal law or the federal Constitution. In this way the federal courts would crowd state courts from the field of law, rendering the people dependent on the central government rather than their states for the adjudication of disputes and the keeping of public order.

Moreover, a number of other powers granted to the federal government were causes of concern to Anti-Federalists. Perhaps most important among them was the central government's new power to fund its own armed forces. To the Anti-Federalists this constituted establishment of a standing army, with all the dangers to liberty implied thereby. In addition, the Constitution allowed the central government to control the state militia. That, in the Anti-Federalist view, turned the militia into a mere creature of the central government—a kind of standing army in waiting—and thus no longer capable of checking federal power.

But the most common targets of Anti-Federalist invective were the Constitution's Necessary and Proper and Supremacy Clauses. The first of these clauses allowed the federal Congress to make all laws necessary and proper to carry into execution the powers granted to the United States by the Constitution. Anti-Federalists argued that this made federal officers judges in their own cases. Who was to say, for example, what laws would be "necessary and proper" to see to the common defense? Unimpressed by Federalists' claims that the Constitution delegated only certain, specified powers to the central government, the Anti-Federalists argued that the Necessary and Proper Clause in effect granted unlimited power to those who wished to use it, including the power to usurp the proper role of the states as the primary source of law.

Similarly, the Supremacy Clause, in placing the laws of the United States above the laws of the states, eliminated the states' ability to defend their own interests and the interests of their citizens. According to Anti-Federalists, the Supremacy Clause in effect banned the states from interfering with any law or judgment made by the federal government. Again, this fact made the central government judge in its own case. States could not counteract an order of the central government; thus federal officers were placed above the power of any state to hold them accountable for their actions.

Anti-Federalists argued that these aspects of the Constitution rendered nugatory its attempts to hold federal powers within limits. No outside force or authority save God Himself could limit the central government's exercise of power. That being the case, internal limits on power such as the separation of powers could be of no avail. It would be in the self-interest of every officer of the central government to expand the powers of his office at the expense of the states. While there might be competition among federal branches over power, all would agree that state powers could be usurped with impunity. The only check remaining would be the displeasure of the people. And that displeasure, in Anti-Federalist eyes, could not be turned into effective action in a nation as large as the United States.

REPRESENTATION

It has often been remarked that Federalists viewed representation as a kind of filter that would sort out those with the greatest virtue and wisdom for public service. Anti-Federalists, on the other hand, saw representation as a kind of mirror reflecting as closely as possible the experience and interests of the people as a whole. This distinction is largely accurate. Anti-Federalists' fear of political elites and aristocracies of any kind (including aristocracies of talent) led them to reject the Federalist model, in which the people, incapable of ruling themselves, were deemed capable of choosing rulers who in turn would serve the people well.

Anti-Federalists argued that representation in Congress could not possibly be adequate to fulfill its proper mission, which was to keep elected officials responsible to their constituents. Because even the popular branch of the legislature was small (members of the Senate were to be appointed by state legislatures through the next century), Congress could not represent all the varied interests existing in the United States. Some men—whether fishermen, farmers of a particular kind, or some other group—effectively would not be represented. These men might vote, but they would have no chance, given the mathematics of the situation, actually to elect someone who would protect their interests.

Moreover, Anti-Federalists argued, a nation the size of the United States could not possibly be well served by a single legislature. This legislature would necessarily be geographically closer to some parts of the country than others, and national Congressmen could not possibly know the circumstances of all the people. Ignorance and favoritism fostered by the new, remote national government would replace common interests and fairness engendered by the old, familiar state governments.

Anti-Federalists demanded representatives who would act as much as possible according to the wishes of their constituents. Indeed, some of the more radical among Anti-Federalists criticized representation itself as a poor substitute for direct voting in the localities on all issues of major importance. Many Anti-Federalists were not merely afraid of federal power breaking the bonds of the Constitution and oppressing the people; they also were afraid that the federal government would prevent democratic majorities in the states and localities from putting their political will into action.

Even at a time when state legislatures were failing to enforce contracts, interfering with commerce for their own ends, and engaging in schemes to pay public debts with devalued currency, Anti-Federalists were jealous of the sovereign, that is unchecked, rights of states. Was not the Constitution written in large part to take from states the ability to levy tariffs on goods from other states, to interfere with contractual rights, and to float their currencies? Each of these restrictions violated the right of the people to use government to accomplish the ends the people had chosen, whatever those ends might be.

One must remember that government, in the view of most Anti-Federalists, was essentially a tool for putting the public's will into action. As we have seen, they demanded homogeneous communities, joined by common backgrounds, beliefs and circumstances, so that political action would be less necessary to maintain public order. But they also demanded this homogeneity so that public action would be more effective—that political officers might be kept responsive to clear expressions of public opinion. If the public were too divided, they reasoned, no clear direction could be established and the state would founder in indecision.

Some Anti-Federalists, such as "A [Maryland] Farmer," even objected to organized religion, because it motivated men to actions not necessarily in the community's political interest. A number of Anti-Federalist writings evidence the prejudice that the will of the people—provided "the people" be defined as a local group—could not be wrong. That such a view contradicts Americans' traditional attachment to limited government and common law rights seems not to have occurred to the most radical among them. But this radical interpretation of the requirements for rule by consent was uncommon or, at any rate, muted even among Anti-Federalists. Indeed, readers should take note of the strong Anti-Federalist concern to protect inherited, common law rights. Anti-Federalists' greatest victory in the ratification debates in this regard came when their Federalist opponents agreed to attach a Bill of Rights, which protected such rights, to the new Constitution as soon as the first Congress convened.

THE BILL OF RIGHTS

Given the extent of administrative centralization achieved by the federal government during the twentieth century, one is tempted to argue that the Anti-Federalists were right to oppose ratification of the Constitution. One also is tempted to conclude that Americans, when they agreed to go beyond a confederation to a compound republic, in effect fooled themselves in thinking there could be more than one sovereign for any length of time. One way or another, one sovereign or the other will win the contest and reduce its rival to its own mere tool. The Anti-Federalists were right to point out this danger.

That conclusion, however, is unwarranted by the facts. A significant number of Anti-Federalists (including a number, such as Richard Henry Lee, whose work is included in this volume) became supporters of the Constitution once assured that a Bill of Rights would be added to it. These men concluded that explicit statements of the rights and prerogatives properly beyond the cognizance of the federal government, accompanied by an explicit statement that powers not delegated to that federal government were reserved to the states or to the people, would be sufficient to render the new union safe for states, localities, and people.

It was assumed that states already respected important rights to the extent and in the manner most appropriate to their circumstances, and if more protection was wanted, the people of the state could provide it at will. But the federal government could be trusted to respect the rights of neither individuals nor states and thus required a Bill of Rights to keep it within its bounds. The states were organic units and so could be trusted to deal properly with the people of whom they were constituted, but the federal government was an artificial construct, so those put in charge of it must be constrained from using it to cause harm to the people.

Regrettably, Americans, or at any rate American lawyers and judges, have come to view the Bill of Rights as a charter of absolute individualist freedoms, creating around every American an inviolable wall of constitutional protection against anyone or anything, including state and local as well as federal officials who would seem to violate the sanctity of individual autonomy. It is important to note, however, that the first ten amendments passed in the first Congress, all of which had been demanded by the Anti-Federalists, were intended to protect both individuals and states against *federal* intrusions.

The First Amendment, for example, stated, among other things, that "Congress shall make no law respecting an establishment of religion" or infringing on religious free-exercise. The clear intent of this provision was to keep the federal government from interfering with state laws regarding religions and their establishment. The worry was not that the states would use public authority and tax dollars to favor one religion over others; many did exactly that and the practice was considered fine and proper. The worry was that the federal government would set up a national church interfering with churches favored in particular states or localities and/or interfering with religious free-exercise in one or more states.

The Second Amendment also was aimed primarily at protecting state and local institutions from federal interference. This amendment, protecting the right of citizens to keep and bear arms, sought to protect state and local militia from being outlawed or undermined by any central government bent on replacing militia with a standing army. In effect, this amendment sought to prevent the federal government from eliminating an institution that served to check federal power.

The Third Amendment forbade the quartering of troops in the people's houses in time of peace or unlawfully in time of war. This amendment was the consequence, in part at least, of memories of British attempts to frighten colonists into submission in the days leading up to the War for Independence. The amendment aimed to prevent the federal government from using a standing army to cow the people into obedience to tyranny.

The Fourth through Eighth amendments all protected specific common law procedures the Federalists had argued were not in danger under the new Constitution. Anti-Federalists insisted, however, on these explicit statements forbidding unreasonable searches and seizures, forced confessions, confiscation of property, and other violations of critically important common law rights. Particularly crucial to the Anti-Federalists was the right to trial by juries of the vicinage.

Unfortunately, judges over the last century or so have increasingly come to ignore the last two amendments of the Bill of Rights—the Ninth, which declared that failure to enumerate other rights may not be taken to mean that these rights were unimportant or not retained by the people; and the Tenth, which expressly reserved all powers not specifically granted to the federal government to the states and localities (thus making clear what many Federalists had claimed from the start: that the Necessary and Proper Clause must be construed very narrowly, allowing only those actions obviously necessary as a practical matter in carrying out delegated powers). Taken together, these two amendments constituted a clear statement that the federal government could properly exercise only those powers specifically granted to it by the Constitution.

All of these amendments aimed to constrain the central government, so that it would not use the additional powers granted to it by the Constitution to subvert the rights of individuals, communities, or states. The goal was not to construct a nation of radical individualists, answerable to no one. Rather, the goal was to protect state sovereignty and, through it, the local communities in which virtue and duty were prominent aspects of life, and in which ordered liberty was practiced on a daily basis.

The sovereign status of the states would be eroded over time, in particular by the federal courts. But in the republic's early years this sovereignty was defended with vigor. Early on, the federal Supreme Court declared that a citizen of one state could sue another state. The Court held that sovereign immunity could apply only to one, true sovereign—the federal government. The outcry was immediate and great. The Eleventh Amendment was quickly passed banning such suits against sovereign states. Georgia, the aggrieved state, passed a law making the bringing of any suit against it by a citizen of a different state a hanging offense. To this day, moreover, an individual may be prosecuted for the same acts by the state and the federal government. This is not deemed to be "double jeopardy" (a violation of common law rights), because, theoretically at least, the defendant is being charged by two different sovereigns. Thus the form, though not the substance, of co-sovereignty survives to this day.

CONCLUSION

Amid their cries of "conspiracy," Anti-Federalists made a number of important criticisms of the Constitution. And their efforts resulted in the addition of several protections of local liberties. In judging the wisdom of their views, one should not forget the Anti-Federalists' almost unquestioning confidence in local majorities; many refused to concede the moral and practical limits of the popular will. But the Anti-Federalists were right about one thing: republican government must rest, in the end, on the virtue of the people. Recognition of this fact, so rare today, was all but universal during the founding era. And, in the end, the Anti-Federalist protection of state rights failed for the same reason federalism itself failed: the loss of virtue among the people. Once the people wanted help from the government more than they feared harm from it, there was no stopping the accumulation of overwhelming power in the hands of the central administration. No parchment barriers, even in a Bill of Rights, could contain the desire for power and office, once the people demanded government do things for them rather than refrain from taking away their liberties.

It has often been argued that the Civil War destroyed the old Constitution. That war established that the federal government could and would force recalcitrant states and localities to obey its will. It also produced constitutional amendments enabling Congress to interfere on a regular basis with state affairs. One cannot reasonably argue that this horrible war did not bring in its aftermath significant administrative centralization. But one also should note that, before the war, the people already had begun looking to the federal government to make their lives easier and more prosperous—in the form of "internal improvements" like bridges, dams, and roads.

It may be the case that state and local liberty cannot be reconciled with a vigorous central government. The essays in this volume present strong arguments in favor of this conjecture. One thing seems clear, however: only a people committed more to virtue and freedom than to material benefits will enjoy any of them for long. On that question, too, essays in this volume present helpful commentary.

NOTE ON THE TEXT

Since its publication in 1981, Herbert J. Storing's, seven-volume *Complete Anti-Federalist* has served as the primary sourcebook for most research on its subject. Additional materials from this crucial era in American thought have appeared in works edited by Sandoz and by Hyneman and Lutz. But the Storing work has generally been viewed as definitive.[1] The three most commonly used abridgements of Anti-Federalist writings, for example, have taken their respective materials exclusively from Storing.[2]

The present work differs from other single-volume collections of Anti-Federalist writings in two significant aspects. First, this volume presents in their entirety the best of the Anti-Federalist

---

[1] Ellis Sandoz, ed., *Political Sermons of the American Founding Era* (Indianapolis, LibertyPress, 1991); Charles S. Hyneman and Donald S. Lutz, *American Political Writing during the Founding Era* (Indianapolis: LibertyPress, 1983). Bernard Bailyn's forecast multi-volume *Pamphlets of the American Revolution* appears to have expired after one volume (Cambridge, Mass: Harvard University Press, 1965). A multi-volume *Documentary History of the Ratification of the Constitution*, (State Historical Society of Wisconsin, 1976-97) is underway but, due to its idiosyncratic organization, of limited use.

[2] *The Complete Anti-Federalist: An Abridgement of the Seven Volume Set of the Complete Anti-Federalist*, ed. by Herbert J. Storing and abridged by Murray Dry (University of Chicago Press, 1985); *The Essential Anti-Federalist*, ed. by W.B. Allen and Gordon Lloyd (University Press of America, 1985), *The Anti-Federalist Papers and the Constitutional Convention Debates*, ed. by Ralph Ketcham (Mentor, 1986).

writings and speeches. The other single volumes contain many of the authors included here but only in excerpted form. The student of the period consulting those volumes cannot, therefore, follow the full arguments of these important critics of the Constitution. That fact, in our opinion, rendered those volumes of limited value. The student may resort, of course, to Storing's work, but, due to its size and expense, doing so is not convenient. These facts suggested to us the project that has resulted in this book.

Second, this volume is set from primary sources researched in public, university, and private libraries. The other single volumes used material from Storing and thus reproduced his deficiencies. True, this volume, too, has bracketed blank spaces, but far fewer than Storing's. In addition, and perhaps most significant (and exciting), this book presents important pieces that, since their original publication, have not been available or not easily obtained. Storing suggests, for example, that the last essay of A [Maryland] Farmer was never written. But the essay has been found and is here included. Important passages from Impartial Examiner Storing could not decipher are also published here. Finally, Storing did not include significant portions of Patrick Henry's most important speeches; these sections are here included. Improvements in copying technology, combined with the tireless efforts of series editor Christopher B. Briggs, have indeed made this volume unique in the literature of American political thought.

The newly discovered final installment of A [Maryland] Farmer is of particular interest. In this piece, the Farmer applies his criticisms of complex governments to the proposed federal contitution. Where before we had principally this author's theoretical objections to complex government, we now have his criticisms of specific sections of the proposed Constitution. These sections, he argues, tend to undermine responsible government.

In general, this volume leaves intact the grammar, punctuation, and spelling of the original sources published here. The purpose has been to provide the reader with the flavor of eighteenth-century American writing. However, in the interests of clarity, the editor has corrected obvious errors made by the original printers and standardized the use of quotations and quotation marks. Footnotes from the original material are denoted by asterisk, the editor's by number. In addition, square brackets containing either a space or the editor's best guess as to the missing words denote any material illegible in the original text. Material in square brackets in the original sources—for example, the reporter's interpolations in the speeches of Patrick Henry— have been enclosed in brackets ({ }).

NOTES PERTAINING TO SPECIFIC TEXTS ARE AS FOLLOWS:

CENTINEL:

All but Letter II first appeared in the Philadelphia *Independent Gazetteer*. Letter II first appeared in the Philadelphia *Freeman's Journal*. Errata printed in subsequent editions of the *Gazetteer* for Letters XI and XV have been incorporated into the letters.

FEDERAL FARMER:

These letters, originally published in the Poughkeepsie *Country Journal*, were subsequently published as pamphlets. The pamphlets were used in making this volume.

LETTER FROM RICHARD HENRY LEE:

The edition of the *Virginia Gazzette* in which this letter first appeared is unavailable. Text here is taken from the *New York Journal*, 22 and 24 December 1787.

Letters of Cato

The Letters of Cato appeared in the New-York Journal *between September 1787 and January 1788. The issue containing the first letter also contained the proposed text of the Constitution. Named after Marcus Porcius Cato, Roman statesman, orator, and defender of the Roman Republic, Cato's letters are generally thought to have been written by New York Governor George Clinton, a leading Anti-Federalist. Not among the most rhetorically powerful or best reasoned Anti-Federalist writings, these letters clearly present the Anti-Federalist conviction that ambition and greed would be neither tamed nor checked by the Constitution's political machinery. Only in the states, where the people knew and watched their representatives, could power be exercised and liberty retained.*

New-York Journal

---

27 SEPTEMBER 1787

LETTER I

Cato begins by reminding Americans that they have fought hard to found a free republic. They should not allow current problems to push them into rashly adopting a new form of government which might destroy their hard-won liberties. Essays in The Federalist *of particular relevance: 1, 2.*

To the CITIZENS *of the* STATE *of* NEW-YORK.

THE Convention, who sat at Philadelphia, have at last delivered to Congress that system of general government, which they have declared best calculated to promote your safety and happiness as citizens of the United States. This system, though not handed to you formally by the authority of government, has obtained an intro-duction through divers channels; and the minds of you all, to whose observation it has come, have no doubt been contemplating it; and alternate joy, hope, or fear have preponderated, as it conformed to, or differed from, your various ideas of just government.

Government, to an American, is the science of his political safety—this then is a moment to you the most important—and that in various points—to your reputation as members of a great nation—to your immediate safety, and to that of your posterity. In your private concerns and affairs of life you deliberate with caution, and act with prudence; your public concerns require a caution and prudence, in a ratio, suited to the difference and dignity of the sub-ject. The disposal of your reputation, and of your lives and property, is more momentous than a contract for a farm, or the sale of a bale of goods; in the former, if you are negligent or inattentive, the ambi-tious and despotic will entrap you in their toils, and bind you with the cord of power from which you, and your posterity, may never be freed; and if the possibility should exist, it carries along with it con-sequences that will make your community totter to its center: in the latter, it is a mere loss of a little property, which more circumspec-tion, or assiduity, may repair.

Without directly engaging as an advocate for this new form of national government, or as an opponent—let me conjure you to con-sider this a very important crisis of your safety and character—You have already, in common with the rest of your countrymen, the cit-izens of the other states, given to the world astonishing evidences of your greatness—you have fought under peculiar circumstances, and was successful against a powerful nation on a speculative ques-tion—you have established an original compact between you and your governors, a fact heretofore unknown in the formation of the governments of the world—your experience has informed you, that there are defects in the federal system, and, to the astonishment of mankind, your legislatures have concerted measures for an alteration, with as much case as an individual would make a disposition of his ordinary domestic affairs, this alteration now lies before you, for your consideration; but beware how you determine—do not, because you admit that something must be done, adopt any thing— teach the members of that convention, that you are capable of a supervision of their conduct. The same medium that gave you this system, if it is erroneous, while the door is now open, can make amendments, or give you another, if it is required.—Your fate, and that of your posterity, depends on your present conduct—do not give the latter reason to curse you, nor yourselves cause of reprehension; as individuals you are ambitious of leaving behind you a good name, and it is the reflection, that you have done right in this life, that blunts the sharpness of death; the same principles would be a consolation to you, as patriots, in the hour of dissolution, that you would leave to your children a fair political inheritance, untouched by the vultures of power, which you had acquired by *an unshaken* perseverance in the cause of liberty—but how miserable the alternative—you would deprecate the ruin you had brought on yourselves—be the curse of posterity, and the scorn and scoff of nations.

Deliberate, therefore, on this new national government with coolness; analize it with criticism; and reflect on it with candour: if you find that the influence of a powerful few, or the exercise of a standing army, will always be directed and exerted for your welfare alone, and not to the agrandizement of themselves, and that it will secure to you and your posterity happiness at home, and national dignity and respect from abroad, adopt it—if it will not, reject it with indignation—better to be where you are, for the present, than insecure forever afterwards. Turn your eyes to the United Netherlands, at this moment, and view their situation; compare it with what yours may be, under a government substantially similar to theirs.

Beware of those who wish to influence your passions, and to make you dupes to their resentments and little interests—personal invectives can never persuade, but they always fix prejudices which candor might have removed—those who deal in them have not your happiness at heart. Attach yourselves to measures, not to men.

This form of government is handed to you by the recommendations of a man who merits the confidence of the public; but you ought to recollect, that the wisest and best of men may err, and their errors, if adopted, may be fatal to the community; therefore, in principles of *politics*, as well as in religious faith, every man ought to think for himself.

Hereafter, when it will be necessary, I shall make such observations, on this new constitution, as will tend to promote your welfare, and be justified by reason and truth.

CATO.

New-York Journal

11 OCTOBER 1787

LETTER II

Cato criticizes the convention that drafted the Constitution for exceeding its mandate. That convention was authorized only to propose amendments to the Articles of Confederation. The people remain sovereign, however, and should not allow usurpers to rush their consideration of this new form of government. Essays in The Federalist *of particular relevance: 22, 39, 40.*

To the CITIZENS *of the* STATE *of* NEW-YORK.
Remember, O my friends! the laws, the rights,
The generous plan of power deliver'd down,
By your renown'd Forefathers;
So dearly bought, the price of so much blood!
O let it never perish in your hands!
But piously transmit it to your children.

THE object of my last address to you was to engage your dispassionate consideration of the new Federal government; to caution you against precipitancy in the adoption of it; to recommend a correction of its errors, if it contained any; to hint to you the danger of an easy perversion of some of its powers; to solicit you to separate yourselves from party, and to be independent of and uninfluenced by any in your principles of politics: and, that address was closed with a promise of future observations on the same subject which should be justified by reason and truth. Here I intended to have rested the introduction, but a writer under the signature of CÆSAR, in Mr. Childs's paper of the 1st instant, who treats you with passion, insult, and threat has anticipated those observations which would otherwise have remained in silence until a future period. It would be criminal in me to hesitate a moment to appear as your advocate in so interesting a cause, and to resist the influence of such doctrines as this Cæsar holds.—I shall take no other cognizance of his remarks on the *questionable* shape of my future, or the *equivocal* appearance of my past reflections, than to declare, that in my past I did not mean to be misunderstood (for Cæsar himself declares, that it is obviously the language of distrust) and that in my future there will not be the semblance of doubt. But, what is the language of Cæsar—he redicules your prerogative, power, and majesty—he talks of this *proferred constitution* as the tender mercy of a benevolent sovereign to deluded subjects, or, as his tyrant name-sake, of his proferred grace to the virtuous Cato:—he shuts the door of free deliberation and discussion, and declares, that you must receive this government in manner and form as it is *proferred*—that you cannot revise nor amend it, and lastly, to close the scene, he insinuates, that it will be more healthy for you that the American Fabius should be induced to accept of the presidency of this new government than that, in case you do not acquiesce, he should be solicited to command an army to impose it on you. Is not your indignation roused at this absolute, imperious stile?—For what did you open the veins of your citizens and expend their treasure?—For what did you throw off the yoke of Britain and call yourselves independent?—Was it from a disposition fond of change, or to procure new masters?—if those were your motives, you have your reward before you—go,—retire into silent obscurity, and kiss the rod that scourges you—bury the prospects you had in store, that you and your posterity would participate in the blessings of freedom, and the employments of your country—let the rich and insolent alone be your rulers—perhaps you are designed by providence as an emphatic evidence of the mutability of human affairs, to have the shew of happiness only, that your misery may seem the sharper, and if so, you must submit. But, if you had nobler views, and you are not designed by heaven as an example—are you now to be derided and insulted?—Is the power of thinking, on the only subject important to you, to be taken away? and if per chance you should happen to dissent from Cæsar, are you to have Cæsar's principles crammed down your throats with an army?—God forbid!

In democratic republics the people collectively are considered as the sovereign—all legislative, judicial, and executive power, is inherent in and derived from them. As a people, your power and authority have sanctioned and established the present government—your executive, legislative, and judicial acknowledge it by their public acts—you are again solicited to sanction and establish the future one—yet this Cæsar mocks your dignity and laughs at the majesty of the people. Cæsar, with his usual dogmatism, enquires, if I had talents to throw light on the subject of legislation, why did I not offer them when the Convention was in session?—he is answered in a moment—I thought with him and you, that the wisdom of America, in that Convention, was drawn as it were to a Focus—I placed an unbounded confidence in some of the characters who were members of it, from the services they had rendered their country, without adverting to the ambitious and interested views of others. I was willingly led to expect a model of perfection and security that would have astonished the world. Therefore, to have offered observation, on the subject of legislation, under these impressions, would have discovered no less arrogance than Cæsar. The Convention too, when in session, that their doors to the observations of the community, and their members were under an obligation of secrecy—Nothing transpired—to have suggested remarks on unknown and anticipated principles would have been like a man groping in the dark, and solely in the extreme. I confess, however, I have been disappointed, and Cæsar is candid enough to make the same declaration, for he thinks it *might* have been more perfect.

But to call in dispute, at this time, and in the manner Cæsar does, the right of free deliberation on this subject, is like a man's propounding a question to another, and telling him, at the same time, that if he does not answer agreeable to the opinion of the propounder, he will exert force to make him of the same sentiment:—to exemplify this, it will be necessary to give you a short history of the rise and progress of the Convention, and the conduct of Congress thereon. The states in Congress suggested, that the articles of confederation had provided for making alterations in the confederation—that there were defects therein, and as a mean to remedy which, a Convention of delegates, appointed by the different states, was resolved expedient to be held for the sole and express purpose of revising it, and reporting to Congress and the different legislatures such alterations and provisions therein as should (when agreed to in Congress and confirmed by the several states) render the federal constitution adequate to the exigencies of government. This resolution is sent to the different states, and the legislature of this state, with others, appoint, in conformity thereto, delegates for the purpose, and in the words mentioned in that resolve, as by the resolution of Congress, and the concurrent resolutions of the senate and assembly of this state, subjoined will appear. For the sole and express purpose aforesaid a Convention of delegates is formed at Philadelphia:—what have they done? have they revised the confederation, and has Congress agreed to their report?—neither is the fact.—This Convention have exceeded the authority given to them, and have transmitted to Congress a new political fabric; essentially and fundamentally distinct and different from it, in which the different states do not retain separately their sovereignty and independency, united by a confederated league—but one entire sovereignty—a consolidation of them into one government—in which new provisions and powers are not made and vested in Congress, but in an assembly, senate, and president, who are not known in the articles of confederation.—Congress, without agreeing to, or approving of, this system *proferred* by the Convention, have sent it to the different legislatures, not for their confirmation, but to submit it to the people; not in conformity to their own resolution, but in conformity to the resolution of the Convention made and provided in that case. Was it then, from the face of the foregoing facts, the intention of Congress, and of this and the other states, that the essence of our present national government should be annihilated, or that it should be retained and only had an increase of substantial necessary power? Congress, sensible of this latter principle, and that the Convention had taken on themselves a power which neither they nor the other states had a right to delegate to them, and that they could not agree to, and approve of this consolidated system, nor the states confirm it—have been silent on its character; and though many have dwelt on their unanimity, it is no less than the unanimity of opinion that it originated in an assumption of power, which your voice alone can sanctify. This new government, therefore, founded in usurpation, is referred to your opinion as the origin of power not heretofore delegated, and, to this end, the exercise of the prerogative of free examination is essentially necessary; and yet you are unhesitatingly to acquiesce, and if you do not, the American Fabius, if we may believe Cæsar, is to command an army to impose it. It is not my view to rouse your passions, I only wish to excite you to, and assist you in, a cool and deliberate discussion of the subject, to urge you to behave like sensible freemen. Think, speak, act, and assert your opinions and rights—let the same good sense govern you with respect to the adoption of a future system for the administration of your public affairs that influenced you in the formation of the present.—Hereafter I do not intend to be diverted by either Cæsar, or any other—My object is to take up this new form of national government—compare it with the experience and the opinions of the most sensible and approved political authors—and to show that its principles, and the exercise of them, will be dangerous to your liberty and happiness.

CATO.

New-York Journal

25 OCTOBER 1787

LETTER III

Cato argues that the Constitution would end up consolidating all state powers in itself. This would be disastrous; America and its people are too varied in their natures and interests to be well and freely governed by a single, centralized state. Essays in The Federalist *of particular relevance: 2, 14, 45, 46.*

To the CITIZENS *of the* STATE *of* NEW-YORK.

IN the close of my last introductory address, I told you, that my object in future would be to take up this new form of national government, to compare it with the experience and opinions of the most sensible and approved political authors, and to show you that its principles, and the exercise of them will be dangerous to your liberty and happiness.

Although I am conscious that this is an arduous undertaking, yet I will perform it to the best of my ability.

The freedom, equality, and independence which you enjoyed by nature, induced you to consent to a political power. The same principles led you to examine the errors and vices of a British superintendence, to divest yourselves of it, and to reassume a new political shape. It is acknowledged that there are defects in this, and another is tendered to you for acceptance; the great question then, that arises on this new political principle, is, whether it will answer the ends for which it is said to be offered to you, and for which all men engage in political society, to wit, the mutual preservation of their lives, liberties, and estates.

The recital, [or] premises on which this new form of government is erected, declares a consolidation or union of all the thirteen parts, or states, into one great whole, under the firm of the United States, for all the various and important purposes therein set forth.—But whoever seriously considers the immense extent of territory comprehended within the limits of the United States, together with the variety of its climates, productions, and commerce, the difference of extent, and number of inhabitants in all; the dissimilitude of interest, morals, and policies, in almost every one, will receive it as an intuitive truth, that a consolidated republican form of government therein, can never *form a perfect union, establish justice, insure domestic tranquility, promote the general welfare, and secure the blessings of liberty to you and your posterity,* for to these objects it must be directed: this is kindred legislature therefore, composed of interests opposite and dissimilar in their nature, will in its exercise, emphatically be, like a house divided against itself.

The governments of Europe have taken their limits and form from adventitious circumstances, and nothing can be argued on the motive of agreement from them; but these adventitious political principles, have nevertheless produced effects that have attracted the attention of philosophy, which has established axioms in the science of politics therefrom, as irrefragable as any in Euclid. It is natural, says Montesquieu, *to a republic to have only a small territory, otherwise it cannot long fulfill: in a large one, there are men of large fortunes, and consequently of less moderation; there are too great deposits to intrust in the hands of a single subject, an ambitious person soon becomes sensible that he may be happy, great, and glorious by oppressing his fellow citizens, and that he might raise himself to grandeur, on the ruins of his country. In large republics, the public good is sacrificed to a thousand views; in a small one the interest of the public is easily perceived, better understood, and more within the reach of every citizen; abuses have a less extent, and of course are less protected*—he also shews you, that the duration of the republic of Sparta, was owing to its having continued with the same extent of territory after all its wars; and that the ambition of Athens and Lacodemon to command and direct the union, lost them their liberties, and gave them a monarchy.

From this picture, what can you promise yourselves, on the score of consolidation of the United States, into one government—impracticability in the just exercise of it—your freedom insecure—even this form of government limited in its continuance—the employments of your country disposed of to the opulent, to whose contumely you will continually be an object—you must risque much, by indispensibly placing trusts of the greatest magnitude, into the hands of individuals, whose ambition for power, and agrandisement, will oppress and grind you—where, from the vast extent of your territory, and the complication of interests, the science of government will become intricate and perplexed, and too misterious for you to understand, and observe; and by which you are to be conducted into a monarchy, either limited or despotic; the latter, Mr. Locke remarks, *is a government derived from neither nature, nor compact.*

Political liberty, the great Montesquieu again observes, *consists in security, or at least in the opinion we have of security;* and this *security* therefore, or the *opinion*, is best obtained in moderate governments, where the mildness of the laws, and the equality of the manners, beget a confidence in the people, which produces this security, or the opinion. This moderation in governments, depends in a great measure on their limits, connected with their political distribution.

The extent of many of the states in the Union, is at this time, almost too great for the superintendence of a republican form of government, and must one day or other, revolve into more vigorous ones, or by separation be reduced into smaller, and more useful, as well as moderate ones. You have already observed the feeble efforts of Massachusetts against their insurgents; with what difficulty did they quell that insurrection; and is not the province of Main at this moment, on the eve of separation from her. The reason of these things is, that for the security of the *property* of the community, in which expressive term Mr. Lock makes life, liberty, and estate, to consist—the wheels of a free republic are necessarily slow in their operation; hence in large free republics, the evil sometimes is not only begun, but almost completed, before they are in a situation to turn the current into a contrary progression: the extremes are also too remote from the usual seat of government, and the laws therefore too feeble to afford protection to all its parts, and insure *domestic tranquility* without the aid of another principle. If, therefore, this state, and that of N. Carolina, had an army under their controul, they never would have lost Vermont, and Frankland, nor the state of Massachusetts suffer an insurrection, or the dismemberment of her fairest district, but the exercise of a principle which would have prevented these things, if we may believe the experience of ages, would have ended in the destruction of their liberties.

Will this consolidated republic, if established, in its exercise beget such confidence and compliance, among the citizens of these states, as to do without the aid of a standing army—I deny that it will.—The mal-contents in each state, who will not be a few, nor the least important, will be exciting factions against it—the fear of a dismemberment of some of its parts, and the necessity to enforce the execution of revenue laws (a fruitful source of oppression) on the extremes and in the other districts of the government, will incidentally, and necessarily require a permanent force, to be kept on foot—will not political security, and even the opinion of it, be extinguished? can mildness and moderation exist in a government, where the primary incident in its exercise must be force? will not violence destroy confidence, and can equality subsist, where the extent, policy, and practice of it, will naturally lead to make odious distinctions among citizens?

The people, who may compose this national legislature from the southern states, in which, from the mildness of the climate, the fertility of the soil, and the value of its productions, wealth is rapidly acquired, and where the same causes naturally lead to luxury, dissipation, and a passion for aristocratic distinctions, where slavery is encouraged, and liberty of course, less respected, and protected; who know not what it is to acquire property by their own toil, nor to economise with the savings of industry—will these men therefore be as tenacious of the liberties and interests of the more northern states, where freedom, independence, industry, equality, and frugality, are natural to the climate and soil, as men who are your own citizens, legislating in your own state, under your inspection, and whose manners, and fortunes, bear a more equal resemblance to your own?

It may be suggested, in answer to this, that whoever is a citizen of one state, is a citizen of each, and that therefore he will be as interested in the happiness and interest of all, as the one he is delegated from; but the argument is fallacious, and, whoever has attended to the history of mankind, and the principles which bind them together as parents, citizens, or men, will readily perceive it. These principles are, in their exercise, like a pebble cast on the calm surface of a river, the circles begin in the center, and are small, active, and forcible, but as they depart from that point, they lose their force, and vanish into calmness.

The strongest principle of union resides within our domestic walls. The ties of the parent exceed that of any other; as we depart from home, the next general principle of union is amongst citizens of the same state, where acquaintance, habits, and fortunes, nourish affection, and attachment; enlarge the circle still further, &, as citizens of different states, though we acknowledge the same national denomination, we lose the ties of acquaintance, habits, and fortunes, and thus, by degrees, we lessen in our attachments, till, at length, we no more than acknowledge a sameness of species. Is it therefore, from certainty like this, reasonable to believe, that inhabitants of Georgia, or New-Hampshire, will have the same obligations towards you as your own, and preside over your lives, liberties, and property, with the same care and attachment? Intuitive reason, answers in the negative.

In the course of my examination of the principals of consolidation of the states into one general government, many other reasons against it have occurred, but I flatter myself, from those herein offered to your consideration, I have convinced you that it is both presumptious and impracticable consistent with your safety. To detain you with further remarks, would be useless—I shall however, continue in my following numbers, to anilise this new government, pursuant to my promise.

CATO.

New-York Journal

8 NOVEMBER 1787

LETTER IV

Turning to the presidency, Cato argues that the Constitution's four year term is too long for an official who would be both powerful and susceptible to corruption. The president's cabinet would also become dangerous, eventually forming a monarch's court. Essays in The Federalist *of particular relevance: 67, 70, 71, 76, 77.*

To the CITIZENS *of the* STATE *of* NEW-YORK.

ADMITTING, however, that the vast extent of America, together with the various other reasons which I offered you in my last number, against the practicability of the just exercise of the new government are insufficient to convince you; still it is an undeniable truth, that its several parts are either possessed of principles, which you have heretofore considered as ruinous, and that others are omitted which you have established as fundamental to your political security, and must in their operation, I will venture to assert—fetter your tongues and minds, enchain your bodies, and ultimately extinguish all that is great and noble in man.

In pursuance of my plan, I shall begin with observations on the executive branch of this new system; and though it is not the first in order, as arranged therein, yet being the *chief*, is perhaps entitled by the rules of rank to the first consideration. The executive power as described in the 2d article, consists of a president and vice-president, who are to hold their offices *during* the term of four years; the same article has marked the manner and time of their election, and established the qualifications of the president; it also provides against the removal, death, or inability of the president and vice-president—regulates the salary of the president, delineates his duties and powers; and lastly, declares the causes for which the president and vice-president shall be removed from office.

Notwithstanding the great learning and abilities of the gentlemen who composed the convention, it may be here remarked with deference, that the construction of the first paragraph of the first section of the second article, is vague and inexplicit, and leaves the mind in doubt, as to the election of a president and vice-president, after the expiration of the election for the first term of four years—in every other case, the election of these great officers is expressly provided for; but there is no explicit provision for their election in case of the expiration of their offices, subsequent to the election which is to set this political machine in motion—no certain and express terms as in your state constitution, that *statedly* once in every four years, and as often as these offices shall become vacant, by expiration or otherwise, as is therein expressed, an election shall be held as follows, &c.—this inexplicitness perhaps may lead to an establishment for life.

It is remarked by Montesquieu, in treating of republics, that *in all magistracies, the greatness of the power must be compensated by the brevity of the duration; and that a longer time than a year, would be dangerous.* It is therefore obvious to the least intelligent mind, to account why, great power in the hands of a magistrate, and that power connected, with a considerable duration, may be dangerous to the liberties of a republic—the deposit of vast trusts in the hands of a single magistrate, enables him in their exercise, to create a numerous train of dependants—this tempts his *ambition,* which in a republican magistrate is also remarked, *to be pernicious* and the duration of his office for any considerable time favours his views, gives him the means and time to perfect and execute his designs—*he therefore fancies that he may be great and glorious by oppressing his fellow citizens, and raising himself to permanent grandeur on the ruins of his country.*—And here it may be necessary to compare the vast and important powers of the president, together with his continuance in office with the foregoing doctrine—his eminent magisterial situation will attach many adherents to him, and he will be surrounded by expectants and courtiers—his power of nomination and influence on all appointments—the strong posts in each state comprised within his superintendance, and garrisoned by troops under his direction—his controul over the army, militia, and navy—the unrestrained power of granting pardons for treason, which may be used to screen from punishment, those whom he had secretly instigated to commit the crime, and thereby prevent a discovery of his own guilt—his duration in office for four years: these, and various other principles evidently prove the truth of the position—that if the president is possessed of ambition, he has power and time sufficient to ruin his country.

Though the president, during the sitting of the legislature, is assisted by the senate, yet he is without a constitutional council in their recess—he will therefore be unsupported by proper information and advice, and will generally be directed by minions and favorites, or a council of state will grow out of the principal officers of the great departments, the most dangerous council in a free country.

The ten miles square, which is to become the seat of government, will of course be the place of residence for the president and the great officers of state—the same observations of a great man will apply to the court of a president possessing the powers of a monarch, that is observed of that of a monarch—*ambition with idleness—baseness with pride—the thirst of riches without labour—aversion to truth—flattery—treason—perfidy—violation of engagements—contempt of civil duties—hope from the magistrates weakness; but above all, the perpetual ridicule of virtue*—these, he remarks, are the characteristics by which the courts in all ages have been distinguished.

The language and the manners of this court will be what distinguishes them from the rest of the community, not what assimilates them to it, and in being remarked for a behaviour that shews they are not *meanly born*, and in adulation to people of fortune and power.

The establishment of a vice president is as unnecessary as it is dangerous. This officer, for want of other employment, is made president of the senate, thereby blending the executive and legislative powers, besides always giving to some one state, from which he is to come, an unjust pre-eminence.

It is a maxim in republics, that the representative of the people should be of their immediate choice; but by the manner in which the president is chosen he arrives to this office at the fourth or fifth hand, nor does the highest votes, in the way he is elected, determine the choice—for it is only necessary that he should be taken from the highest of five, who may have a plurality of votes.

Compare your past opinions and sentiments with the present proposed establishment, and you will find, that if you adopt it, that it will lead you into a system which you heretofore reprobated as odious. Every American whig, not long since, bore his emphatic testimony against a monarchical government, though limited, because of the dangerous inequality that it created among citizens as relative to their rights and property; and wherein does this president, invested with his powers and prerogatives, essentially differ from the king of Great-Britain (save as to name, the creation of nobility and some immaterial incidents, the offspring of absurdity and locality) the direct prerogatives of the president, as springing from his political character, are among the following:—It is necessary, in order to distinguish him from the rest of the community, and enable him to keep, and maintain his court, that the compensation for his services; or in other words, his revenue should be such as to enable him to appear with the splendor of a prince; he has the power of receiving ambassadors from, and a great influence on their appointments to foreign courts; as also to make treaties, leagues, and alliances with foreign states, assisted by the senate, which when made, become the supreme law of the land: he is a constituent part of the legislative power; for every bill which shall pass the house of representatives and senate, is to be presented to him for approbation; if he approves of it, he is to sign it, if he disapproves, he is to return it with objections, which in many cases will amount to a compleat negative; and in this view he will have a great share in the power of making peace, coining money, &c. and all the various objects of legislation, expressed or implied in this Constitution: for though it may be asserted that the king of Great-Britain has the express power of making peace or war, yet he never thinks it prudent so to do without the advice of his parliament from whom he is to derive his support, and therefore these powers, in both president and king, are substantially the same: he is the generalissimo of the nation, and of course, has the command & controul of the army, navy and militia; he is the general conservator of the peace of the union—he may pardon all offences, except in cases of impeachment, and the principal fountain of all offices & employments. Will not the exercise of these powers therefore tend either to the establishment of a vile and arbitrary aristocracy, or monarchy? The safety of the people in a republic depends on the share or proportion they have in the government; but experience ought to teach you, that when a man is at the head of an elective government invested with great powers, and interested in his re-election, in what circle appointments will be made; by which means *an imperfect aristocracy* bordering on monarchy may be established.

You must, however, my countrymen, beware, that the advocates of this new system do not deceive you, by a fallacious resemblance between it and your own state government, which you so much prize; and if you examine, you will perceive that the chief magistrate of this state, is your immediate choice, controuled and checked by a just and full representation of the people, divested of the perogative of influencing war and peace, making treaties, receiving and lending embassies, and commanding standing armies and navies, which belong to the power of the confederation, and will be convinced that this government is no more like a true picture of your own, than an Angel of darkness resembles an Angel of light.

Cato.

New-York Journal

22 NOVEMBER 1787

LETTER V

Cato criticizes the Constitution for failing to separate fully the new government's legislative, executive, and judicial functions. This failure leaves American liberty at the mercy of the rulers. The danger will be increased by a federal legislature that is too small to represent the interests of all the people. Essays in The Federalist *of particular relevance: 47-51, 56, 57, 58.*

To the CITIZENS *of the State of* NEW-YORK.

IN my last number I endeavored to prove that the language of the article relative to the establishment of the executive of this new government was vague and inexplicit, that the great powers of the President, connected with his duration in office would lead to oppression and ruin. That he would be governed by favorites and flatterers, or that a dangerous council would be collected from the great officers of state;—that the ten miles square, if the remarks of one of the wisest men, drawn from the experience of mankind, may be credited, would be the asylum of the base, idle, avaricious and ambitious, and that the court would possess a language and manners different from yours; that a vice-president is as unnecessary, as he is dangerous in his influence—that the president cannot represent you, because he is not of your own immediate choice, that if you adopt this government, you will incline to an arbitrary and odious aristocracy or monarchy—that the president possessed of the power, given him by this frame of government differs but very immaterially from the establishment of monarchy in Great-Britain, and I warned you to beware of the fallacious resemblance that is held out to you by the advocates of this new system between it and your own state governments.

And here I cannot help remarking, that inexplicitness seems to pervade this whole political fabric: certainty in political compacts, which Mr. Coke *calls the mother and nurse of repose and quietness*, the want of which induced men to engage in political society, has ever been held by a wise and free people as essential to their security; as on the one hand it fixes barriers which the ambitious and tyrannically disposed magistrate dare not overleap, and on the other, becomes a wall of safety to the community—otherwise stipulations between the governors and governed are nugatory; and you might as well deposit the important powers of legislation and execution in one or a few and permit them to govern according to their disposition and will; but the world is too full of examples, which prove that *to live by one man's will became the cause of all men's misery.* Before the existence of express political compacts it was reasonably implied that the magistrate should govern with wisdom and justice, but mere implication was too feeble to restrain the unbridled ambition of a bad man, or afford security against negligence, cruelty, or any other defect of mind. It is alledged that the opinions and manners of the people of America, are capable to resist and prevent an extension of prerogative or oppression; but you must recollect that opinion and manners are mutable, and may not always be a permanent obstruction against the encroachments of government; that the progress of a commercial society begets luxury, the parent of inequality, the foe to virtue, and the enemy to restraint; and that ambition and voluptuousness aided by flattery, will teach magistrates, where limits are not explicitly fixed to have separate and distinct interests from the people, besides it will not be denied that government assimilates the manners and opinions of the community to it. Therefore, a general presumption that rulers will govern well is not a sufficient security.—You are then under a sacred obligation to provide for the safety of your posterity, and would you now basely desert their interests, when by a small share of prudence you may transmit to them a beautiful political patrimony, which will prevent the necessity of their travelling through seas of blood to obtain that, which your wisdom might have secured:—It is a duty you owe likewise to your own reputation, for you have a great name to lose; you are characterised as cautious, prudent and jealous in politics; whence is it therefore, that you are about to precipitate yourselves into a sea of uncertainty, and adopt a system so vague, and which has discarded so many of your valuable rights:—Is it because you do not believe that an American can be a tyrant? If this be the case you rest on a weak basis, Americans are like other men in similar situations, when the manners and opinions of the community are changed by the causes I mentioned before, and your political compact inexplicit, your posterity will find that great power connected with ambition, luxury, and flattery, will as readily produce a Caesar, Caligula, Nero, and Domitian in America, as the same causes did in the Roman empire.

But the next thing to be considered in conformity to my plan, is the first article of this new government, which comprises the erection of the house of representatives and senate, and prescribes their various powers and objects of legislation. The most general objections to the first article, are that bi-ennial elections for representatives are a departure from the safe democratical principles of annual ones—that the number of representatives are too few; that the apportionment and principles of increase are unjust; that no attention has been paid to either the numbers or property in each state in forming the senate; that the mode in which they are appointed and their duration, will lead to the establishment of an aristocracy; that the senate and president are improperly connected, both as to appointments, and the making of treaties, which are to become the supreme law of the land; that the judicial in some measure, to wit, as to the trial of impeachments is placed in the senate a branch of the legislative, and some times a branch of the executive: that Congress have the improper power of making or altering the regulations prescribed by the different legislatures, respecting the time, place, and manner of holding elections for representatives; and the time and manner of choosing senators; that standing armies may be established, and appropriation of money made for their support, for two years; that the militia of the most remote state may be marched into those states situated at the opposite extreme of this continent; that the slave trade, is to all intents and purposes permanently established; and a slavish capitation, or poll-tax, may at any time be levied—these are some of the many evils that will attend the adoption of this government.

But with respect to the first objection, it may be remarked that a well digested democracy has this advantage over all others, to wit; that it affords to many the opportunity to be advanced to the supreme command, and the honors they thereby enjoy fills them with a desire of rendering themselves worthy of them; hence this desire becomes part of their education, is matured in manhood, and produces an ardent affection for their country, and it is the opinion of the great Sidney, and Montesquieu that this is in a great measure produced by annual election of magistrates.

If annual elections were to exist in this government, and learning and information to become more prevalent, you never will want men to execute whatever you could design—Sidney observes *that a well governed state it as fruitful to all good purposes as the seven headed-serpent is said to have been in evil; when one head is cut off, many rise up in the place of it.* He remarks further, that *it was also thought, that free cities by frequent elections of magistrates became nurseries of great and able men, every man endeavoring to excel others, that he might be advanced to the honor he had no other title to, than what might arise from his merit, or reputation,* but the framers of this *perfect government*, as it is called, have departed from this democratical principle, and established bi-ennial elections; for the house of representatives, who are to be chosen by the people, and sextennial for the senate, who are to be chosen by the legislatures of the different states, and have given to the executive the unprecendented power of making temporary senators, in case of vacancies, by resignation or otherwise, and so far forth establishing a precedent for virtual representation (though in fact, their original appointment is virtual) thereby influencing the choice of the legislatures, or if they should not be so complaisant as to conform to his appointment—offence will be given to the executive and the temporary members, will appear ridiculous by rejection; this temporary member, during his time of appointment, will of course act by a power derived from the executive, and for, and under his immediate influence.

It is a very important objection to this government, that the representation consists of so few; too few to resist the influence of corruption, and the temptation to treachery, against which all governments ought to take precautions—how guarded you have been on this head, in your own state constitution, and yet the number of senators and representatives proposed for this vast continent, does not equal those of your own state; how great the disparity, if you compare them with the aggregate numbers in the United States. The history of representation in England, from which we have taken our model of legislation, is briefly this, before the institution of legislating by deputies, the whole free part of the community usually met for that purpose; when this became impossible, by the increase of numbers the community was divided into districts, from each of which was sent such a number of deputies as was a complete representation of the various numbers and orders of citizens within them; but can it be asserted with truth, that six men can be a complete and full representation of the numbers and various orders of the people in this state? Another thing may be suggested against the small number of representatives is, that but few of you will have the chance of sharing even in this branch of the legislature; and that the choice will be confined to a very few; the more complete it is, the better will your interests be preserved, and the greater the opportunity you will have to participate in government, one of the principal securities of a free people; but this subject has been so ably and fully treated by a writer under the signature of Brutus, that I shall content myself with referring you to him thereon, reserving further observations on the other objections I have mentioned, for my future numbers.

CATO.

New-York Journal

------

13 DECEMBER 1787

LETTER VI

Cato mistakenly argues that the Constitution's "3/5 rule," appor-
tioning representatives to slave-holding states, applies to women ad
children as well, thus corrupting the representation. He also argues
that the new government will be expensive and will use its taxing
power to oppress the people and set up an aristocracy of office-hold-
ers. Essays in The Federalist *of particular relevance: 13, 30-32,*
35, 36, 54.

To the PEOPLE *of the State of* NEW-YORK.

THE next objection that arises against this proffered constitution
is, that the apportionment of representatives and direct taxes are
unjust.—The words as expressed in this article are, "representatives and direct taxes shall be apportioned among the several
states, which may be included in this union, according to their
respective numbers, which shall be determined by adding to the
whole number of free persons, including those bound to service for
a term of years, and excluding Indians not taxed three-fifths of all
other persons." In order to elucidate this, it will be necessary to
repeat the remark in my last number, that the mode of legislation in
the infancy of free communities was by the collective body, and this
consisted of free persons, or those whose age admitted them to the
rights of mankind and citizenship—whose sex made them capable
of protecting the state, and whose birth may be denominated Free
Born, and no traces can be found that ever women, children, and
slaves, or those who were not sui juris, in the early days of legislation, meeting with the free members of the community to deliberate on public measures; hence is derived this maxim in free
governments, that representation ought to bear a proportion to the
number of free inhabitants in a community; this principle your own

state constitution, and others, have observed in the establishment of a future census, in order to apportion the representatives, and to increase or diminish the representation to the ratio of the increase or diminution of electors. But, what aid can the community derive from the assistance of women, infants, and slaves, in their deliberation, or in their defence? and what motive therefore could the convention have in departing from the just and rational principle of representation, which is the governing principle of this state and of all America.

The doctrine of taxation is a very important one, and nothing requires more wisdom and prudence than the regulation of that portion, which is taken from, and of that which is left to, the subject—and if you anticipate, what will be the enormous expence of this new government added also to your own, little will that portion be which will be left to you. I know there are politicians who believe, that you should be loaded with taxes, in order to make you industrious, and, perhaps, there were some of this opinion in the convention, but it is an erroneous principle—For, what can inspire you with industry, if the greatest measures of your labours are to be swallowed up in taxes? The advocates for this new system hold out an idea, that you will have but little to pay, for, that the revenues will be so managed as to be almost wholly drawn from the source of trade or duties on imports, but this is delusive—for this government to discharge all its incidental expences, besides paying the interests on the home and foreign debts, will require more money than its commerce can afford; and if you reflect one moment, you will find, that if heavy duties are laid on merchandize, as must be the case, if government intend to make this the prime medium to lighten the people of taxes, that the price of the commodities, useful as well as luxurious, must be increased; the consumers will be fewer; the merchants must import less; trade will languish, and this source of revenue in a great measure be dried up; but if you examine this a little further, you will find, that this revenue, managed in this way, will come out of you and be a very heavy and ruinous one, at least—The merchant no more than advances the money for you to the public, and will not, nor cannot pay any part of it himself, and if he pays more duties, he will sell his commodities at a price portionably raised—thus the laborer, mechanic, and farmer, must feel it in the purchase of their utensils and clothing—wages, &c. must rise with the price of things, or they must be ruined, and that must be the case with the farmer, whose produce will not increase, in the ratio, with labour, utensils, and clothing; for that he must sell at the usual price or lower, perhaps, caused by the decrease of trade; the consequence will be, that he must mortgage his farm, and then comes inevitable bankruptcy.

In what manner then will you be eased, if the expences of government are to be raised solely out of the commerce of this country; do you not readily apprehend the fallacy of this argument. But government will find, that to press so heavily on commerce will not do, and therefore must have recourse to other objects; these will be a capitation or poll-tax, window lights, &c. &c. and a long train of impositions which their ingenuity will suggest; but will you submit to be numbered like the slaves of an arbitrary despot; and what will be your reflections when the tax-master thunders at your door for the duty on that light which is the bounty of heaven. It will be the policy of the great landholders who will chiefly compose this senate, and perhaps a majority of this house of representatives, to keep their lands free from taxes; and this is confirmed by the failure of every attempt to lay a land-tax in this state; hence recourse must and will be had to the sources I mentioned before. The burdens on you will be insupportable—your complaints will be inefficacious—this will beget public disturbances, and I will venture to predict, without the spirit of prophecy, that you and the government, if it is adopted, will one day be at issue on this point. The force of government will be exerted, thus will call for an increase of revenue, and will add fuel to the fire. The result will be, that either you will revolve to some other form, or that government will give peace to the country, by destroying the opposition. If government therefore can, notwithstanding every opposition, raise a revenue on such things as are odious and burdensome to you, they can do anything.

But why should the number of individuals be the principle to apportion the taxes in each state, and to include in that number, women, children and slaves. The most natural and equitable principle of apportioning taxes, would be in a ratio to their property, and a reasonable impost in a ratio to their trade; but you are told to look for the reason of these things in accommodation; but this much admired principle, when striped of its mistery, will in this case appear to be no less than a basis for an odious poll-tax—the offspring of despotic governments, a thing so detestable, that the state of Maryland, in their bill of rights, declares, "that the levying taxes by the poll, is grievous and oppressive, and ought to be abolished."—A poll-tax is at all times oppressive to the poor, and their greatest misfortune will consist in having more prolific wives than the rich.

In every civilized community, even in those of the most democratic kind, there are principles which lead to an aristocracy—these are superior talents, fortunes, and public employments. But in free governments, the influence of the two former is resisted by the equality of the laws, and the latter by the frequency of elections, and the chance that every one has in sharing in public business; but when this natural and artificial eminence is assisted by principles interwoven in this government—when the senate, so important a branch of the legislature, is so far removed from the people, as to have little or no connexion with them; when their duration in office is such as to have the resemblance to perpetuity, when they are connected with the executive, by the appointment of all officers, and also, to become a judiciary for the trial of officers of their own appointments: added to all this, when none but men of oppulence will hold a seat, what is there left to resist and repel this host of influence and power. Will the feeble efforts of the house of representatives, in whom your security ought to subsist, consisting of about seventy-three, be able to hold the balance against them, when, from the fewness of the number in this house, the senate will have in their power to poison even a majority of that body by douceurs of office for themselves or friends. From causes like this both Montesquieu and Hume have predicted the decline of the British government into that of an absolute one; but the liberties of this country, it is probable if this system is adopted, will be strangled in their birth; for whenever the executive and senate can destroy the independence of the majority in the house of representatives, then where is your security?—They are so intimately connected, that their interests will be one and the same; and will the slow increase of numbers be able to afford a repelling principle? but you are told to adopt this government first, and you will always be able to alter it afterwards; this would be first submitting to be slaves and then taking care of your liberty; and when your chains are on, then to act like freemen.

Complete acts of legislation, which are to become the supreme law of the land, ought to be the united act of all the branches of government; but there is one of the most important duties may be managed by the senate and executive alone, and to have all the force of the law paramount without the aid or interference of the house of representatives; that is the power of making treaties. This power is a very important one, and may be exercised in various ways, so as to affect your person and property, and even the domain of the nation. By treaties you may defalcate part of the empire; engagements may be made to raise an army, and you may be transported to Europe, to fight the wars of ambitious princes; money may be contracted for, and you must pay it; and a thousand other obligations may be entered into; all which will become the supreme law of the land, and you are bound by it. If treaties are erroneously or wickedly made who is there to punish—the executive can always cover himself with the plea, that he was advised by the senate, and the senate being a collective body are not easily made accountable for mal-administration. On this account we are in a worse situation than Great-Britain, where they have secured by a ridiculous fiction, the King from accountability, by declaring; that he can do no wrong; by which means the nation can have redress against his minister but with us infalibility pervades every part of the system, and neither the executive nor his council who are a collective body, and his advisers, can be brought to punishment for mal-administration.

Cato.

New-York Journal

3 JANUARY 1788

LETTER VII

Cato's last letter begins with criticism of the Senate's executive powers. The Senate's power to try impeachments and to advise and consent on treaties links it too closely to the President, destroying the protections of a separation of powers. In addition, Congress's power to determine the time, place, and manner of its own elections will allow its members to perpetuate themselves in office. Essays in The Federalist *of particular relevance: 59-61, 64-66.*

To the CITIZENS of the State of NEW-YORK.

THAT the senate and president are further improperly connected, will appear, if it is considered, that their dependence on each other will prevent either from being a check upon the other; they must act in concert, and whether the power and influence of the one or the other is to prevail, will depend on the character and abilities of the men who hold those offices at the time. The senate is vested with such a proportion of the executive, that it would be found necessary that they should be constantly sitting. This circumstance did not escape the convention, and they have provided for the event, in the 2d article, which declares, that the executive may, on extraordinary occasions, *convene both houses or either of them.* No occasion can exist for calling the assembly without the senate; the words *or either of them,* must have been intended to apply only to the senate. Their wages are already provided for; and it will be therefore readily observed, that the partition between a perpetuation of their sessions and a perpetuation of their offices, in the progress of the government, will be found to be but thin and feeble. Besides, the senate, who have the sole power to try all impeachments, in case of the impeachment of the president, are to determine, as judges, the propriety of the advice they gave him, as

senators. Can the senate in this, therefore, be an impartial judicature. And will they not rather serve as a screen to great public
defaulters?

Among the many evils that are incorporated in this new system
of government, is that of congress having the power of making or
altering the regulations prescribed by the different legislatures,
respecting the time, place, and manner of holding elections for representatives, and the time, and manner of choosing senators. If it
is enquired, in what manner this regulation may be exercised to
your injury—the answer is easy.

By the first article the house of representatives shall consist of
members, chosen every second year by the people of the several
states, who are qualified to vote for members of their several state
assemblies; it can therefore readily be believed, that the different
state legislatures, provided such can exist after the adoption of
this government, will continue those easy and convenient modes for
the election of representatives for the national legislature, that are
in use, for the election of members of assembly for their own states;
but the congress have, by the constitution, a power to make other
regulations, or alter those in practice, prescribed by your own state
legislatures; hence, instead of having the places of elections in the
precincts, and brought home almost to your own doors. Congress
may establish a place, or places, at either the extremes, center, or
outer parts of the states; at a time and season too, when it may be
very inconvenient to attend; and by these means destroy the rights
of election; but in opposition to this reasoning, it is asserted, that it
is a necessary power because the states might omit making rules
for the purpose, and thereby defeat the existence of that branch of
the government; this is what logicians call *argumentum absurdum,*
for the different states, if they will have any security at all in this
government, will find it in the house of representatives, and they,
therefore, would not be very ready to eradicate a principle in which
it dwells, or involve their country in an instantaneous revolution.
Besides, if this was the apprehension of the framers, and the
ground of that provision, why did not they extend this controuling
power to the other duties of the several state legislatures. To exemplify this the states are to appoint senators, and electors for choos-

ing of a president; but the time is to be under the direction of congress. Now, [suppose they] were to omit the appointment of senators and electors, though congress was to appoint the time, which might well be apprehended [as] the omission of regulations for the election of members of the house of representatives, provided they had that power; or suppose they were not to meet at all: of course, the government cannot proceed in its exercise. And from this motive, or apprehension, congress ought to have taken these duties, entirely in their own hands, and, by a decisive declaration, annihilated them, which they in fact have done by leaving them without the means of support, or at least resting on their bounty. To this, the advocates for this system oppose the common, empty declamation that there is no danger that congress will abuse this power; but such language, as relative to so important a subject, is mere vapour and found without sense. Is it not in their power, however, to make such regulations as may be inconvenient to you? It must be admitted, because the words are unlimited in their sense. It is a good rule, in the construction of a contract, to suppose, that what may be done will be; therefore, in considering this subject, you are to suppose, that in the exercise of this government, a regulation of congress will be made, for holding an election for the whole state at Poughkeepsie, at New-York, or, perhaps, at Fort-Stanwix: who will then be the actual electors for the house of representatives? Very few more than those who may live in the vicinity of these places. Could any others afford the expence and time of attending? And would not the government by this means have it in their power to put whom they pleased in the house of representatives? You ought certainly to have as much or more [distrust] with respect to the exercise of these powers by congress, than congress ought to have with respect to the exercise of those duties which ought to be entrusted to the several states, because over them congress can have a legislative controuling power.

Hitherto we have tied up our rulers in the exercise of their duties by positive restrictions—if the cord has been drawn too tight, loosen it to the necessary extent, but do not entirely unbind them.—I am no enemy to placing a reasonable confidence in them; but such an unbounded one as the advocates and framers of this new system advise you to, would be dangerous to your liberties; it has been the ruin of other governments, and will be yours, if you adopt with all its latitudinal powers—unlimited confidence in governors as well as individuals is frequently the parent of deception.—What facilitated the corrupt designs of Philip of Macedon, and caused the ruin of Athens, but the unbounded confidence in their statesmen and rulers? Such improper confidence Demosthenes was so well convinced had ruined his country, that in his second Phillipic oration he remarks—"that there is one common bulwark with which men of prudence are naturally provided, the guard and security of all people, particularly of free states, against the assaults of tyrants—What is this? Distrust. Of this be mindful; to this adhere; preserve this carefully, and no calamity can affect you.—Montesquieu observes, that "the course of government is attended with an insensible descent to evil, and there is no reascending to good without very great efforts." The plain inference from this doctrine is, that rulers in all governments will erect an interest separate from the ruled, which will have a tendency to enslave them. There is therefore no other way of interrupting this insensible descent and warding off the evil as long as possible, than by establishing principles of distrust in your constituents, and cultivating the sentiment among yourselves. But let me enquire of you, my countrymen, whether the freedom and independence of elections is a point of magnitude. If it is, what kind of a spirit of amity, deference and concession, is that which has put it in the power of Congress at one stroke to prevent your interference in government and do away your liberties for ever? Does either the situation or circumstances of things warrant it?

CATO.

Letters of Centinel

The Letters of Centinel first appeared in the Philadelphia Inde-pendent Gazetteer *and the Philadelphia* Freeman's Journal *between October 1787 and April 1788.*[1] *Several were widely reprinted; and the first two also appeared as special editions or broadsides. Current scholarly opinion points to Samuel Bryan, son of Judge George Bryan, a leader of Pennsylvania Anti-Federalists, as the author of Centinel's letters. Throughout these letters, Centinel seeks to live up to his name by warning Americans of dangers to their liberties posed by the Federalists and their new Constitution. Centinel's first letter was widely cited for its attack on political checks and balances. Subsequent letters were less successful.*

Independent Gazetteer

5 OCTOBER 1787

LETTER I

Centinel begins by praising Pennsylvania's respect for common law rights, including freedom of the press and freedom against unreasonable search and seizure. Americans should not risk their established rights by too easily substituting dependence on

[1]All but the second letter first appeared in the *Gazetteer*. Most were then published in the *Freeman's Journal*. Two other sets of "Centinel" letters, one dealing specifically with Pennsylvania elections and the other, under the title "Centinel Revived," dealing with state politics and proposed amendments to the Constitution, are not included here.

mechanical checks and balances for the direct responsibility of representatives to the people. Essays in The Federalist *of particular relevance: 48-50, 83, 84.*

Mr. Oswald,
As the Independent Gazetteer seems free for the discussion of all public matters, I expect you will give the following a place in your next.

To the Freemen of Pennsylvania.
   Friends, Countrymen and *Fellow Citizens,*
Permit one of yourselves to put you in mind of certain *liberties* and *privileges* secured to you by the constitution of this commonwealth, and to beg your serious attention to his uninterested opinion upon the plan of federal government submitted to your consideration, before you surrender these great and valuable privileges up forever. Your present frame of government, secures to you a right to hold yourselves, houses, papers and possessions free from search and seizure, and therefore warrants granted without oaths or affirmations first made, affording sufficient foundation for them, whereby any officer or messenger may be commanded or required to search your houses or seize your persons or property, not particularly described in such warrant, shall not be granted. Your constitution further provides "that in controversies respecting property, and in suits between man and man, the parties have a right *to trial by jury, which ought to be held sacred.*" It also provides and declares, "*that the people have a right of* FREEDOM OF SPEECH, *and of* WRITING *and* PUBLISHING *their sentiments, therefore* THE FREEDOM OF THE PRESS OUGHT NOT TO BE RESTRAINED." The constitution of Pennsylvania is *yet* in existence, *as yet* you have the right to *freedom of speech*, and of *publishing your sentiments*. How long those rights will appertain to you, you yourselves are called upon to say, whether your *houses* shall continue to be your *castles;* whether your *papers*, your *persons* and your *property*, are to be held sacred and free from *general warrants*, you are now to determine. Whether the *trial by jury* is to continue as your birth-

right, the freemen of Pennsylvania, nay, of all America, are now called upon to declare.

Without presuming upon my own judgement, I cannot think it an unwarrantable presumption to offer my private opinion, and call upon others for their's; and if I use my pen with the boldness of a freeman, it is because I know that *the liberty of the press yet remains unviolated,* and *juries yet are judges.*

The late Convention have submitted to your consideration on a plan of a new, federal government—The subject is highly interesting to your future welfare—Whether it be calculated to promote the great ends of civil society, *viz.* the happiness and prosperity of the community; it behoves you well to consider, uninfluenced by the authority of names. Instead of that frenzy of enthusiasm, that has actuated the citizens of Philadelphia, in their approbation of the proposed plan, before it was possible that it could be the result of a rational investigation into its principles; it ought to be dispassionately and deliberately examined, and its own intrinsic merit the only criterion of your patronage. If ever free and unbiassed discussion was proper or necessary, it is on such an occasion.—All the blessings of liberty and the dearest privileges of freemen, are now at stake and dependent on your present conduct. Those who are competent to the task of developing the principles of government, ought to be encouraged to come forward, and thereby the better enable the people to make a proper judgment; for the science of government is so abstruse, that few are able to judge for themselves; without such assistance the people are too apt to yield an implicit assent to the opinions of those characters, whose abilities are held in the highest esteem, and to those in whose integrity and patriotism they can confide; not considering that the love of domination is generally in proportion to talents, abilities, and superior acquirements; and that the men of the greatest purity of intention may be made instruments of despotism in the hands of the *artful and designing.* If it were not for the stability and attachment which time and habit gives to forms of government, it would be in the power of the enlightened and aspiring few, if they should combine, at any time to destroy the best establishments, and even make the people the instruments of their own subjugation.

The late revolution having effaced in a great measure all former habits, and the present institutions are so recent, that their exists not that great reluctance to innovation, so remarkable in old communities, and which accords with reason, for the most comprehensive mind cannot foresee the full operation of material changes on civil polity; it is the genius of the common law to resist innovation.

The wealthy and ambitious, who in every community think they have a right to lord it over their fellow creatures, have availed themselves, very successfully, of this favorable disposition; for the people thus unsettled in their sentiments, have been prepared to accede to any extreme of government; all the distresses and difficulties they experience, proceeding from various causes, have been ascribed to the impotency of the present confederation, and thence they have been led to expect full relief from the adoption of the proposed system of government; and in the other event, immediately ruin and annihilation as a nation. These characters flatter themselves that they have lulled all distrust and jealousy of their new plan, by gaining the concurrence of the two men in whom America has the highest confidence, and now triumphantly exult in the completion of their long meditated schemes of power and aggrandisement. I would be very far from insinuating that the two illustrious personages alluded to, have not the welfare of their country at heart; but that the unsuspecting goodness and zeal of the one, has been imposed on, in a subject of which he must be necessarily inexperienced, from his other arduous engagements; and that the weakness and indecision attendant on old age, has been practised on in the other.

I am fearful that the principles of government inculcated in Mr. Adams's treatise, and enforced in the numerous essays and paragraphs in the news-papers, have misled some well designing members of the late Convention.—But it will appear in the sequel, that the construction of the proposed plan of government is infinitely more extravagant.

I have been anxiously expecting that some enlightened patriot would, ere this, have taken up the pen to expose the futility, and counteract the baneful tendency of such principles. Mr. Adams's *sine qua non* of a good government is three balancing powers, whose repelling qualities are to produce an equilibrium of interests, and thereby promote the happiness of the whole community. He asserts that the administrators of every government, will ever be actuated by views of private interest and ambition, to the prejudice of the public good; that therefore the only effectual method to secure the rights of the people and promote their welfare, is to create an opposition of interests between the members of two distinct bodies, in the exercise of the powers of government, and balanced by those of a third. This hypothesis supposes human wisdom competent to the talk of instituting three co-equal orders in government, and a corresponding weight in the community to enable them respectively to exercise their several parts, and whose views and interests should be so distinct as to prevent a coalition of any two of them for the destruction of the third. Mr. Adams, although he has traced the constitution of every form of government that ever existed, as far as history affords materials, has not been able to adduce a single instance of such a government; he indeed says that the British constitution is such in theory, but this is rather a confirmation that his principles are chimerical and not to be reduced to practice. If such an organization of power were practicable, how long would it continue? not a day—for there is so great a disparity in the talents, wisdom and industry of mankind, that the scale would presently preponderate to one or the other body, and with every accession of power the means of further increase would be greatly extended. The state of society in England is much more favorable to such a scheme of government than that of America. There they have a powerful hereditary nobility, and real distinctions of rank and interests; but even there, for want of that perfect equallity of power and distinction of interests, in the three orders of government, they exist but in name; the only operative and efficient check, upon the conduct of administration, is the sense of the people at large.

Suppose a government could be formed and supported on such principles, would it answer the great purposes of civil society; If the administrators of every government are actuated by views of private interest and ambition, how is the welfare and happiness of the community to be the result of such jarring adverse interests?

Therefore, as different orders in government will not produce the good of the whole, we must recur to other principles. I believe it will be found that the form of government, which holds those entrusted with power, in the greatest responsibility to their constituents, the best calculated for freemen. A republican, or free government, can only exist where the body of the people are virtuous, and where property is pretty equally divided, in such a government the people are the sovereign and their sense or opinion is the criterion of every public measure; for when this ceases to be the case, the nature of the government is changed, and an aristocracy, monarchy or despotism will rise on its ruin. The highest responsibility is to be attained, in a simple struction of government, for the great body of the people never steadily attend to the operations of government, and for want of due information are liable to be imposed on.—If you complicate the plan by various orders, the people will be perplexed and divided in their sentiments about the source of abuses or misconduct, some will impute it to the senate, others to the house of representatives, and so on, that the interposition of the people may be rendered imperfect or perhaps wholly abortive. But if, imitating the constitution of Pennsylvania, you vest all the legislative power in one body of men (separating the executive and judicial) elected for a short period, and necessarily excluded by rotation from permanency, and guarded from precipitancy and surprise by delays imposed on its proceedings, you will create the most perfect responsibility, for then, whenever the people feel a grievance they cannot mistake the authors, and will apply the remedy with certainty and effect, discarding them at the next election. This tie of responsibility will obviate all the dangers apprehended from a single legislature, and will the best secure the rights of the people.

Having promised thus much, I shall now proceed to the examination of the proposed plan of government, and I trust, shall make it appear to the meanest capacity, that it has none of the essential requisites of a free government, that it is neither founded on those balancing restraining powers, recommended by Mr. Adams and attempted in the British constitution, or possessed of that responsibility to its constituents, which, in my opinion, is the only effectual security for the liberties and happiness of the people; but on the contrary, that it is a most daring attempt to establish a despotic aristocracy among freemen, that the world has ever witnessed.

I shall previously consider the extent of the powers intended to be vested in Congress, before I examine the construction of the general government.

It will not be controverted that the legislative is the highest delegated power in government, and that all others are subordinate to it. The celebrated *Montesquieu* establishes it as a maxim, that legislation necessarily follows the power of taxation. By sect. 8, of the first article of the proposed plan of government, "the Congress are to have power to lay and collect taxes, duties, imposts and excises, to pay the debts and provide for the common defence and *general welfare* of the United States; but all duties, imposts and excises, shall be uniform throughout the United States." Now what can be more comprehensive than these words; not content by other sections of this plan, to grant all the great executive powers of a confederation, and a STANDING ARMY IN TIME OF PEACE, that grand engine of oppression, and moreover the absolute controul over the commerce of the United States and all external objects of revenue, such as unlimited imposts upon imports, &c.—they are to be vested with every species of *internal* taxation;—whatever taxes, duties and excises that they may deem requisite for the *general welfare*, may be imposed on the citizens of these states, levied by the officers of Congress, distributed through every district in America; and the collection would be enforced by the standing army, however grievous or improper they may be. The Congress may construe every purpose for which the state legislatures now lay taxes, to be for the *general welfare*, and thereby seize upon every object of revenue.

The judicial power by 1st sect. of article 3 ["]shall extend to all cases, in law and equity, arising under this constitution, the laws of the United States, and treaties made or which shall be made under their authority; to all cases affecting ambassadors, other public ministers and consuls; to all cases of admiralty and maritime jurisdiction, to controversies to which the United States shall be a party, to controversies between two or more states, between a state and citizens of another state, between citizens of different states, between citizens of the same state claiming lands under grants of different states, and between a state, or the citizens thereof, and foreign states, citizens or subjects."

The judicial power to be vested in one Supreme Court, and in such Inferior Courts as the Congress may from time to time ordain and establish.

The objects of jurisdiction recited above, are so numerous, and the shades of distinction between civil causes are oftentimes so slight, that it is more than probable that the state judicatories would be wholly superceded, for in contests about jurisdiction, the federal court, as the most powerful, would ever prevail. Every person acquainted with the history of the courts in England, knows by what ingenious sophisms they have, at different periods, extended the sphere of their jurisdiction over objects out of the line of their institution, and contrary to their very nature; courts of a criminal jurisdiction obtaining cognizance in civil causes.

To put the omnipotency of Congress over the state government and judicatories out of all doubt, the 6th article ordains that "this constitution and the laws of the United States which shall be made in pursuance thereof, and all treaties made, or which shall be made under the authority of the United States, shall be the *Supreme law of the land,* and the judges in every state shall be bound thereby, any thing in the constitution or laws of any state to the contrary notwithstanding."

By these sections the all prevailing power of taxation, and such extensive legislative and judicial powers are vested in the general government, as must in their operation, necessarily absorb the state legislatures and judicatories; and that such was in the contemplation of the framers of it, will appear from the provision made for such event, in another part of it; (but that, fearful of alarming the people by so great an innovation, they have suffered the forms of the separate governments to remain, as a blind). By sect. 4th of the 1st article, "the times, places and manner of holding elections for senators and representatives, shall be prescribed in each state by the legislature thereof; *but the Congress may at any time, by law, make or alter such regulations, except as to the place of abusing senators.*" The plain construction of which is, that when the state legislatures drop out of sight, from the necessary operation of this government, then Congress are to provide for the election and appointment of representatives and senators.

If the foregoing be a just comment—if the United States are to be melted down into one empire, it becomes you to consider, whether such a government, however constructed, would be eligible in so extended a territory; and whether it would be practicable, consistent with freedom? It is the opinion of the greatest writers, that a very extensive country cannot be governed on democratical principles, on any other plan, than a confederation of a number of small republics, possessing all the powers of internal government, but united in the management of their foreign and general concerns.

It would not be difficult to prove, that any thing short of despotism, could not bind so great a country under one government; and that whatever plan you might, at the first setting out, establish, it would issue in a despotism.

If one general government could be instituted and maintained on principles of freedom, it would not be so competent to attend to the various local concerns and wants, of every particular district; as well as the peculiar governments, who are nearer the scene, and possessed of superior means of information, besides, if the business of the *whole* union is to be managed by one government, there would not be time. Do we not already see, that the inhabitants in a number of larger states, who are remote from the seat of government, are loudly complaining of the inconveniencies and disadvantages they are subjected to on this account, and that, to enjoy the comforts of local government, they are separating into smaller divisions.

Having taken a review of the powers, I shall now examine the construction of the proposed general government.

Art. 1 sect. 1. "All legislative powers herein granted shall be vested in a Congress of the United States, which shall consist of a senate and house of representatives." By another section, the president (the principal executive officer) has a conditional controul over their proceedings.

Sec. 2. "The house of representatives shall be composed of members chosen every second year, by the people of the several states. The number of representatives shall not exceed one for every 30,000 inhabitants."

The senate, the other constituent branch of the legislature, is formed by the legislature of each state appointing two senators, for the term of six years.

The executive power by Art. 2, Sec. 1. is to be vested in a president of the United States of America, elected for four years: Sec. 2. gives him power, by and with the consent of the senate to make treaties, provided two thirds of the senators present concur; and he shall nominate, and by and with the advice and consent of the senate, shall appoint ambassadors, other public ministers and consuls, judges of the Supreme Court, and all other officers of the United States, whose appointments are not herein otherwise provided for, and which shall be established by law, &c. And by another section he has the absolute power of granting reprievs and pardons for treason and all other high crimes and misdemeanors, except in case of impeachment.

The foregoing are the outlines of the plan.

Thus we see, the house of representatives, are on the part of the people to balance the senate, who I suppose will be composed of the *better sort*, the *well born*, &c. The number of the representatives (being only one for every 30,000 inhabitants) appears to be too few, either to communicate the requisite information, of the wants, local circumstances and sentiments of so extensive an empire, or to prevent corruption and undue influence, in the exercise of such great powers; the term for which they are to be chosen, too long to preserve a due dependence and accountability to their constituents; and the mode and places of their election not sufficiently ascertained, for as Congress have the controul over both, they may govern the choice, by ordering the *representatives* of a *whole* state, to be *elected* in *one* place, and that too may be the most *inconvenient*.

The senate, the great efficient body in this plan of government, is constituted on the most unequal principles. The smallest state in the union has equal weight with the great States of Virginia, Massachusetts, or Pennsylvania.—The Senate, besides its legislative functions, has a very considerable share in the Executive; none of the principal appointments to office can be made without its advice and consent. The term and mode of its appointment, will lead to permanency; the members are chosen for six years, the mode is under the controul of Congress, and as there is no exclusion by rotation, they may be continued for life, which, from their extensive means of influence, would follow of course. The President, who would be a mere pageant of state, unless he coincides with the views of the Senate, would either become the head of the aristocratic junto in that body, or its minion; besides, their influence being the most predominant, could the best secure his re election to office. And from his power of granting pardons, he might screen from punishment the most reasonable attempts on the liberties of the people, when instigated by the Senate.

From this investigation into the organization of this government, it appears that it is devoid of all responsibility or accountability to the great body of the people, and that so far from being a regular balanced government, it would be in practice a *permanent* ARISTOCRACY.

The framers of it; actuated by the true spirit of such a government, which ever abominates and suppresses all free enquiry and discussion, have made no provision for the *liberty of the press*, that grand *palladium of freedom*, and *scourge of tyrants;* but observed a total silence on that head. It is the opinion of some great writers, that if the liberty of the press, by an institution of religion, or otherwise, could be rendered *sacred*, even in *Turkey*, that despotism would fly before it. And it is worthy of remark, that there is no declaration of personal rights, premised in most free constitutions; and that trial by *jury* in *civil* cases is taken away; for what other construction can be put on the following, viz. Article III. Sect. 2d. "In all cases affecting ambassadors, other public ministers and consuls, and those in which a State shall be party, the Supreme Court shall have *original* jurisdiction. In all the other cases above mentioned, the Supreme Court shall have *appellate* jurisdiction, both as to *law and fact?*" It would be a novelty in jurisprudence, as well as evidently improper to allow an appeal from the verdict of a jury, on the matter of fact; therefore, it implies and allows of a dismission of the jury in civil cases, and especially when it is considered, that jury trial in criminal cases is expressly stipulated for, but not in civil cases.

But our situation is represented to be so *critically* dreadful, that, however reprehensible and exceptionable the proposed plan of government may be, there is no alternative, between the adoption of it and absolute ruin.—My fellow citizens, things are not at that crisis, it is the argument of tyrants; the present distracted state of Europe secures us from injury on that quarter, and as to domestic dissentions, we have not so much to fear from them, as to precipitate us into this form of government, without it is a safe and a proper one. For remember, of all *possible* evils, that of *despotism* is the *worst* and the most to be *dreaded*.

Besides, it cannot be supposed, that the first essay on so difficult a subject, is so well digested, as it ought to be;—if the proposed plan, after a mature deliberation, should meet the approbation of the respective States, the matter will end; but if it should be found to be fraught with dangers and inconveniencies, a future general Convention being in possession of the objections, will be the better enabled to plan a suitable government.

"WHO'S HERE SO BASE, THAT WOULD A BOND-MAN BE?
IF ANY, SPEAK; FOR HIM HAVE I OFFENED.
WHO'S HERE SO VILE, THAT WILL NOT LOVE HIS COUNTRY?
IF ANY, SPEAK; FOR HIM HAVE I OFFENDED."

CENTINEL.

Freeman's Journal

24 OCTOBER 1787

LETTER II

Centinel warns that the new government's powers will extend beyond those explicitly delegated to it, and will allow it to violate freedom of the press. In addition, federal courts will exercise extensive jurisdiction, without guaranteeing jury trials in civil cases. Centinel wrongly asserts that the Constitution gives federal courts jurisdiction over controversies between states and their own citizens. Essays in The Federalist *of particular relevance: 44, 82-84.*

To the PEOPLE *of* PENNSYLVANIA.

FRIENDS, COUNTRYMEN, *AND* FELLOW-CITIZENS,

AS long as the liberty of the press continues unviolated, and the people have the right of expressing and publishing their sentiments upon every public measure, it is next to impossible to enslave a free nation. The state of society must be very corrupt and base indeed, when the people in possession of such a monitor as the press, can be induced to exchange the heaven-born blessings of liberty for the galling chains of despotism.—Men of an aspiring and tyrannical disposition, sensible of this truth, have ever been inimical to the press, and have considered the shackling of it, as the first step towards the accomplishment of their hateful domination, and the entire suppression of all liberty of public discussion, as necessary to its support.—For even a standing army, that grand engine of oppression, if it were as numerous as the abilities of any nation could maintain, would not be equal to the purposes of despotism over an enlightened people.

The abolition of that grand palladium of freedom, the liberty of the press, in the proposed plan of government, and the conduct of its authors, and patrons, is a striking exemplification of their observations. The reason assigned for the omission of a *bill of rights*, securing the *liberty of the press*, and *other invaluable personal rights*, is an insult on the understanding of the people.

The injunction of secrecy imposed on the members of the late Convention during their deliberations, was obviously dictated by the genius of Aristocracy; it was deemed impolitic to unfold the principles of the intended government to the people, as this would have frustrated the object in view.

The projectors of the new plan, supposed that an ex parte discussion of the subject, was more likely to obtain unanimity in the Convention; which would give it such a sanction in the public opinion, as to banish all distrust, and lead the people into an implicit adoption of it without examination.

The greatest minds are forcibly impressed by the immediate circumstances with which they are connected; the particular sphere men move in, the prevailing sentiments of those they converse with, have an insensible and irresistible influence on the wisest and best of mankind, so that when we consider the abilities, talents, ingenuity and consummate address of a number of the members of the late Convention, whose principles are despotic, can we be surprised that men of the best intentions have been misled in the difficult science of government? Is it derogating from the character of the *illustrious and highly revered* WASHINGTON, to suppose him fallible on a subject that must be in a great measure novel to him?— As a patriotic hero, he stands unequalled in the annals of time.

The new plan was accordingly ushered to the public with such a splendor of names, as inspired the most unlimited confidence; the people were disposed to receive upon trust, without any examination on their part, what would have proved either a *blessing* or a *curse* to them and their posterity.—What astonishing infatuation to stake their happiness on the wisdom and integrity of any set of men! In matters of infinitely smaller concern, the dictates of prudence are not disregarded! The celebrated Montesquieu, in his Spirit of Laws, says, that "slavery is ever preceded by sleep." And again, in his account of the rise and fall of the Roman Empire, page 97, "That it may be advanced as a general rule, that in a free State, whenever a perfect calm is visible, the spirit of liberty no longer subsists." And Mr. [Dickinson], in his Farmer's Letters,

No. XI.[,] lays it down as a maxim, that "A perpetual jealousy respecting liberty is absolutely requisite in all free States."

"Happy are the men, and happy the people, who grow wise by the misfortunes of others. Earnestly, my dear countrymen, do I beseech the author of all good gifts, that you may grow wise in this manner, and I beg leave to recommend to you in general, as the best method of obtaining this wisdom, diligently to study the histories of other countries. You will there find all the arts, that can possibly be practiced by cunning rulers, or false patriots among yourselves, so fully delineated, that changing names, the account would serve for your own times."

A *few* citizens of Philadelphia (too few, for the honour of human nature) who had the wisdom to think *consideration* ought to precede *approbation*, and the fortitude to avow that they would take time to judge for themselves on so momentous an occasion, were stigmatized as enemies to their country; as monsters, whose existence ought not to be suffered, and the destruction of them and their houses recommended, as meritorious.—The authors of the new plan, conscious that it would not stand the test of enlightened patriotism, tyrannically endeavoured to preclude all investigation.—If their views were laudable; if they were honest,—the contrary would have been their conduct, they would have invited the freest discussion. Whatever specious reasons may be assigned for secrecy during the framing of the plan, no good one can exist, for leading the people blind-folded into the implicit adoption of it. Such an attempt does not augur the public good—It carries on the face of it an intention to juggle the people out of their liberties.

The virtuous and spirited exertions of a few patriots, have at length roused the people from their fatal infatuation to a due sense of the importance of the measure before them. The glare and fascination of names is rapidly abating, and the subject begins to be canvassed on its own merits; and so serious and general has been the impression of the objections urged against the new plan, on the minds of the people, that its advocates, finding mere declamation and scurrility will no longer avail, are reluctantly driven to defend it on the ground of argument. Mr. *Wilson*, one of the deputies of this State in the late Convention, has found it necessary to come forward. From so able a lawyer, and so profound a politician, what might not be expected, if this act of Convention be the heavenly dispensation which some represent it. Its divinity would certainly be illustrated by one of the principal instruments of the Revelation; for this gentleman has that transcendent merit!—But if, on the other hand, this able advocate has failed to vindicate it from the objections of its adversaries, must we not consider it is as the production of *frail* and *interested* men.

Mr. *Wilson* has recourse to the most flimsey sophistry in his attempt to refute the charge that the new plan of general government will supersede and render powerless the state governments. His quibble upon the term *Corporation*, as sometimes equivalent to communities which possess sovereignty, is unworthy of him. The same comparison in the case of the British parliament assuming to tax the colonies, is made in the Xth of the Farmer's Letters, and was not misunderstood in 1768 by any. He says that the existence of the proposed federal plan depends on the existence of the State governments, as the senators are to be appointed by the several legislatures, who are also to nominate the electors who chuse the President of the United States; and that hence all fears of the several States being melted down into one empire, are groundless and imaginary.—But who is so dull as not to comprehend, that the *semblance* and *forms* of an ancient establishment, may remain, after the *reality* is gone.—*Augustus*, by the aid of a great army, assumed despotic power, and notwithstanding this, we find even under Tiberius, Caligula and Nero, princes who disgraced human nature by their excesses, the shadows of the ancient constitution held up to amuse the people. The senate sat as formerly; consuls, tribunes of the people, censors and other officers were annually chosen as before, and the forms of republican government continued. Yet all this was in *appearance* only.—Every *senatus consultum* was dictated by him or his ministers, and every Roman found himself constrained to submit in all things to the despot.

Mr. *Wilson* asks, "What controul can proceed from the federal government to shackle or destroy that *sacred palladium* of national freedom, the *liberty of the press?*" What!—Cannot Congress, when possessed of the immense authority proposed to be devolved, restrain the printers, and put them under regulation.—Recollect that the omnipotence of the federal legislature over the State establishments is recognized by a special article, viz.—"that this Constitution, and the laws of the United States which shall be made in pursuance thereof, and all treaties made, or which shall be made, under the authority of the United States, shall be the *Supreme law* of the land; and the judges in every State shall be bound thereby, any thing in the *Constitutions* or laws of any State to the contrary notwithstanding."—After such a declaration, what security does the *Constitutions* of the several States afford for the *liberty of the press and other invaluable personal rights*, not provided for by the new plan?—Does not this sweeping clause subject every thing to the controul of Congress?

In the plan of Confederation of 1778, now existing, it was thought proper by Article the 2d, to declare that "each State retains its sovereignty, freedom and independence, and every power, jurisdiction and right, which is not by this Confederation expressly delegated to the United States in Congress assembled." *Positive* grant was not *then* thought sufficiently descriptive and restraining upon Congress, and the omission of such a declaration *new*, when such great devolutions of power are proposed, manifests the design of reducing the several States to shadows. But Mr. Wilson tells you, that every right and power not specially granted to Congress is considered as withheld. How does this appear? Is this principle established by the proper authority? Has the Convention made such a stipulation? By no means. Quite the reverse; the *laws* of Congress are to be "the *supreme law* of the land, any thing in the *Constitutions* or laws of any State to the contrary notwithstanding"; and consequently, would be *paramount* to all *State* authorities. The lust of power is so universal, that a speculative unascertained rule of construction would be a *poor* security for the liberties of the people.

Such a body as the intended Congress, unless particularly inhibited and restrained, must grasp at omnipotence, and before long swallow up the Legislative, the Executive, and the Judicial powers of the several States.

In addition to the respectable authorities quoted in my first number, to shew that the right of *taxation* includes all the powers of government, I beg leave to adduce the Farmer's Letters, see particularly letter 9th, in which Mr. Dickinson has clearly proved, that if the British Parliament assumed the power of taxing the colonies, *internally*, as well as *externally*, and it should be submitted to, the several colony legislatures would soon become contemptible, and before long fall into disuse.—Nothing, says he, would be left for them to do, higher than to frame bye-laws for empounding of cattle or the yoking of hogs.

By the proposed plan, there are divers cases of judicial authority to be given to the courts of the United States, besides the two mentioned by Mr. *Wilson.*—In maritime causes about property, jury trial has not been usual; but in suits in *equity*, with all due deference to Mr. *Wilson's* professional abilities, (which he calls to his aid) jury trial, as to facts, is in full exercise. Will this jurisperitus say that if the question in equity should be, did *John Doe* make a will, that the chancellor of England would decide upon it? He well knows that in this case, there being no mode of jury trial before the chancellor, the question would be referred to the court of king's bench for discussion according to the common law, and when the judge in equity should receive the verdict, the fact so established, could never be reexamined or controverted. *Maritime* causes and those appertaining, to a court of equity, are, however, but two of the many and extensive subjects of federal cognizance mentioned in the plan. This jurisdiction will embrace all suits arising under the laws of impost, excise and other revenue of the United States. In England if goods be seized, if a ship be prosecuted for noncompliance with, or breach of the laws of the customs, or those for regulating trade, in the court of exchequer, the claimant is secured of the transcendent privilege of Englishmen, *trial by a jury of his peers.* Why not in the United States of America? This jurisdiction also goes to all cases under the laws of the United States, that is to say, under all statutes and ordinances of Congress. How far this may extend, it is easy to foresee; for upon the decay of the state powers of legislation, in consequence of the loss of the *purse strings*, it will be found necessary for the federal legislature to make laws upon every subject of legislation. Hence the state courts of justice, like the barony and hundred courts of England, will be eclipsed and gradually fall into disuse.

The jurisdiction of the federal court goes, likewise, to the laws to be created by treaties, made by the President and Senate, (a species of legislation) with other nations; "to all cases affecting foreign ministers and consuls; to controversies wherein the United States shall be a party; to controversies between citizens of different states," as when an inhabitants of *New York* has a demand on an inhabitant of *New Jersey*.—This last is a very invidious jurisdiction, implying an improper distrust of the impartiality and justice of the tribunals of the states. It will include all legal debates between foreigners in Britain, or elsewhere, and the people of this country.—A reason hath been assigned for it, viz. "That large tracts of land, in neighbouring states, are claimed under royal or other grants, disputed by the states where the lands lie, so that justice cannot be expected from the state tribunals."—Suppose it were proper indeed to provide for such case, why include all cases, and for all time to come? Demands as to land for 21 years would have satisfied this. A London merchant shall come to America, and sue for his supposed debt, and the citizen of this country shall be deprived of jury trial, and subjected to an appeal (tho' nothing but the *fact* is disputed) to a court 500 or 1000 miles from home; when if this American has a claim upon an inhabitant of England, his adversary is secured of the privilege of jury trial.—This jurisdiction goes also to controversies between any state and its citizens; which, though *probably* not intended, may hereafter be set up as a ground to divest the states, severally, of the trial of criminals; inasmuch as every charge of felony or misdemeanour, is a controversy between the state and a citizen of the same: that is to say, the state is plaintiff and the party accused is defendant in the prosecution. In all doubts about jurisprudence, as was observed before, the paramount courts of Congress will decide, and the judges of the state, being *sub graviere irge*,[1] under the paramount law, must acquiesce.

1. Should "irge" be read as "lege" or as "loi," this phrase means "beneath a higher law."

Mr. *Wilson* says, that it would have been impracticable to have made a general rule for jury trial in the civil cases assigned to the federal judiciary, because of the want of uniformity in the mode of jury trial, as practiced by the several states. This objection proves too much, and therefore amounts to nothing. If it precludes the mode of common law in civil cases, it certainly does in criminal. Yet in these we are told "the oppression of government is effectually barred by declaring that in all criminal cases *trial by jury* shall be preserved." Astonishing, that provision could not be made for a jury in civil controversies, of 12 men, whose verdict should be unanimous, *to be taken from the vicinage;* a precaution which is omitted to trial of crimes, which may be any where in the state within which they have been committed. So that an inhabitant of *Kentucky* may be tried for treason at *Richmond.*

The abolition of jury trial in civil cases, is the more considerable, as at length the courts of Congress will supersede the state courts, when such mode of trial will fall into disuse among the people of the United States.

The northern nations of the European continent, have all lost this invaluable privilege: *Sweden*, the last of them, by the artifices of the *aristocratic* senate, which depressed the king and reduced the house of commons to insignificance. But the nation a few years ago, preferring the absolute authority of a monarch to the *vexatitus* domination of the *well-born* few, an end was suddenly put to their power.

"The policy of this right of juries, (says judge Blackstone) to decide upon *fact*, is founded on this: That if the power of judging were entirely trusted with the magistrates, or any select body of men, named by the executive authority, their decisions, in spite of their own natural integrity, would have a biass towards those of their own rank and dignity; for it is not to be expected, that the *few* should be attentive to the rights of the *many*. This therefore preserves in the hands of the people, that share which they ought to have in the administration of justice, and prevents the encroachments of the more powerful and wealthy citizens."

The attempt of governor *Colden*, of New-York, before the revolution to re-examine the *facts* and re-consider the *damages*, in the case of *Forsey* against *Cunningham*, produced about the year 1764, a flame of patriotic and successful opposition, that will not be easily forgotten.

To manage the various and extensive judicial authority, proposed to be vested in Congress, there will be one or more inferior courts immediately requisite in each state; and laws and regulations must be forthwith provided to direct the judges—here is a wide door for inconvenience to enter. Contracts made under the acts of the states respectively, will come before courts acting under new laws and new modes of proceeding, not thought of when they were entered into.—An inhabitant of Pennsylvania residing at Pittsburgh, finds the goods of his debtor, who resides in Virginia, within the reach of his attachment; but no writ can be had to authorise the marshal, sheriff, or other officer of Congress, to seize the property, about to be removed, nearer than 200 miles: suppose that at Carlisle, for instance, such a writ may be had, mean while the object escapes. Or if an inferior court, whose judges have ample salaries, be established in every county, would not the expense be enormous? Every reader can extend in his imagination, the instances of difficulty which would proceed from this needless interference with the judicial rights of the separate states, and which as much as any other circumstance in the new plan, implies that the dissolution of their forms of government is designed.

Mr. *Wilson* skips very lightly over the danger apprehended from the standing army allowed by the new plan. This grand machine of power and oppression, may be made a fatal instrument to overturn the public liberties, especially as the fund to support the troops may be granted for *two* years, whereas in Britain, the grants ever since the revolution in 1688, have been *from year to year.* A standing army with regular provision of pay and contingencies, would afford a strong temptation to some ambitious man to step up into the throne, and to seize absolute power. The keeping on foot a hired military force *in time of peace,* ought not to be gone into, unless *two thirds* of the members of the federal legislature agree to the necessity of the measure, and adjust the numbers employed. Surely Mr. *Wilson* is not serious when he adduces the instance of the troops now stationed on the Ohio, as a proof of the propriety of a standing army.—They are a mere occasional armament for the purpose of restraining divers hostile tribes of savages. It is contended that under the present confederation, Congress possess the power of raising armies at pleasure; but the opportunity, which the states severally have of withholding the supplies necessary to keep these armies on foot, is a sufficient check on the *present* Congress.

Mr. *Wilson* asserts, that never was charge made with less reason, than that which predicts the institution of a *baneful aristocracy* in the federal Senate.—In my first number; I stated that this body would be a very unequal representation of the several states, that the members being appointed for the long term of six years, and there being no exclusion by rotation, they might be continued for life, which would follow of course from their extensive means of influence, and that possessing a considerable share in the *executive* as well as *legislative*, it would become a *permanent aristocracy*, and swallow up the other orders in the government.

That these fears are not imaginary, a knowledge of the history of other nations, where the powers of government have been injudiciously placed, will fully demonstrate. Mr. *Wilson* says, "the senate branches into two characters; the one legislative and the other executive. In its legislative character it can effect no purpose, without the co-operation of the house of representatives, and in its executive character it can accomplish no object without the concurrence of the president. Thus fettered, I do not know any act which the senate can of itself perform, and such dependence necessarily precludes every idea of influence and superiority." This I confess is very specious, but experience demonstrates, that checks in government, unless accompanied with *adequate* power and *independently* placed, prove *merely nominal*, and will be *inoperative*. Is it probable, that the president of the United States, limited as he is in power, and dependent on the will of the senate, in appointments to office, will either have the *firmness* or *inclination* to exercise his prerogative of a conditional controul upon the proceedings of that body, however, injurious they may be to the public welfare: it will be his interest to coincide with the views of the senate, and thus become the head of the aristocratic junto. The king of England is a constituent part in the legislature, but although an hereditary monarchy in possession of the whole executive power, including the unrestrained appointment to offices, and an immense revenue, enjoys but in *name* the prerogative of a negative upon the parliament. Even the king of England, circumstanced as he is, has not dared to exercise it for near a century past. The check of the house of representatives upon the senate will likewise be rendered nugatory for want of due weight in the democratic branch, and from their constitution *they* may become so *independent* of the *people* as to be indifferent of its interests: may as Congress would have the controul over the mode and place of their election, by ordering the representatives of a *whole* state to be elected at *one* place, and that too the most *inconvenient*, the ruling power may govern the *choice*, and thus the house of representatives may be composed of the *creatures* of the senate. Still the *semblance* of checks, may remain but without *operation*.

This mixture of the legislative and executive moreover highly tends to corruption. The chief improvement in government, in modern times, has been the compleat separation of the great distinctions of power; placing the *legislative* in different hands from those which hold the *executive;* and again severing the *judicial* part from the ordinary *administrative*. "When the legislative and executive powers (says Montesquieu) are united in the same person, or in the same body of magistrates, there can be no liberty."

Mr. *Wilson* confesses himself, not satisfied with the organization of the federal senate, and apologizes for it, by alledging a sort of compromise. It is well known, that some members of convention, apprized of the mischiefs of such a compound of authority, proposed to assign the supreme executive powers to the president and a small council, made personally responsible for every appointment to office, or other act, by having their opinions recorded; and that without the concurrence of the majority of the quorum of this council, the president should not be capable of taking any step. Such a check upon the chief magistrate would admirably secure the power of pardoning, now proposed to be exercised by the president alone, from abuse. For as it is placed he may shelter the traitors whom he himself or his coadjutors in the senate, have excited to plot against the liberties of the nation.

The delegation of the power of taxation to Congress, as far as duties on imported commodities, has not been objected to. But to extend this to excises, and every species of internal taxation, would necessarily require so many ordinances of Congress, affecting the body of the people, as would perpetually interfere with the State laws and personal concerns of the people. This alone would directly tend to annihilate the particular governments; for the people fatigued with the operations of two masters would be apt to rid themselves of the weaker. But we are cautioned against being alarmed with imaginary evils, for Mr. *Wilson* has predicted that the great revenue of the United States, will be raised by impost. Is there any ground for this? Will the impost supply the sums necessary to pay the interest and principal of the foreign loan, to defray the great additional expence of the new constitution; for the policy of the new government will lead it to institute numerous and lucrative civil offices, to extend its influence and provide for the swarms of expectants; (the people having in fact no controul upon its disbursements) and to afford pay and support for the proposed standing army, that darling and long wished for object of the *well-born* of America; and which, if we may judge from the principles of the intended government, will be no trifling establishment, for cantonments of troops in every district of America, will be necessary to compel the submission of the people to the arbitrary dictates of the ruling powers? I say will the impost be adequate? By no means.—To answer these there must be excises and other indirect duties imposed, and as land taxes will operate too equally to be agreeable to the wealthy aristocracy in the senate who will be possessed of the government, *poll taxes* will be substituted as provided for in the new plan; for the doctrine then will be, *that slaves ought to pay for wearing their beads.*

As the taxes necessary for these purposes, will drain your pockets of every penny, what is to become of that virtuous and meritorious class of citizens the public creditors. However well disposed the people of the United States may be to do them justice, it would not be in their power; and, *after waiting year after year*, without prospect of the payment of the interest or principal of the debt, they will be constrained to sacrifice their certificates in the purchase of waste lands in the far distant wilds of the western territory.

From the foregoing illustration of the powers proposed to be devolved to Congress, it is evident, that the general government would necessarily annihilate the particular governments, and that the security of the personal rights of the people by the state constitutions is superseded and destroyed; hence results the necessity of such security being provided for by a bill of rights to be inserted in the new plan of federal government. What excuse can we then make for the omission of this grand palladium, this barrier between *liberty* and *oppression*. For universal experience demonstrates the necessity of the most express declarations and restrictions, to protect the rights and liberties of mankind, from the silent, powerful and ever active conspiracy of those who govern.

The new plan, it is true, does propose to secure the people of the benefit of personal liberty by the *habeas corpus;* and trial by jury for all crimes, except in case of impeachment: but there is no declaration, that all men have a natural and unalienable right to worship Almighty God, according to the dictates of their own consciences and understanding; and that no man ought, or of right can be compelled to attend any religious worship, or erect or support any place of worship, or maintain any ministry, contrary to, or against his own free will and consent; and that no authority can or ought to be vested in, or assumed by any power whatever, that shall in any case interfere with, or in any manner controul, the right of conscience in the free exercise of religious worship; that the trial by jury in civil causes as well as criminal, and the modes prescribed by the common law for safety of life in criminal prosecutions shall be held sacred; that the requiring of excessive bail, imposing of excessive fines and cruel and unusual punishments be forbidden; that monopolies in trade or arts, other than to authors of books or inventors of useful arts, for a reasonable time, ought not to be suffered; that the right of the people to assemble peaceably for the purpose of consulting about public matters, and petitioning or remonstrating to the federal legislature ought not to be prevented; that *the liberty of the press be held sacred;* that the people have a right to hold themselves, their houses, papers and possessions free from search or seizure; and that therefore warrants without oaths or affirmations first made, affording a sufficient foundation for them, and whereby any officer or messenger may be commanded or required to search suspected places, or to seize any person or his property, not particularly described, are contrary to that right and ought not to be granted; and that standing armies in time of peace are dangerous to liberty, and ought not to be permitted but when absolutely necessary; all which is omitted to be done in the proposed government.

But Mr. *Wilson* says, the new plan does not arrogate perfection, for it provides a mode of alteration and correction, if found necessary. This is one among the numerous deceptions attempted on this occasion. True, there is a mode prescribed for this purpose. But it is barely possible that amendments may be made. The fascination of power must first cease, the nature of mankind undergo a revolution, that is not to be expected on this side of eternity. For to effect this (Art. 6.) it is provided, that if *two thirds* of both houses of the federal legislature shall propose them; or when two thirds of the several states by their legislatures, shall apply for them, the federal assembly shall call a convention for proposing amendments, which when ratified by three fourths of the state legislatures, or conventions, as Congress shall see best, shall controul and alter the proposed confederation. Does history abound with examples of a voluntary relinquishment of power, however injurious to the community? No; it would require a general and successful rising of the people to effect any thing of this nature.—This provision therefore is mere sound.

The opposition to the new plan (says Mr. Wilson) proceeds from interested men, *viz.* the officers of the state governments. He had before denied that the proposed transfer of powers to Congress would annihilate the state governments. But he here lays aside the masque, and avows the fact. For, the truth of the charge against *them* must entirely rest on such consequence of the new plan. For if the state establishments are to remain unimpaired, why should officers peculiarly connected with them, be interested to oppose the adoption of the new plan? Except the collector of the impost, judge of the admiralty, and the collectors of excise (none of whom have been reckoned of the opposition) they would otherwise have nothing to apprehend.—But the charge is unworthy and may with more propriety be retorted on the expectants of office and emolument under the intended government.

The opposition is not so partial and interested as Mr. *Wilson* asserts. It consists of a respectable yeomanry throughout the union, of characters far removed above the reach of his unsupported assertions. It comprises many worthy members of the late convention, and a majority of the present Congress, for a motion made in that honorable body, for their *approbation* and *recommendation* of the new plan, was after two days animated discussion, prudently withdrawn by its advocates, and a simple *transmission** of the plan to the several states could only be obtained; yet this has been palmed upon the people as the approbation of Congress; and to strengthen the deception, the bells of the city of Philadelphia were rung for a whole day.

Are Mr. *W.*——*n*, and many of his coadjutors in the late C——n, the disinterested patriots they would have us believe? Is their conduct any recommendation of their plan of government? View them the foremost and loudest on the floor of Congress, in our Assembly, at town meetings, in founding its eulogiums:—View them preventing investigation and discussion, and in the most despotic manner endeavouring to compel its adoption by the people, with such precipitancy as to preclude the possibility of a due consideration, and then say whether the motives of these men can be pure.

**Upon the last motion being made, those who had strenuously and successfully opposed Congress giving any countenance of approbation or recommendation to this system of oppression, said,—"We have no objection to transmit the new plan of government to the several states, that they may have an opportunity of judging for themselves on so momentous a subject." Whereupon it was unanimously agreed to, in the following words. viz. "Congress having received the report of the Convention lately assembled in Philadelphia,* Resolved unanimously, *That the said report, with the resolutions and letter accompanying the same, be transmitted to the several legislatures, in order to be submitted to a convention of delegates, chosen in each state by the people thereof, in conformity to the resolves of the Convention, made and provided in that case."*

My fellow citizens, such false detestable *patriots* in every nation, have led their blind confiding country, shouting their applauses, into the jaws of *despotism* and *ruin*. May the wisdom and virtue of the people of America, save them from the usual fate of nations.

CENTINEL.

Independent Gazetteer

8 NOVEMBER 1787

LETTER III

Centinel warns his readers not to allow those who will benefit from the new Constitution to rush others into adopting it. Federalists will sit in the new Congress, to which they have given the power to set the time, place, and manner of elections, as well as power over state militias. Slaveholders, moreover, have secured a provision allowing the continued importation of slaves. Essays in The Federalist *of particular relevance: 1, 29, 42, 59, 60.*

To the PEOPLE of PENNSYLVANIA.
John 3d, verse 20th—*"For every one that doeth evil, hateth the light, neither cometh to the light, lest his deeds should be reproved. But there is nothing covered that shall not be revealed; neither hid that shall not be known. Therefore whatever ye have spoken in darkness. Shall be heard in the light: and that which ye have spoken in the ear in closets, shall be proclaimed on the housetops."* St. Luke, chap. xii, 2d and 3d verses:
Friends, Countrymen, and Fellow Citizens!
THE formation of a good government, is the greatest effort of human wisdom, actuated by disinterested patriotism; but such is the cursed nature of ambition, so prevalent among men, that it would sacrifice every thing to its selfish gratification; hence the fairest opportunities of advancing the happiness of humanity, are so

far from being properly improved, that they are too often converted to the votaries of power and domination, into the means of obtaining their nefarious ends. It will be the misfortune of America of adding to the number of examples of this kind, if the proposed plan of government should be adopted; but I trust, short as the time allowed you for consideration is, you will be so fully convinced of the truth of this, as to escape the impending danger; it is only necessary to strip the monster of its assumed garb, and to exhibit it in its native colours, to excite the universal abhorrence and rejection of every virtuous and patriotic mind.

For the sake of my dear country, for the honor of human nature, I hope and am persuaded, that the good sense of the people will enable them to rise superior to the most formidable conspiracy against the liberties of a free and enlightened nation, that the world has ever witnessed. How glorious would be the triumph! How it would immortalise the present generation in the annals of freedom!

The establishment of a government, is a subject of such momentous and lasting concern, that it should not be gone into without the clearest conviction of its propriety; which can only be the result of the fullest discussion; the most thorough investigation and dispassionate consideration of its nature, principles and construction. You are now called upon to make this decision, which involves in it, not only your fate, but that of your posterity for ages to come. Your determination will either ensure the possession of those blessings, which render life desirable, or entail those evils which make existence a curse:—that such are the consequences of a wise or improper organization of government, the history of mankind abundantly testifies. If you viewed the magnitude of the object in its true light, you would join with me in sentiment, that the new government ought not to be implicitly admitted. Consider then duly before you leap, for after the rubicon is once passed, there will be no retract.

If you were even well assured that the utmost purity of intention predominated in the production of the proposed government, such is the imperfection of human reason and knowledge, that it would not be wise in you to adopt it with precipitation in toto, for all former experience must teach you the propriety of a revision on such occasions, to correct the errors, and supply the deficiencies, that may appear necessary. In every government whose object is the public welfare, the laws are subjected to repeated revisions, in some by different orders in the governments, in others by an appeal to the judgment of the people and deliberative forms of procedure. A knowledge of this, as well as of other states, will show that in every instance where a law has been passed without the usual precautions, it has been productive of great inconvenience and evils, and frequently has not answered the end in view, a supplement becoming necessary to supply its deficiencies.

What then are we to think of the motives and designs of those men who are urging the implicit and immediate adoption of the proposed government; are they fearful, that if you exercise your good sense and discernment, you will discover the masqued aristocracy, that they are attempting to smuggle upon you, under the suspicious garb of republicanism?—When we find that the principal agents in this business, are the very men who fabricated the form of government, it certainly ought to be conclusive evidence of their invidious design to deprive us of our liberties—The circumstances attending this matter, are such as should in a peculiar manner excite your suspicion; it might not be useless to take a review of some of them.

In many of the states, particularly in this and the northern states, there are aristocratic junto's of the *well-born few*, who had been zealously endeavouring since the establishment of their constitutions, to humble that offensive *upstart, equal liberty;* but all their efforts were unavailing, the *ill-bred churl* obstinately kept his assumed station.

However, that which could not be accomplished in the several states, is now attempting through the medium of the future Congress.—Experience having shewn great defects in the present confederation, particularly in the regulation of commerce and marritime affairs; it became the universal wish of America to grant further powers, so as to make the federal government adequate to the ends of its institution. The anxiety on this head was greatly encreased, from the impoverishment and distress occasioned by the excessive importations of foreign merchandise and luxuries and consequent drain of specie, since the peace: thus the people were in the disposition of a drowning man, eager to catch at any thing that promised relief, however delusory. Such an opportunity for the acquisition of *undue* power, has never been viewed with indifference by the ambitious and designing in any age or nation, and it has accordingly been [too] successfully improved by such men among us. The deputies from this state (with the exception of two) and most of those from the other states in the union, were unfortunately of this complexion, and many of them of such superior endowments, that in an *exparte* discussion of the subject by specious glosses, they have gained the concurrence of some well-disposed men, in whom their country has great confidence, which has given a great sanction to their theme of power.

A comparison of the authority under which the convention acted, and their form of government will shew that they have despised their delegated power, and assumed sovereignty; that they have entirely annihilated the old confederation, and the particular governments of the several states, and instead thereof have established one general government that is to pervade the union; constituted on the most *unequal* principles, destitute of accountability to its constituents, and as despotic in its nature, as the Venetian aristocracy; a government that will give full scope to the magnificent designs of the *well-born;* a government where tyranny may glut its vengeance on the *low born,* unchecked by *an odious bill of rights:* as has been fully illustrated in my two preceding numbers; and yet as a blind upon the understandings of the people, they have continued the forms of the particular governments, and termed the whole a confederation of the United States, pursuant to the sentiments of that profound, but corrupt politician Machiavel, who advises any one who would change the constitution of a state, to keep as much as possible to the old forms; for then the people seeing the same officers, the same formalities, courts of justice and other outward appearances, are insensible of the alteration, and believe themselves in possession of their old government. Thus Cæsar, when he seized the Roman liberties, caused himself to be chosen dictator (which was an ancient office) continued the senate, the consuls, the tribunes, the censors, and all other offices and forms of the commonwealth; and yet changed Rome from the most free, to the most tyrannical government in the world.

The convention, after vesting all the great and efficient powers of sovereignty in the general government, insidiously declare by section 4th of article 4th, "that the United States shall guarantee to every state in this union, a republican *form* of government"; but of what avail will be the *form*, without the *reality* of freedom.

The late convention in the majesty of its assumed omnipotence, have not even condescended to submit the plan of the new government to the consideration of the people, the true source of authority; but have called upon them by their several constitutions, to 'assent to and ratify'* in toto, what they have been pleased to decree; just as the grand monarque of France requires the parliament of Paris to register his edicts without revision or alteration, which is necessary previous to their execution.

The authors and advocates of the new plan, conscious that its establishment can only be obtained from the ignorance of the people of its true nature, and their unbounded confidence in some of the men concurring; have hurried on its adoption with a precipitation that betrays their design: before many had seen the new plan, and before any had time to examine it; they by their ready minions, attended by some well-disposed but mistaken persons, obtained the subscriptions of the people to papers expressing their entire approbation of, and their wish to have it established: thus precluding them from any consideration: but left the people should discover the juggle, the elections of the state conventions, are urged on at very early days; the proposition of electing the convention for this state in nine days after the date of the resolution for all counties east of Bedford, and supported by three or four of the deputies of the convention, and who were also members of the then assembly, is one of the most extravagant instances of this kind; and even this was only prevented by the secession of nineteen virtuous and

*See resolution of Convention accompanying the instrument of the proposed government.

enlightened members.* In order to put the matter beyond all recal, they have proceeded a step further, they have made the deputies nominated for the state convention for this city and elsewhere, pledge their sacred honor, previous to their election, that they would implicitly adopt the proposed government, in toto; thus short as the period is before the final fiat is to be given, consideration is rendered nugatory, and conviction of its dangers or impropriety unavailable. A good cause does not stand in need of such means; it scorns all indirect advantages and borrowed helps, and trusts alone to its own native merit and intrinsic strength: the lion is never known to make use of cunning, nor can a good cause suffer by a free and thorough examination—It is knavery that seeks disguise. Actors do not care that any one should look into the tiring room, nor jugglers or sharpers into their hands or boxes.

Every exertion has been made to suppress discussion by shackling the press; but as this could not be effected in *this* state, the people are warned not to listen to the adversaries of the proposed plan, left they should impose upon them, and thereby prevent the adop-

*The message of the President and Council, sent into the present General Assembly, on the 27th of October last, discloses another imposition. The Board send to the House the official transmission of the proposed constitution of the United States, inclosed in a letter from the President of Congress, which proves that the paper produced to the last House on the day before the final rising of the fame, was a surreptitious copy of the vote of Congress, obtained for the purpose of deluding the Legislature into the extravagance of directing an election of Convention within *nine* days.

The provision made by the Convention of Pennsylvania, which sat in 1776 for amending the constitution, is guarded with admirable wisdom and caution. A Council of Censors is to be holden every seven years, which shall have power (two-thirds of the whole number elected agreeing) to propose amendments of the same government, and to call a Convention to adopt and establish these propositions; but the alterations must be "promulgated *at least* fix months before the day appointed for the *election* of such Convention, for the *previous consideration* of the people, that they may have an opportunity of instructing their delegates on the subject." The present measures explain the conduct of a certain party of the Censors, who sat in 1784, (much fewer than two thirds of the whole) that proposed to abolish the 47th article of the constitution, whereby the manner of amending the same was regulated.

tion of this blessed government. What figure would a lawyer make in a court of justice, if he should desire the judges not to hear the counsel of the other side, lest they should perplex the cause and mislead the court? Would not every bystander take it for granted, that he was conscious of the weakness of his client's cause, and that it could no otherwise be defended, than by not being understood?

All who are friends to liberty are friends to reason, the champion of liberty, and none are foes to liberty but those who have truth and reason for their foes. He who has dark purposes to serve, must use dark means: light would discover him, and reason expose him: he must endeavor to shut out both, and make them look frightful by giving them ill names.

Liberty only flourishes where reason and knowledge are encouraged; and wherever the latter are stifled, the former is extinguished. In Turkey printing is forbid, enquiry is dangerous, and free speaking is capital; because they are all inconsistent with the nature of the government. Hence it is that the Turks are all stupidly ignorant and are all slaves.

I shall now proceed in the consideration of the construction of the proposed plan of government.—By section 4th of article 1st of the proposed government it is declared, "that the times, places, and manner of holding elections for senators and representatives shall be prescribed in each state by the legislature thereof; *but the Congress may at any time by law make or alter such regulations, except as to the place of chusing senators.*" Will not this section put it in the power of the future Congress to abolish the suffrage by ballot, so indispensible in a free government—Montesquieu in his spirit of laws vol. 1 page 12, says "that in a democracy there can be no exercise of sovereignty, but by the suffrages of the people, which are their will; now the sovereigns will is the sovereign himself. The laws therefore which establish the right of suffrage, are fundamental to this government. In fact it is as important to regulate in a republic, in what manner, by whom, and concerning what, suffrages are to be given, as it is in a monarchy to know who is the Prince and after what manner he ought to govern." This valuable privilege of voting by ballot, ought not to rest on the discretion of the government, but be irrevocably established in the constitution.

Will not the above quoted section, also authorise the future Congress, to lengthen the term for which the senators and representatives are to be elected, from 6 and 2 year respectively, to any period, even for life? As the parliament of England voted themselves from trienniel to septeniel; and as the long parliament under Charles the 1st became perpetual?

Section 8th of article 1st, vests Congress with power "to provide for calling forth the militia to execute the laws of the union, suppress insurrections and repel evasions; to provide for organizing, arming, and diciplining the militia, and for governing such part of them as may be employed in the service of the United States, reserving to the states respectively, the appointment of the officers, and the authority of training the militia according to the discipline prescribed by Congress."—This section will subject the citizens of these states to the most arbitary military discipline, even death may be inflicted on the disobedient; in the character of militia, you may be dragged from your families and homes to any part of the continent and for any length of time, at the discretion of the future Congress; and as militia you may be made the unwilling instruments of oppression, under the direction of unwilling instruments of oppression, under the direction of government; there is no exemption upon account of conscientious scruples of bearing arms; no equivalent to be received in lieu of personal services. The militia of Pennsylvania may be marched to Georgia or New-Hampshire however incompatible with their interests or consciences;—in short they may be made as meer machines as Prussian soldiers.

Section the 9th begins thus.—"The migration or importation of such persons, as any of the states, now existing, shall think proper to admit, shall not be prohibited by Congress, prior to the year 1808, but a duty or tax may be imposed on such importation not exceeding ten dollars for each person." And by the fifth article this restraint is not to be removed by any future convention. We are told that the objects of this article, are slaves, and that it is inserted to secure to the southern states, the right of introducing negroes for twenty one years to come, against the declared sense of the other states to put an end to an odious traffic in the human species; which is especially scandalous and inconsistent in a people, who

have asserted their own liberty by the sword, and which dangerously enfeebles the districts, wherein the laborers are bondmen.
The words dark and ambiguous; such as no plain man of common
sense would have used, are evidently chosen to conceal from
Europe, that in this enlightened country, the practice of slavery has
its advocates among men in the highest stations. When it is recollected that no poll tax can be imposed on *five* negroes, above what
three whites shall be charged; when it is considered, that the
impost on the consumption of Carolina field negroes, must be trifling, and the excise, nothing, it is plain that the proportion of contributions, which can be expected from the southern states under
the new constitution, will be very unequal, and yet they are to be
allowed to enfeeble themselves by the further importation of
negroes till the year 1808. Has not the concurrence of the five
southern states (in the convention) to the new system, been purchased too dearly by the rest, who have undertaken to make good
their deficiences of revenue, occasioned by their wilful incapacity,
without an equivalent?

The general acquiescence of one description of citizens in the proposed government, surprises me much; if so many of the Quakers
have become indifferent to the sacred rights of conscience, so amply
secured by the constitution of this commonwealth; if they are satisfied, to rest this inestimable privilege on the discretion of the
future government; yet in a political light they are not acting
wisely; in the state of Pennsylvania, they form so considerable a
portion of the community, as must ensure them great weight in the
government; but in the scale of general empire, they will be lost in
the ballance.

I intended in this number to have shewn from the nature of
things, from the opinions of the greatest writers and from the peculiar circumstances of the United States, the impracticability of
establishing and maintaining one government on the principles of
freedom in so extensive a territory; to have shewn, if practicable,
the inadequacy of such government, to provide for its many and
various concerns; and also to have shewn that a confederation of
small republics, possessing all the powers of internal government,
and united in the management of their general and foreign con-

cerns, is the only system of government, by which so extensive a country can be governed consistent with freedom; but a writer under the signature of Brutus, in the New York paper, which has been re-published by Messrs. Dunlap and Claypoole, has done this in so masterly a manner, that it would be superfluous in me to add any thing on this subject.

My fellow citizens, as a lover of my country, as the friend to mankind, whilst it is yet safe to write, and whilst it is yet in your power to avoid it, I warn you of the impending danger. To this remote quarter of the world, has liberty fled—Other countries now subject to slavery, were once as free as we yet are; therefore for your own sakes, for the sake of your posterity, as well as for that of the oppressed of all nations, cherish this remaining asylum of liberty.

CENTINEL.

Independent Gazetteer

30 NOVEMBER 1787

LETTER IV

Centinel addresses the core weakness of government under the Articles of Confederation: the central government cannot collect enough tax dollars to meet its obligations. This problem, according to Centinel, arises primarily from difficult economic times and could be solved by allowing the current Congress to tax commerce and regulate trade with foreign nations. The solution is not a new Constitution. Essays in The Federalist *of particular relevance: 21, 22.*

To the PEOPLE of PENNSYLVANIA.

Friends, Countrymen and fellow Citizens[,]

THAT the present confederation is inadequate to the objects of the
union, seems to be universally allowed. The only question is, what
additional powers me wanting to give due energy to the federal
government? We should, however, be careful in forming our opinion
on this subject, not to impute the temporary and extraordinary
difficulties that has hitherto imposed the execution of the confederation, to defects in the system itself. Taxation is in every government, a very delicate and difficult subject; hence it has been the
policy of all wise statesmen, as far as circumstances permitted, to
lead the people by small beginnings and almost imperceptible
degrees, into the habits of taxation; where the contrary conduct has
been pursued, it has ever failed of full success, not unfrequently
proving the ruin of the projectors. The imposing of a burdensome
tax at once on a people, without the usual gradations, is the severest test that any government can be put to, despotism itself has
often proved unequal to the attempt. Under this conviction, let us
take a review of our situation before and since the revolution. From
the first settlement of the country until the commencement of the
late war, the taxes were so light and trivial as to be scarcely felt
by the people; when we engaged in the expensive contest with
Great Britain, the Congress sensible of the difficulty of levying the
monies necessary to its support, by *direct* taxation, had recourse
to an anticipation of the public resources, by emitting bills of credit,
and thus postponed the necessity of taxation for several years; this
means was pursued to a most ruinous length; but about the year
80 or 81, it was wholly exhausted, the bills of credit had suffered
such a depreciation from the excessive quantities in circulations,
that they ceased to be useful as a medium. The country at this
period, was very much impoverished and exhausted; commerce had
been suspended for near six years; the husbandman, for want of a
market, limited his crops to his own subsistence; the frequent calls
of the militia and long continuance in actual service, the devastations of the enemy, the subsistance of our own armies, the evils of
the depreciation of the paper money, which fell chiefly upon the
patriotic and virtuous part of the community, had all concurred to

produce great distress throughout America. In this situation of affairs, we still had the same powerful enemy to contend with, who had even more numerous and better appointed armies in the field than at any former time. Our allies were applied to in this exigence, but the pecuniary assistance that we could procure from them, was soon exhausted; the only resource now remaining, was to obtain by direct taxation, the monies necessary for our defence; the history of mankind does not furnish a similar instance of an attempt to levy such enormous taxes at once, of a people so wholly unprepared and uninured to them—the lamp of sacred liberty must indeed have burned with unsullied lustre, every sordid principle of the mind must have been then extinct, when the people not only submitted to the grievous impositions, but cheerfully exerted themselves to comply with the calls of their country; their abilities however, were not equal to furnish the necessary sums—indeed the requisition of the year 1782, amounted to the whole income of their farms and other property, including the means of their subsistance; perhaps the strained exertions of *two* years, would not have sufficed to the discharge of this requisition; how then can we impute the difficulties of the people to a due compliance with the requisitions of Congress to a defect in the confederation, for any government, however energetic, in similar circumstances, would have experienced the same fate. If we review the proceedings of the states, we shall find that they gave every sanction and authority to the requisitions of Congress; that their laws could confer, that they attempted to collect the sums called for in the same manner as is proposed to be done in future by the general government, instead of the state legislatures.

It is a maxim that a government, ought to be cautious not to govern over much, for when the cord of power is drawn too tight, it generally proves its destruction, the impracticability of complying with the requisitions of Congress has lessened the sense of obligation and duty in the people, and thus weakened the ties of the union; the opinion of power in a free government is much more efficatious than the exercise of it; it requires the maturity of time and repeated practice to give due energy and certainty to the operations of government, especially to such as affect the purses of the people.

The thirteen Swiss Cantons confederated by more general and weaker ties than these United States are by the present articles of confederation, have not experienced the necessity of strengthening their union by vesting their general diet with further or greater powers; this national body has only the management of their foreign concerns and in case of a war can only call by requisition on the several Cantons for the necessary supplies, who are sovereign and independent in every internal and local exercise of government—and yet this rope of sand, as our confederation has been termed, which is so similar to that, has held together for ages without any apparent charm.

I am persuaded that a due consideration, will evince, that the present inefficacy of the requisions of Congress, is not owing to a defect in the confederation, but the peculiar circumstances of the times.

The wheels of the general government having been thus clogged and the arrearages of taxes still accumulating, it may be asked what prospect is their of the government resuming its proper tone, unless more compulsory powers are granted? To this it may be answered; that the produce of imports on commerce which all agree to vest in Congress, together with the immense tracts of land at their disposal, will rapidly lessen and eventually discharge the present incumbrances; when this takes place, the mode by requision will be found perfectly adequate to the extraordinary exigencies of the union, Congress have lately sold land to the amount of eight millions of dollars, which is a considerable portion of the whole debt.

It is to be lamented that the interested and designing have availed themselves so successfully of the present crisis, and under the specious pretence of having discovered a panacea for all the ills of the people, they are about establishing a system of government, that will prove more destructive to them, than the wooden horse filled with soldiers did in ancient times to the city of Troy; this horse was introduced by their hostile enemy the Grecians, by a prostitution of the sacred rights of their religion; in like manner, my fellow citizens are aspiring despots among yourselves prostituting the name of a Washington to cloak their designs upon your liberties.

I would ask how is the proposed government to shower down those treasures upon every class of citizens as is so industriously inculcated and so fondly believed? Is it by the addition of numerous and expensive establishments? Is it by doubling our judiciaries, instituting federal courts in every county of every state? Is it by a superb presidential court? Is it by a large standing army? In those is it by putting it in the power of the future government to levy money at pleasure, and placing this government so independent of the people as to enable the administration to gratify every corrupt passion of the mind, to riot on your spoils, without check or controul?

A transfer to Congress of the power of imposing imports on commerce and the unlimited regulation of trade, I believe is all that is wanting to render America as prosperous as it is in the power of any form of government to render her; this properly understood would meet the views of all the honest and well meaning.

What gave birth to the late Continental Convention? Was it not the situation of our commerce, which lay at the mercy of every foreign power, who from motives of interest or enmity could restrict and controul it, without risquing a retaliation on the part of America, as Congress was impotent on this subject? Such indeed was the case with respect to Britain, whole hostile regulations gave such a stab to our navigation as to threaten its annihilation, it became the interest of even the American merchant to give a preference to foreign bottoms; hence the distress of our seamen, shiprights, and every mechanic art dependent on navigation.

By these regulations too we were limited in markets for our produce, our vessels were excluded from their West-India Islands, many of our staple commodities were denied entrance in Britain; hence the husbandmen were distressed by the demand for their crops being lessened and their prices reduced. This is the source to which may be traced every evil we experience, that can be relieved by a more energetic government. Recollect the language of complaint for years past, impare the recommendations of Congress founded on such complaints, pointing out the remedy, examine the reasons assigned by the different states for appointing delegates to the late Convention, view the powers vested in that body; they all harmonize in one sentiment, that the due regulation of trade and navigation was the anxious wish of every class of citizens, was the great object of calling the Convention.

This object being provided for, by the proposed Constitution, the people overlook and are not sensible of the needless sacrifice they are making for it.—Of what avail will be a prosperous state of commerce, when the produce of it will be at the absolute disposal of an arbitrary and unchecked government, who may levy at pleasure the most oppressive taxes; who may destroy every principle of freedom; who may even destroy the privilege of complaining.

If you are in doubt about the nature and principles of the proposed government, view the conduct of its authors and patrons, that affords the best explanation, the most striking comment.

The evil genius of darkness presided at its birth, it came forth under the veil of mystery, its true features being carefully concealed, and every deceptive art has been and is practising to have this spurious brat received as the genuine offspring of heaven-born liberty. So fearful are its patrons that you should discern the imposition, that they have hurried on its adoption, with the greatest precipitation; they have endeavored also to preclude an investigation, they have endeavored to intimidate all opposition; by such means as [these] have they surreptitiously procured a Convention in this state, favorable to their views; and here again investigation and discussion are abridged, the final question is moved before the subject has been under consideration; an appeal to the people is precluded even in the last report, lest their eyes should be opened; the Convention have denied the minority the privilege of entering the reasons of their dissent on its journals—Thus despotism is already triumphant[,] and the genius of liberty is on the eve of her exit, is about bidding an eternal adieu to this once happy people.

After so recent a triumph over British despots, after such torrents of blood and treasure have been spent, after involving ourselves in the distresses of an arduous war, and incurring such a debt, for the express purpose of asserting the rights of humanity, it is truly astonishing that a set of men among ourselves, should have the effrontery to attempt the destruction of our liberties. But in this enlightened age to hope to dupe the people by the arts they are practising, is full more extraordinary.

How do the advocates of the proposed government, combat the objections urged against it? Not even by an attempt to disprove them, for that would the more fully confirm their truth, but by a species of reasoning that is very congenital to that contempt of the understandings of the people, that they so eminently possess, and which policy cannot even prevent frequent [ebullitions] of; they seem to think that the oratory and fascination of great names and mere sound will suffice to ensure success; that the people may be diverted from a consideration of the merits of the plan, by bold assertions and mere declamation. Some of their writers for instance, paint the distresses of every class of citizens with all the glowing language of eloquence, as if this was a demonstration of the excellence, or even the safety of the new plan, which, notwithstanding the reality of this distress, may be a system of tyranny and oppression; other writers tell you of the great men who composed the late convention, and give you a pompous display of their virtues, instead of a justification of the plan of government; and others again urge the tyrant's plea, they endeavor to make it a case of necessity, now is the critical moment; they represent the adoption of this government as our only alternative, as the last opportunity we shall have of peaceably establishing a government; they assert it to be the best system that can be formed, and that if we reject it, we will have a worse one or none at all, nay that if we presume to propose alterations, we shall get into a labyrinth of difficulties from which we cannot be extricated, as no two states will agree in amendments, that therefore it would involve us in irreconcilable discord. But they all seduously avoid the fair field of argument, a rational investigation into the origination of the proposed government. I hope the good sense of the people will detect the fallacy of such conduct, will discover the base juggle and with becoming resolution relent the imposition.

That the powers of Congress ought to be strengthened, all allow, but is this a conclusive proof of the necessity to adopt the proposed plan; is it a proof that because the late convention, in the first essay upon so arduous and difficult a subject, harmonised in their ideas, that a future convention will not, or that after a full investigation and mature consideration of the objections, they will not plan a better government and one more agreeable to the sentiments of America, or is it any proof that they can never again agree in any plan? The late convention must indeed have been inspired, as some of its advocates have asserted, to admit the truth of these positions, or even to admit the possibility of the proposed government, being such a one as America ought to adopt; for this body went upon original ground, foreign from their intentions or powers, they must therefore have been wholly uninformed of the sentiments of their constituents in respect to this form of government, as it was not in their contemplation when the convention was appointed to erect a new government, but to strengthen the old one. Indeed they seem to have been determined to monopolize the exclusive merit of the discovery, or rather as if darkness was essential to its success they precluded all communication with the people, by closing their doors; thus the well disposed members unassisted by public information and opinion, were induced by those arts that are now practising on the people, to give their sanction to this system of despotism.

Is there any reason to presume that a new Convention will not agree upon a better plan of government? Quite the contrary, for perhaps there never was such a coincidence on any occasion as on the present, the opponents to the proposed plan, at the same time in every part of the continent, harmonised in the same objections; such an uniformity of opposition is without example and affords the strongest demonstration of its solidity. Their objections too are not local, are not confined to the interests of any one particular state to the prejudice of the rest, but with a philanthropy and liberality that reflects lustre on humanity, that dignifies the character of America, they embrace the interests and happiness of the whole union, they do not even condescend to minute blemishes, but shew that the main pillars of the fabric are bad, that the essential principles of liberty and safety are not to be found in it, that despotism will be the necessary and inevitable consequence of its establishment.

CENTINEL.

Independent Gazetteer

4 DECEMBER 1787

LETTER V

Centinel relies on the famous Baron Montesquieu in arguing that only a despotism could govern an empire as large as America. Because the Constitution would consolidate the states into one large nation, the result would be just that—despotism. Essays in The Federalist *of particular relevance: 9, 10, 14, 17-20.*

To the PEOPLE of PENNSYLVANIA.

Friends, Countrymen, and Fellow-Citizens,

MR. WILSON in a speech delivered in our Convention on Saturday the 24th instant, has conceded, nay forceably proved, that one consolidated government, will not answer for so extensive a territory as the United States includes, that slavery would be the necessary fate of the people under such a government; his words are so remarkable, that I cannot forbear reciting them, they are as follows, viz. "The extent of country for which the new constitution was required, produced another difficulty in the business of the federal convention. It is the opinion of some celebrated writers, that to a small territory, the democratical, to a middling territory, (as Montesquieu has termed it) the monarchical, and, to an extensive territory, the despotic form of government, is best adapted. Regarding then, the wide and almost unbounded jurisdiction of the United States, at first view, the hand of despotism seemed necessary to controul, connect, and protect it; and hence the chief embarrasment rose. For, we knew that, although our constituents would chearfully submit to the legislative restraints of a free government, they would spurn at every attempt to shackle them with despotic power." See page 5 of the printed speech. And again in page 7, he says "Is it probable that the dissolution of the state governments,

and the establishment of one consolidated empire, would be eligible
in its nature, and satisfactory to the people in its administration? I
think not, as I have given reasons to shew that so extensive a territory could not be governed, connected, and preserved, but by the
supremacy of despotic power. All the exertions of the most potent
emperors of Rome were not capable of keeping that empire
together, which, in extent, was far inferior to the dominion of
America."

This great point having been now confirmed by the concession
of Mr. Wilson, though indeed it was self evident before, and the
writers against the proposed plan of government, having proved
to demonstration, that the powers proposed to be vested in Congress, will necessarily annihilate and absorb, the state Legislatures
and judiciaries and produce from their wreck one consolidated government, the question is determined. Every man therefore who has
the welfare of his country at heart, every man who values his own
liberty and happiness, in short, every description of persons, except
those aspiring despots who hope to benefit by the mysery and vassalage of their countrymen, must now concur in rejecting the proposed system of government, must now unite in branding its
authors with the stigma of eternal infamy. The anniversary of this
great escape from the fangs of despotism, ought to be celebrated
as long as liberty shall continue to be dear to the citizens of
America.

I will repeat some of my principal arguments, and add some further remarks, on the subject of consolidation.

The Legislative is the highest delegated power in government,
all others are subordinate to it. The celebrated Montesquieu establishes it as a maxim, that legislation necessarily follows the power
of taxation. By the 8th sect. of article the 1st of the proposed government, "the Congress are to have power to lay and collect taxes,
duties, imposts, and excises, to pay the debts and provide for the
common defence and *general welfare* of the United States." Now,
what can be more comprehensive than these words? Every species
of taxation, whether external or internal are included. Whatever
taxes, duties, and excises that the Congress may deem necessary to
the *general welfare* may be imposed on the citizens of these states

and levied by their officers. The congress are to be the absolute judges of the propriety of such taxes, in short they may construe every purpose for which the state legislatures now lay taxes, to be for the *general welfare*, they may seize upon every source of taxation, and thus make it impracticable for the states to have the smallest revenue, and if a state should presume to impose a tax or excise that would interfere with a federal tax or excise, congress may soon terminate the contention, by repealing the state law, by virtue of the following section—"To make all laws which shall be necessary and proper for carrying into execution the foregoing powers and all other powers vested by this constitution in the government of the United States, or in any department thereof." Indeed every law of the States may be controuled by this power. The legislative power granted for these sections is so unlimited in its nature, may be so comprehensive and boundless in its exercise, that this alone would be amply sufficient to carry the coup de grace to the state governments, to swallow them up in the grand vortex of general empire. But the legislative has an able auxiliary in the judicial department, for a reference to my second number will shew that this may be made greatly instrumental in effecting a consolidation; as the federal judiciary would absorb all others. Lest the foregoing powers should not suffice to consolidate the United States into one empire, the Convention as if determined to prevent the possibility of a doubt, as if to prevent all clashing by the opposition of state powers, as if to preclude all struggle for state importance, as if to level all obstacles to the supremacy of universal sway, which in so extensive a territory, would be an iron-handed despotism, have ordained by article the 6th, "That this constitution, and the laws of the United States, which shall be made in pursuance thereof, and all treaties made, or which shall be made, under the authority of the United States, shall be the *supreme law of the land; and the judges in every state shall be bound thereby any thing in the constitution or laws of any state to the contrary notwithstanding.*"

The words "pursuant to the constitution" will be no restriction to the authority of congress; for the foregoing sections gives them unlimited legislation; their unbounded power of taxation does alone include all others, as whoever has the purse strings will have full

dominion. But the convention has super added another power, by
which the congress may stamp with the sanction of the constitution every possible law; it is contained in the following clause—"To
make all laws which shall be necessary and proper for carrying into
execution the foregoing powers, and all other powers vested by this
constitution in the government of the United States, or in any
department or officer thereof[.]" Whatever law congress may deem
necessary and proper for carrying into execution any of the powers vested in them, may be enacted; and by virtue of this clause,
they may controul and abrogate any and every of the laws of the
state governments, on the allegation that they interfere with the
execution of any of their powers, and yet these laws will "be made
in pursuance of the constitution," and of course will "be the
supreme law of the land, and the judges in every state shall be
bound thereby, any thing in the *constitution* or *laws* to the contrary
notwithstanding."

There is no reservation made in the whole of this plan in favor of
the rights of the separate states. In the present plan of confederation made in the year 1778, it was thought necessary by article the
2d to declare that "each state retains its sovereignty, freedom and
independence, and every power, jurisdiction and right, which is
not by this confederation *expressly* delegated to the United States
in Congress assembled." *Positive* grant was not *then* thought sufficiently descriptive and restrictive upon congress, and the omission
of such a declaration *now*, when such great devolutions of power are
proposed, manifests the design of consolidating the states.

What restriction does Mr. Wilson pretend there is in the new constitution to the supremacy of despotic sway over the United
States? What barrier does he assign for the security of the state
governments? Why truly a mere cobweb of a limit! by interposing
the shield of what will become mere *form*, to check the *reality* of
power. He says, that the existence of the state governments are
essential to the organization of congress, that the *former* is made
the necessary basis of the latter, for the federal senators and president are to be appointed by the state legislatures; and that hence
all fears of a consolidation are groundless and imaginary. It must be
confessed, as reason and argument would have been foreign to the

defence of the proposed plan of government, Mr. Wilson has displayed much ingenuity on this occasion, he has involved the subject in all the mazes of sophistry, and by subtil distinctions, he has established principles and positions, that exist only in his own fertile imagination. It is a solecism in politics for two co-ordinate sovereignties to exist together, you must separate the sphere of their jurisdiction, or after running the race of dominion for some time, one would necessarily triumph over the other; but in the mean time the subjects of it would be harrassed with double impositions to support the contention; however the strife between congress and the states could not be of long continuance, for the former has a decisive superiority in the outset, and has moreover the power by the very constitution itself to terminate it, when expedient.

At this necessary connexion, as it has been termed, between the state governments and the general government, has been made a point of great magnitude by the advocates of the new plan, as it is the only obstacle alleged by them against a consolidation, it ought to be well considered. It is declared by the proposed plan, that the federal senators and the electors who chuse the president of the United States, shall be appointed by the state legislatures for the long period of six and four years respectively;—how will this connexion prevent the state legislatures being divested of every important, every efficient power? may not they, will not they dwindle into mere boards of appointment, as has ever happened in other nations to public bodies, who, in similar circumstances, have been so weak as to part with the essentials of power? Does not history abound with such instances? And this may be the mighty amount of this inseparable connexion, which is so much dwelt upon as the security of the state governments. Yet even this shadow of a limit against consolidation, may be annihilated by the imperial fiat, without any violation of even the forms of the constitution, section 4th of article the 1st has made a provision for this, when the people are sufficiently fatigued with the useless expence of maintaining the *forms* of departed power and security, and when they shall pray to be relieved from the imposition. This section cannot be too often repeated, as it gives such a latitude to the designing, as it revokes every other part of the constitution that may be tolerable, and as it may enable the administration under it, to complete the system of despotism; it is in the following words, viz. "The times, places and manner holding elections for senators and representatives, shall be prescribed in each state by the legislature thereof; *but the Congress may at any time by law make or after such regulations, except as to the place of chusing senators.*" The only apparent restriction in this clause, is as to the *place* of appointing senators, but even this may be rendered of no avail, for as the Congress have the controul over the time of appointment of both senators and representatives, they may under the presence of an apprehension of invasion, upon the presence of the turbulence of what they may stile a faction, and indeed presences are never wanting to the designing, they may postpone the time of the election of the senators and the representatives from period to perpetuity; thus they may and if they may, they certainly will from the lust of dominion, so inherent in the mind of man, relieve the people from the trouble of attending elections by condescending to create themselves. Has not Mr. Wilson avowed it in fact? Has he not said in the Convention, that it was necessary that Congress should possess this power as the means of its own preservation, otherwise says he, an invasion, a civil war, a faction, or a secession of a minority of the assembly might prevent the representation of a state in Congress.

The advocates of the proposed government must be hard driven, when they represent, that because the legislatures of this and the other states have exceeded the due bounds of power, notwithstanding every guard provided by their constitutions; that because the lust of arbitrary sway is so powerful as sometimes to get the better of every obstacle; that therefore we should give full scope to it, for that all restriction would be useless and nugatory. And further, when they tell you that a good administration will atone for all the defects in the government, which, say they, you must necessarily have, for how can it be otherwise, your rulers are to be taken from among yourselves. My fellow citizens, these aspiring despots, must indeed have a great contempt for your understanding, when they hope to gull you out of your liberties by such reasoning; for what is the primary object of government, but to check and controul the ambitious and designing, how then can moderation and virtue be expected from men, who will be in possession of absolute sway, who will have the United States at their disposal? They would be more than men, who could resist such temptation! their being taken from among the people, would be no security; tyrants are of native growth in all countries, the greatest bashaw in Turky has been one of the people, as Mr. Wilson tells you the president-general will be. What consolation would this be, when you shall be suffering under his oppression.

CENTINEL.

Independent Gazetteer

26 DECEMBER 1787

LETTER VI

In passages strikingly similar to several found in The Federalist, *Centinel argues that all men seek dominion and thus that any people seeking to retain its liberties must distrust its governors—or, in this case, those advocating a new government. Essays in* The Federalist *of particular relevance: 10, 51.*

To the PEOPLE of PENNSYLVANIA.

"Man is the glory, jest, and riddle of the world." —POPE

INCREDIBLE transition! the people who, seven years ago, deemed every earthly good, every other consideration, as worthless, when placed in competition with liberty, that heaven-born blessing, that zest of all others; the people, who, actuated by this noble ardor of patriotism, rose superior to every weakness of humanity, and shone with such dazzling lustre amidst the greatest difficulties; who, emulous of eclipsing each other in the glorious assertion of the dignity of human nature, courted every danger, and were ever ready, when necessary, to lay down their lives at the altar of liberty: I say the people, who exhibited so lately a spectacle, that commanded the admiration, and drew the plaudits of the most distant nations, are now reversing the picture, are now lost to every noble principle, are about to sacrifice that inestimable jewel liberty, to the genius of despotism. A *golden phantom* held out to them, by the crafty and aspiring despots among themselves, is alluring them into the fangs of arbitrary power; and so great is their infatuation, that it seems, as if nothing short of the reality of misery necessarily attendant on slavery, will rouse them from their false confidence, or convince them of the direful deception; but then alas! it will be too late, the chains of despotism will be fast rivetted and all escape precluded.

For years past, the harpies of power have been industriously inculcating the idea that all our difficulties proceed from the impotency of Congress, and have at length succeeded to give to this sentiment almost universal currency and belief: the devastations, losses and burthens occasioned by the late war; the excessive importations of foreign merchandise and luxuries, which have drained the country of its specie and involved it in debt, are all overlooked, and the inadequacy of the powers of the present confederation is erroneously supposed to be the only cause of our difficulties; hence persons of every description are revelling in the anticipation of the halcyon days, consequent on the establishment of the new constitution.—What gross deception and fatal delusion! Although very considerable benefit might be derived from strengthening the hands of Congress, so as to enable them: to regulate commerce, and counteract the adverse restrictions of other nations, which would meet with the concurrence of all persons; yet this benefit, is accompanied in the new constitution with the scourge of despotic power, that will render the citizens of America tenants at will of every species of property, of every enjoyment, and make them the meer drudges of government. The gilded bait conceals corrosives that will eat up their whole substance.

Since the late able discussion, all are now sensible of great defects in the new constitution, are sensible that power is thereby granted without limitation or restriction; yet such is the impatience of the people to reap the golden harvest of regulated commerce, that they will not take time to secure their liberty and happiness, nor even to secure the benefit of the expected wealth; but are weakly trusting their every concern to the discretionary disposal of their future rulers: are content to risque every abuse of power, because they are promised a good administration, because moderation and self-denial are the characteristic features of men in possession of absolute sway. What egregious folly! What superlative ignorance of the nature of power does such conduct discover!

History exhibits this melancholy truth, that slavery has been the lot of nearly the whole of mankind in all ages, and, that the very small portion who have enjoyed the blessings of liberty, have soon been reduced to the common level of slavery and misery. The cause of this general vassalage may be traced to a principle of human nature, which is more powerful and operative than all the others combined; it is that lust of dominion that is inherent in every mind, in a greater or less degree; this is so universal and ever active a passion as to influence all our ancestors; the different situation and qualifications of men only modifies and varies the complexion and operation of it.

For this darling pre-eminence and superiority, the merchant, already possessed of a competency, adventures his all in the pursuit of greater wealth; it is for this, that men of all descriptions, after having amassed fortunes, still persevere in the toils of labour; in short, this is the great principle of exertion in the votaries of riches, learning, and fame.

In a savage state, pre-eminence is the result of bodily strength and intrepidity, which compels submission from all such as have the misfortune to be less able; therefore the great end of civil government is to protect the weak from the oppression of the powerful, to put every man upon the level of equal liberty; but here again the same lust of dominion by different means frustrates almost always this salutary intention. In a polished state of society, wealth, talents, address and intrigue are the qualities that attain superiority in the great sphere of government.

The most striking illustration of the prevalence of this lust of dominion is, that the most strenuous assertors of liberty in all ages, after successfully triumphing over tyranny, have themselves become tyrants, when the unsuspicious confidence of an admiring people have entrusted them with unchecked power. Rare are the instances of self denial, or consistency of conduct in the votaries of liberty, when they have become possessed of the reins of authority; it has been the peculiar felicity of this country, that her *great Deliverer* did not prove a *Cromwell* nor a *Monk*.

Compare the declarations of the most zealous assertors of *religious* liberty, whilst under the lash of persecution, with their conduct when in power; you will find that even the benevolence and humility inculcated in the gospels, prove no restraint upon this love of domination—The mutual contentions of the several facts of religion in England some ages since, are sufficient evidence of this truth.

The annals of mankind demonstrate the precarious tenure of privileges and property dependent upon the will and pleasure of rulers; these illustrate the fatal danger of relying upon the moderation and self-denial of men exposed to the temptations that the Congress under the new constitution will be. The lust of power or dominion is of that nature, as seeks to overcome every obstacle, and does not remit its exertions, whilst any object of conquest remains, nothing short of the plenitude of dominion, will satisfy this cursed demon: Therefore, liberty is only to be preserved by a due responsibility in the government, and by the constant attention of the people; whenever that responsibility has been lessened, or this attention remitted, in the same degree has arbitrary sway prevailed.

The celebrated *Montesquieu* has warned mankind of the danger of an implicit reliance on rulers; he says, that "a perpetual *jealousy* respecting liberty, is absolutely requisite in all free states," and again, "that slavery is ever preceded by sleep."

I shall conclude this number with an extract from a speech delivered by Lord *George Digby*, afterwards *Earl of Bristol*, in the *English* Parliament, on the triennial bill in the year 1641, viz. "It hath been a maxim among the wisest legislators that whoever means to settle good laws, must proceed in them, with a minister opinion of all mankind; and suppose that whosoever is not wicked, it is for want only of the opportunity. It is that opportunity of being ill, Mr. Speaker, that we must take away, if ever, we mean to be happy, which can never be done, but by *the frequency of parliaments.*

"No state can wisely be confident of any public minister's continuing good, longer than the red is rod over him.

"Let me appeal to all those that were present in this house at the agitation of the *petition of right*: And let them tell themselves truly of whose promotion to the management of public affairs do they think the generality would, at that time, have had better hopes, than of Mr. *Noy*, and Sir *Thomas Wentworth*; both having been at that time and in that business as I have heard, most keen and active patriots, and the latter of them, to the eternal aggravation of his infamous treachery to the commonwealth be it spoken, the first mover, and insister to have this clause added to the *petition of right*, viz.

"That for the comfort and safety of his subjects, his Majesty would be pleased to declare his will and pleasure, that all his ministers should serve him according to the laws and statutes of the realm.

"And yet, Mr. Speaker, to whom now can all the inundations upon our *liberties*, under presence of law, and the late ship-wreck at once of all our property be attributed more than to *Noy*, and all those other mischiefs whereby this monarchy hath been brought almost to the brink of destruction, so much to any as to that *grand apostate* to the commonwealth, the now Lieutenant of Ireland, Sir Thomas Wentworth? Let every man but consider those men as once they were." British Liberties, page 184 and 185.

CENTINEL.

Independent Gazetteer

29 DECEMBER 1787

LETTER VII

In an essay filled with rhetorical flourishes, Centinel argues that the common people are already rejecting the new Constitution as a plot against their liberties. Essays in The Federalist *of particular relevance: 1, 2, 38, 85.*

To the PEOPLE of PENNSYLVANIA.

Friends and Fellow-Citizens!

THE admiring world lately beheld the sun of liberty risen to meridian splendour in this western hemisphere, whose chearing rays began to dispel the glooms of even transatlantic despotism: the patriotic mind, enraptured with the glowing scene, fondly anticipated an universal and eternal day to the orb of freedom, but the horison is already darkened and the glooms of slavery threaten to fix their empire. How transitory are the blessings of this life! Scarcely have four years elapsed since these United States, rescued from the domination of foreign despots by the unexampled heroism and perseverance of its citizens, at such great expence of blood and treasure, when they are about to fall a prey to the machinations of a profligate junto at home, who seizing the favorable moment, when the temporary and extraordinary difficulties of the people have thrown them off their guard, and lulled that jealousy of power so essential to the preservation of freedom, have been too successful in the sacrilegious attempt; however I am confident that this formidable conspiracy will end in the confusion and infamy of its authors; that if necessary, the avenging sword of an abused people will humble these aspiring despots to the dust, and that their fate, like that of Charles the First of England, will deter such attempts in future, and prove the confirmation of the liberties of America until time shall be no more.

One would imagine by the insolent conduct of these harpies of power, that they had already triumphed over the liberties of the people, that the chains were rivetted and tyranny established. They tell us all further opposition will be vain, as this state has passed the rubicon. Do they imagine the freemen of Pennsylvania will be thus trepaned out of their liberties; that they will submit without a struggle? They must indeed be inebriated with the lust of dominion to indulge such chimerical ideas. Will the act of one sixth of the people, and this too founded on deception and surprise, bind the community? Is it thus that the altar of liberty, so recently crimsoned with the blood of our worthies, is to be prostrated and despotism reared on its ruins? Certainly not. The solemn mumery that has been acting in the name of the people of Pennsylvania will be treated with the deserved contempt; it has served indeed to expose the principles of the men concerned, and to draw a line of discrimination between the real and affected patriots.

Impressed with an high opinion of the understanding and spirit of my fellow citizens, I have in no stage of this business entertained a doubt of its eventual defeat; the momentary delusion, arising from an unreserved confidence placed in some of the characters whose names sanctioned this scheme of power, did not discourage me: I foresaw that this blind admiration would soon be succeeded by rational investigation, which, stripping the monster of its gilded covering, would discover its native deformity.

Already the enlightened pen of patriotism, aided by an able public discussion, has dispelled the mist of deception, and the great body of the people are awakened to a due sense of their danger, and are determined to assert their liberty, if necessary by the sword, but this mean need not be recurred to, for who are their enemies? A junto composed of the lordly and high minded gentry, of the profligate and the needy office-hunters; of men principally who in the late war skulked from the common danger. Would such characters dare to face the majesty of a free people? No.—All the conflict would be between the offended justice and generosity of the people, whether these sacrilegious invaders of their dearest rights should suffer the merited punishment, or escape with an infamous contempt?

However, as additional powers are necessary to Congress, the people will no doubt see the expediency of calling a convention for this purpose as soon as may be, by applying to their representatives in assembly, at their next session, to appoint a suitable day for the election of such Convention.

CENTINEL.

Independent Gazetteer

2 JANUARY 1788

LETTER VIII

Centinel accuses the Federalists of plotting to protect and increase their own riches at the expense of public liberty. Essays in The Federalist *of particular relevance: 1, 2, 38.*

To the People of Pennsylvania.

Fellow Citizens,

Under the benign influence of liberty, this country, so recently a rugged wilderness and the abode of savages and wild beasts, has attained to a degree of improvement and greatness, in less than two ages, of which history furnishes no parallel: It is here that human nature may be viewed in all its glory; man assumes the station designed him by the creation; a happy equality and independency pervades the community; it is here the human mind, untrammeled by the restraints of arbitrary power, expands every faculty: as the field to fame and riches is open to all, it stimulates universal exertion, and exhibits a lively picture of emulation, industry and happiness. The unfortunate and oppressed of all nations, fly to this grand asylum, where liberty is ever protected, and industry crowned with success.

But as it is by comparison only that men estimate the value of any good, they are not sensible of the worth of those blessings they enjoy, until they are deprived of them; hence from ignorance of the horrors of slavery, nations, that have been in possession of that rarest of blessings, liberty, have so easily parted with it: when groaning under the yoke of tyranny what perils would they not encounter, what consideration would they not give to regain the inestimable jewel they had lost; but the jealousy of despotism guards every avenue to freedom, and confirms its empire at the expence of the devoted people, whose property is made instrumental to their misery, for the rapacious hand of power seizes upon every thing; dispair presently succeeds, and every noble faculty of the mind being depressed, and all motive to industry and exertion being removed, the people are adapted to the nature of the government, and drag out a listless existence.

If ever America should be enslaved it will be from this state, that they are not sensible of their peculiar felicity, that they are not aware of the value of the heavenly boon, committed to their care and protection, and if the present conspiracy fails, as I have no doubt will be the case, it will be the triumph of reason and philosophy, as these United States have never felt the iron hand of power, or experienced the wretchedness of slavery.

The conspirators against our liberties have presumed too much on the maxim that nations do not take the alarm, until they feel oppression; the enlightened citizens of America have on two memorable occasions convinced the tyrants of Europe that they are endued with the faculty of foresight, that they will jealously guard against the first introduction of tyranny, however speciously glossed over, or whatever appearance it may assume: It was not the mere amount of *the duty on stamps*, or *tea* that America opposed, they were considered as signals of approaching despotism, as precedents whereon the superstructure of arbitrary sway was to be reared.

Notwithstanding such illustrious evidence of the good sense and spirit of the people of these United States, and contrary to all former experience of mankind, which demonstrates that it is only by gradual and imperceptible degrees that nations have hitherto been enslaved, except in case of conquest by the sword; the authors of the present conspiracy are attempting to seize upon absolute power at one grasp, impatient of dominion they have adopted a decisive line of conduct, which, if successful, would obliterate every trace of liberty. I congratulate my fellow citizens that the infatuated confidence of their enemies has so blended their ambition, that their defeat must be certain and easy, if imitating the refined policy of successful despots, they had attacked the citadel of liberty by sap, and gradually undermined its outworks, they would have stood a fairer chance of effecting their design; but in this enlightened age thus rashly to attempt to carry the fortress by storm, is folly indeed. They have even exposed some of their batteries prematurely, and thereby unfolded every latent view, for the unlimited power of taxation would alone have been amply sufficient for every purpose; by a proper application of this, the will and pleasure of the rulers would of course have become the supreme law of the land; therefore there was no use in portraying the ultimate object, by superadding the form to reality of supremacy in the following clause, viz. that which empowers the new congress to make all laws that may be necessary and proper for carrying into execution any of their powers, by virtue of which every possible law will be constitutional, as they are to be the sole judges of the propriety of such laws, that which ordains that their acts shall be the supreme law of the lands any thing in the laws or constitution of any state to the contrary notwithstanding; that which gives Congress the absolute controul over the time and mode of its appointment and election, whereby, independent of any other means, they may establish hereditary despotism; that which authorises them to keep on foot at all times a standing army; and that which subjects the militia to absolute command—and to accelerate the subjugation of the people, trial by jury in civil cases and the liberty of the press are abolished.

So flagrant, so audacious a conspiracy against the liberties of a free people is without precedent. Mankind in the darkest ages have never been so insulted; even then, tyrants found it necessary to pay some respect to the habits and feelings of the people, and nothing but the name of a Washington could have occasioned a moment's hesitation about the nature of the new plan, or saved its authors from the execration and vengeance of the people, which eventually will prove an aggravation of their treason; for America will resent the imposition practised upon the unsuspicious zeal of her *illustrious deliverer*, and vindicate her character from the aspertions of these enemies of her happiness and fame.

The advocates of this plan have artfully attempted to veil over the true nature and principles of it with the names of those respectable characters that by consummate cunning and address they have prevailed upon to sign it, and what ought to convince the people of the deception and excite their apprehensions, is that with every advantage which education, the science of government and of law, the knowledge of history and superior talents and endowments, furnish the authors and advocates of this plan with, they have from its publication exerted all their power and influence to prevent all discussion of the subject, and when this could not be prevented they have constantly avoided the ground of argument and recurred to declamation, sophistry and personal abuse, but principally relied upon the magic of names. Would this have been their conduct, if their cause had been a good one? No, they would have invited investigation and convinced the understandings of the people.

But such policy indicates great ignorance of the good sense and spirit of the people, for if the sanction of every convention throughout the union was obtained by the means these men are practising; yet their triumph would be momentary, the favorite object would still elude their grasp; for a good government founded on fraud and deception could not be maintained without an army sufficiently powerful to compel submission, which the *well born* of America could not speedily accomplish. However the complexion of several of the more considerable states does not promise even this point of success. The Carolinas, Virginia, Maryland, New-York and New-Hampshire have by their wisdom in taking a longer time to deliberate, in all probability saved themselves from the disgrace of becoming the dupes of this gilded bait, as experience will evince that it need only be properly examined to be execrated and repulsed.

The merchant, immersed in schemes of wealth, seldom extends his views beyond the immediate object of gain; he blindly pursues his seeming interest, and sees not the latent mischief; therefore it is, that he is the last to take the alarm when public liberty is threatened. This may account for the infatuation of some of our merchants, who, elated with the imaginary prospect of an improved commerce under the new government, overlook all danger; they do not consider that commerce is the hand-maid of liberty, a plant of free growth that withers under the hand of despotism, that every concern of individuals will be sacrificed to the gratification of the men in power, who will institute injurious monopolies and shackle commerce with every device of avarice; and that property of every species will be held at the will and pleasure of rulers.

If the nature of the case did not give birth to these well-founded apprehensions, the principles and characters of the authors and advocates of the measure ought. View the monopolising spirit of the principal of them. See him converting a bank, instituted for common benefit, to his own and creatures emolument, and by the aid thereof, controuling the credit of the state, and dictating the measures of government. View the vassalage of our merchants, the thraldom of the city of Philadelphia, and the extinction of that spirit of independency in most of its citizens so essential to freedom. View this Collosus attempting to grasp the commerce of America and meeting with a sudden repulse, in the midst of his immense career, receiving a shock that threatens his very existence. View the desperate fortunes of many of his co-adjutors and dependants, particularly the bankrupt situation of the principal instrument under the *great man* in promoting the new government, whose superlative arrogance, ambition and repacity, would need the spoils of thousands to gratify; view his towering aspect, he would have no bowels of compassion for the oppressed, he would *overlook* all their sufferings. Recollect the strenuous and unremitted exertions of these men, for years past, to destroy our admirable constitution, whose object is to secure equal liberty and advantages to all, and the great obstacle in the way of their ambitious schemes, and then answer, whether these apprehensions are chimerical, whether such characters will be less ambitious, less avaritious, more moderate, when the privileges, property, and every concern of the people of the United States shall lie at their mercy, when they shall be in possession of absolute sway?

CENTINEL.

Independent Gazatteer

8 JANUARY 1788

LETTER IX

Centinel details a Federalist plot to inflate perceptions of support for their Constitution and to keep Anti-Federalist writings from circulating through the mails. According to Centinel, defenders of Pennsylvania's free constitution actually oppose the new federal document. Essays in The Federalist *of particular relevance: 1, 38, 85.*

To the People of Pennsylvania.

Fellow Citizens,

You have the peculiar felicity of living under the most perfect system of local government in the world; prize then this invaluable blessing as it deserves: Suffer it not to be wrested from you, and the scourge of despotic power substituted in its place, under the specious pretence of vesting the general government of the United States with necessary power; that this would be the inevitable consequence of the establishment of the new constitution, the least consideration of its nature and tendency is sufficient to convince every unprejudiced mind. If you were sufficiently impressed with your present favored situation, I should have no doubt of a proper dicision of the question in discussion.

The highest illustration of the excellence of the constitution of this commonwealth, is, that from its first establishment, the ambitious and profligate have been united in a constant conspiracy to destroy it; so sensible are they that it is their great enemy, that it is the great palladium of equal liberty, and the property of the people from the rapacious hand of power: The annals of mankind do not furnish a more glorious instance of the triumph of patriotism over the lust of ambition aided by most of the wealth of the state. The few generally prevail over the many by uniformity of council, unremitted and persevering exertion, and superior information and address; but in Pennsylvania the reverse has happened; here the *well-born* have been baffled in all their efforts to prostrate the altar of liberty for the purpose of substituting their own insolent sway that would degrade the freemen of this state into servile dependence upon the *lordly* and *great*: However, it is not the nature of ambition to be discouraged; it is ever ready to improve the first opportunity to rear its baneful head and with irritated fury to wreak its vengeance on the votaries of liberty. The present conspiracy is a continental exertion of the *well born* of America to obtain that darling domination, which they have not been able to accomplish in their respective states. Of what complexion were the deputies of this state in the general convention? *Six* out of *eight* were the inveterate enemies of our inestimable constitution, and the principals of that faction that for ten years past have kept the people in continual alarm for their liberties. Who are the advocates of the new constitution in this state? They consist of the same faction, with the addition of a few deluded well-meaning men, but whose number is daily lessening.

These conspirators have come forward at a most favorable conjuncture, when the state of public affairs has lulled all jealousy of power: Emboldened by the sanction of the august name of a *Washington*, that they have prostituted to their purpose, they have presumed to overleap the usual gradations to absolute power, and have attempted to seize at once upon the supremacy of dominion. The new instrument of government does indeed make a fallacious parade of some remaining privileges, and insults the understandings of the people with the semblance of liberty in some of its artful and deceptive clauses: which form but a flimsy veil over the reality of tyranny, so weakly endeavored to be concealed from the eye of freedom. For, of what avail are the few inadequate stipulations in favor of the rights of the people, when they may be effectually counteracted and destroyed by virtue of other clauses; when these enable the rulers to renounce all dependence on their constituents, and render the latter tenants at will of every concern? The new constitution is in fact a *carte blanche*, a surrender at discretion to the will and pleasure of our rulers; as this has been demonstrated to be the case, by the investigation and discussion that have taken place, I trust the same good sense and spirit which have hitherto enabled the people to triumph over the wiles of ambition, will be again exerted for their salvation. The accounts from various parts of the country correspond with my warmest hopes, and justify my early predictions of the eventual defeat of this scheme of power and office making.

The genius of liberty has sounded the alarm, and the dormant spirit of her votaries is reviving with enthusiastic ardor; the like unanimity which formerly distinguished them in their conflict with foreign despots, promises to crown their virtuous opposition on the present occasion, with signal success. The structure of despotism that has been reared in this state, upon deception and surprise, will vanish like the baseless fabric of a dream and leave not a trace behind.

The parasites and tools of power in Northampton county ought to take warning from the fate of the Carlisle junto, left like them, they experience the resentment of an injured people. I would advise them not to repeat the imposition of a set of fallacious resolutions as the sense of that county, when in fact, it was the act of a despicable few, with Alexander Paterson at their head, whose achievements at Wyoming, as the meaner instrument of unfeeling avarice, have rendered infamously notorious; but yet, like the election of a Mr. Sedgwick for the little town of Stockbridge, which has been adduced as evidence of the unanimity of the western counties of Massachusetts state in favor of the new constitution, when the fact is far otherwise, this act of a few individuals will be sounded forth over the continent as a testimony of the zealous attachment of the county of Northampton to the new constitution. By such wretched and momentary deceptions do these harpies of power endeavor to give the complexion of strength to their cause. To prevent the detection of such impositions, to prevent the reflection of the rays of light from state to state, which, producing general illumination, would dissipate the mist of deception, and thereby prove fatal to the new constitution, all intercourse between the patriots of America is as far as possible cut off; whilst on the other hand, the conspirators have the most exact information, a common concert is every where evident, they move in unison. There is so much mystery in the conduct of these men, such systematic deception, and fraud characterises all their measures, such extraordinary solicitude shown by them to precipitate and surprise the people into a blind and implicit adoption of this government, that it ought to excite the most alarming apprehensions in the minds of all those who think their privileges, property and welfare worth securing.

It is a fact that can be established, that during almost the whole of the time that the late convention of this state were assembled, the newspapers published in New York, by Mr. Greenleaf, which contains the essays written there against the new government, such as the patriotic ones of Brutus, Cincinnatus, Cato, &c. sent as usual by the printer of that place, to the printers of this city, miscarried in their conveyance, which prevented the republication in this state of many of these pieces, and since that period great irregularity prevails; and I stand informed that the printers in New York complain that the free and independent newspapers of this city do not come to hand; whilst on the contrary, we find the devoted vehicles of despotism pass uninterrupted. I would ask what is the meaning of the new arrangement at the Post-Office, which abridges the circulation of newspapers at this momentous crisis, when our every concern is dependent upon a proper decision of the subject in discussion—No trivial excuse will be admitted; the Centinel will, as from the first approach of despotism, warn his countrymen of the insidious and base stratagems that are practising to hoodwink them out of their liberties.

The more I consider the manoevres that are practising, the more am I alarmed—foreseeing that the juggle cannot long be concealed, and that the spirit of the people will not brook the imposition, they have guarded as they suppose against any danger arising from the opposition of the people, and rendered their struggles for liberty impotent and ridiculous. What otherwise is the meaning of disarming the militia, for the purpose as it is said, of repairing their musquets at such a particular period? Does not the timing of the measure determine the intention? I was ever jealous of the select militia, consisting of infantry and troops of horse, instituted in this city and in some of the counties, without the sanction of law, and officered principally by the devoted instruments of the *well born*, although the illustrious patriotism of one of them, has not corresponded with the intention of appointing him. Are not these corps provided to suppress the first efforts of freedom, and to check the spirit of the people until a regular and sufficiently powerful military force shall be embodied to rivet the chains of slavery on a deluded nation. What confirms these apprehensions is the declaration of a certain Major, an active instrument in this business, and the echo of the principal conspirators, who has said, he should deem the cutting off of five thousand men, as a small sacrifice, a cheap purchase for the establishment of the new constitution.

CENTINEL.

Independent Gazatteer

12 JANUARY 1788

LETTER X

Centinel again details the plottings of Federalist leaders, asserting that the people have discovered their machinations and will reject their Constitution. Essays in The Federalist *of particular relevance: 1, 38.*

TO THE PEOPLE OF PENNSYLVANIA.

Fellow Citizens,

WHAT illustrious evidence and striking demonstration does the present momentous discussion afford of the inestimable value of the liberty of the press? No doubt now remains, but that it will prove the rock of our political salvation. Despotism, with its innumerable host of evils, by gliding through the mist of deception, had gained some of the principal works, had made a lodgement in the very citadel of liberty before it was discovered, and was near carrying the fortress by surprise: at this ment alarming crisis the centries from the watch-towers sounded the alarm, and aroused the dormant votaries of liberty to a due sense of their danger; who, with an alacrity and spirit suited to the exigence, answered to the call, repulsed the enemy, dislodged it from most of its acquisitions, and nothing is now wanting to a total rout and compleat defeat, but a general discharge from the artillery of freedom. As the shades of night fly the approach of the radiant sun, so does despotism before the majesty of enlightened truth; wherever free discussion is allowed, this is invariably the consequence. Since the press has been unshackled in Pennsylvania; what an astonishing transition appears in the sentiments of the people! Infatuation is at an end, execration and indignation have succeeded to blind admiration and mistaken enthusiasm. The rampant insolence of the conspirators is prostrated, black dispair has taken possession of many of them, their countenances proclaim their defeat, and express serious apprehension for their personal safety from the rising resentment of injured freemen.

James, the Caledonian,[1] lieutenant general of the myrmidons of power, under Robert,[2] the cofferer, who, with his aid-du-camp, *Gouvero*,[3] the cunning-man, has taken the field in Virginia: I say James, in this exigence, summonses grand council of his partizans in this city, and represents, in the most pathetic moving language, the deplorable situation of affairs, stimulates them to make a vigorous effort to recover the ground they have lost and establish their empire; that for this purpose, a generous contribution must be made by all those who expect to taste the sweets of power, or share in the fruits of dominion, in order to form a fund adequate to the great design, that may put them in possession of the darling object: then recommends that a committee be appointed of those who are gifted with Machiavelian talents, of those who excel in ingenuity, artifice, sophistry and the refinements of falsehood, who can assume the pleasing appearance of truth and bewilder the people in all the mazes of error; and as the task will be arduous, and requires vari-

1. James Wilson
2. Robert Morris
3. Gouverneur Morris

ous abilities and talents, the business ought to be distributed, and different parts assigned to the members of the committee, as they may be respectively qualified; some by ingenious sophisms to explain away and counteract those essays of patriotism that have struck such general conviction; some to manufacture extracts of letters and notes from correspondents, to give the complexion of strength to their cause, by representing the unanimity of all corners of America in favor of the new constitution; and others to write reams of letters to their tools in every direction, furnishing them with the materials of propagating error and deception; in short that this committee ought to make the press groan and the whole country reverberate with their productions. Thus to overpower truth and liberty by the din of empty sound and the delusion of falsehood.

The conspirators, deceived by their first success, grounded on the unreserved confidence of the people, do not consider that with the detection of their views, all chance of success is over; that suspicion once awakened, is not so soon to be lulled, but with eagle-eye will penetrate all their wiles, and detect their every scheme, however deeply laid, or speciously glossed. The labours of their committee will be unavailing, the point of deception is passed, the rays of enlightened patriotism have diffused general illumination. However, this new effort will serve to shew the perseverance of ambition and the necessity of constant vigilance in the people for the preservation of their liberty.

Already we recognize the ingenuity and industry of this committee; the papers teem with paragraphs, correspondents, &c. that exhibit a picture which bears no resemblance to the original; if we view this mirror for the representation of the sentiments of the people, a perfect harmony seems to prevail, every body in every place are charmed with the new-Constitution, consider it as a gift from heaven, as their only salvation, &c. &c. &c. and I am informed expresses are employing to waft the delusion to the remotest corners; such a scene of bustle, lying, and activity, was never exhibited since the days of Adam. The contributions to the grand fund are so great, that it is whispered a magazine of all the apparatus of war is to be immediately provided, and if all other means fail, force

is to be recurred to, which they hope will successfully terminate the
disagreeable discussion of the rights of mankind, of equal liberty,
&c. and thus establish a due subordination to the *well born few.*

CENTINEL.

Independent Gazetteer

16 JANUARY 1788

LETTER XI

*Centinel argues that neither anarchy nor a split of the United States
into competing confederacies would be likely, should the new Constitution be rejected. Moreover, neither threatened outcome should be
feared as much as the despotism inevitable under the proposed Constitution. Essays in* The Federalist *of particular relevance: 6-10.*

TO THE PEOPLE OF PENNSYLVANIA.

Fellow-Citizens,

THE arguments upon which the advocates of the new constitution
the most dwell, are the distresses of the community, the evils of
anarchy, and the horrible consequences that would ensue from the
dissolution of the union of the states, and the institution of separate confederacies or republics: The unanimity of the federal convention, and the sanction of great names, can be no further urged as
an argument after the exposition made by the attorney-general of
Maryland, who was a member of that convention; he has opened
such a scene of discord and accommodation of republicanism to
despotism as must excite the most serious apprehensions in every
patriotic mind. The first argument has been noticed in the preceding essays; wherein it is shewn that this is not the criterion
whereby to determine the merits of the new constitution; that
notwithstanding the reality of the distresses of the people, the new
constitution may not only be inadequate as a remedy, but destruc-

tive of liberty, and the completion of misery: The remaining two arguments will be discussed in this number; their futility elucidated; and thus the medium of deception [being] dissipated, the public attention, with undiverted unfinished force, will be directed to the proper object, will be confined to the consideration of the nature and construction of the plan of government itself, the question will then [be], whether this plan be calculated for our welfare, or misery; whether it is the temple of liberty, or the structure of despotism? and as the former, or the latter, shall appear to be the case, to adopt, or reject it accordingly, otherwise to banish the demon of domination by suitable amendments and qualifications.

The evils of anarchy have been pourtrayed with all imagery of language, in the glowing colours of eloquence; the affrighted mind is thence led to clasp the new constitution as the instrument of deliverance, as the only avenue to safety and happiness: To avoid the possible and transitory evils at one extreme, it is seduced into the certain and permanent misery necessarily attendant on the other. A state of anarchy from its very nature, can never be of long continuance; the greater its violence, the shorter the duration; order and security are immediately sought by the distracted people beneath the shelter of equal laws, and the salutary restraints of regular government; and if this be not attainable absolute power is assumed by the *one*, or the *few*, who shall be the most enterprising and successful. If anarchy, therefore, were the inevitable consequence of rejecting the new constitution, it would be infinitely better to incur it; for even then there would be at least the chance of a good government rising out of licentiousness; but to rush at once into despotism, because there is a bare possibility of anarchy ensuing from the rejection, or from what is yet more visionary, the small delay that would be occasioned by a revision and correction of the proposed system of government, is so superlatively weak, so fatally blind, that it is astonishing any person of common understanding should suffer such an imposition to have the least influence on his judgement; still more astonishing, that so flimsy and deceptive a doctrine should make converts among the enlightened freemen of America, who have so long enjoyed the blessings of liberty; but when I view among such converts, men otherwise *pre-eminent*, it raises a blush for the weakness of humanity, that these her brightest ornaments should be so dim-lighted to what is self-evident to most men, that such imbecility of judgement should appear where so much perfection was looked for; this ought to teach us to depend more on our own judgement and the nature of the case, than upon the opinions of the greatest and best of men, who, from *constitutional* infirmities, or *particular* situations may sometimes view an object through a delusive medium; but the opinions of great men are more frequently the dictates of ambition, or private interest.

The source of the apprehensions of this so much dreaded anarchy would upon investigation be found to arise from the artful suggestions of designing men, and not from a rational probability grounded on the actual state of affairs; the least reflection is sufficient to detect the fallacy to shew that there is no one circumstance to justify the prediction of such an event: On the contrary, a short time will evince to the utter dismay and confusion of the conspirators, that a perseverance in cramming down their scheme of power upon the freemen of this state, will inevitably produce *an anarchy* destructive of their darling domination, and *may* kindle a flame prejudicial to their safety; they should be cautious not to trespass too far on the forbearance of freemen, when wresting their dearest concerns; but prudently retreat from the gathering storm.

The other spectre that has been raised to terrify and alarm the people out of the exercise of their judgement on this great occasion, is the dread of our splitting into separate confederacies or republics, that might become rival powers and consequently liable to mutual wars from the usual motives of contention. This is an event still more improbable than the foregoing; it is a presumption unwarranted, either by the situation of affairs, or the sentiments of the people; no disposition leading to it exists; the advocates of the new constitution seem to view such a separation with horror, and its opponents are strenuously contending for a confederation that shall embrace all America under its comprehensive and salutary protection. This hobgoblin appears to have sprung from the deranged brain of *Publius*, a New-York writer, who, mistaking sound for argument, has with Herculean labour accumulated myriads of unmeaning sentence, and *mechanically* endeavored to force conviction by a torrent of misplaced words; he might have spared his readers the fatigue of wading through his long-winded disquisitions on the direful effects of the contentions of inimical states, as totally inapplicable to the subject he was *professedly* treating; this writer has devoted much time, and wasted more paper in combating chimeras of his own creation: However, for the sake of argument, I will admit, that the necessary consequence of rejecting, or delaying the establishment of the new constitution, would be the dissolution of the union, and the institution of even rival and inimical republics; yet ought such an apprehension, if well founded, to drive us into the fangs of despotism: Infinitely preferable would be occasional wars to such an event; the forms although a severe scourge, is transient in its continuous and in its operation partial, but a small proportion of the community are exposed to its greatest horrors, and yet fewer experience its greatest evils; the latter is permanent and universal misery, without remission or exemption: as passing clouds obscure for a time the splendour of the sun, so do wars interrupt the welfare of mankind; but despotism is a settled gloom that totally extinguishes happiness, not a ray of comfort can penetrate to cheer the dejected mind; the goad of power with unabating rigor insists upon the utmost exaction, like a merciless task master, is continually inflicting the lash, and is never satiated with the feast of unfeeling domination, or the most abject servility.

The celebrated Lord Kaims whose disquisitions on human nature evidence extraordinary strength of judgement and depth of investigation, says that a continual *civil* war, which is the most destructive and horrible scene of human discord, is preferable to the uniformity of wretchedness and misery attendant upon despotism;—of all *possible* evils, as I observed in my first number, *this* is the worst and the most to be *dreaded*.

I congratulate my fellow-citizens that a good government, the greatest earthly blessing, may be so easily obtained, that our circumstances are so favorable that nothing but the folly of the conspirators can produce anarchy or civil war, which would presently terminate in their destruction and the permanent harmony of the state alone, interrupted by their ambitious machinations.

In a former number I stated a charge of a very heinous nature, and highly prejudicial to the public welfare, and at this great crisis peculiarly alarming and threatening to liberty; I mean the suppression of the circulation of the newspapers from state to state by the of—c—rs of the P—t-O—ce, who in violation of their duty and integrity have prostituted their of–ces to forward the nefarious design of enslaving their countrymen, by thus cutting off all communication by the usual vehicle between the patriots of America;— I find that notwithstanding that public appeal, they persevere in this villainous and daring practice. The newspapers of the other states that contain any useful information, are still withheld from the printers of this state, and I see by the annunciation of the Editor of Mr. Greenleaf's patriotic New-York paper, that the printers of that place are still treated in like manner; this informs his readers that but two southern papers have come to hand, and that they contain no information, which he affects to ascribe to the negligence of the p—t boy, not caring to quarrel with the p—t m–t-r g——l.

CENTINEL.

Independent Gazetteer

23 JANUARY 1788

LETTER XII

Centinel again attacks Federalists for interfering with the distribution of Anti-Federalist newspapers. He goes on to call the new Constitution "a many headed hydra of despotism" worse than any single tyrant. Essays in The Federalist *of particular relevance: 1, 38.*

TO THE PEOPLE OF PENNSYLVANIA.
   Fellow Citizens,
CONSCIOUS guilt has taken the alarm, thrown out the signal of distress, and even appealed to the generosity of patriotism. The

authors and abettors of the new constitution shudder at the term *conspirators* being applied to them, as it designates their true character, and seems prophetic of the catastrophe: they read their fate in the epithet.

In dispair they are weakly endeavouring to screen their criminality by interposing the shield of the virtues of a Washington, in representing his concurrence in the proposed system of government, as evidence of the purity of their intentions; but this impotent attempt to degrade the brightest ornament of his country to a base level with themselves, will be considered as an aggravation of their treason, and an insult on the good sense of the people, who have too much discernment not to make a just discrimination between the honest mistaken zeal of the patriot, and the flagitious machinations of an ambitious junto, and will resent the imposition that Machiavelian arts and consummate cunning have practised upon our *illustrious chief*.

The term *conspirators* was not, as has been alledged, rashly or inconsiderately adopted; it is the language of dispassionate and deliberate reason, influenced by the purest patriotism: the consideration of the nature and construction of the new, constitution naturally suggests the epithet; its justness is strikingly illustrated by the conduct of the patrons of this plan of government, but if any doubt had remained whether this epithet is merited, it is now removed by the very uneasiness it occasions; this is a confirmation of its propriety. Innocence would have nothing to dread from such a stigma, but would triumph over the shafts of malice.

The conduct of men is the best clue to their principles. The system of deception that has been practised; the constant solicitude shewn to prevent information diffusing its salutary light, are evidence of a conspiracy beyond the arts of sophistry to palliate, or the ingenuity of falsehood to invalidate: the means practised to establish the new constitution are demonstrative of the principles and designs of its authors and abettors.

At the time, says Mr. Martin (deputy from the state of Maryland in the general convention) when the public prints were announcing our perfect unanimity, discord prevailed to such a degree, that the minority were upon the point of appealing to the public against the machinations of ambition. By such a base imposition, repeated in every newspaper and reverberated from one end of the union to the other, was the people lulled into a false confidence, into an implicit reliance upon the wisdom and patriotism of the convention; and when ambition, by her deceptive wiles, had succeeded to usher forth the new system of government with apparent unanimity of sentiment, the public delusion was compleat. The most extravagant fictions were palmed upon the people, the seal of divinity was even ascribed to the new constitution; a felicity more than human was to ensue from its establishment;—overlooking the real cause of our difficulties and burthens, which have their proper remedy, the people were taught that the new constitution would prove a mine of wealth and prosperity equal to every want, or the most sanguine desire; that it would effect what can only be produced by the exertion of industry and the practice of economy.

The conspirators, aware of the danger of delay, that allowing time for a rational investigation would prove fatal to their designs, precipitated the establishment of the new constitution with all possible celerity; in Massachusetts the deputies of that convention, who are to give the final fiat in behalf of that great state to a measure upon which their dearest concerns depend, were elected by express in the first moments of blind enthusiasm; similar conduct has prevailed in the other states as far as circumstances permitted.

If the foregoing circumstances did not prove a conspiracy, there are others that must strike conviction in the most unsuspicious. Attempts to prevent discussion by shackling the press ought ever to be a signal of alarm to freemen, and considered as an annunciation of meditated tyranny; this is a truth that the uniform experience of mankind has established beyond the possibility of doubt. Bring the conduct of the authors and abettors of the new constitution to this test, let this be the criterion of their criminality, and every patriotic mind must unite in branding them with the stigma of conspirators against the public liberties.—No stage of this business but what has been marked with every exertion of influence and device of ambition to suppress information and intimidate public discussion; the virtue and firmness of some of the printers, rose superior to the menaces of violence, and the lucre of private interest; when every means failed to shackle the press, the free and independent papers were attempted to be demolished by withdrawing all the subscriptions to them within the sphere of the influence of the conspirators; fortunately for the cause of liberty and truth, these daring high handed attempts have failed except in one instance, where from a peculiarity of circumstances, ambition has triumphed. Under the flimsy pretence of vindicating the character of a contemptible drudge of party rendered ridiculous by his superlative folly in the late convention, of which the statement given in the Pennsylvania Herald, was confessedly a faithful representation, this newspaper has been silenced* by some hundreds of its subscribers (who it seems are generally among the devoted tools of party, or those who are obliged from their thraldom to yield implicit assent to the mandates of the junto) withdrawing their support from it; by the stroke the conspirators have suppressed the publication of the most valuable debates of the late convention, which would have been given in course by the Editor of that paper, whose stipend now ceasing, he cannot afford without compensation the time and attention necessary to this business.

Every patriotic person who had an opportunity of hearing that illustrious advocate of liberty and his country, Mr. Findley, must sensibly regret that his powerful arguments are not to extend beyond the confined walls of the State-House where they could have so limitted an effect; that the United States could not have been his auditory through the medium of the press. I anticipate the answer of the conspirators; they will tell you that this could not be their motive for silencing this paper, as the whole of the debates were taken down in short hand by another person and published, but the public are not to be so easily duped, they will not receive a spurious as an equivalent for a genuine production; equal solicitude was expressed for the publication of the former as for the suppression of the latter—the public will judge of the motives.

That investigation into the nature and construction of the new constitution, which the conspirators have so long and zealously struggled against, has, notwithstanding their partial success, so

*The Herald it is said is to be discontinued the 23d instant, (the Editor is already dismissed.)

far taken place as to ascertain the enormity of their criminality. That system which was pompously displayed as the perfection of government, proves upon examination to be the most odious system of tyranny that was ever projected, a many headed hydra of despotism, whose complicated and various evils would be infinitely more oppressive and afflictive than the scourge of any single tyrant: the objects of dominion would be tortured to gratify the calls of ambition and the cravings of power of rival despots contending for the sceptre of superiority; the devoted people would experience a distraction of misery.

No wonder then that such a discovery should excite uneasy apprehensions in the minds of the conspirators, for such an attempt against the public liberties is unprecedented in history, it is a crime of the blackest dye, as it strikes at the happiness of millions and the dignity of human nature, as it was intended to deprive the inhabitants of so large a portion of the globe of the choicest blessing of life and the oppressed of all nations of an asylum.

The explicit language of the Centinel during the empire of delusion was not congenial to the feelings of the people, but truth when it has free scope is all powerful, it enforces conviction in the most prejudiced mind; he foresaw the consequence of an exertion of the good sense and understanding of the people, and predicted the defeat of the measure he ventured to attack, when it was deemed sacred by most men and the certain ruin of any who should dare to lisp a word against it: he has persevered through every discouraging appearance, and has now the satisfaction to find his countrymen are aware of their danger and are taking measures for their security.

Since writing the foregoing, I am informed that the Printer of the Pennsylvania Herald is not quite decided whether he will drop his paper; he wishes, and perhaps will be enabled, to persevere;—however, the conspirators have effected their purpose; the editor is dismissed and the debates of the convention thereby suppressed.

CENTINEL.

Independent Gazetteer

30 JANUARY 1788

LETTER XIII

Centinel engages the arguments of "Conciliator," who had urged people to trust the new Congress to correct any defects in the Constitution. According to Centinel, trusting Congress would place the people's liberty at the mercy of their rulers and potential tyrants. Essays in The Federalist *of particular relevance: 1, 43, 85.*

TO THE PEOPLE OF PENNSYLVANIA.

Fellow-Citizens,

THE conspirators are putting your good sense, patriotism and spirit to the severest test. So bold a game of deception, so decisive a stroke for despotic power, was never before attempted among enlightened freemen. Can there be apathy so indifferent as not to be rouzed into indignation, or prejudice so blind, as not to yield to the glaring evidence of a flagitious conspiracy against the public liberties! The audacious and high-handed measures practised to suppress information, and intimidate discussion, would in any other circumstances than the present, have kindled a flame fatal to such daring invaders of our dearest privileges.

The conspirators having been severely galled and checked in their career by the artillery of freedom, have made more vigorous and successful efforts to silence her batteries, while falsehood with all her delusions is making new and greater exertions in favor of ambition. On the one hand, every avenue to information is as far as possible cut off, the usual communication between the states through the medium of the press, is in a great measure destroyed, by a new arrangement at the Post-Office, scarcely a newspaper is suffered to pass* by this conveyance, and the arguments of a

*For the truth of this charge I appeal to the Printers.

Findley, a Whitehill and a Smilie, that bright constellation of patriots are suppressed, and a spurious publication substituted; and on the other hand the select committee are assiduously employed in manufacturing deception in all its ensnaring colours, and having an adequate fund at their command, they are deluging the country with their productions. The only newspaper that circulates extensively out of the city is kept running over with deceptive inventions. Doctor Puff the paragraphist, has scarcely slept since his appointment, having received orders to work double tides; beneath his creative pen thousands of correspondents rise into view, who all harmonize in their sentiments and information about the new-constitution; but the chief reliance is on James the Caledonian, who can to appearance distroy all distinction between liberty and despotism, and make the latter pass for the former, who can bewilder truth in all the mazes of sophistry, and render the plainest propositions problematical—He cameleon-like can vary his appearance at pleasure, and assume any character for the purposes of deception. In the guise of a *Conciliator*, in the Independent Gazetteer, he professes great candour and moderation, admits some of the principal objections to the new constitution to be well founded, and insidiously proposes a method to remove them, which is to consider the first Congress under the new constitution as a convention, competent to supply all defects in the system of government. This is really a discovery that does honor to his invention. What! a legislative declaration or law a basis upon which to rest our dearest liberties. Does he suppose the people have so little penetration as not to see through so flimsey a delusion, that such a security would amount to no more than the will and pleasure of their rulers, who might repeal this *fundamental* sanction whenever ambition stimulated?—in the feigned *character* of a *freeman*, he combats the weighty arguments of the minority of the late convention, by a meer play upon words, carefully avoiding the real merits of the question; and we moreover trace him in a variety of miscellaneous productions in every shape and form, he occasionally assists Doctor Puff in the fabrication of extracts of letters, paragraphs, correspondents, &c. &c.

So gifted and with such a claim of merit from his extraordinary and unwearied exertions in the cause of despotism, who so suitable or deserving of the office of Chief Justice of the United States. How congenial would such a post be to the principles and disposition of James! Here he would be both Judge and jury, sovereign arbiter in law and equity. In this capacity he may satiate his vengeance on patriotism for the opposition given to his projects of dominion: Here he may gratify his superlative arrogance and contempt of mankind, by trampelling upon his fellow creatures with impunity; here he may give the finishing stroke to liberty, and silence the offensive complaints of violated justice and innocence, by adding the sanction of his office to the rapacity of power and the wantonness of oppression; there will be no intervening jury to shield the innocent, or procure redress to the injured.

Fellow-citizens, although the conspirators and their abettors are not sufficiently numerous to endanger our liberties by an open and forcible attack on them, yet when the characters of which they are composed and the methods they are practicing, are considered, it ought to occasion the most serious alarm, and stimulate to an immediate, vigorous and united exertion of the patriotic part of the community for the security of their rights and privileges. Societies ought to be instituted in every county and a reciprocity of sentiments and information maintained between such societies, whereby the patriots throughout Pennsylvania, being mutually enlightened and invigorated, would form an invincible bulwark to liberty, and by unity of council and exertion might the better procure and secure to themselves and to unborn ages the blessings of a good federal government. Nothing but such a system of conduct can frustrate the machinations of an ambitious junto, who, versed in Machiavelian arts, can varnish over with the semblance of freedom the most despotic instrument of government ever projected, who cannot only veil over their own ambitious purposes, but raise an outcry against the real patriots for interested views when they are advocating the cause of liberty and of their country by opposing a scheme of arbitrary power and office-making; who can give the appearance of economy to the introduction of a numerous and permanent standing army and the institution of lucrative, needless offices to provide for the swarms of gaping, almost famished expectants, who have been campaigning it for ten years without success against our inestimable state constitution, as a reward for their persevering toils, but particularly for their zeal on the present occasion, and also as a phalanx to tyranny; and who notwithstanding the testimony of uniform experience evinces the necessity of restrictions on those entrusted with power, and a due dependence of the deputy on the constitution being maintained to ensure the public welfare; who notwithstanding the fate that liberty has ever met from the remissness of the people and the persevering nature of ambition who ever on the watch; grasps at every avenue to supremacy. I say, notwithstanding such evidence before them of the folly of mankind so often duped by similar arts; the conspirators have had the address to inculcate the opinion that forms of government are no security for the public liberties, that the administration is every thing, that although there would be no responsibility under the new constitution, no restriction on the powers of the government, whose will and pleasure would be literally the law of the land, yet that we should be perfectly safe and happy, that as our rulers would be made of the same corrupt materials as ourselves, they certainly could not abuse the trust reposed in them, but would be the most self denying order of beings ever created; with your purses at their absolute disposal, and your liberties at their discretion, they would be proof against the charms of money and the allurements of power; however, if such Utopian ideas should prove chimerical and the people should find the yoke too heavy, they might at pleasure alleviate or even throw it off. In short, the conspirators have displayed so much ingenuity on this occasion, that if it had not been for the patriotism and firmness of some of the printers, which gave an opportunity to enlightened truth to come forward, and by her invincible powers to detect the sophistry, and expose the fallacy of such impositions, liberty must have been overcome by the wiles of ambition, and this land of freemen have become the miserable abode of slaves.

CENTINEL.

Independent Gazetteer

5 FEBRUARY 1788

LETTER XIV

Centinel cites prominent Anti-Federalist Luther Martin, a dissenting member of the Constitutional Convention, in arguing that the new Congress's taxing power is absolute and will result in the consolidation of all government in the center. Essays in The Federalist *of particular relevance: 30-36.*

TO THE PEOPLE OF PENNSYLVANIA.

Fellow-Citizens,

I AM happy to find the comment that I have made upon the nature and tendency of the new constitution, and my suspicions of the principles and designs of its authors, are fully confirmed by the evidence of the Honorable LUTHER MARTIN, Esquire, late deputy in the general convention. He has laid open the conclave, exposed the dark scene within, developed the mystery of the proceedings, and illustrated the machinations of ambition. His public spirit has drawn upon him the rage of the conspirators, for daring to remove the veil of secrecy, and announcing to the public the meditated, gilded mischief: all their powers are exerting for his destruction; the mint of calumny is assiduously engaged in coining scandal to blacken his character, and thereby to invalidate his testimony; but this illustrious patriot will rise superior to all their low arts, and be the better confirmed in the good opinion and esteem of his fellow-citizens, upon whose gratitude he has an additional claim by standing forth their champion at a crisis when most men would have shrunk from such a duty. Mr. Martin has appealed to general Washington for the truth of what he has advanced, and undaunted by the threats of his and his country's enemies, is nobly persevering in the cause of liberty and mankind. I would earnestly recommend it to all well meaning persons to read his communication, as the

most satisfactory and certain method of forming a just opinion on
the present momentous question, particularly the three or four last
continuances, as they go more upon the general principles and tendency of the new constitution. I have in former numbers alluded to
some passages in this publication; I shall in this number quote some
few others, referring to the work itself for a more lengthy detail.
The following paragraphs are extracted from the continuances
republished in the Independent Gazetteer of the 25th January, and
the Pennsylvania Packet of the 1st [of] February instant, viz.

"By the eighth section of this article, Congress is to have power
to lay and collect taxes, duties, imposts, and excises.—When we
met in convention after our adjournment, to receive the report of
the committee of detail, the members of that committee were
requested to inform us what powers were meant to be vested in
Congress by the [word *duties* in this section, since the] word
imposts extended to duties on goods imported, and by another part
of the system no duties on exports were to be laid.—In answer to
this inquiry we were informed, that it was meant to give the general government the power of laying stamp duties on paper, parchment and vellum. We then proposed to have the power inserted in
express words, lest disputes hereafter might arise on the subject,
and that the meaning might be understood by all who were to be
affected by it; but to this it was objected, because it was said that
the word stamp would probably sound odiously in the ears of many
of the inhabitants, and be a cause of objection. By the power of
imposing stamp duties the Congress will have a right to declare
that no wills, deeds, or other instruments of writing, shall be good
and valid, without being stamped—that without being reduced to
writing and being stamped, no bargain, sale, transfer of property, or
contract of any kind or nature whatsoever shall be binding; and also
that no exemplifications of records, depositions, or probates [of] any
[kind shall] be received in evidence, unless they have the same
solemnity—They may likewise oblige all proceedings of a judicial
nature to be stamped to give their effect—those stamp duties may
be imposed to any amount they please, and under the pretence of
securing the collection of these duties, and to prevent the laws
which imposed them from being evaded, the Congress may bring

the decision of all questions relating to the conveyance, disposition and rights of property and every question relating to contracts between man and man into the courts of the general government.— Their inferior courts in the first instance and the superior court by appeal. By the power to lay and collect imposts, they may impose duties on any or every article of commerce imported into these states to what amount they please. By the power to lay excises, a power very odious in its nature, since it authorises officers to go into your houses, your kitchens, your cellars, and to examine into your private concerns; the Congress may impose duties on every article of use or consumption, on the food that we eat—on the liquors we drink—on the cloaths we wear—on the glass which enlighten our houses—or the hearths necessary for our warmth and comfort. By the power to lay and collect taxes, they may proceed to direct taxation on every individual either by a capitation tax on their heads, or an assessment on their property. By this part of the section, therefore, the government has a power to lay what duties they please on goods imported—to lay what duties they please afterwards on whatever we use or consume—to impose stamp duties to what amount they please, and in whatever cases they please—afterwards to impose on the people direct taxes, by capitation tax, or by assessment, to what amount they choose, and thus to sluice them at every vein as long as they have a drop of blood, without any controul, limitation or restraint—while all the officers for collecting these taxes, stamp duties, imposts and excises, are to be appointed by the general government, under its direction, not accountable to the states; nor is there even a security that they shall be citizens of the respective states, in which they are to exercise their offices; at the same time the construction of every law imposing any and all these taxes and duties, and directing the collection of them, and every question arising thereon, and on the conduct of the officers appointed to execute these laws, and to collect these taxes and duties so various in their kinds, are taken away from the courts of justice of the different states, and confined to the courts of the general government, there to be heard and determined by judges holding their offices under the appointment, not of the states, but of the general government.

"Many of the members, and myself in the number, thought that the states were much better judges of the circumstances of their citizens, and what sum of money could be collected from them by direct taxation, and of the manner in which it could be raised, with the greatest case and convenience to their citizens, than the general government could be; and that the general government ought not in any case to have the power of laying direct taxes, but in that of the delinquency of a state. Agreeable to this sentiment, I brought in a proposition on which a vote of the convention was taken. The proposition was as follows: 'And whereever the legislature of the United States shall find it necessary that revenue should be raised by direct taxation, having apportioned the same by the above rule, requisitions shall be made of the respective states to pay into the continental treasury their respective quotas within a time in the said requisition to be specified, and in case of any of the states, failing to comply with such requisition, then and then only, to have power to devise and pass acts directing the mode and authorising the collection of the same.' Had this proposition been acceded to, the dangerous and oppressive power in the general government of imposing direct taxes on the inhabitants, which it now enjoys in all cases, would have been only vested in it in case of the non-compliance of a state, as a punishment for its delinquency, and would have ceased that moment that the state complied with the requisition— But the proposition was rejected by a majority, consistent with their aim and desire of encreasing the power of the general government as far as possible, and destroying the powers and influence of the states—And though there is a provision that all duties, imposts and excises shall be uniform, that is, to be laid to the same amount on the same articles in each state, yet this will not prevent Congress from having it in their power to cause them to fall very unequal and much heavier on some states than on others, because these duties may be laid on articles but little or not at all used in some states, and of absolute necessity for the use and consumption of others, in which case the first would pay little or no part of the revenue arising therefrom, while the whole or nearly the whole of it would be paid by the lasts to wit, the states which use and consume the articles on which the imposts and excises are laid."

Another extract, viz.

"But even this provision apparently for the security of the state governments, inadequate as it is, is entirely left at the mercy of the general government, for by the fourth section of the first article, it is expressly provided, that the congress shall have a power to make and alter all regulations concerning the time and manner of holding elections for senators; a provision expressly looking forward to and I have no doubt designed for the utter extinction and abolition of all state governments; nor will this I believe be doubted by any person, when I inform you that some of the warm advocates and patrons of the system in convention, strenuously opposed the choice of the senators by the state legislatures, insisting that the state governments ought not to be introduced in any manner so as to be component parts of, or instruments for carrying into execution the general government—Nay, so far were the friends of the system from pretending that they meant it or considered it as a federal system, that on the question being proposed, 'that a union of the states, merely federal, ought to be the sole object of the exercise of the powers vested in the convention [']; it was negatived by a majority of the members, and it was resolved, 'that a national government ought to be formed'; afterwards the word 'national' was struck out by them, because they thought the word might tend to alarm—and although now they who advocate the system, pretend to call themselves federalists; in convention the distinction was just the reverse—those who opposed the system, were there considered and stiled the federal party, those who advocated it, the anti-federal.

"Viewing it as a national not a federal government, as calculated and designed not to protect and preserve, but to abolish and annihilate the state governments, it was opposed for the following reasons:—It was said that this continent was much too extensive for one national government, which should have sufficient power and energy to pervade and hold in obedience and subjection all its parts, consistent with the enjoyment and preservation of liberty—That the genius and habits of the people of America were opposed to such a government—That during their connexion with Great-Britain they had been accustomed to have all their concerns transacted within a narrow circle, their colonial districts—They had been accustomed to have their seats of government near them, to which they might have access, without much inconvenience when their business should require it—That at this time we find if a county is rather large, the people complain of the inconvenience, and clamour for a division of their county, or for a removal of the place where their courts are held, so as to render it more central and convenient—That in those states, the territory of which is extensive, as soon as the population encreases remote from the seat of government, the inhabitants are urgent for a removal of the seat of their government, or to be erected into a new state—As a proof of this, the inhabitants of the western parts of Virginia and North Carolina, of Vermont and the province of Main, were instances, even the inhabitants of the western parts of Pennsylvania, who it was said already seriously look forward to the time when they shall either be erected into a new state, or have their seat of government removed to the Susquehanna. If the inhabitants of the different states consider it as a grievance to attend a county court or the fear of their own government, when a little inconvenient, can it be supposed they would ever submit to have a national government established, the seat of which would be more than a thousand miles removed from some of them? It was insisted that governments of a republican nature, are those best calculated to preserve the freedom and happiness of the citizen. That governments of this kind, are only calculated for a territory but small in its extent—That the only method by which an extensive continent like America could be connected and united together consistent with the principles of freedom, must be by having a number of strong and energetic state governments for securing and protecting the rights of the individuals forming those governments, and for regulating all their concerns; and a strong energetic federal government over those states for the protection and preservation, and for regulating the common concerns of the states.—It was further insisted, that even if it was possible to effect a total abolition of the state governments at this time, and to establish one general government over the people of America, it could not long subsist, but in a little time would again be broken into a variety of governments of a smaller extent, similar in some manner to the present situation of this continent; the principal difference in all probability would be that the governments, so established; being effected by some violent convulsion, might not be formed on principles so favorable to liberty as those of our present state governments—That this ought to be an important consideration to such of the states who had excellent governments, which was the case with Maryland and most others, whatever it might be to persons who disapproving of their particular state government, would be willing to hazard every thing to overturn and destroy it. These reasons, Sir, influenced me to vote against two branches in the legislature, and against every part of the system which was repugnant to the principles of a federal government—Nor was there a single argument urged, or reason assigned, which to my mind was satisfactory, to prove that a good government on federal principles was unattainable, the whole of their arguments only proving, what none of us controverted, that our federal government as originally formed was defective and wanted amendment—However, a majority of the convention hastily and inconsiderately, without condescending to make a fair trial, in their great wisdom, decided that a kind of government which a Montesquieu and a Price have declared the best calculated of any to preserve internal liberty, and to enjoy external strength and security, and the only one by which a large continent can be connected and united consistent with the principles of liberty was totally impracticable, and they acted accordingly."

After such information, what are we to think of the declarations of Mr. Wilson, who assured our state convention, that it was neither the intention of the authors of the new constitution, nor its tendency to establish a consolidated or national government, founded upon the destruction of the state governments, that such could not have been the design of the general convention he said was certain, because the testimony of experience, the opinions of the most celebrated writers, and the nature of the case demonstrated in the clearest manner, that so extensive a territory as these United States includes, could not be governed by any other mode than a confederacy of republics consistent with the principles of freedom, and that their own conviction was, that nothing short of the

supremacy of despotism could connect and bind together this country under ONE GOVERNMENT? Has any one a doubt now
remaining of the guilt of the conspirators!

The O——rs of the P—t O——ce, fearful of the consequences of
their conduct, are taking measures to invalidate the charge made
against them. As this is a matter of the highest importance to the
public, it will be necessary to state the charge and the evidence. In
two of my former numbers, I asserted that the patriotic newspapers of this city and that of New-York miscarried in their passage,
whilst the vehicles of despotism, meaning those newspapers in
favor of the new constitution, passed as usual; and it was particularly asserted that the patriotic essays of Brutus, Cincinnatus,
Cato, &c. published at New-York, were withheld during the greatest part of the time that our state convention sat; and in a late number, I further asserted that since the late arrangement at the P—t
O——ce, scarcely a newspaper was suffered to pass by the usual
conveyance, and for the truth of this last charge I appealed to the
printers; however I understand this last is not denied or controverted. When the dependence of the printers on the P—t O——ce
is considered, the injury they may sustain by incurring the displeasure of these of——rs, and when to this is added that of the complexion of the printers in respect to the new constitution, that most
of them are zealous in promoting its advancement, it can scarcely be
expected that they would volunteer it against the P—t O——rs, or
refuse their names to a certificate exculpating the of——rs; accordingly we find that most of the printers have signed a certificate that
the newspapers arrived as usual prior to the first of January, when
the new arrangement took place; however, the printer of the Freeman's Journal when applied to, had the spirit to refuse his name to
the establishment of a falsehood, and upon being called upon to
specify the missing papers, particularly during the sitting of the
state convention, he pointed out and offered to give a list of a considerable number, instancing no less than seven successive Greenleaf's patriotic New-York papers, besides others occasionally
with-held from him; Colonel Oswald was out of town when his family was applied to, or I have no doubt he would have observed a similar conduct. But there is a fact that will invalidate any certificate

that can be procured on this occasion, and is alone demonstrative of the suppression of the patriotic newspapers. The opponents to the new constitution in this state were anxious to avail themselves of the well-written essays of the New-York patriots, such as Brutus, Cincinnatus, Cato, &c. and with that view were attentive to have them republished here as soon as they came to hand, and especially during the sitting of our state convention, when they would have been the most useful to the cause of liberty by operating on the members of that convention; a recurrence to the free papers of this city at that period, well shew a great chasm in these republications, owing to the miscarriage of Greenleaf's New-York papers; agreeable to my affections it will appear, that for the greatest part of the time that our state convention sat, scarcely any of the numbers of Brutus, Cincinnatus, Cato, &c. were republished in this city; the fifth number of Cincinnatus that contained very material information about the finances of the union, which strikes at some of the principal arguments in favor of the new constitutions which was published at New-York the 29th November, was not republished here until the 15th December, following [two or three] days after the convention rose, and so of most of the other numbers of this and the other signatures; so great was the desire of the opponents here to republish them, that the fourth number of Cincinnatus was republished so lately as in Mr. Bailey's last paper, which with other missing numbers were procured by private hands from New-York, and in two or three instances, irregular numbers were republished. The new arrangement at the P—t O——ce, novel in its nature, and peculiarly injurious by the suppression of information at this great crisis of public affairs, is a circumstance highly presumptive of the truth of the other charge.

CENTINEL.

Independent Gazetteer

22 FEBRUARY 1788

LETTER XV

Centinel laments that the people's accustomed suspicion of political change is being undermined. He dismisses Massachusetts's ratification of the Constitution as the result of panic over public unrest and urges a calm adherence to old forms. Essays in The Federalist of particular relevance: 1, 16, 43.

To the People of Pennsylvania.

Fellow-Citizens,

THERE are few of the maxims or opinions we hold, that are the result of our own investigation or observation, and even those we adopt from others are seldom on a conviction of their truth or propriety, but from the facination of example and the influence of what is or appears to be the general sentiments. The science of government being the most abstruse and unobvious of all others, mankind are more liable to be imposed upon by the artful and designing in systems and regulations of government, than on any other subject: hence a jealousy of innovation confirmed by uniform experience prevails in most communities; this reluctance to change, has been found to be the greatest security of free governments, and the principal bulwark of liberty; for the aspiring and ever-restless spirit of ambition would otherwise, by her deceptive wiles and ensnaring glosses, triumph over the freest and most enlightened people. It is the peculiar misfortune of the people of these United States, at this awful crisis of public affairs, to have lost this useful; this absolutely necessary jealousy of innovation in government, and thereby to lie at the mercy and be exposed to all the artifices of ambition, without this usual shield to protect them from imposition. The conspirators, well aware of their advantage, have seized the favorable moment, and by the most unparalleled arts of deception; have obtained the sanction of the conventions of several states to the most tyrannic system of government ever projected.

The magic of great names, the delusion of falsehood, the suppression of information, precipitation and fraud have been the instruments of this partial success, the pillars whereon the structure of tyranny has been so far raised. Those influential vehicles, the newspapers with few exceptions, have been devoted to the cause of despotism, and by the subserviency of the P——O——; the usefulness of the patriotic newspapers has been confined to the places of their publication, whilst falsehood and deception have had universal circulation, without the opportunity of refutation. The feigned unanimity of one part of America; has been represented to produce the acquiescence of another, and so mutually to impose upon the whole by the force of example.

The adoption of the new constitution by the convention of the state of Massachusetts, by a majority of nineteen out of near four hundred members, and that too qualified by a number of propositions of amendment, cannot afford the conspirators much cause for triumph, and especially when all the circumstances under which it has been obtained, are considered. The late alarming disorders which distracted that state, and even threatened subversion of all order and government, and were with difficulty suppressed, occasioned the greatest consternation among all men of property and rank: in this disposition even the most high toned and arbitrary government became desirable as a security against licentiousness and agrarian laws; consequently the new constitution was embraced with eagerness by men of these descriptions, who, in every community, form a powerful interest, and added to the conspirators, office-hunters, &c. &c. made a formidable and numerous party in favor of the new constitution. The elections of the members of convention were moreover made in the first moments of blind enthusiasm, when every artifice was practised to prejudice the people against all those who had the enlightened patriotism to oppose this system of tyranny: thus was almost every man of real ability, who was in opposition, excluded from a seat in the convention; consequently the contest was very unequal; well-meaning, though uninformed men, were opposed to great learning, eloquence and sophistry in the shape of lawyers, doctors and divines, who were capable and seemed disposed to delude by deceptive glosses and specious reasoning; indeed, from the specimens we have seen of the discussion on this occasion, every enlightened patriot must regret that the cause of liberty has been so weakly, although zealously advocated, that its champions were so little illuminated. In addition to these numerous advantages in the convention, the friends of the new constitution had the weight and influence of the town of Boston to second their endeavors, and yet, notwithstanding all this, were near losing the question, although delusively qualified. Is this any evidence of the excellency of the new constitution? Certainly not. Nor can it have any influence in inducing the remaining states to accede. They will examine and judge for themselves, and from their wisdom in taking due time for deliberation, I have no doubt will prove the salvation of the liberties of the United States.

CENTINEL.

Independent Gazetteer

26 FEBRUARY 1788

LETTER XVI

Centinel attacks the Federalists for using the new Constitution to erase their own debts. The Constitution's ban on ex post facto laws, combined with its failure to hold onto debts owed to the United States, will eliminate individual and state debts owed to the Confederacy. Essays in The Federalist *of particular relevance: 1, 42, 43.*

To The People of Pennsylvania.

Fellow-Citizens,

The new constitution instead of being the panecea or cure of every grievance so delusively represented by its advocates will be found upon examination-like Pandora's box, replete with every evil. The most specious clauses of this system of ambition and iniquity contain latent mischief, and premedated villainy. By section 9th of the 1st article, "No *ex post facto* law shall be passed," This sounds very well upon a superficial consideration, and I dare say has been read by most people with approbation. Government undoubtedly ought to avoid retrospective laws as far as may be, as they are generally injurious and fraudulent: Yet there are occasions when such laws are not only just but highly requisite. An ex post facto law is a law made after the fact, so that the Congress under the new constitution are precluded from all controul over transactions prior to its establishment. This prohibition would skreen the numerous public defaulters, as no measure could be constitutionally taken to compel them to render an account and restore the public money; the unaccounted millions lying in their hands would become their private property. Hitherto these characters from their great weight and numbers have had the influence to prevent an investigation of their accounts, but if this constitution be established, they may set the public at defiance, as they would be completely exonerated of all demands of the United States against them. This is not a strained construction of this section, but the proper evident meaning of the words, which not even the ingenuity, or sophistry of the *Caledonian,* can disguise from the meanest capacity. However if this matter admitted of any doubt, it would be removed by the following consideration, viz. that the new constitution is founded upon a dissolution of the present articles of confederation and is an original compact between those states, or rather those individuals who accede to it; consequently all contracts, debts and engagements in favor or against the United States, under the *old* government, are cancelled unless they are provided for in the *new* constitution. The framers of this constitution appear to have been aware of such consequence by stipulating in article 6th, that all debts contracted, and engagements entered into before the adoption of this constitution shall be valid *against* the United States under the new constitution, but there is no provision that the debts, &c. due *to* the United States, shall be valid or recoverable. This is a striking omission, and must have been designed, as debts of the latter description would naturally occur and claim equal attention with the former. This article implied, cancels all debts due to the United States prior to the establishment of the new constitution. If equal provision had been made for the debts due *to* the United States, as *against* the United States, the ex post facto clause would not have so pernicious an operation.

The immaculate convention, that is said to have possessed the fullness of patriotism, wisdom and virtue, contained a number of the principal public defaulters; and these were the most influential members, and chiefly instrumental in the framing of the new constitution: There were several of this description in the deputation from the state of Pennsylvania, who have long standing and immense accounts to settle, and MILLIONS perhaps to refund. The late Financier alone, in the capacity of chairman of the commercial committee of Congress, early in the late war, was entrusted with millions of public money, which to this day remain unaccounted for, nor has he settled his accounts as Financier. The others may also find it a convenient method to balance accounts with the public; they are sufficiently known and therefore need not be designated— This will account for the zealous attachment of such characters to the new constitution and their dread of investigation and discussion. It may be said that the new Congress would rather break through the constitution than suffer the public to be defrauded of so much treasure, when the burthens and distresses of the people are so very great; but this is not to be expected from the characters of which that Congress would in all probability be composed, if we may judge from the predominant influence and interest these defaulters now possess in many of the states. Besides, should Congress be disposed to violate the fundamental articles of the constitution for the sake of public justice, they would be prevented in so doing by their oaths*, but even if this should not prove an obstacle, if it can be supposed that any set of men would perjure themselves for the public good, and combat an host of enemies on such terms, still it would be of no avail, as there is a further barrier interposed between the public and these defaulters, namely, the supreme court of the union, whose province it would be to determine the constitutionality of any law that may be controverted; and supposing no bribery or corrupt influence practised on the bench of judges, it would be their sworn duty to refuse their sanction to laws made in the face and contrary to the letter and spirit of the constitution, as any law to compel the settlement of accounts and payment of monies depending and due under the old confederation would be. The 1st section of 3d article gives the supreme court cognizance of not only the laws, but of all cases arising under the constitution, which empowers this tribunal to decide upon the construction of the constitution itself in the last resort. This is so extraordinary, so unprecedented an authority, that the intention in vesting of it must have been to put it out of the power of Congress, even by breaking through the constitution, to compel these defaulters to restore the public treasure.

In the present circumstances these sections of the new constitution would be also productive of great injustice between the respective states; the delinquent states would be exonerated from all existing demands against them on account of the great arrearages of former requisitions, as they could not be constitutionally compelled to discharge them. And as the majority of the states are in this predicament, and have an equal voice in the senate, it would be their interest, and in their power by not only the constitution,

---

*Article VI. "The senators and representatives beforementioned and the members of the several state legislatures, and all executive and judicial officers, both of the United States and of the several states, shall be bound by oath to support this constitution." Were ever public defaulters so effectually skreened! Not only the administrators of the general government, but also of the state governments, are prevented by oath from doing justice to the public; and the legislature of Pennsylvania could not without perjury insist upon the delinquent states discharging their arrears.

but by a superiority of votes to prevent the levying of such arrearages; besides, the constitution, moreover, declares; that all taxes;
&c. shall be uniform throughout the United States; which is an
additional obstacle against noticing them.

The state of Pennsylvania in [such cases], would have no credit
for her extraordinary exertions [and] punctuality heretofore; but
would be taxed equally with those states which, for years past,
have not contributed any thing to the common expences of the
union; indeed, some of the states have paid nothing since the
revolution.

CENTINEL.

Independent Gazetteer

24 MARCH 1788

LETTER XVII

*Centinel charges the Federalists with getting rich off public service
and seeking to protect their ill-gotten gains through the new Constitution. Essays in* The Federalist *of particular relevance: 1, 42, 43.*

TO THE PEOPLE OF PENNSYLVANIA.
   Fellow-Citizens,
IN my last number I exposed the villainous intention of the framers
of the new constitution, to defraud the public out of the millions
lying in the hands of individuals by the construction of this system,
which would, if established, cancel all debts now due to the United
States. I also shewed that thereby the delinquent states would be
exonerated of all arrearages due by them on former requisitions of
Congress; and to prove that the cancelling of the public dues was
premeditated in regard to individuals, I stated that the general convention contained a number of the principal public defaulters, and
that these were the most influential members, and chiefly instru-

mental in framing the new constitution: In answer to which, the conspirators have, by bold assertions, spurious vouchers, and insufficient certificates, endeavoured to exculpate one member, and to alleviate the weight of the charge of delinquency against another. In the face of a resolution of Congress of the 20th June, 1785, declaring their intention of appointing 3 commissioners, to settle and adjust the receipts and expenditures of the late financier; the conspirators have asserted, that his accounts were finally settled in November, 1784, for which they pretend to have vouchers, and by a pompous display of certain resolutions of Congress, respecting a particular charge of fraud against him, as commercial agent to the United States, they vainly hope to divert the public attention from his great delinquency, in never accounting for the millions of public money, entrusted to him in that line. When we consider the immense sums of money taken up by Mr. M——s, as commercial agent, to import military supplies, and even to trade in behalf of the United States, at a time when the risque was so great, that individuals would not venture their property: that all these transactions were conducted under the private firm of W——g and M——, which afforded unrestrained scope to peculation and embezzlement of the public property, by enabling Mr. M——s to throw the loss of all captures by the enemy, at that hazardous period, on the public, and converting most of the safe arrivals (which were consequently very valuable) into his private property; and when we add to these considerations, the principles of the MAN, his bankrupt situation at the commencement of the late war, and the immense wealth he has dazzled the world with since, can it be thought unreasonable to conclude, that the principal source of his affluence was the commercial agency of the United States, during the war, not that I would derogate from his successful ingenuity in his numerous speculations in the paper monies, Havannah monopoly and job, or in the sphere of financiering.

The certificate published in behalf of general M—ffl—n, the quarter master gen—l, will not satisfy a discerning public, or acquit him of the charge of delinquency, as this certificate was procured to serve an electioneering purpose, up on a superficial and hasty inspection of his general account, unchecked by the accounts of his deputies, whose receipts and expenditures had not been examined, and consequently, by errors, collusion between him and them, or otherwise g——l M—ffl—n may retain a large balance in his hands; in such case a *quietus* may have been thought expedient to continue his affluence.

For the honor of human nature, I wish to draw a veil over the situation and conduct of another weighty character, whose name has given a false lustre to the new constitution, and been the occasion of sullying the laurels of a *Washington*, by inducing him to acquiesce in a system of despotism and villainy, at which enlightened patriotism shudders.

The discovery of the intended fraud, which for magnitude and audacity, is unparalleled, must open the eyes of the deluded to the true character and principles of the men who had assumed the garb of patriotism, with an insidious design of enslaving and robbing their fellow-citizens—of establishing those odious distinctions between the well born and the great body of the people, of degrading the latter to the level of slaves, and elevating the former to the rank of nobility.

The citizens of this state, which is in advance in its payments to the federal treasury, whilst some of the others have not paid a farthing since the war, ought in a peculiar manner to resent the intended imposition, and make its authors experience their just resentment; it is incumbent upon them in a particular manner, to exert themselves to frustrate the measures of the conspirators, and set an example to those parts of the union, who have not enjoyed the blessing of a free press on this occasion, but are still enveloped in the darkness of delusion, and enthralled by the fascination of names.

Could it have been supposed seven years ago, that, before the wounds received in the late conflict for liberty were scarcely healed, a post master-general and his deputies would have had the daring presumption to convert an establishment intended to promote and secure the public welfare into an engine of despotism, by suppressing all those newspapers that contain the essays of patriotism and real intelligence, and propagating instead thereof falsehoods and delusion? Such a supposition at that time, would have been treated as chimerical; but how must our indignation rise when we find this flagitious practice is persevered in, after being publicly detected! Must not the bribe from the conspirators be very great to compensate the post master-general and his deputies, for the loss of character and infamy consequent upon such conduct, and for the danger they incur of being impeached and turned out of office?

The scurrilous attack of the *little Fiddler* upon Mr. Workman of the university, on a suspicion, perhaps, unfounded of his being the author of a series of essays under the signature of *Philadelphiensis*, is characteristical of the man; he has ever been the base parasite and tool of the wealthy and great, at the expence of truth, honor, friendship, treachery to benefactors, nay to the nearest relatives; all have been sacrificed by him at the shrine of the great: he ought however, to have avoided a contrast with so worthy and highly respected a character as Mr. Workman, who had an equal right with himself to offer his sentiments on the new constitution; and if he viewed it as a system of despotism, and had talents to unfold its nature and tendency, he deserves the thanks of every patriotic American, if he has exerted them under the character of Philadelphiensis.—His not being above four years in the country can be no objection; the celebrated Thomas Paine wrote his Common Sense before he had been two years in America, which was not the less useful or acceptable upon that account. The public have nothing to do with the author of a piece; it is the merits of the writing that are alone to be considered.—Mr. Workman, prior to his coming to America, was a professor in an eminent academy in Dublin.—Little Francis should have been cautious in giving provocation, for insignificance alone could have preserved him the smallest remnant of character; I hope he will take the hint, or such a scene will be laid open as will disgrace even his patrons; the suit of cloaths, and the quarter cask of wine, will not be forgot.

CENTINEL.

Independent Gazetteer

9 APRIL 1788

ESSAY XVIII

Centinel closes by accusing the Federalists of attempting to silence their opposition. In this attempt to make support for the Constitution seem unanimous, the Federalists have violated freedom of the press. Essays in The Federalist *of particular relevance: 1, 84.*

To the PEOPLE of PENNSYLVANIA.

Fellow-Citizens,

THE measures that are pursuing to effect the establishment of the new constitution, are so repugnant to truth, honor, and the well-being of society, as would disgrace any cause. If the nature and tendency of this system were to be judged of by the conduct of its framers and patrons, what a picture of ambition and villainy would present itself to our view! From the specimens they have already given, anticipation may easily realise the consequences that would flow from the new constitution, if established; may bid adieu to all the blessings of liberty, to all the fruits of the late glorious assertion of the rights of human nature, made at the expence of so much blood and treasure. Yet such is the infatuation of many well meaning persons, that they view with indifference the attrocious villainy which characterises the proceedings of the advocates of the new system: The daring, and in most parts of the United States, the successful methods practised to shackle the press, and destroy the freedom of discussion; the silencing the Pennsylvania Herald, to prevent the publication of the invaluable debates of the late convention of this state; the total suppression of real intelligence, and of the illuminations of patriotism through the medium of the post-office; the systematic fraud and deception that pervade the union; the stigmatising, and by every art which ambition and malice can suggest, labouring to villify, intimidate and trample under foot every disinterested patriot, who preferring his country's good to every other consideration, has the courage to stand forth the champion of liberty and the people; and the intercepting of private confidential letters passing from man to man, violating the sacredness of a seal, and thus infringing one of the first privileges of freemen—that of communicating with each other: I say all these are overlooked by the infatuated admirers of the new system, who, deluded by the *phantom* of wealth and prosperity, profit not by the admonitory lesson which such proceedings afford, are deaf to the calls of patriotism, and would rush blindly into the noose of ambition.

However, to the honor of Pennsylvania, a very large majority of her citizens view the subject in its true light, and spurn the shackles prepared for them. They will in due time convince the aspiring despots and avaricious office-hunters, that their dark intrigues, and deep concerted schemes of power and aggrandisement, are ineffectual, that they are neither to be duped nor dragooned out of their liberties. The conspirators, I know, insolently boast that their strength in the other states will enable them to crush the opposition in this; but let them not build upon that which is in its nature precarious and transient, which must fail them the moment the delusion is dispelled: Their success in the other states is the fruit of deceptions that cannot be long supported. Indeed the audacity and villainy of the conspirators on the one hand, and the frantic enthusiasm, and easy credulity of the people on the other, in some of the states, however well attested and recorded in the faithful page of history, will be treated by posterity as fabulous.

The great artifice that is played off on this occasion, is the persuading the people of one place, that the people every where else are nearly unanimous in favor of the new system, and thus endeavouring by the facination of example and force of general opinion to prevail upon the people every where to acquiesce in what is represented to them as the general sentiment.

Thus as one means of deception has failed them, they have adopted another, always avoiding rational discussion. When the glare of great names, the dread of annihilation if the new system was rejected, or the adoption of it even delayed, were dissipated by the artillery of truth and reason; they have recurred to the one now practising, the intimidating and imposing influence of imaginary numbers and unanimity that are continually reverberated from every part of the union, by the tools and vehicles of the would-be despots; and in which they have had astonishing success. The people in the Eastern states have been taught to believe that it is all harmony to the Southward; and in the Southern states they are discouraged from opposition by the unanimity of the Eastern and Northern states; nay, what will appear incredible, considering the distance, a gentleman of veracity just returned from New-York, assures that the conspirators have had the address to inculcate an opinion there that all opposition had ceased in this state, notwithstanding the evidence of the contrary is so glaring here; this gentleman further informs, that so entirely devoted is the post-office, that not a single newspaper is received by the printers of that place from this city or elsewhere; and a Boston newspaper come by private hand, announces the public, that for some months past, the printers there have received no newspapers to the Southward of New-Haven, in Connecticut, where the press is muzzled, and consequently, cannot injure the cause; that all intelligence of the occurrences in the other states is withheld from them; and that they know more of the state of Europe, than of their own country.

Notwithstanding many thousand copies of the Reasons of Dissent of the minority of the late convention of this state were printed and forwarded in every direction, and by various conveyances, scarcely any of these got beyond the limits of this state, and most of them not until a long time after their publication. The printer of these Reasons, by particular desire, addressed a copy of them to every printer in the union, which he sent to the Post-office to be conveyed in the mail as usual, long before the *new arrangement*, as it is called, took place; and yet we since find that none of them reached the place of their destination. This is a full demonstration of the subserviency of the Post Office, and a striking evidence of the vigilance that has been exerted to suppress information. It is greatly to be regretted that the opposition in Massachusetts were denied the benefits of our discussion, that the unanswerable dissent of our minority did not reach Boston in time to influence the decision of the great question by their convention, as it would in all probability have enabled patriotism to triumph; not that I would derogate from the good sense and public spirit of that state, which I have no doubt would in common circumstances have shone with equal splendor, but this was far from being the case; the new constitution was viewed in Massachusetts through the medium of SHAYS, the terrors of HIS insurrection had not subsided; a government that would have been execrated at another time was embraced by many as a refuge from anarchy, and thus liberty deformed by mad riot and dissention, lost her ablest advocates.

As the liberties of all the states in the union are struck at in common with those of Pennsylvania, by the conduct of the Post-Master General and deputies, I trust that the example which her Legislature* has set by instructing her delegates in Congress on this subject, will be followed by the others, that with one accord they will hurl their vengeance on the venal instruments of ambition, who have presumed to prostrate one of the principal bulwarks of liberty. In a confederated government of such extent as the United States, the freest communication of sentiment and information should be maintained, as the liberties, happiness and welfare of the union depend upon a concert of counsels; the signals of alarm whenever ambition should rear its baneful head, ought to be uniform: without this communication between the members of the confederacy the freedom of the press, if it could be maintained in so severed a situation, would cease to be a security against the encroachments of tyranny. The truth of the foregoing position is strikingly illustrated on the present occasion; for want of this inter-community of sentiment and information, the liberties of this country are brought to an awful crisis; ambition has made a great stride towards dominion; has succeeded thro' the medium of muzzled presses to delude a great body of the people in the other states, and threatens to overwhelm the enlightened opposition in this by *external* force. Here, indeed, notwithstanding every nerve was strained, by the conspirators, to muzzle or demolish every newspaper that allowed free discussion, two printers have asserted the

The application to Congress from our Legislature, was made upon the complaint of all the printers of newspapers in the city of Philadelphia.

independency of the press, whereby the arts of ambition have been detected, and the new system has been pourtrayed in its native villainy; its advocates have long since abandoned the field of argument, relinquished the unequal contest, and truth and patriotism reigns triumphant in this state; but the conspirators trust to their success in the other states for the attainment of their darling object, and therefore all their vigilance is exerted to prevent the infectious spirit of freedom and enlightened patriotism communicating to the rest of the union—all intercourse is as far as possible cut off.

To rectify the erroneous representation made in the other states of the sentiments of the people in this respecting the new constitution, I think it my duty to state the fact as it really is:—Those who favor this system of tyranny are most numerous in the city of Philadelphia, where, perhaps, they may be a considerable majority; in the most eastern counties they compose about one fourth of the people, but in the middle, northern and western counties not above a twentieth part; so that upon the whole the friends to the new constitution in this state are about one-sixth of the people. The following circumstance is an evidence of the spirit and decision of the opposition:—An individual unadvisedly and without conceit, and contrary to the system of conduct generally agreed upon, went to the expence of printing and circulating an address to the Legislature, reprobating in the strongest terms the new constitution, and praying that the deputies of this state in the federal Convention, who in violation of their duty acceded to the new constitution, be called to account for their daring procedure; this address or petition was signed by upwards of four thousand citizens in only two counties, viz. Franklin and Cumberland, and if the time had admitted, prior to the adjournment of the Legislature, there is reason to believe that this high-toned application would have been subscribed by five-sixth of the freemen of this state. The advocates of the new constitution, availing themselves of this partial measure of two counties, have asserted it to be the result of a general exertion, which is so evidently false that it can only deceive people at a distance from us, for the counties over the mountain are nearly unanimous in the opposition; in Fayette at a numerous county meeting, there appeared to be but two persons in favor of the constitution; in Bedford county in the mountains, there are not above twenty; in Huntingdon adjoining, about 30; in Dauphin, in the middle country, not 100; in Berks, a large eastern county that has near 5000 taxable inhabitants, not more than 50, and so of several others, and yet no petitions were circulated or signed in those counties.— The system of conduct alluded to is the forming societies in every county in the state, who have committees of correspondence; these are now engaged in planning a uniform exertion to emancipate this state from the thraldom of despotism; a convention of deputies from every district will in all probability be agreed upon, as the most eligible mode of combining the strength of the opposition, which is increasing daily both in numbers and spirit.

The Centinel, supported by the dignity of the cause he advocates, and sensible that his well-meant endeavors have met the approbation of the community, views with ineffable contempt the impotent efforts of disappointed ambition to depreciate his merit and stigmatize his performances, and without pretending to the spirit of divination, he thinks he may predict that the period is not far distant when the authors and *wilful* abettors of the new constitution will be viewed with detestation by every good man, whilst the Centinels of the present day will be honored with the esteem and confidence of a grateful people.

Great pains have been taken to discover the author of these papers, with a view, no doubt, to villify his private character, and thereby lessen the usefulness of his writings, and many suppose they have made the discovery, but in this they are mistaken. The Centinel submits his performances to the public judgement, and challenges fair argumentation; the information he has given from time to time, has stood the test of the severest scrutiny, and thus his reputation as a writer, is established beyond the injury of his enemies. If it were in the least material to the argument, or answered any one good purpose, he would not hesitate a moment in using his own signature; as it would not, but on the contrary, point where the shafts of malice could be levelled with most effect, and thus divert the public attention from the proper object, to a personal altercation, he from the first determined that the prying eye of party or curiosity, should never be gratified with his real name, and to that end to be the sole depository of the secret. He has been thus explicit to prevent the repetition of the weakness of declaring off, when charged with being the author, and to put the matter upon its true footing; however, it may flatter his vanity, that these papers should be ascribed to an illustrious patriot, whose public spirit and undaunted firmness of mind, eclipse the most shining ornaments of the Roman commonwealth, in its greatest purity and glory, whose persevering exertions for the public welfare, have endeared him to his country whilst it has made every knave and aspiring despot, his inveterate enemy, and who has never condescended, to deny any writings that have been ascribed to him, or to notice the railings of party.

CENTINEL.

Letters from the Federal Farmer

"Observation Leading to a Fair Examination of the System of Government, Proposed by the Late Convention; and to Several Essential and Necessary Alterations in It. In a number of Letters from the Federal Farmer to the Republican." These letters first appeared in the Poughkeepsie Country Journal *between October 1787 and January 1788. Five letters were initially published and enjoyed considerable success in pamphlet form. After a break of some ten weeks, "An Additional Number of Letters From the Federal Farmer" appeared and ran through January 1788. The Letters presented here are taken from the in pamphlet versions.*

Letters from the Federal Farmer, often associated with Virginia statesman Richard Henry Lee, are now generally thought to have been written by Melancton Smith, a wealthy merchant and Alexander Hamilton's most able Anti-Federalist opponent in the New York ratifying convention. Well written and reasoned, they constitute one of the more moderate sets of essays criticizing the proposed Constitution. They focus on the need for improvements, in particular the addition of a federal bill of rights, to protect Americans' inherited liberties.

---

8 OCTOBER 1787

LETTER I

The Federal Farmer sets the stage by arguing that American political and social stability are in no immediate danger. Any significant political change should be examined in light of the many blessings the people have to loose. The question is whether the con-

solidated government that the Constitution will form would serve
the people's freedom and happiness as well as the current structure.
Essays in The Federalist *of particular relevance: 1, 2, 17, 85.*

DEAR SIR,
MY letters to you last winter, on the subject of a well balanced
national government for the United States, were the result of a free
enquiry; when I passed from that subject to enquiries relative to
our commerce, revenues, past administration, &c. I anticipated the
anxieties I feel, on carefully examining the plan of government proposed by the convention. It appears to be a plan retaining some federal features; but to be the first important step, and to aim strongly
at one consolidated government of the United States. It leaves the
powers of government, and the representation of the people, so
unnaturally divided between the general and state governments,
that the operations of our system must be very uncertain. My uniform federal attachments, and the interest I have in the protection
of property, and a steady execution of the laws, will convince you,
that, if I am under any bias at all, it is in favor of any general system
which shall promise those advantages. The instability of our laws
increases my wishes for firm and steady government; but then, I
can consent to no government, which, in my opinion, is not calculated equally to preserve the rights of all orders of men in the community. My object has been to join with those who have
endeavoured to supply the defects in the forms of our governments
by a steady and proper administration of them. Though I have long
apprehended that fraudalent debtors, and embarrassed men, on the
one hand, and men, on the other, unfriendly to republican equality,
would produce an uneasiness among the people, and prepare the
way, not for cool and deliberate reforms in the governments, but for
changes calculated to promote the interests of particular orders of
men. Acquit me, sir, of any agency in the formation of the new system; I shall be satisfied with seeing, if it shall be adopted with a prudent administration. Indeed I am so much convinced of the truth
of Pope's maxim, that "That which is best administered is best,"
that I am much inclined to subscribe to it from experience. I am
not disposed to unreasonably contend about forms. I know our sit-

uation is critical, and it behoves us to make the best of it. A federal government of some sort is necessary. We have suffered the present to languish; and whether the confederation was capable or not originally of answering any valuable purposes, it is now but of little importance. I will pass by the men, and states, who have been particularly instrumental in preparing the way for a change, and perhaps, for governments not very favourable to the people at large. A constitution is now presented which we may reject, or which we may accept with or without amendments, and to which point we ought to direct our exertions is the question. To determine this question with propriety; we must attentively examine the system itself, and the probable consequences of either step. This I shall endeavour to do, so far as I am able, with candor and fairness; and leave you to decide upon the propriety of my opinions, the weight of my reasons, and how far my conclusions are well drawn. Whatever may be the conduct of others, on the present occasion, I do not mean hastily and positively to decide on the merits of the constitution proposed. I shall be open to conviction and always disposed to adopt that which, all things considered, shall appear to me to be most for the happiness of the community. It must be granted, that if men hastily and blindly adopt a system of government, they will as hastily and as blindly be led to alter or abolish it; and changes must ensue, one after another, till the peaceable and better part of the community will grow weary with changes, tumults and disorders, and be disposed to accept any government however despotic, that shall promise stability and firmness.

The first principal question that occurs, is, Whether, considering our situation, we ought to precipitate the adoption of the proposed constitution? If we remain cool and temperate, we are in no immediate danger of any commotions; we are in a state of perfect peace, and in no danger of invasions; the state governments are in the full exercise of their powers; and our governments answer all present exigencies, except the regulation of trade, securing credit, in some cases, and providing for the interest, in some instances, of the public debts; and whether we adopt a change three or nine months hence, can make but little odds with the private circumstances of individuals; their happiness and prosperity, after all, depend principally upon their own exertions. We are hardly recovered from a long and distressing war: The farmers, fishmen, &c. have not fully repaired the waste made by it. Industry and frugality are again assuming their proper station. Private debts are lessened, and public debts incurred by the war have been, by various ways, diminished; and the public lands have now become a productive source for diminishing them much more. I know uneasy men, who with very much to precipitate, do not admit all these facts; but they are facts well known to all men who are thoroughly informed in the affairs of this country. It must, however, be admitted, that our federal system is defective, and that some of the state governments are not well administered; but, then, we impute to the defects in our governments many evils and embarassments which are most clearly the result of the late war. We must allow men to conduct on the present occasion, as on all similar one's. They will urge a thousand pretences to answer their purposes on both sides. When we want a man to change his condition, we describe it as wretched, miserable, and despised; and draw a pleasing picture of that which we would have him assume. And when we wish the contrary, we reverse our descriptions. Whenever a clamor is raised, and idle men get to work, it is highly necessary to examine facts carefully, and without unreasonably suspecting men of falshood, to examine, and enquire attentively, under what impressions they act. It is too often the case in political concerns that men state facts not as they are, but as they wish them to be; and almost every man, by calling to mind past scenes, will find this to be true.

Nothing but the passions of ambitious, impatient, or disorderly men, I conceive, will plunge us into commotions, if time should be taken fully to examine and consider the system proposed. Men who feel easy in their circumstances, and such as are not sanguine in their expectations relative to the consequences of the proposed change, will remain quiet under the existing governments. Many commercial and monied men, who are uneasy, not without just cause, ought to be respected; and by no means, unreasonably disappointed in their expectations and hopes; but as to those who expect employments under the new constitution; as to those weak and ardent men who always expect to be gainers by revolutions, and whose lot it generally is to get out of one difficulty into another, they are very little to be regarded; and as to those who designedly avail themselves of this weakness and ardor, they are to be despised. It is natural for men, who wish to hasten the adoption of a measure, to tell us, now is the crisis—now is the critical moment which must be seized or all will be lost; and to shut the door against free enquiry, whenever conscious the thing presented has defects in it, which time and investigation will probably discover. This has been the custom of tyrants, and their dependants in all ages. If it is true, what has been so often said, that the people of this country cannot change their condition for the worse, I presume it still behoves them to endeavour deliberately to change it for the better. The fickle and ardent, in any community are the proper tools for establishing despotic government. But it is deliberate and thinking men, who must establish and secure governments on free principles. Before they decide on the plan proposed, they will enquire whether it will probably be a blessing or a curse to this people.

The present moment discovers a new face in our affairs. Our object has been all along, to reform our federal system, and to strengthen our governments—to establish peace, order and justice in the community—but a new object now presents. The plan of government now proposed is evidently calculated totally to change, in time, our condition as a people. Instead of being thirteen republics, under a federal head, it is clearly designed to make us one consolidated government. Of this, I think, I shall fully convince you, in my following letters on this subject. This consolidation of the states has been the object of several men in this country for some time past. Whether such a change can ever be effected, in any manner; whether it can be effected without convulsions and civil wars; whether such a change will not totally destroy the liberties of this country—time only can determine.

To have a just idea of the government before us, and to shew that a consolidated one is the object in view, it is necessary not only to examine the plan, but also its history, and the politics of its particular friends.

The confederation was formed when great confidence was placed in the voluntary exertions of individuals, and of the respective states; and the framers of it, to guard against usurpation, so limited, and checked the powers, that, in many respects, they are inadequate to the exigencies of the union. We find, therefore, members of congress urging alterations in the federal system almost as soon as it was adopted. It was early proposed to vest congress with powers to levy an impost, to regulate trade, &c. but such was known to be the caution of the states in parting with power, that the vestment even of these, was proposed to be under several checks and limitations. During the war, the general confusion, and the introduction of paper money, infused in the minds of people vague ideas respecting government and credit. We expected too much from the return of peace, and of course we have been disappointed. Our governments have been new and unsettled; and several legislatures, by making tender, suspension, and paper money laws, have given just cause of uneasiness to creditors. By these and other causes, several orders of men in the community have been prepared, by degrees, for a change of government; and this very abuse of power in the legislatures, which in some cases has been charged upon the democratic part of the community, has furnished aristocratical men with those very weapons, and those very means, with which, in great measure, they are rapidly effecting their favourite object. And should an oppressive government be the consequence of the proposed change, prosperity may reproach not only a few overbearing, unprincipled men, but those parties in the states which have misused their powers.

The conduct of several legislatures, touching paper money, and tender laws, has prepared many honest men for changes in government, which otherwise they would not have thought of—when by the evils, on the one hand, and by the secret instigations of artful men, on the other, the minds of men were become sufficiently uneasy, a bold step was taken, which is usually followed by a revolution, or a civil war. A general convention for mere commercial purposes was moved for—the authors of this measure saw that the people's attention was turned solely to the amendment of the federal system; and that, had the idea of a total change been started, probably no state would have appointed members to the convention. The idea of destroying ultimately, the state government, and forming one consolidated system, could not have been admitted—a convention, therefore, merely for vesting in congress power to regulate trade was proposed. This was pleasing to the commercial towns; and the landed people had little or no concern about it. September, 1786, a few men from the middle states met at Annapolis, and hastily proposed a convention to be held in May, 1787, for the purpose, generally, of amending the confederation—this was done before the delegates of Massachusetts, and of the other states arrived—still not a word was said about destroying the old constitution, and making a new one—The states still unsuspecting, and not aware that they were passing the Rubicon, appointed members to the new convention, for the sole and express purpose or revising and amending the confederation—and, probably, not one man in ten thousand in the United States, till within these ten or twelve days, had an idea that the old ship was to be destroyed, and he put to the alternative of embarking in the new ship presented, or of being left in danger of sinking—The States, I believe, universally supposed the convention would report alterations in the confederation, which would pass an examination in congress, and after being agreed to there, would be confirmed by all the legislatures, or be rejected. Virginia made a very respectable appointment, and placed at the head of it the first man in America. In this appointment there was a mixture of political characters; but Pennsylvania appointed principally those men who are esteemed aristocratical. Here the favourite moment for changing the government was evidently discerned by a few men, who seized it with address. Ten other states appointed, and tho' they chose men principally connected with commerce and the judicial department yet they appointed many good republican characters—had they all attended we should now see, I am persuaded, a better system presented. The non-attendance of eight or nine men, who were appointed members of the convention, I shall ever consider as a very unfortunate event to the United States.—Had they attended, I am pretty clear that the result of the convention would not have had that strong tendency to aristocracy now discernable in every part of the plan. There would not have been so great an accumulation of powers, especially as to the internal police of this country in a few hands as the constitution reported proposes to vest in them—the young visionary men, and the consolidating aristocracy, would have been more restrained than they have been. Eleven states met in the convention, and after four months close attention presented the new constitution, to be adopted or rejected by the people. The uneasy and fickle part of the community may be prepared to receive any form of government; but I presume the enlightened and substantial part will give any constitution presented for their adoption a candid and thorough examination; and silence those designing or empty men, who weakly and rashly attempt to precipitate the adoption of a system of so much importance—We shall view the convention with proper respect—and, at the same time, that we reflect there were men of abilities and integrity in it, we must recollect how disproportionately the democratic and aristocratic parts of the community were represented—Perhaps the judicious friends and opposers of the new constitution will agree, that it is best to let it rely solely on its own merits, or be condemned for its own defects.

In the first place, I shall premise, that the plan proposed is a plan of accommodation—and that it is in this way only, and by giving up a part of our opinions, that we can ever expect to obtain a government founded in freedom and compact. This circumstance candid men will always keep in view, in the discussion of this subject.

The plan proposed appears to be partly federal, but principally however, calculated ultimately to make the states one consolidated government.

The first interesting question, therefore suggested, is, how far the states can be consolidated into one entire government on free principles. In considering this question extensive objects are to be taken into view, and important changes in the forms of government to be carefully attended to in all their consequences. The happiness of the people at large must be the great object with every honest statesman, and he will direct every movement to this point. If we are so situated as a people, as not to be able to enjoy equal happiness and advantages under one government, the consolidation of the states cannot be admitted.

There are three different forms of free government under which the United States may exist as one nation; and now is, perhaps, the time to determine to which we will direct our views. 1. Distinct republics connected under a federal head. In this case the respective state governments must be the principal guardians of the peoples rights, and exclusively regulate their internal police; in them must rest the balance of government. The congress of the states, or federal head, must consist of delegates amenable to, and removable by the respective states: This congress must have general directing powers; powers to require men and monies of the states; to make treaties; peace and war; to direct the operations of armies, &c. Under this federal modification of government, the powers of congress would be rather advisory or recommendatory than coercive. 2. We may do away the federal state governments, and form or consolidate all the states into one entire government, with one executive, one judiciary, and one legislature, consisting of senators and representatives collected from all parts of the union: In this case there would be a compleat consolidation of the states. 3. We may consoldate the states as to certain national objects, and leave them severally distinct independent republics, as to internal police generally. Let the general government consist of an executive, a judiciary, and balanced legislature, and its powers extend exclusively to all foreign concerns, causes arising on the seas to commerce, imports, armies, navies, Indian affairs, peace and war, and to a few internal concerns of the community; to the coin, post-offices, weights and measures, a general plan for the militia, to naturalization, *and, perhaps to bankruptcies*, leaving the internal police of the community, in other respects, exclusively to the state governments; as the administration of justice in all causes arising internally, the laying and collecting of internal taxes, and the forming of the militia according to a general plan prescribed. In this case there would be a compleat consolidation, *quoad* certain objects only.

Touching the first, or federal plan, I do not think much can be said in its favor: The sovereignity of the nation, without coercive and efficient powers to collect the strength of it, cannot always be depended on to answer the purposes of government; and in a congress of representatives of foreign states, there must necessarily be an unreasonable mixture of powers in the same hands.

As to the second, or compleat consolidating plan, it deserves to be carefully considered at this time by every American: If it be impracticable, it is a fatal error to model our governments, directing our views ultimately to it.

The third plan, or partial consolidation, is, in my opinion, the only one that can secure the freedom and happiness of this people. I once had some general ideas that the second plan was practicable, but from long attention, and the proceedings of the convention, I am fully satisfied, that this third plan is the only one we can with safety and propriety proceed upon. Making this the standard to point out, with candor and fairness, the parts of the new constitution which appear to be improper, is my object. The convention appears to have proposed the partial consolidation evidently with a view to collect all powers ultimately, in the United States into one entire government; and from its views in this respect, and from the tenacity of the small states to have an equal vote in the senate, probably originated the greatest defects in the proposed plan.

Independent of the opinions of many great authors, that a free elective government cannot be extended over large territories, a few reflections must evince, that one government and general legislation alone never can extend equal benefits to all parts of the United States: Different laws, customs, and opinions exist in the different states, which by a uniform system of laws would be unreasonably invaded. The United States contain about a million of square miles, and in half a century will, probably, contain ten millions of people; and from the center to the extremes is about 800 miles.

Before we do away the state governments or adopt measures that will tend to abolish them, and to consolidate the states into one entire government several principles should be considered and facts ascertained:—These, and my examination into the essential parts of the proposed plan, I shall pursue in my next.
Your's, &c.

THE FEDERAL FARMER.

9 OCTOBER 1787

LETTER II

The Federal Farmer next addresses the issue of full and fair repre-
sentation. The federal legislature must be large enough to include
representatives of all classes and interests if it is to be truly repre-
sentative. Under the new Constitution it is not. The psychological
and geographical distance of the new government from most of the
people will leave it without their confidence and unquestioning sup-
port, forcing it to oppress the people or to allow its laws to be
ignored. Essays in The Federalist *of particular relevance: 14, 55-57.*

DEAR SIR,

THE essential parts of a free and good government are a full and
equal representation of the people in the legislature, and the jury
trial of the vicinage in the administration of justice—a full and equal
representation, is that which possesses the same interests, feelings,
opinions, and views the people themselves would were they all
assembled—a fair representation, therefore, should be so regulated,
that every order of men in the community, according to the common course of elections, can have a share in it—in order to allow professional men, merchants, traders, farmers, mechanics, &c. to bring
a just proportion of their best informed men respectively into the
legislature, the representation must be considerably numerous—We
have about 200 state senators in the United States, and a less number than that of federal representatives cannot, clearly, be a full representation of this people, in the affairs of internal taxation and
police, were there but one legislature for the whole union. The representation cannot be equal, or the situation of the people proper for
one government only—if the extreme parts of the society cannot
be represented as fully as the central—It is apparently impracticable that this should be the case in this extensive country—it would
be impossible to collect a representation of the parts of the country
five, six, and seven hundred miles from the seat of government.

Under one general government alone, there could be but one judiciary, one supreme and a proper number of inferior courts. I think it would be totally impracticable in this case to preserve a due administration of justice, and the real benefits of the jury trial of the vicinage—there are now supreme courts in each state in the union, and a great number of county and other courts subordinate to each supreme court—most of these supreme and inferior courts are itinerant, and hold their sessions in different parts every year of their respective states, counties and districts—with all these moving courts, our citizens, from the vast extent of the country, must travel very considerable distances from home to find the place where justice is administered. I am not for bringing justice so near to individuals as to afford them any temptation to engage in law suits; though I think it one of the greatest benefits in a good government, that each citizen should find a court of justice within a reasonable distance, perhaps, within a day's travel of his home; so that, without great inconveniences and enormous expense, he may have the advantages of his witnesses and jury—it would be impracticable to derive these advantages from one judiciary—the one supreme court at most could only set in the centre of the union, and move once a year into the centre of the eastern and southern extremes of it—and, in this case, each citizen, on an average, would travel 150 or 200 miles to find this court—that, however, inferior courts might be properly placed in the different counties, and districts of the union, the appellate jurisdiction would be intolerable and expensive.

If it were possible to consolidate the states, and preserve the features of a free government, still it is evident that the middle states, the parts of the union, about the seat of government, would enjoy great advantages, while the remote states would experience the many inconveniences of remote provinces. Wealth, offices, and the benefits of government would collect in the centre: and the extreme states; and their principal towns, become much less important.

There are other considerations which tend to prove that the idea of one consolidated whole, on free principles, is ill-founded—the laws of a free government rest on the confidence of the people, and operate gently—and never can extend the influence very far—if they are executed on free principles, about the centre, where the benefits of the government induce the people to support it voluntarily; yet they must be executed on the principles of fear and force in the extremes—This has been the case with every extensive republic of which we have any accurate account.

There are certain unalienable and fundamental rights, which in forming the social compact, ought to be explicitly ascertained and fixed—a free and enlightened people, in forming this compact, will not resign all their rights to those who govern, and they will fix limits to their legislators and rulers, which will soon be plainly seen by those who are governed, as well as by those who govern: and the latter will know they cannot be passed unperceived by the former, and without giving a general alarm—These rights should be made the basis of every constitution; and if a people be so situated, or have such different opinions that they cannot agree in ascertaining and fixing them, it is a very strong argument against their attempting to form one entire society, to live under one system of laws only.—I confess, I never thought the people of these states differed essentially in these respects; they having derived all these rights from one common source, the British systems; and having in the formation of their state constitutions, discovered that their ideas relative to these rights are very similar. However, it is now said that the states differ so essentially in these respects, and even in the important article of the trial by jury, that when assembled in convention, they can agree to no words by which to establish that trial, or by which to ascertain and establish many other of these rights, as fundamental articles in the social compact. If so, we proceed to consolidate the states on no solid basis whatever.

But I do not pay much regard to the reasons given for not bottoming the new constitution on a better bill of rights. I still believe a complete federal bill of rights to be very practicable. Nevertheless I acknowledge the proceedings of the convention furnish my mind with many new and strong reasons, against a complete consolidation of the states. They tend to convince me, that it cannot be carried with propriety very far—that the convention have gone much farther in one respect than they found it practicable to go in another; that is, they propose to lodge in the general government very extensive powers—*powers* nearly, if not altogether, complete and unlimited, over the purse and the sword. But, in its organization, they furnish the strongest proof that the proper limbs, or parts of a government, to support and execute those powers on proper principles (or in which they can be safely lodged) cannot be formed. These powers must be lodged somewhere in every society; but then they should be lodged where the strength and guardians of the people are collected. They can be wielded, or safely used, in a free country only by an able executive and judiciary, a respectable senate, and a secure, full, and equal representation of the people. I think the principles I have premised or brought into view, are well founded—I think they will not be denied by any fair reasoner. It is in connection with these, and other solid principles, we are to examine the constitution. It is not a few democratic phrases, or a few well formed features, that will prove its merits; or a few small omissions that will produce its rejection among men of sense; they will enquire what are the essential powers in a community, and what are nominal ones; where and how the essential powers shall be lodged to secure government, and to secure true liberty.

In examining the proposed constitution carefully, we must clearly perceive an unnatural separation of these powers from the substantial representation of the people. The state government will exist, with all their governors, senators, representatives, officers and expences; in these will be nineteen twentieths of the representatives of the people; they will have a near connection, and their members an immediate intercourse with the people; and the probability is, that the state governments will possess the confidence of the people, and be considered generally as their immediate guardians.

The general government will consist of a new species of executive, a small senate, and a very small house of representatives. As many citizens will be more than three hundred miles from the seat of this government as will be nearer to it, its judges and officers cannot be very numerous, without making our governments very expensive. Thus will stand the state and the general governments, should the constitution be adopted without any alterations in their organization; but as to powers, the general government will possess all essential ones, at least on paper, and those of the states a mere shadow of power. And therefore, unless the people shall make some great exertions to restore to the state governments their powers in matters of internal police; as the powers to lay and collect, exclusively, internal taxes, to govern the militia, and to hold the decisions of their own judicial courts upon their own laws final, the balance cannot possibly continue long; but the state governments must be annihilated, or continue to exist for no purpose.

It is however to be observed, that many of the essential powers given the national government are not exclusively given; and the general government may have prudence enough to forbear the exercise of those which may still be exercised by the respective states. But this cannot justify the impropriety of giving powers, the exercise of which prudent men will not attempt, and imprudent men will, or probably can, exercise only in a manner destructive of free government. The general government, organized as it is, may be adequate to many valuable objects, and be able to carry its laws into execution on proper principles in several cases; but I think its warmest friends will not contend, that it can carry all the powers proposed to be lodged in it into effect, without calling to its aid a military force, which must very soon destroy all elective governments in the country, produce anarchy, or establish despotism. Though we cannot have now a complete idea of what will be the operations of the proposed system, we may, allowing things to have their common course, have a very tolerable one. The powers lodged in the general government, if exercised by it, must intimately effect the internal police of the states, as well as external concerns; and there is no reason to expect the numerous state governments, and their connections, will be very friendly to the execution of federal laws in those internal affairs, which hitherto have been under their own immediate management. There is more reason to believe, that the general government, far removed from the people, and none of its members elected oftener than once in two years, will be forgot or neglected, and its laws in many cases disregarded, unless a multitude of officers and military force be continually kept in view, and employed to enforce the execution of the laws, and to make the government feared and respected. No position can be truer than this.

That in this country either neglected laws, or a military execution of them, must lead to a revolution, and to the destruction of freedom. Neglected laws must first lead to anarchy and confusion; and a military execution of laws is only a shorter way to the same point—despotic government.

Your's, &c.

THE FEDERAL FARMER.

10 OCTOBER 1787

LETTER III

The Federal Farmer asserts that he hopes the Constitution will be adopted, but with alterations to correct several flaws: the House of Representatives is too small to represent the democratic part of society. The Senate is too aristocratic. The federal government's power of internal taxation on goods (as opposed to external taxation on trade) will spawn an overpowering federal bureaucracy. And the federal judiciary will fail to protect jury trials and the common law. Essays in The Federalist *of particular relevance: 30-36, 55-57, 62, 63, 83.*

DEAR SIR,

THE great object of a free people must be so to form their government and laws, and so to administer them, as to create a confidence in, and respect for the laws; and thereby induce the sensible and virtuous part of the community to declare in favor of the laws, and to support them without an expensive military force. I wish, though I confess I have not much hope, that this may be the case with the laws of congress under the new constitution. I am fully convinced that we must organize the national government on different principals, and make the parts of it more efficient, and secure in it more effectually the different interests in the community; or else leave in the state governments some powers proposed to be lodged in it—at least till such an organization shall be found to be practicable. Not sanguine in my expectations of a good federal administration, and satisfied, as I am, of the impracticability of consolidating the states, and at the same time of preserving the rights of the people at large, I believe we ought still to leave some of those powers in the state governments, in which the people, in fact, will still be represented—to define some other powers proposed to be vested in the general government, more carefully, and to establish a few principles to secure a proper exercise of the powers given it. It is not my object to multiply objections, or to contend about inconsiderable powers or amendments. I wish the system adopted with a few alterations; but those, in my mind, are essential ones; if adopted without, every good citizen will acquiesce, though I shall consider the duration of our governments, and the liberties of this people, very much dependant on the administration of the general government. A wise and honest administration, may make the people happy under any government; but necessity only can justify even our leaving open avenues to the abuse of power, by wicked, unthinking, or ambitious men, I will examine, first, the organization of the proposed government, in order to judge; 2d, with propriety, what powers are improperly, at least prematurely lodged in it. I shall examine, 3d, the undefined powers; and 4th, those powers, the exercise of which is not secured on safe and proper ground.

First. As to the organization—the house of representatives, the democrative branch, as it is called, is to consist of 65 members: that is, about one representative for fifty thousand inhabitants, to be chosen biennially—the federal legislature may increase this number to one for each thirty thousand inhabitants, abating fractional numbers in each state.—Thirty-three representatives will make a quorum for doing business, and a majority of those present determine the sense of the house.—I have no idea that the interests, feelings, and opinions of three or four millions of people, especially touching internal taxation, can be collected in such a house.—In the nature of things, nine times in ten, men of the elevated classes in the community only can be chosen—Connecticut, for instance, will have five representatives—not one man in a hundred of those who form the democrative branch in the state legislature, will, on a fair computation, be one of the five.—The people of this country, in one sense, may all be democratic; but if we make the proper distinction between the few men of wealth and abilities, and consider them, as we ought, as the natural aristocracy of the country, and the great body of the people, the middle and lower classes, as the democracy, this federal representative branch will have but very little democracy in it, even this small representation is not secured on proper principles.—The branches of the legislature are essential parts of the fundamental compact, and ought to be so fixed by the people, that the legislature cannot alter itself by modifying the elections of its own members. This, by a part of Art. 1, Sect. 4, the general legislature may do, it may evidently so regulate elections as to secure the choice of any particular description of men.—It may make the whole state one district—make the capital, or any places in the state, the place or places of election—it may declare that the five men (or whatever the number may be the state may chuse) who shall have the most votes shall be considered as chosen.—In this case it is easy to perceive how the people who live scattered in the inland towns will bestow their votes on different men—and how a few men in a city, in any order or profession, may unite and place any five men they please highest among those that may be voted for—and all this may be done constitutionally, and by those silent operations, which are not immediately perceived by the people in general.—I know it is urged, that the general legislature will be disposed to regulate elections on fair and just principles:—This may be true—good men will generally govern well with almost any constitution: but why in laying the foundation of the social system, need we unnecessarily leave a door open to improper regulations?—This is a very general and unguarded clause, and many evils may flow from that part which authorises the congress to regulate elections.—Were it omitted, the regulations of elections would be solely in the respective states, where the people are substantially represented; and where the elections ought to be regulated, otherwise to secure a representation from all parts of the community, in making the constitutions, we ought to provide for dividing each state into a proper number of districts, and for confining the electors in each district to the choice of some men, who shall have a permanent interest and residence in it; and also for this essential object, that the representative elected shall have a majority of the votes of those electors who shall attend and give their votes.

In considering the practicability of having a full and equal representation of the people from all parts of the union, not only distances and different opinions, customs and views, common in extensive tracts of country, are to be taken into view, but many differences peculiar to Eastern, Middle, and Southern States. These differences are not so perceivable among the members of congress, and men of general information in the states, as among the men who would properly form the democratic branch. The Eastern states are very democratic, and composed chiefly of moderate freeholders; they have but few rich men and no slaves; the Southern states are composed chiefly of rich planters and slaves; they have but few moderate freeholders, and the prevailing influence, in them is generally a dissipated aristocracy: The Middle states partake partly of the Eastern and partly of the Southern character.

Perhaps, nothing could be more disjointed, unweildly and incompetent to doing business with harmony and dispatch, than a federal house of representatives properly numerous for the great objects of taxation, &c. collected from the federal states; whether such men would ever act in concert; whether they would not worry along a few years, and then be the means of separating the parts of the union, is very problematical?—View this system in whatever form we can, propriety brings us still to this point, a federal government possessed of general and complete powers, as to those national objects which cannot well come under the cognizance of the internal laws of the respective states, and this federal government, accordingly, consisting of branches not very numerous.

The house of representatives is on the plan of consolidation, but the senate is entirely on the federal plan; and Delaware will have as much constitutional influence in the senate, as the largest state in the union: and in this senate are lodged legislative, executive and judicial powers: Ten states in this union urge that they are small states, nine of which were present in the convention.—They were interested in collecting large powers into the hands of the senate, in which each state still will have its equal share of power. I suppose it was impracticable for the three large states, as they were called, to get the senate formed on any other principles: But this only proves, that we cannot form one general government on equal and just principles—and proves, that we ought not to lodge in it such extensive powers before we are convinced of the practicability of organizing it on just and equal principles. The senate will consist of two members from each state, chosen by the state legislatures, every sixth year. The clause referred to, respecting the elections of representatives, empowers the general legislature to regulate the elections of senators also, "except as to the places of chusing senators."—There is, therefore, but little more security in the elections than in those of representatives: Fourteen senators make a quorum for business, and a majority of the senators present give the vote of the senate, except in giving judgment upon an impeachment, or in making treaties, or in expelling a member, when two-thirds of the senators present must agree—The members of the legislature are not excluded from being elected to any military offices, or any civil offices, except those created, or the emoluments of which shall be increased by themselves: two-thirds of the members present, of either house, may expel a member at pleasure. The senate is an independant branch of the legislature, a court for trying impeachments, and also a part of the executive, having a negative in the making of all treaties, and in appointing almost all officers.

The vice president is not a very important, if not an unnecessary part of the system—he may be a part of the senate at one period, and act as the supreme executive magistrate at another—The election of this officer, as well as of the president of the United States seems to be properly secured; but when we examine the powers of the president, and the forms of the executive, we shall perceive that the general government, in this part, will have a strong tendency to aristocracy, or the government of the few. The executive is, in fact, the president and senate in all transactions of any importance; the president is connected with, or tied to the senate; he may always act with the senate, but never can effectually counteract its views: The president can appoint no officer, civil or military, who shall not be agreeable to the senate; and the presumption is, that the will of so important a body will not be very easily controuled, and that it will exercise its powers with great address.

In the judicial department, powers ever kept distinct in well balanced governments, are no less improperly blended in the hands of the same men—in the judges of the supreme court is lodged the law, the equity and the fact. It is not necessary to pursue the minute organical parts of the general government proposed.—There were various interests in the convention, to be reconciled, especially of large and small states; of carrying and non-carrying states; and of states more and states less democratic—vast labour and attention were by the convention bestowed on the organization of the parts of the constitution offered; still it is acknowledged there are many things radically wrong in the essential parts of this constitution—but it is said that these are the result of our situation: On a full examination of the subject, I believe it; but what do the laborious inquiries and determination of the convention prove? If they prove anything, they prove that we cannot consolidate the states on proper principles: The organization of the government presented proves, that we cannot form a general government in which all power can be safely lodged; and a little attention to the parts of the one proposed will make it appear very evident, that all the powers proposed to be lodged in it, will not be then well deposited, either for the purposes of government, or the preservation of liberty. I will suppose no abuse of power in those cases, in which the abuse of it is not well guarded against—I will suppose the words authorizing the general government to regulate the elections of its own members struck out of the plan, or free district elections, in each state, amply secured.—That the small representation provided for shall be as fair and equal as it is capable of being made—I will suppose the judicial department regulated on pure principles, by future laws, as far as it can be by the constitution, and consist with the situation of the country—still there will be an unreasonable accumulation of powers in the general government if all be granted, enumerated in the plan proposed. The plan does not present a well balanced government: The senatorial branch of the legislative and the executive are substantially united, and the president, or the state executive magistrate, may aid the senatorial interest when weakest, but never can effectually support the democratic, however it may be opposed;—the excellency, in my mind, of a well-balanced government is that it consists of distinct branches, each sufficiently strong and independant to keep its own station, and to aid either of the other branches which may occasionally want aid.

The convention found that any but a small house of representatives would be expensive, and that it would be impracticable to assemble a large number of representatives. Not only the determination of the convention in this case, but the situation of the states, proves the impracticability of collecting, in any one point, a proper representation.

The formation of the senate, and the smallness of the house, being, therefore, the result of our situation, and the actual state of things, the evils which may attend the exercise of many powers in this national government may be considered as without a remedy.

All officers are impeachable before the senate only—before the men by whom they are appointed, or who are consenting to the appointment of these officers. No judgment of conviction, on an impeachment, can be given unless two thirds of the senators agree. Under these circumstances the right of impeachment, in the house, can be of but little importance; the house cannot expect often to convict the offender; and, therefore, probably, will but seldom or never exercise the right. In addition to the insecurity and inconveniences attending this organization beforementioned, it may be observed, that it is extremely difficult to secure the people against the fatal effects of corruption and influence. The power of making any law will be in the president, eight senators, and seventeen representatives, relative to the important objects enumerated in the constitution. Where there is a small representation a sufficient number to carry any measure, may, with ease, be influenced by bribes, offices and civilities; they easily form private juntoes, and out-door meetings, agree on measures, and carry them by silent votes.

Impressed, as I am, with a sense of the difficulties there are in the way of forming the parts of a federal government on proper principles, and seeing a government so unsubstantially organized, after so arduous an attempt has been made, I am led to believe, that powers ought to be given to it with great care and caution.

In the second place it is necessary, therefore, to examine the extent, and the probable operations of some of those extensive powers proposed to be vested in this government. These powers, legislative, executive, and judicial, respect internal as well as external objects. Those respecting external objects, as all foreign concerns, commerce, imposts, all causes arising on the seas, peace and war, and Indian affairs, can be lodged no where else, with any propriety, but in this government. Many powers that respect internal objects ought clearly to be lodged in it; as those to regulate trade between the states, weights and measures, the coin or current monies, post-offices, naturalization, &c. These powers may be exercised without essentially effecting the internal police of the respective states: But powers to lay and collect internal taxes, to form the militia, to make bankrupt laws, and to decide on appeals, questions arising on the internal laws of the respective states, are of a very serious nature, and carry with them almost all other powers. These taken in connection with the others, and powers to raise armies and build navies, proposed to be lodged in this government, appear to me to comprehend all the essential powers in this community, and those which will be left to the states will be of no great importance.

A power to lay and collect taxes at discretion, is, in itself, of very great importance. By means of taxes, the government may command the whole or any part of the subject's property. Taxes may be of various kinds; but there is a strong distinction between external and internal taxes. External taxes are import duties, which are laid on imported goods; they may usually be collected in a few seaport towns, and of a few individuals, though ultimately paid by the consumer; a few officers can collect them, and they can be carried no higher than trade will bear, or smuggling permit—that in the very nature of commerce, bounds are set to them. But internal taxes, as poll and land taxes, excises, duties on all written instruments, &c. may fix themselves on every person and species of property in the community; they may be carried to any lengths, and in proportion as they are extended, numerous officers must be employed to assess them, and to enforce the collection of them. In the United Netherlands the general government has compleat powers, as to external taxation; but as to internal taxes, it makes requisitions on the provinces. Internal taxation in this country is more important, as the country is so very extensive. As many assessors and collectors of federal taxes will be above three hundred miles from the seat of the federal government as will be less. Besides, to lay and collect taxes, in this extensive country, must require a great number of congressional ordinances, immediately operating upon the body of the people; these must continually interfere with the state laws, and thereby produce disorder and general dissatisfaction, till the one system of laws or the other, operating on the same subjects, shall be abolished. These ordinances alone, to say nothing of those respecting the milita, coin, commerce, federal judiciary, &c. &c. will probably soon defeat the operations of the state laws and governments.

Should the general government think it politic, as some administration (if not all) probably will, to look for a support in a system of influence, the government will take every occasion to multiply laws, and officers to execute them, considering these as so many necessary props for its own support. Should this system of policy be adopted, taxes more productive than the impost duties will, probably, be wanted to support the government, and to discharge foreign demands, without leaving any thing for the domestic creditors. The internal sources of taxation then must be called into operation, and internal tax laws and federal assessors and collectors spread over this immense country. All these circumstances considered, is it wise, prudent, or safe, to vest the powers of laying and collecting internal taxes in the general government, while imperfectly organized and inadequate; and to trust to amending it hereafter, and making it adequate to this purpose? It is not only unsafe but absurd to lodge power in a government before it is fitted to receive it? It is confessed that this power and representation ought to go together. Why give the power first? Why give the power to the few, who, when possessed of it, may have address enough to prevent the increase of representation? Why not keep the power, and, when necessary, amend the constitution, and add to its other parts this power, and a proper increase of representation at the same time? Then men who may want the power will be under strong inducements to let in the people, by their representatives, into the government, to hold their due proportion of this power. If a proper representation be impracticable, then we shall see this power resting in the states, where it at present ought to be, and not inconsiderately given up.

When I recollect how lately congress, conventions, legislatures, and people contended in the cause of liberty, and carefully weighed the importance of taxation, I can scarcely believe we are serious in proposing to vest the powers of laying and collecting internal taxes in a government so imperfectly organized for such purposes. Should the United States be taxed by a house of representatives of two hundred members, which would be about fifteen members for Connecticut, twenty-five for Massachusetts, &c. still the middle and lower classes of people could have no great share, in fact, in taxation. I am aware it is said, that the representation proposed by the new constitution is sufficiently numerous; it may be for many purposes; but to suppose that this branch is sufficiently numerous to guard the rights of the people in the administration of the government, in which the purse and sword is placed, seems to argue that we have forgot what the true meaning of representation is. I am sensible also, that it is said that congress will not attempt to lay and collect internal taxes; that it is necessary for them to have the power, though it cannot probably be exercised.—I admit that it is not probable that any prudent congress will attempt to lay and collect internal taxes, especially direct taxes: but this only proves, that the power would be improperly lodged in congress, and that it might be abused by imprudent and designing men.

I have heard several gentlemen, to get rid of objections to this part of the constitution, attempt to construe the powers relative to direct taxes, as those who object to it would have them; as to these, it is said, that congress will only have power to make requisitions, leaving it to the states to lay and collect them. I see but very little colour for this construction, and the attempt only proves that this part of the plan cannot be defended. By this plan there can be no doubt, but that the powers of congress will be complete as to all kinds of taxes whatever—Further, as to internal taxes, the state governments will have concurrent powers with the general government, and both may tax the same objects in the same year; and the objection that the general government may suspend a state tax, as a necessary measure for the promoting the collection of a federal tax, is not without foundation.—As the states owe large debts, and have large demands upon them individually, there clearly will be a propriety in leaving in their possession exclusively, some of the internal sources of taxation, at least until the federal representation shall be properly encreased: The power in the general government to lay and collect internal taxes, will render its powers respecting armies, navies and the militia, the more exceptionable. By the constitution it is proposed that congress shall have power "to raise and support armies, but no appropriation of money to that use shall be for a longer term than two years; to provide and maintain a navy; to provide for calling forth the militia to execute the laws of the union; suppress insurrections, and repel invasions: to provide for organizing, arming, and disciplining the militia"; reserving to the states the right to appoint the officers, and to train the militia according to the discipline prescribed by congress; congress will have unlimited power to raise armies, and to engage officers and men for any number of years; but a legislative act applying money for their support can have operation for no longer term than two years, and if a subsequent congress do not within the two years renew the appropriation, or further appropriate monies for the use of the army, the army will be left to take care of itself. When an army shall once be raised for a number of years, it is not probable that it will find much difficulty in getting congress to pass laws for applying monies to its support. I see so many men in America fond of a standing army, and especially among those who probably will have a large share in administering the federal system; it is very evident to me, that we shall have a large standing army as soon as the monies to support them can be possibly found. An army is not a very agreeable place of employment for the young gentlemen of many families. A power to raise armies must be lodged some where; still this will not justify the lodging this power in a bare majority of so few men without any checks; or in the government in which the great body of the people, in the nature of things, will be only nominally represented. In the state governments the great body of the people, the yeomanry, &c. of the country, are represented: It is true they will chuse the members of congress, and may now and then chuse a man of their own way of thinking; but it is not impossible for forty, or thirty thousand people in this country, one time in ten to find a man who can possess similar feelings, views, and interests with themselves: Powers to lay and collect taxes and to raise armies are of the greatest moment; for carrying them into effect, laws need not be frequently made, and the yeomanry, &c. of the country ought substantially to have a check upon the passing of these laws; this check ought to be placed in the legislatures, or at least, in the few men the common people of the country, will, probably, have in congress, in the true sense of the word, "from among themselves." It is true, the yeomanry of the country possess the lands, the weight of property, possess arms, and are too strong a body of men to be openly offended—and, therefore, it is urged, they will take care of themselves, that men who shall govern will not dare pay any disrespect to their opinions. It is easily perceived, that if they have not their proper negative upon passing laws in congress, or on the passage of laws relative to taxes and armies, they may in twenty or thirty years be by means imperceptible to them, totally deprived of that boasted weight and strength: This may be done in a great measure by congress, if disposed to do it, by modelling the militia. Should one fifth or one eighth part of the men capable of bearing arms, be made a select militia, as has been proposed, and those the young and ardent part of the community, possessed of but little or no property, and all the others put upon a plan that will render them of no importance, the former will answer all the purposes of an army, while the latter will be defenceless. The state must train the militia in such form and according to such sys-

tems and rules as congress shall prescribe: and the only actual influence the respective states will have respecting the militia will be
in appointing the officers. I see no provision made for calling out the
posse comitatus for executing the laws of the union, but provision is
made for congress to call forth the militia for the execution of
them—and the militia in general, or any select part of it, may be
called out under military officers, instead of the sheriff to enforce an
execution of federal laws, in the first instance, and thereby introduce an entire military execution of the laws. I know that powers to
raise taxes, to regulate the military strength of the community on
some uniform plan, to provide for its defence and internal order, and
for duly executing the laws, must be lodged somewhere; but still we
ought not so to lodge them, as evidently to give one order of men
in the community, undue advantages over others; or commit the
many to the mercy, prudence, and moderation of the few. And so far
as it may be necessary to lodge any of the peculiar powers in the
general government, a more safe exercise of them ought to be
secured, by requiring the consent of two-thirds or three-fourths of
congress thereto—until the federal representation can be
increased, so that the democratic members in congress may stand
some tolerable chance of a reasonable negative, in behalf of the
numerous, important, and democratic part of the community.

I am not sufficiently acquainted with the laws and internal police
of all the states to discern fully, how general bankrupt laws, made
by the union, would effect them, or promote the public good. I
believe the property of debtors, in the several states, is held
responsible for their debts in modes and forms very different. If
uniform bankrupt laws can be made without producing real and
substantial inconveniences, I wish them to be made by congress.

There are some powers proposed to be lodged in the general government in the judicial department, I think very unnecessarily, I
mean powers respecting questions arising upon the internal laws of
the respective states. It is proper the federal judiciary should have
powers co-extensive with the federal legislature—that is, the
power of deciding finally on the laws of the union. By Art. 3, Sec. 2.
the powers of the federal judiciary are extended (among other
things) to all cases between a state and citizens of another state—

between citizens of different states—between a state or the citizens thereof, and foreign states, citizens or subjects. Actions in all these cases, except against a state government, are now brought and finally determined in the law courts of the states respectively and as there are no words to exclude these courts of their jurisdiction in these cases, they will have concurrent jurisdiction with the inferior federal courts in them; and, therefore, if the new constitution be adopted without any amendment in this respect, all those numerous actions, now brought in the state courts between our citizens and foreigners, between citizens of different states, by state governments against foreigners, and by state governments against citizens of other states, may also be brought in the federal courts; and an appeal will lay in them from the state courts or federal inferior courts to the supreme judicial court of the union. In almost all these cases, either party may have the trial by jury in the state courts; except paper money and tender laws, which are wisely guarded against in the proposed constitution; justice may be obtained in these courts on reasonable terms; they must be more competent to proper decisions on the laws of their respective states, than the federal states can possibly be. I do not, in any point of view, see the need of opening a new jurisdiction in these causes— of opening a new scene of expensive law suits, of suffering foreigners, and citizens of different states, to drag each other many hundred miles into the federal courts. It is true, those courts may be so organized by a wise and prudent legislature, as to make the obtaining of justice in them tolerably easy; they may in general be organized on the common law principles of the country: But this benefit is by no means secured by the constitution. The trial by jury is secured only in those few criminal cases, to which the federal laws will extend—as crimes committed on the seas, against the laws of nations, treason and counterfeiting the federal securities and coin: But even in these cases, the jury trial of the vicinage is not secured—particularly in the large states, a citizen may be tried for a crime committed in the state, and yet tried in some states 500 miles from the place where it was committed; but the jury trial is not secured at all in civil causes. Though the convention have not established this trial, it is to be hoped that congress, in putting the new system into execution, will do it by a legislative act, in all cases in which it can be done with propriety. Whether the jury trial is not excluded the supreme judicial court is an important question. By Art. 3, Sec. 2, all cases affecting ambassadors, other public ministers, and consuls, and in those cases in which a state shall be party, the supreme court shall have jurisdiction. In all the other cases beforementioned, the supreme court shall have appellate jurisdiction, both as to *law and fact,* with such exception, and under such regulations as the congress shall make. By court is understood a court consisting of judges; and the idea of a jury is excluded. This court, or the judges, are to have jurisdiction on appeals, in all the cases enumerated, as to law and fact; the judges are to decide the law and try the fact, and the trial of the fact being assigned to the judges by the constitution, a jury for trying the fact is excluded; however, under the exceptions and powers to make regulations, congress may, perhaps, introduce the jury, to try the fact in most necessary cases.

There can be but one supreme court in which the final jurisdiction will centre in all federal causes—except in cases where appeals by law shall not be allowed: The judicial powers of the federal courts extend in law and equity to certain cases: and, therefore, the powers to determine on the law, in equity, and as to the fact, all will concentrate in the supreme court:—These powers, which by this constitution are blended in the same hands, the same judges, are in Great-Britain deposited in different hands—to wit, the decision of the law in the law judges, the decision in equity in the chancellor, and the trial of the fact in the jury. It is a very dangerous thing to vest in the same judge power to decide on the law, and also general powers in equity; for if the law restrain him, he is only to step into his shoes of equity, and give what judgment his reason or opinion may dictate; we have no precedents in this country, as yet, to regulate the divisions in equity as in Great Britain; equity, therefore, in the supreme court for many years will be mere discretion. I confess in the constitution of this supreme court, as left by the constitution, I do not see a spark of freedom or a shadow of our own or the British common law.

This court is to have appellate jurisdiction in all the other cases before mentioned: Many sensible men suppose that cases before mentioned respect, as well the criminal cases as the civil ones mentioned antecedently in the constitution, if so an appeal is allowed in criminal cases—contrary to the usual sense of law. How far it may be proper to admit a foreigner or the citizen of another state to bring actions against state governments, which have failed in performing so many, promises made during the war is doubtful: How far it may be proper so to humble a state, as to oblige it to answer to an individual in a court of law, is worthy of consideration; the states are now subject to no such actions; and this new jurisdiction will subject the states, and many defendants to actions, and processes, which were not in the contemplation of the parties, when the contract was made; all engagements existing between citizens of different states, citizens and foreigners, states and foreigners; and states and citizens of other states were made the parties contemplating the remedies then existing on the laws of the states—and the new remedy proposed to be given in the federal courts, can be founded on no principle whatever.

Your's, &c,

THE FEDERAL FARMER.

12 OCTOBER 1787

LETTER IV

The Federal Farmer criticizes the Constitution as as being too vague. Its provisions regarding taxation, appointments, delegated powers, and individual and state rights are unclear, thereby failing to protect common law liberties, including jury trials. Essays in The Federalist *of particular relevance: 44, 84.*

DEAR SIR,

IT will not be possible to establish in the federal courts the jury trial of the vicinage so well as in the state courts.

Third, there appears to me to be not only a premature deposit of some important powers in the general government—but many of those deposited there are undefined, and may be used to good or bad purposes as honest or designing men shall prevail. By Art. 1, Sec. 2, representatives and direct taxes shall be apportioned among the several states, &c.—same art. sect. 8, the congress shall have powers to lay and collect taxes, duties, &c. for the common defence and general welfare, but all duties, imposts and excises, shall be uniform throughout the United States: By the first recited clause, direct taxes shall be apportioned on the states. This seems to favour the idea suggested by some sensible men and writers that congress, as to direct taxes, will only have power to make requisitions; but the latter clause, power to lay and collect taxes, &c. seems clearly to favour the contrary opinion, and, in my mind, the true one, the congress shall have power to tax immediately individuals, without the intervention of the state legislatures, in fact the first clause appears to me only to provide that each state shall pay a certain portion of the tax, and the latter to provide that congress shall have power to lay and collect taxes, that is to assess upon, and to collect of the individuals in the state, the states quota; but these still I consider as undefined powers, because judicious men understand them differently.

It is doubtful whether the vice-president is to have any qualifications; none are mentioned; but he may serve as president, and it may be inferred, he ought to be qualified therefore as the president; but the qualifications of the president are required only of the person to be elected president. By art. 2, sect. 2, "But the congress may by law vest the appointment of such inferior officers as they think proper in the president alone, in the courts of law, or in the heads of the departments": Who are inferior officers? May not a congress disposed to vest the appointment of all officers in the president, under this clause, vest the appointment of almost every officer in the president alone, and destroy the check mentioned in the first part of the clause, and lodged in the senate. It is true, this check is badly lodged, but then some check upon the first magistrate in appointing officers, ought it appears by the opinion of the convention, and by the general opinion, to be established in the constitution. By art. 3, sect. 2, the supreme court shall have appellate jurisdiction as to law and facts with such exceptions, &c. to what extent is it intended the exceptions shall be carried—Congress may carry them so far as to annihilate substantially the appellate jurisdiction, and the clause be rendered of very little importance.

4th. There are certain rights which we have always held sacred in the United States, and recognized in all our constitutions, and which, by the adoption of the new constitution in its present form, will be left unsecured. By article 6, the proposed constitution, and the laws of the United States, which shall be made in pursuance thereof; and all treaties made, or which shall be made under the authority of the United States, shall be the supreme law of the land; and the judges in every state shall be bound thereby; anything in the constitution or laws of any state to the contrary notwithstanding.

It is to be observed that when the people shall adopt the proposed constitution it will be their last and supreme act; it will be adopted not by the people of New Hampshire, Massachusetts, &c., but by the people of the United States; and wherever this constitution, or any part of it, shall be incompatible with the ancient customs, rights, the laws or the constitutions heretofore established in the United States, it will entirely abolish them and do them away: And not only this, but the laws of the United States which shall be; made in pursuance of the federal constitution will be also supreme laws, and wherever they shall be incompatible with those customs, rights, laws or constitutions heretofore established, they will also entirely abolish them and do them away.

By the article before recited, treaties also made under the authority of the United States, shall be the supreme law: It is not said that these treaties shall be made in pursuance of the constitution—nor are there any constitutional bounds set to those who shall make them: The president and two-thirds of the senate will be empowered to make treaties indefinitely, and when these treaties shall be made, they will also abolish all laws and state constitutions incompatible with them. This power in the president and senate is absolute, and the judges will be bound to allow full force to whatever rule, article or thing the president and senate shall establish by treaty, whether it be practicable to set any bounds to those who make treaties, I am not able to say; if not, it proves that this power ought to be more safely lodged.

The federal constitution, the laws of congress made in pursuance of the constitution, and all treaties must have full force and effect in all parts of the United States; and all other laws, rights and constitutions which stand in their way must yield: It is proper the national laws should be supreme, and superior to state or district laws; but then the national laws ought to yield to unalienable or fundamental rights—and national laws, made by a few men, should extend only to a few national objects. This will not be the case with the laws of congress: To have any proper idea of their extent, we must carefully examine the legislative, executive and judicial powers proposed to be lodged in the general government, and consider them in connection with a general clause in art. 1, sect. 8, in these words (after enumerating a number of powers) "To make all laws which shall be necessary and proper for carrying into execution the foregoing powers, and all other powers vested by this constitution in the government of the United States, or in any department or officer thereof."—The powers of this government as has been observed, extend to internal as well as external objects, and to those objects to which all others are subordinate; it is almost impossible to have a just conception of their powers, or of the extent and number of the laws which may be deemed necessary and proper to carry them into effect, till we shall come to exercise those powers and make the laws. In making laws to carry those powers into effect, it is to be expected, that a wise and prudent congress will pay respect to the opinions of a free people, and bottom their laws on those principles which have been considered as essential and fundamental in the British, and in our government: But a congress of a different character will not be bound by the constitution to pay respect to those principles.

It is said that when people make a constitution, and delegate powers, that all powers are not delegated by them to those who govern, is reserved in the people; and that the people, in the present case, have reserved in themselves, and in their state governments, every right and power not expressly given by the federal constitution to those who shall administer the national government. It is said, on the other hand, that the people, when they make a constitution, yield all power not expressly reserved to themselves. The truth is, in either case, it is mere matter of opinion, and men usually take either side of the argument, as will best answer their purposes: But the general presumption being, that men who govern, will in doubtful cases, construe laws and constitutions most favourably for increasing their own powers; all wise and prudent people, in forming constitutions, have drawn the line, and carefully described the powers parted with and the powers reserved. By the state constitutions, certain rights have been reserved in the people; or rather, they have been recognized and established in such a manner, that state legislatures are bound to respect them, and to make no laws infringing upon them. The state legislatures are obliged to take notice of the bills of rights of their respective states. The bills of rights, and the state constitutions, are fundamental compacts only between those who govern, and the people of the same state.

In the year 1788 the people of the United States made a federal constitution, which is a fundamental compact between them and their federal rulers; these rulers, in the nature of things, cannot be bound to take notice of any other compact. It would be absurd for them, in making laws, to look over thirteen, fifteen, or twenty state constitutions, to see what rights are established as fundamental, and must not be infringed upon, in making laws in the society. It is true, they would be bound to do it if the people, in their federal compact, should refer to the state constitutions, recognize all parts not inconsistent with the federal constitution, and direct their federal rulers to take notice of them accordingly; but this is not the case, as the plan stands proposed at present; and it is absurd, to suppose so unnatural an idea is intended or implied. I think my opinion is not only founded in reason, but I think it is supported by the report of the convention itself. If there are a number of rights established by the state constitutions, and which will remain sacred, and the general government is bound to take notice of them—it must take notice of one as well as another; and if unnecessary to recognize or establish one by the federal constitution, it would be unnecessary to recognize or establish another by it. If the federal constitution is to be construed so far in connection with the state constitution, as to leave the trial by jury in civil causes, for instance, secured; on the same principles it would have left the trial by jury in criminal causes, the benefits of the writ of habeas corpus, &c. secured; they all stand on the same footing; they are the common rights of Americans, and have been recognized by the state constitutions: But the convention found it necessary to recognize or re-establish the benefits of that writ, and the jury trial in criminal cases. As to *expost facto* laws, the convention has done the same in one case, and gone further in another, It is a part of the compact between the people of each state and their rulers, that no *expost facto* laws shall be made. But the convention, by Art. 1, Sect. 10, have put a sanction upon this part even of the state compacts. In fact, the 9th and 10th Sections in Art. 1, in the proposed constitution, are no more nor less, than a partial bill of rights; they establish certain principles as part of the compact upon which the federal legislators and officers can never infringe. It is here wisely stipulated, that the federal legislature shall never pass a bill of attainder, or *expost facto* law; that no tax shall be laid on articles exported, &c. The establishing of one right implies the necessity of establishing another and similar one.

On the whole, the position appears to me to be undeniable, that this bill of rights ought to be carried farther, and some other principles established, as a part of this fundamental compact between the people of the United States and their federal rulers.

It is true, we are not disposed to differ much, at present, about religion; but when we are making a constitution, it is to be hoped, for ages and millions yet unborn, why not establish the free exercise of religion, as a part of the national compact. There are other essential rights, which we have justly understood to be the rights of freemen; as freedom from hasty and unreasonable search warrants, warrants not founded on oath, and not issued with due caution, for searching and seizing men's papers, property, and persons. The trials by jury in civil causes, it is said, varies so much in the several states, that no words could be found for the uniform establishment of it. If so, the federal legislation will not be able to establish it by any general laws. I confess I am of opinion it may be established, but not in that beneficial manner in which we may enjoy it, for the reasons beforementioned. When I speak of the jury trial of the vicinage, or the trial of the fact in the neighborhood, I do not lay so much stress upon the circumstance of our being tried by our neighbours: in this enlightened country men may be probably impartially tried by those who do not live very near them: but the trial of facts in the neighbourhood is of great importance in other respects. Nothing can be more essential than the cross examining witnesses, and generally before the triers of the facts in question. The common people can establish facts with much more ease with oral than written evidence; when trials of facts are removed to a distance from the homes of the parties and witnesses, oral evidence becomes intolerably expensive, and the parties must depend on written evidence, which to the common people is expensive and almost useless; it must be frequently taken ex porte, and but very seldom leads to the proper discovery of truth.

The trial by jury is very important in another point of view. It is essential in every free country, that common people should have a part and share of influence, in the judicial as well as in the legislative department. To hold open to them the offices of senators, judges, and offices to fill which an expensive education is required, cannot answer any valuable purposes for them; they are not in a situation to be brought forward and to fill those offices; these, and most other offices of any considerable importance, will be occupied by the few. The few, the well born, &c. as Mr. Adams calls them, in judicial decisions as well as in legislation, are generally disposed, and very naturally too, to favour those of their own description.

The trial by jury in the judicial department, and the collection of the people by their representatives in the legislature, are those fortunate inventions which have procured for them, in this country, their true proportion of influence, and the wisest and most fit means of protecting themselves in the community. Their situation, as jurors and representatives, enables them to acquire information and knowledge in the affairs and government of the society; and to come forward, in turn, as the centinels and guardians of each other.

I am very sorry that even a few of our countrymen should consider jurors and representatives in a different point of view, as ignorant, troublesome bodies, which ought not to have any share in the concerns of government.

I confess I do not see in what cases the congress can, with any pretence of right, make a law to suppress the freedom of the press; though I am not clear, that congress is restrained from laying any duties whatever on printing, and from laying duties particularly heavy on certain pieces printed, and perhaps congress may require large bonds for the payment of these duties. Should the printer say, the freedom of the press was secured by the constitution of the state in which he lived, congress might, and perhaps, with great propriety, answer, that the federal constitution is the only compact existing between them and the people; in this compact the people have named no others, and therefore congress, in exercising the powers assigned them, and in making laws to carry them into execution, are restrained by nothing beside the federal constitution, any more than a state legislature is restrained by a compact between the magistrates and people of a county, city, or town of which the people, in forming the state constitution, have taken no notice.

It is not my object to enumerate rights of inconsiderable importance; but there are others, no doubt, which ought to be established as a fundamental part of the national system.

It is worthy of observation, that all treaties are made by foreign nations with a confederacy of thirteen states—that the western country is attached to thirteen states—thirteen states have jointly and severally engaged to pay the public debts.—Should a new government be formed of nine, ten, eleven, or twelve states, those treaties could not be considered as binding on the foreign nations who made them. However, I believe the probability to be, that if nine states adopt the constitution, the others will.

It may also be worthy our examination, how far the provision for amending this plan, when it shall be adopted, is of any importance. No measures can be taken towards amendments, unless two-thirds of the congress, or two-thirds of the legislature of the several states shall agree.—While power is in the hands of the people, or democratic part of the community, more especially as at present, it is easy, according to the general course of human affairs, for the few influential men in the community, to obtain conventions, alterations in government, and to persuade the common people that they may change for the better, and to get from them a part of the power: But when power is once transferred from the many to the few, all changes become extremely difficult; the government, in this case, being beneficial to the few, they will be exceedingly artful and adroit in preventing any measures which may lead to a change; and nothing will produce it, but great exertions and severe struggles on the part of the common people. Every man of reflection must see, that the change now proposed, is a transfer of power from the many to the few, and the probability is, the artful and ever active aristocracy, will prevent all peaceful measures for changes, unless when they shall discover some favorable moment to increase their own influence. I am sensible, thousands of men in the United States, are disposed to adopt the proposed constitution, though they perceive it to be essentially defective, under an idea that amendments of it, may be obtained when necessary. This is a pernicious idea, it argues a servility of character totally unfit for the support of free government; it is very repugnant to that perpetual jealousy respecting liberty, so absolutely necessary in all free states, spoken of by Mr. Dickinson.—However, if our countrymen are so soon changed, and the language of 1774, is become odious to them, it will be in vain to use the language of freedom, or to attempt to rouse them to free enquiries: But I shall never believe this is the case with them, whatever present appearances may be, till I shall have very strong evidence indeed of it.

Your's &c.

THE FEDERAL FARMER.

15 OCTOBER 1787

LETTER V

The Federal Farmer again complains that the democratic or common element is not sufficiently represented in the new Constitution. This leaves the new government unbalanced and should be corrected through moderate efforts, avoiding the pitfalls of both levelling and aristocracy. Essays in The Federalist *of particular relevance: 57, 58.*

DEAR SIR,

THUS I have examined the federal constitution as far as a few days leisure would permit. It opens to my mind a new scene; instead of seeing powers cautiously lodged in the hands of numerous legislators, and many magistrates, we see all important powers collecting in one centre, where a few men will possess them almost at discretion. And instead of checks in the formation of the government, to secure the rights of the people against the usurpations of those they appoint to govern, we are to understand the equal division of lands among our people, and the strong arm furnished them by nature and situation, are to secure them against those usurpations. If there are advantages in the equal division of our lands, and the strong and manly habits of our people, we ought to establish governments calculated to give duration to them, and not governments which never can work naturally, till that equality of property, and those free and manly habits shall be destroyed; these evidently are not the natural basis of the proposed constitution. No man of reflection, and skilled in the science of government, can suppose these will move on harmoniously together for ages, or even for fifty years. As to the little circumstances commented upon, by some writers, with applause—as the age of a representative, of the president, &c.—they have, in my mind, no weight in the general tendency of the system.

There are, however, in my opinion, many good things in the proposed system. It is founded on elective principles, and the deposits
of powers in different hands, is essentially right. The guards
against those evils we have experienced in some states in legislation are valuable indeed; but the value of every feature in this system is vastly lessened for the want of that one important feature
in a free government, a representation of the people. Because we
have sometimes abused democracy, I am not among those men who
think a democratic branch a nuisance; which branch shall be sufficiently numerous to admit some of the best informed men of each
order in the community into the administration of government.

While the radical defects in the proposed system are not so soon
discovered, some temptations to each state, and to many classes of
men to adopt it, are very visible. It uses the democratic language
of several of the state constitutions, particularly that of Massachusetts; the eastern states will receive advantages so far as the regulation of trade, by a bare majority, is committed to it: Connecticut
and New Jersey will receive their share of a general impost: The
middle states will receive the advantages surrounding the seat of
government; The southern states will receive protection, and have
their negroes represented in the legislature, and large back countries will soon have a majority in it. This system promises a large
field of employment to military gentlemen, and gentlemen of the
law; and in case the government shall be executed without convulsions, it will afford security to creditors, to the clergy, salary-men
and others depending on money payments. So far as the system
promises justice and reasonable advantages, in these respects, it
ought to be supported by all honest men; but whenever it promises
unequal and improper advantages to any particular states, or
orders of men, it ought to be opposed.

I have, in the course of these letters observed, that there are
many good things in the proposed constitution, and I have endeavored to point out many important defects in it. I have admitted that
we want a federal system—that we have a system presented, which,
with several alterations may be made a tolerable good one—I have
admitted there is a well founded uneasiness among creditors and

mercantile men. In this situation of things, you ask me what I think
ought to be done? My opinion in this case is only the opinion of an
individual, and so far only as it corresponds with the opinions of the
honest and substantial part of the community, is it entitled to consideration. Though I am fully satisfied that the state conventions
ought most seriously to direct their exertions to altering and amending the system proposed before they shall adopt it—yet I have not
sufficiently examined the subject, or formed an opinion, how far it
will be practicable for those conventions to carry their amendments.
As to the idea, that it will be in vain for those conventions to attempt
amendments, it cannot be admitted; it is impossible to say whether
they can or not until the attempt shall be made; and when it shall
be determined, by experience, that the conventions cannot agree in
amendments, it will then be an important question before the people
of the United States, whether they will adopt or not the system
proposed in its present form. This subject of consolidating the states
is new: and because forty or fifty men have agreed in a system, to
suppose the good sense of this country, an enlightened nation, must
adopt it without examination, and though in a state of profound
peace, without endeavouring to amend those parts they perceive are
defective, dangerous to freedom, and destructive of the valuable
principles of republican government—is truly humiliating. It is true
there may be danger in delay; but there is danger in adopting the
system in its present form; and I see the danger in either case will
arise principally from the conduct and views of two very unprincipled parties in the United States—two fires, between which the
honest and substantial people have long found themselves situated.
One party is composed of little insurgents, men in debt, who want no
law, and who want a share of the property of others; these are called
levellers, Shayites, &c. The other party is composed of a few, but
more dangerous men, with their servile dependents; these avari-
ciously grasp at all power and property; you may discover in all the
actions of these men, an evident dislike to free and equal government, and they will go systematically to work to change, essentially,
the forms of government in this country; these are called aristocrats,
m——ites, &c. &c. Between these two parties is the weight of the
community; the men of middling property, men not in debt on the

one hand, and men, on the other, content with republican governments, and not aiming at immense fortunes, offices, and power. In
1786, the little insurgents, the levellers, came forth, invaded the
rights of others, and attempted to establish governments according
to their wills. Their movements evidently gave encouragement to
the other party, which, in 1787, has taken the political field, and with
its fashionable dependants, and the tongue and the pen, is endeavoring to establish in a great haste, a politer kind of government.
These two parties, which will probably be opposed or united as it
may suit their interests and views, are really insignificant, compared
with the solid, free, and independent part of the community. It is
not my intention to suggest, that either of these parties, and the real
friends of the proposed constitution, are the same men. The fact is,
these aristocrats support and hasten the adoption of the proposed
constitution, merely because they think it is a stepping stone to their
favorite object. I think I am well founded in this idea; I think the
general politics of these men support it, as well as the common
observation among them, That the proffered plan is the best that
can be got at present, it will do for a few years, and lead to something better. The sensible and judicious part of the community will
carefully weigh all these circumstances; they will view the late convention as a respectable body of men—America probably never will
see an assembly of men, of a like number, more respectable. But the
members of the convention met without knowing the sentiments of
one man in ten thousand in these states respecting the new ground
taken. Their doings are but the first attempts in the most important scene ever opened. Though each individual in the state conventions will not, probably, be so respectable as each individual in
the federal convention, yet as the state conventions will probably
consist of fifteen hundred or two thousand men of abilities, and
versed in the science of government, collected from all parts of the
community and from all orders of men, it must be acknowledged
that the weight of respectability will be in them—In them will be
collected the solid sense and the real political character of the country. Being revisers of the subject, they will possess peculiar advantages. To say that these conventions ought not to attempt, coolly and
deliberately, the revision of the system, or that they cannot amend

it, is very foolish or very assuming. If these conventions, after examining the system, adopt it, I shall be perfectly satisfied, and wish to
see men make the administration of the government an equal blessing to all orders of men. I believe the great body of our people to be
virtuous and friendly to good government, to the protection of liberty and property; and it is the duty of all good men, especially of
those who are placed as sentinels to guard their rights—it is their
duty to examine into the prevailing politics of parties, and to disclose
them—while they avoid exciting undue suspicions, to lay facts
before the people, which will enable them to form a proper judgment. Men who wish the people of this country to determine for
themselves, and deliberately to fit the government to their situation,
must feel some degree of indignation at those attempts to hurry
the adoption of a system, and to shut the door against examination.
The very attempts create suspicions, that those who make them
have secret views, or see some defects in the system, which, in the
hurry of affairs, they expect will escape the eye of a free people.

What can be the views of those gentlemen in Pennsylvania, who
precipitated decisions on this subject? What can be the views of
those gentlemen in Boston, who countenanced the Printers in shut-
ting up the press against a fair and free investigation of this important system in the usual way. The members of the convention have
done their duty—why should some of them fly to their states—
almost forget a propriety of behaviour, and precipitate measures
for the adoption of a system of their own making? I confess candidly, when I consider these circumstances in connection with the
unguarded parts of the system I have mentioned, I feel disposed
to proceed with very great caution, and to pay more attention than
usual to the conduct of particular characters. If the constitution
presented be a good one, it will stand the test with a well informed
people: all are agreed that there shall be state conventions to examine it; and we must believe it will be adopted, unless we suppose it
is a bad one, or that those conventions will make false divisions
respecting it. I admit improper measures are taken against the
adoption of the system as well for it—all who object to the plan proposed ought to point out the defects objected to, and to propose
those amendments with which they can accept it, or to propose

some other system of government, that the public mind may be known, and that we may be brought to agree in some system of government, to strengthen and execute the present, or to provide a substitute. I consider the field of enquiry just opened, and that we are to look to the state conventions for ultimate decisions on the subject before us; it is not to be presumed, that they will differ about small amendments, and lose a system when they shall have made it substantially good; but touching the essential amendments, it is to be presumed the several conventions will pursue the most rational measures to agree in and obtain them; and such defects as they shall discover and not remove, they will probably notice, keep them in view as the ground work of future amendments, and in the firm and manly language which every free people ought to use, will suggest to those who may hereafter administer the government that it is their expectation, that the system will be so organized by legislative acts, and the government so administered, as to render those defects as little injurious as possible. Our countrymen are entitled to an honest and faithful government; to a government of laws and not of men; and also to one of their chusing—as a citizen of the country, I wish to see these objects secured, and licentious, assuming, and overbearing men restrained; if the constitution or social compact be vague and unguarded, then we depend wholly upon the prudence, wisdom and moderation of those who manage the affairs of government; or on what, probably, is equally uncertain and precarious, the success of the people oppressed by the abuse of government, in receiving it from the hands of those who abuse it, and placing it in the hands of those who will use it well.

In every point of view, therefore, in which I have been able, as yet, to contemplate this subject, I can discern but one rational mode of proceeding relative to it: and that is to examine it with freedom and candour, to have state conventions some months hence, which shall examine coolly every article, clause, and word in the system proposed, and to adopt it with such amendments as they shall think fit. How far the state conventions ought to pursue the mode prescribed by the federal convention of adopting or rejecting the plan in toto, I leave it to them to determine. Our examination of the subject hitherto has been rather of a general nature. The republican characters in the several states, who wish to make this plan more adequate to security of liberty and property, and to the duration of the principles of a free government, will, no doubt, collect their opinions to certain points, and accurately define those alterations and amendments they wish; if it shall be found they essentially disagree in them, the conventions will then be able to determine whether to adopt the plan as it is, or what will be proper to be done.

Under these impressions, and keeping in view the improper and unadvisable lodgment of powers in the general government, organized as it at present is, touching internal taxes, armies and militia, the elections of its own members, causes between citizens of different states, &c. and the want of a more perfect bill of rights, &c. I drop the subject for the present, and when I shall have leisure to revise and correct my ideas respecting it, and to collect into points the opinions of those who wish to make the system more secure and safe, perhaps I may proceed to point out particularly for your consideration, the amendments which ought to be ingrafted into this system, not only in conformity to my own, but the deliberate opinions of others—you will with me perceive, that the objections to the plan proposed may, by a more leisure examination be set in a stronger point of view, especially the important one, that there is no substantial representation of the people provided for in a government in which the most essential powers, even as to the internal police of the country, is proposed to be lodged.

I think the honest and substantial part of the community will wish to see this system altered, permanency and consistency given to the constitution we shall adopt; and therefore they will be anxious to apportion the powers to the features and organizations of the government, and to see abuse in the exercise of power more effectually guarded against. It is suggested, that state officers, from interested motives will oppose the constitution presented—I see no reason for this, their places in general will not be effected, but new openings to offices and places of profit must evidently be made by the adoption of the constitution in its present form.

Your's, &c.

THE FEDERAL FARMER.

"An Additional Number of Letters from The FEDERAL FARMER"

25 DECEMBER 1787

LETTER VI

In the first of his Additional Letters, the Federal Farmer argues that free governments must recognize men's natural rights, as the Magna Charta and subsequent British declaratory documents had done. He goes on to outline the central government's powers under the Articles of Confederation and the structure of state governments, all of which protect common law rights. Essays in The Federalist *of particular relevance: 2, 51, 78, 84.*

DEAR SIR,

MY former letters to you, respecting the constitution proposed, were calculated merely to lead to a fuller investigation of the subject; having more extensively considered it, and the opinions of others relative to it, I shall, in a few letters, more particularly endeavour to point out the defects, and propose amendments. I shall in this make only a few general and introductory observations, which, in the present state of the momentous question, may not be improper; and I leave you, in all cases, to decide by a careful examination of my works, upon the weight of my arguments, the propriety of my remarks, the uprightness of my intentions, and the extent of my candor—I presume I am writing to a man of candor and reflection, and not to an ardent, peevish, or impatient man.

When the constitution was first published, there appeared to prevail a misguided zeal to prevent a fair unbiassed examination of a subject of infinite importance to this people and their posterity— to the cause of liberty and the rights of mankind—and it was the duty of those who saw a restless ardor, or design, attempting to mislead the people by a parade of names and misrepresentations, to endeavour to prevent their having their intended effects. The only way to stop the passions of men in their career is, coolly to state facts, and deliberately to avow the truth—and to do this we are frequently forced into a painful view of men and measures.

Since I wrote to you in October, I have heard much said, and seen many pieces written, upon the subject in question; and on carefully examining them on both sides, I find much less reason for changing my sentiments, respecting the good and defective parts of the system proposed than I expected—The opposers, as well as the advocates of it, confirm me in my opinion, that this system affords, all circumstances considered, a better basis to build upon than the confederation. And as to the principal defects, as the smallness of the representation, the insecurity of elections, the undue mixture of powers in the senate, the insecurity of some essential rights, &c. the opposition appears, generally, to agree respecting them, and many of the ablest advocates virtually to admit them—Clear it is, the latter do not attempt manfully to defend these defective parts, but to cover them with a mysterious veil; they concede, they retract; they say we could do no better; and some of them, when a little out of temper, and hard pushed, use arguments that do more honor to their ingenuity, than to their candor and firmness.

Three states have now adopted the constitution without amendments; these, and other circumstances, ought to have their weight in deciding the question, whether we will put the system into operation, adopt it, enumerate and recommend the necessary amendments, which afterwards, by three-fourths of the states, may be ingrafted into the system, or whether we will make the amendments prior to the adoption—I only undertake to shew amendments are essential and necessary—how far it is practicable to ingraft them into the plan, prior to the adoption, the state conventions must determine. Our situation is critical, and we have but our choice of evils—We may hazard much by adopting the constitution in its present form—we may hazard more by rejecting it wholly—we may hazard much by long contending about amendments prior to the adoption. The greatest political evils that can befal us, are discords and civil wars—the greatest blessings we can wish for, are peace, union, and industry, under a mild, free, and steady government. Amendments recommended will tend to guard and direct the administration—but there will be danger that the people, after the system shall be adopted, will become inattentive to amendments—Their attention is now awake—the discussion of the subject, which has already taken place, has had a happy effect—it has called forth the able advocates of liberty, and tends to renew, in the minds of the people, their true republican jealousy and vigilance, the strongest guard against the abuses of power; but the vigilance of the people is not sufficiently constant to be depended on—fortunate it is for the body of a people, if they can continue attentive to their liberties, long enough to erect for them a temple, and constitutional barriers for their permanent security: when they are well fixed between the powers of the rulers and the rights of the people, they become visible boundaries, constantly seen by all, and any transgression of them is immediately discovered: they serve as centinels for the people at all times, and especially in those unavoidable intervals of inattention.

Some of the advocates, I believe, will agree to recommend *good* amendments; but some of them will only consent to recommend indefinite, specious, but unimportant ones; and this only with a view to keep the door open for obtaining, in some favourable moment, their main object, a complete consolidation of the states, and a government much higher toned, less republican and free than the one proposed. If necessity, therefore, should ever oblige us to adopt the system, and recommend amendments, the true friends of a federal republic must see they are well defined, and well calculated, not only to prevent our system of government moving further from republican principles and equality, but to bring it back nearer to them—they must be constantly on their guard against the address, flattery, and manœuvres of their adversaries.

The gentlemen who oppose the constitution, or contend for amendments in it, are frequently, and with much bitterness, charged with wantonly attacking the men who framed it. The unjustness of this charge leads me to make one observation upon the conduct of parties, &c. Some of the advocates are only pretended federalists; in fact they wish for an abolition of the state governments. Some of them I believe to be honest federalists, who wish to preserve *substantially* the state governments united under an efficient federal head; and many of them are blind tools without any object. Some of the opposers also are only pretended federalists, who want no federal government, or one merely advisory. Some of them are the true federalists, their object, perhaps, more clearly seen, is the same with that of the honest federalists; and some of them, probably, have no distinct object. We might as well call the advocates and opposers tories and whigs, or any thing else, as federalists and anti-federalists. To be for or against the constitution, as it stands, is not much evidence of a federal disposition; if any names are applicable to the parties, on account of their general politics, they are those of republicans and anti-republicans. The opposers are generally men who support the rights of the body of the people, and are properly republicans. The advocates are generally men not very friendly to those rights, and properly anti-republicans.

Had the advocates left the constitution, as they ought to have done, to be adopted or rejected on account of its own merits or imperfections, I do not believe the gentlemen who framed it would ever have been even alluded to in the contest by the opposers. Instead of this, the ardent advocates begun by quoting names as incontestible authorities for the implicit adoption of the system, without any examination—treated all who opposed it as friends of anarchy; and with an indecent virulence addressed M–n G—y, L—e, and almost every man of weight they could find in the opposition by name. If they had been candid men they would have applauded the moderation of the opposers for not retaliating in this pointed manner, when so fair an opportunity was given them; but the opposers generally saw that it was no time to heat the passions; but, at the same time, they saw there was something more than mere zeal in many of their adversaries; they saw them attempting to mislead the people, and to precipitate their divisions, by the sound of names, and forced to do it, the opposers, in general terms, alledged those names were not of sufficient authority to justify the hasty adoption of the system contended for. The convention, as a body, was undoubtedly respectable; it was, generally, composed of members of the then and preceding Congresses as a body of respectable men we ought to view it. To select individual names, is an invitation to personal attacks, and the advocates, for their own sake, ought to have known the abilities, politics, and situation of some of their favourite characters better, before they held them up to view in the manner they did, as men entitled to our implicit political belief: they ought to have known, whether all the men they so held up to view could, for their past conduct in public offices, be approved or not by the public records, and the honest part of the community. These ardent advocates seem now to be peevish and angry, because, by their own folly, they have led to an investigation of facts and of political characters, unfavourable to them, which they had not the discernment to foresee. They may well apprehend they have opened a door to some Junius, or to some man, after his manner, with his polite addresses to men by name, to state serious facts, and unfold the truth; but these advocates may rest assured, that cool men in the opposition, best acquainted with the affairs of the country, will not, in the critical passage of a people from one constitution to another, pursue inquiries, which, in other circumstances, will be deserving of the highest praise. I will say nothing further about political characters, but examine the constitution; and as a necessary and previous measure to a particular examination. I shall state a few general positions and principles, which receive a general assent and briefly notice the leading features of the confederation, and several state conventions, to which, through the whole investigation, we must frequently have recourse, to aid the mind in its determinations.

We can put but little dependance on the partial and vague information transmitted to us respecting antient governments; our situation as a people is peculiar: our people in general have a high sense of freedom; they are high spirited, though capable of deliberate measures; they are intelligent, discerning, and well informed; and it is to their condition we must mould the constitution and laws. We have no royal or noble families, and all things concur in favour of a government entirely elective. We have tried our abilities as freemen in a most arduous contest, and have succeeded; but we now find the main spring of our movements were the love of liberty, and a temporary ardor, and not any energetic principle in the federal system.

Our territories are far too extensive for a limited monarchy, in which the representatives must frequently assemble, and the laws operate mildly and systematically. The most elligible system is a federal republic, that is, a system in which national concerns may be transacted in the centre, and local affairs in state or district governments.

The powers of the union ought to be extended to commerce, the coin, and national objects; and a division of powers, and a deposit of them in different hands, is safest.

Good government is generally the result of experience and gradual improvements, and a punctual execution of the laws is essential to the preservation of life, liberty, and property. Taxes are always necessary, and the power to raise them can never be safely lodged without checks and limitation, but in a full and substantial representation of the body of the people; the quantity of power delegated ought to be compensated by the brevity of the time of holding it, in order to prevent the possessors increasing it. The supreme power is in the people, and rulers possess only that portion which is expressly given them; yet the wisest people have often declared this is the case on proper occasions, and have carefully formed stipulation to fix the extent, and limit the exercise of the power given.

The people by Magna Charta, &c. did not acquire powers, or receive privileges from the king, they only ascertained and fixed those they were entitled to as Englishmen; the title used by the king "we grant," was mere form. Representation, and the jury trial, are the best features of a free government ever as yet discovered, and the only means by which the body of the people can have their proper influence in the affairs of government.

In a federal system we must not only balance the parts of the same government, as that of the state, or that of the union; but we must find a balancing influence between the general and local governments—the latter is what men or writers have but very little or imperfectly considered.

A free and mild government is that in which no laws can be made without the formal and free consent of the people, or of their constitutional representatives; that is, of a substantial representative branch. Liberty, in its genuine sense, is security to enjoy the effects of our honest industry and labours, in a free and mild government, and personal security from all illegal restraints.

Of rights, some are natural and unalienable, of which even the people cannot deprive individuals: Some are constitutional or fundamental; these cannot be altered or abolished by the ordinary laws; but the people, by express acts, may alter or abolish them—These, such as the trial by jury, the benefits of the writ of habeas corpus, &c. individuals claim under the solemn compacts of the people, as constitutions, or at least under laws so strengthened by long usuage as not to be repealable by the ordinary legislature—and some are common or mere legal rights, that is, such as individuals claim under laws which the ordinary legislature may alter or abolish at pleasure.

The confederation is a league of friendship among the states or sovereignties for the common defence and mutual welfare—Each state expressly retains its sovereignty, and all powers not expressly given to congress—All federal powers are lodged in a congress of delegates annually elected by the state legislatures, except in Connecticut and Rhode-Island, where they are chosen by the people—Each state has a vote in congress, pays its delegates, and may instruct or recall them; no delegate can hold any office of profit, or serve more than three years in any six years—Each state may be represented by not less than two, or more than seven delegates.

Congress (nine states agreeing) may make peace and war, treaties and alliances, grant letters of marque and reprisal, coin money, regulate the alloy and value of the coin, require men and monies of the states by fixed proportions, and appropriate monies, form armies and navies, emit bills of credit, and borrow monies.

Congress (seven states agreeing) may send and receive ambassadors, regulate captures, make rules for governing the army and navy, institute courts for the trial of piracies and felonies committed on the high seas, and for settling territorial disputes between the individual states, regulate weight and measures, post-offices, and Indian affairs.

No state, without the consent of congress, can send or receive embassies, make any agreement with any other state, or a foreign state, keep up any vessels of war or bodies of forces in time of peace, or engage in war, or lay any duties which may interfere with the treaties of congress. Each state must appoint regimental officers, and keep up a well regulated militia—Each state may prohibit the importation or exportation of any species of goods.

The free inhabitants of one state are intitled to the privileges and immunities of the free citizens of the other states—Credit in each state shall be given to the records and judicial proceedings in the others.

Canada, acceding, may be admitted, and any other colony may be admitted by the consent of nine states.

Alterations may be made by the agreement of congress, and confirmation of all the state legislatures.

The following, I think, will be allowed to be unalienable or fundamental rights in the United States:—

No man, demeaning himself peaceably, shall be molested on account of his religion or mode of worship—The people have a right to hold and enjoy their property according to known standing laws, and which cannot be taken from them without their consent, or the consent of their representatives; and whenever taken in the pressing urgencies of government, they are to receive a reasonable compensation for it—Individual security consists in having free recourse to the laws—The people are subject to no laws or taxes not assented to by their representatives constitutionally assembled—They are at all times intitled to the benefits of the writ of habeas corpus, the trial by jury in criminal and civil causes—They have a right, when charged, to a speedy trial in the vicinage; to be heard by themselves or counsel, not to be compelled to furnish evidence against themselves, to have witnesses face to face, and to confront their adversaries before the judge—No man is held to answer a crime charged upon him till it be substantially described to him; and he is subject to no unreasonable searches or seizures of his person, papers or effects—The people have a right to assemble in an orderly manner, and petition the government for a redress of wrongs—The freedom of the press ought not to be restrained—No emoluments, except for actual service—No hereditary honors, or orders of nobility, ought to be allowed—The military ought to be subordinate to the civil authority, and no soldier be quartered on the citizens without their consent—The militia ought always to be armed and disciplined, and the usual defence of the country—The supreme power is in the people, and power delegated ought to return to them at stated periods, and frequently—The legislative, executive, and judicial powers, ought always to be kept distinct—others perhaps might be added.

The organization of the state governments—Each state has a legislature, an executive, and a judicial branch—In general legislators are excluded from the important executive and judicial offices—Except in the Carolinas there is no constitutional distinction among Christian sects—The constitutions of New York, Delaware, and Virginia, exclude the clergy from offices civil and military—the other states do nearly the same in practice.

Each state has a democratic branch elected twice a year in Rhode Island and Connecticut, biennially in South Carolina, and annually in the other states—There are about 1500 representatives in all the states, or one to each 1700 inhabitants, reckoning five blacks for three whites—The states do not differ as to the age or moral characters of the electors or elected, nor materially as to their property.

Pennsylvania has lodged all her legislative powers in a single branch, and Georgia has done the same; the other eleven states have each in their legislatures a second or senatorial branch. In forming this they have combined various principles, and aimed at several checks and balances. It is amazing to see how ingenuity has worked in the several states to fix a barrier against popular instability. In Massachusetts the senators are apportioned on districts according to the taxes they pay, nearly according to property. In Connecticut the freemen, in September, vote for twenty counsellers, and return the names of those voted for in the several towns; the legislature takes the twenty who have the most votes, and give them to the people, who, in April, chuse twelve of them, who, with the governor and deputy governor, form the senatorial branch. In Maryland the senators are chosen by two electors from each county; these electors are chosen by the freemen, and qualified as the members in the democratic branch are: In these two cases checks are aimed at in the mode of election. Several states have taken into view the periods of service, age, property, &c. In South-Carolina a senator is elected for two years, in Delaware three, and in New-York and Virginia four, in Maryland five, and in the other states for one. In New-York and Virginia one-fourth part go out yearly. In Virginia a senator must be twenty-five years old, in South Carolina thirty. In New-York the electors must each have a free-hold worth 250 dollars, in North-Carolina a freehold of fifty acres of land; in the other states the electors of senators are qualified as electors of representatives are. In Massachusetts a senator must have a freehold in his own right worth 1000 dollars, or any estate worth 2000, in New-Jersey any estate worth 2666, in South Car-olina worth 1300 dollars, in North-Carolina 300 acres of land in fee, &c. The numbers of senators in each state are from ten to thirty-one, about 160 in the eleven states, about one to 14000 inhabitants.

Two states, Massachusetts and New-York, have each introduced into their legislatures a third, but incomplete branch. In the former, the governor may negative any law not supported by two-thirds of the senators, and two-thirds of the representatives: in the latter, the governor, chancellor, and judges of the supreme court may do the same.

Each state has a single executive branch. In the five eastern states the people at large elect their governors; in the other states the legislatures elect them. In South Carolina the governor is elected once in two years; in New-York and Delaware once in three, and in the other states annually. The governor of New-York has no executive council, the other governors have. In several states the governor has a vote in the senatorial branch—the governors have similar powers in some instances, and quite dissimilar ones in oth-ers. The number of executive counsellers in the states are from five to twelve. In the four eastern states, New-Jersey, Pennsylva-nia, and Georgia, they are of the men returned legislators by the people. In Pennsylvania the counsellers are chosen triennially, in Delaware every fourth year, in Virginia every three years, in South-Carolina biennially, and in the other states yearly.

Each state has a judicial branch; each common law courts, supe-rior and inferior; some chancery and admiralty courts: The courts in general fit in different places in order to accommodate the citizens.

The trial by jury is had in all the common law courts, and in some of the admiralty courts. The democratic freemen principally form the juries; men destitute of property, of character, or under age, are excluded as in elections. Some of the judges are during good behaviour, and some appointed for a year, and some for years; and all are dependant on the legislatures for their salaries—Particulars respecting this department are too many to be noticed here.

THE FEDERAL FARMER.

31 DECEMBER 1787

LETTER VII

The Federal Farmer argues that free governments depend on persuasion and the people's confidence. To win the people's confidence government must fully serve all classes and interests. The new government's legislature will be too small and distant from the people to fulfill this function. Essays in The Federalist *of particular relevance: 10, 55-57.*

DEAR SIR,

IN viewing the various governments instituted by mankind, we see their whole force reducible to two principles—the important springs which alone move the machines, and give them their intended influence and controul, are force and persuasion: by the former men are compelled, by the latter they are drawn. We denominate a government despotic or free, as the one or other principle prevails in it. Perhaps it is not possible for a government to be so despotic, as not to operate persuasively on some of its subjects; nor is it, in the nature of things, I conceive, for a government to be so free, or so supported by voluntary consent, as never to want force to compel obedience to the laws. In despotic govern-

ments one man, or a few men, independant of the people, generally
make the laws, command obedience, and inforce it by the sword:
one-fourth part of the people are armed, and obliged to endure the
fatigues of soldiers, to oppress the others and keep them subject
to the laws. In free governments the people, or their representatives, make the laws; their execution is principally the effect of voluntary consent and aid; the people respect the magistrate, follow
their private pursuits, and enjoy the fruits of their labour with very
small deductions for the public use. The body of the people must
evidently prefer the latter species of government; and it can be only
those few who may be well paid for the part they take in enforcing
despotism, that can, for a moment, prefer the former. Our true
object is to give full efficacy to one principle, to arm persuasion on
every side, and to render force as little necessary as possible. Persuasion is never dangerous not even in despotic governments; but
military force, if often applied internally, can never fail to destroy
the love and confidence, and break the spirits, of the people and to
render it totally impracticable and unnatural for him or them who
govern, and yield to this force against the people, to hold their
places by the people's elections.

I repeat my observation, that the plan proposed will have a
doubtful operation between the two principles; and whether it will
preponderate towards persuasion or force is uncertain.

Government must exist—If the persuasive principle be feeble,
force is infallibly the next resort. The moment the laws of congress
shall be disregarded they must languish, and the whole system be
convulsed—that moment we must have recourse to this next
resort, and all freedom vanish.

It being impracticable for the people to assemble to make laws,
they must elect legislators, and assign men to the different departments of the government. In the representative branch we must
expect chiefly to collect the confidence of the people, and in it to find
almost entirely the force of persuasion. In forming this branch,
therefore, several important considerations must be attended to.
It must possess abilities to discern the situation of the people and of
public affairs, a disposition to sympathize with the people, and a
capacity and inclination to make laws congenial to their circum-

stances and condition: it must afford security against interested combinations, corruption and influence; it must possess the confidence, and have the voluntary support of the people.

I think these positions will not be controverted, nor the one I formerly advanced, that a fair and equal representation is that in which the interests, feelings, opinions and views of the people are collected, in such manner as they would be were the people all assembled. Having made these general observations, I shall proceed to consider further my principal position, viz. that there is no substantial representation of the people provided for in a government, in which the most essential powers, even as to the internal police of the country, are proposed to be lodged; and to propose certain amendments as to the representative branch: 1st, That there ought to be *an increase of the numbers of representatives:* And, 2dly, That the elections of them ought to be better secured.

1. The representation is unsubstantial and ought to be increased. In matters where there is much room for opinion you will not expect me to establish my positions with mathematical certainty: you must only expect my observations to be candid, and such as are well founded in the mind of the writer. I am in a field where doctors disagree; and as to genuine representation, though no feature in government can be more important, perhaps, no one has been less understood, and no one that has received so imperfect a consideration by political writers. The ephori in Sparta, and the tribunes in Rome, were but the shadow: the representation in Great-Britain is unequal and insecure. In America we have done more in establishing this important branch on its true principles, than, perhaps, all the world besides: yet even here, I conceive, that very great improvements in representation may be made. In fixing this branch, the situation of the people must be surveyed, and the number of representatives and forms of election apportioned to that situation. When we find a numerous people settled in a fertile and extensive country, possessing equality, and few or none of them oppressed with riches or wants, it ought to be the anxious care of the constitution and laws, to arrest them from national depravity, and to preserve them in their happy condition. A virtuous people make just laws, and good laws tend to preserve

unchanged a virtuous people. A virtuous and happy people by laws uncongenial to their characters, may easily be gradually changed into servile and depraved creatures. Where the people, or their representatives, make the laws, it is probable they will generally be fitted to the national character and circumstances, unless the representation be partial, and the imperfect substitute of the people. However, the people may be electors, if the representation be so formed as to give one or more of the natural classes of men in the society an undue ascendency over the others, it is imperfect: the former will gradually become masters, and the latter slaves. It is the first of all among the political balances, to preserve in its proper station each of these classes. We talk of balances in the legislature, and among the departments of government; we ought to carry them to the body of the people. Since I advanced the idea of balancing the several orders of men in a community, in forming a genuine representation, and seen that idea considered as chemerical, I have been sensibly struck with a sentence in the marquis Beccaria's treatise: this sentence was quoted by congress in 1774, and is as follows:—"In every society there is an effort continually tending to confer on one part the height of power and happiness, and to reduce the others to the extreme of weakness and misery; the intent of good laws is to oppose this effort, and to diffuse their influence universally and equally." Add to this Montesquieu's opinion, that "in a free state every man, who is supposed to be a free agent, ought to be concerned in his own government: therefore, the legislative should reside in the whole body of the people, or their representatives." It is extremely clear that these writers had in view the several orders of men in society, which we call aristocratical, democratical, merchantile, mechanic, &c. and perceived the efforts they are constantly from interested and ambitious views, disposed to make to elevate themselves and oppress others. Each order must have a share in the business of legislation actually and efficiently. It is deceiving a people to tell them they are electors, and can chuse their legislators if they cannot, in the nature of things chuse men from among themselves, and genuinely like themselves. I wish you to take another idea along with you; we are not only to balance these natural efforts, but we are also to guard against accidental combinations; combinations founded in the connections of offices and private interests, both evils which are increased in proportion as the number of men, among which the elected must be, are decreased. To set this matter in a proper point of view, we must form some general ideas and descriptions of the different classes of men, as they may be divided by occupations and politically: the first class is the aristocratical. There are three kinds of aristocracy spoken of in this country—the first is a constitutional one, which does not exist in the United States in our common acceptation of the word. Montesquieu, it is true, observes, that where a part of the persons in a society, for want of property, age, or moral character, are excluded any share in the government, the others, who alone are the constitutional electors and elected, form this aristocracy; this, according to him, exists in each of the United States, where a considerable number of persons, as all convicted of crimes, under age, or not possessed of certain property, are excluded any share in the government;—the second is an aristocratic faction; a junto of unprincipled men, often distinguished for their wealth or abilities, who combine together and make their object their private interests and aggrandizement; the existence of this description is merely accidental, but particularly to be guarded against. The third is the natural aristocracy; this term we use to designate a respectable order of men, the line between whom and the natural democracy is in some degree arbitrary; we may place men on one side of this line, which others may place on the other, and in all disputes between the few and the many, a considerable number are wavering and uncertain themselves on which side they are, or ought to be. In my idea of our natural aristocracy in the United States, I include about four or five thousand men; and among these I reckon those who have been placed in the offices of governors, of members of Congress, and state senators generally, in the principal officers of Congress, of the army and militia, the superior judges, the most eminent professional men, &c. and men of large property—the other persons and orders in the community form the natural democracy; this includes in general the yeomanry, the subordinate officers, civil and military, the fishermen, mechanics and traders, many of the merchants and professional men. It is easy to perceive that men of these two classes, the aristocratical, and democratical, with views equally honest, have sentiments widely different, especially respecting public and private expences, salaries, taxes, &c. Men of the first class associate more extensively, have a high sense of honor, possess abilities, ambition, and general knowledge; men of the second class are not so much used to combining great objects; they possess less ambition, and a larger share of honesty: their dependence is principally on middling and small estates, industrious pursuits, and hard labour, while that of the former is principally on the emoluments of large estates, and of the chief offices of government. Not only the efforts of these two great parties are to be balanced, but other interests and parties also, which do not always oppress each other merely for want of power, and for fear of the consequences; though they, in fact, mutually depend on each other: yet such are their general views, that the merchants alone would never fail to make laws favourable to themselves and oppressive to the farmers, &c.; the farmers alone would act on like principles; the former would tax the land, the latter the trade. The manufacturers are often disposed to contend for monopolies, buyers make every exertion to lower prices, and sellers to raise them; men who live by fees and salaries endeavour to raise them, and the part of the people who pay them, endeavour to lower them; the public creditors to augment the taxes, and the people at large to lessen them. Thus, in every period of society, and in all the transactions of men, we see parties verifying the observation made by the Marquis; and those classes which have not their centinels in the government, in proportion to what they have to gain or lose, must infallibly be ruined.

Efforts among parties are not merely confined to property; they contend for rank and distinctions; all their passions in turn are enlisted in political controversies—Men, elevated in society, are often disgusted with the changeableness of the democracy, and the latter are often agitated with the passions of jealousy and envy: the yeomanry possess a large share of property and strength, are nervous and firm in their opinions and habits—the mechanics of towns are ardent and changeable, honest and credulous, they are inconsiderable for numbers, weight and strength, not always sufficiently stable for the supporting free governments: the fishing interest partakes partly of the strength and stability of the landed, and partly of the changeableness of the mechanic interest. As to merchants and traders, they are our agents in almost all money transactions; give activity to government, and possess a considerable share of influence in it. It has been observed by an able writer, that frugal industrious merchants are generally advocates for liberty. It is an observation, I believe, well founded, that the schools produce but few advocates for republican forms of government; gentlemen of the law, divinity, physic, &c. probably form about a fourth part of the people; yet their political influence, perhaps, is equal to that of all the other descriptions of men; if we may judge from the appointments to Congress, the legal characters will often, in a small representation, be the majority; but the more the representatives are encreased, the more of the farmers, merchants, &c. will be found to be brought into the government.

These general observations will enable you to discern what I intend by different classes, and the general scope of my ideas, when I contend for uniting and balancing their interests, feelings, opinions, and views in the legislature; we may not only so unite and balance these as to prevent a change in the government by the gradual exaltation of one part to the depression of others, but we may derive many other advantages from the combination and full representation; a small representation can never be well informed as to the circumstances of the people, the members of it must be too far removed from the people, in general, to sympathize with them, and too few to communicate with them: a representation must be extremely imperfect where the representatives are not circumstanced to make the proper communications to their constituents, and where the constituents in turn cannot, with tolerable convenience, make known their wants, circumstances, and opinions, to their representatives: where there is but one representative to 30,000 or 40,000 inhabitants, it appears to me, he can only mix, and be acquainted with a few respectable characters among his constituents, even double the federal representation, and then there must be a very great distance between the representatives and the people in general represented. On the proposed plan, the state of Delaware, the city of Philadelphia, the state of Rhode Island, the province of Main, the county of Suffolk in Massachusetts will have one representative each; there can be but little personal knowledge, or but few communications between him and the people at large of either of those districts. It has been observed, that mixing only with the respectable men, he will get the best information and ideas from them; he will also receive impressions favourable to their purposes particularly. Many plausible shifts have been made to divert the mind from dwelling on this defective representation, these I shall consider in another place.

Could we get over all our difficulties respecting a balance of interests and party efforts, to raise some and oppress others, the want of sympathy, information and intercourse between the representatives and the people, an insuperable difficulty will still remain, I mean the constant liability of a small number of representatives to private combinations, the tyranny of the one, or the licentiousness of the multitude, are, in my mind, but small evils, compared with the factions of the few. It is a consideration well worth pursuing, how far this house of representatives will be liable to be formed into private juntos, how far influenced by expectations of appointments and offices, how far liable to be managed by the president and senate, and how far the people will have confidence in them. To obviate difficulties on this head, as well as objections to the representative branch, generally, several observations have been made—these I will now examine, and if they shall appear to be unfounded, the objections must stand unanswered.

That the people are the electors, must elect good men, and attend to the administration.

It is said that the members of Congress, at stated periods, must return home, and that they must be subject to the laws they may make, and to a share of the burdens they may impose.

That the people possess the strong arm to overawe their rulers, and the best checks in their national character against the abuses of power, that the supreme power will remain in them.

That the state governments will form a part of, and a balance in the system.

That Congress will have only a few national objects to attend to, and the state governments many and local ones.

That the new Congress will be more numerous than the present, and that any numerous body is unwieldy and mobbish.

That the states only are represented in the present Congress, and that the people will require a representation in the new one, that in fifty or an hundred years the representation will be numerous.

That congress will have no temptation to do wrong; and that no system to enslave the people is practible.

That as long as the people are free they will preserve free governments; and that when they shall become tired of freedom, arbitrary government must take place.

These observations I shall examine in the course of my letters; and I think not only shew that they are not well founded, but point out the fallacy of some of them; and shew that others do not very well comport with the dignified and manly sentiments of a free and enlightened people.

THE FEDERAL FARMER.

3 JANUARY 1788

LETTER VIII.

The Federal Farmer compares the growth of liberty in England after the disaster of the Norman conquest with the turmoil in ancient Greece and Rome. England's people secured their liberty where the Greeks and Romans failed because England had both equal (that is, fair) laws and equal (that is widespread and proportionate) representation.

DEAR SIR,

BEFORE I proceed to examine the objections, I beg leave to add a valuable idea respecting representation, to be collected from De Lome, and other able writers, which essentially tends to confirm my positions: They very justly impute the establishment of general and equal liberty in England to a balance of interests and powers among the different orders of men; aided by a series of fortunate events, that never before, and possibly never again will happen.

Before the Norman conquest the people of England enjoyed much of this liberty. The first of the Norman kings, aided by foreign mercenaries and foreign attendants, obnoxious to the English, immediately laid arbitrary taxes, and established arbitrary courts, and severely oppress[ed] all orders of people: The barons and people, who recollected their former liberties, were induced, by those oppressions, to unite their efforts in their common defence: Here it became necessary for the great men, instead of deceiving and depressing the people, to enlighten and court them: the royal power was too strongly fixed to be annihilated, and rational means were, therefore directed to limiting it within proper bounds. In this long and arduous task, in this new species of contents, the barons and people succeeded, because they had been freemen, and knew the value of the object they were contending for; because they were the people of a small island—one people who found it practicable to meet and deliberate in one assembly, and act under one system of resolves, and who were not obliged to meet in different provincial assemblies, as is the case in large countries, as was the case in France, Spain, &c. where their determinations were inconsistent with each other, and where the king could play off one assembly against another.

It was in this united situation the people of England were for several centuries, enabled to combine their exertions, and by compacts, as Magna Charta, a bill of rights, &c. were able to limit, by degrees, the royal prerogatives, and establish their own liberties. The first combination was, probably, the accidental effect of pre-existing circumstances; but there was an admirable balance of interests in it, which has been the parent of English liberty, and excellent regulations enjoyed since that time. The executive power having been uniformly in the king, and he the visible head of the nation, it was chimerical for the greatest lord or most popular leader, consistent with the state of the government, and opinion of the people, to seriously think of becoming the king's rival, or to aim at even a share of the executive power; the greatest subject's prospect was only in acquiring a respectable influence in the house of commons, house of lords, or in the ministry; circumstances at once made it the interests of the leaders of the people to stand by them. Far otherwise was it with the ephori in Sparta, and tribunes in Rome. The leaders in England have led the people to freedom, in almost all other countries to servitude. The people in England have made use of deliberate exertions, their safest and most efficient weapons. In other countries they have often acted like mobs, and been enslaved by their enemies, or by their own leaders. In England, the people have been led uniformly, and systematically by their representatives to secure their rights by compact, and to abolish innovations upon the government: they successively obtained Magna Charta, the powers of taxation, the power to propose laws, the habeas corpus act, bill of rights, &c. they, in short, secured general and equal liberty, security to their persons and property; and, as an everlasting security and bulwark of their liberties, they fixed the democratic branch in the legislature, and jury trial in the execution of the laws, the freedom of the press, &c.

In Rome, and most other countries, the reverse of all this is true. In Greece, Rome, and wherever the civil law has been adopted, torture has been admitted. In Rome the people were subject to arbitrary confiscations, and even their lives would be arbitrarily disposed of by consuls, tribunes, dictators, masters, &c. half of the inhabitants were slaves, and the other half never knew what equal liberty was; yet in England the people have had king, lords, and commons; in Rome they had consuls, senators and tribunes: why then was the government of England so mild and favourable to the body of the people, and that of Rome an ambitious and oppressive aristocracy? Why in England have the revolutions always ended in stipulations in favour of general liberty, equal laws, and the common rights of the people and in most other countries in favour only of a few influential men? The reasons, in my mind, are obvious: In England the people have been substantially represented in many aspects; in the other countries it has not been so. Perhaps a small degree of attention to a few simple facts will illustrate this.—In England, from the oppressions of the Norman kings to the revolution in 1688, during which period of two or three hundred years, the English liberties were ascertained and established, the aristocratic part of that nation was substantially represented by a very large number of nobles, possessing similar interests and feelings with those they represented. The body of the people, about four or five millions, then mostly a frugal landed people, were represented by about five hundred representatives, taken not from the order of men which formed the aristocracy, but from the body of the people, and possessed of the same interests and feelings. De Lome, speaking of the British representation, expressly founds all his reasons on this union; this similitude of interests, feelings, views and circumstances. He observes, the English have preserved their liberties, because they and their leaders or representatives have been strictly united in interests, and in contending for general liberty. Here we see a genuine balance founded in the actual state of things. The whole community, probably, not more than two-fifths more numerous than we now are, were represented by seven or eight hundred men; the barons stipulated with the common people, and the king with the whole. Had the legal distinction between lords and commons been broken down, and the people of that island been called upon to elect forty-five senators, and one hundred and twenty representatives, about the proportion we propose to establish, their whole legislature evidently would have been of the natural aristocracy, and the body of the people would not have had scarcely a single sincere advocate; their interests would have been neglected, general and equal liberty forgot, and the balance lost; contests and conciliations, as in most other countries, would have been merely among the few, and as it might have been necessary to serve their purposes, the people at large would have been flattered or threatened, and probably not a single stipulation made in their favour.

In Rome the people were miserable, though they had three orders, the consuls, senators and tribunes, and approved the laws, and all for want of a genuine representation. The people were too numerous to assemble, and do any thing properly themselves; the voice of a few, the dupes of artifice, was called the voice of the people. It is difficult for the people to defend themselves against the arts and intrigues of the great, but by selecting a suitable number of men fixed to their interests to represent them, and to oppose ministers and senators. And the people's all depends on the number of the men selected, and the manner of doing it. To be convinced of this, we need only attend to the reason of the case, the conduct of the British commons, and of the Roman tribunes: equal liberty prevails in England, because there was a representation of the people, in fact and reality, to establish it; equal liberty never prevailed in Rome, because there was but the shadow of a representation. There were consuls in Rome annually elected to execute the laws, several hundred senators represented the great families; the body of the people annually chose tribunes from among themselves to defend them and to secure their rights; I think the number of tribunes annually chosen never exceeded ten. This representation, perhaps, was not proportionally so numerous as the representation proposed in the new plan; but the difference will not appear to be so great, when it shall be recollected, that these tribunes were chosen annually; that the great patrician families were not admitted to these offices of tribunes, and that the people of Italy who elected the tribunes were a long while, if not always, a small people compared with the people of the United States. What was the consequence of this triffling representation? The people of Rome always elected for their tribunes men conspicuous for their riches, military commands, professional popularity, &c. great commoners, between whom and the noble families there was only the shadowy difference of legal distinction. Among all the tribunes the people chose for several centuries, they had scarcely five real friends to their interests. These tribunes lived, felt and saw, not like the people, but like the great patrician families, like senators and great officers of state, to get into which it was evident, by their conduct, was their sole object. These tribunes often talked about the rights and prerogatives of the people, and that was all; for they never even attempted to establish equal liberty: so far from establishing the rights of the people, they suffered the senate, to the exclusion of the people, to engross the powers of taxation; those excellent and almost only real weapons of defence even the people of England possess. The tribunes obtained that the people should be eligible to some of the great offices of state, and marry, if they pleased, into the noble families; these were advantages in their nature, confined to a few elevated commoners, and of triffling importance to the people at large. Nearly the same observations may be made as to the ephori of Sparta.

We may amuse ourselves with names; but the fact is, men will be governed by the motives and temptations that surround their situation. Political evils to be guarded against are in the human character, and not in the name of patrician or plebian. Had the people of Italy, in the early period of the republic, selected yearly, or biennially, four or five hundred of their best informed men, emphatically from among themselves, these representatives would have formed an honest respectable assembly, capable of combining in them the views and exertions of the people, and their respectability would have procured them honest and able leaders, and we should have seen equal liberty established. True liberty stands in need of a fostering hand; from the days of Adam she has found but one temple to dwell in securely; she has laid the foundation of one, perhaps her last, in America; whether this is to be compleated and have duration, is yet a question. Equal liberty never yet found many advocates among the great: it is a disagreeable truth, that power perverts mens views in a greater degree, than public employments inform their understandings—they become hardened in certain maxims, and more lost to fellow feelings. Men may always be too cautious to commit alarming and glaring iniquities but they, as well as systems, are liable to be corrupted by slow degrees. Junius well observes, we are not only to guard against what men will do, but even against what they may do. Men in high public offices are in stations where they gradually lose sight of the people, and do not often think of attending to them, except when necessary to answer private purposes.

The body of the people must have this true representative security placed some where in the nation; and in the United States, or in any extended empire, I am fully persuaded can be placed no where, but in the forms of a federal republic, where we can divide and place it in several state or district legislatures, giving the people in these the means of opposing heavy internal taxes and oppressive measures in the proper stages. A great empire contains the amities and animosities of a world within itself. We are not like the people of England, one people compactly settled on a small island, with a great city filled with frugal merchants, serving as a common centre of liberty and union: we are dispersed, and it is impracticable for any but the few to assemble in one place: the few must be watched, checked, and often resisted—tyranny has ever shewn a predilection to be in close amity with them, or the one man. Drive it from kings and it flies to senators, to dicemvirs, to dictators, to tribunes, to popular leaders, to military chiefs, &c.

De Lome well observes, that in societies, laws which were to be equal to all are soon warped to the private interests of the administrators, and made to defend the usurpations of a few. The English, who had tasted the sweets of equal laws, were aware of this, and though they restored their king, they carefully delegated to parliament the advocates of freedom.

I have often lately heard it observed, that it will do very well for a people to make a constitution, and ordain, that at stated periods they will chuse, in a certain manner, a first magistrate, a given num-

ber of senators and representatives, and let them have all power
to do as they please. This doctrine, however it may do for a small
republic, as Connecticut, for instance, where the people may chuse
so many senators and representatives to assemble in the legislature, in an eminent degree, the interests, the views, feelings, and
genuine sentiments of the people themselves, can never be admitted in an extensive country; and when this power is lodged in the
hands of a few, not to limit the few, is but one step short of giving
absolute power to one man—in a numerous representation the
abuse of power is a common injury, and has no temptation—among
the few, the abuse of power may often operate to the private emolument of those who abuse it.

THE FEDERAL FARMER.

4 JANUARY 1788

LETTER IX

*The Federal Farmer argues that the small size of the new legisla-
ture will make it aristocratic. Natural aristocrats will be best
known by the people and so will be most likely to be elected and re-
elected. The distance between natural aristocrat legislators and the
people will breed corruption. Essays in* The Federalist *of particular relevance: 55-57.*

DEAR SIR,
THE advocates of the constitution say we must trust to the administration, and elect good men for representatives[.] I admit, that in
forming the social compact, we can fix only general principles, and,
of necessity, must trust something to the wisdom and integrity of
the administration. But the question is, do we not trust too much,
and to men also placed in the vortex of temptation, to lay hold of
proffered advantages for themselves and their connections, and to
oppress the body of the people.

It is one thing to authorise a well organized legislature to make laws, under the restraints of a well guarded constitution, and another to assemble a few men, and to tell them to do what they please. I am not the more shaken in my principles, or disposed to despair of the cause of liberty, because some of our able men have adopted the yielding language of non-resistance, and writers dare insult the people with the signatures of Cæsar, Mark Antony, and of other tyrants; because I see even moderate and amiable men, forced to let go of monarchy in 1775, still in love with it, to use the simile of our countrymen, when the political pot boils, the skum will often get uppermost and make its appearance. I believe the people of America, when they shall fully understand any political subject brought before them, will talk in a very different stile, and use the manly language of freedom.

But "the people must elect good men":—Examine the system, Is it practicable for them to elect fit and proper representatives where the number is so small? "But the people may chuse whom they please." This is an observation, I believe, made without due attention to facts and the state of the community. To explain my meaning, I will consider the descriptions of men commonly presented to the people as candidates for the offices of representatives—we may rank them in three classes: 1. The men who form the natural aristocracy, as before defined. 2. Popular demagogues: these men also are often politically elevated, so as to be seen by the people through the extent of large districts; they often have some abilities, without principle, and rise into notice by their noise and arts. 3. The substantial and respectable part of the democracy, they are a numerous and valuable set of men, who discern and judge well, but from being generally silent in public assemblies are often overlooked: they are the most substantial and best informed men in the several towns, who occasionally fill the middle grades of offices, &c. who hold not a splendid, but a respectable rank in private concerns: these men are extensively diffused through all the counties, towns and small districts in the union; even they, and their immediate connections, are raised above the majority of the people, and as representatives are only brought to a level with a more numerous part of the community, the middle orders, and a degree nearer the mass of the people. Hence it is that the best practical representation, even in a small state, must be several degrees more aristrocratical than the body of the people. A representation so formed as to admit but few or none of the third class, is, in my opinion, not deserving of the name—even in armies, courts-martial are so formed as to admit subaltern officers into them. The true idea is, so to open and enlarge the representation as to let in a due proportion of the third class with those of the first. Now, my opinion is, that the representation proposed is so small as that ordinarily very few or none of them can be elected; and, therefore, after all the parade of words and forms the government must possess the soul of aristocracy, or something worse, the spirit of popular leaders.

I observed in a former letter, that the state of Delaware, of Rhode-Island, the Province of Main, and each of the great counties in Massachusetts &c. would have one member, and rather more than one when the representatives shall be increased to one for each 30,000 inhabitants. In some districts the people are more dispersed and unequal than in others: In Delaware they are compact, in the Province of Main dispersed; how can the elections in either of those districts be regulated so as that a man of the third class can be elected?—Exactly the same principles and motives, the same uncontroulable circumstances, must govern the elections as in the choice of the governors. Call upon the people of either of those districts to chuse a governor, and it will, probably, never happen that they will not bestow a major part, or the greatest number, of their votes on some very conspicuous or very popular character. A man that is known among a few thousands of people, may be quite unknown among thirty or forty thousand. On the whole, it appears to me to be almost a self-evident position, that when we call on thirty or forty thousand inhabitants to unite in giving their votes for one man, it will be uniformly impracticable for them to unite in any men, except those few who have became eminent for their civil or military rank, or their popular legal abilities: it will be found totally impracticable for men in the private walks of life, except in the profession of the law, to become conspicuous enough to attract the notice of so many electors and have their suffrages.

But if I am right, it is asked why so many respectable men advocate the adoption of the proposed system. Several reasons may be
given—many of our gentlemen are attached to the principles of
monarchy and aristocracy; they have an aversion to democratic
republics. The body of the people have acquired large powers and
substantial influence by the revolution. In the unsettled state of
things, their numerous representatives, in some instances, misused
their powers and have induced many good men suddenly to adopt
ideas unfavourable to such republics, and which ideas they will dis-
card on reflection. Without scrutinizing into the particulars of the
proposed system, we immediately perceive that its general tendency is to collect the powers of government, now in the body of the
people in reality, and to place them in the higher orders and fewer
hands; no wonder then that all those of and about these orders are
attached to it; they feel there is something in this system advantageous to them. On the other hand, the body of the people evidently
feel there is something wrong and disadvantageous to them; both
descriptions perceive there is something tending to bestow on the
former the height of power and happiness, and to reduce the latter
to weakness, insignificance, and misery. The people evidently feel
all this though they want expressions to convey their ideas. Further, even the respectable part of the democracy, have never yet
been able to distinguish clearly where the fallacy lies; they find
there are defects in the confederation; they see a system presented,
they think something must be done; and, while their minds are in
suspence, the zealous advocates force a reluctant consent. Nothing
can be a stronger evidence of the nature of this system, than the
general sense of the several orders in the community respecting
its tendency, the parts taken generally by them proves my position,
that notwithstanding the parade of words and forms, the government must possess the soul of aristocracy.

Congress, heretofore, have asked for moderate additional powers, the cry was give them—be federal, but the proper distinction
between the cases that produce this disposition, and the system
proposed, has not been fairly made and seen in all its consequences.
We have seen some of our state representations too numerous and

without examining a medium we run into the opposite extreme. It is true, the proper number of federal representatives, is matter of opinion in some degree: but there are extremes which we immediately perceive, and others, which we clearly discover on examination. We should readily pronounce a representative branch of 15 members small in a federal government, having complete powers as to taxes, military matters, commerce, the coin, &c. &c. On the other hand, we should readily pronounce a federal representation as numerous as those of the several states, consisting of about 500 representatives, unwieldly and totally improper. It is asked, has not the wisdom of the convention found the medium? perhaps not: The convention was divided on this point of numbers, at least some of its ablest members urged, that instead of 65 representatives there ought to be 130 in the first instance: They fixed one representative for each 40,000 inhabitants, and at the close of the work, the president suggested, that the representation appeared to be too small and without debate, it was put as, not exceeding one for each 30,000. I mention these facts to shew, that the convention went on no fixed data. In this extensive country it is difficult to get a representation sufficiently numerous: Necessity, I believe, will oblige us to sacrifice in some degree the true genuine principles of representation. But this sacrifice ought to be as little as possible: How far we ought to increase the representation I will not pretend to say; but that we ought to increase it very considerably, is clear—to double it at least, making full allowances for the state representations: and this we may evidently do and approach accordingly towards safety and perfection without encountering any inconveniences. It is with great difficulty the people can unite these different interests and views even tolerably, in the state senators, who are more than twice as numerous as the federal representatives, as proposed by the convention; even these senators are considered as so far removed from the people, that they are not allowed immediately to hold their purse strings.

The principle objections made to the increase of the representation are, the expence and difficulty in getting the members to attend. The first cannot be important; the last if founded, is against any federal government. As to the expence, I presume, the house of representatives will not be in sessions more than four months in the year. We find by experience, that about two-thirds of the members of representative assemblies usually attend; therefore, of the representation proposed by the convention, about forty five members probably will attend, doubling their number, about 90 will probably attend: their pay, in one case, at four dollars a day each (which is putting it high enough) will amount to, yearly, 21,600 dollars; in the other case, 43,200 dollars difference 21,600 dollars,—reduce the state representatives from 1500 down to 1000, and thereby save the attendance of two thirds of the 500, say three months in a year, at one dollar and a quarter a day each, 3,125 dollars. Thus we may leave the state representations sufficient large, and yet save enough by the reduction nearly to support exceeding well the whole federal representation I propose. Surely we never can be so unwise as to sacrifice, essentially, the all-important principles of representation for so small a sum as 21,000 dollars a year for the United States; a single company of soldiers would cost this sum. It is a fact that can easily be shewn, that we expend three times this sum every year upon useless inferior offices and very triffling concerns. It is also a fact which can be shewn, that the United States in the late war suffered more by a faction in the federal government, than the pay of the federal representation will amount to for twenty years.

As to the attendance—Can we be so unwise as to establish an unsafe and inadequate representative branch, and give it as a reason, that we believe only a few members will be induced to attend; we ought certainly to establish an adequate representative branch, and adopt measures to induce an attendance; I believe that a due proportion of 130 or 140 members may be induced to attend: there are various reasons for the non-attendance of the members of the present congress; it is to be presumed that these will not exist under the new system.

To compensate for the want of a genuine representation in a government, where the purse and sword, and all important powers, are proposed to be lodged, a variety of unimportant things are enumerated by the advocates of it.

In the second place, it is said the members of congress must return home, and share in the burdens they may impose; and, therefore, private motives will induce them to make mild laws, to support liberty, and ease the burdens of the people: this brings us to a mere question of interest under this head. I think these observations will appear, on examination, altogether fallacious; because this individual interest, which may coincide with the rights and interests of the people, will be far more than balanced by opposite motives and opposite interests. If, on a fair calculation, a man will gain more by measures oppressive to others than he will lose by them, he is interested in their adoption. It is true, that those who govern, generally, by increasing the public burdens increase their own share of them; but by this increase they may, and often do, increase their salaries, fees, and emoluments, in a ten-fold proportion, by increasing salaries, forming armies and navies, and by making offices—If it shall appear the members of congress will have these temptations before them, the argument is on my side—they will view the account, and be induced continually to make efforts advantageous to themselves and connections, and oppressive to others.

We must examine facts—Congress, in its present form, have but few offices to dispose of worth the attention of the members, or of men of the aristocracy; yet, from 1774 to this time, we find a large proportion of those offices assigned to those who were or had been members of congress, and though the states chuse annually sixty or seventy members, many of them have been provided for: but few men are known to congress in this extensive country, and, probably, but few will be to the president and senate, except those who have or shall appear as members of congress, or those whom the members may bring forward. The states may now chuse yearly ninety-one members of congress; under the new constitution they will have it in their power to chuse exactly the same number, perhaps afterwards, one hundred and fifteen, but these must be chosen once in two and six years; so that, in the course of ten years together, not more than two-thirds so many members of congress will be elected and brought into view, as there now are under the confederation in the same term of time: but at least there will be five, if not ten times, as many offices and places worthy the attention of the members, under the new constitution, as there are under the confederation: therefore, we may fairly presume, that a very great proportion of the members of congress, especially the influential ones, instead of returning to private life, will be provided for with lucrative offices, in the civil or military department, and not only the members, but many of their sons, friends, and connection. These offices will be in the constitutional disposition of the president and senate, and, corruption out of the question, what kind of security can we expect in a representation, so many of the members of which may rationally feel themselves candidates for these offices?—let common sense decide. It is true, that members chosen to offices must leave their seats in congress, and to some few offices they cannot be elected till the time shall be expired for which they were elected members; but this scarcely will effect the biass arising from the hopes and expectations of office.

It is not only in this point of view, the members of congress, by their efforts, may make themselves and friends powerful and happy, while the people may be oppressed: but there is another way in which they may soon warp laws, which ought to be equal, to their own advantages, by those imperceptible means, and on those doubtful principles which may not alarm. No society can do without taxes; they are the efficient means of safety and defence, and they too have often been the weapons by which the blessings of society have been destroyed. Congress will have power to lay taxes at pleasure for the general welfare; and if they mis-judge of the general welfare, and lay unnecessary oppressive taxes, the constitution will provide, as I shall hereafter shew, no remedy for the people or states—the people must bear them, or have recourse, not to any constitutional checks or remedies, but to that resistance which is the last resort, and founded in self-defence.

It is well stipulated, that all duties, imposts, and excises shall be equal; and that direct taxes shall be apportioned on the several states by a fixed rule, but nothing further. Here commences a dangerous power in matters of taxation, lodged without any regard to the balance of interests of the different orders of men, and without any regard to the internal policy of the states. Congress having assigned to any state its quota, say to New-Jersey, 80,000 dollars in a given tax, congress will be entirely at liberty to apportion that sum on the counties and towns, polls, lands, houses, labour, &c. and appoint the assessors and collectors in that state in what manner they please; there will be nothing to prevent a system of tax laws being made, unduly to ease some descriptions of men and burden others; though such a system may be unjust and injudicious, though we may complain, the answer will be, congress have the power delegated by the people, and, probably, congress has done what it thought best.

By the confederation taxes must be quotaed on the several states by fixed rules, as before mentioned: but then each state's quota is apportioned on the several numbers and classes of citizens in the state, by the state legislature, assessed and collected by state laws. Great pains have been taken to counfound the two cases, which are as distinct as light and darkness; this I shall endeavour to illustrate, when I come to the amendment respecting internal taxes. I shall only observe, at present, that in the state legislatures the body of the people will be genuinely represented, and in congress not; that the right of resisting oppressive measures is inherent in the people, and that a constitutional barrier should be so formed, that their genuine representatives may stop an oppressive ruinous measure in its early progress, before it shall come to maturity, and the evils of it become in a degree fixed.

It has lately been often observed, that the power or body of men intrusted with the national defence and tranquility, must necessarily possess the purse unlimitedly, that the purse and sword must go together—this is new doctrine in a free country, and by no means tenable. In the British government the king is particularly intrusted with the national honor and defence, but the commons solely hold the purse. I think I have amply shewn that the representation in congress will be totally inadequate in matters of taxation, &c. and, therefore, that the ultimate controul over the purse must be lodged elsewhere.

We are not to expect even honest men rigidly to adhere to the line of strict impartiality, where the interest of themselves or friends is particularly concerned; if we do expect it, we shall deceive ourselves, and make a wrong estimate of human nature.

But it is asked how shall we remedy the evil, so as to complete and perpetuate the temple of equal laws and equal liberty? Perhaps we never can do it. Possibly we never may be able to do it in this immense country, under any one system of laws however modified; nevertheless, at present, I think the experiment worth a making. I feel an aversion to the disunion of the states, and to separate confederacies; the states have sought and bled in a common cause, and great dangers too may attend these confederacies. I think the system proposed capable of very considerable degrees of perfection, if we pursue first principles. I do not think that De Lome, or any writer I have seen, has sufficiently pursued the proper inquiries and efficient means for making representation and balances in government more perfect; it is our task to do this in America. Our object is equal liberty, and equal laws diffusing their influence among all orders of men; to obtain this we must guard against the biass of interest and passions, against interested combinations, secret or open; we must aim at a balance of efforts and strength.

Clear it is, by increasing the representation we lessen the prospects of each member of congress being provided for in public offices; we proportionably lessen official influence, and strengthen his prospects of becoming a private citizen, subject to the common burdens, without the compensation of the emoluments of office. By increasing the representation we make it more difficult to corrupt and influence the members; we diffuse them more extensively among the body of the people, perfect the balance, multiply information, strengthen the confidence of the people, and consequently support the laws on equal and free principles. There are two other ways, I think, of obtaining in some degree the security we want; the one is, by excluding more extensively the members from being appointed to offices; the other is, by limiting some of their powers; but these two I shall examine hereafter.

THE FEDERAL FARMER.

7 JANUARY 1788

LETTER X

The Federal Farmer points to full representation in state govern-
ments as the only force protecting the people's rights. Under the
new Constitution, states will be unable to prevent federal
encroachment on these rights. Essays in The Federalist *of partic-*
ular relevance: 2, 45, 46, 51, 78, 84.

DEAR SIR,

IT is said that our people have a high sense of freedom, possess
power, property, and the strong arm; meaning, I presume, that the
body of the people can take care of themselves, and awe their
rulers; and, therefore, particular provision in the constitution for
their security may not be essential. When I come to examine these
observations, they appear to me too triffling and loose to deserve a
serious answer.

To palliate for the smallness of the representation, it is observed,
that the state governments in which the people are fully represented, necessarily form a part of the system. This idea ought to
be fully examined. We ought to enquire if the convention have made
the proper use of these essential parts; the state governments then
we are told will stand between the arbitrary exercise of power and
the people: true they may, but armless and helpless, perhaps, with
the privilege of making a noise when hurt—this is no more than
individuals may do. Does the constitution provide a single check for
a single measure, by which the state governments can constitutionally and regularly check the arbitrary measures of congress?
Congress may raise immediately fifty thousand men, and twenty
millions of dollars in taxes, build a navy, model the militia, &c. and
all this constitutionally. Congress may arm on every point, and the
state governments can do no more than an individual, by petition to
congress, suggest their measures are alarming and not right.

I conceive the position to be undeniable, that the federal government will be principally in the hands of the natural aristocracy, and the state governments principally in the hands of the democracy, the representatives of the body of the people. These representatives in Great-Britain hold the purse, and have a negative upon all laws. We must yield to circumstances, and depart something from this plan, and strike out a new medium, so as to give efficacy to the whole system, supply the wants of the union, and leave the several states, or the people assembled in the state legislatures, the means of defence.

It has been often mentioned, that the objects of congress will be few and national, and require a small representation; that the objects of each state will be many and local, and require a numerous representation. This circumstance has not the weight of a feather in my mind. It is certainly unadvisable to lodge in 65 representatives, and 26 senators, unlimited power to establish systems of taxation, armies, navies, model the militia, and to do every thing that may essentially tend soon to change, totally, the affairs of the community and to assemble 1500 state representatives, and 160 senators, to make sense laws, and laws to regulate the descent and conveyance of property, the administration of justice between man and man, to appoint militia officers, &c.

It is not merely the quantity of information I contend for. Two taxing powers may be inconvenient; but the point is, congress, like the senate of Rome, will have taxing powers, and the people no check—when the power is abused, the people may complain and grow angry, so may the state governments; they may remonstrate and counteract, by passing laws to prohibit the collection of congressional taxes; but these will be acts of the people, acts of sovereign power, the denier resort unknown to the constitution; acts operating in terrorum, acts of resistence, and not the exercise of any constitutional power to stop or check a measure before matured: a check properly is the stopping, by one branch in the same legislature, a measure proposed by the other in it. In fact the constitution provides for the states no check, properly speaking, upon the measures of congress—Congress can immediately enlist soldiers, and apply to the pockets of the people.

These few considerations bring us to the very strong distinction between the plan that operates on federal principles, and the plan that operates on consolidated principles. A plan may be federal or not as to its organization; each state may retain its vote or not; the sovereignty of the state may be represented, or the people of it. A plan may be federal or not as to its operations—federal when it requires men and monies of the states, and the states as such make the laws for raising the men and monies—Not federal, when it leaves the states governments out of the question, and operates immediately upon the persons and property of the citizens. The first is the case with the confederation, the second with the new plan: in the first the state governments may be check, in the last none at all. This distinction I shall pursue further hereafter, under the head before mentioned, of amendments as to internal taxes. And here I shall pursue a species of checks which writers have not often noticed.

To excuse the smallness of the representation, it is said the new congress will be more numerous than the old one. This is not true; and for the facts I refer you to my letter of the 4th instant, to the plan and confederation[;] besides there is no kind of similitude between the two plans. The confederation is a mere league of the states, and congress is formed with the particular checks, and possess the united powers, enumerated in my letter of the 25th ult. The new plan is totally a different thing: a national government to many purposes administered, by men chosen for two, four, and six years, not recallable, and among whom there will be no rotation; operating immediately in all money and military matters, &c. on the persons and property of the citizens—I think, therefore, that no part of the confederation ought to be adduced for supporting or injuring the new constitution. It is also said that the constitution gives no more power to congress than the confederation, respecting money and military matters; that congress, under the confederation, may require men and monies to any amount, and the states are bound to comply. This is generally true; but, I think, I shall in a subsequent letter satisfactorily prove, that the states have well founded checks for securing their liberties.

I admit the force of the observation, that all the federal powers, by the confederation, are lodged in a single assembly; however, I think much more may be said in defence of the leading principles of the confederation. I do not object to the qualifications of the electors of representatives, and I fully agree that the people ought to elect one branch.

Further, it may be observed, that the present congress is principally an executive body, which ought not to be numerous; that the house of representatives will be a mere legislative branch, and being the democratic one, ought to be numerous. It is one of the greatest advantages of a government of different branches, that each branch may be conveniently made conformable to the nature of the business assigned it, and all be made conformable to the condition of the several orders of the people. After all the possible checks and limitations we can devise, the powers of the union must be very extensive; the sovereignty of the nation cannot produce the object in view, the defence and tranquility of the whole, without such powers, executive and judicial. I dislike the present congress a single, assembly, because it is impossible to fit it to receive those powers: the executive and judicial powers, in the nature of things, ought to be lodged in a few hands, the legislature in many hands; therefore want of safety, and unavoidable hasty measures, out of the question, they never can all be lodged in one assembly properly—it, in its very formation, must imply a contradiction.

In objection to increasing the representation, it has also been observed, that it is difficult to assemble a hundred men or more without making them tumultuous and a mere mob; reason and experience do not support this observation. The most respectable assemblies we have any knowledge of and the wisest, have been those, each of which consisted of several hundred members; as the senate of Rome, of Carthage, of Venice, the British Parliament, &c. &c. I think I may without hazarding much, affirm, that our more numerous state assemblies and conventions have universally discovered more wisdom, and as much order, as the less numerous ones: There must be also a very great difference between the characters of two or three hundred men assembled from a single state, and the characters of the number or half the number assembled from all the united states.

It is added, that on the proposed plan the house of representatives in fifty or a hundred years, will consist of several hundred members: The plan will begin with sixty-five, and we have no certainty that the number ever will be encreased, for this plain reason—that all that combination of interests and influence which has produced this plan, and supported so far, will constantly oppose the increase of the representation, knowing that thereby the government will become more free and democratic: But admitting, after a few years, there will be a member for each 30,000 inhabitants, the observation is trifling, the government is in a considerable measure to take its tone from its early movements, and by means of a small representation it may in half of 50 or 100 years, get moved from its basis, or at least so far as to be incapable of ever being recovered. We ought, therefore, on every principle now to fix the government on proper principles, and fit to our present condition—when the representation shall become too numerous, alter it; or we may now make provision, that when the representation shall be increased to a given number, that then there shall be one for each given number of inhabitants, &c.

Another observation is, that congress will have no temptations to do wrong—the men that make it must be very uninformed, or suppose they are talking to children. In the first place, the members will be governed by all those motives which govern the conduct of men, and have before them all the allurements of offices and temptations, to establish unequal burdens, before described. In the second place, they and their friends, probably, will find it for their interests to keep up large armies, navies, salaries, &c. and in laying adequate taxes. In the third place, we have no good grounds to presume, from reason or experience, that it will be agreeable to their characters or views, that the body of the people should continue to have power effectually to interfere in the affairs of government. But it is confidently added, that congress will not have it in their power to oppress or enslave the people, that the people will not bear it. It is not supposed that congress will act the tyrant immediately, and in the face of day light. It is not supposed congress will adopt important measures, without plausible pretences, especially those which may tend to alarm or produce opposition. We are to consider the natural progress of things: that men unfriendly to republican equality will go systematically to work, gradually to exclude the body of the people from any share in the government, first of the substance, and then of the forms. The men who will have these views will not be without their agents and supporters. When we reflect, that a few years ago we established democratic republics, and fixed the state governments as the barriers between congress and the pockets of the people; what great progress has been made in less than seven years to break down those barriers, and essentially to change the principles of our governments, even by the armless few: is it chimerical to suppose that in fifteen or twenty years to come, that much more can be performed, especially after the adoption of the constitution, when the few will be so much better armed with power and influence, to continue the struggle? probably, they will be wise enough never to alarm, but gradually prepare the minds of the people for one specious change after another, till the final object shall be obtained. Say the advocates, these are only possibilities—they are probabilities, a wise people ought to guard against; and the address made use of to keep the evils out of sight, and the means to prevent them, confirm my opinion.

But to obviate all objections to the proposed plan in the last resort: it is said our people will be free, so long as they possess the habits of freemen, and when they lose them, they must receive some other forms of government. To this I shall only observe, that this is very humiliating language, and can, I trust, never suit a manly people, who have contended nobly for liberty, and declared to the world they will be free.

I have dwelt much longer than I expected upon the increasing the representation, the democratic interest in the federal system; but I hope the importance of the subject will justify my dwelling upon it. I have pursued it in a manner new, and I have found it necessary to be somewhat prolix, to illustrate the point I had in view. My idea has ever been, when the democratic branch is weak and small, the body of the people have no defence, and every thing to fear; if they expect to find genuine political friends in kings and nobles, in great and powerful men, they deceive themselves. On the other hand, fix a genuine democratic branch in the government, solely to hold the purse, and with the power of impeachment, and to propose and negative laws, cautiously limit the king and nobles, or the executive and the senate, as the case may be, and the people, I conceive, have but little to fear, and their liberties will be always secure.

I think we are now arrived to a new æra in the affairs of men, when the true principles of government will be more fully unfolded than heretofore, and a new world, as it were, grow up in America. In contemplating representation, the next thing is the security of elections. Before I proceed to this, I beg leave to observe, that the pay of the representatives of the people is essentially connected with their interests.

Congress may put the pay of the members unreasonably high, or so low as that none but the rich and opulent can attend; there are very strong reasons for supposing the latter, probably, will be the case, and a part of the same policy, which uniformly and constantly exerts itself to transfer power from the many to the few. Should the pay be well fixed, and made alterable by congress, with the consent of a majority of the state legislatures, perhaps, all the evils to be feared on this head might, in the best practicable manner, be guarded against, and proper security introduced. It is said the state legislatures fix their own pay—the answer is, that congress is not, nor can it ever be well formed on those equal principles the state legislatures are. I shall not dwell on this point, but conclude this letter with one general observation, that the check I contend for in the system proposed, do not in the least, any of them tend to lessen the energy of it; but giving grounds for the confidence of the people, greatly to increase its real energy, by insuring their constant and hearty support.

THE FEDERAL FARMER.

10 JANUARY 1788

LETTER XI

The Federal Farmer argues that the Constitution's bicameralism is illusory. The Senate will draw its members from the same pool as the House of Representatives. Senators will serve excessively long terms and will not be subject to recall, rendering them too distant from the people. And there will be no check on abuses of power within the legislative branch. Essays in The Federalist *of particular relevance: 51-55, 62, 63.*

DEAR SIR,

I SHALL now add a few observations respecting the organization of the senate, the manner of appointing it, and its powers.

The senate is an assembly of 26 members, two from each state, though the senators are apportioned on the federal plan, they will vote individually; they represent the states, as bodies politic, sovereign to certain purposes; the states being sovereign and independent, are all considered equal, each with the other in the senate. In this we are governed solely by the ideal equalities of sovereignties; the federal and state governments forming one whole, and the state governments an essential part, which ought always to be kept distinctly in view, and preserved: I feel more disposed, on reflection, to acquiesce in making them the basis of the senate, and thereby to make it the interest and duty of the senators to preserve distinct, and to perpetuate the respective sovereignties they shall represent.

As to the appointments of senators, I have already observed, that they must be appointed by the legislatures, by concurrent acts, and each branch have an equal share of power, as I do not see any probability of amendments, if advisable, in these points, I shall not dwell upon them.

The senate, as a legislative branch, is not large, but as an executive branch quite too numerous. It is not to be presumed that we can form a genuine senatorial branch in the United States, a real representation of the aristocracy and balance in the legislature, any more than we can form a genuine representation of the people. Could we separate the aristocratical and democratical interests; compose the senate of the former, and the house of assembly of the latter, they are too unequal in the United States to produce a balance. Form them on pure principles, and leave each to be supported by its real weight and connections, the senate would be feeble, and the house powerful:—I say, on pure principles; because I make a distinction between a senate that derives its weight and influence from a pure source, its numbers and wisdom, its extensive property, its extensive and permanent connections; and a senate composed of a few men, possessing small property, small and unstable connections, that derives its weight and influence from a corrupt or pernicious source; that is, merely from the power given it by the constitution and laws, to dispose of the public offices, and the annexed emoluments, and by those means to interest officers, and the hungry expectants of offices, in support of its measures. I wish the proposed senate may not partake too much of the latter description.

To produce a balance and checks, the constitution proposes two branches in the legislature; but they are so formed, that the members of both must generally be the same kind of men—men having similar interests and views, feelings and connections—men of the same grade in society, and who associate on all occasions (probably, if there be any difference, the senators will be the most democratic.) Senators and representatives thus circumstanced, as men, though convened in two rooms, to make laws, must be governed generally by the same motives and views, and therefore pursue the same system of politics; the partitions between the two branches will be merely those of the building in which they fit: there will not be found in them any of those genuine balances and checks, among the real different interests, and efforts of the several classes of men in the community we aim at; nor can any such balances and checks be formed in the present condition of the United States in any considerable degree of perfection: but to give them the greatest degree of perfection practicable, we ought to make the senate

respectable as to numbers, the qualifications of the electors and of
the elected; to increase the numbers of the representatives, and so
to model the elections of them, as always to draw a majority of them
substantially from the body of the people. Though I conclude the
senators and representatives will not form in the legislature those
balances and checks which correspond with the actual state of the
people; yet I approve of two branches, because we may notwithstanding derive several advantages from them. The senate, from
the mode of its appointment, will probably be influenced to support the state governments, and, from its periods of service will
produce stability in legislation, while frequent elections may take
place in the other branch. There is generally a degree of competition between two assemblies even composed of the same kind of
men; and by this, and by means of every law's passing a revision in
the second branch, caution, coolness, and deliberation are produced
in the business of making laws. By means of a democratic branch we
may particularly secure personal liberty; and by means of a senatorial branch we may particularly protect property. By the division,
the house becomes the proper body to impeach all officers for misconduct in office, and the senate the proper court to try them; and
in a country where limited powers must be lodged in the first magistrate, the senate, perhaps, may be the most proper body to be
found to have a negative upon him in making treaties, and in managing foreign affairs.

  Though I agree the federal senate, in the form proposed, may be
useful to many purposes, and that it is not very necessary to alter
the organization, modes of appointment, and powers of it in several respects; yet, without alterations in others, I sincerely believe
it will, in a very few years, become the source of the greatest evils.
Some of these alterations, I conceive, to be absolutely necessary,
and some of them at least advisable.

  1. By the confederation the members of congress are chosen
annually. By art. 1. sect. 2. of the constitution, the senators shall be
chosen for six years. As the period of service must be, in a considerable degree, matter of opinion on this head, I shall only make a
few observations, to explain why I think it more advisable to limit
it to three or four years.

The people of this country have not been accustomed to so long appointments in their state governments, they have generally adopted annual elections. The members of the present congress are chosen yearly, who, from the nature and multipicity of their business, ought to be chosen for longer periods then the federal senators—Men six years in office absolutely contract callous habits, and cease, in too great a degree, to feel their dependance, and for the condition of their constituents. Senators continued in offices three or four years, will be in them longer than any popular erroneous opinions will probably continue to actuate their electors—men appointed for three or four years, will generally be long enough in office to give stability, and amply to acquire political information. By a change of legislators, as often as circumstances will permit, political knowledge is diffused more extensively among the people, and the attention of the electors and elected more constantly kept alive; circumstances of infinite importance in a free country. Other reasons might be added, but my subject is too extensive to admit of my dwelling upon less material points.

2. When the confederation was formed, it was considered essentially necessary that the members of congress should at any time be recalled by their respective states, when the states should see fit, and others be sent in their room. I do not think it less necessary that this principle should be extended to the members of congress under the new constitution, and especially to the senators. I have had occasion several times to observe, that let us form a federal constitution as extensively, and on the best principles in our power, we must, after all, trust a vast deal to a few men, who, far removed from their constituents, will administer the federal government; there is but little danger these men will feel too great a degree of dependance: the necessary and important object to be attended to, is to make them feel dependant enough. Men elected for several years, several hundred miles distant from their states, possessed of very extensive powers, and the means of paying themselves, will not, probably, be oppressed with a sense of dependance and responsibility.

The senators will represent sovereignties, which generally have, and always ought to retain, the power of recalling their agents; the principle of responsibility is strongly felt in men who are liable to be recalled and censured for their misconduct; and, if we may judge from experience, the latter will not abuse the power of recalling their members; to possess it, will, at least be a valuable check. It is in the nature of all delegated power, that the constituents should retain the right to judge concerning the conduct of their represen-tatives; they must exercise the power, and their decision itself, their approving or disapproving that conduct implies a right, a power to continue in office, or to remove from it. But whenever the substitute acts under a constitution, then it becomes necessary that the power of recalling him be expressed. The reasons for lodging a power to recall are stronger, as they respect the senate, than as they respect the representatives; the latter will be more frequently elected, and changed of course, and being chosen by the people at large, it would be more difficult for the people than for the legisla-tures to take the necessary measures for recalling: but even the people, if the powers will be more beneficial to them than injuri-ous, ought to possess it. The people are not apt to wrong a man who is steady and true to their interests; they may for a while be misled by party representations, and leave a good man out of office unheard; but every recall supposes a deliberate decision, and a fair hearing; and no man who believes his conduct proper, and the result of honest views, will be the less useful in his public character, on account of the examination his actions may be liable to; and a man conscious of the contrary conduct, ought clearly to be restrained by the apprehensions of a trial. I repeat it, it is interested combi-nations and factions we are particularly to guard against in the fed-eral government, and all the rational means that can be put into the hands of the people to prevent them, ought to be provided and furnished for them. Where there is a power to recall, trusty cen-tinels among the people, or in the state legislatures, will have a fair opportunity to become useful. If the members in congress from the states join in such combinations, or favour them, or pursue a pernicious line of conduct, the most attentive among the people, or in the state legislatures, may formally charge them before their constituents: the very apprehensions of such constitutional charges may prevent many of the evils mentioned, and the recalling the members of a single state, a single senator, or representative, may often prevent many more; nor do I, at present, discover any danger in such proceedings, as every man who shall move for a recall will put his reputation at stake, to shew he has reasonable grounds for his motion; and it is not probable such motions will be made unless there be good apparent grounds for succeeding; nor can the charge or motion be any thing more than the attack of an individual or individuals, unless a majority of the constituents shall see cause to go into the enquiry. Further, the circumstance of such a power being lodged in the constituents, will tend continually to keep up their watchfulness, as well as the attention and dependance of the federal senators and representatives.

3. By the confederation it is provided, that no delegate shall serve more than three years in any term of six years, and thus, by the forms of the government, a rotation of members is produced: a like principle has been adopted in some of the state governments, and also in some antient and modern republics. Whether this exclusion of a man for a given period, after he shall have served a given time, ought to be ingrafed into a constitution or not, is a question, the proper decision materially depends upon the leading features of the government: some governments are so formed as to produce a sufficient fluctuation and change of members of course, in the ordinary course of elections, proper numbers of new members are, from time to time, brought into the legislature, and a proportionate number of old ones go out, mix, and become diffused among the people. This is the case with all numerous representative legislatures, the members of which are frequently elected, and constantly within the view of their constituents. This is the case with our state governments, and in them a constitutional rotation is unimportant. But in a government consisting of but a few members, elected for long periods, and far removed from the observation of the people, but few changes in the ordinary course of elections take place among the members; they become in some measure a fixed body, and often inattentive to the public good, callous, selfish, and the fountain of corruption. To prevent these evils, and to force a principle of pure animation into the federal government, which will be formed much in this last manner mentioned, and to produce attention, activity,

and a diffusion of knowledge in the community, we ought to establish among others the principle of rotation. Even good men in office, in time, imperceptibly lose sight of the people, and gradually fall into measures prejudicial to them. It is only a rotation among the members of the federal legislature I shall contend for: judges and officers at the heads of the judicial and executive departments, are in a very different situation, their offices and duties require the information and studies of many years for performing them in a manner advantageous to the people. These judges and officers must apply their whole time to the detail business of their offices, and depend on them for their support then they always act under masters or superiors, and may be removed from office for misconduct; they pursue a certain round of executive business: their offices must be in all societies confined to a few men, because but few can become qualified to fill them: and were they by annual appointments, open to the people at large, they are offices of such a nature as to be of no service to them; they must leave these offices in the possession of the few individuals qualified to fill them, or have them badly filled. In the judicial and executive departments also, the body of the people possess a large share of power and influence, as jurors and subordinate officers, among whom there are many and frequent rotations. But in every free country the legislatures are all on a level, and legislation becomes partial whenever, in practice, it rests for any considerable time in a few hands. It is the true republican principle to diffuse the power of making the laws among the people, and so to modify the forms of the government as to draw in turn the well informed of every class into the legislature.

To determine the propriety or impropriety of this rotation, we must take the inconveniencies as well as the advantages attending it into view: on the one hand, by this rotation, we may sometimes exclude good men from being elected. On the other hand, we guard against those pernicious connections, which usually grow up among men left to continue long periods in office, we increase the number of those who make the laws and return to their constituents; and thereby spread information, and preserve a spirit of activity and investigation among the people: hence a balance of interests and exertions are preserved, and the ruinous measures of factions rendered more impracticable. I would not urge the principle of rotation, if I believed the consequence would be an uninformed federal legislature; but I have no apprehension of this in this enlightened country. The members of congress, at any one time, must be but very few, compared with the respectable well informed men in the United States; and I have no idea there will be any want of such men for members of congress, though by a principle of rotation the constitution should exclude from being elected for two years those federal legislators, who may have served the four years immediately preceding, or any four years in the six preceeding years. If we may judge from experience and fair calculations, this principle will never operate to exclude at any one period a fifteenth part, even of those men who have been members of congress. Though no man can fit in congress, by the confederation, more than three years in any term of six years, yet not more than three, four, or five men in any one state, have been made ineligible at any one period; and if a good man happen to be excluded by this rotation, it is only for a short time. All things considered, the inconveniencies of the principle must be very inconsiderable compared with the many advantages of it. It will generally be expedient for a man who has served four years in congress to return home, mix with the people, and reside some time with them: this will tend to reinstate him in the interests, feelings, and views similar to theirs, and thereby confirm in him the essential qualifications of a legislator. Even in point of information, it may be observed, the useful information of legislators is not acquired merely in studies in offices, and in meeting to make laws from day to day; they must learn the actual situation of the people, by being among them, and when they have made laws, return home, and observe how they operate. Thus occasionally to be among the people, is not only necessary to prevent or banish the callous habits and self interested views of office in legislators, but to afford them necessary information, and to render them useful: another valuable end is answered by it, sympathy, and the means of communication between them and their constituents, is substantially promoted, so that on every principle legislators, at certain periods, ought to live among their constituents.

Some men of science are undoubtedly necessary in every legislature; but the knowledge, generally, necessary for men who make laws, is a knowledge of the common concerns, and particular circumstances of the people. In a republican government seats in the legislature are highly honorable; I believe but few do, and surely none ought to consider them as places of profit and permanent support. Were the people always properly attentive, they would, at proper periods, call their law makers home, by sending others in their room: but this is not often the case, and therefore, in making constitutions, when the people are attentive, they ought cautiously to provide for those benefits, those advantageous changes in the administration of their affairs, which they are often apt to be inattentive to in practice. On the whole, to guard against the evils, and to secure the advantages I have mentioned, with the greatest degree of certainty, we ought clearly, in my opinion, to increase the federal representation, to secure elections on proper principles, to establish a right to recall members, and a rotation among them.

4. By the art. 2. sect. 2., treaties must be made with the advice and consent of the senate, and two-thirds of those present must concur: also, with consent of the senate, almost all federal officers, civil and military, must be appointed. As to treaties I have my doubts; but as to the appointments of officers, I think we may clearly shew the senate to be a very improper body indeed to have any thing to do with them. I am not perfectly satisfied, that the senate, a branch of the legislature, and court for trying impeachments, ought to have a controuling power in making all treaties; yet, I confess, I do not discern how a restraint upon the president in this important business, can be better or more safely lodged: a power to make and conclude all treaties is too important to be vested in him alone, or in him and an executive council, only sufficiently numerous for other purpose, and the house of representatives is too numerous to be concerned in treaties of peace and of alliance. This power is now lodged in congress, to be exercised by the consent of nine states. The federal senate, like the delegations in the present congress, will represent the states, and the consent of two-thirds of that senate will bear some similitude to the consent of nine

states. It is probable the United States will not make more than one treaty, on an average, in two or three years, and this power may always be exercised with great deliberation: perhaps the senate is sufficiently numerous to be trusted with this power, sufficiently small to proceed with secrecy, and sufficiently permanent to exercise this power with proper consistency and due deliberation. To lodge this power in a less respectable and less numerous body might not be safe; we must place great confidence in the hands that hold it, and we deceive ourselves if we give it under an idea that we can impeach, to any valuable purpose, the man or men who may abuse it.

On a fair construction of the constitution, I think the legislature has a proper controul over the president and senate in settling commercial treaties. By art. 1. sect. 2. the legislature will have power to regulate commerce with foreign nations, &c. By art. 2. sect. 2. the president, with the advice and consent of two-thirds of the senate, may make treaties. These clauses must be considered together, and we ought never to make one part of the same instrument contradict another, if it can be avoided by any reasonable construction. By the first recited clause, the legislature has the power, that is, as I understand it, the sole power to regulate commerce with foreign nations, or to make all the rules and regulations respecting trade and commerce between our citizens and foreigners: by the second recited clause, the president and senate have power generally to make treaties.—There are several kinds of treaties—as treaties of commerce, of peace, of alliance, &c. I think the words to "make treaties," may be consistently construed, and yet so as it shall be left to the legislature to confirm commercial treaties; they are in their nature and operation very distinct from treaties of peace and of alliance; the latter generally require secrecy, it is but very seldom they interfere with the laws and internal police of the country; to make them is properly the exercise of executive powers and the constitution authorises the president and senate to make treaties, and gives the legislature no power, directly or indirectly, respecting these treaties of peace and alliance. As to treaties of commerce, they do not generally require secrecy, they almost always involve in them legislative powers, interfere with the laws and internal police of the country, and operate immediately on persons and property, especially in the commercial towns: (they have in Great-Britain usually been confirmed by parliament;) they consist of rules and regulations respecting commerce; and to regulate commerce, or to make regulations respecting commerce, the federal legislature, by the constitution, has the power. I do not see that any commercial regulations can be made in treaties, that will not infringe upon this power in the legislature: therefore, I infer, that the true construction is, that the president and senate shall make treaties; but all commercial treaties shall be subject to be confirmed by the legislature. This construction will render the clauses consistent, and make the powers of the president and senate, respecting treaties, much less exceptionable.

THE FEDERAL FARMER.

12 JANUARY 1788

LETTER XII

The Federal Farmer criticizes the new Congress's power over the time, place, and manner of elections. Rules on these matters should be written into the Constitution, with state legislatures alone exercising any discretion. In addition, legislative districts under the new Constitution will be too large, preventing people from personally knowing those they elect. Essays in The Federalist *of particular relevance: 59-61.*

DEAR SIR,
ON carefully examining the parts of the proposed system, respecting the elections of senators, and especially of the representatives, they appear to me to be both ambiguous and very defective. I shall endeavour to pursue a course of reasoning, which shall fairly lead to establishing the impartiality and security of elections, and then to point out an amendment in this respect.

It is well observed by Montesquieu, that in republican governments, the forms of elections are fundamental; and that it is an
essential part of the social compact, to ascertain by whom, to whom,
when, and in what manner suffrages are to be given.

Wherever we find the regulation of elections have not been carefully fixed by the constitution, or the principles of them, we constantly see the legislatures new modifying its own form, and
changing the spirit of the government to answer partial purposes.

By the proposed plan it is fixed, that the qualifications of the electors of the federal representatives shall be the same as those of
the electors of state representatives; though these vary some in the
several states the electors are fixed and designated.

The qualifications of the representatives are also fixed and designated, and no person under 25 years of age, not an inhabitant of
the state, and not having been seven years a citizen of the United
States, can be elected; the clear inference is, that all persons 25
years of age, and upwards, inhabitants of the state, and having
been, at any period or periods, seven years citizens of the United
States, may be elected representatives. They have a right to be
elected by the constitution, and the electors have a right to chuse
them. This is fixing the federal representation, as to the elected, on
a very broad basis: it can be no objection to the elected, that they
are Christians, Pagans, Mahometans, or Jews; that they are of any
colour, rich or poor, convict or not: Hence many men may be elected,
who cannot be electors. Gentlemen who have commented so largely
upon the wisdom of the constitution, for excluding from being
elected young men under a certain age, would have done well to
have recollected, that it positively makes pagans, convicts, &c. eligible. The people make the constitution; they exclude a few persons,
by certain descriptions, from being elected, and all not thus
excluded are clearly admitted. Now a man 25 years old, an inhabitant of the state, and having been a citizen of the states seven years,
though afterwards convicted, may be elected, because not within
any of the excluding clauses; the same of a beggar, an absentee, &c.

The right of the electors, and eligibility of the elected being fixed
by the people, they cannot be narrowed by the state legislatures, or
congress: it is established, that a man being (among other qualifi-

cations) an inhabitant of the state, shall be eligible. Now it would be narrowing the right of the people to confine them in their choice to a man, an inhabitant of a particular county or district in the state. Hence it follows, that neither the state legislatures or congress can establish district elections; that is, divide the state into districts, and confine the electors of each district to the choice of a man resident in it. If the electors could be thus limited in one respect, they might in another be confined to chuse a man of a particular religion, of certain property, &c. and thereby half of the persons made eligible by the constitution be excluded. All laws, therefore, for regulating elections must be made on the broad basis of the constitution.

Next, we may observe, that representatives are to be chosen by the people of the state. What is a choice by the people of the state? If each given district in it choose one, will that be a choice within the meaning of the constitution? Must the choice be by plurality of votes, or a majority? In connection with these questions, we must take the 4th sect. art. 1. where it is said the state legislatures shall prescribe the times, places, and manner of holding elections; but congress may make or alter such regulations. By this clause, I suppose, the electors of different towns and districts in the state may be assembled in different places, to give their votes; but when so assembled, by another clause they cannot, by congress or the state legislatures, be restrained from giving their votes for any man an inhabitant of the state, and qualified as to age, and having been a citizen the time required. But I see nothing in the constitution by which to decide, whether the choice shall be by a plurality or a majority of votes: this, in my mind, is by far the most important question in the business of elections. When we say a representative shall be chosen by the people, it seems to imply that he shall be chosen by a majority of them; but states which use the same phraseology in this respect, practice both ways. I believe a majority of the states, chuse by pluralities, and, I think it probable, that the federal house of representatives will decide that a choice of its members by pluralities is constitutional. A man who has the most votes is chosen in Great-Britain. It is this, among other things, that gives every man fair play in the game of influence and corruption. I believe that not much stress was laid upon the objection that congress may assemble the electors at some out of the way place. However, the advocates seem to think they obtain a victory of no small glory and importance, when they can shew, with some degree of colour, that the evils is rather a possibility than a probability.

When I observed that the elections were not secured on proper principles, I had an idea of far more probable and extensive evils, secret mischiefs, and not so glaring transgressions, the exclusions of proper district elections, and of the choice by a majority.

It is easy to perceive that there is an essential difference between elections by pluralities and by majorities, between choosing a man in a small or limited district, and choosing a number of men promiscuously by the people of a large state; and while we are almost secure of judicious unbiassed elections by majorities in such districts, we have no security against deceptions, influence and corruption in states or large districts in electing by pluralities. When a choice is made by a plurality of votes, it is often made by a very small part of the electors, who attend and give their votes, when by a majority, never by so few as one half of them. The partialities and improprieties attending the former mode may be illustrated by a case that lately happened in one of the middle states.—Several representatives were to be chosen by a large number of inhabitants compactly settled, among whom there were four or five thousand voters. Previous to the time of election a number of lists of candidates were published, to divide and distract the voters in general— about half a dozen men of some influence, who had a favourite list to carry, met several times, fixed their list, and agreed to hand it about among all who could probably be induced to adopt it, and to circulate the other lists among their opponents, to divide them. The poll was opened, and several hundred electors, suspecting nothing, attended and put in their votes; the list of the half dozen was carried, and men were found to be chosen, some of whom were very disagreeable to a large majority of the electors; though several hundred electors voted, men on that list were chosen who had only 45, 43, 44, &c. votes each; they had a plurality, that is, more than any other persons: the votes generally were scattered, and those who made even a feeble combination succeeded in placing highest upon the list several very unthought of and very unpopular men. This evil never could have happened in a town where all the voters meet in one place, and consider no man as elected unless he have a majority, or more than half of all the votes; clear it is, that the men on whom thus but a small part of the votes are bestowed, cannot possess the confidence of the people, or have any considerable degree of influence over them.

But as partial, as liable to secret influence, and corruption as the choice by pluralities may be, I think, we cannot avoid it, without essentially increasing the federal representation, and adopting the principles of district elections. There is but one case in which the choice by the majority is practicable, and that is, where districts are formed of such moderate extent that the electors in each can conveniently meet in one place, and at one time, and proceed to the choice of a representative; when, if no man have a majority, or more than half of all the votes the first time, the voters may examine the characters of those brought forward, accommodate, and proceed to repeat their votes till some one shall have that majority. This, I believe, cannot be a case under the constitution proposed in its present form. To explain my ideas, take Massachusetts, for instance, she is entitled to eight representatives, she has 370,000 inhabitants, about 46,000 to one representative; if the elections be so held that the electors throughout the state meet in their several towns or places, and each elector puts in his vote for eight representatives, the votes of the electors will ninety-nine times in a hundred, be so scattered that on collecting the votes from the several towns or places, no men will be found, each of whom have a majority of the votes, and therefore the election will not be made. On the other hand, there may be such a combination of votes, that in thus attempting to chuse eight representatives, the electors may chuse even fifteen. Suppose 10,000 voters to attend and give their votes, each voter will give eight votes, one for each of eight representatives; in the whole 80,000 votes will be given—eight men, each having 5,001 votes, in the whole 40,008 will have each a majority, and be chosen—39,092 votes will be bestowed on other men, and if they all be bestowed on seven men, they may have each a considerable majority, and also be chosen. This indeed is a very rare combination: but the bestowing all the votes pretty equally upon nine, ten, or eleven men, and chusing them all, is an event too probable not to be guarded against.

If Massachusetts be divided into eight districts, each having about 46,000 inhabitants, and each district directed to chuse one representative, it will be found totally impracticable for the electors of it to meet in one place; and, when they meet in several towns and places in the district, they will vote for different men, and nineteen times in twenty, so scatter their votes, that no one man will have a majority of the whole and be chosen: we must, therefore, take the man who has the most votes, whether he has three quarters, one quarter, or one tenth part of the whole; the inconveniencies of scattering votes will be increased, as men not of the district, as well as those that are in it, may be voted for.

I might add many other observations to evince the superiority and solid advantages of proper district elections, and a choice by a majority, and to prove, that many evils attend the contrary practice: these evils we must encounter as the constitution now stands.

I see no way to fix elections on a proper footing, and to render tolerably equal and secure the federal representation, but by increasing the representation, so as to have one representative for each district in which the electors may conveniently meet in one place, and at one time, and chuse by a majority. Perhaps this might be effected pretty generally, by fixing one representative for each twelve thousand inhabitants; dividing, or fixing the principles for dividing the states into proper districts; and directing the electors of each district to the choice, by a majority, of some men having a permanent interest and residence in it. I speak of a representation tolerably equal, &c. because I am still of opinion, that it is impracticable in this extensive country to have a federal representation sufficiently democratic, or substantially drawn from the body of the people: the principles just mentioned may be the best practical ones we can expect to establish. By thus increasing the representation, we not only make it more democratical and secure, strengthen the confidence of the people in it, and thereby render it more nervous and energetic; but it will also enable the people essentially to change, for the better, the principles and forms of elections. To pro-

vide for the people's wandering throughout the state for a representative, may sometimes enable them to elect a more brilliant or
an abler man, than by confining them to districts, but generally this
latitude will be used to pernicious purposes, especially connected
with the choice by plurality; when a man in the remote part of the
state, perhaps, obnoxious at home, but ambitious and intriguing,
may be chosen to represent the people in another part of the state
far distant, and by a small part of them, or by a faction, or by a combination of some particular description of men among them. This
has been long the case in Great-Britain, it is the case in several of
the states, nor do I think that such pernicious practices will be
merely possible in our federal concerns, but highly probable. By
establishing district elections, we exclude none of the best men
from being elected; and we fix what, in my mind, is of far more
importance than brilliant talents, I mean a sameness, as to residence and interests, between the representative and his constituents; and by the election by a majority, he is sure to be the man,
the choice of more than half of them.

The federal representatives are to be chosen every second year
(an odd mode of expression). In all the states, except South-Carolina, the people, the same electors, meet twice in that time to elect
state representatives. For instance, let the electors in Massachusetts, when they meet to chuse state representatives, put in their
votes for eight federal representatives, the number that state may
chuse, (merely for distinction sake, we may call these the votes of

Though it is impossible to put elections on a proper footing as the
constitution stands, yet I think regulations respecting them may be
introduced of considerable service: it is not only, therefore, important to enquire how they may be made, but also what body has the
controuling power over them. An intelligent, free and unbiassed
choice of representatives by the people is of the last importance: we
must then carefully guard against all combinations, secret arts,
and influence to the contrary. Various expedients have been
adopted in different countries and states to effect genuine elections;
as the constitution now stands, I confess, I do not discover any better than those adopted in Connecticut, in the choice of counsellers,
before mentioned.

nomination), and return a list of the men voted for, in the several towns and places, to the legislature, or some proper body; let this list be immediately examined and published, and some proper number, say 15 or 20, who shall have the most votes upon the list, be sent out to the people; and when the electors shall meet the next year to chuse state representatives, let them put in their votes for the eight federal representatives, confining their votes to the proper number so sent out; and let the eight highest of those thus voted for in the two votes (which we may call, by way of distinction, votes of election), be the federal representatives: thus a choice may be made by the people, once in two years, without much trouble and expence, and, I believe, with some degree of security. As soon as the votes of nomination shall be collected and made known, the people will know who are voted for, and who are candidates for their votes the succeeding year; the electors will have near a year to enquire into their characters and politics, and also into any undue means if any were taken, to bring any of them forward; and such as they find to be the best men, and agreeable to the people, they may vote for in giving the votes of election. By these means the men chosen will ultimately always have a majority, or near a majority, of the votes of the electors, who shall attend and give their votes. The mode itself will lead to the discovery of truth and of political characters, and to prevent private combinations, by rendering them in a great measure of no effect. As the choice is to be made by the people, all combinations and checks must be confined to their votes. No supplying the want of a majority by the legislatures, as in Massachusetts in the choice of senators, &c. can be admitted: the people generally judge right when informed, and, in giving their votes the second time, they may always correct their former errors.

I think we are all sufficiently acquainted with the progress of elections to see, that the regulations, as to times, places, and the manner merely of holding elections, may, under the constitution, easily be made useful or injurious. It is important then to enquire, who has the power to make regulations, and who ought to have it. By the constitution, the state legislatures shall prescribe the times, places, and manner of holding elections, but congress may make or

alter such regulations. Power in congress merely to alter those regulations, made by the states, could answer no valuable purposes;
the states might make, and congress alter them *ad infinitum:* and
when the state should cease to make, or should annihilate its regulations, congress would have nothing to alter. But the states shall
make regulations, and congress may make such regulations as the
clause stands: the true construction is, that when congress shall see
fit to regulate the times, places, and manner of holding elections,
congress may do it, and state regulations, on this head, must cease;
for if state regulations could exist, after congress should make a
system of regulations, there would, or might, be two incompatible
systems of regulations relative to the same subject.

It has been often urged, that congress ought to have power to
make these regulations, otherwise the state legislatures, by
neglecting to make provision for elections, or by making improper
regulations, may destroy the general government. It is very
improbable that any state legislature will adopt measures to
destroy the representation of its own constituents in congress especially when the state must, represented in congress or not, pay its
proportion of the expence of keeping up the government, and even
of the representatives of the other states, and be subject to their
laws. Should the state legislatures be disposed to be negligent, or to
combine to break up congress, they have a very simple way to do it,
as the constitution now stands—they have only to neglect to chuse
senators, or to appoint the electors of the president, and vice-president: there is no remedy provided against these last evils: nor is it
to be presumed, that if a sufficient number of state legislatures to
break up congress, should, by neglect or otherwise, attempt to do it,
that the people, who yearly elect those legislatures, would elect
under the regulations of congress. These and many other reasons
must evince, that it was not merely to prevent an annihilation of the
federal government that congress has power to regulate elections.

It has been urged also, that the state legislatures chuse the federal senators, one branch, and may injure the people, who chuse the
other, by improper regulations; that therefore congress, in which
the people will immediately have one, the representative branch,
ought to have power to interfere in behalf of the people, and rec-

tify such improper regulations. The advocates have said much about the opponents dwelling upon possibilities; but to suppose the people will find it necessary to appeal to congress to restrain the oppressions of the state legislatures, is supposing a possibility indeed. Can any man in his senses suppose that the state legislatures, which are so numerous as almost to be the people themselves, all branches of them depending yearly, for the most part, on the elections of the people, will abuse them in regulating federal elections, and make it proper to transfer the power to congress, a body, one branch of which is chosen once in six years by these very legislatures, and the other biennially and not half so numerous as even the senatorial branches in those legislatures?

Senators are to be chosen by the state legislatures, where there are two branches the appointment must be, I presume, by a concurrent resolution, in passing which, as in passing all other legislative acts each branch will have a negative; this will give the senatorial branch just as much weight in the appointment as the democratic: the two branches form a legislature only when acting separately, and therefore, whenever the members of the two branches meet, mix and vote individually in one room, for making an election, it is expressly so directed by the constitutions. If the constitution, by fixing the choice to be made by the legislatures, has given each branch an equal vote, as I think it has, it cannot be altered by any regulations.

On the whole, I think, all general principles respecting electors ought to be carefully established by the constitution, as the qualifications of the electors and of elected: the number of the representatives, and the inhabitants of each given district, called on to chuse a man from among themselves by a majority of votes; leaving it to the legislature only so to regulate, from time to time, the extent of the districts so as to keep the representatives proportionate to the number of inhabitants in the several parts of the country; and so far as regulations as to elections cannot be fixed by the constitution, they ought to be left to the state legislatures, they coming far nearest to the people themselves; at most, congress ought to have power to regulate elections only where a state shall neglect to make them.

THE FEDERAL FARMER.

14 JANUARY 1788

LETTER XIII

*The Federal Farmer turns his attention to federal offices, arguing
that members of Congress should not be eligible or participate in
appointments for such posts. Legislators will find it in their interest to build a large class of dependent office holders that will
infringe on the people's rights and pocketbooks. Essays in* The Federalist *of particular relevance: 66, 67, 76.*

DEAR SIR,

IN this letter I shall further examine two clauses in the proposed
constitution respecting appointments to office.—By art. 2. sect. 2.
the president shall nominate, and by and with the advice and consent of the senate, shall appoint ambassadors, other public ministers and consuls, judges of the supreme court, and all other officers
of the United States, whose appointments, &c. By art. 1, sect. 6.
No senator or representative shall, during the term for which he
was elected, be appointed to any civil office under the authority of
the United States, which shall have been created, or the emoluments whereof shall have been increased during such.

  Thus the president must nominate, and the senate concur in the
appointment of all federal officers, civil and military, and the senators and representatives are made ineligible only to the few civil
offices abovementioned. To preserve the federal government pure
and uncorrupt, peculiar precautions relative to appointments to
office will be found highly necessary from the very forms and character of the government itself. The honours and emoluments of
public offices are the objects in all communities, that ambitious and
necessitous men never lose sight of. The honest, the modest, and
the industrious part of the community content themselves, generally, with their private concerns; they do not solicit those offices
which are the perpetual source of cabals, intrigues, and contests
among men of the former description, men embarrassed, intriguing,

and destitute of modesty. Even in the most happy country and virtuous government, corrupt influence in appointments cannot
always be avoided; perhaps we may boast of our share of virtue as
a people, and if we are only sufficiently aware of the influence,
biasses, and prejudices, common to the affairs of men, we may go
far towards guarding against the effects of them.

We all agree, that a large standing army has a strong tendency to
depress and inslave the people; it is equally true that a large body
of selfish, unfeeling, unprincipled civil officers has a like, or a more
pernicious tendency to the same point. Military, and especially civil
establishments, are the necessary appendages of society; they are
deductions from productive labour, and substantial wealth, in proportion to the number of men employed in them; they are oppressive where unnecessarily extended and supported by men
unfriendly to the people; they are injurious when too small, and
supported by men too timid and dependant. It is of the last importance to decide well upon the necessary number of offices, to fill
them with proper characters, and to establish efficiently the means
of punctually punishing those officers who may do wrong.

To discern the nature and extent of this power of appointments,
we need only to consider the vast number of officers necessary to
execute a national system in this extensive country, the prodigious
biasses the hopes and expectations of offices have on their conduct,
and the influence public officers have among the people—these necessary officers, as judges, state's attornies, clerks, sheriffs, &c. in
the federal supreme and inferior courts, admirals and generals,
and subordinate officers in the army and navy ministers, consuls,
&c. sent to foreign countries; officers in the federal city, in the revenue, post office departments, &c. &c. must, probably, amount to
several thousands, without taking into view the very inferior ones.
There can be no doubt but that the most active men in politics, in
and out of congress, will be the foremost candidates for the best of
these offices; the man or men who shall have the disposal of them,
beyond dispute, will have by far the greatest share of active influence in the government; but appointments must be made, and who
shall make them? what modes of appointments will be attended
with the fewest inconveniences? is the question. The senators and

representatives are the law makers, create all offices, and whenever they see fit, they impeach and try officers for misconduct: they ought to be in session but part of the year, and as legislators, they must be too numerous to make appointments, perhaps, a few very important ones excepted. In contemplating the necessary officers of the union, there appear to be six different modes in which, in whole or in part, the appointments may be made, 1. By the legislature; 2. by the president and senate—3. by the president and an executive council—4. by the president alone—5. by the heads of the departments—and 6. by the state governments—Among all these, in my opinion, there may be an advantageous distribution of the power of appointments. In considering the legislators, in relation to the subject before us, two interesting questions particularly arise—1. Whether they ought to be eligible to any offices whatever during the period for which they shall be elected to serve, and even for some time afterwards—and 2. How far they ought to participate in the power of appointments. As to the first, it is true that legislators in foreign countries, or in our state governments, are not generally made ineligible to office: there are good reasons for it; in many countries the people have gone on without ever examining the principles of government. There have been but few countries in which the legislators have been a particular set of men periodically chosen: but the principal reason is, that which operates in the several states, viz. the legislators are so frequently chosen, and so numerous, compared with the number of offices for which they can reasonably consider themselves as candidates, that the chance of any individual member's being chosen, is too small to raise his hopes or expectations, or to have any considerable influence upon his conduct. Among the state legislators, one man in twenty may be appointed in some committee business, &c. for a month or two; but on a fair computation, not one man in a hundred sent to the state legislatures is appointed to any permanent office of profit: directly the reverse of this will evidently be found true in the federal administration. Throughout the United States, about four federal senators, and thirty-three representatives, averaging the elections, will be chosen in a year; these few men may rationally consider themselves as the fairest candidates for a very great number of lucrative offices, which must become vacant in the year, and pretty clearly a majority of the federal legislators, if not excluded, will be mere expectants for public offices. I need not adduce further arguments to establish a position so clear, I need only call to your recollection my observations in a former letter, wherein I endeavoured to shew the fallacy of the argument, that the members must return home and mix with the people. It is said, that men are governed by interested motives, and will not attend as legislators, unless they can, in common with others, be eligible to offices of honor and profit. This will undoubtedly be the case with some men, but I presume only with such men as never ought to be chosen legislators in a free country; an opposite principle will influence good men; virtuous patriots, and generous minds, will esteem it a higher honor to be selected as the guardians of a free people; they will be satisfied with a reasonable compensation for their time and service; nor will they wish to be within the vortex of influence. The valuable effects of this principle of making legislators ineligible to offices for a given time, has never yet been sufficiently attended to or considered; I am assured, that it was established by the convention after long debate, and afterwards, on an unfortunate change of a few members, altered. Could the federal legislators be excluded in the manner proposed, I think it would be an important point gained; as to themselves, they would be left to act much more from motives consistent with the public good.

In considering the principle of rotation I had occasion to distinguish the condition of a legislator from that of mere official man— We acquire certain habits, feelings, and opinions, as men and citizens—others, and very different ones, from a long continuance in office: It is, therefore, a valuable observation in many bills of rights, that rulers ought frequently to return and mix with the people. A legislature, in a free country, must be numerous; it is in some degree a periodical assemblage of the people, frequently formed— the principal officers in the executive and judicial departments, must have more permanency in office. Hence it may be inferred, that the legislature will remain longer uncorrupted and virtuous; longer congenial to the people, than the officers of those departments. If it is not, therefore, in our power to preserve republican principles, for a series of ages, in all the departments of government, we may a long while preserve them in a well formed legislature. To this end we ought to take every precaution to prevent legislators becoming mere office-men; chuse them frequently, make them recallable, establish rotation among them, make them ineligible to offices, and give them as small a share as possible in the disposal of them. Add to this, a legislature, in the nature of things, is not formed for the detail business of appointing officers; there is also generally an impropriety in the same men's making offices and filling them, and a still greater impropriety in their impeaching and trying the officers they appoint. For these, and other reasons, I conclude, the legislature is not a proper body for the appointment of officers in general. But having gone through with the different modes of appointment, I shall endeavour to shew what share in the distribution of the power of appointments the legislature must, from necessity, rather than from propriety, take. 2. Officers may be appointed by the president and senate—this mode, for general purposes, is clearly not defensible. All the reasoning touching the legislature will apply to the senate; the senate is a branch of the legislature, which ought to be kept pure and unbiassed; it has a part in trying officers for misconduct, and in creating offices, it is too numerous for a council of appointment, or to feel any degree of responsibility: if it has an advantage of the legislature, in being the least numerous, it has a disadvantage in being more unsafe: add to this, the senate is to have a share in the important branch of power respecting treaties. Further, this sexennial senate of 26 members, representing 13 sovereign states, will not, in practice, be found to be a body to advise, but to order and dictate in fact; and the president will be a mere *primus inter pares*. The consequence will be, that the senate, with these efficient means of influence, will not only dictate, probably, to the president, but manage the house, as the constitution now stands; and under appearances of a balanced system, in reality, govern alone. There may also, by this undue connection, be particular periods when a very popular president may have a very improper influence upon the senate and upon the legislature. A council of appointment must very probably fit all, or near all, the year—the senate will be too important and too expensive a body for this. By giving the senate, directly or indirectly, an undue influence over the representatives, and the improper means of fettering, embarrassing, or controuling the president or executive, we give the government, in the very out set, a fatal and pernicious tendency to that middle undesirable point—aristocracy. When we, as a circumstance not well to be avoided, admit the senate to a share of power in making treaties, and in managing foreign concerns, we certainly progress full far enough towards this most undesirable point in government. For with this power, also, I believe, we must join that of appointing ambassadors, other foreign ministers, and consuls, being powers necessarily connected.—In every point of view, in which I can contemplate this subject, it appears extremely clear to me, that the senate ought not generally to be a council of appointment. The legislature, after the people, is the great fountain of power, and ought to be kept as pure and uncorrupt as possible, from the hankerings, biasses, and contagion of offices—then the streams issuing from it, will be less tainted with those evils. It is not merely the number of impeachments, that are to be expected to make public officers honest and attentive in their business. A general opinion must pervade the community, that the house, the body to impeach them for misconduct, is disinterested, and ever watchful for the public good; and that the judges who shall try impeachments, will not feel a shadow of biass. Under such circumstances, men will not dare transgress, who, not deterred by such accusers and judges, would repeatedly misbehave. We have already suffered many and extensive evils, owing to the defects of the confederation, in not providing against the misconduct of public officers. When we expect the law to be punctually executed, not one man in ten thousand will disobey it: it is the probable chance of escaping punishment that induces men to transgress. It is one important mean to make the government just and honest, rigidly and constantly to hold, before the eyes of those who execute it, punishment, and dismission from office, for misconduct. These are principles no candid man, who has just ideas of the essential features of a free government, will controvert. They are, to be sure, at this period, called visionary, speculative and anti-governmental—but in the true stile of courtiers, selfish politicians, and flatterers of despotism—discerning republican men of both parties see their value. They are said to be of no value, by empty boasting advocates for the constitution, who, by their weakness and conduct, in fact, injure its cause much more than most of its opponents. From their high founding promises, men are led to expect a defence of it, and to have their doubts removed. When a number of long pieces appear, they, instead of the defence, &c. they expected, see nothing but a parade of names—volumes written without ever coming to the point—cases quoted between which and ours there is not the least similitude—and partial extracts made from histories and governments, merely to serve a purpose. Some of them, like the true admirers of royal and senatorial robes, would fain prove, that nations who have thought like freemen and philosophers about government, and endeavoured to be free, have often been the most miserable: if a single riot, in the course of five hundred years happened in a free country, if a salary, or the interest of a public or private debt was not paid at the moment, they seem to lay more stress upon these triffles (for triffles they are in a free and happy country) than upon the oppressions of despotic government for ages together. As to the lengthy writer in New-York you mention, I have attentively examined his pieces; he appears to be a candid good-hearted man, to have a good stile, and some plausible ideas; but when we carefully examine his pieces, to see where the strength of them lies; when the mind endeavours to fix on those material parts, which ought to be the essence of all voluminous productions, we do not find them: the writer appears constantly to move on a smooth surface, the part of his work, like the parts of a cob-house, are all equally strong and all equally weak, and all like those works of the boys, without an object; his pieces appear to have, but little relation to the great question, whether the constitution is fitted to the condition and character of this people or not. But to return—3. Officers may be appointed by the president and an executive council—when we have assigned to the legislature the appointment of a few important officers—to the president and senate the appointment of those concerned in managing foreign affairs—to the state governments the appointment of militia officers, and authorise the legislature by legislative acts, to assign to the president alone, to the heads of the deparments, and courts of law respectively, the appointment of many inferior officers; we shall then want to lodge some where a residuum of power, a power to appoint all other necessary officers, as established by law. The fittest receptacle for this residuary power is clearly, in my opinion, the first executive magistrate, advised and directed by an executive council of seven or nine members, periodically chosen from such proportional districts as the union may for the purpose be divided into. The people may give their votes for twice the number of counsellers wanted, and the federal legislature take twice the number also from the highest candidates, and from among them chuse the seven or nine, or number wanted. Such a council may be rationally formed for the business of appointments; whereas the senate, created for other purposes, never can be—Such councils forms a feature in some of the best executives in the union—they appear to be essential to every first magistrate, who may frequently want advice.

To authorise the president to appoint his own council would be unsafe: to give the sole appointment of it to the legislature, would confer an undue and unnecessary influence upon that branch. Such a council for a year would be less expensive than the senate for four months. The president may nominate, and the counsellers always be made responsible for their advice and opinions, by recording and signing whatever they advise to be done. They and the president, to many purposes, will properly form an independent executive branch; have an influence unmixed with the legislative, which the executive never can have while connected with a powerful branch of the legislature. And yet the influence arising from the power of appointments be less dangerous, because in less dangerous hands—hands properly adequate to possess it. Whereas the senate, from its character and situation, will add a dangerous weight to the power itself, and be far less capable of responsibility, than the council proposed. There is another advantage the residuum of power, as to appointments, which the president and council need possess, is less than that the president and senate must have. And as such a council would render the sessions of the senate unnecessary many months in the year, the expenses of the government would not be increased, if they would not be lessened by the institution of such a council. I think I need not dwell upon this article, as the fitness of this mode of appointment will perhaps amply appear by the evident unfitness of the others.

4. Officers may be appointed by the president alone. It has been almost universally found, when a man has been authorized to exercise power alone, he has never done it alone; but, generally, aided his determinations by, and rested on the advice and opinions of others. And it often happens when advice is wanted, the worst men, the most interested creatures, the worst advice is at hand, obtrude themselves, and misdirect the mind of him who would be informed and advised. It is very seldom we see a single executive, depend on accidental advice and assistance; but each single executive has, almost always, formed to itself a regular council, to be assembled and consulted on important occasions; this proves that a select council of some kind, is, by experience, generally found necessary and useful. But in a free country, the exercise of any considerable branch of power ought to be under some checks and controuls. As to this point, I think the constitution stands well, the legislature may, when it shall deem it expedient, from time to time, authorise the president alone to appoint particular inferior officers, and when necessary to take back the power. His power, therefore, in this respect, may always be increased or decreased by the legislature, as experience, the best instructor, shall direct: always keeping him, by the constitution, within certain bounds.

THE FEDERAL FARMER.

17 JANUARY 1788

LETTER XIV

The Federal Farmer details the new legislature's role in making appointments, then goes on to describe the executive power. He praises the choice of a single executive, but argues against presidential eligibility for re-election on the grounds that this will pro-

duce corruption. Essays in The Federalist *of particular relevance:*
66, 67, 70-72, 76.

DEAR SIR,

TO continue the subject of appointments:—Officers, in the fifth
place, may be appointed by the heads of departments or courts of
law. Art. 2. sect. 2 respecting appointments, goes on.—"But congress may by law vest the appointment of such inferior officers as
they think proper in the president alone, in the courts of law, or in
the heads of departments." The probability is, as the constitution
now stands, that the senate, a branch of the legislature, will be
tenacious of the power of appointment, and much too sparingly part
with a share of it to the courts of law, and heads of departments.
Here again the impropriety appears of the senate's having, generally, a share in the appointment of officers. We may fairly presume,
that the judges, and principal officers in the departments, will be
able well informed men in their respective branches of business;
that they will, from experience, be best informed as to proper persons to fill inferior offices in them; that they will feel themselves
responsible for the execution of their several branches of business,
and for the conduct of the officers they may appoint therein.—From
these, and other considerations, I think we may infer, that impartial
and judicious appointments of subordinate officers will, generally,
be made by the courts of law, and the heads of departments. This
power of distributing appointments, as circumstances may require,
into several hands, in a well formed disinterested legislature, might
be of essential service, not only in promoting beneficial appointments, but, also, in preserving the balance in government: a feeble
executive may be strengthened and supported by placing in its
hands more numerous appointments; an executive too influential
may be reduced within proper bounds, by placing many of the inferior appointments in the courts of law, and heads of departments;
nor is there much danger that the executive will be wantonly weakened or strengthened by the legislature, by thus shifting the
appointments of inferior officers, since all must be done by legislative acts, which cannot be passed without the consent of the executive, or the consent of two-thirds of both branches—a good

legislature will use this power to preserve the balance and perpetuate the government. Here again we are brought to our ultima-
tum:—is the legislature so constructed as to deserve our
confidence?

6. Officers may be appointed by the state governments. By art. 1.
sect. 8 the respective states are authorised exclusively to appoint
the militia-officers. This not only lodges the appointments in proper
places, but it also tends to distribute and lodge in different executive hands the powers of appointing to offices, so dangerous when
collected into the hands of one or a few men.

It is a good general rule, that the legislative, executive, and judicial powers, ought to be kept distinct; but this, like other general
rules, has its exceptions; and without these exceptions we cannot
form a good government, and properly balance its parts, and we can
determine only from reason, experience and a critical inspection of
the parts of the government how far it is proper to intermix those
powers. Appointment, I believe, in all mixed governments, have
been assigned to different hands—some are made by the executive,
some by the legislature, some by the judges and some by the people. It has been thought adviseable by the wisest nations, that the
legislature should so far exercise executive and judicial powers as
to appoint some officers, judge of the elections of its members, and
impeach and try officers for misconduct—that the executive should
have a partial share in legislation—that judges should appoint some
subordinate officers, and regulate so far as to establish rules for
their own proceedings. Where the members of the government, as
the house, the senate, the executive, and judiciary, are strong and
complete, each in itself, the balance is naturally produced, each
party may take the powers congenial to it, and we have less need
to be anxious about checks, and the subdivision of powers.

If after making the deductions, already alluded to, from the general power to appoint federal officers the residuum shall be thought
to be too large and unsafe, and to place an undue influence in the
hands of the president and council, a further deduction may be
made, with many advantages, and, perhaps, with but a few inconveniencies; and that is, by giving the appointment of a few great
officers to the legislature—as of the commissioners of the trea-

sury—of the comptroller, treasurer, master coiner, and some of the principal officers in the money department—of the sheriffs or marshalls of the United States—of states attornies, secretary of the home department, and secretary at war, perhaps, of the judges of the supreme court—of major-generals and admirals. The appointments of these officers, who may be at the heads of the great departments of business, in carrying into execution the national system involve in them a variety of considerations; they will not often occur, and the power to make them ought to remain in safe hands. Officers of the above description are appointed by the legislatures in some of the states, and in some not. We may, I believe, presume that the federal legislature will possess sufficient knowledge and discernment to make judicious appointments: however, as these appointments by the legislature tend to increase a mixture of power, to lessen the advantages of impeachments and responsibility, I would by no means contend for them any further than it may be necessary for reducing the power of the executive within the bounds of safety. To determine with propriety how extensive power the executive ought to possess relative to appointments, we must also examine the forms of it, and its other powers; and these forms and other powers I shall now proceed briefly to examine.

By art. 2. sect 1. the executive power shall be vested in a president elected for four years, by electors to be appointed from time to time, in such manner as the state legislatures shall direct—the electors to be equal in numbers to the federal senators and representatives: but congress may determine the time of chusing senators, and the day on which they shall give their votes; and if no president be chosen by the electors, by a majority of votes, the states, as states in congress, shall elect one of the five highest on the list for president. It is to be observed, that in chusing the president, the principle of electing by a majority of votes is adopted; in chusing the vice-president, that of electing by a plurality. Viewing the principles and checks established in the election of the president, and especially considering the several states may guard the appointment of the electors as they shall judge best. I confess there appears to be a judicious combination of principles and precautions. Were the electors more numerous than they will be, in case the representation be not increased, I think, the system would be improved; not that I consider the democratic character so important in the choice of the electors as in the choice of representatives: be the electors more or less democratic, the president will be one of the very few of the most elevated characters. But there is danger, that a majority of a small number of electors may be corrupted and influenced, after appointed electors, and before they give their votes, especially if a considerable space of time elapse between the appointment and voting. I have already considered the advisory council in the executive branch: there are two things further in the organization of the executive, to which I would particularly draw your attention; the first, which, is a single executive, I confess, I approve; the second, by which any person from period to period may be re-elected president, I think very exceptionable.

Each state in the union has uniformly shewn its preference for a single executive, and generally directed the first executive magistrate to act in certain cases by the advice of an executive council. Reason, and the experience of enlightened nations, seem justly to assign the business of making laws to numerous assemblies; and the execution of them, principally, to the direction and care of one man. Independent of practice, a single man seems to be peculiarly well circumstanced to superintend the execution of laws with discernment and decision, with promptitude and unformity: the people usually point out a first man—he is to be seen in civilized as well as uncivilized nations—in republics as well as in other governments. In every large collection of people there must be a visible point, serving as a common centre in the government, towards which to draw their eyes and attachments. The constitution must fix a man, or a congress of men, superior in the opinion of the people to the most popular men in the different parts of the community, else the people will be apt to divide and follow their respective leaders. Aspiring men, armies and navies, have not often been kept in tolerable order by the decrees of a senate or an executive council. The advocates for lodging the executive power in the hands of a number of equals, as an executive council, say, that much wisdom may be collected in such a council, and that it will be safe; but they agree, that it cannot be so prompt and responsible as a single man—they admit that such a council will generally consist of the aristocracy, and not stand so indifferent between it and the people as a first magistrate. But the principal objection made to a single man is, that when possessed of power he will be constantly struggling for more, disturbing the government, and encroaching on the rights of others. It must be admitted, that men, from the monarch down to the porter, are constantly aiming at power and importance, and this propensity must be as constantly guarded against in the forms of the government. Adequate powers must be delegated to those who govern, and our security must be in limiting, defining, and guarding the exercise of them, so that those given shall not be abused, or made use of for openly or secretly seizing more. Why do we believe this abuse of power peculiar to a first magistrate? Is it because in the wars and contests of men, one man has often established his power over the rest? Or are men naturally fond of accumulating powers in the hands of one man? I do not see any similitude between the cases of those tyrants, who have sprung up in the midst of wars and tumults, and the cases of limited executives in established governments; nor shall we, on a careful examination, discover much likeness between the executives in Sweden, Denmark, Holland, &c. which have, from time to time, increased their powers, and become more absolute, and the executives, whose powers are well ascertained and defined, and which remain, by the constitution, only for a short and limited period in the hands of any one man or family. A single man, or family, can long and effectually direct its exertions to one point. There may be many favourable opportunities in the course of a man's life to seize on additional powers, and many more where powers are hereditary; and there are many circumstances favourable to usurpations, where the powers of the man or family are undefined, and such as often may be unduly extended before the people discover it. If we examine history attentively, we shall find that such exertions, such opportunities, and such circumstances as these have attended all the executives which have usurped upon the rights of the people, and which appear originally to have been, in some degree, limited. Admitting that moderate and even well defined powers, long in the hands of the same man or family, will, probably, be unreasonably increased, it will not follow that even extensive powers placed in the hands of a man only for a few years will be abused. The Roman consuls and Carthagenian suffetes possessed extensive powers while in office; but being annually appointed, they but seldom, if ever, abused them. The Roman dictators often possessed absolute power while in office; but usually being elected for short periods of time, no one of them for ages usurped upon the rights of the people. The kings of France, Spain, Sweden, Denmark, &c. have become absolute merely from the encroachments and abuse of power made by the nobles. As to kings, and limited monarchs, generally, history furnishes many more instances in which their powers have been abridged or annihilated by the nobles or people, or both, than in which they have been increased or made absolute; and in almost all the latter cases we find the people were inattentive and fickle, and evidently were not born to be free. I am the more particular respecting this subject, because I have heard many mistaken observations relative to it. Men of property, and even men who hold powers for themselves and posterity, have too much to lose, wantonly to hazard a shock of the political system; the game must be large, and the chance of winning great, to induce them to risque what they have, for the uncertain prospect of gaining more. Our executive may be altogether elective, and possess no power, but as the substitute of the people, and that well limited, and only for a limited time. The great object is, in a republican government, to guard effectually against perpetuating any portion of power, great or small, in the same man or family; this perpetuation of power is totally uncongenial to the true spirit of republican governments: on the one hand the first executive magistrate ought to remain in office so long as to avoid instability in the execution of the laws; on the other, not so long as to enable him to take any measures to establish himself. The convention, it seems, first agreed that the president should be chosen for seven years, and never after to be eligible. Whether seven years is a period too long or not, is rather matter of opinion; but clear it is, that this mode is infinitely preferable to the one finally adopted. When a man shall get the chair, who may be re-elected, from time to time, for life, his greatest object will be to keep it; to gain friends and votes, at any rate; to associate some favourite son with himself, to take the office after him: whenever he shall have any prospect of continuing the office in himself and family, he will spare no artifice, no address, and no exertions, to increase the powers and importance of it; the servile supporters of his wishes will be placed in all offices, and tools constantly employed to aid his views and found his praise. A man so situated will have no permanent interest in the government to lose, by contests and convulsions in the state, but always much to gain, and frequently the seducing and flattering hope of succeeding. If we reason at all on the subject, we must irresistably conclude, that this will be the case with nine tenths of the presidents; we may have, for the first president, and, perhaps, one in a century or two afterwards (if the government should withstand the attacks of others) a great and good man, governed by superior motives; but these are not events to be calculated upon in the present state of human nature.

A man chosen to this important office for a limited period, and always afterwards rendered, by the constitution, ineligible, will be governed by very different considerations: he can have no rational hopes or expectations of retaining his office after the expiration of a known limited time, or of continuing the office in his family, as by the constitution there must be a constant transfer of it from one man to another, and consequently from one family to another. No man will wish to be a mere cypher at the head of the government: the great object of each president then will be, to render his government a glorious period in the annals of his country. When a man constitutionally retires from office, he retires without pain; he is sensible he retires because the laws direct it, and not from the success of his rivals, nor with that public disapprobation which being left out, when eligible, implies. It is said, that a man knowing that at a given period he must quit his office, will unjustly attempt to take from the public, and lay in store the means of support and splendour in his retirement; there can, I think, be but very little in this observation. The same constitution that makes a man eligible for a given period only, ought to make no man eligible till he arrive to the age of forty or forty-five years: if he be a man of fortune, he will retire with dignity to his estate; if not, he may, like the Roman consuls, and other eminent characters in republics, find an honorable support and employment in some respectable office. A man who must, at all events, thus leave his office, will have but few or no temptations to fill its dependant offices with his tools, or any particular set of men; whereas the man constantly looking forward to his future elections, and, perhaps, to the aggrandizement of his family, will have every inducement before him to fill all places with his own props and dependants. As to public monies, the president need handle none of them, and he may always rigidly be made account for every shilling he shall receive.

On the whole, it would be, in my opinion, almost as well to create a limited monarchy at once, and give some family permanent power and interest in the community, and let it have something valuable to itself to lose in convulsions in the state, and in attempts of usurpation, as to make a first magistrate eligible for life, and to create hopes and expectations in him and his family, of obtaining what they have not. In the latter case, we actually tempt them to disturb the state, to foment struggles and contests, by laying before them the flattering prospect of gaining much in them without risking any thing.

The constitution provides only that the president shall hold his office during the term of four years; that, at most, only implies, that one shall be chosen every fourth year; it also provides, that in case of the removal, death, resignation, or inability, both of the president and vice-president, congress may declare what officer shall act as president; and that such officers shall act accordingly, until the disability be removed, *or a president shall be elected*: it also provides that congress may determine the time of chusing electors, and the day on which they shall give their votes. Considering these clauses together, I submit this question—whether in case of a vacancy in the office of president, by the removal, death, resignation, or inability of the president and vice-president, and congress should declare, that a certain officer, as secretary for foreign affairs, for instance, shall act as president, and suffer such officer to continue several years, or even for his life, to act as president, by omitting to appoint the time for chusing electors of another president, it would be any breach of the constitution? This appears to me to be an intended provision for supplying the office of president, not only for any remaining portion of the four years, but in cases of emergency, until another president shall be elected; and that at a period beyond the expiration of the four years: we do not know that it is impossible; we do not know that it is improbable, in case a popular officer should thus be declared the acting president, but that he might continue for life, and without any violent act, but merely by neglects and delays on the part of congress.

I shall conclude my observations on the organization of the legislature and executive, with making some remarks, rather as a matter of amusement, on the branch, or partial negative, in the legislation:—The third branch in the legislature may answer three valuable purposes, to impede in their passage hasty and intemperate laws, occasionally to assist the senate or people, and to prevent the legislature from encroaching upon the executive or judiciary. In Great Britain the king has a complete negative upon all laws, but he very seldom exercises it. This may be well lodged in him, who possesses strength to support it, and whose family has independent and hereditary interests and powers, rights and prerogatives, in the government, to defend: but in a country where the first executive officer is elective, and has no rights, but in common with the people, a partial negative in legislation, as in Massachusetts and New-York, is, in my opinion, clearly best: in the former state, as before observed, it is lodged in the governor alone; in the latter, in the governor, chancellor, and judges of the supreme court—the new constitution lodges it in the president. This is simply a branch of legislative power, and has in itself no relation to executive or judicial powers. The question is, in what hands ought it to be lodged, to answer the three purposes mentioned the most advantageously? The prevailing opinion seems to be in favour of vesting it in the hands of the first executive magistrate. I will not say this opinion is ill founded. The negative, in one case, is intended to prevent hasty laws, not supported and revised by two-thirds of each of the two branches; in the second, it is to aid the weaker branch; and in the third, to defend the executive and judiciary. To answer these ends, there ought, therefore, to be collected in the hands which hold this negative, firmness, wisdom, and strength; the very object of the negative is occasional opposition to the two branches. By lodging it in the executive magistrate, we give him a share in making the laws, which he must execute; by associating the judges with him, as in New York, we give them a share in making the laws, upon which they must decide as judicial magistrates; this may be a reason for excluding the judges: however, the negative in New-York is certainly well calculated to answer its great purposes: the governor and judges united must possess more firmness and strength, more wisdom and information, than either alone, and also more of the confidence of the people; and as to the balance among the departments, why should the executive alone hold the scales, and the judicial be left defenceless? I think the negative in New-York is found best in practice; we see it there frequently and wisely put upon the measures of the two branches; whereas in Massachusetts it is hardly ever exercised, and the governor, I believe, has often permitted laws to pass to which he had substantial objections, but did not make them; he, however, it is to be observed, is annually elected.

THE FEDERAL FARMER.

18 JANUARY 1788

LETTER XV

The Federal Farmer describes the proposed federal judiciary, praising life tenure for judges during good behavior but arguing that there should be some provision for salary adjustments. More worrisome to the Federal Farmer is the Constitution's failure to protect the right to jury trials in civil cases. Essays in The Federalist *of particular relevance: 78-84.*

DEAR SIR,

BEFORE I proceed to examine particularly the powers vested, or which ought to be, vested in each branch of the proposed government, I shall briefly examine the organization of the remaining branch, the judicial, referring the particular examining of its powers to some future letters.

In forming this branch, our objects are—a fair and open, a wise and impartial interpretation of the laws—a prompt and impartial administration of justice, between the public and individuals, and between man and man. I believe, there is no feature in a free government more difficult to be well formed than this, especially in an extensive country, where the courts must be numerous, or the citizens travel to obtain justice.

The confederation impowers congress to institute judicial courts in four cases. 1. For settling disputes between individual states. 2. For determining, finally, appeals in all cases of captures. 3. For the trial of piracies and felonies committed on the high seas: And, 4. For the administration of martial law in the army and navy. The state courts in all other cases possess the judicial powers, in all questions arising on the laws of nations, of the union, and of the states individually—nor does congress appear to have any controul over state courts, judges or officers. The business of the judicial department is, properly speaking, judicial in part, in part executive, done by judges and juries, by certain recording and executive officers, as clerks, sheriffs, &c. they are all properly limbs, or parts, of the judicial courts, and have it in charge, faithfully to decide upon, and execute the laws, in judicial cases, between the public and individuals, between man and man. The recording and executive officers, in this department, may well enough be formed by legislative acts, from time to time: but the offices, the situation, the powers and duties of judges and juries, are too important, as they respect the political system, as well as the administration of justice, not to be fixed on general principles by the constitution. It is true, the laws are made by the legislature; but the judges and juries, in their interpretations, and in directing the execution of them, have a very extensive influence for preserving or destroying liberty, and for changing the nature of the government. It is an observation of an approved writer, that judicial power is of such a nature, that when we have ascertained and fixed its limits, with all the caution and precision we can, it will yet be formidable, somewhat arbitrary and despotic—that is, after all our cares, we must leave a vast deal to the discretion and interpretation—to the wisdom, integrity, and politics of the judges—These men, such is the state even of the best laws, may do wrong, perhaps, in a thousand cases, sometimes with, and sometimes without design, yet it may be impracticable to convict them of misconduct. These considerations shew, how cautious a free people ought to be in forming this, as well as the other branches of their government, especially when connected with other considerations equally deserving of notice and attention. When the legislature makes a bad law, or the first executive magistrates usurps upon the rights of the people, they discover the evil much sooner, than the abuses of power in the judicial department; the proceedings of which are far more intricate, complex, and out of their immediate view. A bad law immediately excites a general alarm; a bad judicial determination, though not less pernicious in its consequences, is immediately felt, probably, by a single individual only, and noticed only by his neighbours, and a few spectators in the court. In this country, we have been always jealous of the legislature, and especially the executive; but not always of the judiciary: but very few men attentively consider the essential parts of it, and its proceedings, as they tend to support or to destroy free government: only a few professional men are in a situation properly to do this; and it is often alledged, that instances have not frequently occurred, in which they have been found very alert watchmen in the cause of liberty, or in the cause of democratic republics. Add to these considerations, that particular circumstances exist at this time to increase our inattention to limiting properly the judicial powers, we may fairly conclude, we are more in danger of sowing the seeds of arbitrary government in this department than in any other. In the unsettled state of things in this country, for several years past, it has been thought, that our popular legislatures have, sometimes, departed from the line of strict justice, while the law courts have shewn a disposition more punctually to keep to it. We are not sufficiently attentive to the circumstances, that the measures of popular legislatures naturally settle down in time, and gradually approach a mild and just medium; while the rigid systems of the law courts naturally become more severe and arbitrary, if not carefully tempered and guarded by the constitution, and by laws, from time to time. It is true, much has been written and said about some of these courts lately, in some of the states; but all has been about their fees, &c. and but very little to the purposes, as to their influence upon the freedom of the government.

By art. 3. sect. 1. the judicial power of the United States shall be vested in one supreme court, and in such inferior courts, as congress may, from time to time, ordain and establish—the judges of them to hold their offices during good behaviour, and to receive, at stated times, a compensation for their services, which shall not be diminished during their continuance in office; but which, I conceive, may be increased. By the same art. sect. 2. the supreme court shall have original jurisdiction, "in all cases affecting ambassadors, and other public ministers, and consuls, and those in which a state shall be a party, and appellate jurisdiction, *both as to law and fact*, in all other federal causes, with such exceptions, and under such regulations, as the congress shall make." By the same section, the judicial power shall extend in law and equity to all the federal cases therein enumerated. By the same section the jury trial, in criminal causes, except in cases of impeachment, is established; but not in civil causes, and the whole state may be considered as the vicinage in cases of crimes. These clauses present to view the constitutional features of the federal judiciary: this has been called a monster by some of the opponents, and some, even of the able advocates, have confessed they do not comprehend it. For myself, I confess, I see some good things in it, and some very extraordinary ones. "There shall be one supreme court." There ought in every government to be one court, in which all great questions in law shall finally meet and be determined: in Great-Britain, this is the house of lords, aided by all the superior judges; in Massachusetts, it is, at present, the supreme judicial court, consisting of five judges; in New-York, by the constitution, it is a court consisting of the president of the senate, the senators, chancellor and judges of the supreme court; and in the United States the federal supreme court, or this court in the last resort, may, by the legislature, be made to consist of three, five, fifty, or any other number of judges. The inferior federal courts are left by the constitution to be instituted and regulated altogether as the legislature shall judge best; and it is well provided, that the judges shall hold their offices during good behaviour. I shall not object to the line drawn between the original and appellate jurisdiction of the supreme court; though should we for safety, &c. be obliged to form a numerous supreme court, and place in it a considerable number of respectable characters, it will be found inconvenient for such a court, originally, to try all the causes affecting ambassadors, consuls, &c. Appeals may be carried up to the supreme court, under such regulations as congress shall make. Thus far the legislature does not appear to be limited to improper rules or principles in instituting judicial courts: indeed the legislature will have full power to form and arrange judicial courts in the federal cases enumerated, at pleasure, with these eight exceptions only. 1. There can be but one supreme federal judicial court. 2. This must have jurisdiction as to law and fact in the appellate causes. 3. Original jurisdiction, when foreign ministers and the states are concerned. 4. The judges of the judicial courts must continue in office during good behaviour—and, 5. Their salaries cannot be diminished while in office. 6. There must be a jury trial in criminal causes. 7.

The trial of crimes must be in the state where committed—and, 8. There must be two witnesses to convict of treason.

In all other respects Congress may organize the judicial department according to their discretion; the importance of this power, among others proposed by the legislature (perhaps necessarily) I shall consider hereafter. Though there must, by the constitution, be but one judicial court, in which all the rays of judicial powers as to law, equity, and fact, in the cases enumerated must meet; yet this may be made by the legislature, a special court, consisting of any number of respectable characters or officers, the federal legislators excepted, to superintend the judicial department, to try the few causes in which foreign ministers and the states may be concerned, and to correct errors, as to law and fact, in certain important causes on appeals. Next below this judicial head, there may be several courts, such as are usually called superior courts, as a court of chancery, a court of criminal jurisdiction, a court of civil jurisdiction, a court of admiralty jurisdiction, a court of exchequer, &c, giving an appeal from these respectively to the supreme judicial court. These superior courts may be considered as so many points to which appeals may be brought up, from the various inferior courts, in the several branches of judicial causes. In all these superior and inferior courts, the trial by jury may be established in all cases, and the law and equity properly separated. In this organization, only a few very important causes, probably, would be carried up to the supreme court.—The superior courts would, finally, settle almost all causes. This organization, so far as it would respect questions of law, inferior, superior, and a special supreme court, would resemble that of New-York in a considerable degree, and those of several other states. This, I imagine, we must adopt, or else the Massachusetts plan; that is, a number of inferior courts, and one superior or supreme court, consisting of three, or five, or seven judges, in which one supreme court all the business shall be immediately collected from the inferior ones. The decision of the inferior courts, on either plan, probably will not much be relied on; and on the latter plan, there must be a prodigious accumulation of powers and business in all cases touching law, equity and facts, and all kinds of causes in a few hands, for whose errors of ignorance or design, there will be no possible remedy. As the legislature may adopt either of these, or any other plan, I shall not dwell longer on this subject.

In examining the federal judiciary, there appears to be some things very extraordinary and very peculiar. The judges or their friends may seize every opportunity to raise the judges salaries; but by the constitution they cannot be diminished. I am sensible how important it is that judges shall always have adequate and certain support; I am against their depending upon annual or periodical grants, because these may be withheld, or rendered too small by the dissent or narrowness of any one branch of the legislature; but there is a material distinction between periodical grants, and salaries held under permanent and standing laws: the former at stated periods cease, and must be renewed by the consent of all and every part of the legislature, the latter continue of course, and never will cease or be lowered, unless all parts of the legislature agree to do it. A man has as permanent an interest in his salary fixed by a standing law, so long as he may remain in office, as in any property he may possess; for the laws regulating the tenure of all property, are always liable to be altered by the legislature. The same judge may frequently be in office thirty or forty years; there may often be times, as in cases of war, or very high prices, when his salary may reasonably be increased one half or more; in a few years money may become scarce again, and prices fall, and his salary, with equal reason and propriety be decreased and lowered: not to suffer this to be done by consent of all the branches of the legislature, is, I believe, quite a novelty in the affairs of government. It is true, by a very force and unnatural construction, the constitution of Massachusetts, by the governor and minority in the legislature, was made to speak this kind of language. Another circumstance ought to be considered; the mines which have been discovered are gradually exhausted, and the precious metals are continually wasting: hence the probability is, that money, the nominal representative of property, will gradually grow scarcer hereafter, and afford just reasons for gradually lowering salaries. The value of money depends altogether upon the quantity of it in circulation, which may be also decreased, as well as encreased, from a great variety of causes.

The supreme court, in cases of appeals, shall have jurisdiction both as to law and fact: that is, in all civil causes carried up the supreme court by appeals, the court, or judges, shall try the fact and decide the law. Here an essential principle of the civil law is established, and the most noble and important principle of the common law exploded. To dwell a few minutes on this material point: the supreme court shall have jurisdiction both as to law and fact. What is meant by court? Is the jury included in the term, or is it not? I conceive it is not included: and so the members of convention, I am very sure, understand it. Court, or curia, was a term well understood long before juries existed; the people, and the best writers, in countries where there are no juries, uniformly use the word court, and can only mean by it the judge or judges who determine causes: also, in countries where there are juries we express ourselves in the same manner; we speak of the court of probate, court of chancery, justices court, alderman's court, &c. in which there is no jury. In our supreme courts, common pleas, &c. in which there are jury trials, we uniformly speak of the court and jury, and consider them as distinct. Were it necessary I might site a multitude of cases from law books to confirm, beyond controversy, this position, that the jury is not included, or a part of the court.

But the supreme court is to have jurisdiction as to law and fact, under such regulations as congress shall make. I confess it is impossible to say how far congress may, with propriety, extend their regulations in this respect. I conceive, however, they cannot by any reasonable construction go so far as to admit the jury, on true common law principles, to try the fact, and give a general verdict. I have repeatedly examined this article: I think the meaning of it is, that the judges in all final questions, as to property and damages, shall have complete jurisdiction, to consider the whole cause, to examine the facts, and on a general view of them, and on principles of equity, as well as law, to give judgment.

As the trial by jury is provided for in criminal causes, I shall confine my observations to civil causes—and in these, I hold it is the

established right of the jury by the common law, and the fundamental laws of this country, to give a general verdict in all cases
when they chuse to do it, to decide both as to law and fact, whenever blended together in the issue put to them. Their right to determine as to facts will not be disputed, and their right to give a
general verdict has never been disputed, except by a few judges
and lawyers, governed by despotic principles. Coke, Hale, Holt,
Blackstone, De Lome, and almost every other legal or political
writer, who has written on the subject, has uniformly asserted this
essential and important right of the jury. Juries in Great-Britain
and America have universally practised accordingly. Even Mans-
field, with all his wishes about him, dare not directly avow the contrary. What fully confirms this point is, that there is no instance to
be found, where a jury was ever punished for finding a general verdict, when a special one might, with propriety, have been found. The
jury trial, especially politically considered, is by far the most important feature in the judicial department in a free country, and the
right in question is far the most valuable part, and the last that
ought to be yielded, of this trial. Juries are constantly and frequently drawn from the body of the people, and freemen of the
country; and by holding the jury's right to return a general verdict
in all cases sacred, we secure to the people at large, their just and
rightful controul in the judicial department. If the conduct of judges
shall be severe and arbitrary, and tend to subvert the laws, and
change the forms of government, the jury may check them, by
deciding against their opinions and determinations, in similar cases.
It is true, the freemen of a country are not always minutely skilled
in the laws, but they have common sense in its purity, which seldom
or never errs in making and applying laws to the condition of the
people, or in determining judicial causes, when stated to them by
the parties. The body of the people, principally, bear the burdens
of the community; they of right ought to have a controul in its
important concerns, both in making and executing the laws, otherwise they may, in a short time, be ruined. Nor is it merely this controul alone we are to attend to: the jury trial brings with it an open
and public discussion of all causes, and excludes secret and arbitrary proceedings. This, and the democratic branch in the legisla-

ture, as was formerly observed, are the means by which the people are let into the knowledge of public affairs—are enabled to stand as the guardians of each others rights, and to restrain, by regular and legal measures, those who otherwise might infringe upon them. I am not unsupported in my opinion of the value of the trial by jury; not only British and American writers, but De Lome, and the most approved foreign writers, hold it to be the most valuable part of the British constitution, and indisputably the best mode of trial ever invented.

It was merely by the intrigues of the popish clergy, and of the Norman lawyers, that this mode of trial was not used in maritime, ecclesiastical, and military courts, and the civil law proceedings were introduced; and, I believe, it is more from custom and prejudice, than for any substantial reasons, that we do not in all the states establish the jury in our maritime as well as other courts.

In the civil law process the trial by jury is unknown; the consequence is, that a few judges and dependant officers, possess all the power in the judicial department. Instead of the open fair proceedings of the common law, where witnesses are examined in open court, and may be cross examined by the parties concerned—where council is allowed, &c. we see in the civil law process judges alone, who always, long previous to the trial, are known and often corrupted by ministerial influence, or by parties. Judges once influenced, soon become inclined to yield to temptations, and to decree for him who will pay the most for their partiality. It is, therefore, we find in the Roman, and almost all governments, where judges alone possess the judicial powers and try all cases, that bribery has prevailed. This, as well as the forms of the courts, naturally lead to secret and arbitrary proceedings—to taking evidence secretly—exparte, &c. to perplexing the cause—and to hasty decisions:—but, as to jurors, it is quite impracticable to bribe or influence them by any corrupt means; not only because they are untaught in such affairs, and possess the honest characters of the common freemen of a country; but because it is not, generally, known till the hour the cause comes on for trial, what persons are to form the jury.

But it is said, that no words could be found by which the states could agree to establish the jury-trial in civil causes. I can hardly believe men to be serious, who make observations to this effect. The states have all derived judicial proceedings principally from one source, the British system; from the same common source the American lawyers have almost universally drawn their legal information. All the states have agreed to establish the trial by jury, in civil as well as in criminal causes. The several states, in congress, found no difficulty in establishing it in the Western Territory, in the ordinance passed in July 1787. We find, that the several states in congress, in establishing government in that territory, agreed, that the inhabitants of it, should always be entitled to the benefit of the trial by jury. Thus, in a few words, the jury trial is established in its full extent; and the convention with as much ease, have established the jury trial in criminal cases. In making a constitution, we are substantially to fix principles.—If in one state, damages on default are assessed by a jury, and in another by the judges—if in one state jurors are drawn out of a box, and in another not—if there be other trifling variations, they can be of no importance in the great question. Further, when we examine the particular practices of the states, in little matters in judicial proceedings, I believe we shall find they differ near as much in criminal processes as in civil ones. Another thing worthy of notice in this place—the convention have used the word equity, and agreed to establish a chancery jurisdiction; about the meaning and extent of which, we all know, the several states disagree much more than about jury trials—in adopting the latter, they have very generally pursued the British plan; but as to the former, we see the states have varied, as their fears and opinions dictated.

By the common law, in Great Britain and America, there is no appeal from the verdict of the jury, as to facts, to any judges whatever—the jurisdiction of the jury is complete and final in this; and only errors in law are carried up to the house of lords, the special supreme court in Great Britain; or to the special supreme courts in Connecticut, New-York, New-Jersey, &c. Thus the juries are left masters as to facts: but, by the proposed constitution, directly the opposite principles is established. An appeal will lay in all appellate causes from the verdict of the jury, even as to mere facts, to the judges of the supreme court. Thus, in effect, we establish the civil law in this point; for if the jurisdiction of the jury be not final, as to facts, it is of little or no importance.

By art. 3. sect. 2. "the judicial power shall extend to all cases in law and equity, arising under this constitution, the laws of the United States," &c. What is here meant by equity? what is equity in a case arising under the constitution? possibly the clause might have the same meaning, were the words "in law and equity," omitted. Cases in law must differ widely from cases in law and equity. At first view, by thus joining the word equity with the word law, if we mean any thing, we seem to mean to give the judge a discretionary power. The word equity, in Great Britain, has in time acquired a precise meaning—chancery proceedings there are now reduced to system—but this is not the case in the United States. In New-England, the judicial courts have no powers in cases in equity, except those dealt out to them by the legislature, in certain limited portions, by legislative acts. In New-York, Maryland, Virginia, and South Carolina, powers to decide, in cases of equity, are vested in judges distinct from those who decide in matters of law: and the states generally seem to have carefully avoided giving unlimitedly, to the same judges, powers to decide in cases in law and equity. Perhaps, the clause would have the same meaning were the words, "this constitution," omitted: there is in it either a careless complex misuse of words, in themselves of extensive signification, or there is some meaning not easy to be comprehended. Suppose a case arising under the constitution—suppose the question judicially moved, whether, by the constitution, congress can suppress a state tax laid on polls, lands, or as an excise duty, which may be supposed to interfere with a federal tax. By the letter of the constitution, congress will appear to have no power to do it: but then the judges may decide the question on principles of equity as well as law. Now, omitting the words, "in law and equity," they may decide according to the spirit and true meaning of the constitution, as collected from what must appear to have been the intentions of the people when they made it. Therefore, it would seem, that if these words mean any thing, they must have a further meaning: yet I will not suppose it intended to lodge an arbitrary power or discretion in the judges, to decide as their conscience, their opinions, their caprice, or their politics might dictate. Without dwelling on this obscure clause, I will leave it to the examination of others.

THE FEDERAL FARMER.

20 JANUARY 1788

LETTER XVI

The Federal Farmer calls for a declaration of rights and a declaration of powers granted to the federal government under the Constitution. In combination these declarations would ensure that state bills of rights would continue to protect individuals and communities, and that the federal government would not exceed those powers specifically granted to it. Essays in The Federalist *of particular relevance: 44, 84.*

DEAR SIR,

HAVING gone through with the organization of the government, I shall now proceed to examine more particularly those clauses which respect its powers. I shall begin with those articles and stipulations which are necessary for accurately ascertaining the extent of powers, and what is given, and for guarding, limiting, and restraining them in their exercise. We often find, these articles and stipulations placed in bills of rights; but they may as well be incorporated in the body of the constitution, as selected and placed by themselves. The constitution, or whole social compact, is but one instrument, no more or less, than a certain number of articles or stipulations agreed to by the people, whether it consists of articles, sections, chapters, bills of rights, or parts of any other denomination, cannot be material. Many needless observations, and idle distinctions, in my opinion, have been made respecting a bill of rights. On the one hand, it seems to be considered as a necessary distinct limb of the constitution, and as containing a certain number of very valuable articles, which are applicable to all societies: and, on the other, as useless, especially in a federal government, possessing only enumerated power—may, dangerous, as individual rights are numerous, and not easy to be enumerated in a bill of rights, and from articles, or stipulations, securing some of them, it may be inferred, that others not mentioned are surrendered. There appears to me to be general indefinite propositions without much meaning—and the man who first advanced those of the latter description, in the present case, signed the federal constitution, which directly contradicts him. The supreme power is undoubtedly in the people, and it is a principle well established in my mind, that they reserve all powers not expressly delegated by them to those who govern; this is as true in forming a state as in forming a federal government. There is no possible distinction but this founded merely in the different modes of proceeding which take place in some cases. In forming a state constitution, under which to manage not only the great but the little concerns of a community: the powers to be possessed by the government are often too numerous to be enumerated; the people to adopt the shortest way often give general powers, indeed all powers, to the government, in some general words, and then, by a particular enumeration, take back, or rather say they however reserve certain rights as sacred, and which no laws shall be made to violate: hence the idea that all powers are given which are not reserved: but in forming a federal constitution, which *ex vi termine,* supposes state governments existing, and which is only to manage a few great national concerns, we often find it easier to enumerate particularly the powers to be delegated to the federal head, than to enumerate particularly the individual rights to be reserved; and the principle will operate in its full force, when we carefully adhere to it. When we particularly enumerate the powers given, we ought either carefully to enumerate the rights reserved, or be totally silent about them; we must either particularly enumerate both, or else suppose the particular enumeration of the powers given adequately draws the line between them and the rights reserved, particularly to enumerate the former and not the latter, I think most advisable: however, as men appear generally to have their doubts about these silent reservations, we might advantageously enumerate the powers given, and then in general words, according to the mode adopted in the 2d art. of the confederation, declare all powers, rights and privileges, are reserved, which are not explicitly and expressly given up. People, and very wisely too, like to be express and explicit about their essential rights, and not to be forced to claim them on the precarious and unascertained tenure of inferences and general principles, knowing that in any controversy between them and their rulers, concerning those rights, disputes may be endless, and nothing certain:—But admitting, on the general principle, that all rights are reserved of course, which are not expressly surrendered, the people could with sufficient certainty assert their rights on all occasions, and establish them with ease, still there are infinite advantages in particularly enumerating many of the most essential rights reserved in all cases; and as to the less important ones, we may declare in general terms, that all not expressly surrendered are reserved. We do not by declarations change the nature of things, or create new truths, but we give existence, or at least establish in the minds of the people truths and principles which they might never otherwise have thought of, or soon forgot. If a nation means its systems, religious or political, shall have duration, it ought to recognize the leading principles of them in the front page of every family book. What is the usefulness of a truth in theory, unless it exists constantly in the minds of the people, and has their assent:— we discern certain rights, as the freedom of the press, and the trial by jury, &c. which the people of England and of America of course believe to be sacred, and essential to their political happiness, and this belief in them is the result of ideas at first suggested to them by a few able men, and of subsequent experience; while the people of some other countries hear these rights mentioned with the utmost indifference; they think the privilege of existing at the will of a despot much preferable to them. Why this difference amongst beings every way formed alike. The reason of the difference is obvious—it is the effect of education, a series of notions impressed upon the minds of the people by examples, precepts and declarations. When the people of England got together, at the time they formed Magna Charta, they did not consider it sufficient, that they were indisputably entitled to certain natural and unalienable rights, not

depending on silent titles, they, by a declaratory act, expressly recognized them, and explicitly declared to all the world, that they
were entitled to enjoy those rights; they made an instrument in
writing, and enumerated those they then thought essential, or in
danger, and this wise men saw was not sufficient; and therefore,
that the people might not forget these rights, and gradually become
prepared for arbitrary government, their discerning and honest
leaders caused this instrument to be confirmed near forty times,
and to be read twice a year in public places, not that it would lose its
validity without such confirmations, but to fix the contents of it in
the minds of the people, as they successively come upon the
stage.—Men, in some countries do not remain free, merely because
they are entitled to natural and unalienable rights; men in all countries are entitled to them, not because their ancestors once got
together and enumerated them on paper, but because, by repeated
negociations and declarations, all parties are brought to realize
them, and of course to believe them to be sacred. Were it necessary,
I might shew the wisdom of our past conduct, as a people, in not
merely comforting ourselves that we were entitled to freedom, but
in constantly keeping in view, in addresses bills of rights, in newspapers, &c. the particular principles on which our freedom must
always depend.

It is not merely in this point of view, that I urge the engrafting in
the constitution additional declaratory articles. The distinction, in
itself just, that all powers not given are reserved, is in effect
destroyed by this very constitution, as I shall particularly demonstrate—and even independent of this, the people, by adopting the
constitution, give many general undefined powers to congress, in
the constitutional exercise of which, the rights in question may be
effected. Gentlemen who oppose a federal bill of rights, or further
declaratory articles, seem to view the subject in a very narrow
imperfect manner. These have for their objects, not only the enumeration of the rights reserved, but principally to explain the general powers delegated in certain material points, and to restrain
those who exercise them by fixed known boundaries. Many expla-
nations and restrictions necessary and useful, would be much less
so, were the people at large all well and fully acquainted with the

principles and affairs of government. There appears to be in the constitution, a studied brevity, and it may also be probable, that several explanatory articles were omitted from a circumstance very common. What we have long and early understood ourselves in the common concerns of the community, we are apt to suppose is understood by others, and need not be expressed; and it is not unnatural or uncommon for the ablest men most frequently to make this mistake. To make declaratory articles unnecessary in an instrument of government, two circumstances must exist; the rights reserved must be indisputably so, and in their nature defined; the powers delegated to the government, must be precisely defined by the words that convey them, and clearly be of such extent and nature as that, by no reasonable construction, they can be made to invade the rights and prerogatives intended to be left in the people.

The first point urged, is, that all power is reserved not expressly given, that particular enumerated powers only are given, that all others are not given, but reserved, and that it is needless to attempt to restrain congress in the exercise of powers they possess not. This reasoning is logical, but of very little importance in the common affairs of men; but the constitution does not appear to respect it even in any view. To prove this, I might cite several clauses in it. I shall only remark on two or three. By article 1, section 9, "No title of nobility shall be granted by congress." Was this clause omitted, what power would congress have to make titles of nobility? in what part of the constitution would they find it? The answer must be, that congress would have no such power—that the people, by adopting the constitution, will not part with it. Why then by a negative clause, restrain congress from doing what it would have no power to do? This clause, then, must have no meaning, or imply, that were it omitted, congress would have the power in question, either upon the principle that some general words in the constitution may be so construed as to give it, or on the principle that congress possess the powers not expressly reserved. But this clause was in the confederation, and is said to be introduced into the constitution from very great caution. Even a cautionary provision implies a doubt, at least, that it is necessary; and if so in this case, clearly it is also alike necessary in all similar ones. The fact appears

to be, that the people in forming the confederation, and the convention, in this instance, acted, naturally, they did not leave the
point to be settled by general principles and logical inferences; but
they settle the point in a few words, and all who read them at once
understand them.

The trial by jury in criminal as well as in civil causes, has long
been considered as one of our fundamental rights, and has been
repeatedly recognized and confirmed by most of the state conventions. But the constitution expressly establishes this trial in criminal, and wholly omits it in civil causes. The jury trial in criminal
causes, and the benefit of the writ of habeas corpus, are already as
effectually established as any of the fundamental or essential rights
of the people in the United States. This being the case, why in
adopting a federal constitution do we now establish these, and omit
all others, or all others, at least with a few exceptions, such as again
agreeing there shall be no ex post facto laws, no titles of nobility,
&c. We must consider this constitution, when adopted, as the
supreme act of the people, and in construing it hereafter, we and
our posterity must strictly adhere to the letter and spirit of it, and
in no instance depart from them: in construing the federal constitution, it will be not only impracticable, but improper to refer to the
state constitutions. They are entirely distinct instruments and inferior acts: besides, by the people's now establishing certain fundamental rights, it is strongly implied, that they are of opinion, that
they would not otherwise be secured as a part of the federal system, or be regarded in the federal administration as fundamental.
Further, these same rights, being established by the state constitutions, and secured to the people, our recognizing them now,
implies, that the people thought them insecure by the state establishments, and extinguished or put afloat by the new arrangement
of the social system, unless re-established.—Further, the people,
thus establishing some few rights, and remaining totally silent
about others similarly circumstanced, the implication indubitably
is, that they mean to relinquish the latter or at least feel indifferent about them. Rights, therefore, inferred from general principles of reason, being precarious and hardly ascertainable in the
common affairs of society, and the people, in forming a federal con-

stitution, explicitly shewing they conceive these rights to be thus circumstanced, and accordingly proceed to enumerate and establish some of them, the conclusion will be, that they have established all which they esteem valuable and sacred. On every principle, then, the people especially having began, ought to go through enumerating, and establish particularly all the rights of individuals, which can by any possibility come in question in making and executing federal laws. I have already observed upon the excellency and importance of the jury trial in civil as well as in criminal causes, instead of establishing it in criminal causes only; we ought to establish it generally;—instead of the clause of forty or fifty words relative to this subject, why not use the language that has always been used in this country, and say, "the people of the United States shall always be entitled to the trial by jury." This would shew the people still hold the right sacred, and enjoin it upon congress substantially to preserve the jury trial in all cases, according to the usage and custom of the country. I have observed before, that it is *the jury trial* we want; the little different appendages and modifications tacked to it in the different states, are no more than a drop in the ocean: the jury trial is a solid uniform feature in a free government; it is the substance we would save, not the little articles of form.

Security against expost facto laws, the trial by jury, and the benefits of the writ of habeas corpus, are but a part of those inestimable rights the people of the United States are entitled to, even in judicial proceedings, by the course of the common law. These may be secured in general words, as in New-York, the Western Territory, &c. by declaring the people of the United States shall always be entitled to judicial proceedings according to the course of the common law, as used and established in the said states. Perhaps it would be better to enumerate the particular essential rights the people are entitled to in these proceedings, as has been done in many of the states, and as has been done in England. In this case, the people may proceed to declare, that no man shall be held to answer to any offence, till the same be fully described to him; nor to furnish evidence against himself: that, except in the government of the army and navy, no person shall be tried for any offence, whereby he may incur loss of life, or an infamous punishment, until

he be first indicted by a grand jury: that every person shall have a
right to produce all proofs that may be favourable to him, and to
meet the witnesses against him face to face: that every person shall
be entitled to obtain right and justice freely and without delay: that
all persons shall have a right to be secure from all unreasonable
searches and seizures of their persons, houses, papers, or possessions; and that all warrants shall be deemed contrary to this right,
if the foundation of them be not previously supported by oath, and
there be not in them a special designation of persons or objects of
search, arrest, or seizure: and that no person shall be exiled or
molested in his person or effects, otherwise than by the judgment of
his peers, or according to the law of the land. A celebrated writer
observes upon this last article, that in itself it may be said to comprehend the whole end of political society. These rights are not necessarily reserved, they are established, or enjoyed but in few
countries: they are stipulated rights, almost peculiar to British and
American laws. In the execution of those laws, individuals, by long
custom, by magna charta, bills of rights &c. have become entitled to
them. A man, at first, by act of parliament, became entitled to the
benefits of the writ of habeas corpus—men are entitled to these
rights and benefits in the judicial proceedings of our state courts
generally: but it will by no means follow, that they will be entitled
to them in the federal courts, and have a right to assert them,
unless secured and established by the constitution or federal laws.
We certainly, in federal processes, might as well claim the benefits
of the writ of habeas corpus, as to claim trial by a jury—the right
to have council—to have witnesses face to face—to be secure
against unreasonable search warrants, &c. was the constitution
silent as to the whole of them:—but the establishment of the former, will evince that we could not claim them without it; and the
omission of the latter, implies they are relinquished, or deemed of
no importance. These are rights and benefits individuals acquire by
compact; they must claim them under compacts, or immemorial
usage—it is doubtful, at least, whether they can be claimed under
immemorial usage in this country; and it is, therefore, we generally claim them under compacts, as charters and constitutions.

The people by adopting the federal constitution, give congress general powers to institute a distinct and new judiciary, new courts, and to regulate all proceedings in them, under the eight limitations mentioned in a former letter; and the further one, that the benefits of the habeas corpus act shall be enjoyed by individuals. Thus general powers being given to institute courts, and regulate their proceedings, with no provision for securing the rights principally in question, may not congress so exercise those powers, and constitutionally too, as to destroy those rights? clearly, in my opinion, they are not in any degree secured. But, admitting the case is only doubtful, would it not be prudent and wise to secure them and remove all doubts, since all agree the people ought to enjoy these valuable rights, a very few men excepted, who seem to be rather of opinion that there is little or nothing in them? Were it necessary I might add many observations to shew their value and political importance.

The constitution will give congress general powers to raise and support armies. General powers carry with them incidental ones, and the means necessary to the end. In the exercise of these powers, is there any provision in the constitution to prevent the quartering of soldiers on the inhabitants? you will answer, there is not. This may sometimes be deemed a necessary measure in the support of armies; on what principle can the people claim the right to be exempt from this burden? they will urge, perhaps, the practice of the country, and the provisions made in some of the state constitutions—they will be answered, that their claim thus to be exempt is not founded in nature, but only in custom and opinion, or at best, in stipulations in some of the state constitutions, which are local, and inferior in their operation, and can have no controul over the general government—that they had adopted a federal constitution—had noticed several rights, but had been totally silent about this exemption—that they had given general powers relative to the subject, which, in their operation, regularly destroyed the claim. Though it is not to be presumed, that we are in any immediate danger from this quarter, yet it is fit and proper to establish, beyond dispute, those rights which are particularly valuable to individuals, and essential to the permanency and duration of free government. An excellent writer observes, that the English, always in possession of their freedom, are frequently unmindful of the value of it: we, at this period, do not seem to be so well off, having, in some instances abused ours; many of us are quite disposed to barter it away for what we call energy, coercion, and some other terms we use as vaguely as that of liberty—There is often as great a rage for change and novelty in politics, as in amusements and fashions.

All parties apparently agree, that the freedom of the press is a fundamental right, and ought not to be restrained by any taxes, duties, or in any manner whatever. Why should not the people, in adopting a federal constitution, declare this, even if there are only doubts about it. But, say the advocates, all powers not given are reserved:—true; but the great question is, are not powers given, in the excercise of which this right may be destroyed? The people's or the printers claim to a free press, is founded on the fundamental laws, that is, compacts, and state constitutions, made by the people. The people, who can annihilate or alter those constitutions, can annihilate or limit this right. This may be done by giving general powers, as well as by using particular words. No right claimed under a state constitution, will avail against a law of the union, made in pursuance of the federal constitution: therefore the question is, what laws will congress have a right to make by the constitution of the union, and particularly touching the press? By art. 1. sect. 8, congress will have power to lay and collect taxes, duties, imposts and excise. By this congress will clearly have power to lay and collect all kind of taxes whatever—taxes on houses, lands, polls, industry, merchandize, &c.—taxes on deeds, bonds, and all written instruments—on writs, pleas, and all judicial proceedings, on licences, naval officers papers, &c. on newspapers, advertisements, &c. and to require bonds of the naval officers, clerks, printers, &c. to account for the taxes that may become due on papers that go through their hands. Printing, like all other business, must cease when taxed beyond its profits; and it appears to me, that a power to tax the press at discretion, is a power to destroy or restrain the freedom of it. There may be other powers given, in the exercise of which this freedom may be effected; and certainly it is of too much importance to be left thus liable to be taxed, and constantly to constructions and inferences. A free press is the channel of communication as to mercantile and public affairs; by means of it the people in large countries ascertain each others sentiments; are enabled to unite, and become formidable to those rulers who adopt improper measures. Newspapers may sometimes be the vehicles of abuse, and of many things not true; but these are but small inconveniencies, in my mind, among many advantages. A celebrated writer, I have several times quoted, speaking in high terms of the English liberties, says, "lastly the key stone was put to the arch, by the final establishment of the freedom of the press." I shall not dwell longer upon the fundamental rights, to some of which I have attended in this letter, for the same reasons that these I have mentioned, ought to be expressly secured, left in the exercise of general powers given they may be invaded: it is pretty clear, that some other of less importance, or less in danger, might with propriety also be secured.

I shall now proceed to examine briefly the powers proposed to be vested in the several branches of the government, and especially the mode of laying and collecting internal taxes.

THE FEDERAL FARMER

23 JANUARY 1788

LETTER XVII

The Federal Farmer criticizes the proposed federal government's power to act on the people directly rather than through the states. By, for example, allowing the federal government to tax individuals rather than requisitioning money from the states, which would then tax the people, the Constitution will reduce the state governments' ability to check federal power. Other checks must be added to prevent tyranny. Essays in The Federalist *of particular relevance: 15-22.*

DEAR SIR,

I BELIEVE the people of the United States are full in the opinion, that a free and mild government can be preserved in their extensive territories, only under the substantial forms of a federal republic. As several of the ablest advocates for the system proposed, have acknowledged this (and I hope the confessions they have published will be preserved and remembered) I shall not take up time to establish this point. A question then arises, how far that system partakes of a federal republic.—I observed in a former letter, that it appears to be the first important step to a consolidation of the states; that its strong tendency is to that point.

But what do we mean by a federal republic? and what by a consolidated government? To erect a federal republic, we must first make a number of states on republican principles; each state with a government organized for the internal management of its affairs: The states, as such, must unite under a federal head, and delegate to it powers to make and execute laws in certain enumerated cases, under certain restrictions; this head may be a single assembly, like the present congress, or the Amphictionic council; or it may conflict of a legislature, with one or more branches; of an executive and of a judiciary. To form a consolidated, or one entire government, there must be no state, or local governments, but all things, persons and property, must be subject to the laws of one legislature alone; to one executive, and one judiciary. Each state government, as the government of New Jersey, &c is a consolidated, or one entire government as it respects the counties, towns, citizens and property within the limits of the state.—The state governments are the basis, the pillar on which the federal head is placed, and the whole together, when formed on elective principles, constitute a federal republic. A federal republic in itself supposes state or local governments to exist, as the body or props, on which the federal head rests, and that it cannot remain a moment after they cease. In erecting the federal government, and always in its councils, each state must be known as a sovereign body; but in erecting this government, I conceive, the legislature of the state, by the expressed or implied assent of the people, or the people of the state, under the direction of the government of it, may accede to the federal compact: Nor do I conceive it to be necessarily a part of a confederacy of states, that each have an equal voice in the general councils. A confederated republic being organized, each state must retain powers for managing its internal police, and all delegate to the union power to manage general concerns: The quantity of power the union must possess is one thing, the mode of exercising the powers given, is quite a different consideration and it is the mode of exercising them, that makes one of the essential distinctions between one entire or consolidated government, and a federal republic; that is, however the government may be organized, if the laws of the union, in most important concerns, as in levying and collecting taxes, raising troops, &c. operate immediately upon the persons and property of individuals, and not on states, extend to organizing the militia, &c. the government, as to its administration, as to making and executing laws, is not federal, but consolidated. To illustrate my idea—the union makes a requisition, and assigns to each state its quota of men or monies wanted; each state, by its own laws and officers, in its own way, furnishes its quota: here the state governments stand between the union and individuals; the laws of the union operate only on states, as such, and federally: Here nothing can be done without the meetings of the state legislatures—but in the other case the union, though the state legislature should not meet for years together, proceeds immediately, by its own laws and officers, to levy and collect monies of individuals, to insist men, form armies, &c. here the laws of the union operate immediately on the body of the people, on persons and property; in the same manner the laws of one entire consolidated government operate.—These two modes are very distinct, and in their operation and consequences have directly opposite tendencies: The first makes the existence of the state governments indispensable, and throws all the detail business of levying and collecting the taxes, &c. into the hands of those governments, and into the hands, of course, of many thousand officers solely created by, and dependent on the state. The last entirely excludes the agency of the respective states, and throws the whole business of levying and collecting taxes, &c. into the hands of many thousand officers solely created by, and dependent upon the union, and makes the existence of the state government of no consequence in the case. It is true, congress in raising any given sum in direct taxes, must by the constitution, raise so much of it in one state, and so much in another, by a fixed rule, which most of the states some time since agreed to: But this does not effect the principle in question, it only secures each state against any arbitrary proportions. The federal mode is perfectly safe and eligible, founded in the true spirit of a confederated republic, there could be no possible exception to it, did we not find by experience, that the states will sometimes neglect to comply with the reasonable requisitions of the union. It being according to the fundamental principles of federal republics, to raise men and monies by requisitions, and for the states individually to organize and train the militia, I conceive there can be no reason whatever for departing from them, except this, that the states sometimes neglect to comply with reasonable requisitions, and that it is dangerous to attempt to compel a delinquent state by force, as it may often produce a war. We ought, therefore, to enquire attentively, how extensive the evils to be guarded against are, and cautiously limit the remedies to the extent of the evils. I am not about to defend the confederation, or to charge the proposed constitution with imperfections not in it, but we ought to examine facts, and strip them of the false colourings often given them by incautious observations, by unthinking or designing men. We ought to premise, that laws for raising men and monies, even in consolidated governments, are not often punctually complied with[.] Historians, except in extraordinary cases, but very seldom take notice of the detail collection of taxes; but these facts we have fully proved, and well attested; that the most energetic governments have relinquished taxes frequently, which were of many years standing. These facts amply prove, that taxes assessed, have remained many years uncollected. I agree there have been instances in the republics of Greece, Holland &c. in the course of several centuries, of states neglecting to pay their quotas of requisitions but it is a circumstance certainly deserving of attention, whether these nations which have depended on requisitions principally for their defence, have not raised men and monies nearly as punctually as entire governments, which have taxed directly; whether we have not found the latter as often distressed for the want of troops and monies as the former. It has been said that the Amphictionic council and the Germanic head, have not possessed sufficient powers to controul the members of the republic in a proper manner. Is this, if true, to be imputed to requisitions? Is it not principally to be imputed to the unequal powers of those members, connected with this important circumstance, that each member possessed power to league itself with foreign powers, and powerful neighbours, without the consent of the head. After all, has not the Germanic body a government as good as its neighbours in general? and did not the Grecian republic remain united several centuries, and form the theatre of human greatness? No government in Europe has commanded monies more plentifully than the government of Holland. As to the United States, the separate states lay taxes directly, and the union calls for taxes by way of requisitions; and is it a fact, that more monies are due in proportion on requisitions in the United States, than on the state taxes directly laid?—It is but about ten years since congress begun to make requisitions, and in that time, the monies, &c. required, and the bounties given for men required of the states, have amounted, specie value, to about 36 millions dollars, about 24 millions of dollars of which have been actually paid; and a very considerable part of the 12 millions not paid, remains so not so much from the neglect of the states, as from the sudden changes in paper money, &c. which in a great measure rendered payments of no service, and which often induced the union indirectly to relinquish one demand, by making another in a different form. Before we totally condemn requisitions, we ought to consider what immense bounties the states gave, and what prodigious exertions they made in the war, in order to comply with the requisitions of congress; and if since the peace they have been delinquent, ought we not carefully to enquire, whether that delinquency is to be imputed solely to the nature of requisitions? ought it not in part to be imputed to two other causes? I mean first, an opinion, that has extensively prevailed, that the requisitions for domestic interest have not been founded on just principles; and secondly, the circumstance, that the government itself, by proposing imposts, &c. has departed virtually from the constitutional system; which proposed changes, like all changes proposed in government, produce an inattention and negligence in the execution of the government in being.

I am not for depending wholly on requisitions; but I mention these few facts to shew they are not so totally futile as many pretend. For the truth of many of these facts I appeal to the public records; and for the truth of the others, I appeal to many republican characters, who are best informed in the affairs of the United States. Since the peace, and till the convention reported, the wisest men in the United States generally supposed, that certain limited funds would answer the purposes of the union: and though the states are by no means in so good a condition as I wish they were, yet, I think, I may very safely affirm, they are in a better condition than they would be had congress always possessed the powers of taxation now contended for. The fact is admitted, that our federal government does not possess sufficient powers to give life and vigor to the political system; and that we experience disappointments, and several inconveniencies; but we ought carefully to distinguish those which are merely the consequences of a severe and tedious war, from those which arise from defects in the federal system. There has been an entire revolution in the United States within thirteen years, and the least we can compute the waste of labour and property at, during that period, by the war, is three hundred million of dollars. Our people are like a man just recovering from a severe fit of sickness. It was the war that disturbed the course of commerce, introduced floods of paper money, the stagnation of credit, and threw many valuable men out of steady business. From these sources our greatest evils arise; men of knowledge and reflection must perceive it;—but then, have we not done more in three or four years past, in repairing the injuries of the war, by repairing houses and estates, restoring industry, frugality, the fisheries, manufactures, &c. and thereby laying the foundation of good government, and of individual and political happiness, than any people ever did in a like time; we must judge from a view of the country and facts, and not from foreign newspapers, or our own, which are printed chiefly in the commercial towns, where imprudent living, imprudent importations, and many unexpected disappointments, have produced a despondency, and a disposition to view every thing on the dark side. Some of the evils we feel, all will agree, ought to be imputed to the defective administration of the governments. From these and various considerations, I am very clearly of opinion, that the evils we sustain, merely on account of the defects of the confederation, are but as a feather in the balance against a mountain, compared with those which would, infallibly, be the result of the loss of general liberty, and that happiness men enjoy under a frugal, free, and mild government.

Heretofore we do not seem to have seen danger any where, but in giving power to congress, and now no where but in congress wanting powers; and, without examining the extent of the evils to be remedied, by one step, we are for giving up to congress almost all powers of any importance without limitation. The defects of the confederation are extravagantly magnified, and every species of pain we feel imputed to them: and hence it is inferred, there must be a total change of the principles, as well as forms of government: and in the main point, touching the federal powers we rest all on a logical inference, totally inconsistent with experience and sound political reasoning.

It is said, that as the federal head must make peace and war, and provide for the common defence, it ought to possess all powers necessary to that end: that powers unlimited, as to the purse and sword, to raise men and monies, and form the militia, are necessary to that end; and, therefore, the federal head ought to possess them. This reasoning is far more specious than solid: it is necessary that these powers so exist in the body politic, as to be called into exercise whenever necessary for the public safety; but it is by no means true, that the man, or congress of men, whose duty it more immediately is to provide for the common defence, ought to possess them without limitation. But clear it is, that if such men, or congress, be not in a situation to hold them without danger to liberty, he or they ought not to possess them. It has long been thought to be a well founded position, that the purse and sword ought not to be placed in the same hands in a free government. Our wise ancestors have carefully separated them—placed the sword in the hands of their king, even under considerable limitations, and the purse in the hands of the commons alone: yet the king makes peace and war, and it is his duty to provide for the common defence of

the nation. This authority at least goes thus far—that a nation, well
versed in the science of government, does not conceive it to be necessary or expedient for the man entrusted with the common
defence and general tranquility, to possess unlimitedly the powers
in question, or even in any considerable degree. Could he, whose
duty it is to defend the public, possess in himself independently, all
the means of doing it consistent with the public good, it might be
convenient: but the people of England know that their liberties
and happiness would be in infinitely greater danger from the king's
unlimited possession of these powers, than from all external enemies and internal commotions to which they might be exposed:
therefore, though they have made it his duty to guard the empire,
yet they have wisely placed in other hands, the hands of their representatives, the power to deal out and controul the means. In Holland their high mightinesses must provide for the common defence,
but for the means they depend, in a considerable degree, upon requisitions made on the state or local assemblies. Reason and facts
evince that however convenient it might be for an executive magistrate, or federal head, more immediately charged with the
national defence and safety, solely, directly, and independently to
possess all the means; yet such magistrate, or head, never ought to
possess them, if thereby the public liberties shall be endangered.
The powers in question never have been, by nations wise and free,
deposited, nor can they ever be, with safety, any where, but in the
principal members of the national system;—where these form one
entire government, as in Great-Britain, they are separated and
lodged in the principal members of it. But in a federal republic,
there is quite a different organization; the people form this kind of
government, generally, because their territories are too extensive
to admit of their assembling in one legislature, or of executing the
laws on free principles under one entire government. They convene
in their local assemblies, for local purposes, and for managing their
internal concerns, and unite their states under a federal head for
general purposes. It is the essential characteristic of a confederated
republic, that this head be dependant on, and kept within limited
bounds by, the local governments; and it is because, in these alone,
in fact, the people can be substantially assembled or represented. It

is, therefore, we very universally see, in this kind of government, the congressional powers placed in a few hands, and accordingly limited, and specifically enumerated: and the local assemblies strong and well guarded, and composed of numerous members. Wise men will always place the controuling power where the people are substantially collected by their representatives. By the proposed system, the federal head will possess, without limitation, almost every species of power that can, in its exercise, tend to change the government, or to endanger liberty; while in it, I think it has been fully shewn, the people will have but the shadow of representation, and but the shadow of security for their rights and liberties. In a confederated republic, the division of representation, &c. in its nature, requires a correspondent division and deposit of powers relative to taxes and military concerns: and I think the plan offered stands quite alone, in confounding the principles of governments in themselves totally distinct. I wish not to exculpate the states for their improper neglects in not paying their quotas of requisitions; but, in applying the remedy, we must be governed by reason and facts. It will not be denied, that the people have a right to change the government when the majority chuse it, if not restrained by some existing compact—that they have a right to displace their rulers, and consequently to determine when their measures are reasonable or not—and that they have a right, at any time, to put a stop to those measures they may deem prejudicial to them, by such forms and negatives as they may see fit to provide. From all these, and many other well founded considerations, I need not mention, a question arises, what powers shall there be delegated to the federal head, to insure safety, as well as energy, in the government? I think there is a safe and proper medium pointed out by experience, by reason, and facts. When we have organized the government, we ought to give power to the union, so far only as experience and present circumstances shall direct, with a reasonable regard to time to come. Should future circumstances, contrary to our expectations, require that further powers be transferred to the union, we can do it far more easily than get back those we may now imprudently give. The system proposed is untried: candid advocates and opposers admit, that it is, in a degree, a mere experiment, and that its organization is weak and imperfect, surely then, the safe ground is cautiously to vest power in it, and when we are sure we have given enough for ordinary exigencies, to be extremely careful how we delegate powers, which, in common cases, must necessarily be useless or abused, and of very uncertain effect in uncommon ones.

By giving the union power to regulate commerce, and to levy and collect taxes by imposts, we give it an extensive authority, and permanent productive funds, I believe quite as adequate to the present demands of the union, as exises and direct taxes can be made to the present demands of the separate states. The state governments are now about four times as expensive as that of the union; and their several state debts added together, are nearly as large as that of the union—Our impost duties since the peace have been almost as productive as the other sources of taxation, and when under one general system of regulations, the probability is, that those duties will be very considerably increased: Indeed the representation proposed will hardly justify giving to congress unlimited powers to raise taxes by imposts, in addition to the other powers the union must necessarily have. It is said, that if congress possess only authority to raise taxes by imposts, trade probably will be over-burdened with taxes, and the taxes of the union be found inadequate to any uncommon exigencies: To this we may observe, that trade generally finds its own level, and will naturally and necessarily heave off any undue burdens laid upon it: further, if congress alone possess the impost, and also unlimited power to raise monies by excises and direct taxes, there must be much more danger that two taxing powers, the union and states, will carry excises and direct taxes to an unreasonable extent, especially as these have not the natural boundaries taxes on trade have. However, it is not my object to propose to exclude congress from raising monies by internal taxes, as by duties, excises, and direct taxes but my opinion is, that congress, especially in its proposed organization, ought not to raise monies by internal taxes, except in strict conformity to the federal plan; that is, by the agency of the state governments in all cases, except where a state shall neglect, for an unreasonable time, to pay its quota of a requisition; and never where so many of the state legislatures as represent a majority of the people, shall formally determine an excise law or requisition is improper, in their next session after the same be laid before them. We ought always to recollect that the evil to be guarded against is found by our own experience, and the experience of others, to be mere neglect in the states to pay their quotas; and power in the union to levy and collect the neglecting states' quotas with interest, is fully adequate to the evil. By this federal plan, with this exception mentioned, we secure the means of collecting the taxes by the usual process of law, and avoid the evil of attempting to compel or coerce a state, and we avoid also a circumstance, which never yet could be, and I am fully confident never can be, admitted in a free federal republic; I mean a permanent and continued system of tax laws of the union, executed in the bowels of the states by many thousand officers, dependent as to the assessing and collecting federal taxes, solely upon the union. On every principle then, we ought to provide, that the union render an exact account of all monies raised by imposts and other taxes; and that whenever monies shall be wanted for the purposes of the union, beyond the proceeds of the impost duties, requisitions shall be made on the states for the monies so wanted; and that the power of laying and collecting shall never be exercised, except in cases where a state shall neglect, a given time, to pay its quota. This mode seems to be strongly pointed out by the reason of the case, and spirit of the government; and I believe, there is no instance to be found in a federal republic, where the congressional powers ever extended generally to collecting monies by direct taxes or excises. Creating all these restrictions, still the powers of the union in matters of taxation, will be too unlimited; further checks, in my mind, are indispensably necessary. Nor do I conceive, that as full a representation as is practicable in the federal government, will afford sufficient security: the strength of the government, and the confidence of the people, must be collected principally in the local assemblies; every part or branch of the federal head must be feeble, and unsafely trusted with large powers. A government possessed of more power than its constituent parts will justify, will not only probably abuse it, but be unequal to bear its own burden; it may as soon be destroyed by the pressure of power, as languish and perish for want of it.

There are two ways further of raising checks, and guarding against undue combinations and influence in a federal system. The first is, in levying taxes, raising and keeping up armies in building navies, in forming plans for the militia, and in appropriating monies for the support of the military, to require the attendance of a large proportion of the federal representatives, as two-thirds or three-fourths of them; and in passing laws, in these important cases, to require the consent of two-thirds or three-fourths of the members present. The second is, by requiring that certain important laws of the federal head, as a requisition or a law for raising monies by excise shall be laid before the state legislatures, and if disapproved of by a given number of them, say by as many of them as represent a majority of the people, the law shall have no effect. Whether it would be adviseable to adopt both, or either of these checks, I will not undertake to determine. We have seen them both exist in confederated republics. The first exists substantially in the confederation, and will exist in some measure in the plan proposed, as in chusing a president by the house, in expelling members; in the senate, in making treaties, and in deciding on impeachments, and in the whole in altering the constitution. The last exists in the United Netherlands, but in a much greater extent. The first is founded on this principle, that these important measures may, sometimes, be adopted by a bare quorum of members, perhaps, from a few states, and that a bare majority of the federal representatives may frequently be of the aristocracy, or some particular interests, connections, or parties in the community, and governed by motives, views, and inclinations not compatible with the general interest.—The last is founded on this principle, that the people will be substantially represented, only in their state or local assemblies; that their principal security must be found in them; and that, therefore, they ought to have ultimately a constitutional controul over such interesting measures.

I have often heard it observed, that our people are well informed, and will not submit to oppressive governments; that the state governments will be their ready advocates, and possess their confidence, mix with them, and enter into all their wants and feelings. This is all true; but of what avail will these circumstances be, if the state governments, thus allowed to be the guardians of the people, possess no kind of power by the forms of the social compact, to stop in their passage, the laws of congress injurious to the people. State governments must stand and see the law take place; they may complain and petition—so may individuals; the members of them, in extreme cases, may resist, on the principles of self-defence—so may the people and individuals.

It has been observed, that the people, in extensive territories, have more power, compared with that of their rulers, than in small states. Is not directly the opposite true? The people in a small state can unite and act in concert, and with vigour; but in large territories, the men who govern find it more easy to unite, while people cannot; while they cannot collect the opinions of each part, while they move to different points, and one part is often played off against the other.

It has been asserted, that the confederate head of a republic at best, is in general weak and dependent;—that the people will attach themselves to, and support their local governments, in all disputes with the union. Admit the fact: is it any way to remove the inconvenience by accumulating powers upon a weak organization? The fact is, that the detail administration of affairs, in this mixed republics, depends principally on the local governments; and the people would be wretched without them: and a great proportion of social happiness depends on the internal administration of justice, and on internal police. The splendor of the monarch, and the power of the government are one thing. The happiness of the subject depends on very different causes: but it is to the latter, that the best men, the greatest ornaments of human nature, have most carefully attended: it is to the former tyrants and oppressors have always aimed.

THE FEDERAL FARMER.

LETTER XVIII

The Federal Farmer concludes with a spirited argument that only universal service in the state militia can prevent the loss of state power and liberties to a federal government backed by a standing army. The aristocracy fostered in the new federal district, combined with a standing army, will destroy liberty if not checked by strong militias. Essays in The Federalist *of particular relevance: 25-29.*

DEAR SIR,

I AM persuaded, a federal head never was formed, that possessed half the powers which it could carry into full effect, altogether independently of the state or local governments, as the one, the convention has proposed, will possess. Should the state legislatures never meet, except merely for chusing federal senators and appointing electors, once in four and six years, the federal head may go on for ages to make all laws relative to the following subjects, and by its own courts, officers, and provisions, carry them into full effect, and to any extent it may deem for the general welfare; that is, for *raising taxes*, borrowing and coining monies, and for applying them—for forming and governing *armies* and *navies* and for directing their operations for regulating commerce with foreign nations, and among the several states, and with the Indian tribes—for regulating *bankruptcies*, weights and measures, post-offices and post-roads, and captures on land and water—for establishing a uniform rule of naturalization, and for promoting the progress of science and useful arts—for defining and punishing piracies and felonies committed on the high seas, the offenses of counterfeiting the securities and current coin of the United States, and offences against the law of nations, and for regulating all maritime concerns—for *organizing, arming* and *disciplining* the militia (the respective states training them, and appointing the officers)—for *calling them forth* when wanted, and for governing them when in the service of the union—for the *sole and exclusive government* of a federal city or town, not exceeding ten miles square, and of places ceded for forts, magazines arsenals, dock-yards, and other needful buildings—for granting letters of marque and reprisal, and making war—for regulating the *times, places,* and *manner of holding elections* for senators and representatives—for making and concluding all treaties, and carrying them into execution—for judicially deciding all questions arising on the constitution laws, and treaties of the union, in law and equity, and questions arising on state laws also, where ambassadors, other public ministers, and consuls where the United States, individual states, or a state, where *citizens of different states* and where foreign states, or a *foreign subject,* are parties or party—for impeaching and trying federal officers—for deciding on elections, and for expelling members, &c. All these enumerated powers we must examine and contemplate in all their extent and various branches, and then reflect, that the federal head will have full power to make all laws whatever respecting them; and for carrying into full effect all powers vested in the union, in any department, or officers of it, by the constitution, in order to see the full extent of the federal powers, which will be supreme, and exercised by that head at pleasure, conforming to the few limitations mentioned in the constitution. Indeed, I conceive, it is impossible to see them in their full extent at present: we see vast undefined powers lodged in a weak organization, but cannot, by the enquiries of months and years, clearly discern them in all their numerous branches. These powers in feeble hands, must be tempting objects for ambition and a love of power and fame.

But, say the advocates, they are all necessary for forming an energetic federal government; all necessary in the hands of the union, for the common defence and general welfare. In these great points they appear to me to go from the end to the means, and from the means to the end, perpetually begging the question. I think in the course of these letters, I shall sufficiently prove, that some of these powers need not be lodged in the hands of the union—that others ought to be exercised under better checks, and in part, by the agency of the starts—some I have already considered, some in

my mind, are not liable to objections, and the others, I shall briefly
notice in this closing letter.

The power to controul the military forces of the country as well
as the revenues of it, requires serious attention. Here again I must
premise, that a federal republic is a compound system, made up of
constituent parts, each essential to the whole: we must then expect
the real friends of such a system will always be very anxious for the
security and preservation of each part and to this end, that each
constitutionally possess its natural portion of power and influence—
and that it will constantly be an object of concern to them, to see
one part armed at all points by the constitution, and in a manner
destructive in the end, even of its own existence, and the others left
constitutionally defenceless.

The military forces of a free country may be considered under
three general descriptions—1. The militia. 2. the navy—and 3. the
regular troops—and the whole ought ever to be, and understood
to be, in strict subordination to the civil authority, and that regular
troops, and select corps, ought not to be kept up without evident
necessity. Stipulations in the constitution to this effect, are perhaps,
too general to be of much service, except merely to impress on the
minds of the people and soldiery, that the military ought ever to be
subject to the civil authority, &c. But particular attention, and
many more definite stipulations, are highly necessary to render the
military safe, and yet useful in a free government; and in a federal
republic, where the people meet in distinct assemblies, many stipulations are necessary to keep a part from transgressing, which
would be unnecessary checks against the whole met in one legislature, in one entire government.—A militia, when properly formed,
are in fact the people themselves, and render regular troops in a
great measure unnecessary. The powers to form and arm the militia, to appoint their officers, and to command their services, are
very important; nor ought they in a confederated republic to be
lodged, solely, in any one member of the government. First, the constitution ought to secure a genuine and guard against a select militia, by providing that the militia shall always be kept well
organized, armed, and disciplined, and include, according to the
past and general usuage of the states, all men capable of bearing

arms; and that all regulations tending to render this general militia useless and defenceless, by establishing select corps of militia, or distinct bodies of military men, not having permanent interests and attachments in the community to be avoided. I am persuaded, I need not multiply words to convince you of the value and solidity of this principle, as it respects general liberty, and the duration of a free and mild government: having this principle well fixed by the constitution, then the federal head may prescribe a general uniform plan, on which the respective states shall form and train the militia, appoint their officers, and solely manage them, except when called into the service of the union, and when called into that service, they may be commanded and governed by the union. This arrangement combines energy and safety in it; it places the sword in the hands of the solid interest of the community, and not in the hands of men destitute of property, of principle, or of attachment to the society and government, who often form the select corps of peace or ordinary establishments: by it, the militia are the people, immediately under the management of the state governments, but on a uniform federal plan, and called into the service, command, and government of the union, when necessary for the common defence and general tranquility. But, say gentlemen, the general militia are for the most part employed at home in their private concerns, cannot well be called out, or be depended upon; that we must have a select militia; that is, as I understand it, particular corps or bodies of young men, and of men who have but little to do at home, particularly armed and disciplined in some measure, at the public expence, and always ready to take the field. These corps, not much unlike regular troops, will ever produce an inattention to the general militia; and the consequence has ever been, and always must be, that the substantial men, having families and property, will generally be without arms, without knowing the use of them, and defenceless; whereas, to preserve liberty, it is essential that the whole body of the people always possess arms, and be taught alike, especially when young, how to use them; nor does it follow from this, that all promiscuously must go into actual service on every occasion. The mind that aims at a select militia, must be influenced by a truly anti-republican principle; and when we see many men disposed to practice upon it, whenever they can prevail, no wonder true republicans are for carefully guarding against it. As a farther check, it may be proper to add, that the militia of any state shall not remain in the service of the union, beyond a given period, without the express consent of the state legislature.

As to the navy, I do not see that it can have any connection with the local governments. The want of employment for it, and the want of monies in the hands of the union, must be its proper limitation. The laws for building or increasing it, as all the important laws mentioned in a former letter, touching military and money matters, may be checked by requiring the attendance of a large proportion of the representatives, and the consent of a large proportion of those present, to pass them as before mentioned.

By art. 1. sect. 8. "Congress shall have *power to provide for* organizing, arming, and disciplining the militia["]: *power to provide for*—does this imply any more than power to prescribe a general uniform plan? And must not the respective states pass laws (but in conformity to the plan) for forming and training the militia.

In the present state of mankind, and of conducting war, the government of every nation must have power to raise and keep up regular troops: the question is, how shall this power be lodged? In an entire government, as in Great Britain, where the people assemble by their representatives in one legislature, there is no difficulty, it is of course properly lodged in that legislature: But in a confederated republic, where the organization consists of a federal head, and local governments, there is no one part in which it can be solely, and safely lodged. By art. 1. sect. 8. "congress shall have power to raise and support armies," &c. By art. 1. sect. 10. "no state, without the consent of congress, shall keep troops, or ships of war, in time of peace." It seems fit the union should direct the raising of troops, and the union may do it in two ways; by requisitions on the states, or by direct taxes—the first is most conformable to the federal plan, and safest; and it may be improved, by giving the union power, by its own laws and officers, to raise the states quota that may neglect, and to charge it with the expence; and by giving a fixed quorum of the state legislatures power to disapprove the requisition. There would be less danger in this power to raise troops, could the state governments keep a proper controul over the purse and over the militia; but after all the precautions we can take, without evidently fettering the union too much, we must give a large accumulation of powers to it, in these and other respects. There is one check, which, I think, may be added with great propriety—that is, no land forces shall be kept up, but by legislative acts annually passed by congress, and no appropriation of monies for their support shall be for a longer term than one year. This is the constitutional practice in Great-Britain, and the reasons for such checks in the United States appear to be much stronger. We may also require that these acts be passed by a special majority, as before mentioned. There is another mode still more guarded, and which seems to be founded in the true spirit of a federal system: it seems proper to divide those powers we can with safety, lodge them in no one member of the government alone; yet substantially to preserve their use, and to ensure duration to the government, by modifying the exercise of them—it is to empower congress to raise troops by direct levies, not exceeding a given number, say 2000 in time of peace, and 12,000 in a time of war, and for such further troops as may be wanted, to raise them by requisitions qualified as before mentioned. By the above recited clause no state shall keep troops, &c. in time of peace—this clearly implies, it may do it in time of war: this must be on the principle, that the union cannot defend all parts of the republic, and suggests an idea very repugnant to the general tendency of the system proposed, which is to disarm the state governments: a state in a long war may collect forces sufficient to take the field against the neighbouring states. This clause was copied from the confederation, in which it was of more importance than in the plan proposed, because under this the separate states, probably, will have but small revenues.

By article 1, section 8, congress shall have power to establish uniform laws on the subject of bankruptcies, throughout the United States. It is to be observed, that the separate states have ever been in possession of the power, and in the use of it, of making bankrupt laws, militia laws, and laws in some other cases, respecting which, the new constitution, when adopted, will give the union power to legislate, &c.—but no words are used by the constitution to exclude the jurisdiction of the several states, and whether they will be excluded or not, or whether they and the union will have concurrent jurisdiction or not, must be determined by inference; and from the nature of the subject; if the power, for instance, to make uniform laws on the subject of bankruptcies, is in its nature indivisible, or in capable of being exercised by two legislatures independently, or by one in aid of the other, then the states are excluded, and cannot legislate at all on the subject, even though the union should neglect or find it impracticable to establish uniform bankrupt laws. How far the union will find it practicable to do this, time only can fully determine. When we consider the extent of the country, and the very different ideas of the different parts in it, respecting credit, and the mode of making men's property liable for paying their debts, we may, I think, with some degree of certainty, conclude that the union never will be able to establish such laws; but if practicable, it does not appear to me, on further reflection, that the union ought to have the power; it does not appear to me to be a power properly incidental to a federal head, and, I believe, no one ever possessed it; it is a power that will immediately and extensively interfere with the internal police of the separate states, especially with their administering justice among their own citizens. By giving this power to the union, we greatly extend the jurisdiction of the federal judiciary, as all questions arising on bankrupt laws, being laws of the union, even between citizens of the same state, may be tried in the federal courts; and I think it may be shewn, that by the help of these laws, actions between citizens of different states, and the laws of the federal city, aided by no overstrained judicial fictions, almost all civil causes may be drawn into those courts. We must be sensible how cautious we ought to be in extending unnecessarily the jurisdiction of those courts, for reasons I need not repeat. This article of power too, will considerably increase, in the hands of the union, an accumulation of powers, some of a federal and some of a unfederal nature, too large without it.

The constitution provides, that congress shall have the sole and exclusive government of what is called the federal city, a place not exceeding ten miles square, and of all places ceded for forts, dockyards, &c. I believe this is a novel kind of provision in a federal republic; it is repugnant to the spirit of such a government, and must be founded in an apprehension of a hostile disposition between the federal head and the state governments; and it is not improbable, that the sudden retreat of congress from Philadelphia, first gave rise to it.—With this apprehension, we provide, the government of the union shall have secluded places, cities, and castles of defence, which no state laws whatever shall invade. When we attentively examine this provision in all its consequences, it opens to view scenes almost without bounds. A federal, or rather a national city, ten miles square, containing a hundred square miles, is about four times as large as London; and for forts, magazines, arsenals, dock-yards, and other needful buildings, congress may possess a number of places or towns in each state. It is true, congress cannot have them unless the state legislatures cede them; but when once ceded, they never can be recovered, and though the general temper of the legislatures may be averse to such cessions, yet many opportunities and advantages may be taken of particular times and circumstances of complying assemblies, and of particular parties, to obtain them. It is not improbable, that some considerable towns or places, in some intemperate moments, or influenced by anti-republican principles, will petition to be ceded for the purposes mentioned in the provision. There are men, and even towns, in the best republics, which are often fond of withdrawing from the government of them, whenever occasion shall present. The case is still stronger; if the provision in question holds out allurements to attempt to withdraw, the people of a state must ever be subject to state as well as federal taxes; but the federal city and places will be subject only to the latter, and to them by no fixed proportion, nor of the taxes raised in them, can the separate states demand any account of congress.—These doors opened for withdrawing from the state governments entirely, may, on other accounts, be very alluring and pleasing to those anti-republican men who prefer a place under the wings of courts.

If a federal town be necessary for the residence of congress and the public officers, it ought to be a small one, and the government of it fixed on republican and common law principles, carefully enumerated and established by the constitution. It is true, the states,

when they shall cede places, may stipulate, that the laws and government of congress in them, shall always be formed on such principles; but it is easy to discern, that the stipulations of a state, or of
the inhabitants of the place ceded, can be of but little avail against
the power and gradual encroachments of the union. The principles
ought to be established by the federal constitution, to which all the
states are parties; but in no event can there be any need of so large
a city and places for forts, &c. totally exempted from the laws and
jurisdictions of the state governments. If I understand the constitution, the laws of congress, constitutionally made, will have complete and supreme jurisdiction to all federal purposes, on every inch
of ground in the United States, and exclusive jurisdiction on the
high seas, and this by the highest authority, the consent of the people. Suppose ten acres at West-Point shall be used as a fort of the
union, or a sea port town as a dock-yard, the laws of the union in
those places respecting the navy, forces of the union, and all federal objects, must prevail, be noticed by all judges and officers, and
executed accordingly: and I can discern no one reason for excluding
from these places, the operation of state laws, as to mere state purposes; for instance, for the collection of state taxes in them, recovering debts, deciding questions of property arising within them on
state laws, punishing, by state laws, theft, trespasses, and offences
committed in them by mere citizens against the state laws.

The city and all the places in which the union shall have this
exclusive jurisdiction, will be immediately under one entire government, that of the federal head; and be no part of any state, and
consequently no part of the United States. The inhabitants of the
federal city and places, will be as much exempt from the laws and
controul of the state governments, as the people of Canada or Nova
Scotia will be. Neither the laws of the states respecting taxes, the
militia, crimes or property, will extend to them; nor is there a single
stipulation in the constitution, that the inhabitants of this city, and
these places, shall be governed by laws founded on principles of
freedom. All questions, civil and criminal, arising on the laws of
these places, which must be the laws of congress, must be decided
in the federal courts; and also, all questions that may, by such judicial fictions as these courts may consider reasonable, be supposed to

arise within this city, or any of these places, may be brought into
these courts; and by a very common legal fiction, any personal contract may be supposed to have been made in any place. A contract
made in Georgia may be supposed to have been made in the federal city, in Pennsylvania; the courts will admit the fiction, and not
in these cases, make it a serious question, where it was in fact made.
Every suit in which an inhabitant of a federal district may be a
party, of course may be instituted in the federal courts—also, every
suit in which it may be alledged, and not denied, that a party in it
is an inhabitant of such a district—also, every suit to which a foreign state or subject, the union, a state, citizens of different states,
in fact, or by reasonable legal fictions, may be a party or parties:
And thus, by means of bankrupt laws, federal districts, &c. almost
all judicial business, I apprehend, may be carried into the federal
courts, without essentially departing from the usual course of judicial proceedings. The courts in Great Britain have acquired their
powers, and extended, very greatly, their jurisdictions by such fictions and suppositions as I have mentioned. The constitution, in
these points, certainly involves in it principles, and almost hidden
cases, which may unfold, and in time exhibit consequences we
hardly think of. The power of naturalization, when viewed in connection with the judicial powers and cases, is, in my mind, of very
doubtful extent. By the constitution itself, the citizens of each state
will be naturalized citizens of every state, to the general purposes
of instituting suits, claiming the benefits of the laws, &c. And in
order to give the federal courts jurisdiction of an action, between
citizens of the same state, in common acceptation, may not a court
allow the plaintiff to say, he is a citizen of one state, and the defendant a citizen of another, without carrying legal fictions so far, by
any means, as they have been carried by the courts of King's Bench
and Exchequer, in order to bring causes within their cognizance—
Further, the federal city and districts, will be totally distinct from
any state, and a citizen of a state will not of course be a subject of
any of them; and to avail himself of the privileges and immunities of
them, must he not be naturalized by congress in them? and may
not congress make any proportion of the citizens of the states naturalized subjects of the federal city and districts, and thereby enti-

tle them to sue or defend, in all cases, in the federal courts? I have my doubts, and many sensible men I find, have their doubts, on these points; and we ought to observe, they must be settled in the courts of law, by their rules, distinctions, and fictions. To avoid many of these intricacies and difficulties, and to avoid the undue and unnecessary extension of the federal judicial powers, it appears to me that no federal districts ought to be allowed, and no federal city or town, except perhaps a small town, in which the government shall be republican, but in which congress shall have no jurisdiction over the inhabitants, but in common with the other inhabitants of the states. Can the union want, in such a town, any thing more than a right to the soil on which it may set its buildings, and extensive jurisdiction over the federal buildings, and property, its own members, officers, and servants in it? As to all federal objects, the union will have complete jurisdiction over them, of course any where, and every where. I still think, that no actions ought to be allowed to be brought in the federal courts, between citizens of different states, at least, unless the cause be of very considerable importance: that no action against a state government, by any citizen or foreigner, ought to be allowed, and no action, in which a foreign subject is party, at least, unless it be of very considerable importance, ought to be instituted in the federal courts—I confess, I can see no reason whatever, for a foreigner, or for citizens of different states, carrying sixpenny causes into the federal courts; I think the state courts will be found by experience, to be bottomed on better principles, and to administer justice better than the federal courts.

The difficulties and dangers I have supposed, will result from so large a federal city, and federal districts, from the extension of the federal judicial powers, &c. are not, I conceive, merely possible, but probable, I think, pernicious political consequences will follow from them, and from the federal city especially, for very obvious reasons, a few of which I will mention.

We must observe, that the citizens of a state will be subject to state as well as federal taxes, and the inhabitants of the federal city and districts, only to such taxes as congress may lay—We are not to suppose all our people are attached to free government, and the principles of the common law but that many thousands of them will prefer a city governed, not on republican principles—This city, and the government of it, must indubitably take their tone from the characters of the men, who from the nature of its situation and institution, must collect there. This city will not be established for productive labour, for mercantile, or mechanic industry; but for the residence of government, its officers and attendants. If hereafter it should ever become a place of trade and industry, in the early periods of its existence, when its laws and government must receive their fixed tone, it must be a mere court, with its appendages, the executive, congress, the law courts, gentlemen of fortune and pleasure, with all the officers, attendants, suitors, expectants and dependants on the whole, however brilliant and honourable this collection may be, if we expect it will have any sincere attachments to simple and frugal republicanism, to that liberty and mild government, which is dear to the laborious part of a free people, we most assuredly deceive ourselves. This early collection will draw to it men from all parts of the country, of a like political description: we see them looking towards the place already.

Such a city, or town, containing a hundred square miles, must soon be the great, the visible, and dazzling centre, the mistress of fashions, and the fountain of politics. There may be a free or shackled press in this city, and the streams which may issue from it may overflow the country, and they will be poisonous or pure, as the fountain may be corrupt or not. But not to dwell on a subject that must give pain to the virtuous friends of freedom, I will only add, can a free and enlightened people create a common head so extensive, so prone to corruption and slavery, as this city probably will be, when they have it in their power to form one pure and chaste, frugal and republican.

Under the confederation congress has no power whereby to govern its own officers and servant[s]; a federal town, in which congress might have special jurisdiction, might be expedient; but under the new constitution, without a federal town, congress will have all necessary powers of course over its officers and servants; indeed it will have a complete system of powers to all the federal purposes mentioned in the constitution; so that the reason for a federal town under the confederation, will by no means exist under the constitution.—Even if a trial by jury should be admitted in the federal city, what man, with any state attachments or republican virtue about him, will submit to be tried by a jury of it.

I might observe more particularly upon several other parts of the constitution proposed; but it has been uniformly my object in examining a subject so extensive, and difficult in many parts to be illustrated, to avoid unimportant things, and not to dwell upon points not very material. The rule for apportioning requisitions on the states, having some time since been agreed to by eleven states, I have viewed as settled. The stipulation that congress, after twenty one years may prohibit the importation of slaves, is a point gained, if not so favourable as could be wished for. As monopolies in trade perhaps can in no case be useful, it might not be amiss to provide expressly against them. I wish the power to reprive and pardon was more cautiously lodged, and under some limitations. I do not see why congress should be allowed to consent that a person may accept a present, office, or title of a foreign prince, &c. As to the state governments, as well as the federal, are essential parts of the system, why should not the oath taken by the officers be expressly to support the whole? As to debts due to and from the union, I think the constitution intends, on examining art. 4. sect. 8. and art. 6 that they shall stand on the same ground under the constitution as under the confederation. In the article respecting amendments, it is stipulated, that no state shall ever be deprived of its equal vote in the senate without its consent; and that alterations may be made by the consent of three-fourths of the states. Stipulations to bind the majority of the people may serve one purpose, to prevent frequent motions for change; but these attempts to bind the majority, generally give occasion for breach of contract. The states all agreed about seven years ago, that the confederation should remain unaltered, unless every state should agree to alterations: but we now see it agreed by the convention, and four states, that the old confederacy shall be destroyed, and a new one, of nine states, be erected, if nine only shall come in. Had we agreed, that a majority should alter the confederation, a majority's agreeing would have bound the rest: but now we must break the old league, unless all the states agree to alter, or not proceed with adopting the constitution. Whether the adoption by nine states will not produce a nearly equal and dangerous division of the people for and against the constitution—whether the circumstances of the country were such as to justify the hazarding a probability of such a situation, I shall not undertake to determine. I shall leave it to be determine hereafter, whether nine states, under a new federal compact, can claim the benefits of any treaties made with a confederation of thirteen, under a distinct compact and form of existence—whether the new confederacy can recover debts due to the old confederacy, or the arrears of taxes due from the states excluded.

It has been well observed, that our country is extensive, and has no external enemies to press the parts together: that, therefore, their union must depend on strong internal ties. I differ with the gentlemen who make these observations only in this, they hold the ties ought to be strengthened by a considerable degree of internal consolidation, and my object is to form them and strengthen them, on pure federal principles. Whatever may be the fate of many valuable and necessary amendments in the constitution proposed, the ample discussion and respectable opposition it will receive will have a good effect—they will operate to produce a mild and prudent administration, and to put the wheels of the whole system in motion on proper principles—they will evince that true republican principles and attachments are still alive and formidable in this country. These, in view, I believe, even men quite disposed to make a bad use of the system will long hesitate before they will resolve to do it. A majority, from a view of our situation, and influenced by many considerations, may acquiese in the adoption of this constitution; but, it is evident that a very great majority of the people of the United States, think it, in many parts, an unnecessary and unadviseable departure from true republican and federal principles.

THE FEDERAL FARMER.

Essays of an Old Whig

Essays of an Old Whig first appeared in Philadelphia's Independent Gazetteer *between October 1787 and February 1788. These well written, somewhat underrated essays were reprinted in Pennsylvania, New York, and Massachusetts. The author remains unknown. However, his choice of pen name and many of his arguments evidence a desire to recall to his readers the "Old Whig" principles that motivated the Glorious Revolution of 1688 and the War for Independence: limited, balanced government protecting inherited rights and local prerogatives.*

Independent Gazetteer

---

12 OCTOBER 1787

ESSAY I

Old Whig begins by warning his readers not to ratify the Constitution in the hope that its defects will be taken care of through subsequent amendments. Amendment is too difficult to count on because it requires a large super majority, and those who attain power under the new Constitution will not want to change it. Essays in The Federalist *of particular relevance: 43, 85.*

Mr. PRINTER,

I AM one of those who have long wished for a federal government, which should have power to protect our trade and provide for the general security of the United States. Accordingly, when the constitution proposed by the late convention made its appearance, I was disposed to embrace it almost without examination: I was determined not to be offended with trifles or to scan it too critically. "We want something: let us try this; experience is the best teacher: if it does not answer our purpose we can alter it; at all events it will serve for a beginning." Such were my reasonings;—but, upon further reflection, I may say that I am shaken with very considerable doubts and scruples, I want a federal constitution; and yet I am afraid to concur in giving my consent to the establishment of that which is proposed. At the same time I really wish to have my doubts removed, if they are not well founded. I shall therefore take the liberty of saying some of them before the public, through the channel of your paper.

In the first place, it appears to me that I was mistaken in supposing that we could so very easily make trial of this constitution and again change it at our pleasure. The conventions of the several states cannot propose any alterations—they are only to give their *assent* and *ratification*. And after the constitution is once ratified, it must remain fixed until two thirds of both the houses of Congress shall deem it necessary to propose amendments; or the legislatures of two thirds of the several states shall make application to Congress for the calling a convention for proposing amendments, which amendments shall not be valid till they are ratified by the legislatures of three fourths of the several states, or by conventions in three fourths thereof, as one or the other mode of ratification may be proposed by Congress.—This appears to me to be only a cunning way of saying that no alteration shall ever be made; so that whether it is a good constitution or a bad constitution, it will remain forever unamended. Lycurgus, when he promulgated his laws to the Spartans, made them swear that they would make no alterations in them until he should return from a journey which he was then about to undertake.—He chose never to return, and therefore no alterations could be made in his laws. The people were made to believe that they could make trial of his laws for a few months or years, during his absence, and as soon as he returned they could continue to observe them or reject at pleasure. Thus this celebrated Republic was in reality established by a

trick. In like manner the proposed constitution holds out a prospect
of being subject to be changed if it be found necessary or convenient
to change it; but the conditions upon which an alteration can take
place, are such as in all probability will never exit. The consequence
will be that, when the constitution is once established, it never can be
altered or amended without some violent convulsion or civil war.

The conditions, I say, upon which any alterations can take place,
appear to me to be such as never will exist—two thirds of both
houses of Congress or the legislatures of two thirds of the states,
must agree in desiring a convention to be called. This will probably
never happen; but if it should happen, then the convention may
agree to the amendments or not as they think right; and after all,
three fourths of the states must ratify the amendments.—Before
all this labyrinth can be traced to a conclusion, ages will revolve, and
perhaps the great principles upon which our late glorious revolution was founded, will be totally forgotten. If the principles of liberty
are not firmly fixed and established in the present constitution, in
vain may we hope for retrieving them hereafter. People once possessed of power are always loth to part with it; and we shall never
find two thirds of a Congress voting or proposing any thing which
shall derogate from their own authority and importance, or agreeing
to give back to the people any part of those privileges which they
have once parted with—so far from it; that the greater occasion
there may be for a reformation, the less likelihood will there be of
accomplishing it. The greater the abuse of power, the more obstinately is it always persisted in. As to any expectation of two thirds
of the legislatures concurring in such a request, it is if possible, still
more remote. The legislatures of the states will be but forms and
shadows, and it will be the height of arrogance and presumption in
them, to turn their thoughts to such high subjects. After this constitution is once established, it is too evident that we shall be obliged
to fill up the offices of assemblymen and councillors, as we do those
of constables, by appointing men to serve whether they will or not,
and fining them if they refuse. The members thus appointed, as soon
as they can hurry through a law or two for repairing highways or
impounding cattle, will conclude the business of their sessions as
suddenly as possible; that they may return to their own business.—

Their heads will not be perplexed with the great affairs of state—
We need not expect two thirds of them ever to interfere in so
momentous a question as that of calling a Continental convention.—
The different legislatures will have no communication with one
another from the time of the new constitution being ratified, to the
end of the world. Congress will be the great focus of power as well as
the great and only medium of communication from one state to
another. The great, and the wise, and the mighty will be in possession of places and offices; they will oppose all changes in favor of
liberty; they will steadily pursue the acquisition of more and more
power to themselves and their adherents. The cause of liberty, if it
be now forgotten, will be forgotten forever.—Even the press which
has so long been employed in the cause of liberty, and to which perhaps the greatest part of the liberty which exists in the world is
owing at this moment; the press may possibly be restrained of its
freedom, and our children may possibly not be suffered to enjoy
this most invaluable blessing of a free communication of each others sentiments on political subjects.—Such at least appear to be
some men's fears, and I cannot find in the proposed constitution any
thing expressly calculated to obviate these fears; so that they may
or may not be realized according to the principles and dispositions of
the men who may happen to govern us hereafter. One thing however
is calculated to alarm our fears on this head;—I mean the fashionable language which now prevails so much and is so frequent in the
mouths of some who formerly held very different opinions;—THAT
COMMON PEOPLE HAVE NO BUSINESS TO TROUBLE THEMSELVES
ABOUT GOVERNMENT. If this principle is just the consequence it is
plain that the common people need no information on the subject of
politics. Newspapers, pamphlets and essays are calculated only to
mislead and inflame them by holding forth to them doctrines which
they have no business or right to meddle with, which they ought to
leave to their superiors. Should the freedom of the press be
restrained on the subject of politics, there is no doubt it will soon
after be restrained on all other subjects, religious as well as civil.
And if the freedom of the press shall be restrained, it will be another
reason to despair of any amendments being made in favor of liberty, after the proposed constitution shall be once established. Add

to this, that under the proposed constitution, it will be in the power of the Congress to raise and maintain a standing army for their support, and when they are supported by an army, it will depend on themselves to say whether any amendments shall be made in favor of liberty.

If these reflections are just it becomes us to pause, and reflect previously before we establish a system of government which cannot be amended; which will entail happiness or misery on ourselves and our children. We ought I say to reflect carefully, we ought not by any means to be in haste; but rather to suffer a little temporary inconvenience, than by any precipitation to establish a constitution without knowing whether it is right or wrong, and which if wrong, no length of time will ever mend. Scarce any people ever deliberately gave up their liberties; but many instances occur in history of their losing them forever by a rash and sudden act, to avoid a pressing inconvenience or gratify some violent passion of revenge or fear. It was a celebrated observation of one of our Assemblies before the revolution, during their struggles with the proprietaries, that "those who would give up essential liberty to purchase a little temporary safety deserve neither liberty nor safety."

For the present I shall conclude with recommending to my countrymen not to be in haste, to consider carefully what we are doing. It is our own concern; it is our own business; let us give ourselves a little time at least to read the proposed constitution and know what it contains; for I fear that many, even of those who talk most about it have not even read it, and many others, who are as much concerned as any of us, have had no opportunity to read it. And it is certainly a suspicious circumstance that some people who are presumed to know most about the new constitution seem bent upon forcing it on their countrymen without giving them time to know what they are doing.

Hereafter I may trouble you further on some other parts of this important subject; but I fear this letter is already too long.

Yours.

AN OLD WHIG.

Independent Gazetteer

17 OCTOBER 1787

ESSAY II

Old Whig responds to an influential speech by the Federalist James Wilson, in which Wilson argued that all powers not delegated to the federal government by the new Constitution are reserved to the states. Old Whig points out that, whereas the Articles of Confederation specifically stated that all powers not delegated are reserved, the Constitution does not. Human nature, combined with the supremacy and necessary and proper clauses, guarantee federal infringement on state prerogatives. Essays in The Federalist *of particular relevance: 33, 44, 84.*

MR. PRINTER,

SINCE writing my last, in which I stated some doubts respecting the new federal constitution and expressed a wish that those doubts might be removed, I have met with the printed speech of *James Wilson*, Esquire.—This speech I find was made for the express purpose of removing objections from the minds of those who doubted, like myself, and wished to be satisfied; and except one or two hard names that have escaped the speaker, it bears the marks of more candor than is to be found in most of the production, which have been ushered into the world in support of the same measure. This speech also deserves the more attention as coming from a man of abilities fresh from *"the impressions of four months constant attention to the subject."* The subject however is one of those which it imports us all very carefully to examine. I have therefore paid very considerable attention to his arguments, at the same time that I have examined with some care the foundation upon which they are built. Still I remain unsatisfied; and the more unsatisfied, as I have been disappointed in my hope of conviction, from a quarter, from which so much was to be expected—You will give me leave therefore to state shortly in your paper, some of those difficulties which still remain with me.

The first principle which the gentleman endeavours to establish in his speech is a very important one, if true; and lays a sure foundation to reason upon, in answer to the objection which is made to the new constitution, from the want of a bill of rights. The principle is this: that "in *delegating federal powers*, the congressional authority is to be collected, *not from tacit implication*, but from *the positive grant* expressed in the instrument of union," "*that everything which is not given is reserved.*" If this be a just representation of the matter, the authority of the several states will be sufficient to protect our liberties from the encroachments of Congress, without any continental bill of rights; *unless* the powers which are *expressly given* to Congress are *too large*.

Without examining particularly at present, whether the powers *expressly* given to Congress are too large or too small, I shall beg leave to consider, whether the author of this speech is sufficiently accurate in his statement of the proposition above referred to.—To strip it of unnecessary words, the position may be reduced to this short sentence, "that every thing which is not *expressly* given to Congress is reserved"; or in other words "that Congress cannot exercise any power or authority that is not in express words delegated to them."—This certainly is the case under the first articles of confederation which hitherto have been the rule and standard of the powers of Congress; for in the second of those articles "each state retains its sovereignty, freedom and independence and every power, jurisdiction and right which is not by this confederation *expressly* delegated to the United States in Congress assembled." It was the misfortune of these articles of confederation that they did not by express words give to Congress power sufficient for the purposes of the union; for Congress could not go beyond those powers so expressly given. The position of the speech, therefore is strictly true if applied to the first articles of confederation; "that every thing which is not expressly given is reserved." We are not however to suppose that the speaker meant insidiously to argue from an article in the old confederation in favor of the new constitution, unless the same thing was also in the new constitution. Let us then fairly examine whether in the proposed new constitution there be any thing from which the gentleman can be justified in his opinion, "that every thing which is not expressly given to Congress is reserved."

In the first place then it is most certain that we find no such clause or article in the new constitution. There is nothing in the new constitution which either in form or substance bears the least resemblance to the second article of the confederation. It might nevertheless be a fair argument to insist upon from the nature of delegated powers, that no more power is given in such cases than is expressly given. Whether or not this ground of argument would be such as we might safely rest our liberties upon; or whether it would be more prudent to stipulate expressly as is done in the present confederation for the reservation of all such powers as are not expressly given, it is hardly necessary to determine at present. It strikes me that by the proposed constitution, so far from the reservation of all powers that are not expressly given, *the future Congress will be fully authorised to assume all such powers as they in their wisdom or wickedness, according as the one or the other may happen to prevail, shall from time to time think proper to assume.*

Let us weigh this matter carefully; for it is certainly of the utmost importance, and, if I am right in my opinion, the new constitution vests Congress with such unlimited powers as ought never to be entrusted to any men or body of men. It is justly observed that the possession of sovereign power is a temptation too great for human nature to resist; and although we have read in history of one or two illustrious characters who have refused to enslave their country when it was in their power;—although we have seen one illustrious character in our own times resisting the possession of power when set in competition with his duty to his country, yet these instances are so very rare, that it would be worse than madness to trust to the chance of their being often repeated.

To proceed then with the enquiry, whether the future Congress will be restricted to those powers which are expressly given to them. I would observe that in the opinion of *Montesquieu,* and of most other writers, ancient as well as modern, the legislature is the sovereign power. It is certainly the most important. If any one

doubts this, let him reflect upon the frequent inroads which the legislature of Pennsylvania has made upon the other branches of government: Inroads which it is much to be feared, if the powers of
government in Pennsylvania should ever in time to come be an
object worth contending about, no council of censors will ever be
able to check or restrain. Let us then see what are the powers
expressly given to the legislature of Congress, and what checks are
interposed in the way of the continental legislature's assuming
what further power they shall think proper to assume.

To this end let us look to the first article of the proposed new constitution, which treats of the legislative powers of Congress; and
to the eighth section which *pretends* to define those powers. We find
here that the congress, in its legislative capacity, shall have the
power "to lay and collect taxes, duties and excises; to borrow
money; to regulate commerce; to fix the rule for naturalization and
the laws of bankruptcy; to coin money; to punish counterfeiters;
establish post offices and post roads; to secure copy rights to
authors; to constitute tribunals; to define and punish piracies, to
declare war; to raise and support armies; to provide and support a
navy; to make rules for the army and navy; to call forth the militia;
to organize, arm and discipline the militia; to exercise absolute
power over a district of ten miles square, independant of all the
state legislatures, and to be alike absolute over all forts, magazines,
arsenals, dockyards and other needful buildings thereunto belonging." This is a short abstract of the powers expressly given to Congress. These powers are very extensive, but I shall not stay at
present to inquire whether these *express* powers were necessary to
be given to Congress? whether they are too great or too small? My
object is to consider that *undefined, unbounded and immense
power* which is comprised in the following clause;—"And, to make
all laws which shall be necessary and proper for carrying into execution the *foregoing powers and all other powers* vested by this
constitution in the government of the United States; or in any
department or offices thereof." Under such a clause as this can any
thing be said to be reserved and kept back from Congress? Can it
be said that the Congress have no power but what is *expressed.*
"To make all laws which shall be necessary and proper" is in other

words to make all such laws which *the Congress shall think neces-sary and proper,*—for who shall judge for the legislature what is necessary and proper?—Who shall set themselves above the sov-ereign?—What inferior legislature shall set itself above the supreme legislature?—To me it appears that no other power on earth can dictate to them or controul them, unless by force; and force either internal or external is one of those calamities which every good man would wish his country at all times to be delivered from.—This generation in America have seen enough of war and its usual concomitants to prevent all of us from wishing to see any more of it;—all except those who make a trade of war. But to the question;—without force what can restrain the Congress from mak-ing such laws as they please? What limits are there to their author-ity?—I fear none at all; for surely it cannot justly be said that they have no power but what is expressly given to them, whereby the very terms of their creation they are vested with the powers of making laws in all cases necessary and proper; when from the nature of their power they must necessarily be the judges, what laws are necessary and proper. The British act of Parliament, declaring the power of Parliament to make laws to bind America in all cases whatsoever, was not more extensive; for it is as true as a maxim, that even the British Parliament neither could nor would pass any law in any case in which they did not either deem it nec-essary and proper to make such law or pretend to deem it so. And in such cases it is not of a farthing consequence whether they really are of opinion that the law is necessary and proper, or only *pretend to think so;* for who can overrule their pretensions?—No one; unless we had a bill of rights to which we might appeal, and under which we might contend against any assumption of undue power and appeal to the judicial branch of the government to protect us by their judgements. This reasoning I fear Mr. Printer is but [too] just; and yet, if any man should doubt the truth of it; let me ask him one other question, what is the meaning of the latter part of the clause which vests the Congress with the authority of making all laws which shall be necessary and proper for carrying into execution ALL OTHER POWERS;—besides the foregoing powers vested, &c. &c. Was it thought that the foregoing powers might perhaps admit of some restraint in *their* construction as to what was necessary and proper to carry them into execution? Or was it deemed right to add still further that they should not be restrained to the powers already named?—besides the powers already mentioned, other powers may be assumed hereafter as contained by implication in this constitution. The Congress shall judge of what is necessary and proper in all these cases and in all other cases;—in short in all cases whatsoever.

Where then is the restraint? How are Congress bound down to the powers expressly given? what is reserved or can be reserved?

Yet even this is not all—as if it were determined that no doubt should remain, by the sixth article of the constitution it is declared that, "this constitution, and the laws of the United States which shall be made in pursuance thereof; and all treaties made, or which shall be made, under the authority of the United States, shall be the supreme law of the land, and the judges in every state shall be bound thereby, *any thing in the constitutions or laws of any state to the contrary notwithstanding.*" The Congress are therefore vested with the supreme legislative power, without controul. In giving such immense, such unlimited powers, was there no necessity of a bill of rights to secure to the people their liberties? Is it not evident that we are left wholly dependent on the wisdom and virtue of the men who shall from time to time be the members of Congress? and who shall be able to say seven years hence, the members of Congress will be wise and good men, or of the contrary character.

As I mean to pursue this subject in some other letters, I shall conclude for the present; and am,

Yours,

AN OLD WHIG.

Independent Gazetteer

20 OCTOBER 1787

ESSAY III

Old Whig emphasizes the need for a federal bill of rights by noting the dangers arising from the federal treaty power and supremacy clause. These constitutional provisions subordinate state law and rights to federal power. Essays in The Federalist *of particular relevance: 44, 64, 84.*

Mr. PRINTER,

"GREAT men are not always wise," they have their seasons of inattention, and their moments of frailty and error, in which it is too evident, they are not wholly exempted from the infirmity of human nature. We ought not therefore implicitly to approve and admire, without examination, every act that proceeds even from the best and wisest of mankind. The proposed new plan of federal government, is undoubtedly the work of some of the ablest and best men in this country; but yet we are not, for that reason only, to believe that it is free from imperfection. The convention themselves inform us that the constitution which they offer to us, is the effect of mutual accommodations and concessions, in which mode it is certain that the best and wisest propositions are not always those which are adopted. Indeed it appears to me that, after all the time which has been spent in this business, the convention at the close of their session have been glad to lay hold of any system in which a majority could possibly concur, so as not to separate without doing any thing; and that the model of government now before us, is at least the work of haste and inattention. To be convinced of this, let us turn again to the sixth article, which I have referred to in the close of my last letter. By this article, not only the "proposed constitution and laws of the United States, which shall be made in pursuance thereof"; but also *"all treaties* made or which shall be made under the authority of the United States, shall be the supreme law of the land; and the judges in every state shall be bound thereby, any thing in the constitutions or laws of any state to the contrary notwithstanding."—The power of making treaties is vested in the president, with the concurrence of two thirds of the senators present; so that the president and two thirds of the senate have power to make laws in the forms of treaties, independent of the legislature itself. If Great Britain, for instance, were willing to enter into a treaty with us, upon terms which would be inconsistent with the liberties of the people and destructive of the very being of a Republic, the consent of our president for the time being, and of two thirds of the senators present, even though the senators present should be but a very small part of the senate, will give such a treaty the validity of a law. What power will there be anywhere to prevent this?— None.—Where all power legislative and executive is vested in one man or one body of men, treaties are made by the same authority which makes the laws; but where the legislature is extinct from the executive, the approbation of the legislature ought to be had, before a treaty should have the force of a law; and even in England the parliament is constantly applied to for their sanction to every treaty which tends to introduce an innovation or the slightest alteration in the laws in being, the law there is not altered by the treaty itself; but by an act of parliament which confirms the treaty, and alters the law so as to accommodate it to the treaty. The King in council has no such power. The only answer which can be made to this objection, which is so obvious, to the power given by the proposed constitution to the executive of making treaties, which shall be the "supreme law of the land," is, that it is not to be supposed they will abuse such power.—But yet we find that men in all ages have abused power, and that it has been the study of patriots and virtuous legislators at all times to restrain power, so as to prevent the abuse of it.—What then ought to be done, it may be asked.— Are treaties to be sent to all the different state legislatures for their approbation? By no means. But no treaty ought to be suffered to alter the law of the land, without the consent of the continental legislatures; the powers of the continental legislatures ought to be exactly defined; and there ought to be a bill of rights firmly established, which neither treaties nor acts of the legislature can alter.

Let us however give fair play to the answer which has been attempted to be given to this Objection. The author of the speech tells us, that a bill of rights would have been superfluous and absurd; because "no powers are given to Congress but what are expressly given"; and "that we shall still enjoy those privileges of which we are not divested either by the intention or the act that brought that body into existence.—For instance, the liberty of the press.—What controul can proceed from the federal government to shackle or destroy that sacred palladium of national freedom?"—What controul!—Suppose that an act of the continental legislature should be passed to restrain the liberty of the press;—to appoint licensers of the press in every town in America;—to limit the number of printers;—and to compel them to give security for their good behaviour, from year to year, as the licenses are renewed: If such a law should be once passed, what is there to prevent the execution of it?—By the sixth article of the proposed constitution, this act of the continental legislature is "the supreme law of the land; and the judges in every state shall be bound thereby, ANY THING IN THE CONSTITUTION OR LAWS OF ANY STATE TO THE CONTRARY NOTWITHSTANDING."—Suppose a printer should be found hardy enough to contravene such a law when made, and to contest the validity of it.—He is prosecuted we will suppose, in this state—he pleads in his defence, that by the constitution of Pennsylvania, it is declared "that the freedom of the press ought not to be restrained."—What will this avail him? The judge will be obliged to declare that "*notwithstanding the constitution of any state*," this act of the continental legislature which restrains the freedom of the press, is "the supreme law; and we must punish you—The bill of rights of Pennsylvania is nothing here. That bill of rights indeed is binding upon the legislature of Pennsylvania, but it is not binding upon the legislature of the continent." Such must be the language and conduct of courts, as soon as the proposed continental constitution shall be adopted.

As to the trial by jury, the question may be decided in a few words. Any future Congress sitting under the authority of the pro-

posed new constitution, may, if they chuse, enact that there shall be
no more trial by jury, in any of the United States; except in the trial
of crimes; and this "SUPREME LAW" will at once annul the trial by
jury, in all other cases. The author of the speech supposes that no
danger "can possibly ensue, since the proceedings of the supreme
court are to be regulated by the Congress, which is a faithful representation of the people; and the oppression of government is
effectually barred; by declaring that in all criminal cases the trial by
jury shall be preserved." Let us examine the last clause of this sentence first.—I know that an affected indifference to the trial by jury
has been expressed, by some persons high in the confidence of the
present ruling party in some of the states;—and yet for my own
part I cannot change the opinion I had early formed of the excellence of this mode of trial even in civil causes. On the other hand I
have no doubt that whenever a settled plan shall be formed for the
extirpation of liberty, the banishment of jury trials will be one of the
means adopted for the purpose.—But how is it that "the oppression
of government is effectually barred by declaring that in all criminal cases the trial by jury shall be preserved."—Are there not a
thousand civil cases in which the government is a party?—In all
actions for penalties, forfeitures and public debts, as well as many
others, the government is a party and the whole weight of government is thrown into the scale of the prosecution yet these are all of
them civil causes.—These penalties, forfeitures and demands of
public debts may be multiplied at the will and pleasure of government.—These modes of harrassing the subject have perhaps been
more effectual than direct criminal prosecutions.—In the reign of
Henry the Seventh of England, Empson and Dudley acquired an
infamous immortality by these prosecutions for penalties and forfeitures:—Yet all these prosecutions were in the form of civil
actions; they are undoubtedly objects highly alluring to a government.—They fill the public coffers and enable government to
reward its minions at a cheap rate.—They are a profitable kind of
revenge and gratify the officers about a court, who study their own
interests more than corporal punishment.—Perhaps they have at
all times been more eagerly pursued than mere criminal prosecutions.—Shall trial by jury be taken away in all these cases and shall

we still be told that "we are effectually secured against the oppressions of government?" At this rate Judges may sit in the United States, as they did in some instances before the war, without a jury to condemn people's property and extract money from their pockets, to be put into the pockets of the judges themselves who condemn them; and we shall be told that we are safe from the oppression of government.—No, Mr. Printer, we ought not to part with the trial by jury; we ought to guard this and many other privileges by a bill of rights, which cannot be invaded. The reason that is pretended in the speech why such a declaration; as a bill of rights requires, cannot be made for the protection of the trial by jury;— "that we cannot with any propriety say 'that the trial by jury shall be as heretofore' in the case of a federal system of jurisprudence," is almost too contemptible to merit notice.—Is this the only form of words that language could afford on such an important occasion? Or if it were to what did these words refer when adopted in the constitutions of the states?—Plainly sir, to the trial by juries as established by the common law of England in the state of its purity;—That common law for which we contented so eagerly at the time of the revolution, and which now after the interval of a very few years, by the proposed new constitution we seem ready to abandon forever; at least in that article which is the most invaluable part of it; the trial by jury.

Still however the great answer to all the objections that are made or can be made to the proposed constitution is this;—that there is no danger in trusting the Congress with any power: They will not abuse it. I shall conclude this letter with asking such as are willing to satisfy themselves with this answer only to look back for ten or twelve years and recollect what a mighty change has taken place in the political opinions of many people since that time. If they have forgotten let me beg of them to read over the publications of the years, 1774, 1775, 1776 and 1777. What was the spirit, what was the complaints of those times from Congress down to the smallest meeting of the people? Our present language will be found to give the lie to our former professions; and we have sinned egregiously in wading thro' such an ocean of blood, if we were not well founded in the pretensions upon which we encountered the hor-

rors of a civil war in establishing the revolution.—If such has been
the change, as a very short examination will convince any man that
has taken place in a few years past, what right have we to trust to
the existence of such pure and immaculate virtue in time to come,
that we should tamely and implicitly surrender our liberties at discretion into the hands of a government whose constituent members
are totally unknown to us. Solomon has told us that no man knows
whether a fool or a wise man is to inherit his estate; neither do we
know whether honest and virtuous men or knaves and tyrants are
to regulate our future councils. Let us then guard ourselves, as far
as we can, against the possibility of being enslaved by wicked men,
whilst the power of guarding ourselves is in our own hands. I know
that the country is distressed; but it is not distressed beyond the
power of remedy.—Let us take care that we do not involve ourselves in slavery, from the distresses of which we can never redeem
ourselves.

Your's, &c.

AN OLD WHIG.

Independent Gazetteer

27 OCTOBER 1787

ESSAY IV

*Old Whig says the people will support a second constitutional con-
vention and will be better served by a modified constitution that
does not consolidate the states into a single, centralized government. He goes on to cite historical examples in arguing that a large
republic is an impossibility, though a republican league could be
forged and maintained. Essays in* The Federalist *of particular relevance: 1, 5, 14, 20.*

Mr. PRINTER,

THIS is certainly a very important crisis to the people of America; experience seems to have convinced every one, that the articles of confederation, under which Congress have hitherto attempted to regulate the affairs of the United States, are insufficient for the purposes intended; that we are a ruined people unless some alteration can be effected. The public mind has therefore been raised to the highest pitch of expectation, and the evident need of relief from the many distresses, public and private, in which we are involved has reduced us to such a state, that we can hardly endure a disappointment. Scarcely any thing that could be proposed by the convention, in this state of people's minds, would fail of being eagerly embraced. Like a person in the agonies of a violent disease, who is willing to swallow any medicine, that gives the faintest hope of relief; the people stood ready to receive the new constitution, in almost any form in which it could be presented to them. The zealous supporters of the proposed constitution, seem to be not unwilling to avail themselves of this disposition: and therefore it is strongly inculcated, that if we do not adopt this constitution, we shall not be able to establish another, but be left to our present weakness, confusion and distress. If I was pursuaded that this is really the case, I hardly know whether I should vote for rejecting any government however unfriendly to the liberties of the people, which promised to give vigour to the councils of this country; for any government is better than none. However, I do not see that it is by any means impracticable, for us yet to correct such errors and imperfections, as appear to exist to the proposed constitution; and whilst there is a possibility of procuring a better constitution, it is the duty of every good man to accomplish it.

By the proposed constitution, every law, before it passes, is to undergo repeated revisions; and the constitution of every state in the union provide, for the reversion of the most trifling laws, either by their passing through different houses of assembly and senate, or by requiring them to be published for the consideration of the people. Why then is a constitution which affects all the inhabitants of the United States, which is to be the foundation of all laws and the source of misery or happiness to one quarter of the globe; why is this to be so hastily adopted or rejected, that it cannot admit of a revision?—If a law to regulate highways, requires to be liesurely considered and undergo the examination of different bodies of men, one after another, before it be passed, why is it that the framing of a constitution for the government of a great people; a work which has been justly considered as the greatest effort of human genius, and which, from the beginning of the world has so often baffled the skill of the wisest men in every age, shall be considered as a thing to be thrown out, in the first shape which it may happen to assume? Where is the impracticability of a revision? Cannot the same power which called the late convention, call another? Are not the people still their own masters? If, when the several state conventions come to consider this constitution, they should not approve of it, in its present form, they may easily apply to Congress and state their objections. Congress may as easily direct the calling another convention, as they did the calling the last. The plan may then be reconsidered, deliberately received and corrected; so as to meet the approbation of every friend to his country. A few months only will be necessary for this purpose; and if we consider the magnitude of the object, we shall deem it well worth a little time and attention— It is much better to pause and reflect beforehand, than to repent when it is too late; when no peaceable remedy will be left us, and unanimity will be forever banished. The struggles of the people against a bad government, when it is once fixed, afford but a gloomy picture in the annals of mankind. They are often unfortunate, they are always destructive of public and private happiness; but the peaceable consent of a people to establish a free and effective government, is one of the most glorious objects that is ever exhibited in the theatre of human affairs. Some I know, have objected, that another convention will not be likely to agree upon any thing—I am far however from being of that opinion. The public voice cries so loudly for a new constitution, that I have no doubt we shall have one of some sort.—My only fear is, that the impatience of the people will lead them to accept the first that is offered them, without examining whether it is right or wrong; and after all, if a new convention cannot agree upon any amendments in the constitution, which is at present proposed, we can still adopt this in its present form; and all further opposition being vain, it is to be hoped we shall be unanimous in endeavouring to make the best of it. The experiment is at least worth trying, and I shall be much astonished, if a new convention called together for the purpose of revising the proposed constitution, do not greatly reform it.

I find that a number of pens are employed, in pointing out the defects in the proposed constitution—Without descending therefore, into minute particulars, I shall confine the remainder of my observations in this letter, to one or two of the most important considerations.

It is beyond a doubt that the new federal constitution, if adopted, will in a great measure destroy, if it do not totally annihilate, the separate governments of the several states. We shall, in effect, become one great Republic.—Every measure of any importance, will be Continental.—What will be the consequence of this? One thing is evident—[that no] Republic [of so] great a magnitude, ever [did], or ever can exist. But a few years elapsed, from the time in which ancient Rome extended her dominions beyond the bounds of Italy, until the downfal of her Republic; and all political writers agree, that a Republican government can exist only in a narrow territory: but a confederacy of different Republics has, in many instances, existed and flourished for a long time together—The celebrated *Helvetian* league, which exists at this moment in full vigor, and with unimpaired strength, whilst its origin may be traced to the confines of antiquity, is one, among many examples on this head; and at the same time furnishes an eminent proof of how much less importance it is, that the constituent parts of a confederacy of Republics may be rightly framed than it is, that the confederacy itself should be rightly organized;—for hardly any two of the Swiss cantons have the same form of government, and they are almost equally divided in their religious principles, which have so often rent asunder the firmest establishments. A confederacy of Republics must be the establishment in America, or we must cease altogether to retain the Republican form of government. From the moment we become one great Republic, either in form or substance, the period is very shortly removed, when we shall sink first into monarchy, and then into despotism.—If there were no other fault in the proposed constitution, it must sink by its own weight. The continent of North-America can no more be governed by one Republic, than the fabled Atlas could support the heavens. Is it not worthy a few months labour, to attempt the rescuing this country from the despotism, which at this moment holds the best and fairest regions of the earth in thraldom and wretchedness?—To attempt the forming a plan of confederation which may enable us at once to support our continental union with vigor and efficacy, and to maintain the rights of the separate states and the invaluable liberty of the subject? These ideas of political felicity, to some people, may seem like the visions of an Utopian fancy; and I am persuaded that some amongst us have as little disposition to realize them, as they have to recollect the principles, which inspired us in our revolt from Great-Britain. But there is at least, this consolation in aiming at excellence, that, if we do not obtain our object, we can make considerable progress towards it.—The science of politics has very seldom had fair play. So much of passion, interest and temporary prospects of gain are mixed in the pursuit, that a government has been much oftener established, with a view to the particular advantages or necessities of a few individuals, than to the permanent good of society. If the men, who, at different times, have been entrusted to form plans of government for the world, had been really actuated by no other views than a regard to the public good, the condition of human nature in all ages would have been widely different, from that which has been exhibited to us in history. In this country perhaps we are possessed of more than our share of political virtue. If we will exercise a little patience, and bestow our best endeavours on the business, I do not think it impossible, that we may yet form a federal constitution, much superior to any form of government, which has ever existed in the world;—but, whenever this important work shall be accomplished, I venture to pronounce, that it will not be done without a *careful attention to the framing of a bill of rights.*

Much has been said and written, on the subject of a bill of rights;—possibly without sufficient attention to the necessity of conveying distinct and precise ideas of the true meaning of a bill of rights. Your readers, I hope, will excuse me, if I conclude this letter with an attempt to throw some light on this subject.

Men when they enter into society, yield up a part of their natural liberty, for the sake of being protected by government. If they yield up all their natural rights they are absolute slaves to their governors. If they yield up less than is necessary, the government is so feeble, that it cannot protect them.—To yield up so much, as is necessary for the purposes of government; and to retain all beyond what is necessary, is the great point, which ought, if possible, to be attained in the formation of a constitution. At the same time that by these means, the liberty of the subject is secured, the government is really strengthened; because wherever the subject is convinced that nothing more is required from him, than what is necessary for the good of the community, he yields a chearful obedience, which is more useful than the constrained service of slaves.—To define what portion of his natural liberty, the subject shall at all times be entitled to retain, is one great end of a bill of rights. To these may be added in a bill of rights some particular engagements of protection, on the part of government, without such a bill of rights, firmly secured the privileges of the subject, the government is always in danger of degenerating into tyranny; for it is certainly true, that "in establishing the powers of government, the rulers are invested with every right and authority, which is not in explicit terms reserved."—Hence it is, that we find the rulers so often lording over the people at their will and pleasure. Hence it is that we find the patriots, in all ages of the world, so very solicitous to obtain explicit engagements from their rulers, stipulating, expressly, for the preservation of particular rights and privileges.

In different nations, we find different grants or reservations of privileges appealed to in the struggles between the rulers and the people, many of which in the different nations of Europe, have long since been swallowed up and lost by time, or destroyed by the arbitrary hand of power. In England we find the people, with the Barons at their head, exacting a solemn resignation of their rights from king John, in their celebrated *magna charta*, which was many times renewed in Parliament, during the reigns of his successors.

The *petition of rights* was afterwards consented to by Charles the first, and contained a declaration of the liberties of the people. The *habeas corpus act*, after the restoration of Charles the Second, *the bill of rights*, which was obtained from the Prince and Princess of Orange on their accession to the throne and the act of settlement, at the accession of the Hanover family, are other instances to shew the care and watchfulness of that nation, to improve every opportunity, of the reign of a weak prince, or the revolution in their government, to obtain the most explicit declarations in favor of their liberties. In like manner the people of this country, at the revolution, having all power in their own hands, in forming the constitutions of the several states, took care to secure themselves by bills of rights, so as to prevent, as far as possible, the encroachments of their future rulers up on the rights of the people. Some of these rights are said to be *unalienable* such as the rights of conscience: yet even these have been often invaded, where they have not been carefully secured by express and solemn bills and declarations in their favor.

Before we establish a government, whose acts will be THE SUPREME LAW OF THE LAND, and whose power will extend to almost every case without exception, we ought carefully to guard ourselves by a BILL OF RIGHTS, against the invasion of those liberties which it is essential for us to retain, which it is of no real use to government to strip us of; but which in the course of human events have been too often insulted with all the wantonness of an idle barbarity.

Your's,

AN OLD WHIG.

Independent Gazetteer

1 NOVEMBER 1787

ESSAY V

Old Whig again argues for a bill of rights, this time on the grounds
that Congress can invade state prerogatives through its taxing and
military powers. He expresses special concern regarding religious
intolerance, which he claims to have been frequent and dangerous
throughout history. In addition, the president's military powers
must be lessened or entrusted to a hereditary monarch whose
secure status will make him less likely to abuse them. Essays in
The Federalist *of particular relevance: 10, 24, 28, 30, 34, 67, 69,*
72-77, 84.

MR. PRINTER,

IN order that people may be sufficiently impressed, with the necessity of establishing a BILL OF RIGHTS in the forming of a new constitution, it is very proper to take a short view of some of those liberties, which it is of the greatest importance for Freemen to retain to themselves, when they surrender up a part of their natural rights for the good of society.

The first of these, which it is of the utmost importance for the people to retain to themselves, which indeed they have not even the right to surrender, and which at the same time it is of no kind of advantages to government to strip them of, is the LIBERTY OF CONSCIENCE. I know that a ready answer is at hand, to any objections upon this head. We shall be told that in this enlightened age, the rights of conscience are perfectly secure: There is no necessity of guarding them: for no man has the remotest thoughts of invading them. If this be the case, I beg leave to reply that now is the very time to secure them.—Wise and prudent men always take care to guard against danger beforehand, and to make themselves safe whilst it is yet in their power to do it without inconvenience or risk.—who shall answer for the ebbings and flowings of opinion, or be able to say what will be the fashionable frenzy of the next generation? It would have been treated as a very ridiculous supposition, a year ago, that the charge of witchcraft would cost a person her life in the city of Philadelphia; yet the fate of the unhappy old woman called *Corbmaker*, who was beaten—repeatedly wounded with knives—mangled and at last killed in our streets, in obedience to the commandment which requires "that we shall not suffer a witch to live," without a possibility of punishing or even of detecting the authors of this inhuman folly, should be an example to warn us how little we ought to trust to the unrestrained discretion of human nature.

Uniformity of opinion in science, morality, politics or religion, is undoubtedly a very great happiness to mankind; and there have not been wanting zealous champions in every age, to promote the means of securing so invaluable a blessing. If in America we have not lighted up fires to consume Heretics in religion, if we have not persecuted unbelievers to promote the unity of the faith, in matters which pertain to our final salvation in a future world, think we have all of us been witness to something very like the same spirit, in matters which are supposed to regard our political salvation in this world. In Boston it seems at this very moment that no man is permitted to publish a doubt of the infalibility of the late convention, without giving up his name to the people, that he may be delivered over to speedy destruction; and it is but a short time since the case was little better in this city. Now this is a portion of the very same spirit, which has so often kindled the fires of the inquisition: and the same Zealot who would hunt a man down for a difference of opinion upon a political question which is the subject of public enquiry, if he should happen to be fired with zeal for a particular species of religion, would be equally intolerant. The fact is, that human nature is still the same that ever it was: the fashion indeed changes; but the seeds of superstition, bigotry and enthusiasm, are too deeply implanted in our minds, ever to be eradicated; and fifty years hence, the French may renew the persecution of the Huguenots, whilst the Spaniards in their turn may become indifferent to their forms of religion. They are idiots who trust their future security to the whim of the present hour. One extreme is always apt to produce the contrary, and those countries, which are now the most lax in their religious notions, may in a few years become the most rigid, just as the people of this country from not being able to bear any continental government at all, are now flying into the opposite extreme of surrendering up all the powers of the different states, to one continental government.

The more I reflect upon the history of mankind, the more I am disposed to think that it is our duty to secure the essential rights of the people, by every precaution; for not an avenue has been left unguarded, through which oppression could possibly enter in any government; without some enemy of the public peace and happiness improving the opportunity to break in upon the liberties of the people; and none have been more frequently successful in the attempt, than those who have covered their ambitious designs under the garb of a fiery zeal for religious orthodoxy. What has happened in other countries and in other ages, may very possibly happen again in our own country, and for ought we know, before the present generation quits the stage of life. We ought therefore in a *bill of rights* to secure, in the first place, by the most express stipulations, the sacred rights of conscience. Has this been done in the constitution, which is now proposed for the consideration of the people of this country?—Not a word on this subject has been mentioned in any part of it; but we are left in this important article, as well as many others, entirely to the mercy of our future rulers.

But supposing our future rulers to be wicked enough to attempt to invade the rights of conscience; I may be asked how will they be able to effect so horrible a design? I will tell you my friends—*The unlimited power of taxation* will give them the command of all the treasures of the continent; *a standing army* will we wholly at their devotion, and the authority which is given them over the *militia*, by virtue of which they may, if they please, change all the officers of the militia on the continent in one day, and put in new officers whom they can better trust; by which they can subject all the militia to strict military laws, and punish the disobedient with death, or otherwise, as they shall think right: by which they can march the militia back and forward from one end of the continent to the other, at their discretion; these powers, if they should ever fall into bad hands, may be abused to the worst of purposes. Let us instance one thing arising from this right of organizing and governing the militia. Suppose a man alledges that he is conscientiously scrupulous of bearing Arms.—By the bill of rights of Pennsylvania he is bound only to pay an equivalent for his personal service.—What is there in the new proposed constitution to prevent his being dragged like a Prussian soldier to the camp and there compelled to bear arms?—This will depend wholly upon the wisdom and discretion of the future legislature of the continent in the framing their militia laws; and I have lived long enough to hear the practice *of commuting personal service for a paltry fine* in time of war and foreign invasion most severely reprobated by some persons who ought to have judged more rightly on the subject—Such flagrant oppressions as these I dare say will not happen at the beginning of the new government; probably not till the powers of government shall be firmly fixed; but it is a duty we owe to ourselves and our posterity if possible to prevent their ever happening. I hope and trust that there are few persons at present hardy enough to entertain thoughts of creating any religious establishment for this country; although I have lately read a piece in the newspaper, which speaks of *religious* as well as civil and military *offices*, as being hereafter to be disposed of by the new government; but if a majority of the continental legislature should at any time think fit to establish a form of religion, for the good people of this continent, with all the pains and penalties which in other countries are annexed to the establishment of a national church, what is there in the proposed constitution to hinder their doing so? Nothing; for we have no bill of rights, and every thing therefore is in their power and at their discretion. And at whose discretion? We know not any more than we know the fates of those generations which are yet unborn.

It is needless to repeat the necessity of securing other personal rights in the forming a new government. The same argument which proves the necessity of securing one of them shews also the necessity of securing others. Without a bill of rights we are totally insecure in all of them; and no man can promise himself with any degree of certainty that his posterity will enjoy the inestimable blessings of liberty of conscience, of freedom of speech and of writing and publishing their thoughts on public matters, of trial by jury, of holding themselves, their houses and papers free from seizure and search upon general suspicion or general warrants; or in short that they will be secured in the enjoyment of life, liberty and property without depending on the will and pleasure of their rulers.

If we pass over the consideration of this subject so essential to the preservation of our liberties, and turn our eyes to the *form* of the government which the Convention have proposed to us, I apprehend that changing the prospect will not wholly alleviate our fears.—A few words on this head, will close the present letter. In the first place the office of President of the United States appears to me to be clothed with such powers as are dangerous. To be the fountain of all honors in the United States, commander in chief of the army, navy and militia, with the power of making treaties and of granting pardons, and to be vested with an authority to put a negative upon all laws, unless two thirds of both houses shall persist in enacting it, and put their names down upon calling the yeas and nays for that purpose, is in reality to be a KING as much *a King as the King of Great-Britain*, and a King too of the worst kind;—an elective King.—If such powers as these are to be trusted in the hands of any man, they ought for the sake of preserving the peace of the community at once to be made hereditary.—Much as I abhor kingly government, yet I venture to pronounce where kings are admitted to rule they should most certainly be vested with hereditary power. The election of a King whether it be in America or Poland, will be a scene of horror and confusion; and I am perfectly serious when I declare that, as a friend to my country, I shall despair of any happiness in the United States until this office is either reduced to a lower pitch of power or made perpetual and hereditary.—When I say that our future President will be as much a king as the king of Great-Britain, I only ask of my readers to look into the constitution of that country, and then tell me what important prerogative the King of Great-Britain is entitled to, which does not also belong to the President during his continuance in office.— The King of Great-Britain it is true can create nobility which our

President cannot; but our President will have the power of making all the *great men,* which comes to the same thing.—All the difference is that we shall be embroiled in contention about the choice of the man, which they are at peace under the security of an hereditary succession.—To be tumbled headlong from the pinnacle of greatness and be reduced to a shadow of departed royalty is a shock almost too great for human nature to endure. It will cost a man many struggles to resign such eminent powers, and ere long, we shall find, some one who will be very unwilling to part with them.— Let us suppose this man to be a favorite with his army, and that they are unwilling to part with their beloved commander in chief; or to make the thing familiar, let us suppose, a future President and commander in chief adored by his army and the militia to as great a degree as our late illustrious commander in chief; and we have only to suppose one thing more, that this man is without the virtue, the moderation and love of liberty which possessed the mind of our late general, and this country will be involved at once in war and tyranny. So far is it from its being improbable that the man who shall hereafter be in a situation to make the attempt to perpetuate his own power, should want the virtues of General Washington; that it is perhaps a chance of one hundred millions to one that the next age will not furnish an example of so disinterested a use of great power. We may also suppose, without trespassing upon the bounds of probability, that this man may not have the means of supporting in private life the dignity of his former station; that like Caesar, he may be at once ambitious and poor, and deeply involved in debt.— Such a man would die a thousand deaths rather than sink from the heights of splendor and power into obscurity and wretchedness. We are certainly about giving our president too much or too little; and in the course of less than twenty years we shall find that we have given him enough to enable him to take all. It would be infinitely more prudent to give him at once as much as would content him, so that we might be able to retain the rest in peace; for if once power is seized by violence not the least fragment of liberty will survive the shock. I would therefore advise my countrymen seriously to ask themselves this question;—Whether they are prepared TO RECEIVE A KING? If they are to say so at once, and make the kingly office hereditary; to frame a constitution that should set bounds to his power, and, as far as possible secure the liberty of the subject. If we are not prepared to *receive a king*, let us call another convention to revise the proposed constitution, and form it anew on the principles of a confederacy of free republics; but by no means, under pretence of a republic, to lay the foundation for a military government, which is the worst of all tyrannies.

Yours, &c.

AN OLD WHIG.

Independent Gazetteer

24 NOVEMBER 1787

ESSAY VI

Old Whig again warns his readers of the ease and frequency with which political bodies increase their powers. He goes on to note that a congress given the power to regulate trade between the states and between the United States and other countries, and to tax international trade would answer the Confederacy's needs. Meanwhile, the proposed Constitution ignores the distinction between internal and external taxation, guaranteeing expansion of federal power at the expense of the states. Essays in The Federalist *of particular relevance: 30-36.*

Mr. PRINTER,

I Think it is an observation of Dean Swift, that, in political matters, all men can feel, though all cannot see. Agreeably to this doctrine we find, that the necessity of giving additional powers to Congress is at length *felt*, by all men, though it was not foreseen by a great number of the people. As the states individually could not protect our trade, foreign nations, friends as well as enemies, have combined against it; and at the same time that our trade is more beneficial to any nation in Europe, than the trade of any nation in Europe is to us, because we export provisions and raw materials and receive manufactures in return: we are not suffered to be the carriers of our own produce—foreign bottoms engross the whole of our carrying trade, and we are obliged to pay them for doing that which it is the interest of every people to do for themselves. Our shipwrights are starved, our seamen driven abroad for want of employ, our timber left useless on our hands, our ironworks, once a very profitable branch of business, now almost reduced to nothing, and our money banished from the country. These with the train of concomitant evils which always attend the loss of trade, or a state of trade which is unprofitable, have justly alarmed us all; and I am firmly pursuaded that scarcely a man of common sense can be found, that does not wish for an efficient federal government, and lament that it has been delayed so long. Yet at the same time it is a matter of immense consequence, in establishing a government which is to last for ages, and which, if it be suffered to depart from the principles of liberty in the beginning, will in all probability, never return to them, that we consider carefully what sort of government we are about to form. Power is very easily encreased; indeed it naturally grows in every government; but it hardly ever lessens.

The misfortunes under which we have for some time laboured, and which still press us severely, would be in a great measure alleviated, if not wholly removed, by devolving upon Congress the power of regulating trade and laying and collecting duties and imposts. If these powers were once fully vested in Congress, trade would immediately assume a new face, money and people would flow in upon us, and the vast tracts of ungranted lands would be a mine of wealth for many years to come. I am pursuaded, that with this addition to the powers of Congress, we should soon find them sufficient for every purpose; and it is very certain that if we did not find them sufficient, we could easily encrease them. But instead of being contented with this, the late convention by their proposed constitution, seem to have resolved to give the new continental government every kind of power whatsoever, throughout the United States. This power I have already attempted to show, is not limited by any stipulations in favour of the liberty of the subject, and it is easy to shew, that it will be equally unchecked by any restraint from the individual states. The treasure of the whole continent will be entirely at their command. "The Congress shall have power to levy and collect taxes, duties, imposts and excises." And what are the individual states to do, or how are they to subsist? may they also lay and collect taxes, duties, imposts and excises? If they should, the miserable subject will be like sheep twice shorne; the skin must follow the fleece. But the fact is, that no individual state can collect a penny, unless by the permission of Congress for the "laws of the United States shall be the supreme law of the land, any thing in the constitution or laws of any state to the contrary, notwithstanding." The laws of the individual states, will be only *Leges sub graviore Lege:* for the power of enacting laws necessarily implies the power of repealing laws; and therefore Congress, being the supreme legislatures, may annul or repeal the laws of the individual states, whenever they please. Not a single source of revenue will remain to any state, which Congress may not stop at their sovereign will and pleasure; for if any state attempt to impose a tax or levy a duty, contrary to the inclination of Congress, they have only to exert their supreme legislative power and the law imposing such tax or duty, is done away in a moment. For instance, it will very soon be found inconvenient to have two sets of excise officers in each town or county in every state, they will be in danger of clashing with each other, it will then be found "necessary and proper for carrying into execution the powers vested by the constitution in the government of the United States, or in some department or officer thereof," to forbid the individual states to levy any more excise. Congress may chuse to impose a stamp-duty. It will be very inconvenient for people to run back and forward to different offices, to procure double stamps, and therefore it will be thought "necessary and proper" to forbid any state to meddle with stamp-duties. The same will be the case with many other taxes. They will be in danger of clashing with each other, if Congress and the several states should happen to lay taxes on the same article. The States therefore individually, will be restrained from imposing any taxes upon such articles as Congress shall think proper to tax. They must then try to find out other articles for taxation, which Congress have not thought proper to touch. This I fear will be a difficult task: for the expensive court to be maintained by the great president, the pay of the standing army and the numerous crouds of hungry expectants, who have lost their all, and it will be said, have lost it by their zeal for the new constitution, must necessarily employ the sharpest wits among their ablest financiers, to devise every possible mode of taxation; and besides, if an individual state should hit upon a new tax that should happen to be productive, there is no doubt but it would soon be taken from it and appropriated to the use of the United States. The inhabitants of the TEN MILE SQUARE, would find ways and means to dispose of all the money that could possibly be raised in every part of the United States. What then will become of the separate governments? They will be annihilated; absolutely annihilated; for no man will ever submit to the wretchedness and contempt of holding any office under them.

The advocates of the proposed constitution, seem to be aware of the difficulty I have hinted at, and therefore it is, I presume, that in conversation as well as in their publications, we are told that under the proposed constitution, "direct taxation will be unnecessary"; that "it is probable the principal branch of revenue will be duties on imports." Some of those who have used such language in public and private, I believe to be very honest men; and I would therefore ask of them, what security they can give us, that the future government of the continent will in any measure confine themselves to the duties upon imports, or that the utmost penny will not be exacted which can possibly be collected either by direct or indirect taxation? How can they answer for the conduct of our future rulers? We have heard enough of these fair promises for the good behaviour of men in office, to learn to doubt of their fulfilment, unless we guard ourselves by much better security, there will be no bounds to the new government. They will not have as much to spare for the separate states to collect as Lazarus picked up of the fragments from the rich man's table. There are mouths at this moment gaping in the United States for all that can possibly be collected;—a confederacy is already formed for dividing the public cake to the last crum; and I wish they may not quarrel for more.

But if I were mistaken in this opinion; if in the language of these gentlemen, it is probable that the principal branch of the public revenue will be duties on imports;—if it is probable that these with the back lands and the post-office will be sufficient, where was the necessity of being in such haste to grant more;—to grant all without limits or restrictions? Men do not usually give up their whole purse where they can pay with part. Why might we not try at least how far the customs and back lands would go before we give all away from the seperate states, without reserving any thing for their support.

The true line of distinction which should have been drawn in describing the powers of Congress, and those of the several states, should have been that between internal and external taxation. I am persuaded that the existence of the several states in their separate capacities, and of the United States in their collective capacity, depends upon the maintaining such distinction. Without the power of imposing duties on foreign commerce and regulating trade, the United States will be weak and contemptible, and, indeed, their union must be speedily dissolved: And on the other hand, if the legislature of the United States shall possess the powers of internal as well as external taxation, the individual states in their separate capacities, will be less than the shadows of a name.

I observe that the late delegates of Connecticut, in their letter to the Governor, speak of the power of direct taxation as an authority which need not be exercised if each state will "furnish the quota." Yet there is no doubt but they may exercise this power if they choose to do it; and they alone will have the right of judging what quotas the several states shall be required to furnish. They may ask as much as they please, and if the states do not furnish all they ask, they may tax at their pleasure; under these circumstances the power of internal taxation will undoubtedly be exercised by the Continental Legislature. If it be said that it is to be expected that the Congress will exercise this power with moderation, I venture to pronounce that those who indulge such hopes, are not acquainted with the principles of human nature. Independent of the multitudinous expectations which the followers of the proposed Constitution entertain in their own favor, which alone, if gratified, would consume the treasures of two such continents as this; there is a spirit of rivalship in power, which will not suffer two suns to shine in the same firmament, one will speedily darken the other, and the individual states will be as totally eclipsed, as the stars in the meridian blaze of the sun. We have seen too much of this spirit in the several states, under the present loose and futile confederation. A jealousy of the powers of Congress in the separate states, which is founded in the same rivalship of power, and which, however contemptible it may appear was alike founded in the principles of human nature, may furnish us an exemplary lesson upon this head: And when we verge to the other extreme by vesting all power in Congress, we shall find them equally jealous of any power in the individual states, and equally possessed of the same spirit of rivalship, which heretofore denied the necessary supplies from the states to Congress.—We shall never be able to support the collective powers of the United States in Congress, and the powers of the individual states in their separate capacities, without drawing the line fairly between them. If we leave the states individually to the mercy of the Continental Government, they will be stript of the last penny which is necessary for their support; if we give all powers to one, there will be nothing left for the others. The loss of dominion, where it is indulged, will swallow up the whole.

But I shall be told that if Congress are left to depend upon requisitions from the individual states for any part of the necessary supplies, the same difficulty will remain which has hitherto existed; and I may be asked, what shall we do if the supplies should fall short? I answer that although nothing but a very serious necessity of money for continental purposes will ever procure supplies upon requisition from the separate states, yet when that necessity exists in any degree that is really alarming to the whole community, I do not think that such supplies are to be dispaired of. We have seen many instances of aid being furnished, even voluntarily upon pressing occasions, which should teach us to rely on the exertions of the states upon occasions of real and not mere imaginary necessity. One thing will certainly follow from the Continental Governments being restrained to external taxation;—that it will be under the necessity of exercising more œconomy than it has done especially during the late war. We have been witnesses of such a profuse expenditure of public money at some period, as these states could never support. This profusion ought to convince us that if all the treasures of the continent are intrusted to the power of Congress, there is too much reason to fear that the whole will be consumed by them, and nothing left to the individual states; and judging them past experience we may venture to presage that the people will be fleeced without mercy, if no check is maintained upon the power of Congress in the articles of taxation.

We ought to be very fully convinced of an absolute necessity existing before we entrust the whole power of taxation to the hands of Congress; and the moment we do so, we ought by consent to annihilate the individual states; for the powers of the individual states will be as effectually swallowed as a drop of water in the ocean; and the next consequence will be a speedy dissolution of our republican form of government.

Yours, &c.

AN OLD WHIG.

Independent Gazetteer

28 NOVEMBER 1787

ESSAY VII

Old Whig appeals to the principles of the War for Independence in arguing that the people retain the right to decide on their own form of government. They should propose amendments to the proposed Constitution in their state conventions, then call a new convention to work out the details. General agreement on the nature of necessary changes, particularly an addition of a federal bill of rights, will render this process manageable and productive. Essays in The Federalist *of particular relevance: 1, 84.*

Mr. PRINTER,

MANY people seem to be convinced that the proposed constitution is liable to a number of important objections; that there are defects in it which ought to be supplied, and errors which ought to be amended; but they apprehend that we must either receive this constitution in its present form, or be left without any continental government whatsoever. To be sure, if this were the case, it would be most prudent for us, like a man who is wedded to a bad wife, to submit to our misfortune with patience, and make the best of a bad bargain. But if we will summon up resolution sufficient to examine into our true circumstances, we shall find that we are not in so deplorable a situation as people have been taught to believe, from the suggestions of interested men, who wish to force down the proposed plan of government without delay, for the purpose of providing offices for themselves and their friends. We shall find, that, with a little wisdom and patience, we have it yet in our power, not only to establish a federal constitution, but to establish a good one.

It is true that the continental convention has directed their proposed constitution to be laid before a convention of delegates to be chosen in each state, "for their assent and ratification," which seems to preclude the idea of any power in the several conventions, of proposing any alterations, or indeed of even rejecting the plan proposed, if they should disapprove of it. Still, however, the question recurs, what authority the late convention had to bind the people of the United States, to any particular form of government, or to forbid them to adopt such form of government as they should think fit. I know it is a language frequent in the mouths of some heaven-born PHAETONS amongst us, who like the son of Apollo, think themselves entitled to guide the charriot of the sun; that common people have no right to judge of the affairs of government; that they are not fit for it; that they should leave these matters to their superiors. This however, is not the language of men of real understanding, even among the advocates for the proposed constitution; but these still recognize the authority of the people, and will admit, at least in words, that the people have a right to be consulted. Then I ask, if the people in the different states have a right to be consulted, in the new form of continental government, what authority could the late convention have to preclude them from proposing amendments to the plan they should offer? Had the convention any right to bind the people to the form of government they should propose? Let us consider this matter.

The late convention were chosen by the general assembly of each state; they had the sanction of Congress;—for what? To consider what alterations were necessary to be made in the articles of confederation. What have they done? They have made a new constitution for the United States. I will not say, that in doing so, they have exceeded their authority; but on the other hand, I trust that no man of understanding amongst them will pretend to say, that any thing they did or could do, was of the least avail to lessen the rights of the people to judge for themselves in the last resort. This right, is perhaps, unalienable, but at all events, there is no pretence for saying that this right was ever meant to be surrendered up into the hands of the late continental convention.

The people have an undoubted right to judge of every part of the government which is offered to them: No power on earth has a right to preclude them; and they may exercise this choice either by themselves or their delegates legally chosen to represent them in the State-Convention.—I venture to say that no man, reasoning upon *revolution* principles, can possibly controvert this right.

Indeed very few go so far as to controvert the right of the people to propose amendments; but we are told that the thing is impracticable; that if we begin to propose amendments there will be no end to them; that the several states will never agree in their amendments; that we shall never unite in any plan; that if we reject this we shall either have a worse or none at all; that we ought therefore to adopt this *at once*, without alteration or amendment.—Now these are very kind gentlemen, who insist upon doing so much good for us, whether we will or not. Idiots and maniacs ought certainly to be restrained from doing themselves mischief, and should be compelled to that which is for their own good. Whether the people of America are to be considered in this light, and treated accordingly, is a question

which deserves, perhaps, more consideration than it has yet
received. A contest between the patients and their doctors, which
are mad or which are fools, might possibly be a very unhappy one. I
hope at least that we shall be able to settle this important business
without so preposterous a dispute. What then would you have us do,
it may be asked? Would you have us adopt the proposed Constitution
or reject it? I answer that I would neither with the one nor the other.
Though I would be far from pretending to dictate to the representatives of the people what steps ought to be pursued, yet a method
seems to present itself so simple, so perfectly calculated to obviate all
difficulties, to reconcile us with one another, and establish unanimity
and harmony among the people of this country, that I cannot forbear
to suggest it. I hope that most of my readers have already anticipated me in what I am about to propose. Whether they have or not,
I shall venture to state it, in the humble expectations that it may
have some tendency to reconcile honest men of all parties with one
another.

The method I would propose is this—

1st. Let the Conventions of each state, as they meet, after considering the proposed Constitution, [state] their objections and propose their amendments.

So far from these objections and amendments clashing with each
other in irreconcileable discord, as it has been too often suggested
they would do, it appears that from what has been hitherto published in the different states in opposition to the proposed Constitution, we have a right to expect that they will harmonize in a very
great degree. The reason I say so, is, that about the same time, in
very different parts of the continent, the very same objections have
been made, and the very same alterations proposed by different
writers, who I verily believe, know nothing at all of each other, and
were very far from acting a premeditated concert, and that others
who have not appeared as writers in the newspapers, in the different states, have appeared to act and speak in perfect unison with
those objections and amendments, particularly in the article of a
Bill of Rights. That in short, the very same sentiments seem to
have been echoed from the different parts of the continent by the
opposers of the proposed Constitution, and these sentiments have

been very little contradicted by its friends, otherwise than by suggesting their fears, that by opposing the Constitution at present proposed, we might be disappointed of any federal government or receive a worse one than the present.—It would be a most delightful surprize to find ourselves all of one opinion at last; and I cannot forbear hoping that when we come fairly to compare our sentiments, we shall find ourselves much more nearly agreed than in the hurry and surprize in which we have been involved on this subject, than we ever suffered ourselves to imagine.

2d. When the Conventions have stated these objections and amendments, let them transmit them to Congress and adjourn, praying that Congress will direct another Convention to be called from the different states, to consider of these objections and amendments, and pledging themselves to abide by whatever decision shall be made by such future Convention on the subject; whether it be to amend the proposed Constitution or to reject any alteration and ratify it as it stands.

3d. If a new Convention of the United States should meet, and revise the proposed Constitution, let us agree to abide by their decision.—It is past a doubt that every good citizen of America pants for an efficient federal government—I have no doubt we shall concur at last in some plan of continental government, even if many people could imagine exceptions to it; but if the exceptions which are made at present, shall be maturely considered and even be pronounced by our future representatives as of no importance; (which I trust they will not) even in that case, I have no doubt that almost every man, will give up his own private opinion and concur in that decision.

4th. If by any means another Continental Convention should fail to meet, then let the Conventions of the several states again assemble and at last decide the great solemn question whether we shall adopt the Constitution now proposed, or reject it? And, whenever it becomes necessary to decide upon this point, one at least who from the beginning has been invariably anxious for the liberty and independence of his country, will concur in adopting and supporting this Constitution, rather than none;—though I confess I could easily imagine, some other form of confederation, which I should think better entitled to my hearty approbation;—and indeed I am not afraid of a worse.

I am, &c.

AN OLD WHIG.

Independent Gazetteer

6 FEBRUARY 1788

ESSAY VIII[1]

Old Whig concludes by arguing that most Americans see the need for a stronger continental government, and that the proposed Constitution itself requires amendments. Because the new government will be powerful and aristocratic, the new rulers will not be inclined to make the necessary changes— particularly given the difficulty of the prescribed amending process. Thus these changes should be made before the Constitution is ratified. Essays in The Federalist *of particular relevance: 23, 85.*

MR. PRINTER,

IT is the fate of political controversies to begin with argument and end with abuse: And hence we find, in many instances, that a subject which for a time, has engaged the most earnest attention of the people, is at length quitted with horror and disgust. The question, however, concerning the total adoption of the plan of government, proposed by the late federal convention, is too important for good men to suffer themselves to be diverted from giving it a full consideration by the bouncing of squibs or the whizzing of political firebrands. I therefore persuade myself that a few candid observations on this subject will yet be heard with attention.

[1]Misnumbered as VII in original.

The real question is this;—Whether the people of this country ought to adopt the proposed constitution in its present form, without limitation or alteration, or whether we ought to insist upon amendments being made previous to its adoption.

Most men seem to agree that amendments ought to be made in the proposed plan in some stage of the business; and all seem agreed that an efficient form of continental government ought to be established. Shall we then first adopt the constitution and afterwards amend it; or shall we first amend it and afterwards adopt it? Let us for a moment consider the propriety of adopting it first, and trusting to its being afterwards amended. These necessary amendments, after the constitution is adopted, can only be made in one or two ways;—either by our future rulers in the continental legislature by their own act—or in the way provided for in the fifth article, by a convention to be called for proposing amendments, whenever two-thirds of both houses shall deem it necessary, or whenever the legislatures of two-thirds of the states shall make application for that purpose, such amendments afterwards to be valid if ratified by the legislatures of three-fourths of the states, or by conventions in three-fourths thereof, if Congress should think proper to call them. This latter mode is so intricate, that an attempt to investigate it is like endeavouring to trace the windings of a labyrinth, and I have therefore observed that people willingly turn aside from the subject, as confused and disgusting. Some former observations on this article I found were very little attended to: However I will attempt once more to find a clue to its mazes, after I shall first have considered that more inviting ground of expectation to which most of those who assume the name of federalists turn their eyes with so much confidence.

First then, the general expectation seems to be that our future rulers will rectify all that is amiss. If a bill of rights is wanting, they will frame a bill of rights. If too much power is vested in them, they will not abuse it; nay, they will divest themselves of it. The very first thing they will do, will be to establish the liberties of the people by good and wholesome ordinances, on so solid a foundation as to baffle all future encroachments from themselves or their successors. Much good no doubt might be done in this way; if Congress should possess the most virtuous inclinations, yet there are some things which it will not be in their power to rectify. For instance; *the appellate jurisdiction both as to law and fact*, which is given to the supreme court of the continent, and which annihilates the trial by jury in all civil causes, the Congress can only modify:—They cannot extinguish this power, so destructive to the principles of real liberty. It would not by any means be extravagant to say, that a new continental convention ought to be called, if it were only for the sake of preserving that sacred palladium—THE INESTIMABLE RIGHT OF TRIAL BY JURY.—But even if we were to delude ourselves so far as to believe that it would be entirely in the power of the future legislature to set every thing right, to build up our liberties against all invasions, and to protect us from every political calamity, still we ought not to repose all our liberty and all our happiness in the virtue of our future rulers. I speak not with reference to any particular set of men. I pretend not to know who will be our rulers one year hence. In the state of Pennsylvania I have seen the administration of our constitution in the hands of its bitterest enemies, during near one half of its existence; and I shall not be at all surprized to find that if the new continental government shall be set a-going, that the jockies who at present have vaulted into the saddle; should be the first to be thrown into the dirt and trampled upon; nor, on the other hand, that some of those who are foremost in contending for a permanent security to the rights of the people, should be in the first rank of oppressors. These things have frequently happened; and the only safe way of reasoning on political subjects is, to consider men, abstractly as men, with like passions and infirmities throughout the world, in every age, and every country;and to believe that the same guards and checks against arbitrary power, which were necessary two thousand years ago, are equally necessary at present, and will be so two thousand years hence. Idolatry is the parent of errors in politics as well as religion;—and an implicit confidence in our rulers now, will be abused as much as implicit confidence in priests ever was in the days of superstition. I know well that instances of political moderation may be found, and a tyrant has before now descended from the plenitude of power, satiated with dominion, or worn out with care; but there is not one instance on record in all history of a number of men voluntarily abandoning the powers of an aristocracy. Look at the Decemviri, look at the thirty tyrants of Athens, look at all the lordly aristocracies that ever existed, and shew me one instance—such an instance cannot be shewn. Nay farther, a single monarch has many times used his power with moderation; but a number of men combined in an aristocracy, never knew what moderation meant. They are all struggling to be most powerful, all aiming to enrich themselves and provide for their friends, and all of them plundering the people. And shall we foolishly, after so many thousand examples, trust to the virtue and moderation of our future rulers, to divest themselves of those powers which may be abused to our prejudice, and are no way useful to our protection? Not to insist upon Swift's ludicrous tale of Jack's hanging himself at the instigation of Humphry Hocus, on the promise of being cut down before he should be dead, and when he had hanged himself, of being left to kick his heels in the air, the moral of which, by the bye, is strictly founded in human nature;—let us attend to a more serious fable.— "A man, says Æsop, coming into a wood, begged the trees to grant him the favor of a handle to his axe. The whole forest consented; upon which he provided himself with a strong handle; which he had no sooner done, than he began to fell the trees without number, then the trees, though too late, repented of their weakness, and an universal groan was heard throughout the forest. At length, when the man came to cut down the tree which had furnished him with the handle, the trunk fell to the ground uttering these words: Fool that I was! I have been the cause of my own destruction." If we perish in America, we shall have no better comfort than the same mortifying reflection, that we have been the cause of our own destruction.

I have said that many of the liberties which, by the proposed constitution, are to be surrendered up into the hands of our rulers, will be of no use towards the protection of the people; and a little reflection will convince us, that it is certainly the case. If, indeed, government were really strengthened by such surrender, if the body of the people were made more secure, or more happy by the means, we ought to make the sacrifice. An individual ought to submit to be tossed about, imprisoned and treated injuriously, if the good of his country should require it; and every individual in the community ought to strip himself of some convenience for the sake of the public good.

I know it is an error not uncommon to believe, that a government is the more powerful in proportion as it is more tyrannical; but this is not the case: so far from it, that it has always been found, that free countries have been able to exert powers far superior to those in which a more absolute government prevailed. For instance, a senate which is master of its own elections, without any or with very little dependence on the people, would not be able to exert as much force as a senate which is freely elected by the people; because the cheerful support which would be yielded in the latter case, would far exceed that which could be exacted by the mere force of authority. Again; how could the stripping people of the right of trial by jury conduce to the strength of the state? Do we find the government in England at all weakened by the people retaining the right of trial by jury? Far from it. Yet these things which merely tend to oppress the people, without conducing at all to the strength of the state, are the last which aristocratic rulers would consent to restore to the people; because they encrease the personal power and importance of the rulers. Judges, unincumbered by juries, have been ever found much better friends to government than to the people. Such judges will always be more desireable than juries to a self-created senate, upon the same principle that a large standing army, and the entire command of the militia and of the purse, is ever desireable to those who wish to enslave the people, and upon the same principle that a bill of rights is their aversion.

In like manner, if we should trace the several branches of the proposed constitution, which are obnoxious to the liberties of the people, we shall find them to consist of such articles as are rather fitted to encrease the powers of the rulers, than the strength of the nation. Union is the great source of strength to a nation, not vassalage. To an aristocratic government vassalage is the great object even at the expence of union among the people. We ought not, therefore, by any means to rely upon the virtue of our future rulers for a reformation of those things which at present are amiss in the proposed constitution. The president and senate will ever be grasping at more and more power until they are completely masters of the people, and the president at last master of all.

Let us then turn to the article in the proposed constitution, which provides for the making alterations at some future period; and let us figure to ourselves the time when two-thirds of both houses of Congress shall think it necessary to call a convention, for two-thirds of the legislatures of the individual states shall apply for the calling of a convention, and when a continental convention shall agree upon amendments, and when the legislatures of three-fourths of the states, or three-fourths of the conventions to be called in the several states, if Congress shall prefer that mode of proceeding, shall ratify such amendments; and again, after all these strainings, and filtrings, and refinings, of the hopes and expectations of the people through the channels of power, when the amendments so asked for, proposed, digested, twistificated, altered, and at last ratified, will be of any essential importance. For my part I would full as soon sit down and take my chance of winning an important privilege to the people, by the casting the dice 'till I could throw sixes an hundred times in succession.—There is no doubt but the thing has been purposely contrived to make alterations extremely difficult; and so it certainly ought to be if the proposed constitution were a good one. I do not therefore so much blame the late federal convention for making their constitution very difficult of alteration, as I insist upon it as an argument in favor of making our amendments beforehand. A machine which cannot be taken to pieces after it is once set a-going, ought to be very well finished at first.

Yet this is not all the difficulty. Inveterate power is at all times very hard to be controuled. Habits, connexions, dependence, and a thousand circumstances in course of time, rivet the chains of slavery 'till we grow either callous to their galling, or too feeble to shake them off, or too listless to resist. Ask the beaten Turk to resume his liberty, or the tired horse to resume his pristine freedom.—As well might you ask the galled sons of America, a few years hence, to assert the native rights of men, if the proposed constitution be once fixed upon us. It will be extremely difficult to change it for the better even in the beginning; but in a little time it will become utterly impossible.

A little prudence, a little patience, and a little serious reflection, would lead us to concur in calling a new convention, to revise the constitution proposed to us. That convention, I have no doubt, if fully, freely, and deliberately chosen, would concur in some essential amendments; and we might yet be a united and a happy people. Yours, &c.

AN OLD WHIG.

Letter of Richard Henry Lee
to Governor Edmund Randolph

This letter was originally printed in the Virginia Gazette *on 16 October 1787. It was widely reprinted and discussed, both before and after publication, as much for its content as for the fame of its author, who held public positions during and after the War for Independence. Lee calls for a new convention to redraft sections of the proposed Constitution, which he fears would establish an oligarchy, leaving American rights undefended. Two critical concerns: the mixing of powers in the president and Senate and the judiciary's failure to protect the local administration of justice, particularly through locally selected juries. The* Virginia Gazette *being unavailable, this letter was set from the* New-York Journal, *which reprinted it on 22 and 24 December 1787. Essays in* The Federalist *of particular relevance: 47, 51, 57, 83.*

New-York Journal

22 DECEMBER 1787

From the Virginia Gazette.
Copy of a Letter from the Hon. Richard Henry Lee, Esq. one of the Delegates from this State in Congress, to his Excellency the Governor.

New-York, Oct. 16, 1787.
Dear Sir,
I was duly honored with your favor of Sept. 17, from Philadelphia, which should have been acknowledged long before now, if the nature of the business that is related to had not required time.

The establishment of the new plan of government, in its present form, is a question that involves such immense consequences to the present times, and to posterity, that it calls for the deepest attention of the best and wisest friends of their country and of mankind; if it be found good after mature deliberation, adopt it; if wrong, amend it at all events, for to say (as many do) that a bad government must be established for fear of anarchy, is really saying, that we must kill ourselves for fear of dying. Experience and the actual state of things. Shew that there is no difficulty in procuring a general convention; the late one being collected without any obstruction. Nor does external war or internal discord, prevent the most cool, collected, full, and fair discussion of this all-important subject. If with infinite ease a convention was obtained to prepare a system, why may not another with equal ease be procured to make proper and necessary amendments? Good government is not the work of a short time, or of sudden thought. From Moses to Montesquieu the greatest geniuses have been employed on this difficult subject, and yet experience has shewn capital defects in the system produced for the government of mankind.—But since it is neither prudent or easy to make frequent changes in government, and as bad governments have been generally found the most fixed; so it becomes of the last consequence to frame the first establishment upon ground the most unexceptionable, and such as the best theories with experience justify; not trusting as our new constitution does, and as many approve of doing, to time and future events to correct errors, that both reason and experience in similar cases, point out in the new system. It has hitherto been supposed a fundamental maxim that in governments rightly balanced, the different branches of legislature should be unconnected, and that the legislative and executive powers should be separate: In the new constitution, the president and senate have all the executive, and two thirds of the legislative power. In some weighty instances (as making all kinds of treaties which are to be the laws of the land) they have the whole legislative and executive powers. They jointly, appoint all officers civil and military, and they (the senate) try all impeachments either of their own members, or of the officers appointed by themselves.

Is there not a most formidable combination of power, thus created in a few, and can the most critic eye, if a candid one, discover responsibility in this potent corps? Or will any sensible man say, that great power without responsibility can be given to rulers with safety to liberty? It is most clear that the parade of impeachment is nothing to them, or any of them; as little restraint is to be found, I presume, from the fear of offending constituents. The president is for four years duration (and Virginia for example) has one vote of thirteen in the choice of him, and this thirteenth vote not of the people, but electors, two removes from the people. The senate is a body of six years duration, and as in choice of president, the largest state has but a thirteenth vote, so is it in the choice of senators.— This latter statement is adduced to shew that responsibility is as little to be apprehended from amenability to constituents, as from the terror of impeachment. You are therefore, sir, well warranted in saying, either a monarchy, or aristocracy will be generated, perhaps the most grievous system of government may arise.—It cannot be denied with truth that this new constitution is, in its first principles, highly and dangerously oligarchic; and it is a point agreed that a government of the few, is, of all governments, the worst. The only check to be found in favour of the democratic principle in this system is, the house of representatives; which I believe may justly be called a mere shread or rag of representation: It being obvious to the least examination that smallness of number and great comparative disparity of power, renders that house of little effect to promote good, or restrain bad government. But what is the power given to this ill-constructed body? To judge of what may be for the general welfare, and such judgments when made, the acts of congress become supreme laws of the land. This seems a power co-extensive with every possible object of human legislation. Yet there is no restraint in form of a bill of rights, to secure (what doctor Blackstone calls) that residuum of human rights, which is not intended to be given up to society, and which indeed is not necessary to be given for any good social purpose. The rights of conscience, the freedom of the press, and the trial by jury are at mercy. It is there stated that in criminal cases, the trial shall be by jury. But how? In the state. What then becomes of the jury of the vicinage or at least from the county in the first instance, the states being from 50 to 700 miles in extent? This mode of trial even in criminal cases may be greatly impaired, and in civil cases the inference is strong, that it may be altogether omitted as the constitution positively assumes it in criminal, and is silent about it in civil causes. Nay it is more strongly discountenanced in civil cases by giving the supreme court in appeals, jurisdiction both as to law and fact.

Judge Blackstone in his learned commentaries (Art. Jury Trial) says, is the most transcendant privilege which any subject can enjoy or wish for, that he cannot be affected either in his property, his liberty, his person, but by the unanimous consent of twelve of his neighbours and equals. A constitution, that I may venture to affirm, has under providence, secured the just liberties of this nation for a long succession of ages. The impartial administration of justice, which secures both our persons and our properties, is the great end of civil society. But if that be entirely entrusted to the magistracy, a select body of men, and those generally selected by the prince, or such as enjoy the highest offices of the state, these decisions, in spite of their own natural integrity, will have frequently an involuntary bias towards those of their own rank and dignity. It is not to be expected from human nature, that the few should always be attentive to the good of the many. The learned judge further says, that "every tribunal selected for the decision of facts is a step towards establishing aristocracy; the most oppressive of all governments." The answer to these objections is, that the new legislature may provide remedies! but as they may, so they may not, and if they did, a succeeding assembly may repeal the provisions. The evil is found resting upon constitutional bottom, and the remedy upon the mutable ground of legislation, revocable at any annual meeting. It is the more unfortunate that this great security of human rights, the trial by jury, should be weakened in this system, as power is unnecessarily given in the second section of the third article, to call people from their own country in all cases of controversy about property between citizens of different states and foreigners, with citizens of the United States, to be tried in a distant court where the congress meets. For although inferior congressional courts may for the above [parties] be instituted in the different states, yet this is a matter altogether in the pleasure of the new legislature, so that if they please not to institute them, or if they do not regulate the right of appeal reasonably, the people will be exposed to endless oppression, and the necessity of submitting in multitudes of cases, to pay unjust demands, rather than follow suitors, through great expence, to far distant tribunals, and to be determined upon there, as it may be, without a jury. In this congressional legislature a bare majority of votes, can enact commercial laws, so that the representatives of the seven northern states, as they will have a majority, can by law create the most oppressive monopoly upon the five southern states, whose circumstances and productions are essentially different from theirs, although not a single man of these voters are the representatives of, or amenable to the people of the southern states. Can such a set of men be, with the least colour of truth, called a representative of those they make laws for? It is supposed that the policy of the northern states, will prevent such abuses.

(*To be Continued.*)

New-York Journal

24 DECEMBER 1787

(*Continued.*)

From the VIRGINIA GAZETTE.
Copy of a Letter from the Hon. Richard Henry Lee, Esq. one of the Delegates from this state in Congress, to his Excellency the Governor.

New-York, Oct. 16, 1787.
DEAR SIR,
BUT how feeble, sir, is policy when opposed to interest among trading people. And what is the restraint arising from policy? Why, that

we may be forced by abuse to become ship builders!—But how long will it be before a people of agriculture can produce ships sufficient to export such bulky commodities as ours and of such extent; and if we had the ships, from whence are the seamen to come? 4000 of whom at left will be necessary in Virginia. In questions so liable to abuse, why was not the necessary vote put to two thirds of the members of the legislature? With the constitution, came from the convention so many members of that body to congress, and of those too, who were among the most fiery zealots for their system, that the votes of three states being of them, two states divided by them, and many others mixed with them, it is easy to see that Congress could have little opinion upon the subject. Some denied our right to make amendments, whilst others more moderate agreed to the right, but denied the expediency of amending; but it was plain that a majority was ready to send it on in terms of approbation—my judgment and conscience forbid the last, and therefore I moved the amendments that I have the honor to send you enclosed herewith and demanded the yeas and nays that they might appear on the journal. This seemed to alarm, and to prevent such appearance on the journal, it was agreed to transmit the constitution without a syllable of approbation or disapprobation, so that the term unanimously only applied to the transmission, as you will observe by attending to the terms of the resolve for transmitting. Upon the whole, sir, my opinion is, that as this constitution abounds with useful regulations, at the same time that it is liable to strong and fundamental objections, the plan for us to pursue, will be to propose the necessary amendment, and express our willingness to adopt it with the amendments, and to suggest the calling of a new convention for the purpose of considering them. To this I see no well founded objection, but great safety and much good to be the probable result. I am perfectly satisfied that you make such use of this letter as you shall think to be for the public good; and now, after begging your pardon for so great a trespass on your patience, and representing my best respects to your lady, I will conclude with assuring you, that I am with the sincerest esteem and regard, dear sir, your most affectionate and obedient servant.

RICHARD HENRY LEE.

POSTSCRIPT.

It having been found from universal experience, that the most express declarations and reservations are necessary to protect the just rights and liberty of mankind from the silent powerful and ever active conspiracy of those who govern; and it appearing to be the sense of the good people of America, by the various bills or declarations of rights whereon the government of the greater number of states are founded. That such precautions are necessary to restrain and regulate the exercise of the great powers given to rulers. In conformity with these principles, and from respect for the public sentiment on this subject, it is submitted,—That the new constitution proposed for the government of the United States be bottomed upon a declaration or bill of rights, clearly and precisely stating the principles upon which this social compact is founded, to wit: That the rights of concience in matters of religion ought not to be violated—That the freedom of the press shall be secured—That the trial by jury in criminal and civil cases, and the modes prescribed by the commonlaw for the safety of life in criminal prosecutions shall be held sacred—That standing armies in times of peace are dangerous to liberty, and ought not to be permitted unless assented to by two thirds of the members composing each house of the legislature under the new constitution—That the elections should be free and frequent—That the right administration of justice should be secured by the independency of the judges— that excessive bail, excessive fines, or cruel and unusual punishments should not be demanded or inflicted—That the right of the people to assemble peaceably for the purpose of petitioning the legislature shall not be prevented—That the citizens shall not be exposed to unreasonable searches, seizure of their persons, houses, papers or property; and it is necessary for the good of society, that the administration of government be conducted with all possible maturity of judgment, for which reason it hath been the practice of civilized nations and so determined by every state in the Union.— That a council of state or privy council should be appointed to advise and assist in the arduous business assigned to the executive power. Therefore let the new constitution be so amended as to admit the appointment of a privy council to consist of eleven members chosen by the president, but responsible for the advice they may give. For which purpose the advice given shall be entered in a council book, and signed by the giver in all affairs of great moment, and that the councellors act under an oath of office. In order to prevent the dangerous blending of the legislative and executive powers, and to secure responsibility—The privy, and not the senate, shall be joined with the president in the appointment of all officers civil and military under the new constitution—That the constitution be so altered as not to admit the creation of a vice president, when duties as assigned may be discharged by the privy council, except in the instance of proceding in the senate, which may be supplied by a speaker chosen from the body of senators by themselves as usual, that so may be avoided the establishment of a great officer of state, who is sometimes to be joined with the legislature, and sometimes administer the government, rendering responsibility difficult, besides giving unjust & needless pre-eminence to that state from whence this officer may have come.—That such parts of the new constitution be amended as provide imperfectly for the trial of criminals by a jury of the vicinage, and so supply the omission of a jury trial in civil causes or disputes about property between individuals, whereby the common law is directed, and as generally it is secured by the several state constitutions. That such parts of the new constitution be amended as permit the vexatious and oppressive callings of citizens from their own country, and all controversies between citizens of different states and between citizens and foreigners, to be tried in a far distant court, and as it may be without a jury, whereby in a multitude of cases, the circumstances of distance and expence, may compel numbers to submit to the most unjust and ill founded demand. That in order to secure the rights of the people more effectually from violation, the power and respectability of the house of representatives be increased, by increasing the number of delegates to that house where the popular interest must chiefly depend for protection—That the constitution be so amended as to increase the number of votes necessary to determine questions in cases where a bare majority may be seduced by strong motives of interest to injure and oppress the minority of the community as in commercical regulations, where advantage may be taken of circumstances to ordain rigid and premature laws that will in effect amount to monopolies, to the great impoverishment of those states whose peculiar situation expose them to such injuries.

Essays of Brutus

The *Essays of Brutus first appeared between October 1787 and April 1788 in the* New-York Journal. *It was during this period that the bulk of* The Federalist *appeared, and Brutus, named after Marcus Junius Brutus, assassin of the emperor Julius Caesar in the name of the Roman Republic, at times directly responds to the arguments of Publius, that other defender of Roman liberty. These powerful and highly influential essays are generally ascribed to Robert Yates, judge, dissenting member of the Constitutional Convention, and ally of New York Governor George Clinton. Among the most powerful and well-reasoned Anti-Federalist writings, the Essays of Brutus provide a close examination of the proposed Constitution and penetrating criticisms of the structure of government it provides. Essay XVI ends with a promise of further discussions, which were never published.*

New-York Journal

18 OCTOBER 1787

ESSAY I

Brutus begins by setting forth the general argument of the essays to follow: The Constitution will consolidate power in the federal government through its supremacy and necessary and proper clauses and through the unbounded federal taxing power. The resulting centralized government will encompass an area too large and

diverse for free government to survive. Essays in The Federalist
of particular relevance: 2, 14, 31-35, 44

To the CITIZENS *of the* STATE *of* NEW-YORK.

WHEN the public is called to investigate and decide upon a question
in which not only the present members of the community are
deeply interested, but upon which the happiness and misery of generations yet unborn is in great measure suspended, the benevolent
mind cannot help feeling itself peculiarly interested in the result.

In this situation, I trust the feeble efforts of an individual, to lead
the minds of the people to a wise and prudent determination, cannot fail of being acceptable to the candid and dispassionate part of
the community. Encouraged by this consideration, I have been
induced to offer my thoughts upon the present important crisis of
our public affairs.

Perhaps this country never saw so critical a period in their political concerns. We have felt the feebleness of the ties by which these
United-States are held together, and the want of sufficient energy
in our present confederation, to manage, in some instances, our general concerns. Various expedients have been proposed to remedy
these evils, but none have succeeded. At length a Convention of the
states has been assembled, they have formed a constitution which
will now, probably, be submitted to the people to ratify or reject,
who are the fountain of all power, to whom alone it of right belongs
to make or unmake constitutions, or forms of government, at their
pleasure. The most important question that was ever proposed to
your decision, or to the decision of any people under heaven, is
before you, and you are to decide upon it by men of your own election, [chosen] specially for this purpose. If the constitution, offered
to [your acceptance], be a wise one, calculated to preserve the
[invaluable blessings] of liberty, to secure the inestimable rights of
mankind, and promote human happiness, then, if you accept it, you
will lay a lasting foundation of happiness for millions yet unborn;
generations to come will rise up and call you blessed. You may
rejoice in the prospects of this vast extended continent becoming
filled with freemen, who will assert the dignity of human nature.
You may solace yourselves with the idea, that society, in this

favoured land, will [full] advance to the highest point of perfection; the human mind will expand in knowledge and virtue, and the golden age be, in some measure, realised. But if, on the other hand, this form of government contains principles that will lead to the subversion of liberty—if it tends to establish a despotism, or, what is worse, a tyrannic aristocracy; then, if you adopt it, this only remaining assylum for liberty will be [shut] up, and posterity will execrate your memory.

Momentous then is the question you have to determine, and you are called upon by every motive which should influence a noble and virtuous mind, to examine it well, and to make up a wise judgment. It is insisted, indeed, that this constitution must be received, be it ever so imperfect. If it has its defects, it is said, they can be best amended when they are experienced. But remember, when the people once part with power, they can seldom or never resume it again but by force. Many instances can be produced in which the people have voluntarily increased the powers of their rulers; but few, if any, in which rulers have willingly abridged their authority. This is a sufficient reason to induce you to be careful, in the first instance, how you deposit the powers of government.

With these few introductory remarks I shall proceed to a consideration of this constitution.

The first question that presents itself on the subject is, whether a confederated government be the best for the United States or not? Or in other words, whether the thirteen United States should be reduced to one great republic, governed by one legislature, and under the direction of one executive and judicial; or whether they should continue thirteen confederated republics, under the direction and controul of a supreme federal head for certain defined national purposes only?

This enquiry is important, because, although the government reported by the convention does not go to a perfect and entire consolidation, yet it approaches so near to it, that it must, if executed, certainly and infallibly terminate in it.

This government is to possess absolute and uncontroulable power, legislative, executive and judicial, with respect to every object to which it extend, for by, the last clause of section 8th, article 1st, it is declared "that the Congress shall have power to make all laws which shall be necessary and proper for carrying into execution the foregoing powers, and all other powers vested by this constitution, in the government of the United States; or in any department or office thereof." And by the 6th article, it is declared "that this constitution, and the laws of the United States, which shall be made in pursuance thereof, and the treaties made, or which shall be made, under the authority of the United States, shall be the supreme law of the land; and the judges in every state shall be bound thereby, any thing in the constitution, or law of any state to the contrary notwithstanding." It appears from these articles that there is no need of any intervention of the state governments, between the Congress and the people, to execute any one power vested in the general government, and that the constitution and laws of every state are nullified and declared void, so far as they are or shall be inconsistent with this constitution, or the laws made in pursuance of it, or with treaties made under the authority of the United States.—The government then, so far as it extends, is a complete one, and not a confederation. It is as much one complete government as that of New-York or Massachusetts, has as absolute and perfect powers to make and execute all laws, to appoint officers, institute courts, declare offences, and annex penalties, with respect to every object to which it extends, as any other in the world. So far therefore as its powers reach, all ideas of confederation are given up and lost. It is true this government is limited to certain objects, or to speak more properly, some small degree of power is still left to the states, but a little attention to the powers vested in the general government, will convince every candid man, that if it is capable of being executed, all that is reserved for the individual states [must] very soon be annihilated, except so far a [s they are] barely necessary to the organization of the general government. The powers of the general legislature extend to every case that is of the least importance—there is nothing valuable to human nature, nothing dear to freemen, but what is within its power. It has authority to make laws which will affect the lives, the liberty, and property of every man in the United States; nor can the constitution or laws of any state, in any way prevent or impede the full and complete execution of every power given. The legislative power is competent to lay taxes, duties, imposts, and excises;— there is no limitation to this power, unless it be said that the clause which directs the use to which those taxes, and duties shall be applied, may be said to be a limitation; but this is no restriction of the power at all, for by this clause they are to be applied to pay the debts and provide for the common defence and general welfare of the United States; but the legislature have authority to contract debts at their discretion; they are the sole judges of what is necessary to provide for the common defence, and they only are to determine what is for the general welfare: this power therefore is neither more nor less, than a power to lay and collect taxes, imposts, and excises, at their pleasure; not only the power to lay taxes unlimited, as to the amount they may require, but it is perfect and absolute to raise them in any mode they please. No state legislature, or any power in the state governments, have any more to do in carrying this into effect, than the authority of one state has to do with that of another. In the business therefore of laying and collecting taxes, the idea of confederation is totally lost, and that of one entire republic is embraced. It is proper here to remark, that the authority to lay and collect tax is the most important of any power that can be granted; it connects with it almost all other powers, or at least will in process of time draw all other after it; it is the great mean of protection, security, and defence, in a good government, and the great engine of oppression and tyranny in a bad one. This cannot fail of being the case, if we consider the contracted limits which are set by this constitution, to the late governments, on this article of raising money. No state can emit paper money—lay any duties, or imposts, on imports, or exports, but by consent of the Congress; and then the net produce shall be for the benefit of the United States. The only mean therefore left, for any state to support its government and discharge its debts, is by direct taxation; and the United States have also power to lay and collect taxes, in any way they please. Every one who has thought on the subject, must be convinced that but small sums of money can be collected in any country, by direct taxes, when the fœderal government begins to exercise the right of taxation in all its parts, the legislatures of the several states shall find it impossible to raise monies to support their governments. Without money they cannot be supported, and they must dwindle away, and, as before observed, their powers absorbed in that of the general government.

It might be here shown, that the power of the federal legislative, to raise and support armies at pleasure, as well in peace as in war, and their controul over the militia, tend, not only to a consolidation of the government, but the destruction of liberty.—I shall not, however, dwell upon these, as a few observations upon the judicial power of this government, in addition to the preceding, will fully evince the truth of the position.

The judicial power of the United States is to be vested in a supreme court, and in such inferior courts as Congress may from time to time ordain and establish. The powers of these courts are very extensive; their jurisdiction comprehends all civil causes, except such as arise between citizens of the same state; and it extends to all cases in law and equity arising under the constitution. One inferior court must be established, I presume, in each state at least, with the necessary executive officers appendant thereto. It is easy to see, that in the common course of things, these courts will eclipse the dignity, and take away from the respectability, of the state courts. These courts will be, in themselves, totally independent of the states, deriving their authority from the United States, and receiving from them fixed salaries; and in the course of human events it is to be expected, that they will swallow up all the powers of the courts in the respective states.

How far the clause in the 8th section of the 1st article may operate to do away all idea of confederated states, and to effect an entire consolidation of the whole into one general government, it is impossible to say. The powers given by this article are very general and comprehensive, and it may receive a construction to justify the passing almost any law. A power to make all laws, which shall be *necessary and proper*, for carrying into execution, all powers vested by the constitution in the government of the United States, or any department or officer thereof, is a power very comprehensive and definite, and may, for ought I know, be exercised in such manner as entirely to abolish the state legislatures. Suppose the legislature of a state should pass a law to raise money to support their government and pay the state debt, may the Congress repeal this law, because it may prevent the collection of a tax which they may think proper and necessary to lay, to provide for the general welfare of the United States? For all laws made, in pursuance of this constitution, are the supreme law of the land, and the judges in every state shall be bound thereby, any thing in the constitution or laws of the different states to the contrary notwithstanding.—By such a law, the government of a particular state might be overturned at one stroke, and thereby be deprived of every means of its support.

It is not meant, by stating this case, to insinuate that the constitution would warrant a law of this kind; or unnecessarily to alarm the fears of the people, by suggesting, that the federal legislature would be more likely to pass the limits assigned them by the constitution, than that of an individual state, further than they are less responsible to the people. But what is meant is, that the legislature of the United States are vested with the great and uncontroulable powers, of laying and collecting taxes, duties, imposts, and excises; of regulating trade, raising and supporting armies, organizing, arming, and disciplining the militia, instituting courts, and other general powers. And are by this clause invested with the power of making all laws, *proper and necessary*, for carrying all these into execution; and they may so exercise this power as entirely to annihilate all the state governments, and reduce this country to one single government. And if they may do it, it is pretty certain they will; for it will be found that the power retained by individual states, small as it is, will be a clog upon the wheels of the government of the United States; the latter therefore will be naturally inclined to remove it out of the way. Besides, it is a truth confirmed by the unerring experience of ages, that every man, and every body of men, invested with power, are ever disposed to increase it, and to acquire a superiority over every thing that stands in their way. This disposition, which is implanted in human nature, will operate in the federal legislature to lessen and ultimately to subvert the state authority, and having such advantages, will most certainly succeed, if the federal government succeeds at all. It must be very evident then, that what this constitution wants of being a complete consolidation of the several parts of the union into one complete government, possessed of perfect legislative, judicial, and executive powers, to all intents and purposes, it will necessarily acquire in its exercise and operation.

Let us now proceed to enquire, as I at first proposed, whether it be best the thirteen United States should be reduced to one great republic, or not? It is here taken for granted, that all agree in this, that whatever government we adopt, it ought to be a free one; that it should be so framed as to secure the liberty of the citizens of America, and such an one as to admit of a full, fair, and equal representation of the people. The question then will be, whether a government thus constituted, and founded on such principles, is practicable, and can be exercised over the whole United States, reduced into one state?

If respect is to be paid to the opinion of the greatest and wisest men who have ever thought or wrote on the science of government, we shall be constrained to conclude, that a free republic cannot succeed over a country of such immense extent, containing such a number of inhabitants, and these encreasing in such rapid progression as that of the whole United States. Among the many illustrious authorities which might be produced to this point, I shall content myself with quoting only two. The one is the baron de Montesquieu, spirit of laws, chap. xvi. vol. 1. "It is natural to a republic to have only a small territory, otherwise it cannot long subsist. In a large republic there are men of large fortunes, and consequently of less moderation; there are trusts too great to be placed in any single subject; he has interest of his own; he soon begins to think that he may be happy, great and glorious, by oppressing his fellow citizens; and that he may raise himself to grandeur on the ruins of his country. In a large republic, the public good is sacrificed to a thousand views; it is subordinate to exceptions, and depends on accidents. In a small one, the interest of the public is easier perceived, better understood, and more within the reach of every citizen; abuses are of less extent, and of course are less protected." Of the same opinion is the marquis Beccarari.

History furnishes no example of a free republic, any thing like the extent of the United States. The Grecian republics were of small extent; so also was that of the Romans. Both of these, it is true, in process of time, extended their conquests over large territories of country; and the consequence was, that their governments were changed from that of free governments to those of the most tyrannical that ever existed in the world.

Not only the opinion of the greatest men, and the experience of mankind, are against the idea of an extensive republic, but a variety of reasons may be drawn from the reason and nature of things, against it. In every government, the will of the sovereign is the law. In despotic governments, the supreme authority being lodged in one, his will is law, and can be as easily expressed to a large extensive territory as to a small one. In a pure democracy the people are the sovereign, and their will is declared by themselves; for this purpose they must all come together to deliberate, and decide. This kind of government cannot be exercised, therefore, over a country of any considerable extent; it must be confined to a single city, or at least limited to such bounds as that the people can conveniently assemble, be able to debate, understand the subject submitted to them, and declare their opinion concerning it.

In a free republic, although all laws are derived from the consent of the people, yet the people do not declare their consent by themselves in person, but by representatives, chosen by them, who are supposed to know the minds of their constituents, and to be possessed of integrity to declare this mind.

In every free government, the people must give their assent to the laws by which they are governed. This is the true criterion between a free government and an arbitrary one. The former are ruled by the will of the whole, expressed in any manner they may agree upon; the latter by the will of one, or a few. If the people are to give their assent to the laws, by persons chosen and appointed by them, the manner of the choice and the number chosen, must be such, as to possess, be disposed, and consequently qualified to declare the sentiments of the people; for if they do not know, or are not disposed to speak the sentiments of the people, the people do not govern, but the sovereignty is in a few. Now, in a large extended country, it is impossible to have a representation, possessing the sentiments, and of integrity, to declare the minds of the people, without having it so numerous and unwieldly, as to be subject in great measure to the inconveniency of a democratic government.

The territory of the United States is of vast extent; it now contains near three millions of souls, and is capable of containing much more than ten times that number. Is it practicable for a country, so large and so numerous as they will soon become, to elect a representation, that will speak their sentiments, without their becoming so numerous as to be incapable of transacting public business? It certainly is not.

In a republic, the manners, sentiments, and interests of the people should be similar. If this be not the case, there will be a constant clashing of opinions; and the representatives of one part will be continually striving against those of the other. This will retard the operations of government, and prevent such conclusions as will promote the public good. If we apply this remark to the condition of the United States, we shall be convinced that it forbids that we should be one government. The United States includes a variety of climates. The productions of the different parts of the union are very variant, and their interests, of consequence, diverse. Their manners and habits differ as much as their climates and productions; and their sentiments are by no means coincident. The laws and customs of the several states are, in many respects, very diverse, and in some opposite; each would be in favor of its own interests and customs, and, of consequence, a legislature, formed of representatives from the respective parts, would not only be too numerous to act with any care or decision, but would be composed of such heterogenous and discordant principles, as would constantly be contending with each other.

The laws cannot be executed in a republic, of an extent equal to that of the United States, with promptitude.

The magistrates in every government must be supported in the execution of the laws, either by an armed force, maintained at the public expence for that purpose; or by the people turning out to aid the magistrate upon his command, in case of resistance.

In despotic governments, as well as in all the monarchies of Europe, standing armies are kept up to execute the commands of

the prince or the magistrate, and are employed for this purpose
when occasion requires: But they have always proved the destruction of liberty, and [as] abhorrent to the spirit of a free republic. In
England, where they depend upon the parliament for their annual
support, they have always been complained of as oppressive and
unconstitutional, and are seldom employed in executing of the laws;
never except on extraordinary occasions, and then under the direction of a civil magistrate.

A free republic will never keep a standing army to execute its
laws. It must depend upon the support of its citizens. But when a
government is to receive its support from the aid of the citizens, it
must be so constructed as to have the confidence, respect, and affection of the people. Men who, upon the call of the magistrate, offer
themselves to execute the laws, are influenced to do it either by
affection to the government, or from fear; where a standing army is
at hand to punish offenders, every man is actuated by the latter
principle, and therefore, when the magistrate casts, will obey: but,
where this is not the case, the government must test for its support upon the confidence and respect which the people have for
their government and laws. The body of the people being attached,
the government will always be sufficient to support and execute
its laws, and to operate upon the fears of any faction which may be
opposed to it, not only to prevent an opposition to the execution of
the laws themselves, but also to compel the most of them to aid the
magistrate; but the people will not be likely to have such confidence
in their rulers, in a republic so extensive as the United States, as
necessary for these purposes. The confidence which the people have
in their rulers, in a free republic, arises from their knowing them,
from their being responsible to them for their conduct, and from the
power they have of displacing them when they misbehave: but in a
republic of the extent of this continent, the people in general would
be acquainted with very few of their rulers: the people at large
would know little of their proceedings, and it would be extremely
difficult to change them. The people in Georgia and New-Hampshire would not know one another's mind, and therefore could not
act in concert to enable them to effect a general change of representatives. The different parts of so extensive a country could not

possibly be made acquainted with the conduct of their representatives, nor be informed of the reasons upon which measures were founded. The consequence will be, they will have no confidence in their legislature, suspect them of ambitious views, be jealous of every measure they adopt, and will not support the laws they pass. Hence the government will be nerveless and inefficient, and no way will be left to render it otherwise, but by establishing an armed force to execute the laws at the point of the bayonet—a government of all others the most to be dreaded.

In a republic of such vast extent as the United States, the legislature cannot attend to the various concerns and wants of its different parts. It cannot be sufficiently numerous to be acquainted with the local condition and wants of the different districts, and if it could, it is impossible it should have sufficient time to attend to and provide for all the variety of cases of this nature, that would be continually arising.

In so extensive a republic, the great officers of government would soon become above the controul of the people, and abuse their power to the purpose of aggrandizing themselves, and oppressing them. The trust committed to the executive offices, in a country of the extent of the United States, must be various and of magnitude. The command of all the troops and navy of the republic, the appointment of officers, the power of pardoning offences, the collecting of all the public revenues, and the power of expending them, with a number of other powers, must be lodged and exercised in every state, in the hands of a few. When these are attended with great honor and emolument, as they always will be in large states, so as greatly to interest men to pursue them, and to be proper objects for ambitious and designing men, such men will be ever restless in their pursuit after them. They will use the power, when they have acquired it, to the purposes of gratifying their own interest and ambition, and it is scarcely possible, in a very large republic, to call them to account for their misconduct, or to prevent their abuse of power.

These are some of the reasons by which it appears, that a free republic cannot long subsist over a country of the great extent of these states. If then this new constitution is calculated to consolidate the thirteen states into one, as it evidently is, it ought not to be adopted.

Though I am of opinion, that it is a sufficient objection to this government, to reject it, that it creates the whole union into one government, under the form of a republic, yet if this objection was obviated, there are exceptions to it, which are so material and fundamental, that they ought to determine every man, who is a friend to the liberty and happiness of mankind, not to adopt it. I beg the candid and dispassionate attention of my countrymen, while I state these objections—they are such as have obtruded themselves upon my mind upon a careful attention to the matter, and such as I sincerely believe are well founded. There are many objections, of small moment, of which I shall take no notice—perfection is not to be expected in any thing that is the production of man—and if I did not in my conscience believe that this scheme was defective in the fundamental principles—in the foundation upon which a free and equal government must rest, I would hold my peace.

BRUTUS.

New-York Journal

1 NOVEMBER 1787

ESSAY II

Brutus calls on Americans to give up only so many of their natural rights as absolutely necessary for the common good and to protect their remaining rights through a federal bill of rights supplementing and supporting state charters. Essays in The Federalist *of particular relevance: 2, 83, 84.*

To the CITIZENS *of the* STATE *of* NEW-YORK.

I FLATTER myself that my last address established this position, that to reduce the Thirteen States into one government, would prove the destruction of your liberties.

But lest this truth should be doubted by some, I will now proceed to consider its merits.

Though it should be admitted, that the argument against reducing all the states into one consolidated government, are not sufficient fully to establish this point; yet they will, at least, justify this conclusion, that in forming a constitution for such a country, great care should be taken to limit and define its powers, adjust its parts, and guard against an abuse of authority. How far attention has been paid to these objects, shall be the subject of future enquiry. When a building is to be erected which is intended to stand for ages, the foundation should be firmly laid. The constitution proposed to your acceptance, is designed not for yourselves alone, but for generations yet unborn. The principles, therefore, upon which the social compact is founded, ought to have been clearly and precisely stated, and the most express and full declaration of rights to have been made—But on this subject there is almost an entire silence.

If we may collect the sentiments of the people of America, from their own most solemn declarations, they hold this truth as self evident, that all men are by nature free. No one man, therefore, or any class of me, have a right, by the law of nature, or of God, to assume or exercise authority over their fellows. The origin of society then is to be sought, not in any natural right which one man has to exercise authority over another, but in the untied consent of those who associate. The mutual wants of men, at first dictated the propriety of forming societies; and when they were established, protection and defence pointed out the necessity of instituting government. In a state of nature every individual pursues his own interest; in this pursuit it frequently happened, that the possessions or enjoyments of one were sacrificed to the views and designs of another; thus the weak were a prey to the strong, the simple and unwary were subject to impositions from those who were more crafty and designing. In this state of things, every individual was insecure; common interest therefore directed, that government should be established, in which the force of the whole community should be collected, and under such directions, as to protect and defend every one who composed it. The common good, therefore, is the end of civil government, and common consent, the foundation on which it is established. To effect this end, it was necessary that a certain portion of natural liberty should be surrendered, in order, that what remained should be preserved: how great a proportion of natural freedom is necessary to be yielded by individuals, when they submit to government, I shall not now enquire. So much, however, must be given up, as will be sufficient to enable those, to whom the administration of the government is committed, to establish laws for the promoting the happiness of the community, and to carry those laws into effect. But it is not necessary, for this purpose, that individuals should relinquish all their natural rights. Some are of such a nature that they cannot be surrendered. Of this kind are the rights of conscience, the right of enjoying and defending life, &c. Others are not necessary to be resigned, in order to attain the end for which government is instituted, these therefore ought not to be given up. To surrender them, would counteract the very end of government, to wit, the common good. From these observations it appears, that in forming a government on its true principles, the foundation should be laid in the manner I before stated, by expressly reserving to the people such of their essential natural rights, as are not necessary to be parted with. The same reasons which at first induced mankind to associate and institute government, will operate to influence them to observe this precaution. If they had been disposed to conform themselves to the rule of immutable righteousness, government would not have been requisite. It was because one part exercised fraud, oppression, and violence on the other, that men came together, and agreed that certain rules should be formed, to regulate the conduct of all, and the power of the whole community lodged in the hands of rulers to enforce an obedience to them. But rulers have the same propensities as other men; they are as likely to use the power with which they are vested for private purposes, and to the injury and oppression of those over whom they are placed, as individuals in a state of nature are to injure and oppress one another. It is therefore as proper that bounds should be set to their authority, as that government should have at first been instituted to restrain private injuries.

This principle, which seems so evidently founded in the reason and nature of things, is confirmed by universal experience. Those who have governed, have been found in all ages ever active to enlarge their powers and abridge the public liberty. This has induced the people in all countries, where any sense of freedom remained, to fix barriers against the encroachments of their rulers. The country from which we have derived our origin, is an eminent example of this. Their magna charta and bill of rights have long been the boast, as well as the security, of that nation. I need say no more, I presume, to an American, than, that this principle is a fundamental one, in all the constitutions of our own states; there is not one of them but what is either founded on a declaration or bill of rights, or has certain express reservation of rights interwoven in the body of them. From this it appears, that at a time when the pulse of liberty beat high, and when an appeal was made to the people to form constitutions for the government of themselves, it was their universal sense, that such declarations should make a part of their frames of government. It is therefore the more astonishing, that this grand security, to the rights of the people, is not to be found in this constitution.

It has been said, in answer to this objection, that such declaration of rights, however requisite they might be in the constitutions of the states, are not necessary in the general constitution, because, "in the former case, every thing which is not reserved is given, but in the latter the reverse of the proposition prevails, and every thing which is not given is reserved." It requires but little attention to discover, that this mode of reasoning is rather specious than solid. The powers, rights, and authority, granted to the general government by this constitution, are as complete, with respect to every object to which they extend, as that of any state government—It reaches to every thing which concerns human happiness—Life, liberty, and property, are under its controul. There is the same reason, therefore, that the exercise of power, in this case, should be restrained within proper limits, as in that of the state governments. To set this matter in a clear light, permit me to instance some of the articles of the bills of rights of the individual states, and apply them to the case in question.

For the security of life, in criminal prosecutions, the bills of rights of most of the states have declared, that no man shall be held to answer for a crime until he is made fully acquainted with the charge brought against him; he shall not be compelled to accuse, or furnish evidence against himself—The witnesses against him shall be brought face to face, and he shall be fully heard by himself or counsel. That it is essential to the security of life and liberty, that trial of facts be in the vicinity where they happen. Are not provisions of this kind as necessary in the general government, as in that of a particular state? The powers vested in the new Congress extend in many cases to life; they are authorised to provide for the punishment of a variety of capital crimes, and no restraint is laid upon them in its exercise, save only, that "the trial of all crimes, except in cases of impeachment, shall be by jury; and such trial shall be in the state where the said crimes shall have been committed." No man is secure of a trial in the county where he is charged to have committed a crime; he may be brought from Niagara to New-York, or carried from Kentucky to Richmond for trial for an offence, supposed to be committed. What security is there, that a man shall be furnished with a full and plain description of the charges against him? That he shall be allowed to produce all proof he can in his favor? That he shall see the witnesses against him face to face, or that he shall be fully heard in his own defence by himself or counsel?

For the security of liberty it has been declared, "that excessive bail should not be required, nor excessive fines imposed, nor cruel or unusual punishments inflicted—That all warrants, without oath or affirmation, to search suspected places, or seize any person, his papers or property, are grievous and oppressive."

These provisions are as necessary under the general government as under that of the individual states; for the power of the former is as complete to the purpose of requiring bail, imposing fines, inflicting punishments, granting search warrants, and seizing persons, papers, or property, in certain cases, as the other.

For the purpose of securing the property of the citizens, it is declared by all the states, "that in all controversies at law, respecting property, the ancient mode of trial by jury is one of the best securities of the rights of the people, and ought to remain sacred and inviolable."

Does not the same necessity exist of reserving this right, under this national compact, as in that of the states? Yet nothing is said respecting it. In the bills of rights of the states it is declared, that a well regulated militia is the proper and natural defence of a free government—That as standing armies in time of peace are dangerous, they are not to be kept up, and that the military should be kept under strict subordination to, and controuled by the civil power.

The same security is as necessary in this constitution, and much more so; for the general government will have the sole power to raise and to pay armies, and are under no controul in the exercise of it; yet nothing of this is to be found in this new system.

I might proceed to instance a number of other rights, which were as necessary to be reserved, such as, that elections should be free, that the liberty of the press should be held sacred; but the instances adduced, are sufficient to prove, that this argument is without foundation.—Besides, it is evident, that the reason here assigned was not the true one, why the framers of this constitution omitted a bill of rights; if it had been, they would not have made certain reservations, while they totally omitted others of more importance. We find they have, in the 9th section of the 1st article, declared, that the writ of habeas corpus shall not be suspended, unless in cases of rebellion—that no bill of attainder, or expost facto law, shall be passed—that no title of nobility shall be granted by the United States, &c. If every thing which is not given is reserved, what propriety is there in these exceptions? Does this constitution any where grant the power of suspending the habeas corpus, to make expost facto laws, pass bills of attainder, or grant titles of nobility? It certainly does not in express terms. The only answer that can be given is, that these are implied in the general powers granted. With equal truth it may be said, that all the powers, which the bills of right, guard against the abuse of, are contained or implied in the general ones granted by this constitution.

So far it is from being true, that a bill of rights is less necessary in the general constitution than in those of the states, the contrary is evidently the fact.—This system, if it is possible for the people of America to accede to it, will be an original compact; and being the last, will, in the nature of things, vacate every former agreement inconsistent with it. For it being a plan of government received and ratified by the whole people, all other forms, which are in existence at the time of its adoption, must yield to it. This is expressed in positive and unequivocal terms, in the 6th article, "That this constitution and the laws of the United States, which shall be made in pursuance thereof, and all treaties made, or which shall be made, under the authority of the United States, shall be the supreme law of the land; and the judges in every state shall be bound thereby, any thing in the *constitution*, or laws of any state, *to the contrary* notwithstanding.

"The senators and representatives before-mentioned, and the members of the several state legislatures, and all executive and judicial officers, both of the United States, and of the several states, shall be bound, by oath or affirmation, to support this constitution."

It is therefore not only necessarily implied thereby, but positively expressed, that the different state constitutions are repealed and entirely done away, so far as they are inconsistent with this, with the laws which shall be made in pursuance thereof, or with treaties made, or which shall be made, under the authority of the United States; of what avail will the constitutions of the respective states be to preserve the rights of its citizens? Should they be plead, the answer would be, the constitution of the United States, and the laws made in pursuance thereof, is the supreme law, and all legislatures and judicial officers, whether of the general or state governments, are bound by oath to support it. No priviledge, reserved by the bills of rights, or secured by the state government, can limit the power granted by this, or restrain any laws made in pursuance of it. It stands therefore on its own bottom, and must receive a construction by itself without any reference to any other—And hence it was of the highest importance, that the most precise and express declarations and reservations of rights should have been made.

This will appear the more necessary, when it is considered, that not only the constitution and laws made in pursuance thereof, but all treaties made, or which shall be made, under the authority of the United States, are the supreme law of the land, and sepersede the constitutions of all the states. The power to make treaties, is vested in the president, by and with the advice and consent of two thirds of the senate. I do not find any limitation, or restriction, to the exercise of this power. The most important article in any constitution may therefore be repealed, even without a legislative act. Ought not a government, vested with such extensive and indefinite authority, to have been restricted by a declaration of rights? It certainly ought.

So clear a point is this, that I cannot help suspecting, that persons who attempt to persuade people, that such reservations were less necessary under this constitution than under those of the states, are wilfully endeavouring to deceive, and to lead you into an absolute state of vassalage.

BRUTUS.

New-York Journal

15 NOVEMBER 1787

ESSAY III

Brutus argues that a proper representation of the people will mirror their characters, interests, and opinions. The Constitution's 3/5 rule granting additional representation to slave holders and the apportionment of Senate seats by state rather than by population make proper representation impossible. Essays in The Federalist *of particular relevance: 54-57, 62, 63.*

To the CITIZENS *of the* STATE *of* NEW-YORK.

IN the investigation of the constitution, under your consideration, great care should be taken, that you do not form your opinions respecting it, from unimportant provisions, or fallacious appearances.

On a careful examination, you will find, that many of its parts, of little moment, are well formed; in these it has a specious resemblance of a free government—but this is not sufficient to justify the adoption of it—the gilded pill, is often found to contain the most deadly poison.

You are not however to expect, a perfect form of government, any more than to meet with perfection in man; your views therefore, ought to be directed to the main pillars upon which a free government is to rest; if these are well placed, on a foundation that will support the superstructure, you should be satisfied, although the building may want a number of ornaments, which, if your particular tastes were gratified, you would have added to it: on the other hand, if the foundation is insecurely laid, and the main supports are wanting, or not properly fixed, however the fabric may be decorated and adorned, you ought to reject it.

Under these impressions, it has been my object to turn your attention to the principal defects in this system.

I have attempted to shew, that a consolidation of this extensive continent, under one government, for internal, as well as external purposes, which is evidently the tendency of this constitution, cannot succeed, without a sacrifice of your liberties; and therefore that the attempt is not only preposterous, but extremely dangerous; and I have shewn, independent of this, that the plan is radically defective in a fundamental principle, which ought to be found in every free government; to wit, a declaration of rights.

I shall now proceed to take a nearer view of this system, to examine its parts more minutely, and shew that the powers are not properly deposited, for the security of public liberty.

The first important object that presents itself in the organization of this government, is the legislature. This is to be composed of two branches; the first to be called the general assembly, and is to be chosen by the people of the respective states, in proportion to the number of their inhabitants, and is to consist of sixty five members, with powers in the legislature to encrease the number, not to exceed one for every thirty thousand inhabitants. The second branch is to be called the senate, and is to consist of twenty-six members, two of which are to be chosen by the legislatures of each of the states.

In the former of these there is an appearance of justice, in the appointment of its members—but if the clause, which provides for this branch, be stripped of its ambiguity, it will be found that there is really no equality of representation, even in this house.

The words are "representatives and direct taxes, shall be apportioned among the several states, which may be included in this union, according to their respective numbers, which shall be determined by adding to the whole number of free persons, including those bound to service for a term of years, and excluding Indians not taxed, three fifths of all other persons."—What a strange and unnecessary accumulation of words are here used to conceal from the public eye, what might have been expressed in the following concise manner. Representatives are to be proportioned among the states respectively, according to the number of freemen and slaves inhabiting them, counting five slaves for three free men.

"In a free state," says the celebrated Montesquieu, "every man, who is supposed to be a free agent, ought to be concerned in his own government, therefore the legislature should reside in the whole body of the people, or their representatives." But it has never been alledged that those who are not free agents, can, upon any rational principle, have any thing to do in government, either by themselves or others. If they have no share in government, why is the number of members in the assembly, to be increased on their account? Is it because in some of the states, a considerable part of the property of the inhabitants consists in a number of their fellow men, who are held in bondage, in defiance of every idea of benevolence, justice, and religion, and contrary to all the principles of liberty, which have been publickly avowed in the late glorious revolution? If this be a just ground for representation, the horses in some of the states, and the oxen in others, ought to be represented—for a great share of property in some of them, consists in these animals; and they have as much controul over their own actions, as these poor unhappy creatures, who are intended to be described in the above recited clause, by the words, "all other persons." By this mode of apportionment, the representatives of the different parts of the union, will be extremely unequal; in some of the southern states, the slaves are nearly equal in number to the free men; and for all these slaves, they will be entitled to a proportionate share in the legislature—this will give them an unreasonable weight in the government, which can derive no additional strength, protection, nor defence from the slaves, but the contrary. Why then should they be represented? What adds to the evil is, that these states are to be permitted to continue the inhuman traffic of importing slaves, until the year 1808—and for every cargo of these unhappy people, which unfeeling, unprincipled, barbarous, and avaricious wretches, may tear from their country, friends and tender connections, and bring into those states, they are to be rewarded by having an increase of members in the general assembly. There appears at the first view a manifest inconsistency, in the apportionment of representatives in the senate, upon the plan of a consolidated government. On every principle of equity, and propriety, representation in a government should be in exact proportion to the numbers, or the aids afforded by the persons represented. How unreasonable, and unjust then is it, that Delaware should have a representation in the senate, equal to Massachusetts, or Virginia? The latter of which contains ten times her numbers, and is to contribute to the aid of the general government in that proportion? This article of the constitution will appear the more objectionable, if it is considered, that the powers vested in this branch of the legislature are very extensive, and greatly surpass those lodged in the assembly, not only for general purposes, but in many instances, for the internal police of the states. The other branch of the legislature, in which, if in either, a feint spark of democracy is to be found, should have been properly organized and established—but upon examination you will find, that this branch does not possess the qualities of a just representation, and that there is no kind of security, imperfect as it is, for its remaining in the hands of the people.

It has been observed, that the happiness of society is the end of government—that every free government is founded in compact;

and that, because it is impracticable for the whole community to assemble, or when assembled, to deliberate with wisdom, and decide with dispatch, the mode of legislating by representation was devised.

The very term, representative, implies, that the person or body chosen for this purpose, should resemble those who appoint them— a representation of the people of America, if it be a true one, must be like the people. It ought to be so constituted, that a person, who is a stranger to the country, might be able to form a just idea of their character, by knowing that of their representatives. They are the sign—the people are the thing signified. It is absurd to speak of one thing being the representative of another, upon any other principle. The ground and reason of representation, in a free government, implies the same thing. Society instituted government to promote the happiness of the whole, and this is the great end always in view in the delegation of powers. It must then have been intended, that those who are placed instead of the people, should possess their sentiments and feelings, and be governed by their interests, or, in other words, should bear the strongest resemblance of those in whose room they are substituted. It is obvious, that for an assembly to be a true likeness of the people of any country, they must be considerably numerous.—One man, or a few men, cannot possibly represent the feelings, opinions, and characters of a great multitude. In this respect, the new constitution is radically defective.—The house of assembly, which is intended as a representation of the people of America, will not, nor cannot, in the nature of things, be a proper one—sixty-five men cannot be found in the United States, who hold the sentiments, possess the feelings, or are acquainted with the wants and interests of this vast country. This extensive continent is made up of a number of different classes of people; and to have a proper representation of them, each class ought to have an opportunity of choosing their best informed men for the purpose; but this cannot possibly be the case in so small a number. The state of New-York, on the present apportionment, will send six members to the assembly: I will venture to affirm, that number cannot be found in the state, who will bear a just resemblance to the several classes of people who compose it. In this assembly, the farmer, mer-

chant, mecanick, and other various orders of people, ought to be represented according to their respective weight and numbers; and
the representatives ought to be intimately acquainted with the
wants, understand the interests of the several orders in the society,
and feel a proper sense and becoming zeal to promote their prosperity. I cannot conceive that any six men in this state can be found
properly qualified in these respects to discharge such important
duties: but supposing it possible to find them, is there the least
degree of probability that the choice of the people will fall upon such
men? According to the common course of human affairs, the natural aristocracy of the country will be elected. Wealth always creates influence, and this is generally much increased by large family
connections: this class in society will for ever have a great number of
dependents; besides, they will always favour each other—it is their
interest to combine—they will therefore constantly unite their
efforts to procure men of their own rank to be elected—they will
concenter all their force in every part of the state into one point, and
by acting together, will most generally carry their election. It is
probable, that but few of the merchants, and those the most opulent and ambitious, will have a representation from their body—
few of them are characters sufficiently conspicuous to attract the
notice of the electors of the state in so limited a representation. The
great body of the yeoman of the country cannot expect any of their
order in this assembly—the station will be too elevated for them to
aspire to—the distance between the people and their representatives, will be so very great, that there is no probability that a farmer,
however respectable, will be chosen—the mechanicks of every
branch, must expect to be excluded from a seat in this Body—It
will and must be esteemed a station too high and exalted to be filled
by any but the first men in the state, in point of fortune; so that in
reality there will be no part of the people represented, but the rich,
such in that branch of the legislature, which is called the democratic.—The well born, and highest orders in life, as they term themselves, will be ignorant of the sentiments of the midling class of
citizens, strangers to their ability, wants, and difficulties, and void of
sympathy, and fellow feeling. This branch of the legislature will not
only be an imperfect representation, but there will be no security

in so small a body, against bribery, and corruption—It will consist at first, of sixty-five and can never exceed one for every thirty thousand and inhabitants; a majority of these, that is, thirty-three, are a quorum, and a majority of which, or seventeen, may pass any law—a majority of the senate, or fourteen, are a quorum, and eight of them pass any law—so that twenty-five men, will have the power to give away all the property of the citizens of these states-what security therefore can there be for the people, where their liberties and property are at the disposal of so few men? It will literally be a government in the hands of the few to oppress and plunder the many. You may conclude with a great degree of certainty, that it, like all others of a similar nature, will be managed by influence and corruption, and that the period is not far distant, when this will be the case, if it should be adopted; for even now there are some among us, whose characters stand high in the public estimation, and who have had a principal agency in framing this constitution, who do not scruple to say, that this is the only practicable mode of governing a people, who think with that degree of freedom which the Americans do—this government will have in their gift a vast number of offices of great honor and emolument. The members of the legislature are not excluded from appointments; and twenty-five of them, as the case may be, being secured, any measure may be carried.

The rulers of this country must be composed of very different materials from those of any other, of which history gives us any account, if the majority of the legislature are not, before many years, entirely at the devotion of the executive—and these states will soon be under the absolute domination of one, or a few, with the fallacious appearance of being governed by men of their own election.

The more I reflect on this subject, the more firmly am I persuaded, that the representation is merely nominal—a mere burlesque; and that no security is provided against corruption and undue influence. No free people on earth, who have elected persons to legislate for them, ever reposed that confidence in so small a number. The British house of commons consists of five hundred and fifty-eight members; the number of inhabitants in Great-Britain, is computed at eight millions—this gives one member for a little more than fourteen thousand, which exceeds double the proportion this country can ever have: and yet we require a larger representation in proportion to our numbers, than Great Britain, because this country is much more extensive, and differs more in its productions, interests, manners, and habits. The democratic branch of the legislatures of the several states in the union consists, I believe at present, of near two thousand; and this number was not thought too large for the security of liberty by the framers of our state constitutions: some of the states may have erred in this respect, but the difference between two thousand, and sixty-five, is so very great, that it will bear no comparison.

Other objections offer themselves against this part of the constitution—I shall reserve them for a future paper, when I shall shew, defective as this representation is, no security is provided, that even this shadow of the right, will remain with the people.

BRUTUS.

New-York Journal

29 NOVEMBER 1787

ESSAY IV

Brutus again argues for an equal and full representation of the people. Without it, the Constitution will bring the tyranny of a few. Its laws will not have the people's confidence, so the government will have to rule by force. Essays in The Federalist *of particular relevance: 51, 54-58.*

To the PEOPLE *of the State of* NEW-YORK.

THERE can be no free government where the people are not possessed of the power of making the laws by which they are governed, either in their own persons, or by others substituted in their stead.

Experience has taught mankind, that legislation by representatives is the most eligible, and the only practicable mode in which the people of any country can exercise this right, either prudently or beneficially. But then, it is a matter of the highest importance, in forming this representation, that it be so constituted as to be capable of understanding the true interests of the society for which it acts, and so disposed as to pursue the good and happiness of the people as its ultimate end. The object of every free government is the public good, and all lesser interests yield to it. That of every tyrannical government, is the happiness and aggrandisement of one, or a few, and to this the public felicity, and every other interest must submit.—The reason of this difference in these governments is obvious. The first is so constituted as to collect the views and wishes of the whole people in that of their rulers, while the latter is so framed as to separate the interests of the governors from that of the governed. The principle of self love, therefore, that will influence the one to promote the good of the whole, will prompt the other to follow its own private advantage. The great art, therefore, in forming a good constitution, appears to be this, so to frame it, as that those to whom the power is committed shall be subject to the same feelings, and aim at the same objects as the people do, who transfer to them their authority. There is no possible way to effect this but by an equal, full and fair representation; this, therefore, is the great desideratum in politics. However fair an appearance any government may make, though it may possess a thousand plausible articles and be decorated with ever so many ornaments, yet if it is deficient in this essential principle of a full and just representation of the people, it will be only like a painted sepulcher— For, without this it cannot be a free government; let the administration of it be good or ill, it still will be a government, not according to the will of the people, but according to the will of a few.

To test this new constitution then, by this principle, is of the last importance—It is to bring it to the touch-stone of national liberty, and I hope I shall be excused, if, in this paper, I pursue the subject commenced in my last number, to wit, the necessity of an equal and full representation in the legislature.—In that, I showed that it was not equal, because the smallest states are to send the same num-

ber of members to the senate as the largest, and, because the
slaves, who afford neither aid or defence to the government, are to
encrease the proportion of members. To prove that it was not a
just or adequate representation, it was urged, that so small a number could not resemble the people, or possess their sentiments and
dispositions. That the choice of members would commonly fall upon
the rich and great, while the middling class of the community would
be excluded. That in so small a representation there was no security
against bribery and corruption.

The small number which is to compose this legislature, will not
only expose it to the danger of that kind of corruption, and undue
influence, which will arise from the gift of places of honor and emolument, or the more direct one of bribery, but it will also subject it
to another kind of influence no less fatal to the liberties of the people,
though it be not so flagrantly repugnant to the principles of rectitude. It is not to be expected that a legislature will be found in any
country that will not have some of its members, who will pursue
their private ends, and for which they will sacrifice the public good.
Men of this character are, generally, artful and designing, and frequently possess brilliant talents and abilities; they commonly act in
concert, and agree to share the spoils of their country among them;
they will keep their object ever in view, and follow it with constancy.
To effect their purpose, they will assume any shape, and, Proteus
like, mould themselves into any form—where they find members
proof against direct bribery or gifts of offices, they will endeavor to
mislead their minds by specious and false reasoning, to impose upon
their unsuspecting honesty by an affectation of zeal for the public
good; they will form juntos, and hold out-door meetings; they will
operate upon the good nature of their opponents, by a thousand little attentions, and seize them into compliance by the earnestness of
solicitation. Those who are acquainted with the manner of conducting business in public assemblies, know how prevalent art and
address are in carrying a measure, even over men of the best intentions, and of good understanding. The firmest security against this
kind of improper and dangerous influence, as well as all other, is a
strong and numerous representation: in such a house of assembly, so
great a number must be gained over, before the private views of

individuals could be gratified that there could be scarce a hope of success. But in the fœderal assemble, seventeen men are all that is necessary to pass a law. It is probable, it will seldom happen that more than twenty-five will be requisite to form a majority, when it is considered what a number of places of honor and emolument will be in the gift of the executive, the powerful influence that great and designing men have over the honest and unsuspecting, by their art and address, their soothing manners and civilities, and their cringing flattery, joined with their affected patriotism; when these different species of influence are combined, it is scarcely to be hoped that a legislature, composed of so small a number, as the one proposed by the new constitution, will long resist their force. A farther objection against the feebleness of the representation is, that it will not possess the confidence of the people. The execution of the laws, in a free government must rest on this confidence, and this must be founded on the good opinion they entertain of the framers of the laws. Every government must be supported, either by the people having such an attachment to it, as to be ready, when called upon, to support it, or by a force at the command of the government, to compel obedience. The latter mode destroys every idea of a free government; for the same force that may be employed to compel obedience to good laws, might, and probably would be used to wrest from the people their constitutional liberties.—Whether it is practicable to have a representation for the whole union sufficiently numerous to obtain that confidence which is necessary for the purpose of internal taxation, and other powers to which this proposed government extends, is an important question. I am clearly of opinion, it is not, and therefore I have stated this in my first number, as one of the reasons against going into so an entire consolidation of the states—one of the most capital errors in the system, is that of extending the powers of the fœderal government to objects to which it is not adequate, which it cannot exercise without endangering public liberty, and which it is not necessary they should possess, in order to preserve the union and manage our national concerns; of this, however, I shall treat more fully in some future paper—But, however this may be, certain it is, that the representation in the legislature is not so formed as to give reasonable ground for public trust.

In order for the people safely to repose themselves on their rulers, they should not only be of their own choice. But it is requisite they should be acquainted with their abilities to manage the public concerns with wisdom. They should be satisfied that those who represent them are men of integrity, who will pursue the good of the community with fidelity; and will not be turned aside from their duty by private interest, or corrupted by undue influence; and that they will have such a zeal for the good of those whom they represent, as to excite them to be deligent in their service; but it is impossible the people of the United States should have sufficient knowledge of their representatives, when the numbers are so few, to acquire any rational satisfaction on either of these points. The people of this state will have very little acquaintance with those who may be chosen to represent them; a great part of them will, probably, not know the characters of their own members, much less that of a majority of those who will compose the fœderal assembly; they will consist of men, whose names they have never heard, and of whose talents and regard for the public good, they are total strangers to; and they will have no persons so immediately of their choice so near them, of their neighbours and of their own rank in life, that they can feel themselves secure in trusting their interests in their hands. The representatives of the people cannot, as they now do, after they have passed laws, mix with the people, and explain to them the motives which induced the adoption of any measure, point out its utility, and remove objections or silence unreasonable clamours against it.—The number will be so small that but a very few of the most sensible and respectable yeomanry of the country can ever have any knowledge of them: being so far removed from the people, their station will be elevated and important, and they will be considered as ambitious and designing. They will not be viewed by the people as part of themselves, but as a body distinct from them, and having separate interests to pursue; the consequence will be, that a perpetual jealousy will exist in the minds of the people against them; their conduct will be narrowly watched; their measures scrutinized; and their laws opposed, evaded, or reluctantly obeyed. This is natural, and exactly corresponds with the conduct of individuals towards those in whose hands they intrust important concerns. If the person confided in, be a neighbour with whom his employer is intimately acquainted, whose talents, he knows, are sufficient to manage the business with which he is charged, his honesty and fidelity unsuspected, and his friendship and zeal for the service of his principal unquestionable, he will commit his affairs into his hands with unreserved confidence, and feel himself secure; all the transactions of the agent will meet with the most favorable construction, and the measures he takes will give satisfaction. But, if the person employed be a stranger, whom he has never seen, and whose character for ability or fidelity be cannot fully learn—If he is constrained to choose him, because it was not in his power to procure one more agreeable to his wishes, he will trust him with caution, and be suspicious of all his conduct.

If then this government should not derive support from the good will of the people, it must be executed by force, or not executed at all; either case would lead to the total destruction of liberty.—The convention seemed aware of this, and have therefore provided for calling out the militia to execute the laws of the union. If this system was so framed as to command that respect from the people, which every good free government will obtain, this provision was unnecessary—the people would support the civil magistrate. This power is a novel one, in free governments—these have depended for the execution of the laws on the Posse Comitatus, and never raised an idea, that the people would refuse to aid the civil magistrate in executing those laws they themselves had made. I shall now dismiss the subject of the incompetency of the representation, and proceed, as I promised, to shew, that, impotent as it is, the people have no security that they will enjoy the exercise of the right of electing this assembly, which, at best, can be considered but as the shadow of representation.

By section 4, article 1, the Congress are authorized, at any time, by law, to make, or alter, regulations respecting the time, place, and manner of holding elections for senators and representatives, except as to the places of choosing senators. By this clause the right of election itself, is, in a great measure, transferred from the people to their rulers.—One would think, that if any thing was necessary to be made a fundamental article of the original compact, it would be, that of fixing the branches of the legislature, so as to put it out of its power to alter itself by modifying the election of its own members at will and pleasure. When a people once resign the privilege of a fair election, they clearly have none left worth contending for.

It is clear that, under this article, the fœderal legislature may institute such rules respecting elections as to lead to the choice of one description of men. The weakness of the representation, tends but too certainly to confer on the rich and *well-born*, all honours; but the power granted in this article, may be so exercised, as to secure it almost beyond a possibility of controul. The proposed Congress may make the whole state one district, and direct, that the capital (the city of New-York, for instance) shall be the place for holding the election; the consequence would be, that none but men of the most elevated rank in society would attend, and they would as certainly choose men of their own class; as it is true what the *Apostle Paul* saith, that "no man ever yet hated his own flesh, but nourisheth and cherisheth it."—They may declare that those members who have the greatest number of votes, shall be considered as duly elected; the consequence would be that the people, who are dispersed in the interior parts of the state, would give their votes for a variety of candidates, while any order, or profession, residing in populous places, by uniting their interests, might procure whom they pleased to be chosen—and by this means the representatives of the state may be elected by one tenth part of the people who actually vote. This may be effected constitutionally, and by one of those silent operations which frequently takes place without being noticed, but which often produces such changes as entirely to alter a government, subvert a free constitution, and rivet the chains on a free people before they perceive they are forged. Had the power of regulating elections been left under the direction of the state legislatures, where the people are not only nominally but substantially represented, it would have been secure; but if it was taken out of their hands, it surely ought to have been fixed on such a basis as to have put it out of the power of the fœderal legislature to deprive the people of it by law. Provision should have been made for marking out the states into districts, and for choosing, by a majority of votes, a person out of each of them of permanent property and residence in the district which he was to represent.

If the people of America will submit to a constitution that will vest in the hands of any body of men a right to deprive them by law of the privilege of a fair election, they will submit to almost any thing. Reasoning with them will be in vain, they must be left until they are brought to reflection by feeling oppression—they will then have to wrest from their oppressors, by a strong hand, that which they now possess, and which they may retain if they will exercise but a moderate share of prudence and firmness.

I know it is said that the dangers apprehended from this clause are merely imaginary, that the proposed general legislature will be disposed to regulate elections upon proper principles, and to use their power with discretion, and to promote the public good. On this, I would observe, that constitutions are not so necessary to regulate the conduct of good rulers as to restrain that of bad ones.— Wise and good men will exercise power so as to promote the public happiness under any form of government. If we are to take it for granted, that those who administer the government under this system, will always pay proper attention to the rights and interests of the people, nothing more was necessary than to say who should be invested with the powers of government, and leave them to exercise it at will and pleasure. Men are apt to be deceived both with respect to their own dispositions and those of others. Though this truth is proved by almost every page of the history of nations, to wit, that power, lodged in the hands of rulers to be used at discretion, is almost always exercised to the oppression of the people, and the aggrandizement of themselves; yet most men think if it was lodged in their hands they would not employ it in this manner.— Thus when the prophet *Elisha* told *Hazael*, "I know the evil that thou wilt do unto the children of Israel; their strong holds wilt thou set on fire, and their young men, wilt thou slay with the sword, and wilt dash their children, and rip up their women with child." Hazael had no idea that he ever should be guilty of such horrid cruelty, and said to the prophet, "Is thy servant a dog that he should do this great thing." Elisha, answered, "The Lord hath shewed me that thou thalt be king of Syria." The event proved, that Hazael only wanted an opportunity to perpetrate these enormities without restraint, and he had a disposition to do them, though he himself knew it not.

BRUTUS.

New-York Journal

13 DECEMBER 1787

ESSAY V

Brutus asserts that the new Congress will exercise unlimited taxing powers by calling them necessary and proper to provide for the common defense. States will be left dependent on the federal government for their financial survival. Only America's historic distinction between internal and external taxation can check federal power. Essays in The Federalist *of particular relevance: 30–36, 44.*

To the PEOPLE *of the State of* NEW-YORK.
IT was intended in this Number to have prosecuted the enquiry into the organization of this new system; particularly to have considered the dangerous and premature union of the President and Senate, and the mixture of legislative, executive, and judicial powers in the Senate.

But there is such an intimate connection between the several branches in whom the different species of authority is lodged, and the powers with which they are invested, that on reflection it seems necessary first to proceed to examine the nature and extent of the powers granted to the legislature.

This enquiry will assist us the better to determine, whether the legislature is so constituted, as to provide proper checks and restrictions for the security of our rights, and to guard against the abuse of power—For the means should be suited to the end; a government should be framed with a view to the objects to which it extends: if these be few in number, and of such a nature as to give but small occasion or opportunity to work oppression in the exercise of authority, there will be less need of a numerous representation, and special guards against abuse, than if the powers of the government are very extensive, and include a great variety of cases. It will also be found necessary to examine the extent of these powers, in order to form a just opinion how far this system can be considered as a confederation, or a consolidation of the states. Many of the advocates for, and most of the opponents to this system, agree that the form of government most suitable for the United States, is that of a confederation. The idea of a confederated government is that of a number of independent states entering into a compact, for the conducting certain general concerns, in which they have a common interest, leaving the management of their internal and local affairs to their separate governments. But whether the system proposed is of this nature cannot be determined without a strict enquiry into the powers proposed to be granted.

This constitution considers the people of the several states as one body corporate, and is intended as an original compact, it will therefore dissolve all contracts which may be inconsistent with it. This not only results from its nature, but is expressly declared in the 6th *article* of it. The design of the constitution is expressed in the preamble, to be, "in order to form a more perfect union, to establish justice, insure domestic tranquility, provide for the common defence, promote the general welfare, and secure the blessings of liberty to ourselves and posterity." These are the ends this government is to accomplish, and for which it is invested, with certain powers, among these is the power "to make all laws which are *necessary and proper* for carrying into execution the foregoing powers, and *all other* powers vested by this constitution in the government of the United States, or in any department or officer thereof." It is a rule in construing a law to consider the objects the legislature had in view in passing it, and to give it such an explanation as to promote their intention. The same rule will apply in explaining a constitution. The great objects then are declared in this preamble in general and indefinite terms to be to provide for the common defence, promote the general welfare, and an express power being vested in the legislature to make all laws which shall be necessary and proper for carrying into execution all the powers vested in the general government. The inference is natural that the legislature will have an authority to make all laws which they shall judge necessary for the common safety, and to promote the general welfare. This amounts to a power to make laws at discretion: No terms can be found more indefinite than these, and it is obvious, that the legislature alone must judge what laws are proper and necessary for the purpose. It may be said, that this way of explaining the constitution, is torturing and making it speak what it never intended. This is far from my intention, and I shall not even insist upon this implied power, but join issue with those who say we are to collect the idea of the powers given from the express words of the clauses granting them; and it will not be difficult to shew that the same authority is expressly given which is supposed to be implied in the forgoing paragraphs.

In the 1st article, 8th section, it is declared, "that Congress shall have power to lay and collect taxes, duties, imposts and excises, to pay the debts, and provide for the common defence, and general welfare of the United States." In the preamble, the intent of the constitution, among other things, is declared to be to provide for the common defence, and promote the general welfare, and in this clause the power is in express words given to Congress "to provide for the common defence, and general welfare."—And in the last paragraph of the same section there is an express authority to make all laws which shall be necessary and proper for carrying into execution this power. It is therefore evident, that the legislature under this constitution may pass any law which they may think proper. It is true the 9th section restrains their power with respect to certain objects. But these restrictions are very limited, some of them improper, some unimportant, and others not easily understood, as I shall hereafter shew. It has been urged that the meaning I give to this part of the constitution is not the true one, that the intent of it is to confer on the legislature the power to lay and collect taxes, &c. in order to provide for the common defence and general welfare. To this I would reply, that the meaning and intent of the constitution is to be collected from the words of it, and I submit to the public, whether the construction I have given it is not the most natural and easy. But admitting the contrary opinion to prevail, I shall nevertheless, be able to shew, that the same powers are substantially vested in the general government, by several other articles in the constitution. It invests the legislature with authority to lay and collect taxes, duties, imposts and excises, in order to provide for the common defence, and promote the general welfare, and to pass all laws which may be necessary and proper for carrying this power into effect. To comprehend the extent of this authority, it will be requisite to examine 1st. what is included in this power to lay and collect taxes, duties, imposts and excises.

2d. What is implied in the authority, to pass all laws which shall be necessary and proper for carrying this power into execution.

3d. What limitation, if any, is set to the exercise of this power by the constitution.

1st. To detail the particulars comprehended in the general terms, taxes, duties, imposts and excises, would require a volume, instead of a single piece in a news-paper. Indeed it would be a task far beyond my ability, and to which no one can be competent, unless possessed of a mind capable of comprehending every possible source of revenue; for they extend to every possible way of raising money, whether by direct or indirect taxation. Under this clause may be imposed a poll-tax, a land-tax, a tax on houses and buildings, on windows and fire places, on cattle and on all kinds of personal property:—It extends to duties on all kinds of goods to any amount, to tonnage and poundage on vessels, to duties on written instruments, newspapers, almanacks, and books:—It comprehends an excise on all kinds of liquors, spirits, wines, cyder, beer, &c. and indeed takes in duty or excise on every necessary or conveniency of life; whether of foreign or home growth or manufactory. In short, we can have no conception of any way in which a government can raise money from the people, but what is included in one or other of these general terms. We may say then that this clause commits to the hands of the general legislature every conceivable source of revenue within the United States. Not only are these terms very comprehensive, and extend to a vast number of objects, but the power to lay and collect has great latitude; it will lead to the passing a vast number of laws, which may affect the personal rights of the citizens of the states, expose their property to fines and confiscation, and put their lives in jeopardy: it opens a door to the appointment of a swarm of revenue and excise officers to pray upon the honest and industrious part of the community, eat up their substance, and not on the spoils of the country.

2d. We will next enquire into what is implied in the authority to pass all laws which shall be necessary and proper to carry this power into execution.

It is, perhaps, utterly impossible fully to define this power. The authority granted in the first clause can only be understood in its full extent, by descending to all the particular cases in which a revenue can be raised; the number and variety of these cases are so endless, and as it were infinite, that no man living has, as yet, been able to reckon them up. The greatest geniuses in the world have been for ages employed in the research, and when mankind had supposed that the subject was exhausted they have been astonished with the refined improvements that have been made in modern times, and especially in the English nation on the subject—If then the objects of this power cannot be comprehended, how is it possible to understand the extent of that power which can pass all laws which shall be necessary and proper for carrying it into execution? It is truly incomprehensible. A case cannot be conceived of, which is not included in this power. It is well known that the subject of revenue is the most difficult and extensive in the science of government. It requires the greatest talents of a statesmen, and the most numerous and exact provisions of the legislature. The command of the revenues of a state gives the command of every thing in it.—He that has the purse will have the sword, and they that have both, have every thing; so that the legislature having every source from which money can be drawn under their direction, with a right to make all laws necessary and proper for drawing forth all the resource of the country, would have, in fact, all power.

Were I to enter into the detail, it would be easy to shew how this power in its operation, would totally destroy all the powers of the individual states. But this is not necessary for those who will think for themselves, and it will be useless to such as take things upon trust, nothing will awaken them to reflection, until the iron hand of oppression compel them to it.

I shall only remark, that this power, given to the federal legislature, directly annihilates all the powers of the state legislatures. There cannot be a greater solecism in politics than to talk of power in a government, without the command of any revenue. It is as absurd as to talk of an animal without blood, or the subsistence of one without food. Now the general government having in their controul every possible source of revenue, and authority to pass any law they may deem necessary to draw them forth, or to facilitate their collection; no source of revenue is therefore left in the hands of any state. Should any state attempt to raise money by law, the general government may repeal or arrest it in the execution, for all their laws will be the supreme law of the land: If then any one can be weak enough to believe that a government can exist without having the authority to raise money to pay a door-keeper to their assembly, he may believe that the state government can exist, should this new constitution take place.

It is agreed by most of the advocates of this new system, that the government which is proper for the United States should be a confederated one; that the respective states ought to retain a portion of their sovereignty, and that they should preserve not only the forms of their legislatures, but also the power to conduct certain internal concerns. How far the powers to be retained by the states, [shall] extend, is the question; we need not spend much time on this subject, as it respects this constitution, for a government without the power to raise money is one only in name. It is clear that the legislatures of the respective states must be altogether dependent on the will of the general legislature, for the means of supporting their government. The legislature of the United States will have a right to exhaust every source of revenue in every state, and to annul all laws of the states which may stand in the way of effecting it; unless therefore we can suppose the state governments can exist without money to support the officers who execute them, we must conclude they will exist no longer than the general legislatures choose they should. Indeed the idea of any government existing, in any respect, as an independent one, without any means of support in their own hands, is an absurdity. If therefore, this constitution has in view, what many of its framers and advocates say it has, to secure and guarantee to the separate states the exercise of certain powers of government it certainly ought to have left in their hands some sources of revenue. It should have marked the line in which the general government should have raised money, and set bounds over which they should not pass, leaving to the separate states other means to raise supplies for the support of their governments, and to discharge their respective debts. To this it is objected, that the general government ought to have power competent to the purposes of the union; they are to provide for the common defence, to pay the debts of the United States, support foreign ministers, and the civil establishment of the union, and to do these they ought to have authority to raise money adequate to the purpose. On this I observe, that the state governments have also contracted debts, they require money to support their civil officers, and how this is to be done, if they give to the general government a power to raise money in every way in which it can possibly be raised, with such a controul over the state legislatures as to prohibit them, whenever the general legislature may think proper, from raising any money. It is again objected that it is very difficult, if not impossible, to draw the line of distinction between the powers of the general and state governments on this subject. The first, it is said, must have the power of raising the money necessary for the purposes of the union, if they are limited to certain objects the revenue may fall short of a sufficiency for the public exigencies, they must therefore have discretionary power. The line may be easily and accurately drawn between the powers of the two governments on this head. The distinction between external and internal taxes, is not a novel one in this country, it is a plain one, and easily understood. The first includes impost duties on all imported goods; this species of taxes it is proper should be laid by the general government; many reasons might be urged to shew that no danger is to be apprehended from their exercise of it. They may be collected in few places, and from few hands with certainty and expedition. But few officers are necessary to be imployed in collecting them, and there is no danger of oppression in laying them, because, if they are laid higher than trade will bear, the merchants will cease importing, or smuggle their goods. We have therefore sufficient security, arising from the nature of the thing, against burdonsome, and intolerable impositions from this kind of tax. But the case is far otherwise with regard to direct taxes; these include poll taxes, land taxes, excises, duties on written instruments, on every thing we eat, drink, or wear; they take hold of every species of property, and come home to every man's house and packet. These are often so oppressive, as to grind the face of the poor, and render the lives of the common people a burden to them. The great and only security the people can have against oppression from this kind of taxes, must rest in their representatives. If they are sufficiently numerous to be well informed of the circumstances, and ability of those who send them, and have a proper regard for the people, they will be secure. The general legislature, as I have shewn in a former paper, will not be thus qualified, and therefore, on this account, ought not to exercise the power of direct taxation. If the power of laying imposts will not be sufficient, some other specific mode of raising a revenue should have been assigned the general government; many may be suggested in which their power may be accurately defined and limited, and it would be much better to give them authority to lay and collect a duty on exports, not to exceed a certain rate per cent, than to have surrendered every kind of resource that the country has, to the complete abolition of the state governments, and which will introduce such an infinite number of laws and ordinances, fines and penalties, courts, and judges, collectors, and excisemen, that when a man can number them, he may enumerate the stars of Heaven.

I shall resume this subject in my next, and by an induction of particulars shew, that this power, in its exercise, will subvert all state authority, and will work to the oppression of the people, and that there are no restrictions in the constitution that will soften its rigour, but rather the contrary.

BRUTUS.

New-York Journal

27 DECEMBER 1787

ESSAY VI

Brutus paints a frightening picture of the lengths to which Congress might go in exercising its taxing power, including operating its own businesses and intruding on commercial and private life. Essays in The Federalist *of particular relevance: 30-36, 44.*

IT is an important question, whether the general government of the United States should be so framed, as to absorb and swallow up the state governments? or whether, on the contrary, the former ought not to be confined to certain defined national objects, while the latter should retain all the powers which concern the internal police of the states?

I have, in my former papers, offered a variety of arguments to prove, that a simple free government could not be exercised over this whole continent and that therefore we must either give up our liberties and submit to an arbitrary one, or frame a constitution on the plan of confederation. Further reasons might be urged to prove this point—but it seems unnecessary, because the principal advocates of the new constitution admit of the position. The question therefore between us, this being admitted, is, whether or not this system is so formed as either directly to annihilate the state governments, or that in its operation it will certainly effect it. If this is answered in the affirmative, then the system ought not to be adopted, without such amendments as will avoid this consequence. If on the contrary it can be shewn, that the state governments are secured in their rights to manage the internal police of the respective states, we must confine ourselves in our enquiries to the organization of the government and the guards and provisions it contains to prevent a misuse or abuse of power. To determine this question, it is requisite, that we fully investigate the nature, and the extent of the powers intended to be granted by this constitution to the rulers.

In my last number I called your attention to this subject, and proved, as I think, uncontrovertibly, that the powers given the legislature under the 8th section of the 1st article, had no other limitation than the discretion of the Congress. It was shewn, that even if the most favorable construction was given to this paragraph, that the advocates for the new constitution could wish, it will convey a power to lay and collect taxes, imposts, duties, and excises, according to the discretion of the legislature, and to make all laws which they shall judge proper and necessary to carry this power into execution. This I shewed would totally destroy all the power of the state governments. To confirm this, it is worth while to trace the operation of the government in some particular instances.

The general government is to be vested with authority to levy and collect taxes, duties, and excises; the separate states have also power to impose taxes, duties, and excises, except that they cannot lay duties on exports and imports without the consent of Congress. Here then the two governments have concurrent jurisdiction; both may lay impositions of this kind. But then the general government have supperadded to this power, authority to make all laws which shall be necessary and proper for carrying the foregoing power into execution. Suppose then that both governments should lay taxes, duties, and excises, and it should fall so heavy on the people that they would be unable, or be so burdensome that they would refuse to pay them both—would it not be necessary that the general legislature should suspend the collection of the state tax? It certainly would. For, if the people could not, or would not pay both, they must be discharged from the tax to the state, or the tax to the general government could not be collected.—The conclusion therefore is inevitable, that the respective state governments will not have the power to raise one shilling in any way, but by the permission of the Congress. I presume no one will pretend, that the states can exercise legislative authority, or administer justice among their citizens for any length of time, without being able to raise a sufficiency to pay those who administer their governments.

If this be true, and if the states can raise money only by permission of the general government, it follows that the state governments will be dependent on the will of the general government for their existence.

What will render this power in Congress effectual and sure in its operation is, that the government will have complete judicial and executive authority to carry all their laws into effect, which will be paramount to the judicial and executive authority of the individual states: in vain therefore will be all interference of the legislatures, courts, or magistrates of any of the states on the subject; for they will be subordinate to the general government, and engaged by oath to support it, and will be constitutionally bound to submit to their decisions.

The general legislature will be empowered to lay any tax they chuse, to annex any penalties they please to the breach of their revenue laws; and to appoint as many officers as they may think proper to collect the taxes. They will have authority to farm the revenues and to vest the farmer general, with his subalterns, with plenary powers to collect them, in any way which to them may appear eligible. And the courts of law, which they will be authorized to institute, will have cognizance of every case arising under the revenue laws, the conduct of all the officers employed in collecting them; and the officers of these courts will execute their judgments. There is no way, therefore, of avoiding the destruction of the state governments, whenever the Congress please to do it, unless the people rise up, and, with a strong hand, resist and prevent the execution of constitutional laws. The fear of this, will, it is presumed, restrain the general government, for some time, within proper bounds; but it will not be many years before they will have a revenue, and force, at their command, which will place them above any apprehensions on that score.

How far the power to lay and collect duties and excises, may operate to dissolve the state governments, and oppress the people, it is impossible to say. It would assist us much in forming a just opinion on this head, to consider the various objects to which this kind of taxes extend, in European nations, and the infinity of laws they have passed respecting them. Perhaps, if liesure will permit, this may be essayed in some future paper.

It was observed in my last number, that the power to lay and collect duties and excises, would invert the Congress with authority to impose a duty and excise on every necessary and convenience of life. As the principal object of the government, in laying a duty or excise, will be, to raise money, it is obvious, that they will fix on such articles as are of the most general use and consumption; because, unless great quantities of the article, on which the duty is laid, is used, the revenue cannot be considerable. We may therefore presume, that the articles which will be the object of this species of taxes will be either the real necessaries of life; or if not these, such as from custom and habit are esteemed so. I will single out a few of the productions of our own country, which may, and probably will, be of the number.

Cider is an article that most probably will be one of those on which an excise will be laid, because it is one, which this country produces in great abundance, which is in very general use, is consumed in great quantities, and which may be said too not to be a real necessary of life. An excise on this would raise a large sum of money in the United States. How would the power, to lay and collect an excise on cider, and to pass all laws proper and necessary to carry it into execution, operate in its exercise? It might be necessary, in order to collect the excise on cider, to grant to one man, in each county, an exclusive right of building and keeping cider-mills, and oblige him to give bonds and security for payment of the excise; or, if this was not done, it might be necessary to license the mills, which are to make this liquor, and to take from them security, to account for the excise; or, if otherwise, a great number of officers must be employed, to take account of the cider made, and to collect the duties on it.

Porter, ale, and all kinds of malt-liquors, are articles that would probably be subject also to an excise. It would be necessary, in order to collect such an excise, to regulate the manufactory of these, that the quantity made might be ascertained, or otherwise security could not be had for the payment of the excise. Every brewery must then be licensed, and officers appointed, to take account of its product, and to secure the payment of the duty, or excise, before it is sold. Many other articles might be named, which would be objects of this species of taxation, but I refrain from enumerating them. It will probably be said, by those who advocate this system, that the observations already made on this head, are calculated only to inflame the minds of the people, with the apprehension of dangers merely imaginary. That there is not the least reason to apprehend, the general legislature will exercise their power in this manner. To this I would only say, that these kinds of taxes exist in Great Britain, and are severely felt. The excise on cider and perry, was imposed in that nation a few years ago, and it is in the memory of every one, who read the history of the transaction, what great tumults it occasioned.

This power, exercised without limitation, will introduce itself into every corner of the city, and country—It will wait upon the ladies at their toilett, and will not leave them in any of their domestic concerns; it will accompany them to the ball, the play, and the assembly; it will go with them when they visit, and will, on all occasions, sit beside them in their carriages, nor will it defect them even at church; it will enter the house of every gentleman, watch over his cellar, wait upon his cook in the kitchen, follow the servants into the parlour, preside over the table, and note down all he eats or drinks; it will attend him to his bedchamber, and watch him while he sleeps; it will take cognizance of the professional mail in his office, or his study; it will watch the merchant in the counting-house, or in his store; it will follow the mechanic to his shop, and in his work, and will haunt him in his family, and in his bed; it will be a constant companion of the industrious farmer in all his labour, it will be with him in the house, and in the field, observe the toil of his hands, and the sweat of his brow; it will penetrate into the most obscure cottage; and finally, it will light upon the head of every person in the United States. To all these different classes of people, and in all these circumstances, in which it will attend them, the language in which it will address them, will be GIVE! GIVE!

A power that has such latitude, which reaches every person in the community to every conceivable circumstance, and lays hold of every species of property they possess and which has no bounds set to it but the discretion of those who exercise it. I say, such a power must necessarily, from its very nature, swallow up all the power of the state governments.

I shall add but one other observation on this head, which is this— It appears to me a solecism, for two men, or bodies of men, to have unlimited power respecting the same object. It contradicts the scripture maxim, which saith, "no man can serve two masters," the one power or the other must prevail, or else they will destroy each other, and neither of them effect their purpose. It may be compared to two mechanic powers, acting upon the same body in opposite directions, the consequence would be, if the powers were equal, the body would remain in a state of rest, or if the force of the one was superior to that of the other, the stronger would prevail, and overcome the resistance of the weaker.

But it is said, by some of the advocates of this system, "That the idea that Congress can levy taxes at pleasure, is false, and the suggestion wholly unsupported: that the preamble to the constitution is declaratory of the purposes of the union, and the assumption of any power not necessary to establish justice, &c. to provide for the common defence, &c. will be unconstitutional. Besides, in the very clause which gives the power of levying duties and taxes, the purposes to which the money shall be appropriated, are specified, viz. to pay the debts, and provide for the common defence and general welfare."* I would ask those, who reason thus, to define what ideas are included under the terms, to provide for the common defence and general welfare? Are these terms definite, and will they be understood in the same manner, and to apply to the same cases by every one? No one will pretend they will. It will then be matter of opinion, what tends to the general welfare; and the Congress will be the only judges in the matter. To provide for the general welfare, is an abstract proposition, which mankind differ in the explanation of, as much as they do on any political or moral proposition that can be proposed; the most opposite measures may be pursued by

*Vide an examination into the leading principles of the federal constitution, printed in Philadelphia, Page 34.

different parties, and both may profess, that they have in view the general welfare; and both sides may be honest in their professions, or both may have sinister views. Those who advocate this new constitution declare, they are influenced by a regard to the general welfare; those who oppose it, declare they are moved by the same principle; and I have no doubt but a number on both sides are honest in their professions; and yet nothing is more certain than this, that to adopt this constitution, and not to adopt it, cannot both of them be promotive of the general welfare.

It is as absurd to say, that the power of Congress is limited by these general expressions, "to provide for the common safety, and general welfare," as it would be to say, that it would be limited, had the constitution said they should have power to lay taxes, &c. at will and pleasure. Were this authority given, it might be said, that under it the legislature could not do injustice, or pursue any measures, but such as were calculated to promote the public good, and happiness. For every man, rulers as well as others, are bound by the immutable laws of God and reason, always to will what is right. It is certainly right and fit, that the governors of every people should provide for the common defence and general welfare; every government, therefore, in the world, even the greatest despot, is limited in the exercise of his power. But however just this reasoning may be, it would be found, in practice, a most pitiful restriction. The government would always say, their measures were designed and calculated to promote the public good; and there being no judge between them and the people, the rulers themselves must, and would always, judge for themselves.

There are others of the favourers of this system, who admit, that the power of the Congress under it, with respect to revenue, will exist without limitation, and contend, that so is ought to be.

It is said, "The power to raise armies, to build and equip fleets, and to provide for their support ought to exist without limitation, because it is impossible to foresee, or to define, the extent and variety of national exigencies, or the correspondent extent and variety of the means which may be necessary to satisfy them."

This, it is said, "is one of those truths which, to correct and unprejudiced minds, carries its own evidence along with it. It rests upon axioms as simple as they are universal: the means ought to be proportioned to the end; the person, from whose agency the attainment of any end is expected, ought to possess the means by which it is to be attained."*

This same writer insinuates, that the opponents to the plan promulgated by the convention, manifests a want of candor, in objecting to the extent of the powers proposed to be vested in this government; because he asserts, with an air of confidence, that the powers ought to be unlimited as to the object to which they extend; and that this position, if not self-evident, is at least clearly demonstrated by the foregoing mode of reasoning. But with submission to this author's better judgment, I humbly conceive his reasoning will appear, upon examination, more specious than solid. The means, says the gentleman, ought to be proportioned to the end; admit the proposition to be true it is then necessary to enquire, what is the end of the government of the United States, in order to draw any just conclusions from it. Is this end simply to preserve the general government, and to provide for the common defence and general welfare of the union only? certainly not[:] for beside this, the state governments are to be supported, and provision made for the managing such of their internal concerns as are allotted to them. It is admitted, "that the circumstances of our country are such, as to demand a compound, instead of a simple, a confederate, instead of a sole government," that the objects of each ought to be pointed out, and that each ought to possess ample authority to execute the powers committed to them. The government then, being complex in its nature, the end it has in view is so also; and it is as necessary, that the state governments should possess the means to attain the ends expected from them, as for the general government. Neither the general government, nor the state governments, ought to be vested with all the powers proper to be exercised for promoting the ends of government. The powers are divided between them—certain ends are to be attained by the one, and other certain ends by the other; and these, taken together, include all the ends of good government. This being the case, the

*Vide the Federalist, No. 23.

conclusion follows, that each should be furnished with the means, to attain the ends, to which they are designed.

To apply this reasoning to the case of revenue; the general government is charged with the case of providing for the payment of the debts of the United States; supporting the general government, and providing for the defence of the union. To obtain these ends, they should be furnished with means. But does it hence follow, that they should command all the revenues of the United States! Most certainly it does not. For if so, it will follow, that no means will be left to attain other ends, as necessary to the happiness of the country, as those committed to their care. The individual states have debts to discharge; their legislatures and executives are to be supported, and provision is to be made for the administration of justice in the respective states. For those objects the general government has no authority to provide; nor is it proper it should. It is clear then, that the states should have the command of such revenues, as to answer the ends they have to obtain. To say, "that the circumstances that endanger the safety of nations are infinite," and from hence to infer, that all the sources of revenue in the states should be yielded to the general government, is not conclusive reasoning: for the Congress are authorized only to controul in general concerns, and not regulate local and internal ones; and these are as essentially requisite to be provided for as those. The peace and happiness of a community is as intimately connected with the prudent direction of their domestic affairs, and the due administration of justice among themselves, as with a competent provision for their defence against foreign invaders, and indeed more so.

Upon the whole, I conceive, that there cannot be a clearer position than this, that the state governments ought to have an uncontroulable power to raise a revenue, adequate to the exigencies of their governments; and, I presume, no such power is left them by this constitution.

BRUTUS.

New-York Journal

3 JANUARY 1788

ESSAY VII

Brutus argues that Congress's need to defend the nation is not absolute. For example, this power properly extends only to the waging of defensive wars. Because its purposes are limited, the federal taxing power also should be limited—in ways that will protect state prerogatives and individual liberties. Essays in The Federalist *of particular relevance: 30-36.*

THE result of our reasoning in the two preceeding numbers is this, that in a confederated government, where the powers are divided between the general and the state government, it is essential to its existence, that the revenues of the country, without which no government can exist, should be divided between them, and so apportioned to each, as to answer their respective exigencies, as far as human wisdom can effect such a division and apportionment.

It has been shewn, that no such allotment is made in this constitution, but that every source of revenue is under the controul of the Congress; it therefore follows, that if this system is intended to be a complex and not a simple, a confederate and not an entire consolidated government, it contains in it the sure seeds of its own dissolution.—One of two things must happen—Either the new constitution will become a mere [nu]dum pactum, and all the authority of the rulers under it be cried down, as has happened to the present confederation—Or the authority of the individual states will be totally supplanted, and they will retain the mere form without any of the powers of government.—To one or the other of these issues, I think, this new government, if it is adopted, will advance with great celerity.

It is said, I know, that such a separation of the sources of revenue, cannot be made without endangering the public safety—"unless (says a writer) it can be shewn that the circumstances which may affect the public safety are reducible within certain determinate limits; unless the contrary of this position can be fairly and rationally disputed; it must be admitted as a necessary consequence, that there can be no limitation of that authority which is to provide for the defence and protection of the community, &c."*

The pretended demonstration of this writer will instantly vanish, when it is considered, that the *protection and defence* of the community is not intended to be entrusted *solely* into the hands of the general government, and by his own confession it ought not to be. It is true this system commits to the general government the protection and defence of the community against foreign force and invasion, against piracies and felonies on the high seas, and against insurrection among ourselves. They are also authorised to provide for the administration of justice in certain matters of a general concern, and in some that I think are not so. But it ought to be left to the state governments to provide for the protection and defence of the citizen against the hand of private violence, and the wrongs done or attempted by individuals to each other.—Protection and defence against the murderer, the robber, the thief, the cheat, and the unjust person, is to be derived from the respective state governments.—The just way of reasoning therefore on this subject is this, the general government is to provide for the protection and defence of the community against foreign attacks, &c. they therefore ought to have authority sufficient to effect this, so far as is consistent with the providing for our internal protection and defence. The state governments are entrusted with the care of administering justice among its citizens, and the management of other internal concerns, they ought therefore to retain power adequate to the end. The preservation of internal peace and good order, and the due administration of law and justice, ought to be the first care of every government.—The happiness of a people depends infinitely more on this than it does upon all that glory and respect which nations acquire by the most brilliant martial achievements—and I believe history will furnish but few examples of nations who have duly

*Federalist, No. 23.

attended to these, who have been subdued by foreign invaders. If a proper respect and submission to the laws prevailed over all orders of men in our country; and if a spirit of public and private justice, œconomy and industry influenced the people, we need not be under any apprehensions but what they would be ready to repel any invasion that might be made on the country. And more than this, I would not wish from them—A defensive war is the only one I think justifiable—I do not make these observations to prove, that a government ought not to be authorised to provide for the protection and defence of a country against external enemies, but to shew that this is not the most important, much less the only object of their care.

The European governments are almost all of them framed, and administered with a view to arms, and war, as that in which their chief glory consists; they mistake the end of government—it was designed to save mens lives, not to destroy them. We ought to furnish the world with an example of a great people, who in their civil institutions hold chiefly in view, the attainment of virtue, and happiness among ourselves. Let the monarchs in Europe, share among them the glory of depopulating countries, and butchering thousands of their innocent citizens, to revenge private quarrels, or to punish an insult offered to a wife, a mistress, or a favorite: I envy them not the honor, and I pray heaven this country may never be ambitious of it. The czar Peter the great, acquired great glory by his arms; but all this was nothing, compared with the true glory which he obtained, by civilizing his rude and barbarous subjects, diffusing among them knowledge, and establishing, and cultivating the arts of life: by the former he desolated countries, and drenched the earth with human blood: by the latter he softened the ferocious nature of his people, and pointed them to the means of human happiness. The most important end of government then, is the proper direction of internal police, and economy; this is the province of the state governments, and it is evident, and is indeed admitted, that these ought to be under their controul. Is it not then preposterous, and in the highest degree absurd, when the state governments are vested with powers so essential to the peace and good order of society, to take from them the means of their own preservation?

The idea, that the powers of congress in respect to revenue ought to be unlimited, "because the circumstance which may affect the public safety are not reducible to certain determinate limits," [is novel], as it relates to the government of the united states. The inconveniencies which resulted from the feebleness of the present confederation was discerned, and felt soon after its adoption. It was soon discovered, that a power to require money, without either the authority or means to enforce a collection of it, could not be relied upon either to provide for the common defence, the discharge of the national debt, or for support of government. Congress therefore, so early as February 1781, recommended to the states to invest them with a power to levy an impost of five per cent ad valorem, on all imported goods, as a fund to be appropriated to discharge the debts already contracted, or which should hereafter be contracted for the support of the war, to be continued until the debts should be fully and finally discharged. There is not the most distant idea held out in this act, that an unlimited power to collect taxes, duties and excises was necessary to be vested in the united states, and yet this was a time of the most pressing danger and distress. The idea then was, that if certain definite funds were assigned to the union, which were certain in their natures, productive, and easy of collection, it would enable them to answer their engagements, and provide for their defence, and the impost of five per cent was fixed upon for the purpose.

This same subject was revived in the winter and spring of 1783, and after a long consideration of the subject, and many schemes were proposed; the result was, a recommendation of the revenue system of April 1783; this system does not suggest an idea that it was necessary to grant the United States unlimitted authority in matters of revenue. A variety of amendments were proposed to this system, some of which are upon the journals of Congress, but it does not appear that any of them proposed to invest the general government with discretionary power to raise money. On the contrary, all of them limit them to certain definite objects, and fix the bounds over which they could not pass. This recommendation was passed at the conclusion of the war, and was founded on an estimate of the whole national debt. It was computed, that one million and an half of dollars, in addition to the impost, was sufficient sum to pay the annual interest of the debt, and gradually to abolish the principal.—Events have proved that their estimate was sufficiently liberal, as the domestic debt appears upon its being adjusted to be less than it was computed, and since this period a considerable portion of the principal of the domestic debt has been discharged by the sale of the western lands. It has been constantly urged by Congress, and by individuals, ever since, until lately, that had this revenue been appropriated by the states, as it was recommended, it would have been adequate to every exigency of the union. Now indeed it is insisted, that all the treasures of the country are to be under the controul of that body, whom we are to appoint to provide for our protection and defence against foreign enemies. The debts of the several states, and the support of the governments of them are to trust to fortune and accident. If the union should not have occasion for all the money they can raise, they will leave a portion for the state, but this must be a matter of mere grace and favor. Doctrines like these would not have been listened to by any state in the union, at a time when we were pressed on every side by a powerful enemy, and were called upon to make greater exertions than we have any reason to expect we shall ever be again. The ability and character of the convention, who framed the proferred constitution, is founded forth and reiterated by every declaimer and writer in its favor, as a powerful argument to induce its adoption. But are not the patriots who guided our councils in the perilous times of the war, entitled to equal respect. How has it happened, that none of these perceived a truth, which it is pretended is capable of such clear demonstration, that the power to raise a revenue should be deposited in the general government without limitation? Were the men so dull of apprehension, so incapable of reasoning as not to be able to draw the inference? The truth is, no such necessity exists. It is a thing practicable, and by no means so difficult as is pretended, to limit the powers of the general government in respect to revenue, while yet they may retain reasonable means to provide for the common defence.

It is admitted, that human wisdom cannot foresee all the variety of circumstances that may arise to endanger the safety of nations—

and it may with equal truth be added, that the power of a nation, exerted with its utmost vigour, may not be equal to repel a force with which it may be assailed, much less may it be able, with its ordinary resources and power, to oppose an extraordinary and unexpected attack;—but yet every nation may form a rational judgment, what force will be competent to protect and defend it, against any enemy with which it is probable it may have to contend. In extraordinary attacks, every country must rely upon the spirit and special exertions of its inhabitants—and these extraordinary efforts will always very much depend upon the happiness and good order the people experience from a wise and prudent administration of their internal government. The states are as capable of making a just estimate on this head, as perhaps any nation in the world.—We have no powerful nation in our neighbourhood; if we are to go to war, it must either be with the Aboriginal natives, or with European nations. The first are so unequal to a contest with this whole continent, that they are rather to be dreaded for the depredations they may make on our frontiers, than for any impression they will ever be able to make on the body of the country. Some of the European nations, it is true, have provinces bordering upon us, but from these, unsupported by their European forces, we have nothing to apprehend; if any of them should attack us, they will have to transport their armies across the atlantic, at immense expence, while we should defend ourselves in our own country, which abounds with every necessary of life. For defence against any assault, which there is any probability will be made upon us, we may easily form an estimate.

I may be asked to point out the sources, from which the general government could derive a sufficient revenue, to answer the demands of the union. Many might be suggested, and for my part, I am not disposed to be tenacious of my own opinion on the subject. If the object be defined with precision, and will operate to make the burden fall any thing nearly equal on the different parts of the union, I shall be satisfied.

There is one source of revenue, which it is agreed, the general government ought to have the sole controul of. This is an impost upon all goods imported from foreign countries. This would, of itself, be very productive, and would be collected with ease and certainty.—It will be a fund too, constantly encreasing—for our commerce will grow, with the productions of the country; and these, together with our consumption of foreign goods, will encrease with our population. It is said, that the impost will not produce a sufficient sum to satisfy the demands of the general government; perhaps it would not. Let some other then, equally well defined, be assigned them—that this is practicable is certain, because such particular objects were proposed by some members of Congress when the revenue system of April 1783, was agitated in that body. It was then moved, that a tax at the rate of [   ] ninetieths of a dollar on surveyed land, and a house tax of half a dollar on a house, should be granted to the United States. I do not mention this, because I approve of raising a revenue in this mode. I believe such a tax would be difficult in its collection, and inconvenient in its operation. But it shews, that it has heretofore been the sense of some of those, who now contend, that the general government should have unlimited authority in matters of revenue, that their authority should be definite and limited on that head.—My own opinion is, that the objects from which the general government should have authority to raise a revenue, should be of such a nature, that the tax should be raised by simple laws, with few officers, with certainty and expedition, and with the least interference with the internal police of the states.—Of this nature is the impost on imported goods—and it appears to me that a duty on exports, would also be of this nature—and therefore, for ought I can discover, this would be the best source of revenue to grant the general government. I know neither the Congress nor the state legislatures will have authority under the new constitution to raise a revenue in this way. But I cannot perceive the reason of the restriction. It appears to me evident, that a tax on articles exported would be as nearly equal as any that we can expect to lay, and it certainly would be collected with more ease and less expence than any direct tax. I do not however, contend for this mode, it may be liable to well founded objections that have not occurred to me. But this I do contend for, that some mode is practicable, and that limits must be marked between the general government, and the states on this head, or if they be

not, either the Congress in the exercise of this power, will deprive
the state legislatures of the means of their existence, or the states
by resisting the constitutional authority of the general government,
will render it nugatory.

BRUTUS.

New-York Journal

10 JANUARY 1788

ESSAY VIII

*Brutus criticizes the ease with which the new federal government
will be able to borrow money and use state militias for its own ends
and suggests solutions to both problems. Essays in* The Federalist
of particular relevance: 12, 13, 29.

THE next powers vested by this constitution in the general government, which we shall consider, are those, which authorise them
to "borrow money on the credit of the United States, and to raise
and support armies." I take these two together and connect them
with the power to lay and collect taxes, duties, imposts and excises,
because their extent, and the danger that will arise from the exercise of these powers, cannot be fully understood, unless they are
viewed in relation to each other.

The power to borrow money is general and unlimitted, and the
clause so often before referred to, authorises the passing any laws
proper and necessary to carry this into execution. Under this
authority, the Congress may mortgage any or all the revenues of
the union, as a fund to loan money upon, and it is probable, in this
way, they may borrow of foreign nations, a principal sum, the interest of which will be equal to the annual revenues of the country.—
By this means, they may create a national debt, so large, as to
exceed the ability of the country ever to sink. I can scarcely con-

template a greater calamity that could befal this country, than to be loaded with a debt exceeding their ability ever to discharge. If this be a just remark, it is unwise and improvident to vest in the general government, a power to borrow at discretion, without any limitation or restriction.

It may possibly happen that the safety and welfare of the country may require, that money be borrowed, and it is proper when such a necessity arises that the power should be exercised by the general government.—But it certainly ought never to be exercised, but on the most urgent occasions, and then we should not borrow of foreigners if we could possibly avoid it.

The constitution should therefore have so restricted, the exercise of this power as to have rendered it very difficult for the government to practise it. The present confederation requires the assent of nine states to exercise this, and a number of the other important powers of the confederacy—and it would certainly have been a wise provision in this constitution, to have made it necessary that two thirds of the members should assent to borrowing money— when the necessity was indispensible, this assent would always be given, and in no other cause ought it to be.

The power to raise armies, is indefinite and unlimitted, and authorises the raising forces, as well in peace as in war. Whether the clause which impowers the Congress to pass all laws which are proper and necessary, to carry this into execution, will not authorise them to impress men for the army, is a question well worthy consideration? If the general legislature deem it for the general welfare to raise a body of troops, and they cannot be procured by voluntary enlistments, it seems evident, that it will be proper and necessary to effect it, that men be impressed from the militia to make up the deficiency.

These powers taken in connection, amount this: that the general government have unlimitted authority and controul over all the wealth and all the force of the union. The advocates for this scheme, would favor the world with a new discovery, if they would shew, what kind of freedom or independency is left to the state governments, when they cannot command any part of the property or of the force of the country, but at the will of the Congress. It seems

to me as absurd, as it would be to say, that I was free and independent, when I had conveyed all my property to another, and was ten-
ant to will to him, and had beside, given an indenture of myself to
serve him during life.—The power to keep up standing armies in
time of peace, has been justly objected, to this system, as dangerous
and improvident. The advocates who have wrote in its favor, have
some of them ridiculed the objection, as though it originated in the
distempered brain of its opponents, and others have taken pains to
shew, that it is a power that was proper to be granted to the rulers
in this constitution. That you may be enabled to form a just opinion on this subject. I shall first make some remarks, tending to
prove, that this power ought to be restricted, and then animadvert
on the arguments which have been adduced to justify it.

I take it for granted, as an axiom in politic, that the people should
never authorise their rulers to do any thing, which if done, would
operate to their injury.

It seems equally clear, that in a case where a power, if given and
exercised, will generally produce evil to the community, and seldom
good—and which, experience has proved, has most frequently been
exercised to the great injury, and very often to the total destruction
of the government; in such a case, I say, this power, if given at all,
should if possible be so restricted, as to prevent the ill effect of its
operation.

Let us then enquire, whether standing armies in time of peace,
would be ever beneficial to our country—or if in some extraordinary cases; they might be necessary; whether it is not true, that
they have generally proved a scourge to a country, and destructive
of their liberty.

I shall not take up much of your time in proving a point, in which
the friends of liberty, in all countries, have so universally agreed.
The following extract from Mr. Pultney's speech; delivered in the
house of commons of Great-Britain, on a motion for reducing the
army, is so full to the point, and so much better than any thing I
can say, that I shall be excused for inserting it. He says, "I have
always been, and always shall be against a standing army of any
kind; to me it is a terrible thing, whether under that of a parlia-

mentary, or any other designation; a standing army is still a standing army by whatever name it is called; they are a body of men distinct from the body of the people, they are governed by different laws, and blind obedience, and an entire submission to the orders of their commanding officer, is their only principle; the nations around us, sir, are already enslaved, and have been enslaved by those very means; by means of their standing armies they have every one lost their liberties; it is indeed impossible that the liberties of the people in any country can be preserved where a numerous standing army is kept up. Shall we then take our measures from the example of our neighbours? No, sir, on the contrary, from their misfortunes we ought to learn to avoid those rocks upon which they have split.

"It signifies nothing to tell me that our army is commanded by such gentlemen as cannot be supposed to join in any measures for enslaving their country; it may be so; I have a very good opinion of many gentlemen now in the army; I believe they would not join in any such measures; but their lives are uncertain, nor can we be sure how long they will be kept in command, they may all be dismissed in a moment, and proper tools of power put in their room. Besides, sir, we know the passions of men, we know how dangerous it is to trust the best of men with too much power. Where was a braver army than that under Jul. Caesar? Where was there ever an army that had served their country more faithfully? That army was commanded generally by the best citizens of Rome, by men of great fortune and figure in their country, yet that army enslaved their country. The affections of the soldiers towards their country, the honor and integrity of the under officers, are not to be depended on. By the military law the administration of justice is so quick, and the punishment so severe, that neither the officer nor soldier dare dispute the orders of his supreme commander; he must not consult his own inclination. If an officer were commanded to pull his own father out of this house, he must do it; he dares not disobey; immediate death would be the sure consequence of the least grumbling: and if an officer were sent into the court of request, accompanied by a body of musketeers with screwed bayonets, and with orders to tell us what we ought to do, and how we were to vote: I know what would be the duty of this house; I know it would be our duty to order the officer to be hanged at the door of the lobby: but I doubt, sir, I doubt much, if such a spirit could be found in the house, or in any house of commons that will ever be in England.

"Sir, I talk not of imaginary things? I talk of what has happened to an English house of commons, from an English army; not only from an English army, but an army that was raised by that very house of commons, an army that was paid by them, and an army that was commanded by generals appointed by them; therefore do not let us vainly imagine, that an army, raised and maintained by authority of parliament, will always be submissive to them. If an army be so numerous as to have it in their power to overawe the parliament, they will be submissive as long as the parliament does nothing to disoblige their favourite general; but when that case happens I am afraid, that in place of the parliament's dismissing the army, the army will dismiss the parliament."—If this great man's reasoning be just, it follows, that keeping up a standing army, would be in the highest degree dangerous to the liberty and happiness of the community—and if so, the general government ought not to have authority to do it; for no government should be empowered to do that which if done, would tend to destroy public liberty.

BRUTUS.

———

New-York Journal

———

17 JANUARY 1788

———

ESSAY IX

———

Brutus laments the Constitution's lack of a bill of rights. Especially troublesome is the failure to prohibit standing armies in peacetime. Such armies breed corruption and will not be properly

checked by the unrepresentative legislature. Essays in The Federalist *of particular relevance: 24-29, 84.*

THE design of civil government is to protect the rights and promote
the happiness of the people.

For this end, rulers are invested with powers. But we cannot
from hence justly infer that these powers should be unlimited.
There are certain rights which mankind possess, over which government ought not to have any controul, because it is not necessary they should, in order to attain the end of its institution. There
are certain things which rulers should be absolutely prohibited
from doing, because, if they should do them, they would work an
injury, not a benefit to the people. Upon the same principles of reasoning, if the exercise of a power, is found generally or in most cases
to operate to the injury of the community, the legislature should
be restricted in the exercise of that power, so as to guard, as much
as possible, against the danger. These principles seem to be the
evident dictates of common sense, and what ought to give sanction
to them in the minds of every American, they are the great principles of the late revolution, and those which governed the framers of
all our state constitutions. Hence we find, that all the state constitutions, contain either formal bills of rights, which set bounds to the
powers of the legislature, or have restrictions for the same purpose in the body of the constitutions. Some of our new political Doctors, indeed, reject the idea of the necessity, or propriety of such
restrictions in any elective government, but especially in the general one.

But it is evident, that the framers of this new system were of a
contrary opinion, because they have prohibited the general government, the exercise of some powers, and restricted them in that
of others.

I shall adduce two instances, which will serve to illustrate my
meaning, as well as to confirm the truth of the preceding remark.

In the 9th section, it is declared, "no bill of attainder shall be
passed." This clause takes from the legislature all power to declare
a particular person guilty of a crime by law. It is proper the legis-

lature should be deprived of the exercise of this power, because it seldom is exercised to the benefit of the community, but generally to its injury.

In the same section it is provided, that "the privilege of the writ of habeas corpus shall not be suspended, unless when in cases of rebellion and invasion, the public safety may require it." This clause limits the power of the legislature to deprive a citizen of the right of habeas corpus, to particular cases viz. those of rebellion and invasion; the reason is plain, because in no other cases can this power be exercised for the general good.

Let us apply these remarks to the case of standing armies in times of peace. If they generally prove the destruction of the happiness and libertys of the people, the legislature ought not to have power to keep them up, or if they had, this power should be so restricted, as to secure the people against the danger arising from the exercise of it.

That standing armies are dangerous to the liberties of a people was proved in my last number—If it was necessary, the truth of the position might be confirmed by the history of almost every nation in the world. A cloud of the most illustrious patriots of every age and country, where freedom has been enjoyed, might be adduced as witnesses in support of the sentiment. But I presume it would be useless, to enter into a laboured argument, to prove to the people of America, a position, which has so long and so generally been received by them as a kind of axiom.

Some of the advocates for this new system controvert this sentiment, as they do almost every other that has been maintained by the best writers on free government.—Others, though they will not expressly deny, that standing armies in times of peace are dangerous, yet join with these in maintaining, that it is proper the general government should be vested with the power to do it. I shall now proceed to examine the arguments they adduce in support of their opinions.

A writer, in favor of this system, treats this objection as a ridiculous one. He supposes it would be as proper to provide against the introduction of Turkish janizaries, or against making the Alcoran a rule of faith.

From the positive, and dogmatic manner, in which this author delivers his opinions, and answers objections made to his sentiments—one would conclude, that he was some pedantic pedagogue who had been accustomed to deliver his dogmas to pupils, who always placed implicit faith in what he delivered.

But, why is this provision so ridiculous? because, says this author, it is unnecessary. But, why is it unnecessary? ["]because, the principles and habits, as well as the power of the Americans are directly opposed to standing armies; and there is as little necessity to guard against them by positive constitutions, as to prohibit the establishment of the Mahometan religion." It is admitted then, that a standing army in time of peace, is an evil. I ask then, why should this government be authorised to do evil? If the principles and habits of the people of this country are opposed to standing armies in time of peace, if they do not contribute to the public good, but would endanger the public liber[ty] and happiness, why should the government be [vested] with the power? No reason can be given, why [rulers] should be authorised to do, what, if done, would oppose the principles and habits of the people, and endanger the public safety, but there is every reason in the world, that they should be prohibited from the exercise of such a power. But this author supposes, that no danger is to be apprehended from the exercise of this power, because, if armies are kept up, it will be by the people themselves, and therefore, to provide against it, would be as absurd as for a man to "pass a law in his family that no troops should be quartered in his family by his consent." This reasoning supposes, that the general government is to be exercised by the people of America themselves— But such an idea is groundless and absurd. There is surely a distinction between the people and their rulers, even when the latter are representatives of the former.—They certainly are not identically the same, and it cannot be disputed, but it may and often does happen, that they do not possess the same sentiments or pursue the same interests. I think I have shewn, that as this government is constituted, there is little reason to expect, that the interest of the people and their rulers will be the same.

Besides, if the habits and sentiments of the people of America are to be relied upon, as the sole security against the encroachment of their rulers, all restrictions in constitutions are unnecessary; nothing more is requisite, than to declare who shall be authorized to exercise the powers of government, and about this we need not be very careful—for the habits and principles of the people will oppose every abuse of power. This I suppose to be the sentiments of this author, as it seems to be of many of the advocates of this new system. An opinion like this, is as directly opposed to the principles and habits of the people of America, as it is to the sentiments of every writer of reputation on the science of government, and repugnant to the principles of reason and common sense.

The idea that there is no danger of the establishment of a standing army, under the new constitution, is without foundation.

It is a well known fact, that a number of those who had an agency in producing this system, and many of those who it is probable will have a principal share in the administration of the government under it, if it is adopted, are avowedly in favour of standing armies. It is a language common among them, "That no people can be kept in order, unless the government have an army to awe them into obedience; it is necessary to support the dignity of government, to have a military establishment." And there will not be wanting a variety of plausible reason to justify the raising one, drawn from the danger we are in from the Indians on our frontiers, or from the European provinces in our neighbourhood. If to this we add, that an army will afford a decent support, and agreeable employment to the young men of many families, who are too indolent to follow occupations that will require care and industry, and too poor to live without doing any business we can have little reason to doubt, but that we shall have a large standing army, as soon as this government can find money to pay them, and perhaps sooner.

A writer, who is the boast of the advocates of this new constitution, has taken great pains to shew, that this power was proper and necessary to be vested in the general government.

He sets out with calling in question the candour and integrity of those who advance the objection, and with insinuating, that it is their intention to mislead the people, by alarming their passions, rather than to convince them by arguments addressed to their understandings.

The man who reproves another for a fault, should be careful that he himself be not guilty of it. How far this writer has manifested a spirit of candour, and has pursued fair reasoning on this subject, the impartial public will judge, when his arguments pass before them in review.

He first attempts to shew, that this objection is futile and disingenuous, because the power to keep up standing armies, in time of peace, is vested, under the present government, in the legislature of every state in the union, except two. Now this is so far from being true, that it is expressly declared, by the present articles of confederation, that no body of forces "shall be kept up by any state, in time of peace, except such number only, as in the judgment of the United States in Congress assembled, shall be deemed requisite to garrison the forts necessary for the defence of such state." Now, was it candid and ingenuous to endeavour to persuade the public, that the general government had no other power than your own legislature have on this head; when the truth is, your legislature have no authority to raise and keep up any forces?

He next tells us, that the power given by this constitution, on this head is similar to that which Congress possess under the present confederation. As little ingenuity is manifested in this representation as in that of the former.

I shall not undertake to enquire whether or not Congress are vested with a power to keep up a standing army in time of peace; it has been a subject warmly debated in Congress, more than once, since the peace; and one of the most respectable states in the union, were so fully convinced that they had no such power, that they expressly instructed their delegates to enter a solemn protest against it on the journals of Congress, should they attempt to exercise it.

But should it be admitted that they have the power, there is such a striking dissimilarity between the restrictions under which the present Congress can exercise it, and that of the proposed government, that the comparison will serve rather to shew the impropriety of vesting the proposed government with the power, than of justifying it.

It is acknowledged by this writer, that the powers of Congress, under the present confederation, amount to little more than that of recommending. If they determine to raise troops, they are obliged to effect it through the authority of the state legislatures. This will, in the first instance, be a most powerful restraint upon them, against ordering troops to be raised. But if they should vote an army, contrary to the opinion and wishes of the people, the legislatures of the respective states would not raise them. Besides, the present Congress hold their places at the will and pleasure of the legislatures of the states who send them, and no troops can be raised, but by the assent of nine states out of the thirteen. Compare the power proposed to be lodged in the legislature on this head, under this constitution, with that vested in the present Congress and every person of the least discernment, whose understanding is not totally blinded by prejudice, will perceive, that they bear no analogy to each other. Under the present confederation, the representatives of nine states, out of thirteen, must assent to the raising of troops, or they cannot be levied: under the proposed constitution, a less number than the representatives of two states, in the house of representatives, and the representatives of three states and an half in the senate, with the assent of the president, may raise any number of troops they please: The present Congress are restrained from an undue exercise of this power, from this consideration, they know the state legislatures, through whose authority it must be carried into effect, would not comply with the requisition for the purpose, if it was evidently opposed to the public good: the proposed constitution authorizes the legislature to carry their determinations into execution, without the intervention of any other body between them and the people. The Congress under the present form are amenable to, and removable by, the legislatures of the respective states, and are chosen for one year only: the proposed constitution does not make the members of the legislature accountable to, or removeable by the state legislatures at all; and they are chosen, the one house for six, and the other for two years; and cannot be removed until their time of service is expired, let them conduct ever so badly.—The public will judge, from the above comparison, how just a claim this writer has to that candour he affects to possess. In the mean time, to convince him, and the advocates for this system, that I possess some share of candor, I pledge myself to give up all opposition to it, on the head of standing armies, if the power to raise them be restricted as it is in the present confederation; and I believe I may safely answer, not only for myself, but for all who make the objection, that they will be satisfied with less.

BRUTUS.

New-York Journal

24 JANUARY 1788

ESSAY X

Brutus uses the examples of Julius Caesar and Oliver Cromwell to show the dangers of standing armies. George Washington was too virtuous to go along with the army's plot to destroy America's liberties, but the people should not count on such virtue in future leaders. Essays in The Federalist *of particular relevance: 24-28.*

To the PEOPLE of the STATE of NEW-YORK.
THE liberties of a people are in danger from a large standing army, not only because the rulers may employ them for the purposes of supporting themselves in any usurpations of power, which they may see proper to exercise, but there is great hazard, that an army will subvert the forms of the government, under whose authority, they are raised, and establish one, according to the pleasure of their leaders.

We are informed, in the faithful pages of history, of such events frequently happening.—Two instances have been mentioned in a former paper. They are so remarkable, that they are worthy of the most careful attention of every lover of freedom.—They are taken from the history of the two most powerful nations that have ever

existed in the world; and who are the most renowned, for the freedom they enjoyed, and the excellency of their constitutions:—I
mean Rome and Britain.

In the first, the liberties of the commonwealth was destroyed,
and the constitution overturned, by an army, lead by Julius Cesar,
who was appointed to the command, by the constitutional authority
of that commonwealth. He changed it from a free republic, whose
fame had sounded, and is still celebrated by all the world, into that
of the most absolute despotism. A standing army effected this
change, and a standing army supported it through a succession of
ages, which are marked in the annals of history, with the most horrid cruelties, bloodshed, and carnage;—The most devilish, beastly,
and unnatural vices, that ever punished or disgraced human nature.

The same army, that in Britain, vindicated the liberties of that
people from the encroachments and despotism of a tyrant king,
assisted Cromwell, their General, in wresting from the people, that
liberty they had so dearly earned.

You may be told, these instances will not apply to our case:—
But those who would persuade you to believe this, either mean to
deceive you, or have not themselves considered the subject.

I firmly believe, no country in the world had ever a more patriotic
army, than the one which so ably served this country, in the late
war.

But had the General who commanded them, been possessed of
the spirit of a Julius Cesar or a Cromwell, the liberties of this country, had in all probability, terminated with the war; or had they
been maintained, might have cost more blood and treasure, than
was expended in the conflict with Great-Britain. When an anoni-
mous writer addressed the officers of the army at the close of the
war, advising them not to part with their arms, until justice was
done them—the effect it had is well known. It affected them like an
electric shock. He wrote like Cesar; and had the commander in
chief, and a few more officers of rank, countenanced the measure,
the desperate resolution had been taken, to refuse to disband.
What the consequences of such a determination would have been,
heaven only knows.—The army were in the full vigor of health and
spirits, in the habit of discipline, and possessed of all our military

stores and apparatus. They would have acquired great accessions of strength from the country.—Those who were disgusted at our republican forms of government (for such there then were, of high rank among us) would have lent them all their aid.—We should in all probability have seen a constitution and laws, dictated to us, at the head of an army, and at the point of a bayonet, and the liberties for which we had so severely struggled, snatched from us in a moment. It remains a secret, yet to be revealed, whether this measure was not suggested, or at least countenanced, by some, who have had great influence in producing the present system.—Fortunately indeed for this country, it had at the head of the army, a patriot as well as a general; and many of our principal officers, had not abandoned the characters of citizens, by assuming that of soldiers, and therefore, the scheme proved abortive. But are we to expect, that this will always be the case? Are we so much better than the people of other ages and of other countries, that the same allurements of power and greatness, which led them aside from their duty, will have no influence upon men in our country? Such an idea, is wild and extravagant.—Had we indulged such a delusion, enough has appeared in a little time past, to convince the most credulous, that the passion for pomp, power and greatness, works as powerfully in the hearts of many of our better sort, as it ever did in any country under heaven.—Were the same opportunity again to offer, we should very probably be grossly disappointed, if we made dependence, that all who then rejected the overture, would do it again.

From these remarks, it appears, that the evils to be feared from a large standing army in time of peace, does not arise solely from the apprehension, that the rulers may employ them for the purpose of promoting their own ambitious views, but that equal, and perhaps greater danger, is to be apprehended from their overturning the constitutional powers of the government, and assuming the power to dictate any form they please.

The advocates for power, in support of this right in the proposed government, urge that a restraint upon the discretion of the legislatures, in respect to military establishments in time of peace, would be improper to be imposed, because they say, it will be necessary to maintain small garrisons on the frontiers, to guard against the depredations of the Indians, and to be prepared to repel any encroachments or invasions that may be made by Spain or Britain.

The amount of this argument striped of the abundant verbages with which the author has dressed it, is this:

It will probably be necessary to keep up a small body of troops to garrison a few posts, which it will be necessary to maintain, in order to guard against the sudden encroachments of the Indians, or of the Spaniards and British; and therefore, the general government ought to be invested with power to raise and keep up a standing army in time of peace, without restraint; at their discretion.

I confess, I cannot perceive that the conclusion follows from the premises. Logicians say, it is not good reasoning to infer a general conclusion from particular premises: though I am not much of a Logician, it seems to me, this argument is very like that species of reasoning.

When the patriots in the parliament in Great-Britain, contended with such force of argument, and all the powers of eloquence, against keeping up standing armies in time of peace, it is obvious, they never entertained an idea, that small garrisons on their frontiers, or in the neighbourhood of powers, from whom they were in danger of encroachments, or guards, to take care of public arsenals would thereby be prohibited.

The advocates for this power farther urge that it is necessary, because it may, and probably will happen, that circumstances will render it requisite to raise an army to be prepared to repel attacks of an enemy, before a formal declaration of war, which in modern times has fallen into disuse. If the constitution prohibited the raising an army, until a war actually commenced, it would deprive the government of the power of providing for the defence of the country, until the enemy were within our territory. If the restriction is not to extend to the raising armies in cases of emergency, but only to the keeping them up, this would leave the matter to the discretion of the legislature; and they might, under the pretence that there was danger of an invasion, keep up the army as long as they judged proper—and hence it is inferred, that the legislature should have authority to raise and keep up an army without any restriction. But from these premises nothing more will follow than this, that the legislature should not be so restrained, as to put it out of their power to raise an army, when such exigencies as are instanced shall arise. But it does not thence follow, that the government should be empowered to raise and maintain standing armies at their discretion as well in peace as in war. If indeed, it is impossible to vest the general government with the power of raising troops to garrison the frontier posts, to guard arsenals, or to be prepared to repel an attack, when we saw a power preparing to make one, without giving them a general and indefinite authority, to raise and keep up armies, without any restriction or qualification, then this reasoning might have weight; but this has not been proved nor can it be.

It is admitted that to prohibit the general government, from keeping up standing armies, while yet they were authorised to raise them in case of exigency, would be an insufficient guard against the danger. A discretion of such latitude would give room to elude the force of the provision.

It is also admitted that an absolute prohibition against raising troops, except in cases of actual war, would be improper; because it will be requisite to raise and support a small number of troops to garrison the important frontier posts, and to guard arsenals; and it may happen, that the danger of an attack from a foreign power may be so imminent, as to render it highly proper we should raise an army, in order to be prepared to resist them. But to raise and keep up forces for such purposes and on such occasions, is not included in the idea, of keeping up standing armies in times of peace.

It is a thing very practicable to give the government sufficient authority to provide for these cases, and at the same time to provide a reasonable and competent security against the evil of a standing army—a clause to the following purpose would answer the end:

As standing armies in time of peace are dangerous to liberty, and have often been the means of overturning the best constitutions of government, no standing army, or troops of any description whatsoever, shall be raised or kept up by the legislature, except so many as shall be necessary for guards to the arsenals of the United States, or for garrisons to such posts on the frontiers, as it shall be deemed absolutely necessary to hold, to secure the inhabitants, and facilitate the trade with the Indians: unless when the United States are threatened with an attack or invasion from some foreign power, in which case the legislature shall be authorised to raise an army to be prepared to repel the attack; provided that no troops whatsoever shall be raised in time of peace, without the assent of two thirds of the members, composing both houses of the legislature.

A clause similar to this would afford sufficient latitude to the legislature to raise troops in all cases that were really necessary, and at the same time competent security against the establishment of that dangerous engine of despotism a standing army.

The same writer who advances the arguments I have noticed, makes a number of other observations with a view to prove that the power to raise and keep up armies, ought to be discretionary in the general legislature; some of them are curious; he instances the raising of troops in Massachusetts and Pennsylvania, to shew the necessity of keeping a standing army in time of peace; the least reflection must convince every candid mind that both these cases are totally foreign to his purpose—Massachusetts raised a body of troops for six months, at the expiration of which they were to disband of course; this looks very little like a standing army. But beside, was that commonwealth in a state of peace at that time? So far from it that they were in the most violent commotions and contests, and their legislature had formally declared that an unnatural rebellion existed within the state. The situation of Pennsylvania was similar; a number of armed men had levied war against the authority of the state, and openly avowed their intention of withdrawing their allegiance from it. To what purpose examples are brought, of states raising troops for short periods in times of war or insurrections, on a question concerning the propriety of keeping up standing armies in times of peace, the public must judge.

It is farther said, that no danger can arise from this power being lodged in the hands of the general government, because the legislatures will be a check upon them, to prevent their abusing it.

This is offered, as what force there is in it will hereafter receive a more particular examination. At present, I shall only remark, that it is difficult to conceive how the state legislatures can, in any case, hold a check over the general legislature, in a constitutional way. The latter has, in every instance to which their powers extend, complete controul over the former. The state legislatures can, in no case, by law, resolution, or otherwise, of right, prevent or impede the general government, from enacting any law, or executing it, which this constitution authorizes them to enact or execute. If then the state legislatures check the general legislatures, it must be by exciting the people to resist constitutional laws. In this way every individual, or every body of men, may check any government, in proportion to the influence they may have over the body of the people. But such kinds of checks as these, though they sometimes correct the abuses of government, oftner destroy all government.

It is further said, that no danger is to be apprehended from the exercise of this power, because it is lodged in the hands of representatives of the people; if they abuse it, it is in the power of the people to remove them, and chuse others who will pursue their interests. Not to repeat what has been said before, That it is unwise in any people, to authorize their rulers to do, what, if done, would prove injurious—I have, in some former numbers, shewn, that the representation in the proposed government will be a mere shadow without the substance. I am so confident that I am well founded in this opinion; that I am persuaded, if it was to be adopted or rejected, upon a fair discussion of its merits, without taking into contemplation circumstances extraneous to it, as reasons for its adoption, nineteen-twentieths of the sensible men in the union would reject it on this account alone; unless its powers were confined to much fewer objects than it embraces.

BRUTUS.

New-York Journal

31 JANUARY 1788

ESSAY XI

Brutus uses English examples to argue that the federal Supreme Court will use its power to interpret the Constitution to extend the Court's jurisdiction at the expense of state powers and liberties. Essays in The Federalist *of particular relevance. 79-82.*

THE nature and extent of the judicial power of the United States, proposed to be granted by this constitution, claims our particular attention.

Much has been said and written upon the subject of this new system on both sides, but I have not met with any writer, who has discussed the judicial powers with any degree of accuracy. And yet it is obvious, that we can form but very imperfect ideas of the manner in which this government will work, or the effect it will have in changing the internal police and mode of distributing justice at present subsisting in the respective states, without a thorough investigation of the powers of the judiciary and of the manner in which they will operate. This government is a complete system, not only for making, but for executing laws. And the courts of law, which will be constituted by it, are not only to decide upon the constitution and the laws made in pursuance of it, but by officers subordinate to them to execute all their decisions. The real effect of this system of government, will therefore be brought home to the feelings of the people, through the medium of the judicial power. It is, moreover, of great importance, to examine with care the nature and extent of the judicial power; because those who are to be vested with it, are to be placed in a situation altogether unprecedented in a free country. They are to be rendered totally independent, both of the people and the legislature, both with respect to their offices and salaries. No errors they may commit can be corrected by any power above them, if any such power there be, nor can they be removed from office for making ever so many erroneous adjudications.

The only causes for which they can be displaced, is conviction of treason, bribery, and high crimes and misdemeanors.

This part of the plan is so modelled, as to authorise the courts, not only to carry into execution the powers expressly given, but where these are wanting or ambiguously expressed, to supply what is wanting by their own decisions.

That we may be enabled to form a just opinion on this subject, I shall, in considering it,

1st. Examine the nature and extent of the judicial powers—and

2d. Enquire, whether the courts who are to exercise them, are so constituted as to afford reasonable ground of confidence, that they will exercise them for the general good.

With a regard to the nature and extent of the judicial powers, I have to regret my want of capacity to give that full and minute explanation of them that the subject merits. To be able to do this, a man should be possessed of a degree of law knowledge far beyond what I pretend to. A number of hard words and technical phrases are used in this part of the system, about the meaning of which gentlemen learned in the law differ.

Its advocates know how to avail themselves of these phrases. In a number of instances, where objections are made to the powers given to the judicial, they give such an explanation to the technical terms as to avoid them.

Though I am not competent to give a perfect explanation of the powers granted to this department of the government, I shall yet attempt to trace some of the leading features of it, from which I presume it will appear, that they will operate to a total subversion of the state judiciaries, if not, to the legislative authority of the states.

In article 3d, sect. 2d, it is said, "The judicial power shall extend to all cases in law and equity arising under this constitution, the laws of the United States, and treaties made, or which shall be made, under their authority, &c."

The first article to which this power extends, is, all cases in law and equity arising under this constitution.

What latitude of construction this clause should receive, it is not easy to say. At first view, one would suppose, that it meant no more than this, that the courts under the general government should exercise, not only the powers of courts of law, but also that of courts of equity, in the manner in which those powers are usually exercised in the different states. But this cannot be the meaning, because the next clause authorises the courts to take cognizance of all cases in law and equity arising under the laws of the United States; this last article, I conceive, conveys as much power to the general judicial as any of the state courts possess.

The cases arising under the constitution must be different from those arising under the laws, or else the two clauses mean exactly the same thing.

The cases arising under the constitution must include such, as bring into question its meaning, and will require an explanation of the nature and extent of the powers of the different departments under it.

This article, therefore, vests the judicial with a power to resolve all questions that may arise on any case on the construction of the constitution, either in law or in equity.

1st. They are authorised to determine all questions that may arise upon the meaning of the constitution in law. This article vests the courts with authority to give the constitution a legal construction, or to explain it according to the rules laid down for construing a law.—These rules give a certain degree of latitude of explanation. According to this mode of construction, the courts are to give such meaning to the constitution as comports best with the common, and generally received acceptation of the words in which it is expressed, regarding their ordinary and popular use, rather than their grammatical propriety. Where words are dubious, they will be explained by the contex. The end of the clause will be attended to, and the words will be understood, as having a view to it; and the words will not be so understood as to bear no meaning or a very absurd one.

2d. The judicial are not only to decide questions arising upon the meaning of the constitution in law, but also in equity.

By this they are empowered, to explain the constitution according to the reasoning spirit of it, without being confined to the words or letter.

"From this method of interpreting laws (says Blackstone) by the reason of them, arises what we call equity"; which is thus defined by Grotius, "the correction of that, wherein the law, by reason of its universality, is deficient; for since in laws all cases cannot be foreseen, or expressed, it is necessary, that when the decrees of the law cannot be applied to particular cases, there should some where be a power vested of [defining] those circumstances, which had they been foreseen the legislator would have expressed; and these are the cases, which according to Grotius, lex non exacte definit, sed arbitrio boni viri permittet."

The same learned author observes, "That equity, thus depending essentially upon each individual case, there can be no established rules and fixed principles of equity laid down, without destroying its very essence, and reducing it to a positive law."

From these remarks, the authority and business of the courts of law, under this clause, may be understood.

They will give the sense of every article of the constitution, that may from time to time come before them. And in their decisions they will not confine themselves to any fixed or established rules, but will determine, according to what appears to them, the reason and spirit of the constitution. The opinions of the supreme court, whatever they may be, will have the force of law; because there is no power provided in the constitution, that can correct their errors, or controul their adjudications. From this court there is no appeal. And I conceive the legislature themselves, cannot set aside a judgment of this court, because they are authorised by the constitution to decide in the last resort. The legislature must be controuled by the constitution, and not the constitution by them. They have therefore no more right to set aside any judgment pronounced upon the construction of the constitution, than they have to take from the president, the chief command of the army and navy, and commit it to some other person. The reason is plain; the judicial and executive derive their authority from the same source, that the legislature do theirs; and therefore in all cases, where the constitution does not make the one responsible to, or controulable by the other, they are altogether independent of each other.

The judicial power will operate to effect, in the most certain, but yet silent and imperceptible manner, what is evidently the tendency of the constitution:—I mean, an entire subversion of the legislative, executive and judicial powers of the individual states. Every adjudication of the supreme court, on any question that may arise upon the nature and extent of the general government, will affect the limits of the state jurisdiction. In proportion as the former enlarge the exercise of their powers, will that of the latter be restricted.

That the judicial power of the United States, will lean strongly in favour of the general government, and will give such an explanation to the constitution, as will favour an extension of its jurisdiction, is very evident from a variety of considerations.

1st. The constitution itself strongly countenances such a mode of construction. Most of the articles in this system, which convey powers of any considerable importance, are conceived in general and indefinite terms, which are either equivocal, ambiguous, or which require long definitions to unfold the extent of their meaning. The two most important powers committed to any government, those of raising money, and of raising and keeping up troops, have already been considered, and shewn to be [unlimitted] by any thing but the discretion of the legislature. The clause which vests the power to pass all laws which are proper and necessary, to carry the powers given into execution, it has been shewn, leaves the legislature at liberty, to do every thing, which in their judgment is best. It is said, I know, that this clause confers no power on the legislature, which they would not have had without it—though I believe this is not the fact, yet, admitting it to be, it implies that the constitution is not to receive an explanation strictly, according to its letter; but more power is implied than is expressed. And this clause, if it is to be considered, as explanatory of the extent of the powers given, rather than giving a new power, is to be understood as declaring, that in construing any of the articles conveying power, the spirit, intent and design of the clause, should be attended to, as well as the words in their common acceptation.

This constitution gives sufficient colour for adopting an equitable construction, if we consider the great end and design it professedly has in view—these appears from its preamble to be, "to form a more perfect union, establish justice, insure domestic tranquillity, provide for the common defence, promote the general welfare, and secure the blessings of liberty to ourselves and posterity." The design of this system is here expressed, and it is proper to give such a meaning to the various parts, as will best promote the accomplishment of the end; this idea suggests itself naturally upon reading the preamble, and will countenance the court in giving the several articles such a sense, as will the most effectually promote the ends the constitution had in view—how this manner of explaining the constitution will operate in practice, shall be the subject of future enquiry.

2d. Not only will the constitution justify the courts in inclining to this mode of explaining it, but they will be interested in using this latitude of interpretation. Every body of men invested with office are tenacious of power; they feel interested, and hence it has become a kind of maxim, to hand down their offices, with all its rights and privileges, unimpared to their successors; the same principle will influence them to extend their power, and increase their rights; this of itself will operate strongly upon the courts to give such a meaning to the constitution in all cases where it can possibly be done, as will enlarge the sphere of their own authority. Every extension of the power of the general legislature, as well as of the judicial powers, will increase the powers of the courts; and the dignity and importance of the judges, will be in proportion to the extent and magnitude of the powers they exercise. I add, it is highly probable the emolument of the judges will be increased, with the increase of the business they will have to transact and its importance. From these considerations the judges will be interested to extend the powers of the courts, and to construe the constitution as much as possible, in such a way as to favour it; and that they will do it, appears probable.

3d. Because they will have precedent to plead, to justify them in it. It is well known, that the courts in England, have by their own authority, extended their jurisdiction far beyond the limits set them in their original institution, and by the laws of the land.

The court of exchequer is a remarkable instance of this. It was originally intended principally to recover the king's debts, and to order the revenues of the crown. It had a common law jurisdiction, which was established merely for the benefit of the king's accomptants. We learn from Blackstone, that the proceedings in this court are grounded on a writ called quo minus, in which the plaintiff suggests, that he is the king's farmer or debtor, and that the defendant hath done him the damage complained of, by which he is less able to pay the king. These suits, by the statute of Rutland, are expressly directed to be confined to such matters as specially concern the king, or his ministers in the exchequer. And by the articuli super cartas, it is enacted, that no common pleas be thenceforth held in the exchequer contrary to the form of the great charter: but now any person may sue in the exchequer. The surmise of being debtor to the king being matter of form, and mere words of course; and the court is open to all the nation.

When the courts will have a president before them of a court which extended its jurisdiction in opposition to an act of the legislature, is it not to be expected that they will extend theirs, especially when there is nothing in the constitution expressly against it? and they are authorised to construe its meaning, and are not under any controul?

This power in the judicial, will enable them to mould the government, into almost any shape they please.—The manner in which this may be effected we will hereafter examine.

BRUTUS.

New-York Journal

7 FEBRUARY 1788

ESSAY XII

Brutus argues that the Supreme Court will use the Constitution's preamble and necessary and proper clause to expand Congress's powers. In addition, the Court will extend its own jurisdiction, taking for itself the power to rule on the validity of state laws. Essays in The Federalist *of particular relevance: 44, 82, 84.*

IN my last, I shewed, that the judicial power of the United States under the first clause of the second section of article eight, would be authorized to explain the constitution, not only according to its letter, but according to its spirit and intention; and having this power, they would strongly incline to give it such a construction as to extend the powers of the general government, as much as possible, to the diminution, and finally to the destruction, of that of the respective states.

I shall now proceed to shew how this power will operate in its exercise to effect these purposes. In order to perceive the extent of its influence, I shall consider,

First. How it will tend to extend the legislative authority.

Second. In what manner it will increase the jurisdiction of the courts, and

Third. The way in which it will diminish, and destroy, both the legislative and judicial authority of the United States.

First. Let us enquire how the judicial power will effect an extension of the legislative authority.

Perhaps the judicial power will not be able, by direct and positive decrees, ever to direct the legislature, because it is not easy to conceive how a question can be brought before them in a course of legal discussion, in which they can give a decision, declaring, that the legislature have certain powers which they have not exercised, and which, in consequence of the determination of the judges, they will be bound to exercise. But it is easy to see, that in their adjudications they may establish certain principles, which being received by the legislature, will enlarge the sphere of their power beyond all bounds.

It is to be observed, that the supreme court has the power, in the last resort, to determine all questions that may arise in the course of legal discussion, on the meaning and construction of the constitution. This power they will hold under the constitution, and independent of legislature. The latter can no more deprive the former of this right, than either of them, or both of them together, can take from the president, with the advice of the senate, the power of making treaties, or appointing ambassadors.

In determining these questions, the court must and will assume certain principles, from which they will reason, in forming their decisions. These principles, whatever they may be, when they become fixed, by a course of decisions, will be adopted by the legislature, and will be the rule by which they will explain their own powers. This appears evident from this consideration, that if the legislature pass laws, which, in the judgment of the court, they are not authorised to do by the constitution, the court will not take notice of them; for it will not be denied, that the constitution is the highest or supreme law. And the courts are vested with the supreme and uncontroulable power, to determine, in all cases that come before them, what the constitution means; they cannot, therefore, execute a law, which, in their judgment, opposes the constitution, unless we can suppose they can make a superior law give way to an inferior. The legislature, therefore, will not go over the limits by which the courts may adjudge they are confined. And there is little room to doubt but that they will come up to those bounds, as often as occasion and opportunity may offer, and they may judge it proper to do it. For as on the one hand, they will not readily pass laws which they know the courts will not execute, so on the other, we may be sure they will not scruple to pass such as they know they will give effect, as often as they may judge it proper.

From these observations it appears, that the judgment of the judicial, on the constitution, will become the rule to guide the legislature in their construction of their powers.

What the principles are, which the courts will adopt, it is impossible for us to say; but taking up the powers as I have explained them in my last number, which they will possess under this clause, it is not difficult to see, that they may, and probably will, be very liberal ones.

We have seen, that they will be authorized to give the constitution a construction according to its spirit and reason, and not to confine themselves to its letter.

To discover the spirit of the constitution, it is of the first importance to attend to the principal ends and designs it has in view. These are expressed in the preamble, in the following words, viz. "We, the people of the United States, in order to form a more perfect union, establish justice, insure domestic tranquility, provide for the common defence, promote the general welfare, and secure the blessings of liberty to ourselves and our posterity, do ordain and establish this constitution," &c. If the end of the government is to be learned from these words, which are clearly designed to declare it, it is obvious it has in view every object which is embraced by any government. The preservation of internal peace—the due administration of justice—and to provide for the defence of the community, seems to include all the objects of government; but if they do not, they are certainly comprehended in the words, "to provide for the general welfare." If it be further considered, that this constitution, if it is ratified, will not be a compact entered into by states, in their corporate capacities, but an agreement of the people of the United States, as one great body politic, no doubt can remain, but that the great end of the constitution, if it is to be collected from the preamble, in which its end is declared, is to constitute a government which is to extend to every case for which any government is instituted, whether external or internal. The courts, therefore, will establish this as a principle in expounding the constitution, and will give every part of it such an explanation, as will give latitude to every department under it, to take cognizance of every matter, not only that affects the general and national concerns of the union, but also of such as relate to the administration of private justice, and to regulating the internal and local affairs of the different parts.

Such a rule of exposition is not only consistent with the general spirit of the preamble, but it will stand confirmed by considering more minutely the different clauses of it.

The first object declared to be in view is, "To form a perfect union." It is to be observed, it is not an union of states or bodies corporate; had this been the case the existence of the state governments, might have been secured. But it is a union of the people of the United States considered as one body, who are to ratify this constitution, if it is adopted. Now to make a union of this kind perfect, it is necessary to abolish all inferior governments, and to give the general one compleat legislative, executive and judicial powers to every purpose. The courts therefore will establish it as a rule in explaining the constitution. To give it such a construction as will best tend to perfect the union or take from the state government every power of either making or executing laws. The second object is "to establish justice." This must include not only the idea of instituting the rule of justice, or of making laws which shall be the measure or rule of right, but also of providing for the application of this rule or of administering justice under it. And under this the courts will in their decisions extend the power of the government to all cases they possibly can, or otherwise they will be restricted in doing what appears to be the intent of the constitution they should do, to wit, pass laws and provide for the execution of them, for the general distribution of justice between man and man. Another end declared is "to insure domestic tranquility." This comprehends a provision against all private breaches of the peace, as well as against all public commotions or general insurrections; and to attain the object of this clause fully, the government must exercise the power of passing laws on these subjects, as well as of appointing magistrates with authority to execute them. And the courts will adopt these ideas in their expositions. I might proceed to the other clause, in the preamble, and it would appear by a consideration of all of them separately, as it does by taking them together, that if the spirit of this system is to be known from its declared end and design in the preamble, its spirit is to subvert and abolish all the powers of the state government, and to embrace every object to which any government extends.

As it sets out in the preamble with this declared intention, so it proceeds in the different parts with the same idea. Any person, who will peruse the 8th section with attention, in which most of the powers are enumerated, will perceive that they either expressly or by implication extend to almost every thing about which any legislative power can be employed. But if this equitable mode of construction is applied to this part of the constitution; nothing can stand before it.

This will certainly give the first clause in that article a construction which I confess I think the most natural and grammatical one, to authorise the Congress to do any thing which in their judgment will tend to provide for the general welfare, and this amounts to the same thing as general and unlimited powers of legislation in all cases.

(*To be continued.*)

New-York Journal

14 FEBRUARY 1788

ESSAY XII

(*Continued.*)

THIS same manner of explaining the constitution, will fix a meaning, and a very important one too, to the 12th clause of the same section, which authorises the Congress to make all laws which shall be proper and necessary for carrying into effect the foregoing powers, &c. A voluminous writer in favor of this system, has taken great pains to convince the public, that this clause means nothing: for that the same powers expressed in this, are implied in other parts of the constitution. Perhaps it is so, but still this will undoubtedly be an excellent auxilliary to assist the courts to discover the spirit and reason of the constitution, and when applied to any and every of the other clauses granting power, will operate powerfully in extracting the spirit from them.

I might instance a number of clauses in the constitution, which, if explained in an *equitable* manner, would extend the powers of the government to every case, and reduce the state legislatures to nothing; but, I should draw out my remarks to an undue length, and I presume enough has been said to shew, that the courts have sufficient ground in the exercise of this power, to determine, that the legislature have no bounds set to them by this constitution, by any supposed right the legislatures of the respective states may have, to regulate any of their local concerns.

I proceed, 2d, To inquire, in what manner this power will increase the jurisdiction of the courts.

I would here observe, that the judicial power extends, expressly, to all civil cases that may arise save such as arise between citizens of the same state, with this exception to those of that description, that the judicial of the United States have cognizance of cases between citizens of the same state, claiming lands under grants of different states. Nothing more, therefore, is necessary to give the courts of law, under this constitution, complete jurisdiction of all civil causes, but to comprehend cases between citizens of the same state not included in the foregoing exception.

I presume there will be no difficulty in accomplishing this. Nothing more is necessary than to set forth, in the process, that the party who brings the suit is a citizen of a different state from the one against whom the suit is brought, & there can be little doubt but that the court will take cognizance of the matter, & if they do, who is to restrain them? Indeed, I will freely confess, that it is my decided opinion, that the courts ought to take cognizance of such causes, under the powers of the constitution. For one of the great ends of the constitution is, "to establish justice." This supposes that this cannot be done under the existing governments of the states; and there is certainly as good reason why individuals, living in the same state, should have justice, as those who live in different states. Moreover, the constitution expressly declares, that "the citizens of each state shall be entitled to all the privileges and immunities of citizens in the several states." It will therefore be no fiction, for a citizen of one state to set forth, in a suit, that he is a citizen of another; for he that is entitled to all the privileges and immunities of a country, is a citizen of that country. And in truth, the citizen of one state will, under this constitution, be a citizen of every state.

But supposing that the party, who alledges that he is a citizen of another state: has recourse to fiction in bringing in his suit, it is well known; that the courts have high authority to plead, to justify them in suffering actions to be brought before them by such fictions. In my last number I stated, that the court of exchequer tried all causes in virtue of such a fiction. The court of king's bench, in England, extended their jurisdiction in the same way. Originally, this court held pleas, in civil cases, only of trespasses and other injuries alledged to be committed *vi et armis*. They might likewise, says Blackstone, upon the division of the *aula regia*, have originally held pleas of any other civil action whatsoever (except in real actions which are now very seldom in use) provided the defendant was an officer of the court, or in the custody of the marshall or prison-keeper of this court, for breach of the peace, &c. In process of time, by a fiction, this court began to hold pleas of any personal action whatsoever; it being surmised, that the defendant has been arrested for a supposed trespass that "he has never committed, and being thus in the custody of the marshall of the court, the plaintiff is at liberty to proceed against him, for any other personal injury: which surmise of being in the marshall's custody, the defendant is not at liberty to dispute." By a much less fiction, may the pleas of the courts of the United States extend to cases between citizens of the same state. I shall add no more on this head, but proceed briefly to remark, in what way this power will diminish, and destroy both the legislative and judicial authority of the states.

It is obvious that these courts will have authority to decide upon the validity of the laws of any of the states, in all cases where they come in question before them. Where the constitution gives the general government exclusive jurisdiction, they will adjudge all laws made by the state, in such cases, *void ab [initio]*. Where the constitution gives them concurrent jurisdiction, the laws of the United States must prevail, because they are the supreme law. In such cases, therefore, the laws of the state legislatures must be repealed, restricted, or so construed, as to give full effect to the laws of the union on the same subject. From these remarks it is easy to see, that in proportion as the general government acquires power and jurisdiction, by the liberal construction which the judges may give the constitution, will those of the states lose its rights, until they become so trifling and unimportant, as not to be worth having. I am much mistaken, if this system will not operate to effect this with as much celerity, as those who have the administration of it will think prudent to suffer it. The remaining objections to the judicial power shall be considered in a future paper.

BRUTUS.

New-York Journal

21 FEBRUARY 1788

ESSAY XIII

Brutus sets forth the argument that will lead to the Eleventh Amendment, which forbids federal court jurisdiction over suits between one state and a citizen of another state. Federal jurisdiction in such matters, according to Brutus, would destroy state sovereignty. Essays in The Federalist *of particular relevance: 82.*

HAVING in the two preceding numbers, examined the nature and tendency of the judicial power, as it respects the explanation of the constitution, I now proceed to the consideration of the other matters, of which it has cognizance.—The next paragraph extends its authority, to all cases, in law and equity, arising under the laws of the United States. This power, as I understand it, is a proper one.

The proper province of the judicial power, in any government, is, as I conceive, to declare what is the law of the land. To explain and enforce those laws, which the supreme power or legislature may pass; but not to declare what the powers of the legislature are. I suppose the cases in equity, under the laws, must be so construed, as to give the supreme court not only a legal, but equitable jurisdiction of cases which may be brought before them, or in other words, so, as to give them, not only the powers which are now exercised by our courts of law, but those also, which are now exercised by our court of chancery. If this be the meaning, I have no other objection to the power, than what arises from the undue extension of the legislative power. For, I conceive that the judicial power should be commensurate with the legislative. Or, in other words, the supreme court should have authority to determine questions arising under the laws of the union.

The next paragraph which gives a power to decide in law and equity, on all cases arising under treaties, is unintelligible to me. I can readily comprehend what [is meant] by deciding a case under a treaty. For as treaties will be the law of the land, every person who have rights or privileges secured by treaty, will have aid of the courts of law, in recovering them. But I do not understand, what is meant by equity arising under a treaty. I presume every right which can be claimed under a treaty, must be claimed by virtue of some article or clause contained in it, which gives the right in plain and obvious words; on at least, I conceive, that the rules for explaining treaties, are so well ascertained, that there is no need of having recourse to an equitable construction. If under this power, the courts are to explain treaties, according to what they conceive are their spirit, which is nothing less than a power to give them whatever extension they may judge proper, it is a dangerous and improper power. The cases affecting ambassadors, public ministers, and consuls—of admiralty and maritime jurisdiction; controversies to which the United States are a party, and controversies between states, it is proper should be under the cognizance of the courts of the union, because none but the general government, can, or ought to pass laws on their subjects. But, I conceive the clause which extends the power of the judicial to controversies arising between a state and citizens of another state, improper in itself, and will, in its exercise, prove most pernicious and destructive.

It is improper, because it subjects a state to answer in a court of law, to the suit of an individual. This is humiliating and degrading to a government, and, what I believe, the supreme authority of no state ever submitted to.

The states are now subject to no such actions. All contracts entered into by individuals with states, were made upon the faith and credit of the states; and the individuals never had in contemplation any compulsory mode of obliging the government to fulfill its engagements.

The evil consequences that will flow from the exercise of this power, will best appear by tracing it in its operation. The constitution does not direct the mode in which an individual shall commence a suit against a state or the manner in which the judgement of the court shall be carried into execution, but it gives the legislature full power to pass all laws which shall be proper and necessary for the purpose. And they certainly must make provision for these purposes, or otherwise the power of the judicial will be nugatory. For, to what purpose will the power of a judicial be, if they have no mode, in which they can call the parties before them? Or of what use will it be, to call the parties to answer, if after they have given judgment, there is no authority to execute the judgment? We must, therefore, conclude, that the legislature will pass laws which will be effectual in this head. An individual of one state will then have a legal remedy against a state for any demand he may have against a state to which he does not belong. Every state in the union is largely indebted to individuals. For the payment of these debts they have given notes payable to the bearer. At least this is the case in this state. Whenever a citizen of another state becomes possessed of one of these notes, he may commence an action in the supreme court of the general government; and I cannot see any way in which he can be prevented from recovering. It is easy to see, that when this once happens, the notes of the state will pass rapidly from the hands of citizens of the state to those of other states.

And when the citizens of other states possess them, they may bring suits against the state for them, and by this means, judgments and executions may be obtained against the state for the whole amount of the state debt. It is certain the state, with the utmost exertions it can make, will not be able to discharge the debt she owes, under a considerable number of years, perhaps with the best management, it will require twenty or thirty years to discharge it. This new system will protract the time in which the ability of the state will enable them to pay off their debt, because all the funds of the state will be transferred to the general government, except those which arise from internal taxes.

The situation of the states will be deplorable. By this system, they will surrender to the general government, all the means of raising money, and at the same time, will subject themselves to suits at law, for the recovery of the debts they have contracted in effecting the revolution.

The debts of the individual states will amount to a sum, exceeding the domestic debt of the United States; these will be left upon them, with power in the judicial of the general government, to enforce their payment, while the general government will possess an exclusive command of the most productive funds, from which the states can derive money, and a command of every other source of revenue paramount to the authority of any state.

It may be said that the apprehension that the judicial power will operate in this manner is merely visionary, for that the legislature will never pass laws that will work these effects. Or if they were disposed to do it, they cannot provide for levying an execution on a state, for where will the officer find property whereon to levy?

To this I would reply, if this is a power which will not or cannot be executed, it was useless and unwise to grant it to the judicial. For what purpose is a power given which it is imprudent or impossible to exercise? If it be improper for a government to exercise a power, it is improper they should be vested with it. And it is unwise to authorise a government to do what they cannot effect.

As to the idea that the legislature cannot provide for levying an execution on a state, I believe it is not well founded. I presume the last paragraph of the 8th section of article 1, gives the Congress express power to pass any laws they may judge proper and necessary for carrying into execution the power vested in the judicial department. And they must exercise this power, or otherwise the courts of justice will not be able to carry into effect the authorities with which they are invested. For the constitution does not direct the mode in which the courts are to proceed, to bring parties before them, to try causes, or to carry the judgment of the courts into execution. Unless they are pointed out by law, how are they to proceed, in any of the cases of which they have cognizance? They have the same authority to establish regulations in respect to these matters, where a state is a party, as where an individual is a party. The only difficulty is, on whom shall process be served, when a state is a party, and how shall execution be levied. With regard to the first, the way is easy, either the executive or legislative of the state may be notified, and upon proof being made of the service of the notice, the court may proceed to a hearing of the cause. Execution may be levied on any property of the state, either real or personal. The treasury may be seized by the officers of the general government, or any lands the property of the state, may be made subject to seizure and sale to satisfy my judgment against it. Whether the estate of any individual citizen may not be made answerable for the discharge of judgments against the state, may be worth consideration. In some corporations this is the case.

If the power of the judicial under this clause will extend to the cases above stated, it will, if executed, produce the utmost confusion, and in its progress, will crush the states beneath its weight. And if it does not extend to these cases, I confess myself utterly at a loss to give it any meaning. For if the citizen of one state, possessed of a written obligation, given in pursuance of a solemn act of the legislature, acknowledging a debt due to the bearer, and promising to pay it, cannot recover in the supreme court, I can conceive of no case in which they can recover. And it appears to me ridiculous to provide for obtaining judgment against a state, without giving the means of levying execution.

BRUTUS.

New-York Journal

28 FEBRUARY 1788

ESSAY XIV

Brutus expresses grave fear that the Supreme Court's power to hear appeals of civil and criminal cases will damage liberty. Double jeopardy may ensue for criminal defendants.[1] And the federal courts' ability to overturn civil decisions will destroy state courts, making justice expensive and inconvenient.[2] Essays in The Federalist *of particular relevance: 79-83.*

THE second paragraph of sect. 2d. art. 3, is in these words: "In all cases affecting ambassadors, other public ministers and consuls, and those in which a state shall be a party, the supreme court shall have original jurisdiction. In all the other cases before mentioned, the supreme court shall have appellate jurisdiction, both as to law and fact, with such exceptions, and under such regulations as the Congress shall make."

Although it is proper that the courts of the general government should have cognizance of all matters affecting ambassadors, foreign ministers, and consuls; yet I question much the propriety of giving the supreme court original jurisdiction in all cases of this kind.

Ambassadors, and other public ministers, claim, and are entitled by the law of nations, to certain privileges, and exemptions, both for their persons and their servants.

---

[1] The Supreme Court subsequently ruled double jeopardy unconstitutional in most cases. But the federal government retains the ability to prosecute individuals under federal law even when they have been tried for the same acts under state law.

[2] This danger was addressed to some extent by subsequent statutes somewhat limiting federal appellate jurisdiction.

The meanest servant of an ambassador is exempted by the law of nations from being sued for debt. Should a suit be brought against such an one by a citizen, through inadvertency or want of information, he will be subject to an action in the supreme court. All the officers concerned in issuing or executing the process will be liable to like actions. Thus may a citizen of a state be compelled, at great expence and inconveniency, to defend himself against a suit, brought against him in the supreme court, for inadvertently commencing an action against the most menial servant of an ambassador for a just debt.

The appellate jurisdiction granted to the supreme court, in this paragraph, has justly been considered as one of the most objectionable parts of the constitution: under this power, appeals may be had from the inferior courts to the supreme, in every case to which the judicial power extends, except in the few instances in which the supreme court will have original jurisdiction.

By this article, appeals will lie to the supreme court, in all criminal as well as civil causes. This I know, has been disputed by some; but I presume the point will appear clear to any one, who will attend to the connection of this paragraph with the one that precedes it. In the former, all the cases, to which the power of the judicial shall extend, whether civil or criminal, are enumerated. There is no criminal matter, to which the judicial power of the United States will extend; but such as are included under some one of the cases specified in this section. For this section is intended to define all the cases, of every description, to which the power of the judicial shall reach. But in all these cases it is declared, the supreme court shall have appellate jurisdiction, except in those which affect ambassadors, other public ministers and consuls, and those in which a state shall be a party. If then this section extends the power of the judicial, to criminal cases, it allows appeals in such cases. If the power of the judicial is not extended to criminal matters by this section, I ask, by what part of this system does it appear, that they have any cognizance of them?

I believe it is a new and unusual thing to allow appeals in criminal matters. It is contrary to the sense of our laws, and dangerous to the lives and liberties of the citizen. As our law now stands, a person charged with a crime has a right to a fair and impartial trial by a jury of his country, and their verdict is final. If he is acquitted no other court can call upon him to answer for the same crime. But by this system, man may have had ever so fair a trial, have been acquitted by ever so respectable a jury of his country; and still the officer of the government who prosecutes, may appeal to the supreme court. The whole matter may have a second hearing. By this means, persons who may have disobliged those who execute the general government, may be subjected to intolerable oppression. They may be kept in long and ruinous confinement, and exposed to heavy and insupportable charges, to procure the attendence of witnesses, and provide the means of their defence, at a great distance from their places of residence.

I can scarcely believe there can be a considerate citizen of the United States, that will approve of this appellate jurisdiction, as extending to criminal cases, if they will give themselves time for reflection.

Whether the appellate jurisdiction as it respects civil matters, will not prove injurious to the rights of the citizens, and destructive of those privileges which have ever been held sacred by Americans, and whether it will not render the administration of justice intolerably burthensome, intricate, and dilatory, will best appear, when we have considered the nature and operation of this power.

It has been the fate of this clause, as it has of most of those, against which unanswerable objections have been offered, to be explained different ways, by the advocates and opponents to the constitution. I confess I do not know what the advocates of the system, would make it mean, for I have not been fortunate enough to see in any publication this clause taken up and considered. It is certain however, they do not admit the explanation which those who oppose the constitution give it, or otherwise they would not so frequently charge them with want of candor, for alledging that it takes away the trial by jury, appeals from an inferior to a superior court, as practised in the civil law courts, are well understood. In these courts, the judges determine both on the law and the fact; and appeals are allowed from the inferior to the superior courts, on the whole merits: the superior tribunal will re-examine all the facts as well as the law, and frequently new facts will be introduced, so as many times to render the cause in the court of appeals very different from what it was in the court below.

If the appellate jurisdiction of the supreme court, be understood in the above sense, the term is perfectly intelligible. The meaning then is, that in all the civil causes enumerated, the supreme court shall have authority to re-examine the whole merits of the case, both with respect to the facts and the law which may arise under it, without the intervention of a jury; that this is the sense of this part of the system appears to me clear, from the express words of it, "in all the other cases before mentioned, the supreme court shall have appellate jurisdiction, both as to law and fact, &c." Who are the supreme court? Does it not consist of the judges? and they are to have the same jurisdiction of the fact as they are to have of the law. They will therefore have the same authority to determine the fact as they will have to determine the law, and no room is left for a jury on appeals to the supreme court.

If we understand the appellate jurisdiction in any other way, we shall be left utterly at a loss to give it a meaning; the common law is a stranger to any such jurisdiction: no appeals can lie from any of our common law courts, upon the merits of the case; the only way in which they can go up from an inferior to a superior tribunal is by habeas corpus before a hearing, or by certiorari, or writ of error, after they are determined in the subordinate courts; but in no case, when they are carried up, are the facts re-examined, but they are always taken as established in the inferior court.

(*To be continued.*)

New-York Journal

6 MARCH 1788

ESSAY XIV

(*Continued.*)

It may still be insisted that this clause does not take away the trial by jury on appeals, but that this may be provided for by the legislature, under that paragraph which authorises them to form regulations and restrictions for the court in the exercise of this power.

The natural meaning of this paragraph seems to be no more than this, that Congress may declare, that certain cases shall not be subject to the appellate jurisdiction, and they may point out the mode in which the court shall proceed in bringing up the causes before them, the manner of their taking evidence to establish the facts, and the method of the courts proceeding. But I presume they cannot take from the court the right of deciding on the fact, any more than they can deprive them of the right of determining on the law, when a cause is once before them; for they have the same jurisdiction as to fact, as they have as to the law. But supposing the Congress may under this clause establish the trial by jury on appeals. It does not seem to me that it will render this article much less exceptionable. An appeal from one court and jury to another court and jury, is a thing altogether unknown in the laws of our state, and in most of the states in the union. A practice of this kind prevails in the eastern states; actions are there commenced in the inferior courts, and an appeal lies from them on the whole merits to the superior courts: the consequence is well known, very few actions are determined in the lower courts; it is rare that a case of any importance is not carried by appeal to the supreme court, and the jurisdiction of the inferior courts is merely nominal; this has proved so burthensome to the people in Massachusetts, that it was one of the principal causes which excited the insurrection in that state, in the year past; very few sensible and moderate men in that state but what will admit, that the inferior courts are almost entirely useless, and answer very little purpose, save only to accumulate costs against the poor debtors who are already unable to pay their just debts.

But the operation of the appellate power in the supreme judicial of the United States, would work infinitely more mischief than any such power can do in a single state.

The trouble and expence to the parties would be endless and intolerable. No man can say where the supreme court are to hold their sessions, the presumption is, however, that it must be at the seat of the general government: in this case parties must travel many hundred miles, with their witnesses and lawyers, to prosecute or defend a suit; no man of midling fortune, can sustain the expence of such a law suit, and therefore the poorer and midling class of citizens will be under the necessity of submitting to the demands of the rich and the lordly, in cases that will come under the cognizance of this court. If it be said, that to prevent this oppression, the supreme court will set in different parts of the union, it may be replied, that this would only make the oppression somewhat more tolerable, but by no means so much as to give a chance of justice to the poor and midling class. It is utterly impossible that the supreme court can move into so many different parts of the Union, as to make it convenient or even tolerable to attend before them with witnesses to try causes from every part of the United States, if to avoid the expence and inconvenience of calling witnesses from a great distance, to give evidence before the supreme court, the expedient of taking the deposition of witnesses in writing should be adopted, it would not help the matter. It is of great importance in the distribution of justice that witnesses should be examined face to face, that the parties should have the fairest opportunity of cross examining them in order to bring out the whole truth; there is something in the manner in which a witness delivers his testimony which cannot be committed to paper, and which yet very frequently gives a complexion to his evidence, very different from what it would bear if committed to writing, besides the expence of taking written testimony would be enormous; those who are acquainted with the costs that arise in the courts, where all the evidence is taken in writing, well know that they exceed beyond all comparison those of the common law courts, where witnesses are examined viva voce.

The costs accruing in courts generally advance with the grade of the court; thus the charges attending a suit in our common please, is much less than those in the supreme court, and these are much lower than those in the court of chancery; indeed the costs in the last mentioned court, are in many cases so exorbitant and the proceedings so dilatory that the suitor had almost as well give up his demand as to prosecute his suit. We have just reason to suppose, that the costs in the supreme general court will exceed either of our courts; the officers of the general court will be more dignified than those of the states, the lawyers of the most ability will practice in them, and the trouble and expence of attending them will be greater. From all these considerations, it appears, that the expence attending suits in the supreme court will be so great, as to put it out of the power of the poor and midling class of citizens to contest a suit in it.

From these remarks it appears, that the administration of justice under the powers of the judicial will be dilatory; that it will be attended with such an heavy expence as to amount to little short of a denial of justice to the poor and midling class of people who in every government stand most in need of the protection of the law; and that the trial by jury, which has so justly been the boast of our fore fathers as well as ourselves is taken away under them.

These extraordinary powers in this court are the more objectionable, because there does not appear the least necessity for them, in order to secure a due and impartial distribution of justice.

The want of ability or integrity, or a disposition to render justice to every suitor, has not been objected against the courts of the respective states: so far as I have been informed, the courts of justice in all the states, have ever been found ready, to administer justice with promptitude and impartiality according to the laws of the land; It is true in some of the states, paper money has been made, and the debtor authorised to discharge his debts with it, at a depreciated value, in others, tender laws have been passed, obliging the creditor to receive on execution other property than money in discharge of his demand, and in several of the stated laws have been made unfavorable to the creditor and tending to render property insecure.

But these evils have not happened from any defect in the judicial departments of the states[;] the courts indeed are bound to take notice of these laws, and so will the courts of the general government be under obligation to observe the laws made by the general legislature; not repugnant to the constitution; but so far have the judicial been from giving undue latitude of construction to laws of this kind, that they have invariably strongly inclined to the other [side]. All the acts of our legislature, which have been charged with being of this complexion, have uniformly received the strictest construction by the judges, and have been extended to no cases but to such as came within the first letter of the law. In this way, have our courts, I will not say evaded the law, but so limited it in its operation as to work the least possible injustice: the same thing has taken place in Rhode-Island, which has justly rendered herself infamous, by her tenaciously adhering to her paper money system. The judges there gave a decision, in opposition to the words of the Statute, on this principle, that a construction according to the words of it, would contradict the fundamental maxims of their laws and constitution.

No pretext therefore, can be formed, from the conduct of the judicial courts which will justify giving such powers to the supreme general court for their decisions have been such as to give just ground of confidence in them, that they will firmly adhere to the principles of rectitude, and there is no necessity of lodging these powers in the courts in order to guard against the evils justly complained of, on the subject of security of property under this constitution. For it has provided, "that no state shall emit bills of credit, or make any thing but gold and silver coin a tender in payment of debts." It has also declared, that "no state shall pass any law impairing the obligation of contracts."—These prohibitions give the most perfect security against those attacks upon property which I am sorry to say some of the states have but too wantonly made, by passing laws sanctioning fraud in the debtor against his creditor.

For "this constitution will be the supreme law of the land and the judges in every state will be bound thereby; any thing in the constitution and laws of any state to the contrary notwithstanding."

The courts of the respective states might therefore have been securely trusted, with deciding all cases between man and man, whether citizens of the same state or of different states, or between foreigners and citizens, and indeed for ought I see every case that can arise under the constitution or laws of the United States, ought in the first instance to be tried in the court of the state, except those which might arise between states, such as respect ambassadors, or other public ministers, and perhaps such as call in question the claim of lands under grants from different states. The state courts would be under sufficient controul, if writs of error were allowed from the state courts to the supreme court of the union, according to the practice of the courts in England and of this state, on all cases in which the laws of the union are concerned, and perhaps to all cases in which a foreigner is a party.

This method would preserve the good old way of administering justice, would bring justice to every man's door, and preserve the inestimable right of trial by jury. It would be following, as near as our circumstances will admit, the practice of the courts in England, which is almost the only thing I would wish to copy in their government.

But as this system now stands, there is to be as many inferior courts as Congress may see fit to appoint, who are to be authorised to originate and in the first instance to try all the cases falling under the description of this article; there is no security that a trial by jury shall be had in these courts, but the trial here will soon become, as it is in Massachusetts' inferior courts, mere matter of form; for an appeal may be had to the supreme court on the whole merits. This court is to have power to determine in law and in equity, on the law and the fact, and this court is exalted above all other power in the government, subject to no controul, and so fixed as not to be removeable, but upon impeachment, which I shall hereafter shew, is much the same thing as not to be removeable at all.

To obviate the objections made to the judicial power it has been said, that the Congress, in forming the regulations and exceptions

which they are authorised to make respecting the appellate jurisdiction, will make provision against all the evils which are apprehended from this article. On this I would remark, that this way of
answering the objection made to the power, implies an admission
that the power is in itself improper without restraint, and if so, why
not restrict it in the first instance.

The just way of investigating any power given to a government,
is to examine its operation supposing it to be put in exercise. If
upon enquiry, it appears that the power, if exercised, would be prejudicial, it ought not to be given. For to answer objections made to
a power given to a government, by saying it will never be exercised, is really admitting that the power ought not to be exercised,
and therefore ought not to be granted.

BRUTUS.

New-York Journal

20 MARCH 1788

ESSAY XV

*Brutus argues that the Constitution lacks sufficient checks on fed-
eral judicial power. While English judges also held life tenure, their
decisions could be overturned by the House of Lords, and English
judges could not declare a law unconstitutional. In addition, federal judges would not be liable to impeachment for judicial error or
lack of capacity, leaving them too free of oversight from the people's
representatives. Essays in* The Federalist *of particular relevance:
79–82.*

I SAID in my last number, that the supreme court under this constitution would be exalted above all other power in the government, and subject to no controul. The business of this paper will be
to illustrate this, and to shew the danger that will result from it. I

question whether the world ever saw, in any period of it, a court of justice invested with such immense powers, and yet placed in a situation so little responsible. Certain it is, that in England, and in the several states, where we have been taught to believe, the courts of law are put upon the most prudent establishment, they are on a very different footing.

The judges in England, it is true, hold their offices during their good behaviour, but then their determinations are subject to correction by the house of lords; and their power is by no means so extensive as that of the proposed supreme court of the union.—I believe they in no instance assume the authority to set aside an act of parliament under the idea that it is inconsistent with their constitution. They consider themselves bound to decide according to the existing laws of the land, and never undertake to controul them by adjudging that they are inconsistent with the constitution—much less are they vested with the power of giv. an *equitable* construction to the constitution.

The judges in England are under the controul of the legislature, for they are bound to determine according to the laws passed by them. But the judges under this constitution will controul the legislature, for the supreme court are authorised in the last report, to determine what is the extent of the powers of the Congress; they are to give the constitution an explanation, and there is no power above them to sit aside their judgment. The framers of this constitution appear to have followed that of the British, in rendering the judges independent, by granting them their offices during good behaviour, without following the constitution of England, in instituting a tribunal in which their errors may be corrected; and without adverting to this, that the judicial under this system have a power which is above the legislative, and which indeed transcends any power before given to a judicial by any free government under heaven.

I do not object to the judges holding their commissions during good behaviour. I suppose it a proper provision provided they were made properly responsible. But I say, this system has followed the English government in this, while it has departed from almost every other principle of their jurisprudence, under the idea, of rendering the judges independent; which, in the British constitution, means no more than that they hold their places during good behaviour, and have fixed salaries, they have made the judges *independent*, in the fullest sense of the word. There is no power above them, to controul any of their decisions. There is no authority that can remove them, and they cannot be controuled by the laws of the legislature. In short, they are independent of the people, of the legislature, and of every power under heaven. Men placed in this situation will generally soon feel themselves independent of heaven itself. Before I proceed to illustrate the truth of these assertions, I beg liberty to make one remark—Though in my opinion the judges ought to hold their offices during good behaviour, yet I think it is clear, that the reasons in favour of this establishment of the judges in England, do by no means apply to this country.

The great reason assigned, why the judges in Britain ought to be commissioned during good behaviour, is this, that they may be placed in a situation, not to be influenced by the crown, to give such decisions, as would tend to increase its powers and prerogatives. While the judges held their places at the will and pleasure of the king, on whom they depended not only for their offices, but also for their salaries, they were subject to every undue influence. If the crown wished to carry a favorite point, to accomplish which the aid of the courts of law was necessary, the pleasure of the king would he signified to the judges. And it required the spirit of a martyr, for the judges to determine contrary to the king's will.—They were absolutely dependent upon him both for their offices and livings. The king, holding his office during life, and transmitting it to his posterity as an inheritance, has much stronger inducements to increase the prerogatives of his office than those who hold their offices for stated periods, or even for life. Hence the English nation gained a great point, in favour of liberty. When they obtained the appointment of the judges, during good behaviour, they got from the crown a concession, which deprived it of one of the most powerful engines with which it might enlarge the boundaries of the royal prerogative and encroach on the liberties of the people. But these reasons do not apply to this country, we have no hereditary monarch; those who appoint the judges do not hold their offices for life, nor do they descend to their children. The same arguments, therefore, which will conclude in favor of the tenor of the judge's offices for good behaviour, lose a considerable part of their weight when applied to the state and condition of America. But much less can it be shewn, that the nature of our government requires that the courts should be placed beyond all account more independent, so much so as to be above controul.

I have said that the judges under this system will be *independent* in the strict sense of the word: To prove this I will shew—That there is no power above them that can controul their decisions, or correct their errors. There is no authority that can remove them from office for any errors or want of capacity, or lower their salaries, and in many cases their power is superior to that of the legislature.

1st. There is no power above them that can correct their errors or controul their decisions—The adjudications of this court are final and irreversible, for there is no court above them to which appeals can lie, either in error or on the merits. In this respect it differs from the courts in England, for there the house of lords is the highest court, to whom appeals, in error, are carried from the highest of the courts of law.

2d. They cannot be removed from office or suffer a dimunition of their salaries, for any error in judgement or want of capacity.

It is expressly declared by the constitution,—"That they shall at stated times receive a compensation for their services which shall not be diminished during their continuance in office."

The only clause in the constitution which provides for the removal of the judges from offices, is that which declares, that "the president, vice-president, and all civil officers of the United States, shall be removed from office, on impeachment for, and conviction of treason, bribery, or other high crimes and misdemeanors." By this paragraph, civil officers, in which the judges are included, are removable only for crimes. Treason and bribery are named, and the rest are included under the general terms of high crimes and misdemeanors.—Errors in judgement, or want of capacity to discharge the duties of the office, can never be supposed to be included in these words, *high crimes and misdemeanors*. A man may mistake a case in giving judgment, or manifest that he is incompetent to the discharge of the duties of a judge, and yet give no evidence of corruption or want of [integrity]. To support the charge, it will be necessary to give in evidence some facts that will shew, that the judges commited the error from wicked and corrupt motives.

3d. The power of this court is in many cases superior to that of the legislature. I have shewed, in a former paper, that this court will be authorised to decide upon the meaning of the constitution, and that, not only according to the natural and ob. meaning of the words, but also according to the spirit and intention of it. In the exercise of this power they will not be subordinate to, but above the legislature. For all the departments of this government will receive their powers, so far as they are expressed in the constitution, from the people immediately, who are the source of power. The legislature can only exercise such powers as are given them by the constitution, they cannot assume any of the rights annexed to the judicial, for this plain reason, that the same authority which vested the legislature with their powers, vested the judicial with theirs— both are derived from the same source, both therefore are equally valid, and the judicial hold their powers independently of the legislature, as the legislature do of the judicial.—The supreme court then have a right, independent of the legislature, to give a construction to the constitution and every part of it, and there is no power provided in this system to correct their construction or do it away. If, therefore, the legislature pass any laws, inconsistent with the sense the judges put upon the constitution, they will declare it void; and therefore in this respect their power is superior to that of the legislature. In England the judges are not only subject to have their decisions set aside by the house of lords, for error, but in cases where they give an explanation to the laws or constitution of the country, contrary to the sense of the parliament, though the parliament will not set aside the judgement of the court, yet, they have authority, by a new law, to explain a former one, and by this means to prevent a reception of such decisions. But no such power is in the legislature. The judges are supreme—and no law, explanatory of the constitution, will be binding on them.

From the preceding remarks, which have been made on the judicial powers proposed in this system, the policy of it may be fully developed.

I have, in the course of my observation on this constitution, affirmed and endeavored to shew, that it was calculated to abolish entirely the state governments, and to melt down the states into one entire government, for every purpose as well internal and local, as external and national. In this opinion the opposers of the system have generally agreed—and this has been uniformly denied by its advocates in public. Some individuals indeed, among them, will confess, that it has this tendency, and scruple not to say, it is what they wish; and I will venture to predict, without the spirit of prophecy, that if it is adopted without amendments, or some such precautions as will ensure amendments immediately after its adoption, that the same gentlemen who have employed their talents and abilities with such success to influence the public mind to adopt this plan, will employ the same to persuade the people, that it will be for their good to abolish the state governments as useless and burdensome.

Perhaps nothing could have been better conceived to facilitate the abolition of the state governments than the constitution of the judicial. They will be able to extend the limits of the general government gradually, and by insensible degrees, and to accomodate themselves to the temper of the people. Their decisions on the meaning of the constitution will commonly take place in cases which arise between individuals, with which the public will not be generally acquainted; one adjudication will form a precedent to the next; and this to a following one. These cases will immediately affect individuals only; so that a series of determinations will probably take place before even the people will be informed of them. In the meantime all the art and address of those who wish for the change will be employed to make converts to their opinion. The people will be told, that their state officers, and state legislatures are a burden and expence without affording any solid advantage, for that all the laws passed by them, might be equally well made by the general legislature. If to those who will be interested in the change, be added, those who will be under their influence, and such who will submit to almost any change of government, which they can be persuaded to believe will ease them of taxes, it is easy to see, the party who will favor the abolition of the state governments would be far from being inconsiderable.—In this situation, the general legislature, might pass one law after another, extending the general and abridging the state jurisdictions, and to sanction their proceedings would have a course of decisions of the judicial to whom the constitution has committed the power of explaining the constitution.—If the states remonstrated, the constitutional mode of deciding upon the validity of the law, is with the supreme court, and neither people, nor state legislatures, nor the general legislature can remove them or reverse their decrees.

Had the construction of the constitution been left with the legislature, they would have explained it at their peril; if they exceed their powers, or sought to find, in the spirit of the constitution, more than was expressed in the letter, the people from whom they derived their power could remove them, and do themselves right; and indeed I can see no other remedy that the people can have against their rulers for encroachments of this nature. A constitution is a compact of a people with their rulers; if the rulers break the compact, the people have a right and ought to remove them and do themselves justice; but in order to enable them to do this with the greater facility, those whom the people chuse at stated periods, should have the power in the last resort to determine the sense of the compact; if they determine contrary to the understanding of the people, an appeal will lie to the people at the period when the rulers are to be elected, and they will have it in their power to remedy the evil; but when this power is lodged in the hands of men independent of the people, and of their representatives, and who are not, constitutionally, accountable for their opinions, no way is left to controul them but *with a high hand and an outstretched arm.*

BRUTUS.

New-York Journal

10 APRIL 1788

ESSAY XVI

Brutus argues that the supreme power in any free government must be responsible to the people. The Constitution's separation of powers makes this responsibility impossible, especially in regard to the federal judiciary. In addition, the Senate, which by its power to try impeachments commands the greatest federal power, is too distant from the people. Senate terms should be shortened to bring senators more in touch with the people. Essays in The Federalist *of particular relevance: 48-51, 62-66, 79.*

WHEN great and extraordinary powers are vested in any man, or body of men, which in their exercise, may operate to the oppression of the people, it is of high importance that powerful checks should be formed to prevent the abuse of it.

Perhaps no restraints are more forcible, than such as arise from responsibility to some superior power.—Hence it is that the true policy of a republican government is, to frame it in such manner, that all persons who are concerned in the government, are made accountable to some superior for their conduct in office.—This responsibility should ultimately rest with the People. To have a government well administered in all its parts, it is requisite the different departments of it should be separated and lodged as much as may be in different hands. The legislative power should be in one body, the executive in another, and the judicial in one different from either— But still each of these bodies should be accountable for their conduct. Hence it is impracticable, perhaps, to maintain a perfect distinction between these several departments—For it is difficult, if not impossible, to call to account the several officers in government, without in some degree mixing the legislative and judicial. The legislature in a free and republic are chosen by the people at stated periods, and their responsibility consists, in their being amenable to the people. When the term, for which they are chosen, shall expire, who will then have opportunity to displace them if they disapprove of their conduct—but it would be improper that the judicial should be elective, because their business requires that they should possess a degree of law knowledge, which is acquired only by a regular education, and besides it is fit that they should be placed, in a certain degree in an independent situation, that they may maintain firmness and steadiness in their decisions. As the people therefore ought not to elect the judges, they cannot be amenable to them immediately, some other mode of amenability must therefore be devised for these, as well as for all other officers which do not spring from the immediate choice of the people: this is to be effected by making one court subordinate to another, and by giving them cognizance of the behaviour of all officers; but on this plan we at last arrive at some supreme, over whom there is no power to controul but the people themselves. This supreme controling power should be in the choice of the people, or else you establish an authority independent, and not amenable at all, which is repugnant to the principles of a free government. Agreeable to these principles I suppose the supreme judicial ought to be liable to be called to account, for any misconduct, by some body of men, who depend upon the people for their places; and so also should all other great officers in the State; who are not made amenable to some superior officers. This policy seems in some measure to have been in view of the framers of the new system, and to have given rise to the institution of a court of impeachments—How far this Court will be properly qualified to execute the trust which will be reposed in them, will be the business of a future paper to investigate. To prepare the way to do this, it shall be the business of this, to make some remarks upon the constitution and powers of the Senate, with whom the power of trying impeachments is lodged.

The following things may be observed with respect to the constitution of the Senate.

1st. They are to be elected by the legislatures of the States and not by the people, and each State is to be represented by an equal number.

2d. They are to serve for six years, except that one third of those first chosen are to go out of office at the expiration of two years, one third at the expiration of four years, and one third at the expiration of six years, after which this rotation is to be preserved, but still every member will serve for the term of six years.

3d. If vacancies happen by resignation or otherwise, during the recess of the legislature of any State, the executive is authorised to make temporary appointments until the next meeting of the legislature.

4. No person can be a senator who has not arrived to the age of thirty years, been nine years a citizen of the United States, and who is not at the time he is elected an inhabitant of the State for which he is elected.

The apportionment of members of Senate among the States is not according to numbers, or the importance of the States; but is equal. This, on the plan of a consolidated government, is unequal and improper; but is proper on the system of confederation—on this principle I approve of it. It is indeed the only feature of any importance in the constitution of a confederated government. It was obtained after a vigorous struggle of that part of the Convention who were in favor of preserving the state governments. It is to be regreted that they were not able to have infused other principles into the plan, to have secured the government of the respective states, and to have marked with sufficient precision the line between them and the general government.

The term for which the senate are to be chosen, is in my judgment too long, and no provision being made for a rotation will, I conceive, be of dangerous consequence.

It is difficult to fix the precise period for which the senate should be chosen. It is a matter of opinion, and our sentiments on the matter must be formed, by attending to certain principles. Some of the duties which are to be performed by the senate, seem evidently to point out the propriety of their term of service being extended beyond the period of that of the assembly. Besides as they are designed to represent the aristocracy of the country, it seems fit they should possess more stability, and so continue a longer period than that branch who represent the democracy. The business of making treaties and some other which it will be proper to commit to the senate, requires that they should have experience, and therefore that they should remain some time in office to acquire it.— But still it is of equal importance that they should not be so long in office as to be likely to forget the hand that formed them, or be insensible of their interests. Men long in office are very apt to feel themselves independent. To form and pursue interests separate from those who appointed them. And this is more likely to be the case with the senate, as they will for the most part of the time be absent from the state they represent, and associate with such company as will possess very little of the feelings of the middling class of people. For it is to be remembered that there is to be a *federal city*, and the inhabitants of it will be the great and the mighty of the earth. For these reasons I would shorten the term of their service to four years. Six years is a long period for a man to be absent from his home, it would have a tendency to wean him from his constituents.

A rotation in the senate, would also in my opinion be of great use. It is probable that senators once chosen for a state will, as the system now stands, continue in office for life. The office will be honorable if not lucrative. The persons who occupy it will probably wish to continue in it, and therefore use all their influence and that of their friends to continue in office.—Their friends will be numerous and powerful, for they will have it in their power to confer great favors; besides it will before long be considered as disgraceful not to be re-elected. It will therefore be considered as a matter of delicacy to the character of the senator not to return him again.—Every body acquainted with public affairs knows how difficult it is to remove from office a person who is long been in it. It is seldom done except in cases of gross misconduct. It is rare that want of competent ability procures it. To prevent this inconvenience I conceive it would be wise to determine, that a senator should not be eligible after he had served for the period assigned by the constitution for a certain number of years; perhaps three would be sufficient. A farther benefit would be derived from such an arrangement; it would give opportunity to bring forward a greater number of men to serve their country, and would return those, who had served, to their state, and afford them the advantage of becoming better acquainted with the condition and politics of their constituents. It farther appears to me proper, that the legislatures should retain the right which they now hold under the confederation, or recalling their members. It seems an evident dictate of reason, that when a person authorises another to do a piece of business for him, he should retain the power to displace him, when he does not conduct according to his pleasure. This power in the state legislatures, under confederation, has not been exercised to the injury of the government, nor do I see any danger of its being so exercised under the new system. It may operate much to the public benefit.

These brief remarks are all I shall make on the organization of the senate. The powers with which they are invested will require a more minute investigation.

This body will possess a strange mixture of legislative, executive and judicial powers, which in my opinion will in some cases clash with each other.

1. They are one branch of the legislature, and in this respect will possess equal powers in all cases with the house of representatives; for I consider the clause which gives the house of representatives the right of originating bills for raising a revenue as merely nominal, seeing the senate we authorised to propose or concur with amendments.

2. They are a branch of the executive in the appointment of ambassadors and public ministers, and in the appointment of all other officers, not otherwise provided for; whether the forming of treaties, in which they are joined with the president, appertains to the legislative or the executive part of the government, or to neither, is not material.

3. They are part of the judicial, for they form the court of impeachments.

It has been a long established maxim, that the legislative, executive and judicial departments in government should be kept distinct. It is said, I know, that this cannot be done. And therefore that this maxim is not just, or at least that it should only extend to certain leading features in a government. I admit that this distinction cannot be perfectly preserved. In a due ballanced government, it is perhaps absolutely necessary to give the executive qualified legislative powers, and the legislative or a branch of them judicial powers in the last resort. It may possibly also, in some special cases, be adviseable to associate the legislature, or a branch of it, with the executive, in the exercise of acts of great national importance. But still the maxim is a good one, and a separation of these powers should be sought as far as is practicable. I can scarcely imagine that any of the advocates of the system will pretend, that it was necessary to accumulate all these powers in the senate.

There is a propriety in the senate's possessing legislative powers; this is the principal end which should be held in view in their appointment. I need not here repeat what has so often and ably been advanced on the subject of a division of the legislative power into two branches—The arguments in favor of it I think conclusive. But I think it equally evident, that a branch of the legislature should not be invested with the power of appointing officers. This power in the senate is very improperly lodged for a number of reasons—These shall be detailed in a future number.

BRUTUS.

Essays of John De Witt

The Essays of John De Witt first appeared in the American Herald *of Boston between October and December 1787. The unknown Anti-Federalist who wrote these essays took his pseudonym to remind Americans of the seventeenth-century Dutch statesman Jan De Witt, who fought a centralizing aristocracy in the name of the people's rights. The author skillfully lays out a common line of Anti-Federalist argument: Americans enjoy many blessings under their current government and so should closely examine any proposed constitution. Examination of this Constitution shows that it would give the central government an overawing military power unchecked by full representation or a bill of rights.*

American Herald

22 OCTOBER 1787

ESSAY I

De Witt begins by describing a nation that is prosperous, free, and at peace. Such inconveniences as do exist are natural in a country that has only recently fought a costly war. With so much to lose, Americans would be foolish to rush to judgment regarding a new form of government. Essays in The Federalist *of particular relevance: 1-5, 85.*

To the FREE CITIZENS of the COMMONWEALTH OF MASSACHUSETTS.

WHOEVER attentively examines the history of America, and compares it with that of other nations, will find its commencement, its growth, and its present situation, without a precedent.

It must ever prove a source of pleasure to the Philosopher, who ranges the explored parts of this inhabitable globe, and takes a comparative view, as well of the rise and fall of those nations, which have been and are gone, as of the growth and present existence of those which are now in being, to close his prospect with this Western world. In proportion as he loves his fellow creatures, he must here admire and approve; for while they have severally laid their foundations in the blood and slaughter of three, four, and sometimes, ten successive generations, from their passions have experience, every misery to which [human] nature is subject, and at this day present striking features of usurped power, unequal justice, and despotic tyranny, America stands completely systemised without any of these misfortunes.—On the contrary, from the first settlement of the country, the necessity of civil associations, founded upon equality, consent, and proportionate justice have ever been universally acknowledged.—The means of education always attended to, and the fountains of science brought within the reach of poverty—Hitherto we have commenced society, and advanced in all respects resembling a family, without partial affections, or even a domestic bickering: And if we consider her as an individual, instead of an undue proportion of violent passions and bad habits; we must set her down possessed of reason, genius and virtue.—I premise these few observations because there are too many among us of narrow minds, who live in the practice of blasting the reputation of their own country.—They hold it as a maxim, that virtues cannot grow in their own soil.—They will appreciate those of a man, they know nothing about, because he is an exotic; while they are sure to depreciate those much more brilliant in their neighbours, because they are really acquainted with and know them.

Civil society is a blessing.—It is here universally known as such.—The education of every child in this country tends to promote it.—There is scarcely a citizen in America who does not wish to bring it, consistent with our situation and circumstances, to its highest state of improvement.—Nay, I may say further, that the people in general aim to effect this point, in a peaceable, laudable, and rational way. These assertions are proved by stubborn facts, and I need only resort to that moment, when, in contest with a powerful enemy, they paid such an unprecedented attention to civilization, as to select from among themselves their different conventions, and form their several constitutions, which, for their beautiful theoretical structure, caught the admiration of our enemies, and secured to us the applause of the world.—We at this day feel the effects of this disposition, and now live under a government of our own choice, constructed by ourselves, upon unequivocal principles, and requires but to be well administered to make us as happy under it as generally falls to the lot of humanity. The disturbances in the course of the years past cannot be placed as an objection to the principle I advance.—They took their rise in idleness, extravagance and misinformation, a want of knowledge of our several finances, a universal delusion at the close of the war, and in consequence thereof, a pressure of embarassments, which checked, and in many cases, destroyed that disposition of forbearance, which ought to be exercised towards each other. These were added to the accursed practice of letting money at usury, and some few real difficulties and grievances, which our late situation unavoidably brought upon us. The issue of them, however, rather proves the position for, a very few irreclaimables excepted, we find even an anxiety to hearken to reason pervading all claims—industry and frugality increasing, and the advantages arising from good, wholesome laws, confessed by every one.—Let who will gain say it, I am confident we are in a much better situation, in all respects, than we were at this period the last year; and as fast as can be expected, consistent with the passions and habits of a free people, of men who will think for themselves, coalescing, as a correspondent observes in a late paper, under a firm, wise and efficient government. The powers vested in Congress have hitherto been found inadequate.—Who are those that have been against investing them? The people of this Commonwealth have very generally supposed it expedient, and the farmer equally with the merchant have taken steps to effect it.—A Convention from the different States for that sole purpose hath been appointed of their most respectable citizens—respectable indeed I may say for their equity, for their literature, and for their love of their country. Their proceedings are now before us for our approbation.—The eagerness with which they have been received by certain classes of our fellow citizens, naturally forces upon us this question? Are we to adopt this Government, without an examination?—Some there are, who, literally speaking, are for pressing it upon us at all events. The name of the man who but lisps a sentiment in objection to it, is to be handed to the printer, by the printer to the publick, and by the publick he is to be led to execution. They are themselves stabbing its reputation. For my part, I am a stranger to the necessity for all this haste! Is it not a subject of some small importance? Certainly it is.——are not your lives, your liberties and properties intimately involved in it?—Certainly they are. Is it a government for a moment, a day, or a year? By no means—but for ages—Altered it may possibly be, but it is easier to correct before it is adopted:—Is it for a family, a state, or a small number of people? It is for a number no less respectable than three millions. Are the enemy at our gates, and have we not time to consider it? Certainly we have. Is it so simple in its form as to be comprehended instantly?—Every letter, if I may be allowed the expression, is an idea. Does it consist of but few additions to our present confederation, and those which have been from time to time described among us, and known to be necessary?—Far otherwise.—It is a compleat system of government, and armed with every power, that a people in any circumstances ought to bestow. It is a path newly struck out, and a new set of ideas are introduced that have neither occurred or been digested.—A government for national purposes, preserving our constitution entire, hath been the only plan hitherto agitated. I do not pretend to say, but it is in theory the most unexceptionable, and in practice will be the most conducive to our happiness of any possible to be adopted:—But it ought to undergo a candid and strict examination. It is the duty of every one in the Commonwealth to communicate his sentiments to his neighbour, divested of passion, and equally so of prejudices. If they are honest and he is a real friend to his country, he will do it and embrace every opportunity to do it. If thoroughly looked into before it is adopted, the people will be more apt to approve of it in practice, and every man is a TRAI-TOR to himself and his posterity, who shall ratify it with his signature, without first endeavouring to understand it.—We are but yet in infancy; and we had better proceed slow than too fast.—It is much easier to dispense powers, than recall them.—The present generation will not be drawn into any system; they are too enlightened; they have not forfeited their right to a share in government, and they ought to enjoy it.

Some are heard to say, "When we consider the men who made it, we ought to take it for sterling, and without hesitation—that they were the collected wisdom of the States, and had no object but the general good."—I do not doubt all this, but facts ought not to be winked out of sight:—They were delegated from different States, and nearly equally represented, though vastly disproportionate both in wealth and numbers. They had local prejudices to combat, and in many instances, totally opposite interests to consult. Their situations, their habits, their extent, and their particular interest, varied each from the other. The gentlemen themselves acknowledge that they have been less rigid upon some points, in consequence of those difficulties than they otherwise should have been.—Others again tell you that the Convention is or will be dissolved; that we must take their proceedings in whole or reject them—But this surely cannot be a reason for their speedy adoption; it rather works the other way. If evils are acknowledged in the composition, we ought, at least, to see whose shoulders are to bear the most; to compare ours with those of other States, and take care that we are not saddled with more than our proportion: That the citizens of Philadelphia are running mad after it, can be no argument for us to do the like:—Their situation is almost contrasted with ours; they suppose themselves a central State; they expect the perpetual residence of Congress, which of itself alone will ensure their aggrandizement: We, on the contrary, are sure to be near one of the extremes; neither the loaves or fishes will be so plenty with us, or shall we be so handy to procure them.

We are told by some people, that upon the adopting this New Government, we are to become every thing in a moment:—Our foreign and domestic debts will be as a feather; our ports will be crowded with the ships of all the world, soliciting our commerce and our produce: Our manufactures will increase and multiply; and, in short, if we STAND STILL, our country, notwithstanding, will be like the blessed Canaan, a land flowing with milk and honey. Let us not deceive ourselves; the only excellency of any government is in exact proportion to the administration of it:—Idleness and luxury will be as much a bane as ever; our passions will be equally at war with us then as now; and if we have men among us trying with all their ability to undermine our present Constitution, these very persons will direct their force to sap the vitals of the new one.—

Upon the whole, my fellow countrymen, I am as much a federal man as any person: In a federal union lies our political salvation— To preserve that union, and make it respectable to foreign opticks, the National Government ought to be armed with all necessary powers; but the subject I conceive of infinite delicacy, and requires both ability and reflection. In discusing points of such moment, America has nothing to do with passions or hard words; every citizen has an undoubted right to examine for himself, neither ought he to be ill treated and abused, because he does not think at the same moment exactly as we do. It is true, that many of us have but our liberties to loose, but they are dearly bought, and are not the least precious in estimation:—In the mean time, is it not of infinite consequence, that we pursue inflexibly that path, which I feel persuaded we are now approaching, wherein we shall discourage all foreign importations; shall see the necessity of greater economy and industry; shall smile upon the husbandman, and reward the industrious mechanick; shall promote the growth of our own country, and wear the produce of our own farms; and, finally, shall support measures in proportion to their honesty and wisdom, without any respect to men. Nothing more is wanted to make us happy at home, and respectable abroad.

JOHN DE WITT.

American Herald

29 OCTOBER 1787

ESSAY II

De Witt argues that a bill of rights is crucial but would be impossible to secure once the Constitution is ratified. The people should give up only those rights needed to maintain peace and public order. Because rulers seek to expand their powers, the people must limit them to delegated by drafting a bill of rights. Essays in The Federalist *of particular relevance: 84, 85.*

To the FREE CITIZENS of the COMMONWEALTH of MASSACHUSETTS.

IN my last address upon the proceedings of the Fœderal Convention, I endeavored to convince you of the importance of the subject, that it required a cool, dispassionate examination, and a thorough investigation, previous to its adoption—that it was not a mere revision and amendment of our first Confederation, but a compleat System for the future government of the United States, and I may now add in preference to, and in exclusion of, all others heretofore adopted.—It is not TEMPORARY; but in its nature, PERPETUAL.—It is not designed that you shall be annually called, either to revise, correct, or renew it; but, that your posterity shall grow up under, and be governed by it, as well as ourselves.—It is not so capable of alterations as you would at the first reading suppose; and I venture to assert, it never can be, unless by force of arms. The fifth article in the proceedings, it is true, expressly provides for an alteration under certain conditions, whenever "it shall be ratified by the Legislatures of three fourths of the several States, or by Conventions in three fourths thereof, as the one or the other mode of ratification may be proposed by Congress."— Notwithstanding which, such are the *"heterogeneous materials from which this System was formed,*" such is the difference of interest, different manners, and different local prejudices, in the different parts of the United States, that to obtain that majority of three fourths to any one single alteration, essentially affecting this or any other State, amounts to an absolute impossibility. The conduct of the Delegates in dissolving the Convention, plainly speaks this language, and no other.—Their sentiments in their Letter to his Excellency the President of Congress are—That this Constitution was the result of a spirit of amity—that the parties came together disposed to concede as much as possible each to the other—that mutual concessions and compromises did, in fact, take place, and all those which could, consistent with the peculiarily of their political situation. Their dissolution enforces the same sentiment, by confining you to the alternative of taking or refusing their doings in the gross. In this view, who is there to be found among us, who can seriously assert, that this Constitution, after ratification and being practiced upon, will be so easy of alteration? Where is the probability that a future Convention, in any future day, will be found possessed of a greater spirit of amity and mutual concession than the present? Where is the probability that three fourths of the States in that Convention, or three fourths of the Legislatures of the different States, whose interests differ scarcely in nothing short of every thing, will be so very ready or willing materially to change any part of this System, which shall be to the emolument of an individual State only? No, my fellow citizens, as you are now obliged to take it in the whole, so you must hereafter administer it in whole, without the prospect of change, unless by again reverting to a state of Nature, which will be ever opposed with success by those who approve of the Government in being.

That the want of a Bill of Rights to accompany this proposed System, is a solid objection to it, provided there is nothing exceptionable in the System itself, I do not assert.—If, however, there is at any time, a propriety in having one, it would not have been amiss here. A people, entering into society, surrender such a part of their natural rights, as shall be necessary for the existence of that society. They are so precious in themselves, that they would never be parted with, did not the preservation of the remainder require it.

They are entrusted in the hands of those, who are very willing to receive them, who are naturally fond of exercising of them, and whose passions are always striving to make a bad use of them.— They are conveyed by a written compact, expressing those which are given up, and the mode in which those reserved shall be secured. Language is so easy of explanation, and so difficult is it by words to convey exact ideas, that the party to be governed cannot be too explicit. The line cannot be drawn with too much precision and accuracy. The necessity of this accuracy and this precision encreases in proportion to the greatness of the sacrifice and the numbers who make it.—That a Constitution for the United States does not require a Bill of Rights, when it is considered, that a Constitution for an individual State would, I cannot conceive.—The difference between them is only in the numbers of the parties concerned; they are both a compact between the Governors and Governed, the letter of which must be adhered to in discussing their powers. That which is not expressly granted, is of course retained.

The Compact itself is a recital upon paper of that proportion of the subject's natural rights, intended to be parted with, for the benefit of adverting to it in case of dispute. Miserable indeed would be the situation of those individual States who have not prefixed to their Constitutions a Bill of Rights, if, as a very respectable, learned Gentleman at the Southward observes, "the People, when they established the powers of legislation under their separate Governments, invested their Representatives with every right and authority which they did not, in explicit terms, reserve; and therefore upon every question, respecting the jurisdiction of the House of Assembly, if the Frame of Government is silent, the jurisdiction is efficient and complete." In other words, those powers which the people by their Constitutions expressly give them, they enjoy by positive grant, and those remaining ones, which they never meant to give them, and which the Constitutions say nothing about, they enjoy by tacit implication, so that by one means and by the other, they became possessed of the whole.—This doctrine is but poorly calculated for the meridian of America, where the nature of compact, the mode of construing them, and the principles upon which society is founded, are so accurately known and universally diffused. That insatiable thirst for unconditional controul over our fellow-creatures, and the facility of sounds to convey essentially different ideas, produced the first Bill of Rights ever prefixed to a Frame of Government. The people, altho' fully feasible that they reserved every tittle of power they did not expressly grant away, yet afraid that the words made use of, to express those rights so granted might convey more than they originally intended, they chose at the same moment to express in different language those rights which the agreement did not include, and which they never designed to part with, endeavoring thereby to prevent any cause for future altercation and the intrusion into society of that doctrine of tacit implication which has been the favorite theme of every tyrant from the origin of all governments to the present day.

The proceedings of the Convention are now handed to you by your Legislature, and the second Wednesday in January is appointed for your final answer. To enable you to give that with propriety; that your future reflections may produce peace, however opposed the present issue of your present conduct may be to your present expectations, you must determine, that, in order to support with dignity the Fœderal Union, it is proper and fit, that the present Confederation shall be annihilated:—That the future Congress of the United States shall be armed with the powers of Legislation, Judgment and Execution:—That annual elections in this Congress shall not be known, and the most powerful body, the Senate, in which a due proportion of representation is not preserved, and in which the smallest State has equal weight with the largest, be the longest in duration:—That it is not necessary for the publick good, that persons habituated to the exercise of power should ever be reminded from whence they derive it, by a return to the station of private citizens, but that they shall at all times at the expiration of the term for which they were elected to an office, be capable of immediate re-election to that same office:—That you will hereafter risque the probability of having the Chief Executive Branch chosen from among you; and that it is wholly indifferent, both to you and your children after you, whether this future Government shall be administered within the territories of your own State, or at the distance of four thousand miles from them.—You must also determine, that they shall have the exclusive power of imposts and the duties on imports and exports, the power of laying excises and other duties, and the additional power of laying internal taxes upon your lands, your goods, your chattels, as well as your persons at their sovereign pleasure:—That the produce of these several funds shall be appropriated to the use of the United States, and collected by their own officers, armed with a military force, if a civil aid should not prove sufficient:—That the power of organizing, arming and disciplining the militia shall be lodged in them, and this thro' fear that they shall not be sufficiently attentive to keeping so respectable a body of men as the yeomanry of this Commonwealth, compleatly armed, organized and disciplined; they shall have also the power of raising, supporting and establishing a standing army in time of peace in your several towns, and I see not why in your several houses:—That should an insurrection or an invasion, however small, take place, in Georgia, the extremity of the Continent, it is highly expedient they should have the power of suspending the writ of Habeas Corpus in Massachusetts, and as long as they shall judge the public safety requires it:—You must also say, that your present Supreme Judicial Court shall be an Inferior Court to a Continental Court, which is to be inferior to the Supreme Court of the United States:—That from an undue biass which they are supposed to have for the citizens of their own States, they shall not be competent to determine title to your real estate, disputes which may arise upon a protested Bill of Exchange, a simple note of hand, or book debt, wherein your citizens shall be unfortunately involved with disputes of such or any other kind, with citizens either of other States or foreign States: In all such cases they shall have a right to carry their causes to the Supreme Court of the United States, whether for delay only or vexation; however distant from the place of your abode, or inconsistent with your circumstances:—That such appeals shall be extended to matters of fact as well as law, and a trial of the cause by jury you shall not have a right to insist upon.— In short, my fellow-citizens, previous to a capacity of giving a compleat answer to these proceedings, you must determine that the Constitution of your Commonwealth, which is instructive, beautiful and consistent in practice, which has been justly admired in

Europe, as a model of perfection, and which the present Convention have affected to imitate, a Constitution which is especially calculated for your territory, and is made conformable to your genius, your habits, the mode of holding your estates, and your particular interests, shall be reduced in its powers to those of a City Corporation:—The skeleton of it may remain, but its vital principle shall be transferred to the new Government: Nay, you must go still further, and agree to invest the new Congress with powers, which you have yet thought proper to withhold from your own present Government.—All these, and more, which are contained in the proceedings of the Fœderal Convention, may be highly proper and necessary.—In this overturn of all individual Governments, in this new-fashioned set of ideas, and in this total dereliction of those sentiments which animated us in 1775, the Political Salvation of the United States may be very deeply interested, but BE CAUTIOUS.

JOHN DE WITT.

American Herald

5 NOVEMBER 1787

ESSAY III

De Witt asserts that there is a simple reason why Federalists demand immediate ratification of the proposed Constitution: they are lying. The new Constitution would not be federal, limited, and balanced, but wholly centralized and dangerous to the people's liberties. Its Senate would be powerful and aristocratic, and its House of Representatives worse, because it would be too small truly to represent the people's interests. Essays in The Federalist *of particular relevance: 17, 44-46, 55-58, 62.*

To the FREE CITIZENS of the COMMONWEALTH of MASSACHUSETTS.

CIVIL LIBERTY, in all countries, hath been promoted by a free discussion of publick measures, and the conduct of publick men. The FREEDOM OF THE PRESS hath, in consequence thereof, been esteemed one of its safe guards. That freedom gives the right, at all times, to every citizen to lay his sentiments, in a decent manner, before the people. If he will take that trouble upon himself, whether they are in point or not, his countrymen are obliged to him for so doing; for, at least, they lead to an examination of the subject upon which he writes.—If any possible situation makes it a duty, it is our present important one, for in the course of sixty or ninety days you are to approve of or reject the present proceedings of your Convention, which, if established, will certainly effect, in a greater or less degree, during the remainder of your lives, those privileges which you esteem dear to you, and not improbably those of your children for succeeding ages. Now therefore is unquestionably the proper time to examine it, and see if it really is what, upon paper, it appears to be. If with your eyes open, you deliberately accept it, however different it may prove in practice from what it appears in theory, you will have nobody to blame but yourselves; and what is infinitely worse, as I have before endeavoured to observe to you, you will be wholly without a remedy. It has many zealous advocates, and they have attempted, at least as far as their modesty would permit, to monopolize our gazettes, with their encomiums upon it. With the people they have to manage, I would hint to them, their zeal is not their best weapon, and exertions of such a kind, artful attempts to seize the moment do seldom tend either to elucidate and explain principles, or ensure success. Such conduct ought to be an additional stimulous for those persons who are not its professed admirers, to speak their sentiments with freedom however unpopular.—Such conduct ought to inspire caution, for as a man is invariably known by his company, so is the tendency of principles known by their advocates—Nay, it ought to lead you to enquire who are its advocates? Whether ambitious men throughout America, waiting with impatience to make it a stepping stone to posts of honour and emolument, are not of this class? Whether men

who openly profess to be tired of republican governments, and sick
to the heart of republican measures; who daily ridicule a government of choice, and pray ardently for one of force, are not of the
same class? And, whether there are not men among us, who disapprove of it only because it is not an absolute monarchy, but who,
upon the whole, are among its advocates?—In such examinations as
these, you cannot mispend a proportion of the sixty days.

All contracts are to be construed according to the meaning of
the parties at the time of making them. By which is meant, that
mutual communications shall take place, and each shall explain to
the other their ideas of the contract before them.—If any unfair
practices are made use of, if its real tendency is concealed by either
party, or any advantage taken in the execution of it, it is in itself
fraudalent and may be avoided. There is no difference in the constitution of government—Consent it is allowed is the spring—The
form is the mode in which the people choose to direct their affairs,
and the magistrates are but trustees to put that mode in force.—It
will not be denied, that this people, of any under Heaven, have a
right of living under a government of their own choosing.—That
government, originally consented to, which is in practice, what it
purports to be in theory, is a government of choice; on the contrary,
that which is essentially different in practice, from its appearance in
theory, however it may be in letter a government of choice, it never
can be so in spirit. Of this latter kind appear to me to be the proceedings of the Fœderal Convention—They are presented as a
Frame of Government purely Republican, and perfectly consistent
with the individual governments in the Union. It is declared to be
constructed for national purposes only, and not calculated to interfere with domestic concerns. You are told, that the rights of the
people are very amply secured, and when the wheels of it are put
in motion, it will wear a milder aspect than its present one.
Whereas the very contrary of all this doctrine appears to be true.
Upon an attentive examination you can pronounce it nothing less,
than a government which in a few years, will degenerate to a compleat Aristocracy, armed with powers unnecessary in any case to
bestow, and which in its vortex swallows up every other Government upon the Continent. In short, my fellow-citizens, it can be said

to be nothing less than a hasty stride to Universal Empire in this Western World, flattering, very flattering to young ambitious minds, but fatal to the liberties of the people. The cord is strained to the very utmost.—There is every spice of the SIC. JUBEO possible in the composition. Your consent is requested, because it is essential to the introduction of it; after having received-confirmation, your complaints may encrease the whistling of the wind, and they will be equally regarded.

It cannot be doubted at this day by any men of common sense, that there is a chram in politicks. That persons who enter reluctantly into office become habituated, grow fond of it, and are loath to resign it.—They feel themselves flattered and elevated, and are apt to forget their constituents, until the time returns that they again feel the want of them.—They uniformly exercise all the powers granted to them, and ninety-nine in a hundred are for grasping at more. It is this passionate thirst for power, which has produced different branches to exercise different departments and mutual checks upon those branches. The aristocratical hath ever been found to have the most influence, and the people in most countries have been particularly attentive in providing checks against it. Let us see if it is the case here.—A President, a Senate, and a House of Representatives are proposed. The Judicial Department is at present out of the question, being seperated excepting in impeachments. The Legislative is divided between the People who are the Democratical, and the Senate who are the Aristocratical part, and the Executive between the same Senate and the President who represents the Monarchical Branch.—In the construction of this System, their interests are put in opposite scales. If they are exactly balanced, the Government will remain perfect; if there is a prepondency, it will finally prevail. After the first four years, each Senator will hold his seat for the term of six years. This length of time will be amply sufficient of itself to remove any checks that he may have upon his independency, from the fear of a future election. He will consider that it is a serious portion of his life after the age of thirty; that places of honour and trust are not generally obtained unsolicited. The same means that placed him there may be again made use of; his influence and his abilities arising from his opportunities, will, during the whole term encrease those means; he will have a compleat negative upon all laws that shall be general, or that shall favor individuals, and a voice in the appointment of all officers in the United States.—Thus habituated to power, and living in the daily practice of granting favors and receiving solicitations, he may hold himself compleatly independent of the people, and at the same time ensure his election. If there remains even a risque, the blessed assistance of a little well-distributed money, will remove it.

With respect to the Executive, the Senate excepting in nomination, have a negative upon the President, and if we but a moment attend to their situation and to his, and to the power of persuasion over the human mind, especially when employed in behalf of friends and favorits, we cannot hesitate to say, that he will be infinitely less apt to disoblige them, than they to refuse him. It is far easier for twenty to gain over one, than one twenty; besides, in the one case, we can ascertain where the denial comes from, and the other we cannot. It is also highly improbable but some of the members, perhaps a major part, will hold their seats during their lives. We see it daily in our own Government, and we see it in every Government we are acquainted with, however many the cautions, and however frequent the elections.

These considerations, added to their share above mentioned in the Executive department must give them a decided superiority over the House of Representatives.—But that superiority is greatly enhanced, when we consider the difference of time for which they are chosen. They will have become adepts in the mystery of administration, while the House of Representatives may be composed perhaps two thirds of members, just entering into office, little used to the course of business, and totally unacquainted with the means made use of to accomplish it.—Very possible also in a country where they are total strangers.—But, my fellow-citizens, the important question here arises, who are this House of Representatives? "A representative Assembly,["] says the celebrated Mr. Adams, ["]is the sense of the people, and the perfection of the portrait, consists in the likeness."—Can this Assembly be said to contain the sense of the people?—Do they resemble the people in any one single feature?—Do you represent your wants, your grievances, your wishes, in person? If that is impracticable, have you a right to send one of your townsmen for that purpose?— Have you a right to send one from your county? Have you a right to send more than one for every thirty thousand of you? Can he be presumed knowing to your different, peculiar situations—your abilities to pay publick taxes, when they ought to be abated, and when encreased? Or is there any possibility of giving him information? All these questions must be answered in the negative. But how are these men to be chosen? Is there any other way than by dividing the State into districts? May not you as well at once invest your annual Assemblies with the power of choosing them—where is the essential difference? The nature of the thing will admit of none. Nay, you give them the power to prescribe the mode. They may invest it in themselves.—If you choose them yourselves, you must take them upon credit, and elect those persons you know only by common fame. Even this privilege is denied you annually, through fear that you might withhold the shadow of controul over them. In this view of the System, let me sincerely ask you, where is the people in this House of Representatives?—Where is the boasted popular part of this much admired System?—Are they not couzin germans in every sense to the Senate? May they not with propriety be termed an Assistant Aristocratical Branch, who will be infinitely more inclined to co-operate and compromise with each other, than to be the careful guardians of the rights of their constituents? Who is there among you would not start at being told, that instead of your present House of Representatives, consisting of members chosen from every town, your future Houses were to consist of but ten in number, and these to be chosen by districts?—What man among you would betray his country and approve of it? And yet how infinitely preferable to the plan proposed?—In the one case the elections would be annual, the persons elected would reside in the center of you, their interests would be yours, they would be subject to your immediate controul, and nobody to consult in their deliberations—But in the other, they are chosen for double the time, during which, however well disposed, they become strangers to the very people choosing them, they reside at a distance from you, you

have no controul over them, you cannot observe their conduct, and
they have to consult and finally be guided by twelve other States,
whose interests are, in all material points, directly opposed to
yours. Let me again ask you, What citizen is there in the Commonwealth of Massachusetts, that would deliberately consent laying
aside the mode proposed, that the several Senates of the several
States, should be the popular Branch, and together, form one
National House of Representatives?—And yet one moment's attention will evince to you, that this blessed proposed Representation of
the People, this apparent faithful Mirror, this striking Likeness, is
to be still further refined, and more Aristocratical four times told.—
Where now is the exact balance which has been so diligently
attended to? Where lies the security of the people? What assur-
ances have they that either their taxes will not be exacted but in
the greatest emergencies, and then sparingly, or that standing
armies will be raised and supported for the very plausible purpose
only of cantoning them upon their frontiers? There is but one
answer to these questions.—They have none. Nor was it intended
by the makers they should have, for meaning to make a different
use of the latter, they never will be at a loss for ways and means to
expend the former. They do not design to beg a second time. Knowing the danger of frequent applications to the people, they ask for
the whole at once, and are now by their conduct, teazing and
absolutely haunting of you into a compliance.—If you choose all
these things should take place, by all means gratify them. Go, and
establish this Government, which is unanimously confessed imperfect, yet incapable of alteration. Intrust it to men, subject to the
same unbounded passions and infirmities as yourselves, possessed
with an insatiable thirst for power, and many of them, carrying in
them vices, tho' tinsel'd and concealed, yet, in themselves, not less
dangerous than those more naked and exposed. But in the mean
time, add an additional weight to the stone that now covers the
remains of the Great WARREN and MONTGOMERY; prepare an
apology for the blood and treasure, profusely spent to obtain those
rights which you now so tamely part with. Conceal yourselves from
the ridicule of your enemies, and bring your New-England spirits
to a level with the contempt of mankind. Henceforth you may fit

yourselves down with propriety, and say, Blessed are they that never expect, for they shall not be disappointed.

JOHN DE WITT.

American Herald

19 NOVEMBER 1787

ESSAY IV

DeWitt criticizes the federal taxing power because, in his view, it will become a tool in Congress's quest for domination. Unlimited taxing power will lead Congress to expand the number of officers in its employ so that it may collect more money and foster a class dependent on its members' continuance in office. These officers will help the legislature take away the people's rights. De Witt concludes with a rousing condemnation of standing armies and a defense of the militia. Essays in The Federalist *of particular relevance: 12, 30-36.*

To the FREE CITIZENS of the COMMONWEALTH of MASSACHUSETTS. Place the Frame of Government proposed, in the most favorable point of view, magnify the priviledges held forth to the people to their fullest extent, and enlarge as much as you please, upon the great checks therein provided, notwithstanding all which, there cannot remain a doubt in the mind of any reflecting man, that it is a System purely Aristocratical, calculated to find employment for men of ambition, and to furnish means of sporting with the sacred principles of human nature. The great object throughout, is the acquisition of property and power, and every possible opportunity has been embraced to make ample provision for supplying a redundancy of the one, to exercise the other in its fullest extent. They have engrossed to themselves the riches of America, and are carefully silent what use they intend to put them to. Powers are there granted, that shall give to persons, greater strangers, and perhaps greater enemies to you than the people of Great-Britain, the right of entry into your habitations without your consent, not a lisp being mentioned as to the mode or time when such powers shall be exercised. They have taken to themselves the Purse and Sword of your country.

Like the performance of a fine painter, the Senate is the subject of the piece painted.—The people with their priviledges, to an attentive observer, may be seen in the back ground, composing an insignificant part of the drapery, but their existence depends upon the freshness of the colours.—Frequent handling, a little exposure, and the smallest inroads of time upon these shades, will soon destroy them, and they will no longer be considered a part of the composition. If this is true—if in any future period, however distant, we are to be governed by One Branch, it surely behoves us to provide for an equal voice in that Branch, that our respective influence shall bear some small proportion to our respective contributions and numbers: Whereas in this System, equality is totally disregarded. Five pounds in the Senate has an equal voice with fifty, and about five hundred thousand of the inhabitants the same number of votes with the remaining three millions. Where then is the probability the rights of the people will find equal security? Is it not demonstrable that your burthens will be great in proportion as your influence in that body that imposes them is small? As it respects this Commonwealth, infinitely better would be our situation in a representation in the British Parliament. The terms offered us by our enemies to place us as we stood in 1763, bear no comparison in their consequences, to those which would flow from the exercise of the powers of this Government by the Senate, as now constructed. If the same proportion in numbers and property had been observed in this Branch as in the House of Representatives (and no reason why it was not hath yet appeared, excepting what the celebrated Southern gentleman is pleased to term a *"necessary compromise between contending interest"*) however successful they might be hereafter in arrogating all the powers of government to themselves, or however severe in executing them, still one gleam of hope with the spirit of consolation would be found in the breast of the subject, that his grievances were proportionate to those of his neighbours; but in the present case, even this satisfaction is denied him—the uncertainty is not left him—his reason [instanter] convinces him it is not so.

It is idle to expect more virtue in an American than in an individual of any other nation.—That in opposition to all other countries, we are disposed in this, to live peaceably with each other, to consult our neighbours interest equally with our own, and to do to others as we should wish they should do to us. This being the case, we should not want any government.—Human nature is the same in all parts of the world, bad is the best: Education and example may tend to check or promote good or bad qualities, and encourage different degrees of vice. Some passions are more encreased by exercise in some countries than in others; but in all, the original stock is the same. We see in America the same vices, as abroad, and we are not backward in the practice of both wit and ingenuity in cultivating them. The pleasure of controul is palatable to all mankind without a single exception from the cradle to the throne. Let our peculiar situations be what they may, our proportion of happiness great, our domestic circles pleasing, our love of money unbounded, without a moment of suspense still we are ready to risque the sacrifice of them all for a share in the exercise of power over our fellow creatures,— for the sake of governing others, instead of being governed ourselves; and the more we examine the conduct of those men who have been intrusted with the administration of governments, the more assured we shall be in our position, that mankind have perhaps in every instance abused the authority vested in them, or attempted the abuse of it. In considering the present Government before us, we therefore certainly ought to look upon those who are to put it in motion, as our enemies—to be careful what we give—to see what use it is to be put to—and where to resort for a remedy, if it is abused.—Every door unguardedly left open, they will take care we never shall hereafter shut—every link in the chain unrevitted, they will provide shall always remain so.—It is of the last importance we set out right, we never can return to our present situation so well prepared to set out again:

This institution once established will not wear wholly out for thousands of years.—It will not be easy for any single State to alter it by force of arms.—To guard against such attempts, will claim the earliest attention of our new Governours.

To you, my fellow-citizens, let me now appeal: To you, who do not expect immediately to taste the sweets that flow from unlimited power, who determine upon principles that are immutable, who are not warped by private interest, and do not see through different mediums on different days—is there any among you who have had leisure to examine this Frame of Government, and without taking into consideration the powers granted therein, can say he approves of it—that he is pleased with the organization of the different branches, in their balances and their checks, that the people are fully and adequately represented, and let Human Nature be as depraved as Hell itself, (and we all know it is) yet the means provided to keep it within bounds are ample for the purposes?—I trust there as not one so passively disposed.—Indeed there cannot be, for it is grossly deficient in all these properties, it fails in a balance, and in a due separation of the different departments—it totally fails in a fair, faithful, honest image of the people, and in an equality of representation, in the only powerful branch in it.—I feel a confidence that the good sense of the people of this Commonwealth, will secure a proper decision upon so important a subject. I feel animated, when I reflect, in what precious estimation they have held their liberties, from the settlement of their country to the present hour—with what ardour they have encountered distress, poverty and death, to preserve and secure them, and with what caution they have parted with even that proportion, which is necessary for the assistance of good order and society.—I go on further to contend, that though its frame was the best ever proposed to a people for their acceptance, and would last properly balanced for ages, yet powers are there given, more than are either fit or necessary in any case to be parted with.

The extent of our country, with all its striking features, while they conspire to promote a fœderal union, are totally inconsistant with the plan of one Universal Empire, involving in it the destruction of the different State Governments.—I appeal to the most flaming zealots for the new Constitution, whether one of them, until the disclosure of the proceedings, entertained an idea, that the Convention would assume the power of internal taxation.—I dare affirm it was not lisped by an individual, throughout the whole Continent. Among all the conversations respecting the sending of members to that Convention; even the claim over the excises was not started.—It was on the contrary, a point universally conceded, that had the impost been vested in Congress by the States at the time proposed, with powers to collect it, there never would have been an occasion for a Convention. That fœderal measures would have taken a favourable turn, and with the proceeds of that revenue, Congress would have been able to have supported her own household, paid the interest of her domestic debt, and the different instalments, and interest of her foreign. But now these same Gentlemen, despising every civil institution yet adopted in America, and finding the form of Government far more grateful to their ambitious spirits than they ever imagined, will tell you, that the existance of the Continent depends upon its adoption—that we are ruined and undone, if we do not cordially embrace it, but if we do, like the ingenious dentist, it will pull from the breast of every citizen, all his jarring, malevolent passions, making us a wise, virtuous and wealthy people, and though they do not in plain words say that the millennium is to commence on its birth day; yet they describe to you, all the blessed effects expectant upon such an æra.

A dry tax is at all times odious. It is not congenial to the feelings of a free people. It is a visible demand upon a man at noon day, of that which he prefers to his life. He is called upon, when the necessity of giving it to support the society he lives in, does not strike him so forceably;—he for ever parts with it with reluctance, and would never consent, but under a conviction, that it is absolutely necessary—that it is his proportion—that it will be properly applied, and is laid upon him by his neighbour, chosen by himself, whom he controuls, and who bears an equal share of the same burthen.—It is a science difficult in its nature, duly to assess it. A man must not only be knowing to the different circumstances of every individual, the value of his real and personal estate but also must be without passions, without prejudices, without connections, making it his whole business. This not being the case, produces heart burnings, evasions, false oaths, unequal assessments, delays of payment, and finally, inability. These inconveniences are still increased by the mode of collecting the tax when so assessed. This trust is placed, in general, in persons who have neither knowledge or discretion equal to the importance of it. An opportunity is put into their hands to gratify all their little prejudices and resentments. They will unreasonably press upon one, and at the same moment indulge another. Unused to handle large sums of money, they cannot help fingering untill they think it their own—They misapply first a small proportion, one extravagance leads to another, until they are in arrears when called upon—and the honest and industrious are obliged again to contribute to supply their deficiencies.—This is the operation of a dry tax in its best situation; and it serves to demonstrate, that taxation and representation are inseperable—that they never can be laid upon the subject but by himself, or his representative, not treble refined, but resident in his vicinity, who shall be conversant both in his ability as to quantum, and propriety as to time. Even then they ought not be resorted to, but in the last extremity, for surely this Commonwealth will not be backward to testify, that notwithstanding they have made the experiment under the most promising circumstances, still woeful experience demonstrates the utter impossibility of raising and collecting monies sufficient for the use of government in such an odious, unequal manner. The five taxes past, in their consequences, have introduced idleness, dissipation, fraud, discontent, brankruptcies, unlawful speculations, stock-jobbing, and every other vice incident to our species, without supplying the Treasury with scarce a farthing. Government have always demonstrated a disposition to ease the people in the payment as much as in their power, notwithstanding which no one single person is satisfied, Government itself almost destroyed in consequence, and the end proposed in no one shape answered. If then, my fellow citizens, it is so easily demonstrated that dry taxes are attended with such fatal consequences when we impose them ourselves, that the evils accompanying the collection of them in the best given circumstances, over-balance all the advantages accruing from the monies raised by such collections.—What reason have you to suppose that a Continental tax will be more beneficial in its consequences, more equal in its assessments, and milder in its mode of collection. A man must be distracted to suppose so, for there are no avenues open for either of those consequences to flow through. In the first instance, the sum will be laid upon you by people that cannot be sufficiently acquainted with your country. A new set of Continental pensioned Assessors will be introduced into your towns, whose interest will be distinct from yours.—They will be joined by another set of Continental Collectors, still less principled and less adequate than the former. Attempts will be made by interested men upon their integrity, and instances of their deviations will be daily before your eyes—At a distance from their employers and removed from the Seat of Government, you will see them exulting with ideas, that they can practice their oppression upon you with impunity, and in their rioting and debauchery they will squander the proceeds of your industry.—The extremes of tyranny are commonly at the extreme parts of the country governed. You must kiss the rod, or they will make you feel it.— According to the spirit of obedience which you manifest; to the ease with which you part with your money, so will the mode of assessing and collecting it be varied from time to time by your new masters. If one man shall not be competent, he shall be attended with an host.—Whether that host shall be the posse of your country or a file of armed soldiers, shall depend upon circumstances. They are to determine, and you are to make no laws inconsistent with such determination, whether such Collectors shall carry with them any paper, purporting their commission, or not—whether it shall be a general warrant, or a special one—whether written or printed— whether any of your goods, or your persons shall be exempt from distress, and in what manner either you or your property is to be treated when taken in consequence of such warrants. They will have the liberty of entering your houses by night as well as by day for such purposes.—All these points are given in letter and in spirit to the New Constitution, and the subject has not a shadow of security that they will not be executed.—Nay, if they ever should mean to exercise the right of taxation at all, I affirm it can be done with success by them in no other way, but in an arbitrary manner, and by previously subduing the spirit and strength of this Commonwealth.

In forming our own Constitution, by persons having one common interest, we deemed it of consequence, to preface such powers, with the mode in which they should be exercised.—We thought it highly proper to declare "That every subject had a right to be secured from all unreasonable searches and seizures of his person, his houses, his papers, and all his possessions—that all warrants were contrary to this right, if the cause or foundation of them be not previously supported by oath or affirmation, and if the order in the warrant to a civil officer, be not accompanied with a special designation," &c. &c. &c.—These checks are omitted, however, in the present proceedings, and the sole reason why appears to be this, that the makers of them know the power itself to be improper, that the people would always be convinced of that impropriety, and would never submit, so long as they could resist.—That of course it must be collected without these checks, or not collected at all.

These are serious thoughts.—They may by some be called bugbears; but they will be verified in the future history of America, with a vengeance.—That it will be in five, ten or fifteen years is not probable. Your rulers will be too knowing, to be over hasty in a display of their strength; they will not loose ground so easily as the Court of Great-Britain did for want of a little well timed policy.—Your chains will be gradual, and gilded. But finally they will be as visible as the Summer's Sun in the Meridian. Where is the Government under Heaven, where every farthing is not taken from the people, that they possibly can part with.—It must be the case here. Their interest will point out to them the policy in accustoming you to contributions, and their curiosity will be early excited to make the experiment to constitute a thermometer for your feelings.—They will have a plausible pretext.—They will tell you your burthens will be less when you get out of debt, and that they are the effect of not adopting it sooner.—They have large demands upon them, and matters of moment to undertake.

The officers of their Government will be encreased an hundred fold, and the liberality with which they have expended their money in salaries plainly evinces the improbability that there ever will be a great sum lying idle in their treasury.

JOHN DE WITT.

(To be continued.)

American Herald

---

3 DECEMBER 1787

(Continued.)

To the FREE CITIZENS of the COMMONWEALTH of MASSACHUSETTS.

The chief blessings of society, like individuals, are fond of association, and have a mutual dependence upon each other. They form links of one chain, and are all actuated by the same cause. Where freedom prevails, industry and science there also prevail. Industry produces wealth, and science preserves freedom in purity. The majority of the people in all such countries become so active in their different pursuits, that they are deprived both of their time and opportunity to inform themselves of the principles of the government by which those great blessings are secured to them, and almost implicitly rely both for the explaining and for the enforcing of those principles upon the patriotism of those, their fellow-citizens, who labour but in the field of enquiry, and who spend their whole time in researches after knowledge. Thanks be to Heaven, that in America, that majority always retaining the power, the others have never dared to enforce their principles, without previous explanation, and it has become natural to mankind, wherever they have a system of any kind, a favorite, if it is as genuine and honest in principle, as in appearance, they leave no active powers of the mind unessayed, in elucidating, explaining and enlarging upon its benefits to those whom they wish should adopt it—all its good qualities are delineated, and every exertion is made to refute all objections offered against it, which exertions will be crowned with success, if the objections in themselves are futile, and will not bear the force of light and argument.

The malevolent passions of the heart are not called in, private faults of individuals are not raked from oblivion and magnified, invidious representations are not made, neither are the slanderous, envenomed darts of malice and envy hurled against those characters, who yesterday were deemed praise-worthy and held sacred for a series of obligations conferred by them upon their country, but today are execrated with passion, because they do not in all points see as other men see. On the contrary, cool reasoning and dispassionate argument, are of themselves sufficient to build up such a system, to unravel all its mysteries, and to present to the people in expressive, legible colours, the blessings that will result from its adoption. Where this mode of conduct is not pursued by its advocates, where instead of cool reasoning upon the subject in question, artful evasions are presented, the system itself is winked out of sight, instead of dispassionate endeavours to remove difficulties arising in honest minds, which are offered with decency to the public in order to be refuted, those who make them are loaded with the opprobious terms of *Insurgents, destroyers of all government, bankrupts, defaulters,* and *anti-federalists,* which is worse than *jacobitism*: Where, instead of promoting free discussions upon the most important subject ever before a community, attempts are made to fetter and suppress such discussions, by THREATNING the Printer and DROPPING the papers that contain them: Where, instead of coming forward like men, in the full exercise of reason, like fellow-citizens warmed with a patriotick ardour for their country, emulous to secure and preserve its sacred principles, and with proper weapons disarming their fellow-citizens of those objections, they blast and asperse their characters (the dernier resort of all supporters of a bad cause) I say the people have a fair, undoubted right to presume those objections unanswerable, the system itself essentially defective, and that its advocates are, by their conduct, endeavouring not to reason, but to surprize the people into a hasty approbation of it.—

That this is the case with the supporters of the proceedings of the Fœderal Convention, far be it from me to declare.—Judge, my fellow-citizens, for yourselves—examine the public prints from the promulgation of this Constitution. Objections there you will find in score—are they offered with decency? Do they attack men or measures? Are they answered in the same manner? And do you discover a desire in those who wish you to embrace this Government, to inform you of its principles, and the consequences which will probably ensue from such principles—why they have taken from you the sinews of your present government, and instead of revising and amending your Confederation; have handed you a new one, contrasted in the plenitude of its powers.—As you answer these questions, so you must make up your opinion upon that which is before you.

They have the power of "organizing, arming and disciplining the militia, and of governing them when in service of the United States, giving to the seperate States the appointment of the officers, and the authority of training the militia according to the discipline prescribed by Congress." Let us enquire, why they have assumed this power, for if it is for the purpose of forming you into one uniform, solid body throughout the United States, making you respectable both at home and abroad—of arming you more compleatly and exercising you oftener—of strengthening the power which is now lodged in your hands, and relying upon you and you solely for aid and support to the civil power in the execution of all the laws of the New Congress, it certainly can be no where better placed under the restrictions therein mentioned, than in that body. But is this probable. Does the complection of the proceedings countenance such a supposition? When they unprecedently claim the power of raising and supporting standing armies; do they tell you for what purposes they are to be raised?—How they are to be employed?—How many they are to consist of, and where to be stationed?—Is this power fettered with any one of these necessary restrictions which will shew they depend upon the militia, and not upon this internal engine of oppression to execute their civil laws. The nature of the demand in itself contradicts such a supposition, and forces you to believe that it is for none of these causes—but rather for the purpose of consolidating and finally destroying your strength, as your respective Governments are to be destroyed.

They well know the impolicy of putting or keeping arms in the hands of a nervous people, at a distance from the Seat of Government, upon whom they mean to exercise the powers granted in that Government.—They have no idea of calling upon the party aggrieved to support and enforce their own grievances. They are aware of the necessity of catching Samson asleep to trim him of his locks. It is asserted by the most respectable writers upon Government, that a well regulated militia, composed of the yeomanry of the country have ever been considered as the bulwark of a free people; and, says the celebrated Mr. HUME, "without it, it is folly to think any free government will have stability or security—When the sword is introduced, as in our constitution (speaking of the British) the person entrusted will always neglect to discipline the militia, in order to have a pretext for keeping up a standing army; and it is evident this is a mortal distemper in the British parliament, of which it must finally inevitably perish."—If they have not the same design, why do they wish a standing army unrestrained? It is universally agreed, that a militia and a standing body of troops never yet flourished in the same soil. Tyrants have uniformly depended upon the latter, at the expence of the former. Experience has taught them, that a standing body of regular forces, where ever they can be compleatly introduced, are always efficacious in enforcing their edicts, however arbitrary, and slaves by profession themselves, are "nothing loath" to break down the barriers of freedom with a *goût*.—No, my fellow-citizens, this plainly shews they do not mean to depend upon the citizens of the States alone to enforce their powers, wherefore it is their policy to neglect them, and lean upon something more substantial and summary. It is true, they have left the appointment of officers in the breast of the several States; but this to me, appears an insult, rather than a priveledge, for what avails this right, if they in their pleasure should choose to neglect to arm, organize and discipline the men over whom such Officers are to be appointed. It is a bait, that you might be led to suppose they did intend to apply to them in all cases, and to pay particular attention to making them the bulwark of this Continent.—And would they not be equal to such an undertaking?—Are they not abundantly able to give security and stability to your government as long as it is free? Are they not the only proper persons to do it? Are they not the most respectable body of yeomanry in that character upon earth? Have they not been deeply engaged in some of the most brilliant actions in America, and more than once decided the fate of armies? In short, do they not preclude the necessity of any standing army whatsoever, unless in case of invasion; and in that case it would be time enough to raise them, for no free government under Heaven, with a well disciplined militia was ever yet subdued by mercenary troops.

The advocates at the present day, for a standing army in the New Congress pretend it is necessary for the respectability of government. I defy them to produce an instance in any country, in the Old or New World, where they have not finally done away the liberties of the people.—Every writer upon government,—Lock, Sidney, Hamden, and a list of others have uniformly asserted, that standing armies are a solecism in any government; that no nation ever supported them, that did not resort to, rely upon, and finally become a prey to them.—No Western Historians have yet been hardy enough to advance principles that look a different way. What historians have asserted, all the Grecian Republicks have verified— They are brought up to obedience and unconditional submission.—With arms in their hands, they are taught to feel the weight of rigid discipline:—They are excluded from the enjoyments which liberty gives to its votaries, they, in consequence, hate and envy the rest of the community in which they are placed, and indulge a malignant pleasure in destroying those privileges to which they never can be admitted.—"Without them,["] says the Marquis of Beccaria, ["]in every society there is an effort constantly tending to confer on one part the height of power, and to reduce the other to the extreme of weakness and misery, and this is of itself sufficient to employ the people's attention." There is no instance of any government being reduced to a confirmed tyranny without military oppression; and the first policy of tyrants has been to annihi-

late all other means of national activity and defence, and to rely
solely upon standing troops.—Repeated were the trials before the
Sovereigns of Europe dared to introduce them upon any pretext
whatever; and the whole record of the transactions of mankind cannot furnish an instance (unless the proceedings of the Convention
may now be called a part of that record) where the motives which
caused their establishment, were not completely disguised.—Pisistratus in Greece, and Dyonysius in Syracuse, Charles in France,
and Henry in England, all cloaked their villainous intentions under
an idea of raising a small body for a guard to their persons; and
Spain, could not succeed in the same nefarious plan, until through
the influence of the ambitious Priest, they were called upon to resist
the progress of the Infidels. "Cæsar, who first attacked the commonwealth with *mines*, very soon opened his *batteries*."—Notwithstanding all these objections to this engine of oppression, which
are made by the most experienced men, and confirmed by every
country, where the rays of freedom ever extended.—Yet in America, which has hitherto been her favorite abode—in this civilized
territory, where property is valuable, and men are found with feelings that will not patiently submit to arbitrary controul—in this
Western region, where, my fellow-countrymen, it is confessedly
proper that you should associate and dwell in society from choice
and reflection, and not be kept together by force and fear, you are
modestly requested to engraft into the component parts of your
Constitution, a STANDING ARMY, without any qualifying
restraints whatever,—certainly to exist somewhere within the
bowels of your country in time of peace. It is very true, that the
celebrated Mr. Wilson, a member of the Convention, and who we
may suppose breathes, in some measure, the spirit of that body,
tells you, it is for the purpose of forming cantonments upon your
frontiers, and for the dignity and safety of your country, as it
respects foreign nations. No man that loves his country could object
to their being raised for the first of these causes, but for the last it
cannot be necessary. GOD has so separated us by an extensive ocean
from the rest of mankind, he hath so liberally endowed us with privileges, and so abundantly taught us to esteem them precious, it
would be impossible, while we retain our integrity and advert to

first principles, for any nation whatever to subdue us. We have succeeded in an opposition to the most powerful people upon the globe;
and the wound that America received in the struggle, where is it?
As speedily healed as the track in the ocean is buried by the succeeding wave. It has scarcely stopped her progress, and our private
dissentions only at this moment, tarnish the lustre of the most illustrious infant nation under Heaven.

You cannot help suspecting this gentleman, when he goes on to
tell you, "that standing armies in time of peace, have always been
a topic of *popular declamation*, but Europe hath found them necessary to maintain the appearance of strength in a season of the
most profound tranquility."—This shews you his opinion, and that
he as one of the Convention, was for unequivocally establishing
them in time of peace; and to object to them is mere popular declamation. But I will not, my countrymen, I cannot believe you to be of
the same sentiment. Where is the standing army in the world, that,
like the musquet they make use of, hath been, in time of peace,
brightned and burnished for the sake only of maintaining an
appearance of strength, without being put to a different use, without having had a pernicious influence upon the morals, the habits,
and the sentiments of society, and finally, taking a chief part in executing its laws. But some say, that there is a controul over them,
and that consists in the appropriation of monies for their support.
Turn your attention to England, and see the popular part of this
constitution by the influence of money, by the influence of military
and revenue officers, brought gravely to give their annual assent to
the existence of a standing army, and for monies to support it. It has
long since been an insult on the good sense of that nation.

It may not be amiss to remind you of that swarm of revenue,
excise, impost and stamp officers, Continental assessors and collectors, that your new Constitution will introduce among you. They
will, of themselves, be a STANDING ARMY to you, and you will
see them at your elections, active and industrous to secure the seats
of those men who put them into office.—They will be very adequate
to give you a surfeit of their company, to make you tired in med-
dling with government, and disposed to become indifferent about

the exercise of it, without the blessed assistance of any military corps.—

Upon the whole, my countrymen, it appears to me, that this power as it now stands, is decidedly improper and dangerous. That Congress ought to have the power of raising armies when invaded by our enemies, is certain; that they ought not to have it for any other cause, is equally so. If they did not or do not mean to employ them in any other way, they ought [in express] terms to say so, in a Bill of Rights. They never ought to exist at all, but in subordination to civil authority. If the people are not in general disposed to execute the powers of government, it is time to suspect there is something wrong in that government, and rather than employ a standing army, they had better have another; for, in my humble opinion, it is yet much too early to set it down for a fact, that mankind cannot be governed, but by force.

JOHN DE WITT.

Address of the Minority of the Pennsylvania Convention

"The Address and Reasons of Dissent of the Minority of the Convention of Pennsylvania to Their Constituents" was first published in the Pennsylvania Packet and Daily Advertiser *on 18 December 1787. The Minority had attempted, unsuccessfully, to have its address printed in the ratifying convention's official journal. Widely reprinted, this address recounts the limits originally put on the Constitutional Convention and the abuses suffered by the minority during the Pennsylvania ratification debate. It also lists a number of specific objections to the proposed Constitution, centering on its failure to protect state and individual prerogatives, and proposes a number of amendments intended to improve that Constitution. Essays in* The Federalist *of particular relevance: 40, 44-46.*

Pennsylvania Packet and Daily Advertiser

---

18 DECEMBER 1787

The Address and Reasons of Dissent of the Minority of the Convention of the State of Pennsylvania to their Constituents.

IT was not until after the termination of the late glorious contest, which made the people of the United States an independent nation, that any defect was discovered in the present confederation. It was formed by some of the ablest patriots in America. It carried us successfully through the war; and the virtue and patriotism of the people, with their disposition to promote the common cause, supplied the want of power in Congress.

The requisition of Congress for the five *per cent.* impost was made
before the peace, so early as the first of February, 1781, but was prevented taking effect by the refusal of one state; yet it is probable
every state in the union would have agreed to this measure at that
period, had it not been for the extravagant terms in which it was
demanded. The requisition was new moulded in the year 1783, and
accompanied with an additional demand of certain supplementary
funds for 25 years. Peace had now taken place, and the United
States found themselves labouring under a considerable foreign and
domestic debt, incurred during the war. The requisition of 1783 was
commensurate with the interest of the debt, as it was then calculated; but it has been more accurately ascertained since that time.
The domestic debt has been found to fall several millions of dollars
short of the calculation, and it has lately been considerably diminished by large sales of the western-lands. The states have been
called on by Congress annually for supplies until the general system of finance proposed in 1783 should take place.

It was at this time that the want of an efficient federal government was first complained of, and that the powers vested in Congress were found to be inadequate to the procuring of the benefits
that should result from the union. The impost was granted by most
of the states, but many refused the supplementary funds; the
annual requisitions were set at nought by some of the states, while
others complied with them by legislative acts, [but] were tardy in
their payments, and Congress found themselves incapable of complying with their engagements, and supporting the federal government. It was found that our national character was sinking in
the opinion of foreign nations. The Congress could make treaties
of commerce, but could not enforce the observance of them. We
were suffering from the restrictions of foreign nations, who had
shackled our commerce, while we were unable to retaliate: and all
now agreed that it would be advantageous to the union to enlarge
the powers of Congress; that they should be enabled in the amplest
manner to regulate commerce, and to lay and collect duties on the
imports throughout the United States. With this view a convention was first proposed by Virginia, and finally recommended by
Congress for the different states to appoint deputies to meet in con-

vention, "for the purposes of revising and amending the present articles of confederation, so as to make them adequate to the exigencies of the union." This recommendation the legislatures of twelve states complied with so hastily as not to consult their constituents on the subject; and though the different legislatures had no authority from their constituents for the purpose, they probably apprehended the necessity would justify the measure; and none of them extended their ideas at that time further than "revising and amending the present articles of confederation." Pennsylvania by the act appointing deputies expressly confined their powers to this object; and though it is probable that some of the members of the assembly of this state had at that time in contemplation to annihilate the present confederation as well as the constitution of Pennsylvania, yet the plan was not sufficiently matured to communicate it to the public.

The majority of the legislature of this commonwealth, were at that time under the influence of the members from the city of Philadelphia. They agreed that the deputies sent by them to convention should have no compensation for their services, which determination was calculated to prevent the election of any member who resided at a distance from the city. It was in vain for the minority to attempt electing delegates to the convention, who understood the circumstances, and the feelings of the people, and had a common interest with them. They found a disposition in the leaders of the majority of the house to chuse themselves and some of their dependants. The minority attempted to prevent this by agreeing to vote for some of the leading members, who they knew had influence enough to be appointed at any rate, in hopes of carrying with them some respectable citizens of Philadelphia, in whose principles and integrity they could have more confidence; but even in this they were disappointed, except in one member; the eighth member was added at a subsequent session of the assembly.

The Continental convention met in the city of Philadelphia at the time appointed. It was composed of some men of excellent characters; of others who were more remarkable for their ambition and cunning, than their patriotism; and of some who had been opponents to the independence of the United States. The delegates from

Pennsylvania were, six of them, uniform and decided opponents to the constitution of this commonwealth. The convention sat upwards of four months. The doors were kept shut, and the members brought under the most solemn engagements of secrecy.* Some of those who opposed their going so far beyond their powers, retired, hopeless, from the convention, others had the firmness to refuse signing the plan altogether; and many who did sign it, did it not as a system they wholly approved, but as the best that could be then obtained, and notwithstanding the time spent on this subject, it is agreed on all hands to be a work of haste and accommodation.

Whilst the gilded chains were forging in the secret conclave, the meaner instruments of despotism without, were busily employed in alarming the fears of the people with dangers which did not exist, and exciting their hopes of greater advantages from the expected plan than even the best government on earth could produce.

The proposed plan had not many hours issued forth from the womb of suspicious secrecy, until such as were prepared for the purpose, were carrying about petitions for people to sign, signifying their approbation of the system, and requesting the legislature to call a convention. While every measure was taken to intimidate the people against opposing it, the public papers seemed with the most violent threats against those who should dare to think for themselves, and *tar and feathers* were liberally promised to all those who would not immediately join in supporting the proposed government be it what it would. Under such circumstances petitions in favour of calling a convention were signed by great numbers in and about the city, before they had leisure to read and examine the system, many of whom, now they are better acquainted with it, and have had time to investigate its principles, are heartily opposed to it. The petitions were speedily handed into the legislature.

Affairs were in this situation when on the 28th of September last a resolution was proposed to the assembly by a member of the house who had been also a member of the federal convention, for calling a state convention, so be elected within *ten* days for the purpose of

* The Journals of the conclave are still concealed.

examining and adopting the proposed constitution of the United States, though at this time the house had not received it from Congress. This attempt was opposed by a minority, who after offering every argument in their power to prevent the precipitate measure, without effect, absented themselves from the house as the only alternative left them, to prevent the measure taking place previous to their constituents being acquainted with the business—That violence and outrage which had been so often threatened was now practised; some of the members were seized the next day by a mob collected for the purpose, and forcibly dragged to the house, and there detained by force whilst the quorum of the legislature, *so formed*, compleated their resolution. We shall dwell no longer on this subject, the people of Pennsylvania have been already acquainted therewith. We would only further observe that every member of the legislature, previously to taking his seat, by solemn oath or affirmation, declares, "that he will not do or consent to any act or thing whatever that shall have a tendency to lessen or abridge their rights and privileges, as declared in the constitution of this state." And that constitution which they are so solemnly sworn to support cannot legally be altered but by a recommendation of the council of censors, who alone are authorised to propose alterations and amendments, and even these must be published at least *six months*, for the consideration of the people.—The proposed system of government for the United States, if adopted, will [alter] and may annihilate the constitution of Pennsylvania; and therefore the legislature had no authority whatever to recommend the calling a convention for that purpose. This proceeding could not be considered as binding on the people of this commonwealth. The house was formed by violence, some of the members composing it were detained there by force, which alone would have vitiated any proceedings, to which they were otherwise competent; but had the legislature been legally formed, this business was absolutely without their power.

In this situation of affairs were the subscribers elected members of the convention of Pennsylvania. A convention called by a legislature in direct violation of their duty, and composed in part of members, who were compelled to attend for that purpose, to consider of a constitution proposed by a convention of the United

States, who were not appointed for the purpose of framing a new form of government, but whose powers were expressly confined to altering and amending the present articles of confederation.—Therefore the members of the continental convention in proposing the plan acted as individuals, and not as deputies from Pennsylvania.* The assembly who called the state convention acted as individuals, and not as the legislature of Pennsylvania; nor could they or the convention chosen on their recommendation have authority to do any [act] or thing, that can alter or annihilate the constitution of Pennsylvania (both of which will be done by the new constitution) nor are their proceedings in our opinion, at all binding on the people.

The election for members of the convention was held at so early a period and the want of information was so great, that some of us did not know of it until after it was over, and we have reason to believe that great numbers of the people of Pennsylvania have not yet had an opportunity of sufficiently examining the proposed constitution—We apprehend that no change can take place that will affect the internal government or constitution of this commonwealth, unless a majority of the people should evidence a wish for such a change; but on examining the number of votes given for members of the present state convention, we find that of upwards of *seventy thousand* freemen who are intitled to vote in Pennsylvania, the whole convention has been elected by about *thirteen thousand* voters, and though *two thirds* of the members of the convention have thought proper to ratify the proposed constitution, yet those *two thirds* were elected by the votes of only *six thousand and eight hundred* freemen.

In the city of Philadelphia and some of the eastern counties, the junto that took the lead in the business agreed to vote for none but

---

* The continental convention in direct violation of the 13th article of the confederation, have declared, "that the ratification of nine states shall be sufficient for the establishment of this constitution, between the states so ratifying the same."—Thus has the plighted faith of the states been sported with! They had solemnly engaged that the confederation now subsisting should be inviolably preserved by each of them, and the union thereby formed, should be perpetual, unless the same should be altered by mutual consent.

such as would solemnly promise to adopt the system in *toto*, without exercising their judgment. In many of the counties the people did not attend the elections as they had not an opportunity of judging of the plan. Others did not consider themselves bound by the call of a set of men who assembled at the state-house in Philadelphia, and assumed the name of the legislature of Pennsylvania; and some were prevented from voting by the violence of the party who were determined at all events to force down the measure. To such lengths did the tools of despotism carry their outrage, that in the night of the election for members of convention, in the city of Philadelphia, several of the subscribers (being then in the city to transact your business) were grossly abused, ill-treated and insulted while they were quiet in their lodgings, though they did not interfere, nor had any thing to do with the said election, but, as they apprehend, because they were supposed to be adverse to the proposed constitution, and would not tamely surrender those sacred rights, which you had committed to their charge.

The convention met, and the same disposition was soon manifested in considering the proposed constitution, that had been exhibited in every other stage of the business. We were prohibited by an express vote of the convention, from taking any question on the separate articles of the plan, and reduced to the necessity of adopting or rejecting *in toto*.—'Tis true the majority permitted us to debate on each article, but restrained us from proposing amendments.—They also determined not to permit us to enter on the minutes our reasons of dissent against any of the articles, nor even on the final question our reasons of dissent against the whole. Thus situated we entered on the examination of the proposed system of government, and found it to be such as we could not adopt, without, as we conceived, surrendering up your dearest rights. We offered our objections to the convention, and opposed those parts of the plan, which, in our opinion, would be injurious to you, in the best manner we were able; and closed our arguments by offering the following propositions to the convention.

1. The right of conscience shall be held inviolable; and neither the legislative, executive nor judicial powers of the United States shall have authority to alter, abrogate, or infringe any part of the

constitution of the several states, which provide for the preservation of liberty in matters of religion.

2. That in controversies respecting property, and in suits between man and man, trial by jury shall remain as heretofore, as well in the federal courts, as in those of the several states.

3. That in all capital and criminal prosecutions, a man has a right to demand the cause and nature of his accusation, as well in the federal courts, as in those of the several states; to be heard by himself and his counsel; to be confronted with the accusers and witnesses; to call for evidence in his favor, and a speedy trial by an impartial jury of his vicinage, without whose unanimous consent, he cannot be found guilty, nor can he be compelled to give evidence against himself; and that no man be deprived of his liberty, except by the law of the land or the judgment of his peers.

4. That excessive bail ought not to be required, nor excessive fines imposed, nor cruel nor unusual punishments inflicted.

5. That warrants unsupported by evidence, whereby any officer or messenger may be commanded or required to search suspected places, or to seize any person or persons, his or their property, not particularly described, are grievous and oppressive, and shall not be granted either by the magistrates of the federal government or others.

6. That the people have a right to the freedom of speech, of writing and publishing their sentiments, therefore, the freedom of the press shall not be restrained by any law of the United States.

7. That the people have a right to bear arms for the defense of themselves and their own state, or the United States, or for the purpose of killing game; and no law shall be passed for disarming the people or any of them, unless for crimes committed, or real danger of public injury from individuals; and as standing armies in the time of peace are dangerous to liberty, they ought not to be kept up: and that the military shall be kept under strict subordination to and be governed by the civil powers.

8. The inhabitants of the several states shall have liberty to fowl and hunt in seasonable times, on the lands they hold, and on all other lands in the United States not inclosed, and in like manner to fish in all navigable waters, and others not private property,

without being restrained therein by any laws to be passed by the legislature of the United States.

9. That no law shall be passed to restrain the legislatures of the several states from enacting laws for imposing taxes, except imposts and duties on goods imported or exported, and that no taxes, except imposts and duties upon goods imported and exported, and postage on letters shall be levied by the authority of Congress.

10. That the house of representatives be properly increased in number; that elections shall remain free; that the several states shall have power to regulate the elections for senators and representatives, without being controuled either directly or indirectly by any interference on the part of the Congress; and that elections of representatives be annual.

11. That the power of organizing, arming and disciplining the militia (the manner of disciplining the militia to be prescribed by Congress) remain with the individual states, and that Congress shall not have authority to call or march any of the militia out of their own state, without the consent of such state, and for such length of time only as such state shall agree.

That the sovereignty, freedom and independency of the several states shall be retained, and every power, jurisdiction and right which is not by this constitution expressly delegated to the United States in Congress assembled.

12. That the legislative, executive, and judicial powers be kept separate; and to this end that a constitutional council be appointed, to advise and assist the president, who shall be responsible for the advice they give, hereby the senators would be relieved from almost constant attendance; and also that the judges be made completely independent.

13. That no treaty which shall be directly opposed to the existing laws of the United States in Congress assembled, shall be valid until such laws shall be repealed, or made conformable to such treaty; neither shall any treaties be valid which are in contradiction to the constitution of the United States, or the constitutions of the several states.

14. That the judiciary power of the United States shall be confined to cases affecting ambassadors, other public ministers and

consuls; to cases of admiralty and maritime jurisdiction; to controversies to which the United States shall be a party; to controversies between two or more states—between a state and citizens of different states—between citizens claiming lands under grants of different states; and between a state or the citizens thereof and foreign states, and in criminal cases, to such only as are expressly enumerated in the constitution, & that the United States in Congress assembled, shall not have power to enact laws, which shall alter the laws of descents and distribution of the effects of deceased persons, the titles of lands or goods, or the regulation of contracts in the individual states.

After reading these propositions, we declared our willingness to agree to the plan, provided it was so amended as to meet those propositions, or something similar to them: and finally moved the convention to adjourn, to give the people of Pennsylvania time to consider the subject, and determine for themselves; but these were all rejected, and the final vote was taken, when our duty to you induced us to vote against the proposed plan, and to decline signing the ratification of the same.

During the discussion we met with many insults, and some personal abuse; we were not even treated with decency, during the sitting of the convention, by the persons in the gallery of the house; however, we flatter ourselves that in contending for the preservation of those invaluable rights you have thought proper to commit to our charge, we acted with a spirit becoming freemen, and being desirous that you might know the principles which actuated our conduct, and being prohibited from inserting our reasons of dissent on the minutes of the convention, we have subjoined them for your consideration, as to you alone we are accountable. It remains with you whether you will think those inestimable privileges, which you have so ably contended for, should be sacrificed at the shrine of despotism, or whether you mean to contend for them with the same spirit that has so often baffled the attempts of an aristocratic faction, to rivet the shackles of slavery on you and your unborn posterity.

Our objections are comprised under three general heads of dissent, viz.

WE Dissent, first, because it is the opinion of the most celebrated writers on government, and confirmed by uniform experience, that a very extensive territory cannot be governed on the principles of freedom, otherwise than by a confederation of republics, possessing all the powers of internal government; but united in the management of their general, and foreign concerns.

If any doubt could have been entertained of the truth of the foregoing principle, it has been fully removed by the concession of *Mr. Wilson*, one of majority on this question, and who was one of the deputies in the late general convention. In justice to him, we will give his own words; they are as follows, viz. "The extent of country for which the new constitution was required, produced another difficulty in the business of the federal convention. It is the opinion of some celebrated writers, that to a small territory, the democratical; to a middling territory (as Montesquieu has termed it) the monarchial; and to an extensive territory, the despotic form of government is best adapted. Regarding then the wide and almost unbounded jurisdiction of the United States, at first view, the hand of despotism seemed necessary to controul, connect, and protect it; and hence the chief embarrassment rose. For, we know that, altho' our constituents would chearfully submit to the legislative restraints of a free governments, they would spure at every attempt to shackle them with despotic power."—And again in another part of his speech he continues.—"Is it probable that the dissolution of the state governments, and the establishment of one *consolidated empire* would be eligible in its nature, and satisfactory to the people in its administration? I think not, as I have given reasons to shew that so extensive a territory could not be governed, connected, and preserved, but by the *supremacy of despotic power*. All the exertions of the most potent emperors of Rome were not capable of keeping that empire together, which in extent was far inferior to the dominion of America."

We dissent, secondly, because the powers vested in Congress by this constitution, must necessarily annihilate and absorb the legislative, executive, and judicial powers of the several states, and produce from their ruins one consolidated government, which from the nature of things will be *an iron banded despotism*, as nothing short of the supremacy of despotic sway could connect and govern these United States under one government.

As the truth of this position is of such decisive importance, it ought to be fully investigated, and if it is founded to be clearly ascertained; for, should it be demonstrated, that the powers vested by this constitution in Congress will have such an effect as necessarily to produce one consolidated government, the question then will be reduced to this short issue, viz. whether satiated with the blessings of liberty; whether repenting of the folly of so recently asserting their unalienable rights, against foreign despots at the expence of so much blood and treasure, and such painful and arduous struggles, the people of America are now willing to resign every privilege of freemen, and submit to the dominion of an absolute government, that will embrace all America in one chain of despotism; or whether they will with virtuous indignation, sparn at the shackles prepared for them, and confirm their liberties by a conduct becoming freemen.

That the new government will not be a confederacy of states, as it ought, but one consolidated government, founded upon the destruction of the several governments of the states, we shall now shew.

The powers of Congress under the new constitution, are complete and unlimited over the *purse* and the *sword*, and are perfectly independent of, and supreme over, the state governments; whose intervention in these great points is entirely destroyed. By virtue of their power of taxation, Congress may command the whole, or any part of the property of the people. They may impose what imposts upon commerce; they may impose what land taxes, poll taxes, excises, duties on all written instruments, and duties on every other article that they may judge proper; in short, every species of taxation, whether of an external or internal nature is comprised in section the 8th, of article the 1st, viz. "The Congress shall have power to lay and collect taxes, duties, imposts, and excises, to pay the debts, and provide for the common defence and general welfare of the United States."

As there is no one article of taxation reserved to the state governments, the Congress may monopolise every source of revenue, and thus indirectly demolish the state governments, for without funds they could not exist, the taxes, duties and excises imposed by Congress may be so high as to render it impracticable to levy further sums on the same articles; but whether this should be the case or not, if the state governments should presume to impose taxes, duties or excises, on the same articles with Congress, the latter may abrogate and repeal the laws whereby they are imposed, upon the allegation that they interfere with the due collection of their taxes, duties or excises, by virtue of the following clause, part of section 8th, article 1st. viz. "To make all laws which shall be necessary and proper for carrying into execution the foregoing powers, and all other powers vested by this constitution in the government of the United States, or in any department or officer thereof[.]"

The Congress might gloss over this conduct by construing every purpose for which the state legislatures now lay taxes, to be for the *"general welfare,"* and therefore as of their judiction.

And the supremacy of the laws of the United States is established by article 6th, viz. "That this constitution and the laws of the United States, which shall be made in pursuance thereof, and *all treaties* made, or which shall be made, under the authority of the United States, shall be the *supreme law of the land;* and *the judges in every state shall be bound thereby; any thing in the constitution or laws of any state to the contrary notwithstanding.*" It has been alledged that the words "pursuant to the constitution," are a restriction upon the authority of Congress; but when it is considered that by other sections they are invested with every efficient power of government, and which may be exercised to the absolute destruction of the state governments, without any violation of even the forms of the constitution, this seeming restriction, as well as every other restriction in it, appears to us to be nugatory and delusive; and only introduced as a blind upon the real nature of the government. In our opinion, "pursuant to the constitution," will be coextensive with the *will* and *pleasure* of Congress, which, indeed, will be the only limitation of their powers.

We apprehend that two co-ordinate sovereignties would be a solecism in politics. That therefore as there is no line of distinction drawn between the general, and state governments; as the sphere of their jurisdiction is undefined, it would be contrary to the nature of things, that both should exist together, one or the other would necessarily triumph in the fullness of dominion. However the contest could not be of long continuance, as the state governments are divested of every means of defence, and will be obliged by "the supreme law of the land" *to yield at discretion.*

It has been objected to this total destruction of the state governments, that the existence of their legislatures is made essential to the organization of Congress; that they must assemble for the appointment of the senators and president general of the United States. True, the state legislatures may be continued for some years, as boards of appointment, merely, after they are divested of every other function, but the framers of the constitution foreseeing that the people will soon be disgusted with this solemn mockery of a government without power and usefulness, have made a provision for relieving them from the imposition, in section 4th, of article 1st, viz. "The times, places, and manner of holding elections for senators and representatives, shall be prescribed in each state by the legislature thereof; *but the Congress may at any time, by law make or alter such regulations; except as to the place of chusing senators.*"

As Congress have the controul over the time of the appointment of the president general, of the senators and of the representatives of the United States, they may prolong their existence in office, for life, by postponing the time of their election and appointment, from period to period, under various pretences, such as an apprehension of invasion, the factious disposition of the people, or any other plausible presence that the occasion may suggest; and having thus obtained life-estates in the government, they may fill up the vacancies themselves, by their controul over the mode of appointment; with this exception in regard to the senators, that as the place of appointment for them, must, by the constitution, be in the particular state, they may depute some body in the respective states, to fill up the vacancies in the senate, occasioned by death, until they can venture to assume it themselves. In this manner, may the only restriction in this clause be evaded. By virtue of the foregoing section, when the spirit of the people shall be gradually broken; when the general government shall be firmly established, and when a numerous standing army shall render opposition vain, the Congress may compleat the system of despotism, in renouncing all dependence on the people, by continuing themselves and children in the government.

The celebrated *Montesquieu*, in his Spirit of Laws, vol. 1, page 12th, says, "That in a democracy there can be no exercise of sovereignty, but by the suffrages of the people, which are their will; now the sovereigns will is the sovereign himself; the laws therefore, which establish the right of suffrage, are fundamental to this government. In fact, it is as important to regulate in a republic in what manner, by whom, and concerning what suffrages are to be given, as it is in a monarchy to know who is the prince, and after what manner he ought to govern." The *time, mode* and *place* of the election of representatives, senators and president general of the United States, ought not to be under the controul of Congress, but fundamentally ascertained and established.

The new constitution, consistently with the plan of consolidation, contains no reservation of the rights and privileges of the state governments, which was made in the confederation of the year 1778, by article the 2d, viz. "That each state retains its sovereignty, freedom, and independence, and every power, jurisdiction and right, which is not by this confederation expressly delegated to the United States in Congress assembled."

The legislative power vested in Congress by the foregoing recited sections, is so unlimited in its nature; may be so comprehensive and boundless its exercise, that this alone would be amply sufficient to annihilate the state governments, and swallow them up in the grand vortex of general empire.

The judicial powers vested in Congress are also so various and extensive, that by legal ingenuity they may be extended to every case, and thus absorb the state judiciaries, and when we consider the decisive influence that a general judiciary would have over the civil polity of the several states, we do not hesitate to pronounce that this power, unaided by the legislative, would effect a consolidation of the states under one government.

The powers of a court of equity, vested by this constitution, in the tribunals of Congress; powers which do not exist in Pennsylvania, unless so far as they can be incorporated with jury trial, would, in this state, greatly contribute to this event. The rich and wealthy suitors would eagerly lay hold of the infinite makes, perplexities and delays, which a court of chancery, with the appellate powers of the supreme court in fact as well as law would furnish him with, and thus the poor man being plunged in the bottomless pit of legal discussion, would drop his demand in despair.

In short, consolidation pervades the whole constitution. It begins with an annuciation that such was the intention. The main pillars of the fabric correspond with it, and the concluding paragraph is a confirmation of it. The preamble begins with the words, "We the people of the United States," which is the style of a compact between individuals entering into a state of society, and not that of a confederation of states. The other features of consolidation, we have before noticed.

Thus we have fully established the position, that the powers vested by this constitution in Congress, will effect a consolidation of the states under one government, which even the advocates of this constitution admit, could not be done without the sacrifice of all liberty.

3. We dissent, Thirdly, Because if it were practicable to govern so extensive a territory as these United States includes, on the plan of a consolidated government, consistent with the principles of liberty and the happiness of the people, yet the construction of this constitution is not calculated to attain the object, for independent of the nature of the case, it would of itself, necessarily produce a despotism, and that not by the usual gradations, but with the celerity that has hitherto only attended revolutions effected by the sword.

To establish the truth of this position, a cursory investigation of the principles and form of this constitution will suffice.

The first consideration that this review suggests, is the emission of a BILL OF RIGHTS ascertaining and fundamentally establishing those unalienable and personal rights of men, without the full, free, and secure enjoyment of which there can be no liberty, and over which it is not necessary for a good government to have the controul. The principal of which are the rights of conscience, personal liberty by the clear and unequivocal establishment of the writ of *habeas corpus*, jury trial in criminal and civil cases, by an impartial jury of the vicinage or county, with the common law proceedings, for the safety of the accused in criminal prosecutions and the liberty of the press, that scourge of tyrants; and the grand bulwark of every other liberty and privilege; the stipulations heretofore made in saving of them in the state constitutions, are entirely superceded by this constitution.

The legislature of a free country should be so formed as to have a competent knowledge of its constituents, and enjoy their confidence. To produce these essential requisites, the representation ought to be fair, equal, and sufficiently numerous, to possess the same interests, feelings, opinions, and views, which the people themselves would possess, were they all assembled; and so numerous as to prevent bribery and undue influence, and so responsible to the people, by frequent and fair elections, as to prevent their neglecting or sacrificing the views and interests of their constituents, to their own pursuits.

We will now bring the legislature under this constitution to the test of the foregoing principles, which will demonstrate, that it is deficient in every essential quality of a just and fare representation.

The house of representatives is to consist of [65] members; that is one for about every 50,000 inhabitants, to be chosen every two years. Thirty-three members will form a quorum for doing business, and 17 of these, being the majority, determine the sense of the house.

The senate, the other constituent branch of the legislature, consists of 26 members, being *two* from each state, appointed by their legislatures every six years—fourteen senators make a quorum; the majority of whom, eight, determines the sense of the body; except in judging on impeachments, or in making treaties, or in expelling a member, when two thirds of the senators present, must concur.

The president is to have the controul over the enacting of laws, so far as to make the concurrence of *two* thirds of the representatives and senators present necessary, if he should object to the laws.

Thus it appears that the liberties, happiness, interests, and great concerns of the whole United States, may be dependent upon the integrity, virtue, wisdom, and knowledge of 25 or 26 men.—How unadequate and unsafe a representation! Inadequate, because the sense and views of 3 or 4 millions of people diffused over so extensive a territory comprising such various climates, products, habits, interests, and opinions, cannot be collected in so small a body; and besides, it is not a fair and equal representation of the people even in proportion to its number, for the smallest state has as much weight in the senate as the largest, and from the smallness of the number to be chosen for both branches of the legislature; and from the mode of election and appointment, which is under the controul of Congress; and from the nature of the thing, men of the most elevated rank in life will alone be chosen. The other orders in the society, such as farmers, traders, and mechanics, who all ought to have a competent number of their best informed men in the legislature, will be totally unrepresented.

The representation is unsafe, because in the exercise of such great powers and trusts, it is so exposed to corruption and undue influence, by the gift of the numerous places of honor and emolument, at the disposal of the executive; by the arts and address of the great and designing; and by direct bribery.

The representation is moreover inadequate and unsafe, because of the long terms for which it is appointed, and the mode of its appointment, by which Congress may not only controul the choice of the people, but may so manage as to divest the people of this fundamental right, and become self elected.

The number of members in the house of representatives *may* be encreased to one for every 30,000 inhabitants. But when we consider, that this cannot be done without the consent of the senate, who from their share in the legislative, in the executive, and judicial departments, and permanency of appointment, will be the great efficient body in this government, and whose weight and predominance would be abridged by an increase of the representatives, we are persuaded that this is a circumstance that cannot be expected. On the contrary, the number of representatives will probably be continued at 65, although the population of the country may swell to treble what it now is; unless a revolution should effect a change.

We have before noticed the judicial power as it would effect a consolidation of the states into one government; we will now examine it, as it would affect the liberties and welfare of the people, supposing such a government were practicable and proper.

The judicial power, under the proposed constitution, is founded on the well-known principles of the *civil law*, by which the judge determines both on law and fact, and appeals are allowed from the inferior tribunals to the superior, upon the whole question; so that *facts* as well as *law*, would be re-examined, and even new facts brought forward in the court of appeals and to use the words of a very eminent Civilian—"The cause is many times another thing before the court of appeals, than what it was at the time of the first sentence."

That this mode of proceeding is the one which must be adopted under this constitution, is evident from the following circumstances:—1st. That the trial by jury, which is the grand characteristic of the common law, is secured by the constitution, only in criminal cases.—2d. That the appeal from both *law* and *fact* is expressly established, which is utterly inconsistent with the principles of the common law, and trials by jury. The only mode in which an appeal from law and fact can be established, is, by adopting the principles and practice of the civil law; unless the United States should be drawn into the absurdity of calling and swearing juries, merely for the purpose of contradicting their verdicts, which would render juries contemptible and worse than useless.—3d. That the courts to be established would decide on all cases *of law and equity*, which is a well known characteristic of the civil law, and these courts would have conusance not only of the laws of the United States and of treaties, and of cases affecting ambassadors, but of all cases of *admiralty and maritime jurisdiction*, which last are matters belonging exclusively to the civil law, in every nation in Christendom.

Not to enlarge upon the loss of the invaluable right of trial by an unbiassed jury, so dear to every friend of liberty, the monstrous expence and inconveniences of the mode of proceeding to be adopted, are such as will prove intolerable to the people of this country. The lengthy proceedings of the civil law courts in the chancery of England, and in the courts of Scotland and France, are such that few men of moderate fortune can endure the expence of; the poor man must therefore submit to the wealthy. Length of purse will too often prevail against right and justice. For instance, we are told by the learned judge *Blackstone*, that a question only on the property of an ox[,] of the value of *three* guineas, originating under the civil law proceedings in Scotland, after many interlocutory orders and sentences below, was carried at length from the court of sessions, the highest court in that part of Great Britain, by way of *appeal* to the house of lords, where the question of law and fact was finally determined. He adds, that no pique or spirit could in the court of king's bench or common pleas at Westminster, have given continuance to such a cause for a tenth part of the time, nor have cost a twentieth part of the expence. Yet the costs in the courts of king's bench and common pleas in England, are infinitely greater than those which the people of this country have ever experienced. We abhor the idea of losing the transcendant privilege of trial by jury, with the loss of which, it is remarked by the same learned author, that in Sweden, the liberties of the commons were extinguished by an aristocratic senate; and that *trial by jury* and the liberty of the people went out together. At the same time we regret the intolerable delay, the enormous expences and infinite vexation to which the people of this country will be exposed from the voluminous proceedings of the courts of civil law, and especially from the appellate jurisdiction, by means of which a man may be drawn from the utmost boundaries of this extensive country to the seat of the supreme court of the nation to contend, perhaps with a wealthy and powerful adversary. The consequence of this establishment will be an absolute confirmation of the power of aristocratical influence in the courts of justice; for the common people will not be able to contend or struggle against it.

Trial by jury in criminal cases may also be excluded by declaring that the libeller for instance shall be liable to an action of debt for a specified sum thus evading the common law prosecution by indictment and trial by jury. And the common course of proceeding against a ship for breach of revenue laws by information (which will be classed among civil causes) will at the civil law be within the resort of a court, where no jury intervenes. Besides, the benefit of jury trial, in cases of a criminal nature, which cannot be evaded, will be rendered of little value, by calling the accused to answer far from home; there being no provision that the trial be by a jury of the neighbourhood or country. Thus an inhabitant of Pittsburgh, on a charge of crime committed on the banks of the Ohio, may be obliged to defend himself at the side of the Delaware, and so *vice versa:* To conclude this head: we observe that the judges of the courts of Congress would not be independent, as they are not debarred from holding other offices, during the pleasure of the president and senate, and as they may derive their support in part from fees, alterable by the legislature.

The next consideration that the constitution presents, is the undue and dangerous mixture of the powers of government: the same body possessing legislative, executive, and judicial powers. The senate is a constituent branch of the legislature, it has judicial power in judging on impeachments, and in this case unites in some measure the characters of judge and party as all the principal officers are appointed by the president-general with the concurrence of the senate and therefore they derive their offices in part from the senate. This may biass the judgments of the senators, and tend to screen great delinquents from punishment. And the senate has, moreover, various and great executive powers, viz. in concurrence with the president-general, they form treaties with foreign nations, that may controul and abrogate the constitutions and laws of the several states. Indeed, there is no power, privilege or liberty of the state governments, or of the people, but what may be affected by virtue of this power. For all treaties, made by them, are to be the "supreme law of the land: any thing in the constitution or laws of any state, to the contrary notwithstanding."

And this great power may be exercised by the president and 10 senators (being two thirds of 14, which is a quorum of that body). What an inducement would this offer to the ministers of foreign powers to compass by bribery *such concessions* as could not otherwise be obtained. It is the unvaried usage of all free states, whenever treaties interfere with the positive laws of the land, to make

the intervention of the legislature necessary to give them operation. This became necessary, and was afforded by the parliament
of Great-Britain, in consequence of the late commercial treaty
between that kingdom and France—As the senate judges on
impeachments, who is to try the members of the senate for the
abuse of this power! And none of the great appointments to office
can be made without the consent of the senate.

Such various, extensive, and important powers combined in one
body of men, are inconsistent with all freedom; the celebrated Montesquieu tells us, that "when the legislative and executive powers
are united in the same person, or in the same body of magistrates,
there can be no liberty, because apprehensions may arise, lest the
same monarch or *senate* should enact tyrannical laws, to execute
them in a tyrannical manner."

"Again, there is no liberty, if the power of judging be not separated from the legislative and executive powers. Were it joined
with the legislative, the life and liberty of the subject would be
exposed to arbitrary controul; for the judge would then be legislator. Were it joined to the executive power, the judge might behave
with all the violence of an oppressor. There would be an end of
every thing, were the same man, or the same body of the nobles,
or of the people, to exercise those three powers; that of enacting
laws; that of executing the public resolutions; and that of judging
the crimes or differences of individuals."

The president general is dangerously connected with the senate; his coincidence with the views of the ruling junto in that body,
is made essential to his weight and importance in the government,
which will destroy the independency and purity in the executive
department, and having the power of pardoning without the concurrence of a council, he may skreen from punishment the most
[treasonable] attempts that may be made on the liberties of the
people, when instigated by his enadjutors in the senate. Instead of
this dangerous and improper mixture of the executive with the
legislative and judicial, the supreme executive powers ought to
have been placed in the president, with a small independent council,
made personally responsible for every appointment to office or
other act, by having their opinions recorded; and that without the

concurrence of the majority of the quorum of this council, the president should not be capable of taking any step.

The power of direct taxation applies to every individual, as congress, under this government, is expressly vested with the authority of laying a capitation or poll tax upon every person to any amount. This is a tax that, however oppressive in its nature, and unequal in its operation, is certain as to its produce and simple in its collection; it cannot be evaded like the objects of imposts or excise, and will be paid, because all that a man hath will he give for his head. This tax is so congenial to the nature of despotism, that it has ever been a favorite under such governments. Some of those who were in the late general convention from this state, have long laboured to introduce a poll-tax among us.

The power of direct taxation will further apply to every individual as congress may tax land, cattle, trades, occupations &c. to any amount, and every object of internal taxation is of that nature that however oppressive, the people will have but this alternative, either to pay the tax, or let their property be taken, for all resistance will be vain. The standing army and select militia would enforce the collection.

For the moderate exercise of this power, there is no controul left in the state governments, whose intervention is destroyed. No relief, or redress of grievances can be extended, as heretofore by them. There is not even a declaration of RIGHTS to which the people may appeal for the vindication of their wrongs in the court of justice. They must therefore, implicitly, obey the most arbitrary laws, as the worst of them will be pursuant to the principles and form of the constitution, and that strongest of all checks upon the conduct of administration, *responsibility to the people*, will not exist in this government. The permanency of the appointments of senators and representatives, and the controul the congress have over their election, will place them independent of the sentiments and resentment of the people, and the administration having a greater interest in the government than in the community, there will be no consideration to restrain them from oppression and tyranny. In the government of this state, under the old confederation, the members of the legislature are taken from among the people, and their interests and welfare are so inseparably connected with those of their constituents, that they can derive no advantage from oppressive laws and taxes, for they would suffer in common with their fellow citizens; would participate in the burthens they impose on the community, as they must return to the common level, after a short period; and notwithstanding every exertion of influence, every means of corruption, a necessary rotation excludes them from permanency in the legislature.

This large state is to have but ten members in that Congress which is to have the liberty, property and dearest concerns of every individual in this vast country at absolute command and even these ten persons, who are to be our only guardians; who are to supercede the legislature of Pennsylvania, will not be of the choice of the people, nor amenable to them. From the mode of their election and appointment they will consist of the lordly and high-minded; of men who will have no congenial feelings with the people, but a perfect indifference for, and contempt of them; they will consist of those harpies of power, that prey upon the very vitals; that riot on the miseries of the community. But we will suppose, although in all probability it may never be realized in fact, that our deputies in Congress have the welfare of their constituents at heart, and will exert themselves in their behalf, what security could even this afford; what relief could they extend to their oppressed constituents? To attain this, the majority of the deputies of the twelve other states in Congress must be alike well disposed; must alike forego the sweets of power, and relinquish the pursuits of ambition which from the nature of things is not to be expected. If the people part with a responsible representation in the legislature, founded upon fair, certain and frequent elections, they have nothing left they can call their own. Miserable is the lot of that people whose every concern depends on the WILL and PLEASURE of their rulers. Our soldiers will become Janissaries, and our officers of government Bashaws; in short, the system of despotism will soon be compleated.

From the foregoing investigation, it appears that the Congress under this constitution will not possess the confidence of the people, which is an essential requisite in a good government; for unless the laws command the confidence and respect of the great body of the people so as to induce them to support them, when called on by the civil magistrate they must be executed by the aid of a numerous standing army, which would be inconsistent with every idea of liberty; for the same force that may be employed to compel obedience to good laws, might and probably would be used to wrest from the people their constitutional liberties. The framers of this constitution appear to have been aware of this great deficiency; to have been sensible that no dependence could be placed on the people for their support; but on the contrary, that the government must be executed by force. They have therefore made a provision for this purpose in a permanent STANDING ARMY, and a MILITIA that may be subjected to as strict discipline and government.

A standing army in the hands of a government placed so independent of the people, may be made a fatal instrument to overturn the public liberties; it may be employed to enforce the collection of the most oppressive taxes, and to carry into execution the most arbitrary measures. An ambitious man who may have the army at his devotion, may step up into the throne, and seize upon absolute power.

The absolute unqualified command that Congress have over the militia may be made instrumental to the destruction of all liberty, both public and private; whether of a personal, civil or religious nature.

First, the personal liberty of every man probably from sixteen to sixty years of age, may be destroyed by the power Congress have in organizing and governing of the militia. As militia they may be subjected to fines to any amount, levied in a military manner; they may be subjected to corporal punishments of the most disgraceful and humiliating kind, and to death itself, by the sentence of a court martial: To this our young men will be more immediately subjected, as a select militia, composed of them, will best answer the purposes of government.

Secondly, The rights of conscience may be violated, as there is no exemption of those persons who are conscientiously scrupulous of bearing arms. These compose a respectable proportion of the community in the state. This is the more remarkable, because even when the distresses of the late war, and the evident disaffection of many citizens of that description, inflamed our passions, and when every person, who was obliged to risque his own life, must have been exasperated against such as on any account kept back from the common danger, yet even then, when outrage and violence might have been expected, the rights of conscience were held sacred.

At this momentous crisis, the framers of our state constitution made the most express and decided declaration and stipulations in favour of the rights of conscience; but now when no necessity exists, those dearest rights of men are left insecure.

Thirdly, The absolute command of Congress over the militia may be destructive of public liberty; for under the guidance of an arbitrary government, they may be made the unwilling instruments of tyranny. The militia of Pennsylvania may be marched to New England or Virginia to quell an insurrection occasioned by the most galling oppression, and aided by the standing army, they will no doubt be successful in subduing their liberty and independency; but in so doing, although the magnanimity of their minds will be extinguished, yet the meaner passions of resentment and revenge will be increased, and these in turn will be the ready and obedient instruments of despotism to enslave the others; and that with an irritated vengeance. Thus, may the militia be made the instruments of crushing the last efforts of expiring liberty, of riveting the chains of despotism on their fellow citizens, and on one another. This power can be exercised not only without violating the constitution but in strict conformity with it; it is calculated for this express purpose, and will doubtless be executed accordingly.

As this government will not enjoy the confidence of the people, but be executed by force, it will be a very expensive and burthensome government. The standing army must be numerous, and as a further support, it will be the policy of this government to multiply officers in every department; judges, collectors, tax gatherers, excisemen and the whole host of revenue officers will swarm over the land, devouring the hard earnings of the industrious. Like the locusts of old, impoverishing and defolating all before them.

We have not noticed the smaller, nor many of the considerable blemishes, but have confined our objections to the great and essential defects; the main pillars of the constitution; which we have shewn to be inconsistent with the liberty and happiness of the people, as its establishment will annihilate the state governments, and produce one consolidated government, that will eventually and speedily issue in the supremacy of despotism.

In this investigation, we have not confined our views to the interests or welfare of this state, in preference to the others. We have overlooked all local circumstances—we have considered this subject on the broad scale of the general good: we have asserted the cause of the present and future ages; the cause of liberty and mankind.

Nathaniel Breading
John Smilie
Richard Baird
Adam Orth
John A. Hanna
John Whitehill
John Harris
Robert Whitehill
John Reynolds
Jonathan Hoge
Nicholas Lutz

John Ludwig
Abraham Lincoln
John Bishop
Joseph Heister
Joseph Powel
James Martin
William Findley
John Baird
James Edgar
William Todd.

The yeas and nays upon the final vote were as follows, viz.

YEAS.
George Latimer
Benjamin Rush
Hilary Baker
James Wilson
Thomas McKean
William McPherson
John Hunn
George Gray
Samuel Ashmead

YEAS.
John Hubley
Jasper Yates
Henry Stagle
Thomas Campbell
Thomas Hartley
David Grier
John Black
Benjamin Pedan
John Arndt

Continued on next page

Continued from previous page

YEAS.

Enoch Edwards
Henry Wynkoop
John Barclay
Thomas Yardley
Abraham Stout
Thomas Bull
Anthony Wayne
William Gibbons
Richard Downing
Thomas Cheyney
John Hannum
Stephen Chambers
Robert Coleman
Sebastian Grass

YEAS.

Stephen Balliott
Joseph Horsefield
David Deshler
William Wilson
John Boyd
Thomas Scott
John Nevill
John Allison
Jonathan Roberts
John Richards
F. A. Muhlenberg
James Morris
Timothy Pickering
Benjamin Elliot

NAYS.

John Whitehill
John Harris
John Reynolds
Robert Whitehill
Jonathan Hoge
Nicholas Lutz
John Ludwig
Abraham Lincoln
John Bishop
Joseph Heister
James Martin
Joseph Powell

NAYS.

William Findley
John Baird
William Todd
James Marshall
James Edgar
Nathaniel Breading
John Smilie
Richard Baird
William Brown
Adam Orth
John Andre Hannah

Philadelphia, Dec. 12, 1787.

Essays by a [Maryland] Farmer

Essays by a Farmer first appeared in the Baltimore Maryland
Gazette *between February and April 1788. Scholars currently
point to John Francis Mercer, a dissenting member of the Constitutional Convention, as the probable author. Emphasizing many
common Anti-Federalist themes, including the objective status and
historical British recognition of natural rights, this farmer strikes
a radical, rationalist note sounded by only a minority of the Constitution's opponents. His references to religion, and to Catholic
Christianity in particular, show a determination to blame political
tyranny on religious belief. His calls for bills of rights seem in
conflict with his demand for direct rule by local landowners. These
essays stop abruptly in the Storing edition but are presented here
in their entirety.*

Maryland Gazette

15 FEBRUARY 1788

ESSAY I

*The Farmer begins by criticizing federalist pamphleteer Aristides
for doubting the need for a bill of rights. The Farmer refers to the
British Glorious Revolution of 1688 as proof that rights are natural
and not merely gifts from the rulers. Important documents like
the English Bill of Rights merely affirm the social compact granting certain powers to the government in exchange for protection of
essential, reserved rights. These rights require increased protection*

*in democratic countries because of the powers majorities can wield in
them. Essay in* The Federalist *of particular relevance: 84.*

WHEN men, to whom the guardianship of public liberty has been
committed, discover a neglect if not contempt for a bill of rights—
when they answer reasons by alledging a fact,—which fact too, is no
fact at all—it becomes a duty to bear testimony against such conduct, for silence and acquiescence in political language are synoni-
mous terms.

If men were as anxious about reality as appearance, we should
have fewer professions of disinterested patriotism—true patriotism
like true piety, is incompatible with an ostentatious personal display.

In a world more cautious than correct, the intrusion of private
names in a public cause, is generally considered as a sacrifice of prudence to vanity, and not unfrequently censured as impertinent—in
either view it is unreasonable to require it—It is more, it is inad-
missible—it would be betraying one of those inestimable rights of
an individual, over which society should have no controul—the freedom of the press—and the only recompence for the treason, would
be a boundless increase of private malice.

That men who profess an attachment to the liberty of the press,
should also require names, is one of those instances of human weakness and inconsistency, that deserves rather pity than resentment.
Political as well as religious freedom has ever been and forever
will be destroyed by that invariable tendency of enthusiasts and
bigots to mark out as objects of public resentment and persecution, those who presume to dispute their opinions or question their
infallibility—and whilst there are men, enthusiasm and bigotry will
prevail—it is the natural predominance of the passions over reason—The citizens of America are not yet so agitated by the phrenzy
of innovation as to forget—that the object of public inquiry is, or
ought to be, *truth*—that to convert *truth* into *falsehood, right* into
wrong, is equally beyond the reach of the *good*, the *bad*, the *great*
and the *humble*—A great name may indeed *impose falsehood* for
truth—*wrong* for *right*—and whenever such voluntarily offer themselves, there may be ground for suspicion—But the people may lis-

ten with safety to those, who assert no other claim to their attention, than the *reason* and *merit* of their remarks.

To assert that bills of rights have always originated from, or been considered as grants of the King or Prince, and that the liberties which they secure are the gracious concessions of the sovereign, betrays an equal ignorance of history and of law, or what in effect amounts to the same thing a violent and precipitate zeal.

I believe no writer in the most venal age, has ever openly asserted this doctrine, but the prostituted, rotten Sir Robert Filmer, and Aristides—And the man who at this day would contend in England that their bill of rights is the grant of the King, would find the general contempt his only security—In saying this, I sincerely regret that the name of Aristides should be joined with that of Sir Robert Filmer, and I freely acknowledge that no contemptible degree of talents, and integrity render him who uses it, much more worthy of the very respectable association he has selected for himself—But the errors of such men alone are dangerous—the man who has too much activity of mind, or restlessness to be quiet, qualities to engage public and private esteem, talents to form and support an opinion, fortitude to avow it, and too much pride to be convinced, will at all times have weight in a free country, (especially where indolence is the general characteristic) though that weight he will always find impaired in proportion as he indulges levity, caprice and passion.

I will confine my inquiry to the English constitution—Example *there,* is in a great measure law *here*—and the authority of an American judge on a point of English law, should be digested with coolness and promulgated with caution, because it is frequently conclusory.

The celebrated and only bill of rights of Great-Britain, which is considered as the supreme law of the land, and not to be questioned or impeached in their courts, was the work of that convention of lords and commons in 1688, which declared that *King James 2d, had abdicated the crown, and that the throne had thereby become vacant,* and who after they had compleated and asserted this glorious declaration of the unalienable rights of their fellow citizens, pursuing the peculiar duty of a convention, conferred the crown of the three kingdoms on an alien and foreigner, William the 3d.

Can any man imagine that this convention could at that time, have considered these rights as the grant of a King, whom they previously declared to have abdicated the throne, or the gracious concessions of a Prince whom they were about to deprive forever of the crown? Or could they have considered this bill of rights as the concession of Prince William, at that time a foreigner and alien, not entitled to hold a foot of land, or any of the common rights of citizenship, and who could afterwards only derive his title to the crown from the same source, which gave authority and sanction to this fundamental and most inestimable law? or, could the British nation at that time, or ever since, have viewed this declaration, as the grant and concession of a King or Prince, when no King or Prince was at that time in existence?—But should there remain any minds yet unsatisfied, I refer such to the debates of that convention, which are preserved in Grey's debates in parliament, and there will be found in them, the principles of equal liberty, the inherent and unalienable rights of men, as amply and ably discussed, and as fully recognized by the authors of that blessing, the artists of that British palladium, as ever they have since been by the animated patriots of America, or the present age.—I also refer them to an inestimable little treatise composed on this occasion by that accomplished lawyer and patriot, afterwards the Lord Somers—High Chancellor of Great-Britain—then a member of the convention, and chiefly instrumental in their great work—a pamphlet that should find a place in the library of every American judge at least—Whoever peruses these, will discover undeniable evidence, that the British convention, considered this their declaration, as the concession of no Prince, but the Prince of Heaven—whom alone they acknowledged as the author of their liberties—they will there find that a bill of rights, is an enumeration of those conditions on which the individuals of the empire agreed to confirm the social compact; and consequently that no power, which they thus conditionally delegated to the majority (in whatever form organized) should be so exercised as to infringe and impair these their natural rights—not vested in SOCIETY, but reserved to each member thereof.

This was not the doctrine of that period alone—it was the common law and constitution of England, so asserted and maintained by the ablest lawyers of every age of the empire.—The petition of right, which came forward in the reign of Charles 1st, said to have been originally penned by the celebrated Lord Coke—although in its title a contradiction in terms, is yet in substance equally strong and clear—asserting the rights of the people to be coeval with the government—We find this principle strenuously and ably maintained through all the works of this great man, and to this doctrine he finally, with the devotion of a freeman, and the fortitude of an Englishman, sacrificed his vanity, his ambition and his avarice— This last act of an aged and venerable judge, has obliterated the errors of a youthful courtier—it has made his peace with posterity, who with gratitude and indulgence has forgiven the conduct of a court lawyer, which she might have punished with detestation, although she could not correct.

Here I cannot but observe what strenuous bill of rights men, all the great luminaries of the English law have been: to Lord Coke and Lord Somers, I will add that ornament of human nature, Sir Matthew Hale, in whom were united true Christian piety, Roman fortitude, and an understanding more than human.

This perfect man although firmly opposed to the violences of the mad fanatics of the age, stood up almost alone in that parliament which restored the regal government, in favor of a bill of rights— but the tide of popular rage, hastening to place the worthless Charles on the throne of his more worthless ancestors, was too strong, and the voice of that man could not be heard, who was the delight of his own and the admiration of succeeding ages.

It is true, that something like the doctrine of Aristides was frequently the language of courtiers and sycophants in the feeble reigns of the arbitrary Stuarts—times of impotent and impudent usurpation—and they grounded their assertions on the form of the statute of magna charta, a statute much estemed for the many valuable rights it ascertains—the enacting words of which imply it to be an act of the King—But Aristides must know that this was the frequent form of the ancient statutes, sometime it is the King alone enacts, sometime the King with advice and consent of the great men and Barons, and sometimes the three estates—Even at this day, the King uses these words in passing laws that bear the same implication; and we see even in America acts of authority issue under the name and signature of the Governor alone, who has not a voice unless the council are divided—But as to the legal and acknowledged authority of the King at the time of enacting magna charta, there can remain but little doubt. Henry Bracton a contemporary lawyer and judge, who has left us a compleat and able treatise on the laws of England, is thus clear and express—*Omnes quidem sub rege, ipse autem sublege*, all are subject to the King, but the King is subject to the law—it will hardly then be imagined, that the supreme law and constitution were the grants and concessions of a Prince, who was thus in theory and practice, subject himself to ordinary acts of legislation—But all these things are so amply discussed and the authorities so accurately collected in the publication of my Lord Somers, that a reference must be much more satisfactory than a repetition.

If I understand Aristides, he says that it would have been considered as an arrogant usurpation of sovereign rights in the members of convention, to have affixed a bill of rights—Can he reconcile this position with another opinion in his remarks, where he maintains that in offering this constitution, they could only act as private individuals, any of whom have a right to propose a constitution to the Americans to adopt at their discretion—In this view they could only have proposed—it is certain they could not have enacted a bill of rights—Nor would there have been any usurpation in *We the people, of the States of New-Hampshire, Massachusetts &c. securing to ourselves and our posterity the following [unalienable] rights &c.* which is the stile of the new constitution—The convention have actually engrafted some of these natural rights, yet no one calls it an usurpation—nor can I believe that any of my fellow-citizens of the United States, would have discovered the least indignation, had they engrafted them all—The universal complaint has been that they have enumerated so few—But says Aristides, it would have been a work of great difficulty, if not impossible to have ascertained them—Are the fundamental rights of mankind at this day unknown? Are they so soon forgot? If they are not imprinted on our hearts, they are in several of the constitutions—Although various in form, they are certainly not contradictory in substance—It did not require the wisdom of a national convention to have reduced them into order, and such as would not have gained the [suffrage] of a majority, would never have been regretted by America—or, I will venture to assert, what I shall never believe, that the majority were very unworthy of the truth reposed in them—Nor yet can I believe, that the late convention were incompetent to a task that has never been undertaken in the separate States without success.

This constitution is to be the act of the individual members of the American empire—the highest source of terrestial power with us—As it is a subsequent act, it not only repeals all prior acts of the same authority where it interferes with them—But being a government of the people of all the States, I do not know what right the citizens of Maryland for instance, have to expect that the citizens of Connecticut or New-Jersey, will be governed by the laws or constitution of Maryland—or what benefit a citizen of Maryland could derive from his bill of rights in a court of the United States, which can only be governed by the constitution and laws of the United States—Nor will it help the question to say, what will certainly be denied, that the future Congress may provide by law for this,—that an ordinary law of the United States can make, is an admission that it can unmake, and to submit the bills of rights of the separate States to the power of every annual national parliment, is a very uncertain tenure indeed.

If a citizen of Maryland can have no benefit of his own bill of rights in the confederal courts, and there is no bill of rights of the United States—how could he take advantage of a natural right founded in reason, could he plead it and produce Locke, Sydney, or Montesquieu as authority? How could he take advantage of any of the common law rights, which have heretofore been considered as the birthright of Englishmen and their descendants, could he plead them and produce the authority of the English judges in his support? Unquestionably not, for the authority of the common law arises from the express adoption by the several States in their respective constitutions, and that in various degrees and under different modifications—If admitted at all, I do not see to what

extent, and if admitted, it must be admitted as unalterable by ordinary acts of legislation; which would be impossible—and it could
never be of use to an individual, but in combating some national law
infringing natural right.—To render this more intelligible—suppose for instance, that an officer of the United States should force
the house, the asylum of a citizen, by virtue of a general warrant, I
would ask, are general warrants illegal by the constitution of the
United States? Would a court, or even a jury, but juries are no
longer to exist, punish a man who acted by express authority, upon
the bare recollection of what once was law and right? I fear not,
especially in those cases which may strongly interest the passions
of government, and in such only have general warrants been used—
Suppose a case that must and will frequently happen, for such happen almost daily in England—That an officer of the customs should
break open the dwelling, and violate the sanctuary of a freeman, in
search for smuggled goods—impost and revenue laws always are
and from necessity must be in their nature oppressive—in their
execution they may and will become intolerable to a free people,
no remedy has been yet found equal to the task of detering and
curbing the insolence of office, but a jury—It has become an invariable maxim of English juries, to give ruinous damages whenever an
officer has deviated from the rigid letter of the law, or been guilty of
any unnecessary act of insolence or oppression—It is true these
damages to the individual, are frequently paid by government,
upon a certificate of the judge that there was probable cause of suspicion—But the same reasons that would induce an English judge
to give this certificate, would probably lead an American judge,
who will be judge and jury too, to spare the public purse, if not
favour a brother officer.

I could proceed with an enumeration of familiar instances that
must and will happen, that would be as alarming as prolix; but it is
not my intention to ring an alarm bell—If I know myself I would
rather conciliate than divide—But says Aristides the government
may establish [juries] for such [cases], though not commanded;
what they will do I will not presume to say; but I can readily and
will hereafter prove that if they do, they will violate the constitu-

tion; and even admitting their power, it would be but a slender thread to [hang] so great a stake upon.

Here I must meet a position that has been ingeniously advanced—That all powers and rights not expressly given, [are] consequently reserved—If this is not downright political nonsense, it is at least, untrue in theory and impossible in practice—until man is gifted with one of the most important attributes of the Deity—that of foreknowledge and prophecy—it will be impossible to limit *affirmatively* legislative power.—When a people part with the legislative power to government, they can no more say, you shall make such and such laws than they can say, such and such events shall happen—law must be regulated by events—All the precaution that is left to human wisdom, is the exertion of a *negative limitation* speaking thus in the language of a bill of rights, no event shall authorize, no plea of necessity shall justify the legislature in making a law to abolish or infringe the freedom of the press, or the liberty of conscience, &c.—And even when these bounds are expressly and clearly assigned, we have to lament that they do not always prove an effectual safeguard against the power of government; but they are the only guard, and why shall we leave our citizens totally defenceless. A gentleman in the Pennsylvania convention, of considerable reputation, said that one form of the constitution—the organization of power, is a bill of rights—he had then a [very sensible], but unformed idea floating in his imagination, [he] however, expressed it inaccurately, and unfortunately [got] on the wrong side of his own question. A proper organization of power would most probably prevent a violation of a bill of rights and prove the best security of political liberty. Such an organization is nothing more than a good machine. A mint or die, that will make money in its proper form, but the quantity of alloy must be regulated by law, or the people may be cheated by a debased currency—The truth is, that the rights of individuals are frequently opposed to the apparent interests of the majority—For this reason the greater the portion of political freedom in a form of government the greater the necessity of a bill of rights—When the natural rights of an individual are opposed to the decided interests or heated passions of a large majority of a democratic government; if these rights are not clearly and expressly ascertained, the individual must be lost; and for the truth of this I appeal to every man who has borne a part in the legislative council of America. In such governments the tyranny of the legislative is most to be dreaded.—In monarchical governments, the feelings of the majority will be most frequently on the side of the individual from the general jealousy inseperably attendant on those forms of government, where the tyranny of the executive prevails. [All] tyranny whether exercised in the garb of a despot, or the plain coat of a quaker, is equally detestable, and should be guarded against.

If a bill of rights was that essential requisite to a good constitution, why was it omitted by a convention of the ablest men in America, a large majority of whom were unquestionably well disposed? This has been a natural inquiry, and perhaps the true reason yet remains to be disclosed. I have been informed that the proposed constitution was carried through its several stages, in a very inoffensive form to the last, and that it did not assume its decided features until the days before the convention rose—the changes then effected produced much difference of opinion—created some warmth and their patience was too much exhausted to make the necessary correspondent alterations and additions. These [same] may, I believe, be depended on, but the inference is [one] offered as conjecture—if true, we may attribute the omission of a bill of rights, and many other imperfections to fatigue rather than design.

From the foregoing observations, many will conclude that I am the determined foe to the new constitution—I am neither its concealed or open enemy—Sorry I am to say that [I] cannot in its present state be its advocate or friend—That it is as far preferable to the present existing confederation (considered as a national government) as substance is preferable to form, is a truth I have as little doubt of, as of its very numerous defects.—The true and only question is, whether any national government whatever, ought to be prefered to a league or confederacy administered by a diet, or congress of diplomatic deputies—And this is a question that will continue to divide the ablest and best men in America—the misfortune is, that experience alone will decide a doubt which perhaps no theory is competent to solve—But that the proposed confederal constitution, cannot be considered as such a diplomatic assembly must appear to all men—It is a national government, and a league between independent States compounded—One of those mixtures of heterogeneous qualities that will forever produce a neutral—a caput [mortuum] —consequently the present Congress is already found to be, but the carcase of a government, and a rotten carcase too.—The momentous subject has led me farther than I intended— My remarks will discover the hurry in which they were written— Had I leisure I would censure freely those [defects] in the proposed system, that must be amended, for [I] have strong doubts whether it can be administered in its present form—In doing this I should, I am persuaded, convince the public that Aristides has generally erred and frequently mistated in his remarks—that he has done so intentionally [I] neither believe myself or would wish the public to believe—to err is the common portion of humanity—and to be misinformed the frequent misfortune of ARISTIDES and

A FARMER.

Maryland Gazette

29 FEBRUARY 1788

ESSAY II

The Farmer again criticizes Aristides's doubts concerning the need for a bill of rights. This time the Farmer argues that representation will not check those wielding federal power. In fact, he argues, representation is inherently aristocratic and will benefit the rich in their conflicts with the poor. In addition, provisions for a standing arming will overwhelm state militias, which alone can defend liberty and which, by fostering republican zeal, are the most effective means of common defense. Essays in The Federalist *of particular relevance: 10, 24, 25, 28, 29, 56, 57, 84.*

A BILL of rights is an useless, if not a dangerous thing; and a standing army, a bugbear, an hobgoblin to freighten children.—This seems to me the doctrine of *Aristides*, and the common language abroad.—What amazing progress in political knowledge have the Americans made in the last ten years! Should they go on improving by such laudable and rapid discoveries, what may we not expect in the course of a few years to come! Nothing less, surely, than a demonstration, that liberty is a visionary phantom, fleeting forever from our embrace—never intended for the possession of mankind, and never existing but in the enthusiastic imaginations of some illustrious madmen.

We talk now with the utmost confidence of our own experience, and an appeal to the history of mankind, is considered as an insult on the sagacity and understanding, of THE CHOICE AND MASTER SPIRITS OF THIS AGE.—

That we are the wisest people under the sun, seems to be no longer disputed, and those whose youthful vanity has been flattered, by a transient public applause, think that because they have come later into the world, they have therefore all the wisdom and experience, of those who have gone before them—This is the opinion of the Americans now.—Machiavelli informs us, that it was the firm persuasion of the Florentines, his countrymen, in his day, and Peter Kolben relates the same thing of the Hottentots when he was amongst them—perhaps the greatest share of confidence is inseperably united with the greatest share of ignorance.

Notwithstanding all this, human nature has always been, and always will continue the same, and so long will it be impossible to put *old* heads upon *young* shoulders.—It is as unnatural to be guided by the experience of others, as for one man to see with another's eyes. This fatal and unalterable law of nature, is founded not less on our presumption and confidence, than on a persuasion, which the young and unexperienced always feel, that there is some peculiar circumstance, that distinguishes their own particular case, from that which a father describes to a son, or an historian to posterity.—Where our vanity is not strong enough to despise, inclination will invent an excuse to avoid the lessons of experience; and where the passions do not entirely command, they are sure to blind the understanding.

Is there one branch of science, literary knowledge, or even art, pleasing or useful to an individual, or society, that has received any improvement from the earliest records of time?—Homer, Theocritus, Pindar and Sophocles are yet unrivalled in poetry.—Thucydides, Polybius and Livy surpass all who have followed them in history.—Demosthenes and Cicero in eloquence.—Socrates, Plato and Plutarch in those moral lessons which form the human heart to virtue.—We penetrate into Grecian forests, and dive into the Tyber to refuse the relics of ancient architecture, painting, sculpture and statuary; and preserve them as the most precious and perfect models of art.—Although, perhaps, gunpowder was unknown, yet they contrived to slaughter men enough without it, and the invention has only put the cowardice of a dastardly slave in uniform, more on a level with the manly exertions of an undisciplined freeman.—The invention of printing, the most important of all modern discoveries, has rather multiplied books than increased knowledge; nor has the discovery of an eighth planet brought with it any remedy for the inclemencies of a cold winter.—Our acquaintance with the skies is as useless as balloons. There is nothing solid or useful that is new—And I will venture to assert, that if every *political institution* is not fully explained by Aristotle, and other ancient writers, yet that, there is no *new* discovery in this the most important of all sciences, for ten centuries back.

Our politicians of an hour, of an empire of a day, boast of government *by representation*, as a most important improvement; and whilst they discant on its excellencies they do not scruple to assert, that it was unknown to the ancients*.—Some, indeed, have confined it to the British and their descendants.

* *Is it not strange to hear the Governor of Connecticut, gravely asserting in their Convention, the novelty of government by representation, and pinning all his hopes of our future happiness, and exemption from evil on this new discovery. And yet the Governor of Connecticut is not only one of the worthiest of our citizens, but rather of uncommon information in a country, where very few are so independent in their fortunes as to afford much time to study.*

Government, by representatives, freely chosen by the body of the people, is as old as the history of mankind, and once formed the basis of every European government now existing; but as it is the most liable to corruption, it has always proved of the shortest duration; it has first degenerated into aristocracy, or the government of a few wealthy individuals, and has terminated regularly by a monarchy and standing army.—The reasoning on this progress is not essential at this moment, but as to the antiquity of government by representation, example must be produced to expose an error as general as it is surprizing.

The first legal government of Athens, the most ancient we have any authentic history of, was by Archons elected by the body of the people, first for one and then for five years. Solon divided the legislative from the executive, as we have done, although not exactly in the same form.—This government lasted a very few years, and was destroyed by Pisistratus, assisted by a small standing force.—The examples drawn from several modern governments of Europe will be presently adduced.—

But before this, it is essential that we examine what is meant by *monarchy* and *aristocracy:*—Unhappily for mankind frequent and ridiculous dispute is the least inconvenience arising from the imperfection of language.—Ambiguity and uncertainty of expression admit the imposition of dangerous doctrine, and produce more misfortune than error—Because in the government, from which we separated, the monarchy and aristocracy were attended with certain hereditary names and titles, we are to be compelled to view the *substance* of those powers as inseperable from those *forms* and *titles.*

Formerly the public authority exercised by one person, whether dignified with the title of Emperor, King, Stadtholder, Doge, &c. was elective, and generally revocable—as for instance, the ancient Emperors of Rome; the Emperors of Germany; the Emperor of Russia; the Kings of Denmark and Sweden; the Stadtholder of Holland; Doge of Genoa, &c.—They were seldom entrusted with any *legislative* power.—These various offices and titles, have all become hereditary, and have generally swallowed up the legislative power; except the Doge, who is only the pageant of the day, decorated with the tinsel trappings of authority, but not entrusted with the most trifling portion of its substance. Three great families have established an *hereditary despotism* over three-fourths of the habitable globe.—The house of HOLSTEIN, who now govern Sweden, Denmark, Norway, Russia, great part of Poland, Germany, and the greatest part of Asia, within two centuries has sprung from a gentleman of less fortune than many Americans now possess.—The house of AUSTRIA, who have usurped the Imperial office of Germany, as a patrimony, and govern a great proportion of Europe, are derived, within a few centuries back, from a poor Count of Hapsburg without fortune or honor—And the mighty race of BOURBON, who possess France, Spain, the two Sicilies, two-thirds of America, and extensive dominions in Asia and Africa, sprung not long since from Hugh Capel, who, if he was not the son of a butcher (as is generally believed) was certainly of very low extraction.— There is not a kingdom in Europe, that does not contain many better families than these,—that is families, that have been longer people of property, and produced more illustrious men; but they are all involved in one common fate, reduced to a despicable slavery by these individuals, whose usurpations have been as successful as rapid, and who hold them in trembling subjection by numerous standing armies.—This is the history of MONARCHY divested of its glitter and pomp.

Where *wealth* is hereditary, *power* is hereditary, for *wealth* is power.—Titles are of very little, or no consequence.—The *rich* are *nobility*, and the *poor plebeans* in all countries.—And on this distinction alone, the true definition of *aristocracy* depends.—An aristocracy is that influence of power, which property may have in government; a *democracy* is the power or influence of the people or numbers, as contradistinguished from property. Machiavelli exposes the futility of an attempt to establish an aristocracy, upon any other principles than the solid distinction of property.—In examining the principles of those aristocracies that now exist, we shall find hereditary wealth the only universally pervading principle and characteristic.

In *England* the aristocracy have hereditary titles, and share in the legislature.—It is preserved by the power of the King to add the most wealthy and able of the commons to this order;—and if that principle, by which George Neville, Duke of Bedford, was degraded from his nobility on account of his poverty, still continued, it would be the most perfect and confirmed aristocracy in the world.—Although this aristocracy is extremely powerful, yet from the happy temperature of the government, by three well consti- tuted estates, it has not proved oppressive: on the contrary, a firm rock, that has preserved this system from every shock of innova- tion.—Were the other two estates even as perfect as the aristoc- racy, the government might last forever.

In *Scotland*, the aristocracy have hereditary titles, but they are almost entirely deprived of any share in the legislature, and their power is much broken by the axe and confiscation.

In *Holland*, the aristocracy is composed of the wealthiest.—They hold their power for life most commonly, though in some instances for a limited time;—and elections are generally, though by no means universally abolished. Their estates are hereditary, but they have no titles.—Such is the aristocracy of America, yet in its infancy, and that of the aristocratic Cantons of Switzerland,—and they are all the most odious, oppressive and abominable aristocratics in the world;—for as their power is exclusively derived from wealth, which is more frequently the reward of iniquity and oppression than merit,—iniquity and oppression will be therefore openly and without shame practised to secure that wealth, which attended by power, defends its possessor from punishment.

In *France* and *Spain*, the aristocracies are decorated with titles, but have no share in the legislature, yet still they are almost as powerful as the former, from their wealth;—but not so oppres- sive.—This wealth they hold by those fundamental laws which secure the descent of property from ancestors to heirs, on the preservation of which the King's safety, in a great measure, depends.—In fine, in all governments by *representation* or *delega- tion of power*, where property is secured by fixed and permanent laws, from the rage of the populace on one side, and the tyranny of a despot on the other, the aristocracy will and must rule; that is a number of the wealthiest individuals, and the heads of great families:—The perfection of all political wisdom is so to temper this aristocracy as to prevent oppression.

Between these two powers, the aristocracy and democracy, that is the *rich* and *poor*, there is a constant warfare.—Sir William Temple observes, that all the disputes, factions and revolutions in government spring from this source,—that the rich want to keep what they have got, and the poor to take it from them;—this is the favourable side of aristocracy, and is true where numbers unqualified by property have too great a weight in government.—Hence in such States, agrarian laws, and an abolition of debts, are always agitated; but this is only the infancy of government.—So long as the rich, only mean honestly to secure what they have lawfully gained, by their own or the industry of their ancestors, the contest is of short duration, and government, at an early period is so far strengthened as to secure property; but it is then, that the corruption of human nature discovers itself—the more we have, this more we want, and the possession of one object, becomes only the means of attaining another.—The aristocracy who move by system and design, and always under the colourable pretext of securing property, act as has been frequently said like the screw in mechanics, always gaining, holding fast what it gains, and never loosing; and in the event has ever proved an overmatch for the multitude, who never act but from their feelings, and are never permitted to feel *until it is too late*; and whose ineffectual violence, being generally attended by the outrages of despair, involves their cause in odium and horror. Hence it is that unsuccessful popular insurrections have always been succeeded by a general disposition favourable to tyranny. A great and good man has said, that an aristocracy in their progress to power is the most correct of all governments—after they have attained it, the most corrupt and abominable on earth.— The honest emoluments of office, are too few to gratify the many, who must be interested in administration in order to render it effectual,—they first connive at each other,—bad laws are made,—the good are perverted and avoided,—in fine, oppression becomes general, and the multitude in a paroxism of despair generally conclude, that it is better to suffer the tyranny of one man, than one hundred.

The only remedy the ingenuity of man has discovered for this evil is—*a properly constituted and independent executive,*—a vindex injuriarum—an avenger of public wrongs; who with the assistance of a third estate, may enforce the rigor of equal law on those who are otherwise above the fear of punishment; and who may expose to public view and inquiry, those who screen their peculations under the sanction of office:—How well the new proposed federal or national government, for it is a government of individuals, not of States, has provided for this great end of all government, by uniting the executive with the aristocracy, or senate, tempting the aristocracy with every executive power that can rouse or stimulate their ambition,—and how the executive will be enabled to discharge its duty against those, without whose consent it cannot act, I leave to the sensible and discerning part of my fellow-citizens. A senate should not only be composed of men of ripe age, where the violent passions have quitted the mental field, overcome by the vigor of judgment, but its chief perfection consists in such organization, that content with more than independence and a very respectable situation, they should be cut off from the active exercise of those powers which gratify personal ambition and tend to self aggrandizement or that of their friends, relatives and dependants:—That this feature of the constitution—that this union of the senate and executive will prove fatal to the liberty and happiness of America, unless corrected, I cannot doubt;—as I shall adduce examples of the same form of government, only not quite so bad as ours, terminating in despotism and a standing army, almost as soon as established.—For once let mankind listen to the counsel of experience:—This form of government is not new, it is the same form as that established in Denmark and Sweden, previous to the late revolutions, and exactly such a form as a number of wealthy and well disposed individuals, deliberately set to work, have made, and forever will make, in every age and every clime.—These examples will shew that ruin comes from a quarter entirely unexpected— they will, I hope, entirely disperse the delusion which now misleads our judgments, when we hug ourselves to the security, that we cannot be betrayed by representatives chosen every two years;—let every man, of any property, who has been active in the late revolution, and who is tolerably apprized of the sentiments of the people at large, scrutinize his own judgment; and let him ask himself whether in even the present disposition of the lower orders of our citizens, who bear with great impatience and reluctance their present inconveniences and incumberances, and those trifling distinctions and [pre-eminences,] which our present disinterested forms of government afford so trifling, that offices almost go a begging,—if in the event of the proposed plan the burthens of government should be encreased, greater distinctions among citizens arise, and emoluments of [office] be augmented—Will not the multitude croud with joy to the standard erected by any man in whom they have the least confidence, who will promise them vengeance on those whom they will consider as the authors of all their misfortunes, and to rid them at once of the evils of complicated government and numerous officers, whom they always think they pay, only to plunder them?

To attempt to form a government composed simply of aristocracy and democracy—where rich and poor are jointly to govern—is long of yore represented in the fable of the league between the wolves and sheep—The sheep were soon compelled to recall the shepherd and his dogs.—

But let us here for a moment return to *Aristides*.—He asks, what European power is without a standing army? and which has lost its liberties by them? Many of his remarks betray a misrecollection of the A, B, C, of politics, and some of the historical questions discover a total absence of memory.—It may be answered, that both political and civil liberty have long since ceased to exist in almost all the countries that now employ standing troops, and that their slavery has in every instance been effected and maintained by the instrumentality and invariable obedience of these living machines to their chief.—I grant that the discontent of the people under the oppressions of a complicated aristocratical government has always paved the way to the despotism of one man;—the progress is natural, troops must be raised in such circumstances to compel an unwilling obedience to the laws—these troops must not be part of the discontented—they cannot be trusted—they must not feel like them, and must therefore have separate interests—

they must be paid and well paid—they must be admitted to a preference and pre-eminence over those whom they subdue—Here are new taxes and new oppressions, which cause insurrections.—A foreign enemy is expected to take advantage of the confusion; the people are not to be trusted—Your liberties (as they will then be called) must be committed to the guardianship of the standing army—a day which, as I am informed, a member in the late convention declared he wished to see—The people look anxiously for the punishment of their oppressors, and they look up to that man who will gratify their revenge on the aristocracy.—All senates have been, and always will be for raising standing troops, notwithstanding they have invariably found to their destruction, that no oaths can prevent them, from following the fortunes of a favourite leader, whose orders their rigid discipline has accustomed them to obey.—

That this is not the painting of a warm imagination, the history of those governments that were far less complicated and onerous than ours must prove, will evidence—Thirteen complicated forms all under one form of government, still more complicated, seem to bid defiance to all *responsibility*, (the only test of good government) as it can never be discovered where the fault lies—the blame will be shifted from the States to Congress—from Congress to the States—from one State to another, and so from one shoulder to another, until investigation is tired—the burthen of double government complete throughout, when we can scarce support its expense single.—This double officering from front to rear, will prove so extremely burthensome, and above all, this double set of laws will afford so plentiful an harvest of oppression and confusion, that I do not see what right we have to expect a more fortunate fate, than those nations who had happier and fairer prospect.

Let us now view the catastrophes of these governments.—First of *Sweden*—previous to the year 1772—the States or legislature was composed of four orders—I. *Nobility*, who were only as we are informed the heads of the wealthiest families represented in a senate by selection—the old nobility having been almost to a man extirpated by that Nero of the North, Christian IId, who made a general massacre of the order assisted by the populace, who hunted them like blood-hounds—II. The *clergy*—III. The *citizens* chosen by the magistrates and common council of each corporation, their number about 150—IV. The *farmers*, chosen in each district by a majority of voices out of the landholders, their number 180.— It would seem as if theory could hardly invent a more perfect *legislature.*—The *executive* was committed to one man, dignified indeed by the title of King, a word to which we attach ideas unauthorized by its meaning—but this King however (who was elected for life) was in fact, hardly more than a president of the senate, without whose concurrence he could exercise none of the important powers belonging to the executive branch:—Although the King and every officer, civil and military, were sworn to support this constitution, yet there was but one military officer found who regarded this oath, when solicited by Gustavus to take a contrary oath to support its usurpation.—This singular man had the courage to declare, that the Prince ought to have no confidence in him, if he should by one oath violate another.—A few grenadiers with bayonets fixed, ordered to the senate-room, and a very few regiments previously prepared, effected the most sudden and unexpected revolution that ever mankind were the melancholy witnesses of.—A few days after the King published that form of government, which it was his *will and pleasure the Swedes and their posterity* should be governed by—The Americans ought to read it—they will find it in William's history of Northern Governments.—In the preface is this remarkable passage: "We, whose names are hereunto subscribed, Senators, States, Counts, Barons, Bishops, Knights, and Nobles, Military Officers, Citizens, and Commons, who are actually here assembled, make known for us and our absent citizens and commons, that many of our citizens under the name of liberty had assumed a power and domination that was insupportable, &c. &c. &c."

In *Denmark*, the revolution in 1666, presents exactly the same story over again.—The constitution was the same as in Sweden precisely, senate, representatives of the people, and an executive elected for life, clogged in the same manner by the senate.—The representatives of the people became at last so tired of the senate, that they made a formal offer of their liberties to Frederick IIId, and actually compelled the senate to give their assent.—This man whose moderation and real disinterested virtue had captivated the affections of all ranks, with the assistance of 24,000 troops, selected chiefly from foreign vagabonds, established the most despotic government, that ever mankind groaned under *for them* and *their posterity*;—and no doubt with the best intentions, as from his declaration we find he believed what Mr. Pope has wrote, and what many good, but mistaken men, both in Europe and America, have thought and now think—

For forms of government let fools contest
That which is best administered, is best.—

and as for the good administration he thought he could very well trust that to *himself* and *his posterity*.

It was thus that the hardy descendants of the Goths and Vandals lost their liberties, and from the boldest and most enterprizing they have degenerated into the most miserable and depressed of mankind, the country depopulated, commerce destroyed, dirty minions, and court-favourites plundering every thing and nothing flourishing but the standing army.—For the truth of this picture I refer to William's history.

In *Holland*, at this moment, the standing troops adhering to the Stadtholder (who from the best accounts proved a traitor to his country last war) in conjunction with those bred under that grand Prince of despots, the late King of Prussia, have disarmed the Burghers, the national militia, and are now changing the forms of government, under the pretext of throwing power into the hands of the States-General, but actually paving the way for the *hereditary despotism* of William of Nassau.

It is so long since the other States of Europe have lost all semblance of liberty, that it may be difficult to trace their revolutions.— In *France* the oppressions of the aristocracy enabled first the politic Lewis IId, and afterwards Lewis XIIIth, and Cardinal Richlieu, by the assistance of the mob and standing army, since become the standing law of France, to destroy every vestige of freedom.

In *Spain* the immense estates, which by the six fortunate marriages of the house of Austria (as they are called) became concentered in the person of Charles Vth.—The mines of the two Indies then lately discovered which became the property of his family, *and above all* the obstinacy of that hardy, disinterested and frugal priest, Ximenes, finished at a blow the power of the Cortes, who were chiefly composed of representatives elected by the people in the several States of Old and New Castile, Arragon, Catalonia, &c.—For *Spain* was at that time divided into as many States almost as we are, and perhaps more independent of each other, having separate legislatives and executives, and *the general power not entrusted with the right of taxation.*—However, a standing army has from that time destroyed all hopes of a revolution in favour of the rights of mankind.

It will be asked how has *England* preserved her liberties, with at least an apparent standing army?—I answer, she did loose them; but as there was no standing army until lately, she regained them again:—She lost them under the Tudors, who broke the then oppressive power of the aristocracy, but the unparalleled avarice of Henry VIIth, the boundless extravagance of Henry VIIIth, the short reign of Edward VIth, (which was but the sickly blaze of a dying candle) the bigotry of that weak woman Mary, who had no other object than religious persecution, and lastly the parsimony of Elizabeth, who had no children of her own to provide for, and who hated her legal successor and his family—all conspired to prevent their establishing a military standing force, sufficient to secure their usurpations; and the nation recovered from their paroxism under the Stuarts, who were too weak and too wicked to command even respect, notwithstanding their dignity.—On the revolution in 1688, the patriots of that day formed some glorious bulwarks, which seem as yet to have secured them from the evils and danger of their present standing army, though still in my opinion, they hold their remaining liberties by a very precarious tenure indeed, as the first enterprizing and popular Prince will most probably convince them.

Let us now examine these defences and compare them with those of the proposed constitution.

In *England,* by their bill of rights, a standing army is declared to be contrary to their constitution, and a militia the only natural and safe defence of a free people—This keeps the jealously of the nation constantly awake, and has proved the foundation of all the other checks.

In the American constitution, there is no such declaration, or check at all.

In *England*, the military are declared by their constitution to be in all cases subordinate to the civil power; and consequently the civil officers have always been active in supporting this pre-eminence.

In the American constitution, there is no such declaration.

In *England*, the mutiny bill can only be passed from year to year, or on its expiration every soldier is as free, and the equal by law of the first general officer of the land.

In America, the articles of war (which is the same thing) has been already considered as *perpetual* (as I am well informed) under even the present Congress, although the constitutions of all the States positively forbid any standing troops at all, much less laws for them.

In England, the appropriation of money for the support of their army must be from year to year; in America it may be for double the period.

How favorable is this contrast to Britain—that Britain which we lavished our blood and treasure to separate ourselves from, as a country of slavery—But we then held different sentiments from those now become so fashionable; for this I appeal to the constitutions of the several States.

In the declaration of rights of *Massachusetts*, Sect. 17.—The people have a right to keep and to bear arms for the common defence. And as in time of peace, armies are dangerous to liberty, they ought not to be maintained without the consent of the legislature, and the military power shall always be held in exact subordination to the civil authority, and be governed by it.

Sect. 27. In time of peace, no soldier ought to be quartered in any house without the consent of the owner; and in time of war, such quarters ought not to be made but by the civil magistrate, in a manner ordained by the legislature.

Declaration of rights of *Pennsylvania*, feet. 13.—That the people have a right to bear arms for the defence of themselves and the State; and as standing armies in the time of peace, are dangerous to liberty, they ought not to be kept up: And that the military should be kept under strict subordination to, and governed by the civil power.

Declaration of rights of *Maryland*, sect. 25.—That a well regulated militia is the proper and natural defence of a free government.

Sect. 26. That standing armies are dangerous to liberty, and ought not to be raised or kept without consent of the legislature.

Sect. 27. That in all cases and at all times the military ought to be under strict subordination to, and control of the civil power.

Sect. 28. That no soldier ought to be quartered in any house in time of peace, without the consent of the owner; and in time of war, in such manner only as the legislature shall direct.

Declaration of rights of *Delaware*, in the same words as *Maryland*.

Declaration of rights of *North-Carolina*, sect. 17.—That the people have a right to hear arms for the defence of the State; and as standing armies in time of peace are dangerous to liberty, they ought not to be kept up; and that the military should be kept under strict subordination to, and governed by the civil power.

Constitution of *South-Carolina*, sect. 42.—That the military be subordinate to the civil power of the State.

But we are told by *Aristides*, that our poverty is our best security against many standing troops.—Are *we then, and our posterity*, always to be poor? This security would certainly cease with our poverty; but the truth is, our poverty instead of preventing will be the first cause of the increase of a standing army.—Our poverty will render the people less able to pay the few troops it is admitted we must keep.—This expense added to the immense public and private debts, which an efficient government seems to be requisite to enforce payment of, together with the onerous and complicated civil governments, both Continental and State, will be product[ive] of future uneasiness and discontent.—The most sanguine among us must expect some turbulence and commotion; let the smallest appearance of commotion peep out again in any part of the Continent, and there is not a rich man in the United States, who will think himself or his property [safe] *until both* are surrounded with standing troops. This is the only public purpose for which *these* men ever did, or ever will willingly contribute their money. But then, according to their laudable custom, they must have interest for their advances;—this increases the public burthens—Commotion followed by commotion, until the spirit of the people is broken, and sunk by the halter, the scaffold, and a regular standing army.—

Yet notwithstanding this I am as sensible as *Aristides*, that a few troops will be necessary for the United States, for those very services which he says it would be oppressive to a free people constantly to execute.—The western territory, [some] guards, arsenals and posts whenever our finances will admit our attention to that safe and honorable defence, a navy—will require a few men in constant pay. But it is this necessity that alone causes all my apprehension. There is no public abuse that does not spring from the necessary use of power,—it is that insensible progress from the use to the abuse that has led mankind through scenes of calamity and woe that make us now think back with horror, from the history of our species. Do we not see at this moment, that even the present Congress have been compelled by necessity to embody and maintain troops in time of peace for these purposes and yet the raising or maintaining one man is as complete a violation of the bill of rights of the several States, as the raising 100,000.—This necessary infraction of the only check that existed, has already taught all America to view the approach of a standing army, with composure and indifference, nay when a limitation of the evil is proposed, *Aristides* [asks] without hesitation—how shall we distinguish between peace and a *threatened war*? Shall we not be surprized, unprepared?

I must confess that from the vigor and resolution with which we began the erection of these fabrics of freedom, I was persuaded that the grave would have closed on my bones, before this question would be publicly proposed in America.—Are we then to look up to a standing army for the defence of this soil from foreign invasion? Have we forgot that a few freemen of Sparta defended their country against a million of Persian slaves? Have not an handful of Swiss farmers, defended their country against the numerous veteran armies, which Burgandy, Austria and Bourbon have led against them? They beat them among their rocks, and then descended into the plains and beat them, and they [will] beat them forever on any ground, to all eternity, whilst they remain free and are defending that freedom.—Did it not [cost] the Spaniards more time and blood to subdue a few republican unarmed Indians, on the little island of Gran [Canaria] than they expended in the destruction of the mighty empires of Mexico and Peru, defended by numerous standing armies? Did their arms meet with any resistance on this Continent until they penetrated to the free republics of Chili?—I had rather trust the defence of a country to the savage valour of a few Shawnesse and Delawares, who live in freedom and [value] the blessing, than to the numerous hosts of civilian slaves that surround the thrones of Delhi, Pekin and [Ispahan]—But a few years have elapsed since that feather of a King, Lewis XIVth, over-run all Holland in a few days, and became master, almost without resistance, of that country which the veteran infantry of Spain, led by the most celebrated Captains, an age of chivalry produced, Alva, Alexander Farneza, and the Marquis Spinola, were forced to gain inch by inch, from a few desperate Burghers. When the French troops came, the people were universally discontented with the oppressions of the rich, as soon as they had reeked a brutal vengeance on the aristocracy, the latent [cou]rage of the nation revived, and Lewis was obliged to scamper off as fast as he came.— Let the [body] of the people be [in]terested in the defence of a *good* government, and my countrymen need not fear being surprized by all the slaves and brutes that the despots of the old and new world can [arm] against them.—There will then need no distinction of a threatened war, and our establishment may at all times be [limited] to the purposes just mentioned.—

But perhaps standing troops may be wanted to suppress [*domestic*] insurrections[?] The people cannot be trusted to [rule] the people, is becoming a [cant] expression; But I fervently hope by no means a general sentiment. I am free to declare, that I never wish to see any measure of government enforced [by] arms, which the yeomanry of the United States will not turn out to support.

My countrymen! never forget this truth, which the sad experience of your fellow-mortals has witnessed with their blood!— Remember it yourselves!—Engrave it on the tender minds of your children, as the first article of their political creed—that, *There is no form of government safe with a standing army*, and there is none that is not safe without.—A people may frequently be so unfortunate as to loose their liberties. They may be so foolish as to give them away, as in Denmark, where not only the senators and representatives of the people, but also every man in the whole empire of the smallest note, or consequence, signed a formal surrender of their liberties on an instrument now kept in the archives of that kingdom—an everlasting monument of—*how catching a thing this signing of names is; or of what is now called—a modest deference for the opinion of others.* But whether they loose them, or give them away, they will soon regain them, or resume them, unless they are prevented by a *standing army*—And also recollect, my fellow-citizens, *That what is doctrine to day, may be treason tomorrow.*

A FARMER.

Maryland Gazette

7 MARCH 1788

ESSAY III

The Farmer argues that those best situated by occupation and belief to defend liberty are natural supporters of confederal rather than national government. Only the desire for pride and splendour could produce a drive for consolidated government. Essays in The Federalist *of particular relevance: 1, 2, 10.*

THERE are but two modes by which men are connected in society, the one which operates on individuals, this always has been, and ought still to be called, *national government;* the other which binds States and governments together (not corporations, for there is no considerable nation on earth, despotic, monarchical, or republican, that does not contain many subordinate corporations with various constitutions) this last has heretofore been denominated a *league or confederacy.*—The term *fœderalists* is therefore improperly applied to themselves, by the friends and supporters of the proposed constitution.—This abuse of language does not help the cause,—every degree of imposition serves only to irritate, but can never convince.—They are *national men,* and their opponents, or at least a great majority of them, are fœderal, in the only true and strict sense of the word.—

Whether any form of *national* government is preferable for the Americans, to a league or confederacy, is a previous question we must first make up our minds upon.—There will then remain still another—Whether, if any, is the one proposed the best, in our circumstances safe, and such a one as we should *unconditionally* receive? and if ever duty required deliberation before decision, it calls for it now, and in terms too strong to be resisted or evaded.— Let the light come in free from every quarter. If reason cannot satisfy, experiment will determine. But even then, is it not the duty of those to whom the happiness of so great a proportion of the human species is entrusted, to conduct that experiment with the utmost coolness and fairness, with all those precautions which the wisdom of antiquity affords, and finally qualified with those securities to our liberty, that, should it prove oppressive or impracticable, ourselves, or at least our posterity, may not be prevented, by the power or influence of a civil or *military oligarchy,* from adopting the alternative?

The advantages or disadvantages of *national government,* open too wide a field of discussion for my leisure or talents.—Some few remarks I shall cursorily offer. That a *national government* will add to the dignity and encrease the splendour of the United States abroad, can admit of no doubt: It is essentially requisite for both. That it will render government, and officers of government, more dignified at home is equally certain. That these objects are more suited to the manners, if not genius and disposition of our people is, I fear, also true. That it is requisite in order to keep us at peace among ourselves, is doubtful. That it is necessary, to prevent foreigners from dividing us, or interfering in our government, I deny positively; and after all, I have strong doubts whether all its advan-

tages are not more *specious* than [*solid*]. We are vain, like other
nations,—we wish to make a [noise in] the world; and feel hurt that
Europeans are not so attentive to America in *peace*, as they were to
America in *war*.—We are also, no doubt, desirous of cutting a figure
in history.—Should we not reflect, that quiet is happiness?—That
[content] and pomp are incompatible?—I have either read or heard
this truth, which the Americans should never forget,—*That the
silence of historians is the surest record of the happiness of the
people*.—The Swiss have been four hundred years the envy of
mankind, and there is yet scarcely an history of their nation. What
is history, but a disgusting and painful detail of the butcheries of
conquerors, and the woeful calamities of the conquered? Many of us
are proud, and are frequently disappointed that office confers neither respect or [distinction]. No man of merit can ever be disgraced
by office. [A rogue] in office may be feared in *some* governments—
he will be respected in none.—After all, what we call respect and
[difference] only arise from contrast of situation, as most of
our [ideas] come by comparison and relation. Where the people
[are free] there can be no great contrast, or distinction among [*honest*] citizens *in* or *out* of office.—In proportion as the people [loose]
their freedom, every gradation of distinction, between the *Governors* and *governed* obtains, until the former become *masters*,
and the latter become *slaves*. In all governments virtue will command reverence—The divine Cato knew every Roman citizen by
name, and never assumed any pre-eminence; yet Cato found, and
his memory will find, respect and reverence in the bosoms of
mankind, until this world returns into that nothing, from whence
Omnipotence called it.—That the people are not at present disposed for, and are actually incapable of, governments of simplicity
and equal rights, I can no longer doubt—But whose fault is it? We
make them bad, by bad governments, and then abuse and despise
them for being so. Our people are capable of being made any thing,
that human nature was or is capable of, if we would only have a little patience and give them good and wholesome institutions; but I
see none such and very little prospect of such.—Alas! I see nothing in my fellow-citizens, that will permit my still fostering the
delusion, that they are now capable of sustaining the weight of

SELF-GOVERNMENT: A burthen to which Greek and Roman shoulders proved unequal.—The honor of supporting the dignity of the human character, seems reserved to the hardy Helvetians alone—If the body of the people will not govern themselves, and govern themselves *well* too, the consequence is unavoidable.—A FEW will, and must govern *them.*—Then it is that government becomes truly a government by *force* only,—where men *relinquish part* of their natural rights to secure the *rest,* instead of an union of will and force, to protect *all* their natural rights, which ought to be the foundation of every rightful social compact.—Whether *national* government will be productive of internal peace, is too uncertain to admit of decided opinion.—I only hazard a conjecture when I say, that our state disputes, *in a confederacy,* would be disputes of levity and passion, which would subside before injury.— The people being free, government having no right to them, but they to government, they would separate and divide as interest or inclination prompted—as they do at this day, and always have done, in Switzerland—In a *national* government, unless cautiously and fortunately administered, the disputes will be the deep-rooted differences of interest, where part of the empire must be injured by the operation of general law; and then should the sword of government be once drawn (which Heaven avert) I fear it will not be sheathed, until we have waded through that series of desolation, which France, Spain, and the other great kingdoms of the world have suffered, in order to bring so many separate States into uniformity, of government and law; in which event the legislative power can only be entrusted to one man (as it is with them) who can have no *local attachments, partial interests,* or *private views* to gratify.

That a *national* government will prevent the influence or danger of foreign intrigue, or secure us from invasion, is in my judgment directly the reverse of the truth:—The only *foreign,* or at *least evil foreign influence,* must be obtained through corruption.—Where the government is lodged in the body of the people, as in Switzerland, they can never be corrupted; for no prince, or people, can have resources enough to corrupt, the *majority of a nation;*—and if they could, the play is not worth the candle.—The facility of corruption is encreased in proportion as power tends by representation or delegation, to a concentration in the *hands of a few.*—The French have kept a minister in Switzerland for 300 years back to persuade them to place power in their General Assembly or Diet.—The Swiss have always proved faithful allies and friends to France,—but have laughed at her political advice—as the assembly of Foxes treated with derision the curtailed Reynard—who advised them to part with their cumbersome quantity of brush.*—As to any nation attacking a number of confederated independent republics, who are always as populous as brave, it is not to be expected, more especially as the wealth of the empire is there universally diffused, and will not be collected into any one overgrown, luxurious and effeminate capital to become a lure to the enterprizing ambitious.—That extensive empire is a misfortune to be deprecated, will not now be disputed.— The balance of power has long engaged the attention of all the European world, in order to avoid the horrid evils of a general government.—The same government pervading a vast extent of territory, terrifies the minds of individuals into meanness and submission.—All human authority, however organized, must have confined limits,—or insolence and oppression will prove the offspring of its grandeur,—and the difficulty or rather impossibility of escape prevents resistance.—Gibbon relates that some Roman Knights who had offended government in Rome were taken up in Asia, in a very few days after.—It was the extensive territory of the Roman republic that produced a Sylla, a Marius, a Caligula, a Nero, and an Eliagabalus.—In small independent States contiguous to each other, the people run away and leave despotism, to reek its vengeance on itself; and thus it is that moderation becomes with them, the law of self-preservation.—These and such reasons founded on the eternal and immutable nature of things have long caused and will continue to cause much difference of sentiment throughout our wide extensive territories—From our divided and dispersed situation, and from the natural moderation of the American character, it has hitherto proved a warfare of argument and reason.

A FARMER.

* See Campbell's present state of Europe.

(*To be continued.*)

Maryland Gazette

18 MARCH 1788

ESSAY III

(*Continued.*)

THUS it was that the opposite qualities of the first confederation were rather caused by than the cause of two parties, which from its first existence began and have continued their operations, I believe, unknown to their country and almost unknown to themselves—as really but few men have the capacity or resolution, to develope the secret causes, which influence their daily conduct.— The old Congress was a national government and an union of States, both brought into one political body, as these opposite powers, I do not mean parties, were so exactly blended and very nearly balanced, like every artificial, operative machine where action is equal to re-action—it stood perfectly still—it would not move at all—Those who were merely confœderal in their views, were for dividing the public debt—those who were for national government, were for encreasing of it—Those who thought any national government would be destructive to the liberties of America, as I imagine, assisted those who thought it our only safety, to put every thing as wrong as possible.—Requisitions were made, which every body knew it was impossible to comply with—either in 82 or 83, ten millions of hard dollars, if not thirteen, were called into the continental treasury, when there could not be half that sum in the whole tract of territory between Nova-Scotia and Florida—The States neglected them in despair—The public honor was tarnished, and our governments abused by their servants and best friends—In fine, it became a cant word—things are not yet bad enough to mend—However, as great part of the important objects of society were entrusted to this mongrel species of general government, the sentiment of pushing it forward became general throughout America, and the late Convention met at Philadelphia under the uniform impression, that such was the desire of their constituents—But even then the advantages and disadvantages of national government operated so strongly, although silently, on each individual, that the conflict was nearly equal—A third or middle opinion, which always arises in such cases, broke off and took the lead—the national party assisted, pursued steadily their object—the fœderal party dropt off, one by one, and finally, when the middle party came to view the offspring which they had given birth to, and in a great measure reared, several of them immediately disowned the child— Such has been hitherto the progress of party, or rather of the human mind dispassionately contemplating our separate and relative situation, and aiming at that perfect completion of social happiness and grandeur, which perhaps can be combined only in idea—Every description of men entertain the same wishes (excepting perhaps a few very bad men of each)—they forever will differ about the mode of accomplishment—and some must be permitted to doubt the practibility.

As our citizens are now apprized of the progress of parties or political opinions on the continent, it is fit they should also be informed of the present state, force and designs of each in order that they may form their decisions with safety to the public and themselves—this shall be given with all the precision and impartiality the author is capable of.

America is at present divided into three classes or descriptions of men, and in a few years there will be but two.

The first class comprehends all those men of fortune and reputation who stepped forward in the late revolution, from opposition to the administration, rather than the government of Great-Britain— All those aristocrats whose pride disdains equal law—Many men of very large fortune, who entertain real or imaginary fears for the security of property—Those young men, who have sacrificed their time and their talents to public service, without any prospect of an adequate pecuniary or honorary reward—All your people of fashion and pleasure who are corrupted by the dissipation of the French, English and American armies; and a love of European manners and luxury—The public creditors of the continent, whose interest has been heretofore sacrificed by their friends, in order to retain their services on this occasion—A large majority of the mercantile people, which is at present a very unformed and consequently dangerous interest—Our old native merchants have been almost universally ruined by the receipt of their debts in paper during the war, and the payment in hard money of what they owed their British correspondents since peace—Those who are not bankrupts, have generally retired and given place to a set of young men, who conducting themselves as rashly as ignorantly, have embarrassed their affairs and lay the blame on the government, and who are really unacquainted with the true mercantile interest of the country—which is perplexed from circumstances rather temporary than permanent—The foreign merchants are generally not to be trusted with influence in our government—they are most of them birds of passage—some perhaps British emissaries encreasing and rejoicing in our political mistakes, and even those who have settled among us with an intention to fix themselves and their posterity in our soil, have brought with them more foreign prejudices, than wealth—time must elapse before the mercantile interest will be so organized as to govern themselves, much less others, with propriety: And lastly, to this class I suppose we may ultimately add the tory *interest* with the exception of very many respectable characters, who reflect with a gratification mixed with disdain, that those principles are now become fashionable for which they have been persecuted and hunted down—which, although by no means so formidable as is generally imagined, is still considerable—They are at present wavering—they are generally, though with very many exceptions, openly for the proposed, but secretly against any American government—*A burnt child dreads the fire*—but should they see any fair prospect [of] confusion arise, these gentry will be off at any moment for these five and twenty years to come—Ultimately should the administration promise stability to the new government, they may be counted on as the Janizaries of power, ready to efface all suspicion by the violence of their zeal—In general, all these various people would prefer a government, as nearly copied after that of Great-Britain, as our circumstances will permit—some would strain these circumstances—others still retain a deep rooted jealousy of the executive branch and strong republican prejudices as they are called—finally, this class contains more aggregate wisdom, and moral virtue than both the other two together—it commands nearly two-thirds of the property and almost one half the numbers of America, and has at present, become almost irresistible from the name of the truly great and amiable man who it has been said, is disposed to patronize it, and from the influence which it has over the second class—This class is nearly at the height of their power, they must decline or moderate, or another revolution will ensue, for the opinion of America is becoming daily more unfavorable to those radical changes which high-toned government requires:—A conflict would terminate in the destruction of this class, or the liberties of their country—May the Guardian Angel of America prevent both!

The second class is composed of those descriptions of men who are certainly more numerous with us than in any other part of the globe—*First, those men* who are so wise as to discover that their ancestors and indeed all the rest of mankind were and are fools. We have a vast over proportion of these great men, who, when you tell them that from the earliest period at which mankind devoted their attention to social happiness, it has been their uniform judgment, that a government over governments cannot exist—*that is two governments* operating on the same individual—assume the smile of confidence and tell you of two people travelling the same road—of a perfect and precise division of the duties of the individual: Still however, the political apothegm is as old as the proverb—*That no man can serve two masters,* and whoever will run their noddles against old proverbs will be sure to break them, however hard they may be, and if they broke only their own, all would be right; but it is very horrible to reflect that all our numskulls must be cracked in concert.—*Second*—The *trimmers* who from sympathetic indecision are always united with, and when not regularly employed, always fight under the banners of these great men. These people are forever at market and when parties are nearly equally divided, they get very well paid for their services. *Thirdly*—The *indolent,* that is almost every second man of independent fortune you meet with in America—*these are quite easy, and can live under any government.* If men can be said to live, who scarcely breathe, and if breathing was attended with any bodily exertion, would give up their small portion of life in despair. These men do not swim with the stream as the trimmers do, but are dragged like mud at the bottom. As they have no other weight than their fat flesh, they are hardly worth mentioning when we speak of the sentiments and opinions of America. As this second class never can include any of the yeomanry of the union, who never affect superior wisdom, and can have no interest but the public good, it can be only said to exist at the birth of government, and as soon as the first and third classes become more decided in their views, this will divide with each and dissipate like a mist, or sink down into what are called moderate men, and become the tools and instruments of others. These people are prevented by a cloud from having *any* view; and if they are not virtuous, they at least preserve the appearance which in this world amounts to the same thing.

At the head of the third class appear the old rigid republicans, who although few in number, are still formidable—Reverence will follow these men in spite of detraction, as long as wisdom and virtue are esteemed among mankind—they are joined by the true *democrats*, who are in general fanatics and enthusiasts, and some few sensible, charming madmen—a decided majority of the *yeomanry* of America will, for a length of years, be ready to support these two descriptions of men; but as this last class is forced to act as a residuary legatee, and receive all the trash and filth—it is in some measure disgraced and its influence weakened, by 3dly. The free-booters and plunderers, who infest all countries and ours perhaps as little as any other whatever—these men have that natural antipathy to any kind or sort of government, that a rogue has to a halter. In number they are few indeed—such characters are the offspring of dissipation and want, and there is not that country in the world where so much real property is shared so equally among so few citizens, or where property is as easily acquired by fair means, very few indeed will resort to foul. Lastly, by the poor *mob*, infœlix pecus! the property of whoever will feed them and take care of them—let them be spared—let the burthen of taxation fit lightly on their shoulders, but alas! this is not their fate—it is here that government forever falls with all its weight—it is here that the proposed government will press where it should scarcely be felt.—

Oves bis mulget in bora, et succus pecori et lac subducitur agais.

If ever a direct tax is laid by the general government, it must, if not from necessity, at least from propriety, be laid on polls—it is the only one I believe to be practicable—there ought then to be some security that they avoid direct taxation where not absolutely indispensible, and some better security than the opinion of *Aristides.*

In this class may be counted men of the greatest mental powers and of as sublime virtue as any in America—they at present command nearly one-third of the property and above half the numbers of the United States, and in either event they must continue to encrease in influence by great desertions from both the other classes.—If the government is adopted, by the numerous, discontented and disappointed, and from that natural jealousy, which Englishmen and their descendants always will retain, of their government and Governors. If the government is not adopted theirs will be the prevalent opinion. The object of this class either is or will be purely fœderal—an union of independent States, not a government of individuals: And should the proposed fœderal plan fail, from the obstinacy of those who will listen to no *conditional* amendments, although such as they cannot disapprove; or should it ultimately in its execution upon a fair trial, disappoint the wishes and expectations of our country: An union purely fœderal is what the reasonable and dispationate patriots of America must bend their views to. My countrymen, preserve your jealousy—reject suspicion, it is the fiend that destroys public and private happiness. I know some weak, but very few if any wicked men in public confidence; and learn this most difficult and necessary lesson:—That on the preservation of parties, public liberty depends. Whenever men are unanimous on great public questions, whenever there is but one party, freedom ceases and despotism commences. The object of a free and wise people should be so to balance parties, that *from the weakness of all you may be governed by the moderation of the combined judgments of the whole, not tyranized over by the blind passions of a few individuals.*

A FARMER.

Maryland Gazette

21 MARCH 1788

ESSAY IV

The Farmer turns to the right to trial by jury. By expressly grant-ing this right only in criminal cases, the Constitution, he argues, effectively refuses it in civil cases. This is particularly dangerous, because juries are the true source of popular government. Further, by protecting the people's property from arbitrary decisions, juries also protect the people's freedom. Essays in The Federalist *of par-ticular relevance: 81, 83.*

I HAVE said that the boasted birthright of Englishmen and their posterity—*the trial by jury in civil cases,* is destroyed under the proposed fœderal constitution;that the hope of its re-establishment by the future Congress is at best doubtful; that its tenure, depend-ing on the fluctuating breath of annual or biennial sessions, is uncer-tain; and finally, I denied the power of reviving it by a *Congressional law* at all, as it would be a violation of the constitution:—It may be expected that in a cause like this, assertion and proof should go hand in hand.

It has ever been contended, at least on one side, that the pro-posed Congress are to exercise *no power not expressly vested in them by the fœderal plan.* This is the position of *Aristides,* and of all the friends of the system.—It is now asked, is the power of establishing juries in *civil* cases by Congress, given in that consti-tution? It must be answered NO, not at least in express words.—Is it then given by *implication?* If so great an authority can be taken from the judges, the judiciary, an independent branch of govern-ment, by the legislature, and vested in a distinct branch, a jury, I do not see in what *judiciary independence* consists.—Can these judi-cial powers, vested in the judges, by the constitution, which gives *them* the cognizance of certain causes, be divested by an *implied* legislative power? If we imply this power, may we not imply any other? And does not the doctrine of *implication* totally defeat the fundamental position of *Aristides*, and the friends of the *new* government? But moreover does not *Aristides*, and every lawyer, know that in the interpretation of all political as well as civil laws, this fundamental maxim must be observed, *That where there are two objects in contemplation of any legislature, the express adoption of one, is the total exclusion of the other*; and that the adoption of juries in *criminal* cases, in every legal interpretation, amounts to an absolute rejection in *civil* cases:—If the right of establishing juries, by a *Congressional* law is admitted at all, it must be admitted, as an *inherent legislative right*, paramount to the constitution, as it is not derived from it, and then the power that can make, can by law unmake; so that referring this power to a source of authority *superior* to the act of government, would leave us without any juries at all (even in *criminal* cases) if Congress should so please; which position can never be the object of either friends or enemies to the system at present.—If it is defective, it is still bad policy to make it worse; but still in every view, we must reflect, that the establishment of trials by jury, belongs to *political*, not to *civil* legislation. It includes the right of organizing government, not of regulating the conduct of individuals, as the following enquiry will prove; we must never give an assembly the power of giving itself power.

As the worth and excellence of this mode of trial, preserved and handed down from generation to generation for near two thousand years, has drawn down the enthusiastic encomiums of the most enlightened lawyers and statesmen of every age; as it has taken deep root in the breast of every freeman, encompassed by the defences of affection and veneration, a repetition of its praises would be as tedious as useless: Some remarks however, still remain to be made, which will place this subject in a more important and conspicuous view.

The trial by jury, is the only remaining power which the Commons of England have retained in their own hands, of all that plenitude of authority and freedom, which rendered their northern progenitors irresistible in war, and flourishing in peace.—The usurpations of *the few*, gradually effected by artifice and force, have robbed *the many*, of that power which once formed the basis of those governments, so celebrated by mankind.—The government of Sparta, the form of which it is said, has continued from the days of Lycurgus to our age, preserving its model amidst those overwhelming tides of revolution and shipwrecks of governments, which Greece has sustained for near three thousand years; the same form of government among the Saxons and other Germans, consisting of King, Lords and Commons, applauded by Tacitus and Machiavelli, were thus distinguished from the present government of England—The power of the Commons resided with them, not in representatives but in the body of the people.—*De minoribus rebus, principes consultant; de majoribus omnes*, are either the words of Tacitus or Cæsar. The administration of *ordinary* affairs was committed to the select men; but all important subjects were deliberated on by the whole body of the people.—Such was the constitution of Sparta, and of England, when Machiavelli gives them as a model, for there can be no doubt but that the *folk-motes* of the Saxons were not formed by representation—The venerable remembrance of which assemblies, hung long about the affections of Englishmen, and it was to restore them that they offered such frequent libations of their noblest blood; but the usurpations of *the few* have been unwearied and irresistible, and the trial by jury is all that now remains to *the many*.

The trial by jury is—the democratic branch of the judiciary power—more necessary than representatives in the legislature; for those usurpations, which silently undermine the spirit of liberty, under the sanction of law, are more dangerous than direct and open legislative attacks; in the one case the treason is never discovered until liberty, and with it the power of defence is lost; the other is an open summons to arms, and then if the people will not defend their rights, they do not deserve to enjoy them.

The *judiciary* power, has generally been considered as a branch of the *executive*, because these two powers, have been so frequently united;—but where united, there is no liberty.—In every *free* State, the judiciary is kept separate, independent, and considered as an intermediate power;—and it certainly partakes more of a legisla-

tive, than an executive nature.—The sound definition which
Delolme applied to one branch may be justly extended to the whole
judiciary,—*That it is a subordinate legislation in most instances,
supplying by analogy, and precedent in each particular case, the
defects of general legislative acts,*—without then the check of the
democratic branch—the *jury*, to ascertain those facts, to which the
judge is to apply the law, and even in many cases to determine the
cause by a *general* verdict—the latitude of judicial power, combined
with the various and uncertain nature of evidence, will render it
impossible to convict a judge of corruption, and ascertain his
guilt.—Remove the fear of punishment, give hopes of impunity, and
vice and tyranny come scowling from their dark abodes in the
human heart.—Destroy juries and every thing is prostrated to
judges, who may easily disguise law, by suppressing and varying
fact:—Whenever therefore the trial by juries has been abolished,
the liberties of the people were soon lost—The judiciary power is
immediately absorbed, or placed under the direction of the executive, as example teaches in most of the States of Europe.—So formidable an engine of power, defended only by the gown and the
robe, is soon seized and engrossed by the power that weilds the
sword.—Thus we find the judiciary and executive branches united,
or the *former* totally dependant on the *latter* in most of the governments in the world.—It is true, where the judges will put on
the sword and weild it with success, they will subject both princes
and legislature to their despotism, as was the case in the memorable usurpation of the Justizia of Arragon, where the judiciary
erected themselves into a frightful tyranny.

Why then shall we risque this important check to judiciary
usurpation, provided by the wisdom of antiquity? Why shall we
rob the Commons of the only remaining power they have been able
to preserve, for their personal exercise? Have they ever abused
it?—I know it has and will be said—they have—that they are too
ignorant—that they cannot distinguish between right and wrong—
that decisions on property are submitted to chance; and that the
last word, commonly determines the cause:—There is some truth in
these allegations—but whence comes it—The Commons are much
degraded in the powers of the mind:—They were deprived of the

use of understanding. when they were robbed of the power of employing it.—Men no longer cultivate, what is no longer useful,—should every opportunity be taken away, of exercising their reason, you will reduce them to that state of mental baseness, in which they appear in nine-tenths of this globe—distinguished from brutes, only by form and the articulation of found—*Give them power and they will find understanding to use it*—But taking juries with all their real and attributed defects, is it not better to submit a cause to an impartial tribunal, who would at least, as soon do you right as wrong—than for every man to become subservient to government and those in power?—Would any man oppose government, where his property would be wholly at the mercy and decision of those that govern?—We know the influence that property has over the minds of men—they will risque their lives rather than their property; and a government, where there is no trial by jury, has an unlimited command over every man who has any thing to loose.—It is by the attacks on private property through the judiciary, that despotism becomes as irresistible as terrible. I could relate numerous examples of the greatest and best men in all countries, who have been driven to despair, by vexations law-suits, commenced at the instigation of the court, of favorites and of minions, and all *from the loss of juries.*—France was reduced to the brink of destruction in one instance.—The Queen mother Louise of Savoy, piqued at the constable of Bourbon, a young and amiable man, who refused to marry her, commenced a suit against him for all his estate—The judges were ready at the beck of the court, and without a shadow of justice deprived him by law of every shilling he was worth; and drove from his country an unfortunate hero, whose mad revenge carried desolation into her bosom.—In Denmark a despicable minion, who came in rags to the court, after the establishment of their new government, which they solicited Frederick the IIId to make for them, acquired an immense fortune by plunder, sheltered by the favour of the Sovereign. At last he fixed his eyes on a most delightful estate, and offered to buy it—The owner did not want money, and could not think of selling the patrimony of an ancient family; this wretch then spirited up law-suits against him, and after the most cruel vexations obliged him to fell the estate for much less than he at first offered him. This unfortunate gentleman was driven from the country which gave him birth, and a once happy society of relations and friends.—Such would have been the fate of England, from those courts without juries, which took cognizance of causes arising in the revenues and imports in Charles the first's time; the court fortunately for the liberties of England, seized the bull by the horns, when they attacked that wonderful man John Hampden. He spent 20,000l. rather than pay an illegal tax of twenty shillings, brought the cause before the Parliament, roused the spirit of the nation, and finally overturned courts, King, and even the constitution for many years. These dreadful examples may teach us the importance of juries in civil cases—they may recal to my countrymen a maxim which their ancestors, as wise, and more virtuous than their posterity, held ever in view—*That if the people creep like tortoises, they will still find themselves too fast in giving away power.*

A FARMER.

———

Maryland Gazette

———

25 MARCH 1788

———

ESSAY V

———

The Farmer holds up Switzerland as the proper model of republican confederacy. The Swiss know the keys to maintaining free government: responsibility and an easy and certain method of changing rulers and measures without significant commotion. Praising Machiavelli, the Farmer argues that vigilance, constant referral of proposals to local landowners, and strong measures to keep the people virtuous are needed because rulers naturally seek to dominate. Essays in The Federalist *of particular relevance: 10, 49-51.*

I HAVE been long since firmly persuaded, that there are no hidden sources of moral agency beyond the reach of investigation.—The all-wise and all-bountiful Author of Nature, could never have created *human reason* unequal to the happy regulation of *human conduct*.—The errors and misfortunes of mankind spring from obvious sources. Religious and political prejudices, formed by education, strengthened by habit, maintained by interest, and consecrated by fear, are forever arming the passions against the judgment.—The celebrated Blaise Pascal (the powers of whose understanding were rather miraculous than surprizing) closed his painful researches after religious truth, with this dogma, as pernicious as untrue,— *"That a religion purely spiritual, was never intended for mankind."* There could be no judgment more unbiassed, for there was no mind so strong, no heart more pure; but bred in the bosom of the church, even her idolatry impressed him with veneration and awe. Notwithstanding his conclusion, the doctrines of Calvin maintain their ground in their primitive simplicity, divested of the aid of ceremony and form. The thunders of the Vatican, which for ages deluged Europe with blood, have dissipated their force, and reason has resumed her spiritual empire. Would to God, that the history of temporal despotism had terminated as favourably for the happiness of mankind!—In the political world, the chains of civil power, upheld by the numerous links of private interest, have proved more equal and permanent in their effects; they have, and I fear forever must, shackle the human understanding; and it is much to be questioned whether the full and free political opinion of any one great luminary of science, has been fairly disclosed to the world.—Even when the great and amiable Montesquieu had hazarded a panegyric on the English constitution, he shrinks back with terror into this degrading apostrophe—*"Think not that I mean to undervalue other governments—I who think an excess of liberty an excess of all things, even of reason itself, a misfortune, and that the happiness of mankind is only to be found in a medium between two extremes."*—The author of the Persian letters, at that moment recollected the afflicting pressure he had felt from the hand of Gallic government, and his pen trembled as he wrote.

Is it then possible that governments of simplicity and equal right, can have been fairly dealt by in theory or practice? The votaries of tyranny and usurpation stand not alone—in bitter opposition; every man of enterprize, of superior talents and fortune, is interested to debase them; their banners have ever been deserted because they never can pay their troops.—The most amiable and sensible of mankind seem to have made a stand in favour of a mixed government founded on the permanent orders and objects of men.— Thither I suspect the American government is now tending. If it must be so—Let it go gently then—with slow and equal steps.— Let each gradation and experiment have a full and fair trial—Let there be no effect without a good, apparent and well considered cause—Let us live all the days of our lives, and as happily as circumstances will permit.—Finally, let moderation be our guide and the influence of manners will conduct us (I hope without injury) to some permanent, fixed establishment, where we may repose awhile, unagitated by alteration or revolution—For in sudden and violent changes, how many of the most worthy of our fellow-citizens must get their bones crashed?

I cannot think that any *able and virtuous citizen,* would in his cool and dispationate moments, wish to blend or risque the fundamental rights of men, with any organization of society that the Americans can or will make for fifty years to come.—Let us keep these rights of individuals—these unalienable blessings reserved and separated from every constitution and form—If they are unmingled, the attentive eyes of every citizen will be kept fixed upon them. We shall watch them as a sacred deposit, and we may carry them uninjured and unimpaired through every vicissitude and change, from the government we have left, into some other that may be established on the fixed and solid principles of reason— [Nor] can there be, I imagine, any *prudent man,* who would trust the whimsical inventions of the day, with that dangerous weapon *a standing army,* in our present unsettled circumstances—striving to substantiate inefficient and unnatural forms—it would wield us into despotism in a moment, and we have surely had throat-cutting enough in our day.

Throughout the world government by representation seems only to have been established to disgrace itself and be abolished—its very principle is charge, and it sets all system at defiance—it perishes by speedy corruption.—The few representatives can always corrupt themselves by legislative speculations, from the pockets of their numerous constituents—quick rotation, like a succession of term tenants on a farm, only encreases the evil by rendering them more rapacious: If the executive is changeable, he can never oppose large decided majorities of influential individuals—or enforce on those powerful men, who may render his next election abortive, the rigor of *equal law, which is the grand and only object of human society*.—If the executive is to be rendered ineligible at a certain period, he will either *not do his duty*, or he will retire into the unprotected situation of a private individual with all the sworn animosities of a powerful majority—aristocracy—junto—the cry of the populace, or perhaps the whole combined to pursue him to the grave, or a public execution. The considerate and good, who adorn private life, and such only can be safely trusted in high public station, will never commit themselves to a situation where a consciencious discharge of duty may embitter the evening of life, if not draw down ruin and infamy on themselves and families.—There never was but one man who stepped from the top to the bottom, without breaking his neck, and that was Sylla; and although it is true that whilst he was up, he broke the hearts of the Romans, yet his dying undisturbed in private life, is one of those miracles that must remain forever unexplained. If the aristocracy, or representation of wealth, (the principle of which order is to keep all things as they are, for by confusion they may lose more than they can gain) is also changeable, there then is nothing fixed and permanent in government.—Legislative tyranny commences, and exhibits a perpetual scene of plunder and confusion, fearlessly practised under the sanction of authority and law. It is true that the influence of manners may and will resist for a time; yet that must give way to a general and prevalent corruption.—Those who are respectable at home and have permanent views in life, and such only can give stability to government, will not suffer themselves to be mounted up on the wheel of fortune, to be let down again as it turns, the mockery of children and fools.—Where representation has been admitted as a component part of government, it has always proved defective, if not destructive. What then must be the consequence where the whole government is founded on representation? Every American can now answer, it will be at best but—*representation of government*—with us the influence of manners has been great—it is indeed declining fast; but aided by the solidity of the judiciary establishments, and the wisest code of civil laws, that ever mankind were blessed with, it has hitherto supported the forms of society: But the people are now weary of their representatives and their governments.—We may trace the progress.—One candidate, to recommend his pretensions, discloses and descants on the errors of the preceding administration—The people believe him and are deceived—they change men; but measures are still the same, or injured by the sudden and violent alteration of system—At least the next candidate asserts it is so—is again believed, and his constituents again deceived; a general disgust and sullen silence ensue; elections are deserted; government is first despised, and then cordially hated.

There can be no fixed and permanent government that does not rest *on the fixed and permanent orders and objects of mankind.*— Government on *paper* may amuse, but we pay dear for the amusement, the only fixed and permanent *order* with us at present are the *YEOMANRY*, and they have no power whatever,—unless the right of changing masters at a certain period, and devolving on their changeable representatives their whole political existence—may be called power—The order of GENTRY, with us, is not a fixed and permanent order at all, and if they attempt to erect themselves into one at present, it is usurpation, and they will be pulled down; and yet, in my opinion, such an order is essential to a perfect government founded on representation.—Every other mode of introducing wealth into power, has proved vicious and [abominable].—With us delegates become by selection, themselves a species of subaltern aristocracy—they intrigue with the senates, who by a refined mode of election are a misbegotten, side blow, representation of wealth, and they both form an imperfect aristocracy, on the worst principles on which that order can be admitted into government—and the democratic influence which is thus amalgomated and not divided, but unformed becomes vicious from its impotence.

These defects spring from our attempting to erect republican fabrics on the ruined and imperfect pillars of an old corrupt monarchy—not less absurd, than to expect the limbs to perform the functions of life, after cutting off the head.—The opposition which brought Charles the first to the block, was composed of some of the ablest and most virtuous characters that ever adorned any age or clime—Hampden, Pym, Selden, Sir Harry Vane, Sydney, Marvell and many others.—They pursued their old model—attempted to form a government by representation which was at first steadied and restrained by the best senate in the world, (the English House of Lords)—the two houses soon disagreed, and there being no third power to interpose, the representatives, voted the House of Lords useless—new modelled the government into a single branch, and then began to plunder most unmercifully—At last Cromwell kicked them all out of doors, and after his tyrannical usurpation and death, the nation were very happy to take shelter again under the regal government, and even restored an unworthy family (which they had irritated beyond forgiveness) to the throne.

A FARMER.

(*To be continued.*)

Maryland Gazette

28 MARCH 1788

ESSAY V

(*Continued.*)

AFTER every consideration I can give this subject, I am satisfied, that *government founded on representation*, indispensibly requires, at least an executive for life, whose person must be sacred from impeachment, and only his ostensible ministers responsible—A senate for life, the vacancies to be filled up and the number occasionally encreased but under a limitation, by the executive—the hand that holds the balance must have the power of adding weight and influence to the lightest scale, and of frequently removing turbulent men into an higher and inoffensive situation:—I am inclined to think that an important portion of American opinion leans that way at this moment—My fear is, that our general government may ultimate in an hereditary authority—if not despotism—to avoid the former, great attention should be paid to the important office of Vice-President—at present but little understood:—A Vice-President to succeed on a vacancy prevents those evils which have ruined Poland and all the northern kingdoms—thus we see the King of the Romans has secured Germany from every evil of elective monarchy, and had the golden bull prevented one of the family or kindred of the reigning Emperor from filling the office of the King of the Romans, this part of the Germanic constitution would have been perfect, and the house of Austria would never have been enabled to usurp the imperial crown as a patrimony and desolate Europe with her ambitious views; she would have continued in that beggarly condition from which Rodolph of Hapsburg raised it—The American constitution is much better guarded but not by any means completely so.

If this is the best we can hope for—if this is the best reward we can expect for the sons of America slain, and the distresses we shall long continue to feel—is it not incumbent on us to examine minutely all its consequences?—Let us view government by representation in its favorite form—The constitution of England—its uncommon success and length of duration there, has drawn on it very unmerited encomiums from the enlightened Genevan Delolme—the only great political writer who does not seem to hold representation in contempt,—indeed the viewing it through this favorable medium has always animated our hopes, and led many sensible Americans to imagine, this old and universal experiment, to be peculiar to that isle—In pursuing my inquiry into the principles and effects of the British government, I shall first grant that it is a rational system, founded on solid, safe principles—and one of the best governments for the higher ranks of mankind in the world—but then I must

insist that it was hardly a government at all, until it became simplified by the introduction and regular formation of the effective
administration of responsible ministers, on its present system—
which we cannot date higher up, than the appointment of Lord
Strafford and others by Charles 1st.*—Moreover I do not know
how far the system of bribery introduced by Sir Robert Walpole,
and the influence of the numerous body of public creditors, are not
now absolutely necessary to its present stability—and after all, I
am not satisfied how such a simplification [as would produce a
responsibility, can be effected in a government, complicated by so]
many subordinate and powerful corporations as the American
States will be—and yet responsibility must be attained and an easy
and certain mode adopted, of changing measures and men without
commotion, or liberty will be lost in the attempt—I am confused
and bewildered when I arrive at this point of reflection, and despotism meets me at every turn.—There are but *two* modes of governing mankind, by just and equal law, enforced impartially on all
ranks of society, or by the sword:—If such laws cannot be obtained,
or the attainment is attended with too much difficulty, the sword
will supply their place; *et inter arma leges silent. When arms command the laws are disobeyed.* Shall we have patience, with the disorders of our complicated machine? As Alexander dissolved the
gordian knot with the sword—so I fear a standing army will sim-
plify the governments of America.—I have said that the government of England afforded firm protection to property—it certainly
does so, comparatively speaking—yet the history of its frequent
revolutions, will discover that even property is insecure there. During the civil wars, in which the Stuarts involved this nation, two-
thirds of the property of the kingdom changed masters; and in those
between Lancaster and York, and before the firm establishment of
the line of Tudor, almost all the old families perished and their property became dissipated:—And yet its protection of property is its
favorable side; turn your eyes to the lower order of citizens, and
they are pressed into the earth by taxation and imposition—very

---

*Before that period they were minions and favorites, who by plundering and
oppressing the people excited constant commotion, and were seldom changed
but with their masters, and by the axe or halter.*

rarely will industry enable the husbandman to rear a family—
where the sons of agriculture are so poorly rewarded, government
must be ulcerated to the heart—the miserable poor who pursue the
dictates of nature and religion, in that connection which is destined
to sweeten the bitter draught of life, are commonly handed from
constable to constable, until their unfortunate birth compels some
parish to own them.—The people of England have always and forever will emigrate—The people of England never repair to arms
to repel foreign invasion—and they never will unless compelled—to
conquer England, it would only seem necessary from past example, to escape their floating defences and land on the island; passing by former invasions and conquests. As late as the year 1745,
Prince Charles Edward, at the head of an undisciplined rabble,
belonging to some Highland clans attached to his family, marched
undisturbed, through the most populous counties into the heart of
the kingdom, and the capital containing 200,000 fighting men trembled for its safety at the approach of an unexperienced boy, followed
by 4 or 5000 half armed peasants—scarcely a man in the kingdom
shouldered a musquet until the danger disappeared, and government owed its safety to the protection of foreign mercenaries, or
rather the weakness and irresolution of the assailant—The fact is,
the people will never fight (if they can help it) for representatives,
taxes and rags.

Let us now contrast this scene with one, where the people *personally* exercise the powers of government—The three small
democratic Cantons of Uri, Schuitz and Underwald, broke the
chains of their former servitude, and laid the foundation of the
Swiss confederacy—they effected the revolution, and in conjunction with the other democratic Cantons and their democratic allies
the Grisons, have supported the grand fabric of Helvetic liberty to
this day. Every Swiss farmer is by birth a legislator, and he
becomes a voluntary soldier to defend his power and his property;
their fathers have been so before them for near 500 years, without
revolution, and almost without commotion—they have been the
secure spectators of the constant and universal destruction of the
human species, which the usurpations of the *few* have ever created, and must I fear forever perpetuate:—Whilst all Europe were

butchering each other for the love of God, and defending the usurpations of the clergy, under the masque of religion, the malignant evil crept into this sacred asylum of liberty; (but where the government resides in the body of the people, they can never be corrupted by the artifice or the wealth of the *few*) they soon banished the dæmon of discord, and Protestant and Papist sat down under the peaceful shade of the same tree, whilst in every surrounding State and kingdom, the son was dragging the father, and brothers, their brothers, to the scaffold, under the sanction of those distinctions:—Thus these happy Helvetians have in peace and security beheld all the rest of Europe become a common slaughterhouse.—A free Swiss acquires from his infancy, a knowledge of the fundamental laws of his country, and the leading principles of their national policy are handed down by tradition from father to son—the first of these is never to trust power to representatives, or a national government. A free Swiss pays no taxes, on the contrary he receives taxes; every male of 16 years, shares near ten shillings sterling annually, which the rich and powerful surrounding monarchies pay for the friendship of these manly farmers. Whenever their societies become too large, as government belongs to the citizens and the citizens are the property of no government, they divide amicably, and each separate part pursues the simple form, recommended by their ancestors and become venerable, by the glorious and happy experience of ages of prosperity—Their frugal establishments are chiefly supported by the pay which the officers of government receive for the services they render individuals. With a country the most unfriendly to industry in the world, they have become in a series of years, passed in uninterrupted but moderate labor, frugality, peace and happiness, the richest nation under the sun. I have seen a computation, by which it appeared, that the interest of the money they have before hand, and that which is due them from the rich nations of Europe, would support themselves and their posterity forever, without farther exertion; and this whilst every other government is actually as much or more in debt than it is worth.

An intelligent author has remarked, that [passing from a democratic to an aristocratic Canton] of Swisserland, you quit the society of men to contemplate the regular labor of brutes; they are compelled indeed in the aristocratic Cantons to be extremely moderate in their government, and to lay few or no taxes, or they would drive their subjects into the neighbouring free States—as it is, they are well cloathed, well fed and taken good care of—The same author remarks, that the line which separates all Swisserland, from the countries around (where men like cattle are the property of their proud Lords and kept chained to the soil) is the line of division between light and darkness—between happiness and horror.

The love of the Switzers for their country is altogether romantic and surpasses the bounds of credibility—those memorable relations authenticated by the common consent of all historians, of their beating on all occasions the flower of the Austrian and French troops (who have invaded them) with numbers so unequal and trifling as scarce to exceed their enemies out-guards; the instances of hundreds of citizens devoting their lives for the safety of their country; of their frequently disdaining life and refusing quarter when overpowered by numbers, have astonished and terrified the neighbouring powers, and seem incomprehensible to a people dispirited by taxes, overloaded with debts and disgusted with government. I cannot omit a striking characteristic, authenticated by Coxe and others, whose authority will not be questioned; they relate that there is a rustic tune familiar in the mountains of Swisserland—it is called the *Rantz des vacqes*—it consists of a few simple notes of native wild melody. The French and Dutch governments have been compelled to forbid under very severe penalties, the playing this woodland music, to those Swiss troops, which they hire for a limited time; the well-known notes revive instantly all the fond images, which were impressed on their youthful bosoms, their friends, their parents, their relations and their beloved country, rush into their imaginations in a full tide of affection—no persuasion can detain them, they desert home in regiments, or if retained by force, they pine away in the deepest melancholy—no instance has yet occurred of Swiss troops serving in any part of Europe, who have not returned, with the diligence and anxiety of affectionate children, on the first appearance of danger to their parent country:—The same amor-patriæ, the same divine love of their country, universally pervades the bosom of every citizen, who in right of his birth, legislates for himself:—Grosley relates that he saw in Rome a poor fellow (who had travelled through great part of Europe and Asia afoot) declaiming to a crowd with the most passionate zeal, in praise of his own country, boasting of her happiness and prefering San Marino to all the world besides—This democratic republic, is a little bee-hive of free citizens, who have made a delicious garden of the top of a bleak barren mountain, situated in the midst of the finest and most fruitful plains of Italy, which tyranny has depopulated around them.—Look into the human breast—We love that power, which we exercise ourselves, but we detest that which others exercise over us, be they Representatives, Lords, or Kings; and to this source we may trace the abuse, which the Americans bestow on their country and their governments.

But we are told that Swisserland, *should be no example for us*— I am very sorry for it—they are the only, the only part of the human species that sustain the dignity of character, belonging to the divine resemblance we bear,—*they are few in number it is said*—This is not true—they are more numerous then we are—*They cover a small spot of territory*—this is also not true—they possess a large tract of country in the very heart of Europe—but this is not all— The Helvetic confederacy, including the three leagues of the Grisons comprehends one hundred perhaps two hundred, independent governments and States—nor is there any reason from their history or present state to doubt, that the same plan of confederation might not be extended with as lasting and happy effects to one thousand independent governments—But it is also said *they are a poor, frugal people*—As to their poverty that is likewise untrue— they have great sums of money before hand and owe not a sixpence—they indeed are a wise and consequently a frugal people—though they still have great estates and even luxury among them too—But should we despise their poverty or their frugality? We who are so many millions worse than nothing? *But still we are told we must not take example from them—we must take example from Holland and Germany*—They had better at once tell us, that we must desert the worship of God and follow that of the devil.

From the first dawn of light, that broke in upon my reason, I became devoted to governments of simplicity and equal right—The names of heroes, whose blood has bedewed the altars of freedom, vibrate like the shock of electricity, on my frame; and when I read the story of Brutus and of Cassius, the most noble and the last of the Romans, tears of admiration gush from my eyes.—Under these impressions which only the grave can erase, I feel unspeakable horror at every step, which removes power and rights, at a greater distance from the body of the people, to whom they belong, and confines them to the hands of *the few*. I have proposed to myself this question: If representatives cannot govern the people—If they abuse the power entrusted to them, shall they devolve this power on a still smaller number, who must be more liable to corruption from the encrease of temptation? Or should they restore it into the hands of the people, from whom they received it? who alone are incorruptible, because the wealth of the few can never bribe the many, against the duty they owe to themselves. If I am told that the people are incapable of governing themselves—I shall answer that they have never been tried in America, except among the native Indians, who are free and happy, and who prove that self-government is the growth of our soil—and I also answer that they are more fit for self-government, than they are at present for any of the safe and solid governments, founded on representation.—When I see all these principles established by the example of the Swiss, who have remained under the simplest of all forms of government for near five hundred years, in uninterrupted tranquility and happiness—whilst every other invention of genius, devise of art, or imposition [of force, has been torn up by the roots, with every] aggravated circumstance of horror—I can no longer doubt—All the mists of theory and speculation vanish before an experiment like this.

The greatest human discernment, ever concentrated in the mind of one man, was the portion of the celebrated Nicholas Machiavelli—a name loaded with abuse by tyrants, flatterers and the mushrooms of science, because he told the truth; because he was a republican and the friend of mankind in times of usurpation; or because, they have never read or do not understand his works.

After every inquiry which the most unbounded information and reflection, with a long experience in high public office afforded, Machiavelli, delivers his deliberate opinion in favour of the body of the people, as the only safe depository of liberty and power—He prefers it to the aristocracy and the Prince; but he does not disgrace the inquiry by mentioning representation. If this was the opinion of Machiavelli, a citizen of Florence, where a numerous populace confined and crowded within the walls of a city, formed the most turbulent republic, that ever disgraced the cause of freedom by cruelty and anarchy—How much more favourably must his decision apply to the yeomanry of America—Landholders and consequently the most independent of mankind, mild by nature, moderate by manners, and persevering in every honest pursuit:—Surely if ever men were worthy of being entrusted with their own rights, the freeholders of America are—*Make them then and their posterity legislators by birth*—I mean not the lowest populace—I mean that class of citizens to whom this country belongs:—Numbers unqualified by property, should have their influence—they should be protected—they might preserve the right of election—But they who hold the property of the soil, are alone entitled to govern it:—To effect this there would need but little change in the present forms—They might all stand—But the laws which pass the legislature before they become binding, should be referred to the different counties and cities—printed reasons drawn by committees, might if necessary, accompany each, together with an annual estimate of public wants and a detail of the expenditures of the former sums granted. Let these laws then be submitted to the free deliberation of the free-holders of the counties and cities—the numbers of the yeas and nays be taken on each by the presiding magistrate, and transmitted to the executive, who may then upon comparing the returns from the several counties and corporations, declare what laws are the will of the people. On the appearance of any sudden danger the two houses or indeed a majority of one house, might invest the Executive with that authority, exigency might require for the safety of the republic, until remedy should be provided by law.

The number of representatives might be decreased and an expence saved—this would at one blow destroy all legislative speculations—the influence of demagogues, or oligarchic juntos must then cease—The assemblage of the freeholders, separate in different counties would prevent disturbance—As no new law could be made in them, little confusion could ensue—After some years or even immediately if confined to future cases the celebrated law of Geneva might be introduced, and no freeholder admitted to the assembly until he had paid his father's debts. Sumptu[ary] laws, permitting the use, but prohibiting the abuse of wealth, might be interposed to guard the public manners.—The Governor and the members of the senate might constitute a council of censors, to punish offenders against the sumptuary laws and the laws of morality, by a removal from office, and even disfranchisement, if necessary, with an appeal to the people of the county where the offender resided, in the latter case and to the people of the State in the former[.—]Seminaries of useful learning, with professor[ships] of political and domestic oeconomy might be established in every county, discarding the philosophy of the moon and skies, we might descend to teach our citizens what is useful in this world—the principles of free government, illustrated by the history of mankind—the sciences of morality, agriculture, commerce, the management of farms and household affairs—The light would then penetrate, where mental darkness now reigns.—Do these things and in a very few years the people instead of abusing, would wade up to their [knees] in blood, to defend their government.

For some years past this has been the darling object of my life—to which all my views have tended—And I now think that nothing intermediate would be lasting or worthy the pursuit—Whenever I fairly lose sight of this—As soon as I turn my back forever on these dear illusions which will be as soon as the proposed fœderal government is adopted—I shall turn all my wishes to that social state, whither that government will lead us, and I both hope and expect that with those amendments and guards, which it seems to be the general disposition to provide—it will gradually maturate in a safe and reasonable government.—Until that adoption I speak to my fellow citizens in the words of the proverb—*Do not that by others, which you can do yourselves.*

A FARMER.

Maryland Gazette

1 APRIL 1788

ESSAY VI

The Farmer responds to the charge of slander against the Federalists, leveled at him by Aristides calling on Aristides to argue facts rather than personalities. The Farmer goes on to argue that Aristides was wrong to say that state courts would enjoy concurrent jurisdiction with federal courts regarding issues involving interpretion of federal laws. Federal supremacy would control in this area. Essays in The Federalist *of particular relevance: 1, 82.*

RETIRED in the country the publication by *Aristides* did not reach the *Farmer* until this moment. The object of the remarks by the *Farmer* was to draw the attention of the public to a question of the greatest magnitude to them and their posterity; and the *cause* in which he has ventured to publish his sentiments is a *cause* of the United States.—The great and manifest defects in the *national* government proposed for America,—the omission of a declaration to ascertain the *rights* of the several *States*, and the *rights* of *individuals*, the primary object of every good and free government, particularly the trial by jury on suit against a *federal* officer for abuse of authority;—the want of proper checks to prevent the abuse, or annihilation of those rights;—the manifest danger to public liberty from a standing army, without limitation of number, in time of peace;—and the pernicious doctrines of *Aristides;* alone induced the *Farmer* to lay his reflections before the tribunal of public opinion.

It would give the *Farmer* real pain to stain a *public* cause with *private* altercation, and he flatters himself that his candid and impartial readers will admit, that his *first* address, which has given so great offence to *Aristides*, and which he calls abuse, slander, calumny, and a wanton and unprovoked attack on his *good name*, was temperate, moderate, and decent, and even respectful to that writer. The *Farmer* took the liberty to condemn and to expose the doctrines and errors of *Aristides*; but with charity he imputed his opinions to defect of judgment, or want of information. A good and virtuous citizen may, from want of understanding, maintain principles incompatible with the public welfare. If his integrity is not accused he should bear admonition or reproof with temper and moderation. If his opinions are censured he should justify or explain them with candor and decency, and should treat his adversary with respect. If his motives of action are questioned, he should defend himself with dignity and manly firmness, without petulance or asperity, or as Aristides recommends, *"he should behave like a gentleman."* *Personalities* are always odious and can only be *excused* by the imputation of political opinions to improper, unworthy or base motives. The *Farmer* could not possibly entertain any *personal* resentment against *Aristides*. A knowledge by light and a very few occasional conversations comprehend all the acquaintance between them. The *Farmer* was disposed to think well of *Aristides* from the report of some few of his acquaintance, and not from his own declaration, however solemn of his immaculate purity, and love of country; for in this degenerate age the integrity and the patriotism of men must be measured by their actions, and not their professions.

The *Farmer* disdains intentionally to *misrepresent Aristides*, he may have been so unfortunate as to have *misunderstood* him. It seems that what the *Farmer* considered as the *opinions* of *Aristides* were only *objections* to a bill of rights by *some [æriel] forms*, which he has pleased to usher into his drama to close the catastrophe, when from the former character he had assumed, he could not so well appear with the *sword* himself. Why did *Aristides* put *groundless* objections in the mouths of any persons, which no persons had ever used? What sense is there in making objections of no weight (and which he himself despised) to a bill of rights, under the covert of persons of his own creating?—If the *Farmer* misunderstood *Aristides*, it might have arose from his combining with his *general* doctrine a report of a declaration by him of the respect and regard he would pay to the Maryland bill of rights in his judicial capacity.—The *Farmer* then firmly believed, and he still believes that *Aristides* thought that bills of rights were considered in Europe as grants of Kings. The *Farmer* knew that this had been the language and argument of a Judge of another State. All the arguments of the *Farmer* went to prove that they were not so considered in Europe, attended with the observation that he never knew the doctrine advanced in print, but by *Filmer* and *Aristides*.

Aristides insinuates that the remarks of the *Farmer* on his opinions proceeded from his desire to *pay* COURT to a gentleman who lately held the highest office in the State. This insinuation is as false as it is mean and illiberal. The *Farmer* can respect and esteem the *public* and *private* virtues of a citizen without degrading himself to the lowest servility of the lowest sycophant. The *Farmer* has never dealt in the fulsome language of modern dedications, and if inclined, he could not direct his flatteries to obtain any office civil or military, under the new government. The *Farmer* has no wish to conceal himself from the apprehension of censure from an impartial public; and from the resentment of *Aristides* it is impossible he can have any thing to fear. A fancied superiority, and insolence of office gave birth to this unwarrantable suggestion.

There may be other reasons why *Aristides* has thought proper to make known his real name to the public than those he has suggested. If his vanity prompted him to believe, that his character would carry respect and authority to his publication, never was any political writer more mistaken. His pamphlet will injure the *cause* he undertakes to defend wherever it appears. It might be expected that *Aristides* would be more competent to understand the part of the new constitution, that establishes the JUDICIARY, than any other. He approves the *whole* system, and yet he knows the *least* of what he ought to understand the *most*. He says the article erecting the *judiciary* has been generally misconceived, and the *Farmer* verily believes by no person more than by *Aristides*. That Farmers and Planters should not comprehend the jurisdiction of the *federal judicial power* might be expected; but that a great *law character*, like *Aristides*, should so egregiously blunder, is very astonishing. A man grossly mistaken in his profession may be justly suspected in other subjects.

Aristides asserts, "that the *inferior federal* courts, and the *State* courts will have *concurrent original* jurisdiction in all the enumerated cases, *wherein an appeal lies to the supreme federal court,* except only the cases created by, or under the proposed constitution."—By the second section of the third article, "The judicial power is to extend to all cases, in law and equity, arising under the *constitution,* or the LAWS of the United States; and to all controversies between citizens of *different* States, and the citizens of any of the United States, and the citizens, or subjects, of *foreign* States"; and by the eighth section of the first article, "The Congress are invested with *power* to levy and collect taxes, duties, imposts, and excises; and to make such *laws* as shall be necessary and proper for carrying into execution these powers." *Aristides* contends that a *federal* officer, say an excise officer, may be sued by a citizen in a *State* court (I suppose any county court as well as the supreme court) for an abuse of his authority; and with confidence he asserts, "That *no sound lawyer, of a good moral reputation* will maintain the contrary opinion"; and he treats with supercilious contempt the objection of want of remedy in a *State* court, and a trial by jury *for* the citizen *against* a *federal* officer, for an abuse of office, "as a ridiculous bugbear, fit only to alarm minds on which no science has ever dawned." Is it not evident that the jurisdiction in the cases *above-mentioned,* is *expressly* given to the *inferior federal* courts, with an appeal, both as to law and *fact,* to the *supreme federal* court?—Is it not clear that it was intended to keep the *federal* and State jurisdictions entirely separate? Were not the *subordinate federal* courts established to protect the continental revenue officers from the *State* jurisdictions?—If an action would lie *against a federal* officer in the *State* courts would it not blend and confound the *two* jurisdictions, and that too without any appeal from the *State* courts?—Is not the *supreme federal* court superior to the *State* courts? Is it not superior to the bills of rights, and the constitutions, of the several States?—If the *State* courts have *concurrent jurisdiction* with the *inferior federal* courts, that is, if any suit of which the *latter* has cognizance by the *new* government, may notwithstanding be instituted in the *former,* is it not self-evident that there may be *different* adjudications on the SAME question; and if decided in the *inferior federal* court with an appeal, if decided in a *State* court without any appeal, to the *supreme federal* court? What would be the effect of opposite decisions by two courts having concurrent jurisdiction?—If an action is commenced in a *State* court, *Aristides* thinks, and justly too, that thence there is no appeal to the *supreme federal* court, but only to their own high court of appeals, as heretofore. With confidence he maintains that as the jurisdiction of the *State* courts is not taken away by an *express* clause, or *necessary implication*, that they will still have cognizance of those cases of which jurisdiction is given to the *inferior federal* courts. The *Farmer* believes there is not another lawyer, or Judge, *of sound judgment in the law*, in all America, that entertains a similar opinion.—The *Farmer* is so bold as to hazard his opinion, contrary to that of *Aristides*, that if a citizen of Georgia, or subject of Great-Britain, has any claim against a citizen of Maryland, or if he has any claim against them, that suits in such cases, after the establishment of the *national* government, can only be commenced and prosecuted in the *inferior federal* courts, because the *State* courts are ousted of their jurisdiction of those cases, by *necessary implication*, from the obvious motives for the establishment of the *federal judiciary*, and the evident absurdities that must flow from a *concurrent jurisdiction* in the SAME cases. Is it not absurd to suppose that the *national* governments intended that the *State* courts should have jurisdiction to decide on the LAWS of the *United States*, whether consonant or repugnant to the *national constitution*; or whether the *federal* officers abuse their authority?—And yet the grave, the solemn, the didactic *Aristides* asserts, "That every *State* Judge will have a *right* to *reject* any *act* handed to him as a *law* of the United States, which HE may conceive repugnant to the constitution." How perverted or confused must be the head of that man who can seriously entertain so ridiculous an opinion! He can never claim from his knowledge of the *national*, or any other government to be one of the Judges of the most inferior of the inferior *federal* courts—*Risum teneatis*. A puisne Judge of a petty State (of Delaware, or Rhode-Island) to have a *right* to declare a LAW of the United States VOID? Will any *sound lawyer*, his moral reputation out of the question, risk his legal character so far as to maintain this assertion?—If *Aristides* has not too much pride to be convinced, if he has the candour he professes, or the legal or political knowledge he wishes the world to believe, he would not obstinately continue in error, but confess, how greatly he has misunderstood the *judiciary* system of the *national* government.

If *Aristides* shall determine to mix *private* resentment with a *public* cause, if he cannot discuss political questions without descending to offensive personalities, or if he wishes to examine into the motives or private reputation of his *adversary*, as he very improperly calls the *Farmer*, he is informed that the *Farmer* has left his *real* name with the Printer.—If *Aristides* can discover ought in the life or manners of the *Farmer*, the detection of which may serve the public cause, or gratify private malice, he has free liberty to publish, to expose it to the world, in the strongest colours;— he will for his own sake confine himself to fact.—Calumniating invective may rouse any temper. *Aristides* has too long held a licentious pen with impunity.

A Farmer.

Maryland Gazette

4 APRIL 1788

ESSAY VII

In an essay spanning several newspaper issues, the Farmer presents equality as the prime good. The equality of nature may legitimately give way only to the equal subordination of all classes to the law, an equality which inequality of property undermines. He goes on to detail the corruption of free government from aristocracy to tyranny, with an attendant corruption of public morals. At lowest stage of corruption the people become susceptible to religious movements like Christianity, which themselves breed only conflict. Religion can be rendered harmless only by free government,

which must be sustained through a balance of local powers. The
Farmer then criticizes all existing American constitutions, calling
for new ones that would eliminate representation in favor of direct
control by local landowners. In the essay's final section, which is
not found in Storing, the Farmer asks whether the proposed con-
stitution will answer the defects of America's state constitutions.
According to the Farmer, the framework will make matters worse
by further complicating political arrangements. Essays in The
Federalist *of particular relevance: 49, 50.*

ARISTIDES with a degree of confidence, which many will deem presumption, insinuates that his arguments can only be combated by
sophistry:—Language expressly calculated to impose on the uninformed mind may be justly suspected; but remarks addressed to the
reason of *those* who are happy in education and leisure for reflection,
can never do injury:—*Sophistry* may blind or mislead the wavering
and inconstant mind, of the humble and unenlightened individual;
but to convince the understanding and rouse the spirit, of the intelligent part of mankind, is the sacred province of *truth* alone.

To examine and elucidate the great and leading principles of government, we must penetrate to the source of human action, and
explore the heart and constitution of man;—a consciousness of the
equal rights of nature, is a component part of that ætherial spirit,
which we dignify with the appellation of soul; the ardent desire
and unceasing pursuit of equality, can therefore be no more
destroyed by human power, than the soul itself; the chains of ter-
restrial despotism may confine, afflict and bow down to the earth,
this mould of flesh; but the soul more free than air, quits this mortal frame, surrounded by ills no longer supportable, and after wit-
nessing the final overthrow of all its hopes in this world, retires
with indignation, into a world unknown.

Let any people be personally and fairly consulted on the form of
that government, which is to rule them and their children, and they
will establish the *law of equality* as its basis;—the unequal division of property silently and gradually undermines this foundation, almost as soon as society is formed; or before a new compact
is confirmed, this equality is materially injured if not destroyed.—

Montesquieu justly observes that men, in the advanced stages of government, quit the equality of nature, from the moment of their birth, never to re-enter it but by the force of equal law;—the law then that is equally enforced on all ranks of society, to which the *great* and the *humble*, are compelled to submit, is the next state of equality, to which this ever active principle of the mind aspires; with this it would be content, as the most perfect state of liberty, which exists only, in a just medium between two extremes; but in the attainment and preservation of this, the efforts of the human understanding never keep pace with the will.

Quicquid delirant reges, plectuntur achivi.

It is the poor people who suffer for the misrule of the great.

Laws are cobwebs, catching only the flies and letting the wasps escape. The great and powerful, can easily bring to justice, the *poor and humble offender*; but who is to lead to punishment the *great*? These lords of the earth, who have extensive and powerful connexions, who aim at no trifling larcenies; but who plunder a people of their liberties and put public revenues into their private purses, under the sanction of laws made by themselves:—These are the men who deprive their fellow mortals of their fondest hopes, and compel them to resort to the supreme aim of a monarch—to the authority of a single person—who exalted far above all may reduce them all, once more to that common level of equal law, of which mankind never lose sight:—*Come we will choose one man to rule over us!* is the cry of a people who are tired of the rule of the *elders*—the meaning of the word senate, is an assembly of elders; but this the last and most fatal step, is never retrieved, until government returns through blood into that original chaos—from the discordant elements of which, new and equal forms of society arise, created upon first principles.

The corruption of the rule of one man is also regular and perhaps like every other progressive step of *mixed government*—unavoidable.—He is at first limited and his hands tied; but as the powerful and strong are alone able to keep him confined—they are the checks which are necessarily imposed.—The elders, or the senate, are always joined in power to guard against his usurpations:—The people in this event, find that instead of a protector of their equal rights, they have elected a patron for the rich and powerful, who, under the sanction of his name and authority, plunder and oppress with still greater security.—If a weak Prince should attempt to curb their insolence, he generally becomes himself the sacrifice to his own temerity—the proud chiefs rebel—put new shackles on their principal;—until at length tired of his own uneasy and dependant situation—disgusted at sheltering evil and his incapacity to do good—Some able and politic chieftain breaks the bonds of restraint; perhaps with the manly boldness of a Gustavus Erickson, he may demand of the representatives of the nation, to take back that power which is only a cloak for vice and which is too weak to do good.—He may request them to deprive him of the authority he had received, or give him that which would enable him to secure the public prosperity and private happiness.—Let him leave the legislature with a stern firmness—retire to an army who adore him, and submission must follow;—or let such a chief pursue the more usual rout to power—let him profit of the discontents of the multitude and he will quickly fasten the cords of authority around the necks of the great.

The chief magistrate is now cloathed with full authority to *do good.*—If he does so, he confirms a solid tyranny for his degenerate successors—For if power does not corrupt him it certainly will those that follow:—In this view, the best elected magistrates have only entailed misery on mankind—the wife and moderate administration of Augustus, (who was appointed commander in chief of the established forces, and was annually elected consul during the whole period of his life) secured the power and gave full scope to the vices of Tiberius, Caligula and Nero in whom the julian line ended:—A veneration for the memory of Titus enabled his brother Domitian to sink the spirit of the world, and the divine Marcus Aurelius found that the lustre of his own virtues would frustrate every endeavour of his disinterested and patriot head, to set aside the election of that monster, his son, or rather his wife's son Commodus; for Marcus Aurelius could never have been the father of such a son—and the latter end of this all-accomplished mortal, was embittered with the prospect, of the misery of his fellow citizens under the administration of a brute—As to hereditary chief magistrates, I perfectly agree with the Marquis Mirabeau, and what he says of France may be justly extended to the whole world—he says, if I recollect right, that in 1100 years there have been but four Princes on the French throne, that did not deserve the gallows.—In England, an Henry IId. was succeeded by a brute, a coward and a fool—Richard, John and Henry—the valiant and just Edward the Ist. made way for the mean and despicable Edward IId—the Great Edward the IIId and his adored son, the Black Prince, crowned the English throne with laurels to be lavished away by the profuse and injudicious hand of Richard IId—and the valiant Henry the Vth. transmitted his glory and authority to be tarnished by his weak son, Henry the sixth.—In fine, there is no general truth more fully established than, that human beings entrusted with power will abuse it—from the Prince who fills the throne, down to the degraded negro, who beats his poor plough-horses and oxen so unmercifully:—There is a humane and benevolent saying of an illustrious *Prince*, the Marshal Vendome, which deserves to be imprinted on our minds in indelible characters.—He said that in a long march he listened attentively to the quarrels between the muleteers and the mules, and that he found the mules always in the right—thus the possession and the abuse of power seem inseperably connected.

The rule of any one man, who is elevated to a preheminence of power, is always surrounded by those vile minions and favorites, who bask in the sunshine of courts—deify the object of their adoration with the venal incense of flattery—intercept every avenue to truth, and who never can be satisfied until they reduce the people to the slavery of the ancient Persians—who, when their Prince ordered them to be well bastinadoed, were obliged to fall down upon their knees and say—*We thank you most gracious Sovereign for deigning to recollect us.*—

But it will be asked can this happen in America?—My countrymen, you will yet discover before your clay is cold, a truth long established by every political enquiry—that in all governments, in which there is sown the smallest seed of the rule of one man, no checks—no bars, can prevent its growing into a monarchy, or a despotism if the empire is extensive—And that to attempt to form a virtuous republic on the unqualified principles of representation is as vain as to expect a carriage to run with wheels only on one side.—Wheels will be added on the other, and the machine once set in motion down hill will never stop until it carries us to the *bottom*—then let us not set off without every necessary check.

It is true the proposed national system guarantees to each State a republican form of government—Whoever will look into Coxe's Northern Travels, will find that in the treaty whereby the three arch-despots of Russia, Germany and Prussia, divided that poor distracted country, Poland—they solemnly guarantee (in express words) to the said Poland—*a republican government forever.*

A Farmer.

(*To be continued.*)

For the Maryland Gazette, &c.

---

8 APRIL 1788

ESSAY VII

(*Continued.*)

The chief who is thus liberated from constitutional restraints, is under no control but the licentiousness of the soldiery:—The prætorian bands of the Roman and the Janizaries of the Turkish empire, have frequently stained the imperial purple with blood, and applied the bow-string to the haughty descendants of Othman—yet they are always the willing instruments of the cruelty of the Prince against all ranks of his subjects.

Here then we arrive at the summit of imperfection in human legislation—the magistrate whose will is law, is no longer restrained by the influence of manners—a regard to reputation or the desire of glory—the three ruling principles that guide the heart to virtue;—his own inclinations become the manners of the empire—establish reputation and fix the standard of fame.—Caius Cæsar, who was declared Imperator or Emperor of the Roman republic (a title in its most extensive signification meaning only a military commander in chief) was devoted to lust—A grave senate of Rome—that senate which twenty or indeed ten years before, had commanded the awe and veneration of mankind, solemnly proposed a law, as Suetonius informs us, to submit their wives and daughters to his embraces— it was his regard for the public reputation that alone forbad this sacrifice of the honor of the empire—the first Cæsar was a compound of the most exalted virtue and deepest vice—but the fact discovers what instantaneous change, the slightest alterations of government may create in the manners of a people—of a most enlightened and virtuous people—for the age of Julius Cæsar, was the age of Cicero, Cato, Brutus, Cassius and of all that noble but unfortunate band of conspirators.—

But this furious passion which has celestial beauty for its object, soon banishes philosophy and moderation—even the glowing idea that gives all that is beautiful and amiable to our arms, makes the senses drunk with passion—What effects then must spring from the *idea realized*—all history informs us—the minds of all men, even the best unrestrained by their own, or the constitution of the State become inebriated with lust, from the times of David, the second chief magistrate of Israel—a man after God's own heart—and his son Solomon—the wife, who had the moderate share of seven hundred wives and three hundred concubines—down to the amorous Charles, (who restored to the English throne, before the republican fever had cooled, or Presbyterian sanctity had relaxed) yet contrived to fill the English peerage with his bastards.—The nation made one jump from the cold pulpit of religion into the hotbed of vice—This irresistible passion marked with celebrity the decemvirate of Rome—a *tyranny* established by the free suffrages of the people, in the infancy and most quiet and virtuous æra of the republic; because they took it into their heads that their old constitution and laws were not good enough, and therefore sent to Greece for new ones:—If in the six and twenty senators of America, some future Appius may be found, I yet trust from the high confidence I repose in my fair countrywomen, that for many years a Virginia will not be wanting to react the Roman tragedy;—but all human virtue is frail—What the senate intended by law for Julius Cæsar, the influence of manners provided for Octavius and his successors—

Matrons and the beauties of the first rank of Rome esteemed it the highest honor to prostitute themselves to the artful Augustus, and even to such an infamous villain as Caligula:—The amorous dispositions of a succession of Princes, have rendered the present of the handkerchief the highest honor, to which female beauty and merit could aspire in the seraglio of Constantinople, and in the courts of the two Lewises—who preceded the present amiable and virtuous monarch of France; yet they were rewarded with implicit obedience, and Lewis the 16th meets with turbulence and resistance in his most meritorious acts:—Virtue only breeds confusion in perverted government.—Whoever will read what the pens of Suetonius and Tacitus have described, will be lost in admiration at the original and surpassing wickedness to which Rome arrived in less than half a century—But can these things happen to the Americans? What distinguishes the Americans, from the French—the Germans—the Turks or the Persians?—America is in a great measure peopled by emigrants from the old countries, now enthralled in slavery—Does crossing the atlantic alter the nature of these people?—Let our countrymen reflect on this awful truth, that nothing creates that wide distinction between them, and the white slaves of the old world, or indeed their black slaves here, but *their government*—Let them consider this well, and they will be rendered cautious how they change it—(bad as it is) for new imported constitutions—Amalgomated as we were with a corrupt old monarchy—with the combined corruptions of three armies—a constant communication with the luxurious and debauched capitals of the old world—we cannot be surprised, that some of our great cities are now ripe for any thing.—These remarks are intended for the thinking part of our citizens, and particularly those who are most active in promoting this revolution.—In the most important characters of this class of men, the author has great confidence:—America has more to dread from the want of information than the want of integrity in her rulers; and her own precipitation is the most dreadful of all. People should be liberal of every thing but power—but to give away an atom of their liberties is as criminal as dishonorable.

However degrading and disgraceful the state of society just described may be—worse as it is far then ten thousand deaths to a feeling and delicate mind—yet to the mass of the people it is not so afflicting as the loss of the other moral virtues, which in large governments, are exchanged for the fashionable vices of him who *presides:*—Under Caligula, the Roman legions were not ashamed to adorn their helmets with cockle-shells in triumph for their expedition against Britain, in which, they never ventured to leave the shores of Gaul—this Prince—the degenerate son of the adored Germanicus, happened to be a poltron.—During the reign of Nero, fiddling—dancing—singing—burning cities—plundering States—perfidy and assassination were the manners of the age, and discover the motley mind of this monster of levity and vice.—Domitian who like every man that from weakness—vicious heart—or the allurements of pleasure, deserts the paths of virtue—hated cordially those examples of merit which he could not imitate. Tacitus informs us, that during his life—*virtue became a death warrant*—Philosophy fled—Pliny sat himself down quietly to compose a grammar—the only work of science then safe—in short, nothing was honourable or profitable but assassinations, informations, and all sorts of corruptions and pollutions.

A FARMER.

(*To be continued.*)

Maryland Gazette

11 APRIL 1788

ESSAY VII

(*Continued.*)

HUMAN misery is wound up to its highest pitch in this last stage of corruption, to which the social union can arrive:—At length the poor, wretched beings, who, let whatever be the change, and in every preceding gradation of government, have invariably fallen from bad to worse—turn their weary eyes, from a world which presents so frightful a prospect—to the world of hope,—the kingdom that is to come hereafter—the only solace and comfort of those who are miserable here;—there all the fond images of equality, which men are fated ever to retain, are once more revived—scenes of never-ending bliss are painted in the most delightful colours—the imagination grows warm with the prospect—mad with the hopes of celestial happiness, the souls of all men seem anxious to take their flight, to their Omnipotent Author—the Sovereign Legislator of nature—who, peerless and above all, dispences equal law to willing minds:—The people flock in crouds to hear preachers—who, exalted by the presence of numerous and passionate audiences, are elevated into flights of native eloquence, surpassing the strains of the most studied oratory:—The people mind nothing but preaching; the things of this miserable world, are despised when put in competition with the joys of Paradise—agriculture is neglected—famine ensues—government is at length roused for want of plunder and a supply of luxuries—the sword of coercion is drawn—but it increases the phrenzy—One martyr makes fifty converts—such was the first rise of the Christian religion, as it is exactly and pathetically described by the historic pen of Ammianus Marcellinus:—The empire torn by intestine convulsions becomes an easy prey to any bold invader.

Thus it is that the barbarity—cruelty and blood which stain the history of religion, spring from the corruption of civil government, and from that never-dying hope and fondness for a state of equality, which constitutes an essential part of the soul of man:—A chaos of darkness obscures the downfal of empire, intermixed with gleams of light, which serve only to disclose scenes of desolation and horror—From the last confusion springs order:—The bold spirits who pull down the ancient fabric—erect a new one, founded on the natural liberties of mankind, and *where civil government is preserved free, there can be no religious tyranny*—the sparks of bigotry and enthusiasm may and will crackle, but can never light into a blaze.—

The truth of these remarks appear from the histories of those two great revolutions of European government, which seem to have convulsed this earth to the centre of its orb, and of which we have com-

pleat record—The Roman and the Gothic, or as it is more commonly
called the feudal constitution:—In the infancy of the Roman republic,
when enterprizing and free, their conquests were rapid, because beneficial to the conquered (who were admitted to a participation of their
liberty) their religion, although devoid, was not only unstained by
persecution, but censurably liberal—they received without discrimination the Gods of the countries they subdued, into the list of their
deities, until Olympus was covered with an army of demigods as
numerous as the legions of Popish Saints; and we find the Grecian
divinities adored with more sincere piety at Rome, than at Athens.—
Rome was then in the zenith of her glory—in the days of her
wretched decline—in the miserable reigns of Caracalla, Eliagabalus
and Commodus.—Ammianus and others, inform us that the Christians were butchered like sheep, for reviving the old exploded doctrine of a future state, in which Emperors and Senators were to be
placed on a level with the poorest and most abject of mankind:—
And in the succeeding despotisms when christianity became the
established religion, it grew immediately as corrupt in its infancy, as
ever it has proved at any period since—the most subtle disquisitions
of a metaphysical nature became the universal rage—the more
incomprehensible—the more obstinately were they maintained, and
in fine, the canonized Austin or Ambrose, (I forget which) closed his
laborious enquiries, with this holy position—*that he believed, because
it was impossible.* At length the great question, whether the three
persons of the divinity, were three or one, became publickly agitated,
and threw all mankind into a flame—Councils after councils, composed of all the wisdom of the divines, were assembled, and at length
the doctrine that three were one prevailed, and such would have
been the determination had it been proposed that three were sixteen—because misery is the foundation, upon which error erects her
tyranny over the vulgar mind.—After this determination the arm of
the Magistrate was called in, and those poor misled Arians who were
still so wicked as to imagine that three must be three, were not only
declared guilty of a most abominable and damnable heresy, but were
thenceforth exterminated by fire and sword.

In the first age of the *Gothic* government, those free and hardy
adventurers, deserted their Idols and embraced the doctrines of

Christianity with ardent sincerity:—The King and a large majority of a nation, would be converted and baptized with as much celerity as the ceremony could be performed—but still liberty in the temporal, secured freedom in the spiritual administration: Christians and Pagan citizens lived together in the utmost harmony—Those bold and hardy conquerors would never listen to Bishops who advised persecution, and held in sovereign contempt all those metaphysical distinctions with which a pure religion has been disgraced, in order to cloak villainous designs and support artful usurpations of civil powers in feeble and turbulent governments. The Gothic institutions were however much sooner corrupted from internal vices than the Roman, and the undeniable reason was, that in the former, government by representation was admitted almost coeval with their first inundations;—whereas with the Romans, the democratic branch of power, exercised by the people personally, rendered them invincible both in war and peace—the virtue of this internal institution could only be subdued by the greatness of its external acquisition—extensive empire ruined this mighty fabric—a superstructure, which overshadowed the then known world, was too mighty for the foundation confined within the walls of a city—the wealth imported by the Scipios from Spain and Afric, and by Flaminius, Lucullus, Sylla and Pompey, from the East, enabled the *few* to corrupt the *many*—a case that can never exist but where the legislative power resides exclusively in the citizens of the town—The Roman republic then became diseased at the heart, but as it was ages in forming, so it required ages of corruption to destroy a robust constitution where every atom was a nerve: It was not so with the Gothic constitution, mortal disease soon made its appearance there—Civil liberty was early destroyed by the insolence and oppressions of the great—The temporal power availed itself of that spiritual influence which nature has given religion over the hearts of men—A religion, the divinity of which is demonstrable by reason alone, unassisted by revelation became the corrupt instrument of usurpation.—Those who were the authors of the disorders which disgraced civil government, cut the reins of ecclesiastical persecution: And an universal and tyrannic confusion was mingled with absurdities that excite both ridicule and horror. We see a Duke of Gandia (who was betrayed and assassinated

by that monster of perfidy Cæsar Borgia, the bastard of the infamous
Pope Alexander the VIth) in the last moments of his existence, begging the cut throat son, that he would intercede with his father, the
Pope, in favour of his poor soul, that it might not be kept long in pur-
gatory, but dispatched as soon as possible to Heaven, to dispute the
infallibility of those vice-gerents of God, who generally patterned
after the devil, was considered as an heresy more damnable than
blaspheming the most high. Religious tyranny continued in this
state, during those convulsions which broke the aristocracies of
Europe, and settled their governments into mixed monarchies: A ray
of light then beamed—but only for a moment—the turbulent state
and quick corruption of mixed monarchy, opened a new scene of religious horror—Pardons for all crimes committed and to be committed, were regulated by ecclesiastical law, with a mercantile
exactitude, and a Christian knew what he must pay for murdering
another better than he now does the price of a pair of boots: At length
some bold spirits began to doubt whether wheat flour, made into
paste, could be actually human flesh, or whether the wine made in the
last vintage could be the real blood of Christ, who had been crucified
upwards of 1400 years—Such was the origin of the Protestant reformation—at the bare mention of such heretical and dangerous doctrine, striking (as they said) at the root of all religion, the sword of
power leaped from its scabbard, the smoke that arose from the
flames, to which the most virtuous of mankind, were without mercy
committed, darkened all Europe for ages; tribunals, armed with
frightful tortures, were every where erected, to make men confess
opinions, and then they were solemnly burned for confessing, whilst
priest and people sang hymns around them; and the fires of persecution are scarcely yet extinguished. *Civil and religious liberty are
inseparably interwoven—whilst government is pure and equal—
religion will be uncontaminated:—The moment government
becomes disordered, bigotry and fanaticism take root and grow—
they are soon converted to serve the purposes of usurpation, and
finally, religious persecution reciprocally supports and is supported
by the tyranny of the temporal powers.*

A FARMER.

(*To be continued.*)

Maryland Gazette

15 APRIL 1788

ESSAY VII

(*Continued.*)

ALTHOUGH both civil and political liberty may be truly said no longer to exist in Europe—yet from one effect of the *feudal institutions*, that enlightened part of the globe, has in a great measure, recovered from the disorders occasioned by their irreparable loss:—What I allude to is the division of that quarter of the world into a multitude of separate States and sovereignties, and that extreme attention to the preservation of each and to the balance of power, which has become a fundamental law of the whole; this secures the influence of political moderation, or a species of *fœderal liberty*, which is the next blessing that government can afford; and certainly were wise men obliged to confine themselves to the choice of one alternative—fœderal or national liberty—they would prefer the former—whilst the influence of that exists, it must support the substance in a great measure of the latter, although the forms should no longer remain—But when that ceases, national liberty, which includes both civil and political freedom, must soon expire.— The history of mankind furnishes a series of invariable and frightful examples of this.—The Roman republic included a variety of other republics, States and Kingdoms living in a perfect liberty, and according to their own laws; this variety and contrariety of interests seemed to promise internal freedom, independant of external influence—But the time of their delirium had arrived—after the conquest of Hannibal and the peace which the first Scipio made with the Carthaginians—that immortal statesman and hero gave his countrymen this remarkable advice—to restore Carthage, as an enemy worthy of Rome—but the opinion of that stupid old fool Cato, the censor, prevailed as more consonant to the vulgar level of mens' judgments, and *delenda est Carthago—Carthage must be destroyed,* became the motto of the day—the consequence of this political advice was, that Carthage being razed to the ground, and no enemy existing contiguous to Rome, which she could dread—not all her internal institutions—not all the variety of interests, which a multitude of almost independent States afforded, could prevent her speedy destruction—*ruit [mole sua]*—*she fell by her own weight*—and their liberty became such liberty as a Nero and the prætorian bands thought fit to distribute.—The Turkish empire is at this day extended over a multitude of kingdoms, States—even democratic and aristocratic republics, oligarchies, and every species of institution which the inventive genius of man has created—but I do not see that it has moderated its despotism.—Spain still contains in her bosom that very extensive and well formed republic Biscay—but the slavery of Spain has since the reign of Charles the Vth, nearly depopulated the finest part of Europe.— France contains an extensive free country, which would not submit to the general government but on conditions that have hitherto secured them a superior degree of happiness—I mean Britany, which was annexed to the crown by the marriage of Anne, of Bretagne, with Lewis the VIIth. There was a democracy until lately within the territory of France, Marseilles—A French gentleman once told me, *we had one republic in France, which made one very great noise, at last the King he did build one little citadel in the middle of it, and then he teach them republicans how to behave themselves*—The melancholy truth is, that the internal institutions of an extensive empire signify nought—the principle that the convenience, the rights and interests of a part must give way to what is called the good of the whole, unhinges every species of just and equal government, because it is a principle that has no limits.

Still however the division of Europe into small independent States, preserves a degree of social happiness very different from what exists in other parts of the world—we find them injured by foreign war—but the moderation of a political influence exempts them from the desolations of those internal commotions which lay waste two extensive empires—Their wars too are becoming more mild and less frequent than formerly, and certainly if they could not be entirely prevented, they might be quickly suppressed by keeping up an annual Congress of diplomatique ministers, instead of their present imperfect mode of negociation, which defective as it is, has notwithstanding rendered peace more durable, and war less destructive; the only satisfactory reason their greatest patriots have given for neglecting, what at first view appears so important an improvement, is that terror with which they justly view, any thing in the shape of general government, which they universally admit to be the greatest curse that can befal mankind:—The enlightened statesmen of the old world, have imprinted on their minds the wisdom of the ancient fable, which I shall now repeat to the Americans—"The lion, the king of the beasts, gave out that he was sick—he confined himself to his den, and his friends did not stick out to say that he must die of that disorder—all the beasts went to pay their court and assist him but the fox—at length the lion appeared abroad and took Reynard roundly to talk, why he had not come to see him, when he was so ill—the fox, who in fable is the emblem of wisdom, made this memorable reply—In truth I did intend to pay my respects to your majesty, *but when I came near your den, I saw all the feet pointing in and none coming out*"—So invariably have powers been travelling to the centre, never again to return to those who bestow them.

At present as a recompence for the evils of occasional broils, Europe has the consolation to reflect, that she is secure from the terrible despotisms which reign over the other three quarters of the globe.—Those States who admit the sanction of the laws of nature and nations form as it were a *great fœderal republic*, and the balance of power, even under an imperfect system, has prevented those great revolutions and shocks which sweeping myriads of mortals at a blow, degrade mankind in the eye of philosophy, to a level with the ants and other insects of the earth—negociation unnerves the arm of conquest, and the genius of a Marlbrough, an Eugene, a Saxe and Turenne, is displayed in harmless counter-marches, which in Asia, or even Europe, some centuries back, would have formed an Alexander, a Cæsar, a Gengis Khan and a Tamerlane.

To this balance of power, France has long owed her safety, and that only can save her at this particular and awful crisis of turbulence; the despotism of Constantinople would soon reign at Paris,

but that the territory of France is not sufficiently large for such a
tyranny, and she is surrounded by numerous, warlike and independant sovereignties—the influence of manners, which their philosophers boast of, as one great security, if not ironically introduced, is
certainly but an empty found—their manners—reputation and
every thing, have been long regulated by the capricious vices of
the Prince who sat on the throne—but France is not sufficiently
extensive to defend her empire by such immense deserts, as surround the despotisms of Turkey, Persia, China and Morocco, and
secure them from foreign conquest—If the Prince, in France, was
to destroy all their fundamental laws, which by what they now call
their constitution, he evidently may do and subject his subjects to
the caprice of a Turkish yoke, which 200,000 standing troops will
accomplish for him whenever he pleases:—The inevitable consequence would be, that he would only subject himself and his slaves
to instant conquest and partition among his neighbours.—No
Prince of France will therefore ever be permitted to attempt this,
whilst the present balance of power remains.

                                                    A FARMER.

(*To be continued.*)

Maryland Gazette

22 APRIL 1788

ESSAY VII

(*Continued.*)

IT remains to apply the foregoing principles to the American
States—It is now evident, that they are not to be fixed as a constellation to give light to revolving ages—they have blazed for a
moment like meteors in a troubled sky: Scarce has peace secured
them the independence they sought, when a mighty revolution is to
annihilate their separate and independant sovereignties, and to

embrace them in the wide arms of one general government; it is impossible that the free citizens of these States could listen for a moment, to such a tremendous and awful change, but from some real defects which they have experienced in their separate constitutions—That there are such cannot be denied—but still the author has no hopes that the citizens of these States will ever be again so happy as they were under the government of Great-Britain and since the revolution—The state of society before the late war was remarkably mild and moderate, and what is uncommon, we rather combatted the theory of tyranny than the practice—since the war we have been much embarrassed by a great encrease of private, and the creation of an enormous public debt, with its attendant paper securities, the corrupting influence of which would contaminate a society of angels; our new elevation among the nations of the earth has opened to our principal citizens unbounded prospects of national splendor and private preferment, which lay dormant in our former dependant situation—all these, and a variety of other causes have combined to disturb the public tranquility and vitiate our social happiness.—We have no opportunity of comparing our situation but with that which existed before the late revolution, and from this we conclude our forms of government are defective, without considering our change of situation, or without reflecting how few countries in the world are so happy as we are at this moment—notwithstanding we are in the most disturbed of all situations of society, that is on the eve of a great revolution; suppose such a change was now impending in any other country in the world—a change opening such unlimited views to some and so detrimental to other individuals, involving the interests and agitating the passions of every citizen—could so much moderation and candor be expected—the general abhorrence which we all entertain of the violences of the mad partizans of the new system, evinces the mild state of our present institutions.

Notwithstanding this, no man is more thoroughly convinced than the Farmer, that there is not a government in the confederacy perfect, or indeed founded on solid fixed principles.—Pennsylvania has the boldest direction to a happy theory of all the new contrivances—but still it is fundamentally defective, and it is said that they are daily weakening in practice the great virtue of their institution, instead of substantiating so glorious an idea—The four New-England States were practically the most solid in their formation, until two of them were spoiled by their nasty new gingerbread work—and yet they originally required amendments—their town meetings, which were the essential pith and marrow of their constitution seem rather to have been regulated by manners, than substantiated by proper and legal powers; as for the others they were all begun in the middle and formed without materials necessary for the work—they remain and must remain governments on paper, substantiated by anarchy and misrule—*New-York* indeed, by an excess of inverted ingenuity, has contrived to make something like a real government, that would for a length of years secure their political freedom—On the other hand *Georgia* is utterly incomprehensible—it appears at first sight all body and no head or feet, and on nearer view it has no body either—it is in fact a lusus naturæ in the political world—However, should they all escape the stroke that now impends, which is hardly to be expected, it is in my opinion utterly impossible for nine out of thirteen to prolong their feeble existence for twenty years without considerable alterations.—I see nothing that could greatly injure New-York, Connecticut or Rhode-Island. Were I to give a model of a perfect government, it would not vary greatly from the Connecticut charter—the amendments would be all in the town-meetings—Rhode-Island lays under a popular odium—all governments have their inconveniences, but I should be apt to ascribe those of Connecticut and Rhode-Island to their paper securities and other evils of the late war.—When parties run high, popular odium is a very uncertain test of truth, and *audi et alteram partem—hear both sides*, is the best maxim of political and moral justice. However, the conduct of Rhode-Island with regard to paper money, as we hear it, is incomprehensible—What shall I say of Pennsylvania? When I view this bold effort of the human understanding, I am struck with admiration and surprize at the masterly hand of him that broke through the mounds of prejudice and education, guided by the glimmering of a distant light; he adventured boldly into the realms of truth, but the brilliant resplendence dazzled his fight—he found himself alone and unsupported, and he retired precipitately to his companions, who were groping in error and darkness—Let Pennsylvania pursue with energy and propriety the ray of light, which beams through the mass of her constitution; let her establish county meetings of *freeholders*, to whom one third of her legislature may refer a contested law for the revision of the great body of the people *by actual vote*—establish county seminaries of learning and similar institutions to promote true patriotism and true knowledge, and she will last the envy of mankind until time shall be no more—As it is she is a child of nature, and strong convulsions must attend her destruction. As to all the other institutions of this continent, they are governments of the people, and yet the people are excluded from all share in the government. They can only be supported by the *few* individuals who are objects of elections, maintaining a disinterested preference of the public good to their private convenience—for it must be ever held in view, that the interest of the *few* is opposed to the public interest, but the interest of the *many*, is the public interest—on which great distinction the weakness of representative government depends—The elected few are tempted to corruption by all the emoluments of government, and by that plunder which public disorder affords—they are screened from punishment by making legislation subservient to their interested purposes, and there is no control but public manners and the propinquity of our independant States, which enforces moderation by interest, emulation and example—Public manners are daily corrupting by a fell avarice, which is the canker worm of public and private virtue—the facility of gratifying avaricious views, by prostituting legislative authority, renders intrigue the only profitable quality in an age of venality. Profit, honor and distinction are all inseparably interwoven, and a man of deep intrigue must be necessarily, the most respected character in perverted governments—if virtue gets into office, rotation wheels it out, hated and despised.—This view which I believe to be in a great measure just; although the principles are but developing, discover our systems to be fundamentally wrong, did not the proposed revolution bear a more fatal testimony; the truth is that we aimed at, and still aim at premature public splendor and private luxury, forgetting that bodies politic, like natural bodies have their duration of manly vigor and the decline of age, prolonged and regulated by the length of years in which they have been arriving at maturity.—We wanted to be every thing at once—that is what we now wish, and in the event we shall be nothing or worse than nothing; we strived to patch up the ruined fabric of the British constitution for our use, and rushing headlong to our object, we did not discover the precipices that lay in our road—we never reflected, that we had none of those distinctions of ranks which preserve that government—that the state of our society was altogether different—and that we had only the wishes, but none of the means.

A Farmer.

(*To be continued.*)

Maryland Gazette

25 APRIL 1788

ESSAY VII

(*Continued.*)

Will then the proposed national government provide a proper remedy for these defects?—I do not hesitate to declare, that in my judgment, without considerable amendments, the remedy will prove infinitely worse than the disease.—In the first place, it is undeniably the worst constitution in North-America, excepting that of Georgia—It has every defect which all the others labour under, and considerably increased; for all the vices of representation become more dangerous in proportion to the extent of territory and variety of interests represented. The qualified negative of the President is more than overbalanced by his junction with the aristocratic branch—indeed the difficulties attending, the making of any government at all, upon republican principles for so extensive a continent, rendered it but a patched up affair even on paper. To

have agreed upon any one plan, was beyond all human calculation—
and their attention to the perfecting of the system was prevented
by a constant endeavour to keep it together—can we then be surprized that it is so defective? The recollection of these difficulties
deter the advocates of the system from any future convention, not
reflecting that a future convention could not destroy what is done,
that if with the full sense of their constituents, they could agree on
no amendments, it would still remain for the States to adopt as it
now stands—but this may be a subject of future consideration.—It
is certain we had better have no general government than a bad
one—We may make one hereafter, but we shall never get rid of
this if we adopt it—Its defects are that it almost entirely neglects
civil liberty, that is the rights of individuals against legislative and
executive encroachments—It is true it has a bill of rights, but then
it is the shortest that ever was seen; although long enough for the
government as originally reported—yet now it appears that they
stumbled over diamonds in order to pick up stones; and it is most
certain that this new system will entirely annihilate that *fœderal
freedom* which would have attoned in a great measure, for the loss
of the forms of both political and civil liberty.—Had the States continued separate, sovereign and independant, they must have bid
an eternal defiance to despotism, and they might have had leisure to
have amended gradually the defects of their several institutions;
as it is, the same authority operating immediately on the individuals of such vast territories; differing materially in national interests
and private manners must from necessity, be either despotic or
ineffectual, and that for the following among many other reasons.—
The misrule and commotions of this general government (and all
governments are unavoidably subject to misrule and its attendant
commotions) will agitate the passions and affect the interests of the
whole mass of national society by the same shock; of course the
fate of the empire must be involved in the good or bad administration of the most complicated and difficult system of government,
that mankind ever yet beheld; but had the States remained separate and sovereign, this misrule if their individuals or even the revolution of a single State, being altogether local, would have left the
others, entirely unagitated, to interpose the voice of reason and

pursue the dictates of justice, which is the great and applauded security and happiness of a confederacy of republics. The examples adduced and the opinions given by Montesquieu, extend only to *unions between States*, not *governments of individuals*—In Montesquieu's time, fœderal had entirely a different meaning from what it has now—The small distinction between a confederacy operating on States collectively in their corporate capacity, and a general or national government exercising legislative, executive and judiciary powers on every citizen of the empire, so trifling to Aristides, that he marches over it without noticing, would probably have brought this great legislator for mankind, to a full stop.—Called upon so solemnly as he is, if the good old Frenchman could come back and see how his works are read and understood in our day, and what principles they are quoted to support, he would certainly take up his books and carry them off with him.—In the new American government there is nothing to prevent despotism, every feature and symptom forebode its rapid approach. In the first place it will not be denied but that a nation must be governed by its own sense of what is right, and then they are free—or they must be governed contrary to their sense, and then it must be by despotic force and they become slaves.—Where the national interests of separate parts an empire differ materially—each part must mutually give up part of its interests and wishes, to constitute an impartial general law—which made by a mutual sacrifice opinion must in its nature be contrary to the sense of the whole—As the people then loose sight of the only means of judging of what is right, that is their own feelings—power becomes transferred on their rulers, without any certain limitation remaining with their constituents, who always displeased even with the most perfect impartiality, which in this case becomes general injustice, must have their senses and their strength destroyed, or they will destroy the government.—Again a nation to be governed according to its own sense of what is right, must have some regular and certain mode of changing the effective administration of their government, or they will be involved in such constant turbulence and commotion, that the quiet slavery of despotism, will appear preferable and be submitted to—a complicated system, which hides from investigation the diseased part, and destroys responsibility (one State changing its representatives for a law which will be popular in other States, who will encourage and support theirs) will soon reduce our people to despair—complicated forms are therefore always simplified by the sword of a despot.—Again our immense territory offers a secure asylum, easily surrounded by solitary wildernesses, in which despotism may safely erect her throne of terrors; we shall not be surrounded by a number of independant States, who may control our government by the influence of a balance of power:—And lastly, what is most dangerous, our state of society demands either absolute freedom or absolute tyranny—we have among us none of those permanent orders and distinct ranks of men, which are the only security of the mixed governments we so much admire.—All are entitled to be equally free, and they will be so, or by one common ruin involve themselves in an equal slavery. In such cases the gradation is an easy, constant, and natural one—Voltaire, with more truth than many are aware of, calls Turkey a great democracy—and any State as large as Turkey, without fixed distinctions of different orders of society, will be ruled by exactly such a government as Turkey— the difference between a pure democracy and a pure despotism is not worth a distinction—Representation will not do—I have not the smallest doubt but that every reflecting merchant in the southern States, and every member that has served them in Congress, would this moment rather entrust the regulation of our commerce to a President and Council, independant of all the States, than to a Senate in which the staple States are out-voted as eight to five—Thus we can even now discover that *the authority of one man is a law fundamental in all large governments*—and that is despotism— To conclude this general government as it now stands, without the necessary checks, will either be unable to move at all, from the stout resistance and alarmed jealousy of the separate States, which may not perhaps be an undesirable event—or secondly, which would be the most dishonorable event, it may frighten us to take shelter again under the wing of Great-Britain—or lastly and worst of all, it may in one day by a vigorous and good administration, lay the foundation of as dreadful a tyranny as ever scourged mankind— How shall we avoid the three—the first and most obvious instruction of wisdom, would be to tread back the hasty and injudicious steps we have taken—recur to first principles, when we are sensible that we labor under any defect, the common lesson of reason is to look for the disease at home and apply a remedy there—Fools and children look abroad for assistance—Americans amend your separate constitutions!—When they are right; you will no longer hanker after these dangerous general governments—Were I assured this could be done now, my decided advice would be to divide the continental debt according to the average revenues of each State since peace—leave a committee of Congress to sell the western territory, and to call a general council when necessary—but break up Congress until the present *esprit du corps* should be thoroughly annihilated—But as I despair of proper State amendments, I would advise our conventions to digest those amendments to the proposed system, which will guard the civil rights of our citizens—agree on those checks on the general government which will prevent their legislating for individuals, but in cases where the State governments are actually deficient and refractory—this may secure our political and fœderal liberty—having done this, let them authorize their former deputies or others to meet those of the other States, revise their work and then adjourn to give them time for fix or eight months; if no amendments can be got, they may if they choose adopt it as it now stands on their second meeting—at present the important States who have adopted, are most anxious for such amendments—will they not rather agree to this proposal, than risque amending after a government should be adopted, which from its great powers and the numerous offices it will have the disposal of, may certainly influence one-fourth of the States to reject any diminution of their authority?—But at all events my countrymen, no standing army—If this government is founded on truth, truth can always defend her own cause against error or design—and now that you may be free and happy is the interest, and I will add, the wish of

A Farmer.

Essays by
the Impartial Examiner

Essays by the Impartial Examiner appeared in the Virginia
Independent Chronicle. *The first essay appeared in three parts in
February and March 1788. The remainder appeared in May and
June of the same year. They contain a number of paragraphs of
great eloquence and insight. The unknown Anti-Federalist writer
of the Impartial Examiner essays bases his arguments on the conviction that those with political office will naturally seek to extend
their powers and can be limited only through express reservations
and limits.*

Virginia Independent Chronicle

---

20 FEBRUARY 1788

ESSAY I

---

*The Impartial Examiner begins with a long, detailed discussion
of the nature of constitutions. Because a new constitution is a new
compact between the people and their government, it must contain
express reservations, or the people will have given up all their
rights—including crucial common law rights such as trial by jury.
The lack of a bill of rights renders a government arbitrary, because,
without such a bill, the will of the rulers is the only check on their
power. Essays in* The Federalist *of particular relevance: 10, 51,
83-85.*

To the free people of VIRGINIA.

Countrymen and Fellow-Citizens,

THAT the subject, which has given rise to the following observations, is of the highest consequence to this country, requires not the aid of logical proof; that it merits the most serious attention of every member of this community, is a fact not to be controverted. Will not a bare mention of the new Fœderal Constitution justify this remark? To foreigners or such, whose local connections form no permanent interest in America, this may be totally indifferent; and to them it may afford mere matter of speculation and private amusement. When such advert to the high and distinguished characters, who have drawn up, and proposed a set of articles to the people of an extensive continent as a form of their future government, an emotion of curiosity may induce them to examine the contents of those articles: and they may, perhaps, from having contemplated on a former situation of those people—that they had struggled against a potent enemy—that they had by their virtuous and patriotic exertions rescued themselves from impending danger—that they had used the like endeavors to establish for themselves a system of government upon free and liberal principles—that they had in pursuance of those endeavors chosen a system, as conducive to the great ends of human happiness, the preservation of their *natural rights* and *liberties*—that this system has prevailed but a few years; and now already a change, a fundamental change therein is meditated:—strangers, I say, having contemplated on these circumstances, may be led to consider this nation, as a restless and dissatisfied people, whose fickle inconsistent minds suffer them not to abide long in the same situation; who perpetually seeking after new things throw away one blessing in pursuit of another: and while they are thus indulging their caprice—lose all, ere any can ripen into maturity. If the unconcerned part of those among us entertain themselves in this manner, can any good American be content to deserve such reflections? Will not all rather feel an honest indignation, if they once perceive their country stamped with a character like this? And yet, may we not justify such conceptions, if we thus precipitate ourselves into a new government before we have sufficiently tried the virtues of the old? So incident is error to the human mind, that it is not to be wondered at indeed, if our present Constitution is incomplete. The best regulated governments have their defects, and might perhaps admit of improvement: but the great difficulty consists in clearly discovering the most exceptionable parts and judiciously applying the amendments. A wise nation will, therefore, attempt innovations of this kind with much circumspection. They will view the political fabric, which they have once reared, as the sacred *palladium* of their happiness;—they will touch it, as a man of tender sensibility toucheth the apple of his own eye,—they will touch it with a light, with a trembling—with a cautious hand,—lest they injure the whole structure in endeavoring to reform any of its parts. In small and trivial points alterations may be attempted with less danger; but—where the very nature, the essence of the thing is to be changed: when the foundation itself is to be transformed, and the whole plan entirely new modelled;—should you not hesitate, O Americans? Should you not pause—and reflect a while on the important step, you are about to take? Does it not behove you to examine well into the nature and tendency of the Constitution now proposed for your adoption? And by comparing it with your present mode of government, endeavor to distinguish which of the two is most eligible? Whether *this* or *that* is best calculated for promoting your happiness? for obtaining and securing those benefits, which are the great object of civil society? Will it be consistent with the duty, which you owe to yourselves, as a nation, or with the affection, which you ought to bear for your posterity, if you rashly or inconsiderately adopt a measure, which is to influence the fate of this country for ages yet to come? How will it accord with your dignity and reputation, as an independent people, if either through an over-weaning fondness for novelty you are suddenly transported on the wings of imagination, and too hastily make up your thoughts on this great subject; or by sinking into a listless inactivity of mind, view it as an indifferent matter unworthy of any deliberate consideration? Will any respect? Will any honor? Will any veneration be due to the memory of yourselves, as ancestors, if millions of beings, who have not yet received their birth, when you are all mouldered into dust, should find themselves fixed in a miserable condition by

one injudicious determination of your's at this period? If you see
no impropriety in these questions, the suggestions contained in
them will not appear altogether unworthy of attention. One
moment's reflection, it is humbly presumed, will render it obvious
that on this occasion they are not impertinently propounded.

In pursuing this address I beg leave to premise that the only true
point of distinction between arbitrary and free governments seems
to be, that in the former the governors are invested with powers
of acting according to their own wills, without any other limits them
what they themselves may understand to be necessary for the general good; whereas in the latter they are intrusted with no such
unlimited authority, but are restrained in their operations to conform to certain fundamental principles, the preservation whereof is
expressly stipulated for in the *civil compact:* and whatever is not so
stipulated for is virtually and impliedly given up. Societies so constituted invest their supreme governors with ample powers of
exerting themselves according to their own judgment in every
thing not inconsistent with or derogatory to those principles; and so
long as they adhere to such restrictions, their deeds ought not to
be rescinded or controuled by any other power whatsoever. Those
principles are certain inherent rights pertaining to all mankind in
a state of natural liberty, which through the weakness, imperfection, and depravity of human nature cannot be secured in that state.
Men, therefore, agree to enter into society, that by the united force
of *many* the rights of *each* individual may be protected and secured.
These are in all just governments laid down as a foundation to the
civil compact, which contains a *covenant* between *each* with *all,*
that they shall enter into one society to be governed by the same
powers; establishes for that purpose the *frame* of government; and
consequently creates a *Convention* between *every* member, binding
those, who shall at any time be intrusted with power, to a faithful
administration of their trust according to the form of the *civil policy,* which they have so constituted, and obliging all to a due obedience therein. There can be no other just origin of civil power, but
some such mutual contract of all the people: and although their
great object in forming society is an intention to secure their natural rights; yet the relations arising from this *political union* create

certain duties and obligations to the state, which require a sacrifice of some portion of those rights and of that exuberance of liberty, which obtains in a state of nature.—This, however, being compensated by certain other adventitious rights and privileges, which are acquired by the social connection; it follows that the advantages derived from a government are to be estimated by the *strength* of the *security*, which is attended at once with the *least sacrifice* and the *greatest acquired benefits*. That government, therefore, which is best adapted for promoting these three *great ends*, must certainly be the best constituted scheme of *civil policy*. Here, then, it may not be improper to remark that persons forming a social community cannot take too much precaution when they are about to establish the plan of their government. They ought to construct it in such a manner as to procure the best possible security for their rights;—in doing this they ought to give up no greater share than what is understood to be absolutely necessary:—and they should endeavor so to organize, arrange and connect it's several branches, that when duly exercised it may tend to promote the *common good* of all, and contribute as many advantages, as the civil institution is capable of. It has been before observed that the only just origin of civil power is a contract entered into by all the people for that purpose.—If this position be true (and, I dare presume, it is not controverted, at least in this country) right reason will always suggest the expediency of adhering to the essential requisites in forming that contract upon true principles. A cautious people will consider all the inducements to enter into the *social state*, from the most important object down to the minutest prospect of advantage. Every motive with them will have its due weight. They will not pay a curious attention to trifles and overlook matters of great consequence:—and in pursuing these steps they will provide for the attainment of *each* point in view with a care—with an earnestness proportionate to its dignity, and according as it involves a *greater* or a *lesser* interest. It is evident, therefore that they should attend most diligently to those sacred rights, which they have received with their birth, and which can neither be retained to themselves, nor transmitted to their posterity, unless they are *expressly reserved*: for it is a maxim, I dare say, universally acknowledged, that when men establish a system of government, in granting the powers therein they are always understood to surrender whatever they do not so expressly reserve. This is obvious from the very design of the civil institution, which is adopted in lieu of the state of natural liberty, wherein each individual, being equally intitled to the enjoyment of all natural rights, and having equally a just authority to exercise full powers of acting, with relation to other individuals, in any manner not injurious to their rights, must, when he enters into society, be presumed to give up all those powers into the hands of the state by submitting his whole conduct to the direction thereof. This being done by every member, it follows, as a regular conclusion, that all such powers, whereof the whole were possessed, so far as they related to each other individually, are of course given up by the mere act of union. If this surrender be made without any reservation, the conclusion is equally plain and regular, *that* each and *all* have given up not only those powers, which relate to others, but likewise every claim, which pertained to themselves, as individuals. For the universality of the grant in this case must necessarily include every *power* of acting, and every *claim* of possessing or obtaining any thing— except according to the regulations of the state. Now a right being properly defined, "a power or claim established by law, to act, or to possess, or to obtain something from others," every natural right is such *power* or *claim* established by the law of nature. Thus, it is manifest, that in a society constituted after this manner, every right whatsoever will be under the power and controul of the civil jurisdiction. This is the leading characteristic of an arbitrary government, and whenever any people establish a system like this, they subject themselves to one, which has not a single property of a free constitution. Hence results the necessity of an *express stipulation* for all such rights as are intended to be exempted from the civil authority.

Permit me now, my country-men, to make a few observations on the proposed Fœderal Constitution. In this attempt the subject, as it is arduous and difficult, naturally impresses the modest mind with dissidence: yet being of the last importance, as involving in it the highest interest, that freemen can have—all that is dear and valuable to the citizens of these United States; a consciousness of the strong claim, which this subject has, to a free and general discussion, has prevailed over that discouraging idea so far as to produce the present address to you. This is done with a reliance on that benevolence and liberality of sentiment, with which you have hitherto been actuated. From these benign qualities, it is hoped, the most favorable indulgence will be granted, and that the zeal, with which this is written, will be allowed in some measure an excuse for its defects. However imperfect, therefore this may be, however inadequate to your own ideas, or to the wishes of him, who offers it to your consideration; you are hereby intreated to let the perusal, with which you may think proper to favor it, be serious, candid, dispassionate—as it relates to a common cause, in which all are alike concerned.

Suffer me, then, in the first place to advert to a part of the sixth article in this constitution. It may, perhaps, appear somewhat irregular, to begin with this article, since it is almost the last proposed: yet, if it be considered that this at once defines the extent of Congressional authority, and indisputably fixes its supremacy, every idea of impropriety on this head will probably vanish. The clause alluded to contains the following words, "This constitution, and the laws of the United States, which shall be made in pursuance thereof, and all treaties made, or which shall be made, under the authority of the United States, shall be the supreme law of the land; and the judges in every state shall be bound thereby; any thing in the constitution or laws of any state to the contrary, notwithstanding." If this constitution should be adopted, here the sovereignty of America is ascertained and fixed in the fœderal body at the same time that it abolishes the present independent sovereignty of each state. Because this government being general, and not confined to any particular part of the continent, but pervading every state and establishing its authority equally in all, its superiority will consequently be recognized in each; and all other powers can operate only in a secondary subordinate degree. For the idea of two sovereignties existing within the same community is a perfect solecism. If they be supposed equal, their operation must be commensurate, and like two mechanical powers of equal *momenta* counteracting each other;—here the force of the one will be destroyed by the force of the other: and so there will be no efficiency in either. If one be greater than the other, they will be similar to two unequal bodies in motion with a given degree of velocity, and impinging each other from opposite points;—the motion of the lesser in this case will necessarily be destroyed by that of the greater: and so there will be efficiency only in the greater. But what need is there for a mathematical deduction to shew the impropriety of two such distinct co-existing sovereignties? The natural understanding of all mankind perceives the apparent absurdity arising from such a supposition: since, if the word means any thing at all, it must mean that *supreme power*, which must reside somewhere instate; or, in other terms, it is the united powers of each individual member of the state collected and consolidated into *one body*. This collection, this union, this supremacy of power can, therefore, exist only in one body. This is obvious to every man: and it has been very properly suggested that under the proposed constitution each state will dwindle into "the insignificance of a town corporate." This certainly will be their utmost consequence; and, as such, they will have no authority to make laws, even for their own private government any farther than the permissive indulgence of Congress may grant them leave. This, Virginians, will be your mighty, your enviable situation after all your struggles for independence! and, if you will take the trouble to examine, you will find that the great, the supereminent authority, with which this instrument of union proposes to invest the fœderal body, is to be created without a single check—without a single article of covenant for the preservation of those inestimable rights, which have in all ages been the glory of freemen. It is true, "the United States shall guarantee to every state in this union a republican form of government": yet they do not guarantee to the different states their present forms of government, or the bill of rights thereto annexed, or any of them; and the expressions are too vague, too indefinite to create such a compact by implication. It is possible that a "republican form" of government may be built upon as absolute principles of despotism as any oriental monarchy ever yet possessed. I presume that the liberty of a nation depends, not on planning the frame of government, which consists merely in fixing and delineating the powers thereof; but on prescribing due limits to those powers, and establishing them upon just principles.

It has been held in a northern state by a zealous advocate for this constitution that there is no necessity for "a bill of rights" in the fœderal government; although at the same time he acknowledges such necessity to have existed when the constitutions of the separate governments were established. He confesses that in these instances the people "invested their representatives with every power and authority, which they did not in explicit terms reserve[,]" but "in delegating fœderal powers," says he, "every thing, which is not given, is reserved." Here is a distinction, I humbly conceive, without a difference, at least in the present enquiry. How far such a discrimination might prevail with respect to the present system of union, it is immaterial to examine; and had the observation been restrained to that alone, perhaps it might be acknowledged to contain some degree of propriety. For under the confederation it is well known that the authority of Congress cannot extend so far as to interfere with, or exercise any kind of coercion on, the powers of legislation in the different states; but the internal police of each is left free, sovereign and independent: so that the liberties of the people being secured as well as the nature of their constitution will admit; and the declaration of rights, which they have laid down as the *basis* of government, having their full force and energy, any farther stipulation on that head might be unnecessary. But, surely, when this doctrine comes to be applied to the *proposed* fœderal constitution, which is framed with such large and extensive powers, as to transfer the individual sovereignty from each state to the *aggregate body*,—a constitution, which delegates to Congress an authority to interfere with, and restrain the legislatures of every state—invests them with supreme powers of legislation throughout all the states—annihilates the separate independency of each; and, in short—swallows up and involves in the plenitude of its jurisdiction all other powers whatsoever:—I shall not be taxed with arrogance in declaring such an argument to be fallacious; and insisting on the necessity of a positive unequivocal declaration in favor of the rights of freemen in this case even more strongly than in the case of their separate governments. For it seems to me that when any civil establishment is formed, the more general its influence, the more extensive the powers, with which it is invested, the greater reason there is to take the necessary precaution for securing a due administration, and guarding against unwarrantable abuses.

(To be continued.)

Virginia Independent Chronicle

27 FEBRUARY 1788

ESSAY I

(Continued.)

SECTION 8th of the first article gives the Congress a power "to lay and collect, taxes, duties, imposts and excises." If it be a true maxim that those, who are entrusted with the exercise of the higher powers of government, ought to observe two essential rules; first in having no other view than the general good of all without any regard to private interest; and secondly, to take equal care of the whole body of the community, so as not to favor one part more than another: it is apparent that under the proposed constitution, this general confederated society, made up of thirteen different states, will have very little security for obtaining an observance, either of the one, or of the other, rule. For being different societies, though blended together in legislation, and having as different interests; no uniform rule for the whole seems to be practicable: and hence, it is to be feared, that the general good may be lost in a mutual attention to private views. From the same causes we may lament the probability of losing the advantage of the second rule; for it may be expected, in like manner, that the general care of the whole will be lost by the separate endeavors of different legislators to favor their own states. So long as mankind continues to be influenced by interest, the surest means of effecting an union of counsels in any assem-

bly is by an union of interests. Now, if it be considered that it is
this concert, that it is this union in promoting the *general good,*
which alone can preserve concord in this great republic, and secure
it success and glory,—unhappy will be the situation of America, if
she once precludes the beneficial effects of such a good understanding. Yet, I apprehend that these evils may result in a great measure
from an exercise of that branch of legislative authority, which
respects internal direct taxation. For in this, it is scarcely probable that the interest, ease or convenience of the several states can
be so well consulted in the fœderal assembly, as in their own respective legislatures. So different are many species of property, so various the productions, so unequal the profits arising, even from the
same species of property, in different states, that no general mode
of contribution can well be adopted in such a manner as at once to
affect all in an equitable degree. Hence may arise disagreeable
objects of contention. A diversity of interests will produce a diversity of schemes. Thus each state, as it is natural, will endeavor to
raise a revenue by such means, as may appear least injurious to its
own interest: a source of dissention manifestly detrimental to that
harmony, which is necessary to support the confederation. I cannot conceive it impracticable to reform the fœderal system in such
a manner as to ensure a compliance with the necessary requisitions of Congress from the different state legislatures. Then all the
several states being left to raise their own share of the revenue, and
being the only proper judges of the mode most convenient to themselves, it is highly probable that this important branch of government would be carried on more generally to the satisfaction of each
state; and would tend to promote a spirit of concord between all
the parts of this great community. Because *each* being thus accom-
modated, and participating the advantages of the union,—*none* subjected to any inconvenience thereby,—*all* would consequently
concur in nourishing an affection for the government, which so
cemented them.

I believe, it is acknowledged that the establishment of excises
has been one of the greatest grievances, under which the English
nation has labored for almost a century and an half. Although this
may seem an œconomical tax, as arising out of manufactures, from

which the *industrious* may derive advantages; and whereof the *wealthy* by consuming the greatest share, will of course contribute the largest proportion of the tax: yet the nature of it being such, as requires severe laws for its execution, it has justly become an object of general detestation. This has induced Judge Blackstone to declare that "the rigour and arbitrary proceedings of excise laws seem hardly compatible with the temper of a free nation." While, therefore, you are freemen—while you are unused to feel any other power, but such as can be exercised within the bounds of moderation and decency, it, doubtless, behoves you to consider whether it is an eligible step to subject yourselves to a new species of authority, which may warrant the most flagrant violations of the sacred rights of habitation. If this branch of revenue takes place, all the consequent rigour of excise laws will necessarily be introduced in order to enforce a due collection. On any charges of offence in this instance you will see yourselves deprived of your boasted trial by jury. The much admired common law process will give way to some quick and summary mode, by which the unhappy defendant will find himself reduced, perhaps to ruin, in less time than a charge could be exhibited against him in the usual course.

It has ever been held that standing armies in times of peace are dangerous to a free country; and no observation seems to contain more reason in it. Besides being useless, as having no object of employment, they are inconvenient and expensive. The soldiery, who are generally composed of the dregs of the people, when disbanded, or unfit for military service, being equally unfit for any other employment, become extremely burthensome. As they are a body of men exempt from the common occupations of social life, having an interest different from the rest of the community, they wanton in the lap of ease and indolence, without feeling the duties, which arise from the political connection, though drawing their subsistence from the bosom of the state. The severity of discipline necessary to be observed reduces them to a degree of slavery: the unconditional submission to the commands of their superiors, to which they are bound, renders them the fit instruments of tyranny and oppression.—Hence they have in all ages afforded striking examples of contributing, more or less, to enslave mankind;—and whoever will take the trouble to examine, will find that by far the greater part of the different nations, who have fallen from the glorious state of liberty, owe their ruin to standing armies. It has been urged that they are necessary to provide against sudden attacks. Would not a well regulated militia, duly trained to discipline, afford ample security? Such, I conceive, to be the best, the surest means of protection, which a free people can have when not actually engaged in war. This kind of defence is attended with two advantages superior to any others; first, when it is necessary to embody an army, they at once form a band of soldiers, whose interests are uniformly the same with those of the whole community, and in whose safety they see involved every thing, that is dear to themselves: secondly, if one army is cut off, another may be immediately raised already trained for military service. By a policy, somewhat similar to this, the Roman empire rose to the highest pitch of grandeur and magnificence.

The supreme court is another branch of fœderal authority, which wears the aspect of imperial jurisdiction, clad in dread array, and spreading its wide domain into all parts of the continent. This is to be co-extensive with the legislature, and, like that, is to swallow up all other courts of judicature.—For what is that judicial power which "shall extend to all cases in law and equity" in some having "original," in all others "appellate jurisdiction," but an establishment universal in its operation? And what is that "appellate jurisdiction both as to law and fact," but an establishment, which may in effect operate as original jurisdiction?—Or what is an appeal to enquire into facts after a solemn adjudication in any court below, but a trial *de novo?* And do not such trials clearly imply an incompetency in the inferior courts to exercise any kind of judicial authority with rectitude? Hence, will not this eventually annihilate their whole jurisdiction? Here is a system of jurisprudence to be erected, no less surprising than it is new and unusual. Here is an innovation, which bears no kind of analogy to any thing, that Englishmen, or Americans, the descendants of Englishmen, have ever yet experienced. Add to all, that this high prerogative court establishes no fundamental rule of proceeding, except that the trial by jury is allowed in some criminal cases. All other cases are left

open—and subject "to such regulations as the Congress shall make."—Under these circumstances I beseech you all, as citizens of Virginia, to consider seriously whether you will not endanger the solemn trial by jury, which you have long revered, as a sacred barrier against injustice—which has been established by your ancestors many centuries ago, and transmitted to you, as one of the greatest bulwarks of civil liberty—which you have to this day maintained inviolate:—I beseech you, I say, as members of this commonwealth, to consider whether you will not be in danger of losing this inestimable mode of trial in all those cases, wherein the constitution does not provide for its security. Nay, does not that very provision, which is made, by being confined to a few particular cases, almost imply a total exclusion of the rest? Let it, then, be a reflection deeply impressed on your minds—that if this noble privilege, which by long experience has been found the most exquisite method of determining controversies according to the scale of equal liberty, should once be taken away, it is unknown what new species of trial may be substituted in its room. Perhaps you may be surprised with some strange piece of judicial polity,—some arbitrary method, perhaps confining all trials to the entire decision of the magistracy, and totally excluding the great body of the people from any share in the administration of public justice.
(To be continued)

Virginia Independent Chronicle

5 MARCH 1788

ESSAY I

(Continued.)
AFTER the most deliberate reflections on this important matter, permit me, my dear countrymen, to declare to you in the most [unfeigned] manner, that not perceiving any thing in the proposed

plan of government, which seems calculated to ensure the happiness of America—I could not, as a fellow-citizen, resist the inclination to impart these sentiments to you. Unmoved by party—rage [unassailed] by passion—uninfluenced by any other interest, but the genuine effusion of zeal for this, our common country, I confess to you in the language of sincerity and candor, that after the first reading of this new code, I could not behold it; but with an eye of disapprobation. Unwilling, however, to reject at first sight an object of such high moment, I resolved to distrust the propriety of a construction passed at so early a period.—This led me to peruse it with the utmost diligence I was capable of; and believe me, the foregoing observations have arisen from the fullest conviction, that the system involves in it the most dangerous principles; and—so far from exalting the *standard* of American liberty, I fear indeed that, should it be adopted, this glorious *work*, which already has cost the lives of many worthy patriots, will ere long be leveled with the dust. Let it not be conjectured from hence that any illiberal conceptions are formed by the writer hereof respecting the intentions of those gentlemen, who have offered this plan of fœderal government. He knows no circumstance inducing him to suppose they had any other object in view but the good of their country.—When we contemplate the great—the magnanimous HERO, who has conducted our armies through all the trying vicissitudes of danger and difficulty,—there is no man so disingenuous—there is no man so ungrateful, as to impute any transactions of his to sinister motives. Every true American is well assured that steadiness of virtue— that benignity of soul have the chief rule in all his actions.—Yet every American, and every other person, are satisfied also that there is no infallibility in human nature.—To be man is to be subject to error. The best, the greatest, the wisest are liable to commit mistakes.—Let it be remembered, then, that this code of government is solemnly proposed to every freeman in America. For what?—For the purpose of binding them without their approbation? No.—For an implicit acceptance? No.—For their adoption merely in compliment to the general convention? No.—What then?—Every man's duty to his country points out to him the end of this proposition. Every man knows that it is for a free, a candid, an impartial discussion and determination thereon; whether they will approve and adopt it; or whether they will disapprove and reject it. Can any citizen, therefore, be so weak? can any be so timid? so pusillanimous, as to acknowledge that he has no right to exercise his own judgment with regard to this matter? If there should be any haughty spirits among us, who think that this subject ought to be handled by none but a few persons of eminent characters, let such recollect that the dignity, the importance of their country should inspire sentiments more exalted than the highest characters—sentiments, that should correspond with the worth of America, not with the consequence of any mere individuals. Will you, then, Virginians, arrogate too much by boldly asserting the privilege to judge for yourselves in what so nearly concerns the cause of liberty? No, no, my countrymen, you will not arrogate too much; you will not: I avow it by the souls of those brave patriots, who fought for the same cause in the late war. You will in this affair act as becomes you. The rank, you hold amongst the nations of the earth, requires this of you. And you will forfeit that rank: you will forfeit the character of *freemen;* and shew that you deserve to be enslaved, if you decline that privilege. The happiness of a multitude of people is certainly the highest advantage, which can be conferred on any society: and if you will contribute a full share of duty to effect this, so shall you obtain a due share of glory. No pomp of character, no sound of names, no distinction of birth—no pre-eminence of any kind, should dispose you to hoodwink your own understandings; and in that state suffer yourselves to be led at the will of any order of men whatsoever. The part you have acted heretofore,—the brave, the noble efforts, you have made, are proof enough of your fortitude, and totally exclude every idea of pusillanimity. Herein you have evinced the highest sense of public virtue: herein you have manifested to the whole world that the cause of liberty has hitherto had the prevailing influence over your hearts. And shall men possessed of these sentiments? shall those valiant defenders of their country, who have not feared to encounter toil and danger in a thousand shapes? who have not startled, even at the prospect of death itself? Shall you, O Virginians; shall you, I say, after exhibiting such bright examples of true patriotic heroism, suddenly become inconsistent with yourselves; and were to maintain a privilege so incontestibly your due?—No, my countrymen;—by no means can I conceive that the laudable vigor, which flamed so high in every breast, can have so far evaporated in the space of five years. I doubt not, but you will in this trying instance acquit yourselves in a manner worthy of your former conduct. It is not to be feared that you need the force of persuasion, to exercise a proper freedom of enquiry into the merits of this proposed plan of government: or that you will not pay a due attention to the welfare of that country, for which you have already so bravely exerted yourselves. Of this I am well assured; and do not wonder when imagination presents to my view the idea of a numerous and respectable body of men reasoning on the principles of this fœderal constitution. If herein I conceive that you are alarmed at the exceedingly high and extensive authority, which it is intended to establish, I cannot but see the strongest reasons for such apprehensions. For a system, which is to supersede the present different governments of the states, by ordaining that "laws made in pursuance thereof shall be supreme, and shall bind the judges in every state, any thing in the constitution or laws of any state to the contrary notwithstanding," must be alarming indeed! What cannot this omnipotence of power effect? How will your bill of rights avail you any thing? By this authority the Congress can make laws, which shall bind all, repugnant to your present constitution—repugnant to every article of your rights; for they are a part of your constitution,—they are the basis of it. So that if you pass this new constitution, you will have a naked plan of government unlimited in its jurisdiction, which not only expunges your bill of rights by rendering ineffectual, all the state governments; but is proposed without any kind of stipulation for any of those natural rights, the security whereof ought to be the end of all governments. Such a stipulation is so necessary, that it is an absurdity to suppose any civil liberty can exist without it. Because it cannot be alledged in any case whatsoever, that a breach has been committed—that a right has been violated; as there will be no standard to resort to—no criterion to ascertain the breach, or even to find whether there has been any violation at all. Hence it is evident that the most flagrant acts of oppression may be inflicted; yet, still there will be no apparent object injured: there will be no unconstitutional infringement. For instance, if Congress should pass a law that persons charged with capital crimes shall not have a *right to demand the cause or nature of the accusation,* shall not be *confronted with the accusers or witnesses, or call for evidence in their own favor;* and a question should arise respecting their authority therein,—can it be said that they have exceeded the limits of their jurisdiction, when *that* has no limits; when no provision has been made for such a right?—When no responsibility on the part of Congress has been required by the constitution? The same observation may be made on any arbitrary or capricious imprisonments *contrary to the law of the land.* The same may be made, if *excessive bail should be required;* if *excessive fines should be imposed;* if *cruel and unusual punishments should be inflicted;* if *the liberty of the press should be restrained;* in a word—if laws should be made totally derogatory to the whole catalogue of rights, which are now secured under your present form of government.

You will, doubtless, consider whether the inconveniencies may not be very disagreeable, and perhaps injurious, to which this country may be subjected by excise laws,—by direct taxation of every kind,—by the establishment of fœderal courts. You will advert to the dangerous and oppressive consequences, that may ensue from the introduction of standing armies in times of peace; those baneful engines of ambition, against which free nations have always guarded with the greatest degree of caution. You will determine likewise as to the propriety of being excluded from keeping ships of war without the consent of Congress. The situation of these states renders a naval force extremely desirable. Being bounded on one side by the sea, their coasts are accessible to every lawless adventurer: and without ships to guard them, they are subject to continual depredations. The expediency of this species of defence is manifest. The great advantages to be derived from it,—the strength,—the consequence, which it adds to a nation, are such, that every well-wisher to this country would rejoice to see as large a navy established, as the circumstances of the state can at any time admit of. This, therefore, seems to be a very improper restraint upon the states,—a restraint, which may perhaps eventually prove very injurious.

Upon the whole, my fellow-citizens, if you judge this proposed constitution to be eligible or ineligible, you will accordingly instruct your delegates when they are about to meet in convention. The wisdom of the legislature has judged it advisable to fix the time for deciding on this momentous business at the distance of several months, that you may become thoroughly acquainted with a subject, which so nearly concerns your greatest interests.

I know it is a favorite topic with the advocates for the new government—that it will advance the dignity of Congress; and that the energy, which is now wanting in the fœderal system, will be hereby rendered efficient. Nobody doubts, but the government of the union is susceptible of amendment. But can any one think that there is no medium between want of power, and the possession of it in an unlimited degree? Between the imbecility of mere recommendatory propositions, and the sweeping jurisdiction of exercising every branch of government over the United States to the greatest extent? Between the present feeble texture of the confœderation, and the proposed nervous ligaments? Is it not possible to strengthen the hands of Congress so far as to enable them to comply with all the exigences of the union—to regulate the great commercial concerns of the continent,—to superintend all affairs, which relate to the United States in their aggregate capacity, without devolving upon that body the supreme powers of government in all its branches? The original institution of Congressional business,—the nature, the end of that institution evince the practicability of such a reform; and shew that it is more honorable, more glorious—and will be more happy for each American state to retain its independent sovereignty. For what can be more truly great in any country than a number of different states in the full enjoyment of liberty—exercising distinct powers of government; yet associated by *one general head,* and under the influence of a mild, just and well-organized confederation duly held *in equilibrio;*—whilst all derive those external advantages, which are the great purposes of the union? This separate independency existing in each—this harmony pervading the whole—this due degree of energy in the fœderal department, all together, will form a beautiful *species* of national grandeur. These will add lustre to every member, and spread a glory all around. These will command the admiration of mankind. These will exhibit a bright *specimen* of real dignity, far superior to that immense devolution of power, under which the sovereignty of each state shall shrink to nothing.

It requires no great degree of knowledge in history to learn what dangerous consequences generally result from large and extensive powers. Every man has a natural propensity to power; and when one degree of it is obtained, *that* seldom fails to excite a thirst for more:—an higher point being gained, still the soul is impelled to a farther pursuit. Thus step by step, in regular progression, she proceeds onward, until the lust of domination becomes the ruling passion, and absorbs all other desires. When any man puts himself under the influence of such a passion, it is natural for him to seek after every opportunity, and to employ every means within reach, for obtaining his purpose. There is something so exceedingly bewitching in the possession of power that hardly a man can enjoy it, and not be affected after an unusual manner. The pomp of superiority carries with it charms, which operate strongly on the imagination. Nay, it is a melancholy reflection that too often the very disposition itself is transformed,—and for the gratification of ambitious views, the mild, the gentle, humane—the virtuous become cruel and violent, losing all sense of honor, probity, humanity and gratitude.—Hence, should it not be a *maxim*, never to be forgotten—that a free people ought to intrust no set of men with powers, that may be abused without controul, or afford opportunities to designing men to carry dangerous measures into execution, without being responsible for their conduct? And as no human foresight can penetrate so far into future events, as to guard always against the effects of vice,—as the securest governments are seldom secure enough;—is it not the greatest imprudence to adopt a system, which has an apparent tendency to furnish ambitious men with the means of exerting themselves—perhaps to the destruction of American liberty?

It is next to impossible to enslave a people immediately after a firm struggle against oppression, while the sense of past injury is recent and strong. But after some time this impression naturally wears off;—the ardent glow of freedom gradually evaporates;—the charms of popular equality, which arose from the *republican plan,* insensibly decline;—the pleasures, the advantages derived from the new kind of government grow stale through use. Such declension in all these vigorous springs of action necessarily produces a supineness. The altar of liberty is no longer watched with such attentive assiduity;—a new train of passions succeeds to the empire of the mind;—different objects of desire take place:—and, if the nation happens to enjoy a series of prosperity, voluptuousness, excessive fondness for riches, and luxury gain admission and establish themselves—these produce venality and corruption of every kind, which open a fatal avenue to bribery. Hence it follows, that in the midst of this general contageon a few men—or one—more powerful than all others, industriously endeavor to obtain all authority; and by means of great wealth—or embezzling the public money,—perhaps totally subvert the government, and erect a system of aristocratical or monarchic tyranny in its room. What ready means for this *work of evil* are numerous standing armies, and the disposition of the great revenue of the United States! Money can purchase soldiers;—soldiers can produce money: and both together can do anything. It is this depravation of manners, this wicked propensity, my dear countrymen, against which you ought to provide with the utmost degree of prudence and circumspection. All nations pass this *paroxism* of vice at some period or other;—and if at that dangerous juncture your government is not secured upon a solid foundation, and well guarded against the machinations of evil men, the liberties of this country will be lost—perhaps forever!

Let us establish a strong fœderal government, which shall render our Congress a great and eminent body, says one. By all means, replies another; and then they will command the attention of all Europe.—Why, pray, what will it avail you in the hour of distress— in the midst of calamity, though all Europe should pay attention to the Congress? What advantage will it be to the citizens of America, should they elevate Congress to the highest degree of grandeur;—should the sound of that grandeur be wasted across the Atlantic, and echoe through every town in Europe? What will the pomp—the splendor of that *dignified body* profit you, I say, if you place yourselves in a situation, which may terminate in wretched-

ness? Of what consequence will that state of congressional preemi-
nence be to you, or to your posterity, if either the one, or the other
should thereby be reduced to a mere herd of—? O great GOD, avert
that dreadful catastrophe.—Let not the day be permitted to dawn,
which shall discover to the world that America remains no longer
a free nation!—O let not this last sacred asylum of persecuted *liberty* cease to afford a resting place for that fair goddess!—Re-ani-
mate each spirit, that languishes in this glorious cause! Shine in
upon us, and illumine all our counsels!—Suffer thy bright ministers of grace to come down and direct us;—and hovering for awhile
on the wings of affection, breathe into our souls true sentiments of
wisdom!—that in this awful, this important moment we may be
conducted safely through the maze of error!—that a firm basis of
national happiness may be established, and flourish in undiminished
glory through all succeeding ages!

Virginia Independent Chronicle

28 MAY 1788

ESSAY II

*In this short essay the Impartial Examiner builds on his first piece
by arguing that an arbitrary government will be tyrannical. If the
rulers have the power to abuse the people, they will. Thus the central issue in examining any proposed Constitution is whether it
binds the rulers to obey the principles of liberty. Essays in* The
Federalist *of particular relevance: 10, 51, 84.*

I HAVE in a former paper endeavored to take a view of the leading
principles of the new *foederal constitution*. In pursuing the design
of that address it was necessary to make some previous remarks on
the nature of civil government in general: This led me to premise

the material discrimination between arbitrary constitutions and the constitution of free governments.

The arbitrary species, or those, which fix no other limits to the *supreme rulers*, but their *own wills*, are totally incompatible with the spirit of civil liberty, and exclude every idea of free government. These may be described by the harsher epithet of *despotism*.

Some men may perhaps fancy a distinction where in reality none exists. They may conceive the possibility of a government being constituted, which may with great propriety be denominated *arbitrary;* and yet consider it not as *despotic*. If, however, it be recollected that the term *despotism* is a relative expression arising from the authority of masters over their servants, which authority is founded in the *will* of the masters, it must plainly appear that every degree of *arbitrary* power is *despotic;* and that tyranny in government, whether it be distinguished by the former, or by the latter, appellation, is its regular and natural production. For whenever a power becomes vested in any *agent*, as unrestrained as the *will* of that *agent*, in him are immediately created the properties of a master; and those, over whom he exercises such power, stand *ipso facto* in the relation of servants.

To some the bare mention of *despotic rule* conveys the most alarming ideas of horror; yet at the same time are they satisfied with [the idea's preparations], as they imagine, [offering some *arbitrary* freedom.] With [fervency] of zeal they urge the expediency of *a plan*, which has for its basis the extended sphere of *human will*. They contend that it is necessary to establish a system, so unrestrained in its nature, in order to effectuate a *strong* and *energetic* government. This desirable object they seem to consider as unattainable by any other means;—and that all institutions, which convey only a limited authority, are inadequate to the purposes of society.

Such a kind of responsibility, as would form a *check* on the *supreme rulers*, is deemed a source of continual impediment; and— to secure any degree of natural liberty, however small a residuum, is, in contemplation of their minds, laying the foundation of a *weak* government, liable to endless confusions, and productive of nothing better than sedition and anarchy. They conceive a fondness for this species of government, because it is framed in the *republican stile*; and, although fraught with the seeds of *despotism*, the apparent *loveliness* of its outward garb hides all the *deformity* of its inward corruptions. Whence it is manifest that distinctions are formed, which are preposterous and merely imaginary.

Nothing, perhaps, has contributed more towards interrupting the repose of mankind than a curious attention to the names and shadows of things, whilst the real essence and substantial parts have been disregarded.

That, which in any particular form has once produced much *evil* and *discontent*, generally stamps a lasting impression on the mind, and is not contemplated but with extreme detestation; although evils of the same nature, when inflicted under a different appearance, are frequently submitted to without repining. Thus, after the expulsion of *Tarquin*, and with him the extinction of regal authority in *Rome*, the name of *King* was ever odius to the *Roman people*; yet did they acquiesce in the exercise of arbitrary transactions under a different form of government. Such were they frequently subjected to through the various stages of their *republic*; until at last the sovereign power was established in the person of a *single man*. This change produced a system of government, unbounded as the *regal sway*, and no less susceptible of *tyrannical* proceedings. They could then respect the name of *emperor*, unlimited as he was, and, though exposed to all the rage of oppression, bow down with reverence, and venerate the *imperial scepter*.

The insidious attempts under a British administration to pervert the former government into a baneful system of tyranny had spread a general alarm throughout America. Opposition to *arbitrary* measures manifested itself among all ranks of people. Diligent inquiries were made to [see] the [schemes] of their enemies; jealousies excited to an unusual degree with respect to their rights and privileges;—whilst exertions were made, which produced the most desirable effects. All these circumstances conspired in exhibiting very favorable prospects, and promised a lasting security to American liberty.

The injuries suffered under a government, which exposed the people of these states to the machinations of wicked and designing ministers, determined them in the choice of a system, which had principally in view the preservation of their *liberty*. Such was its grand object. In pursuit of this plan, as the great means of national happiness, constitutions were formed for the different states upon principles, salutary in their nature; and tending to perpetuate the freedom and independency of each. To these was added a confederation, under which the separate *republics* so constituted might harmonize in all their *general interests*.

Thus were they situated—when a defect was apprehended in this confederation. The ineffectual endeavors to promote some important advantages, and to answer all the exigences of the *union*, indicated a weakness in the general government. A revision was deemed expedient. When, therefore, a new constitution was proposed, it became the duty of every American diligently to enquire, *first*, whether this system was coincident with their *standing maxims of liberty;* and, if so—whether conducive to *good policy.* If found derogatory to the former—any consideration respecting the latter should be unnecessary. This alone should mark it, as dangerous, and unworthy of approbation. The genius [of America] that *no fancied schemes of policy should compensate for the adoption of a plan discordant to her favorite principles of liberty.* This is not a chimerical illusion, but a solid and interesting consideration. A mind thus convicted must act inconsistent with propriety, and contrary to every sentiment of duty, if it would then approve of the plan.

The writer of this address had, therefore, in his first number chiefly intended to take up this matter only so far as related to its principles—and having conceived that these were incompatible with the admired maxims of *American liberty*, his objections on that head were there laid down.

Observing, however, that most of the writers in favor of the plan seem in a great measure to have passed over this *important point*—and recommend it merely from *motives of policy*; it is now intended, as the business of some succeeding papers, to state objections to such of the constituent parts of the plan, abstracted of its principles, as appear, in his opinion, improperly constructed, and calculated to produce ill effects in their operation. These writers seem not to regard any fundamentals in government, provided they can procure a plan, in which they fancy some prospects of immediate benefit are to be discovered. In conformity with the stile of the *proposed constitution*, the favorers of it have, with a peculiarity of self-applause, ascribed to themselves the distinction of fœderalists; while those, who oppose the plan are marked with the epithet of anti-fœderal.

The strong desire, which has been manifested, for a union between the American states, since the revolution, affords an opportunity of making the distinction, as they imagine, to their advantage.—As *fœderalists*, in their opinion, they must be deemed friendly to the *union:*—as *anti-fœderal*, the opposers must, in their opinion too, be considered unfriendly. Thus on the sound of names they build their fame.

For those gentlemen, however, let it be observed that the opponents seem to act on the broader scale of true *fœderal principles*. The advocates for the new code with all sovereignty to be lodged in the hands of Congress. This is not to connect thirteen independent states—but to form one extended empire by compounding the whole, and thus destroying the sovereignty of each. The other party desire a continuance of each distinct sovereignty—and are anxious for such a degree of energy in the general government, as will cement the union in the strongest manner. This they consider as one of the greatest blessings, which can attend their country.

Virginia Independent Chronicle

4 JUNE 1788

ESSAY III

The Impartial Examiner criticizes the Constitutions's federal legislature. The House of Representatives is too small truly to represent Americans' interests. Senators should be directly elected, because states, no longer being sovereign, do not themselves prop-

erly represent the interests of their people. Essays in The Federal-ist *of particular interests: 55, 56, 62, 63.*

BESIDES those inherent rights, which should be established as fun-damental principles, independent of the constitution, there are cer-tain other maxims essential to every free government. These should pervade the whole plan. They should be interwoven with its very texture. And, as it is necessary that the first should be pre-served sacred and inviolate; so ought the last to be regarded as indispensible. These should be the leading properties, the head—the soul of the system; whilst those exist entire, supreme and uncontrouled.

It will not be denied, that *all power is originally vested in the peo-ple, and that it should be exercised either* immediately *by themselves,* or mediately *by their representatives.* These are *maxims,* without the observance of which the liberty of every nation must expire. When the power is exercised by their representatives, it is expedient that the representation be *ample* and *complete.* It should be *ample,* that amongst the *members* there may be a competent knowledge of the *constituents,* their sentiments, connections, views and habits; and that amongst the *constituents* there may generally be a due degree of knowledge respecting the virtues and abilities of the *members.*

In extensive territories, where the people are widely dispersed, and individuals can have very little communication beyond the cir-cle of their own neighbourhood, the representation should also be extensive. In countries thus situated, unless the legislature be numerous, there cannot be expected amongst the *members* thereof a general knowledge of their constituents: and when the *member* to be elected bears a very small proportion to the *number* of electors, it is utterly improbable that the *majority* should have an adequate knowledge of those; who will be elected. So that a great part of the community must in a manner be obliged to submit their most important concerns into the hands of a few persons unknown to themselves, and of whose wisdom, integrity and patriotism they can form no competent judgment.

Again, the representation should be *complete,* that is, it should be such as to comprehend every species of interest within the society. All orders of men, who have any permanent interest in the government, as far as practicable, ought to be represented. Regarding, then, the great diversity, which pervades most communities, from the highest landed concerns through the various stages of mercantile and mechanic interests, we must discover the necessity of an extensive delegation. When, therefore, the number of *representatives* in a legislature is very small, this affords objections, not only because they are not numerous enough to contain a competent knowledge of their constituents: they are inadequate to, and cannot sufficiently respect, all the complicated; variant and opposite interests, which must necessarily subsist in a commonwealth, whose inhabitants are spread over a wide-extended country. The smallness of their number enhances the dignity of their *seats;* and none can expect to obtain a *seat,* except men of the most elevated station. Thus in the beginning of a government so constituted there will be laid a foundation for the exercise of undue influence, whereby every branch of supreme power will be in a manner monopolized by one set of men: and thus the delegation will become partial. For, besides the effect of this undue influence in elections, the dispersed situation of the electors, together with that of the candidates, will ever produce much division amongst the suffrages;—and so the select party, who will be distinguished by their superior wealth, being the leading *junto* in this business, will easily procure a competent number to decide for themselves or their favorites.

Thus it will generally happen, that elections will be determined, not by the majority of the people, but perhaps by an inconsiderable part of them; and the persons chosen will be such, whose situation and rank in life had removed them far from a knowledge of the *great body* of the people. They will consequently be unacquainted with the customs, feelings, opinions and wishes of most of their constituents; and as the constituents will be unacquainted with their representatives,—these will not possess the confidence of *those.* Doubt and distrust will prevail.—That course of congenial sentiment—that reciprocity of common interest between the *legislature* and *bulk* of the nation, which should be the soul of *republicanism,* and are the chief objects of a free, unbiassed and general representation, will not exist in this kind of government. How, then, can it be expected that a strict regard to the *good* of all will mark the public proceedings? Who can really imagine that a *body*, thus constituted and thus invested with sovereign authority, will regularly devote their labors to promote the happiness, prosperity and freedom of a community, over whom they bear the rule—when they view themselves advanced to this state of exaltation—when this high degree of dignity will tempt them to look down with indifference, perhaps contempt, on the inhabitants of a spacious territory, as the subjects of their government—and when they contemplate these, as generally unconnected with themselves in all their most important concerns?—The uniform experience of ages operates against the idea. It may be dangerous to indulge in such a scheme of policy—lest its fairest prospects should prove visionary indeed!—lest in its exercise the directly contrary effects should be produced.

For the foregoing reasons, the legislative powers proposed to be granted according to the new system appear liable to material objections. For herein the number of representatives being too small to encourage the idea of a *full* or *complete* deputation, there is no prospect of securing a due regard to all the different interests necessarily arising amongst the numerous inhabitants of America, spread over a territory so extensive—so vast—so various in climate, products, habits and connections.

That part of the legislature, which is particularly denominated the *house of representatives*, is indeed the only popular branch; and although these officers are to be chosen by the immediate suffrages of the people, yet their dignity being necessarily great in proportion as their number is small, fair and unbiassed elections are scarcely probable, if not impracticable.

In the appointment and constitution of the other branch; the *senate*, we have but the shade of a deputation from the people. The state-legislatures, it seems, are to elect this *body*. The objections, which apply to the *house of representatives*, hold more strongly with regard to this, in as much as longer continuance in office will be productive of more danger; and the mode of appointment, by rendering them more independent of the people, will preclude *these* from having any decisive influence on their conduct.

It is no argument in favor of the manner proposed, that it is the same, by which the members of the present Congress are chosen. The nature and end of the one being totally different from those of the other, if they be duly considered, it may, perhaps, be thought not inexpedient to vary the proceedings respecting them. The Congress under the present confederation are the deputies of sovereign states in the full exercise of independent government. These deputies are appointed by the legislatures thereof, not for the purpose of regulating the internal police of the states, but to superintend their general and foreign affairs so far as all the states are concerned in common. When, therefore, the legislature of any state is actually existing and in the exercise of their office, it seems not improper that such deputies should be appointed by them: for in strictness they appear to be the deputies of the legislature; and are to them immediately amenable. The proposed *senate* are to exercise a share of legislation in the general government, and to participate in the sovereignty of America. Thus circumstanced, they will know not any authority superior to that, whereof they themselves possess a part. They are intended, as such, to be a branch of the representation of the people. To the people they ought to be amenable: and by the people they ought to be chosen.

Virginia Independent Chronicle

11 JUNE 1788

ESSAY IV

The Impartial Examiner objects to the presidential veto, using the trappings of English monarchy as examples of the dangerous powers a veto gives to the executive. Particularly worrisome to the Impartial Examiner is the president's power over the military and over civil appointments. Essays in The Federalist *of particular relevance: 67, 69.*

ALTHOUGH the *senate* and *house of representatives* are to be established, and it seems to be the spirit of the proposed plan of government, that they should be considered as the grand *deputation* of America—the great aggregate *body*, to whom shall be delegated the important trust of *representing* the whole nation—the august, puissant *assembly*, in whom shall reside the full majesty of the people: yet, it seems too, these alone shall not be sufficient to exercise the powers of legislation. It is ordained, as a necessary expedient in the fœderal government, that a *president* of the United States (who is to hold the supreme *executive* power) should also concur in passing every law.

In monarchy, where the established maxim is, that the king should be respected as a great and transcendent personage, who knows no equal—who in his royal political capacity can commit no *wrong*—to whom no evil can be ascribed—in whom exists the height of perfection—who is supreme above all, and accountable to no earthly being, it is consistent with such a maxim, that the *prince* should form a constituent branch of the legislature, and that his power of rejecting whatever has been passed by the other branches should be distinct, and co-extensive with that of either of those branches in rejecting what has been proposed and consented to by the other. It is necessary that the fundamental laws of the realm should ascribe to the king those high and eminent attributes—that he should possess in himself the sovereignty of the nation; and that the regal dignity should distinguish him, as superior to all his subjects, and in his political character endowed with certain inherent qualities, which cannot be supposed to reside in any other individual within the kingdom: otherwise, that constitutional independence, which the laws meant peculiarly to establish in his person, would not be preserved. To this end the king of England is invested with the sole *executive* authority, and a branch of legislative jurisdiction so far as to pass his *negative* on all proceedings of the other two branches, or to confirm them by his *assent*.

This secures to him the intended superiority in the constitution, and gives him the ascendant in government; else his sovereignty would become a shadow—whilst that doctrine, whereby he is declared to be the *head*, the *beginning* and *end* of the great *body politic,* would prove to be nothing more than mere found. This two-fold jurisdiction established in the British monarch being founded on maxims extremely different from those, which prevail in the American States, the writer hereof is inclined to hope that he will not be thought singular, if he conceives an impropriety in assimilating the component parts of the American government to those of the British: and as the reasons, which to the founders of the British constitution were motives superior to all others to induce them thus to give the *executive* a controul over the *legislative,* are so far from existing in this country, that every principle of that kind is generally, if not universally, exploded; so it should appear that the same *public spirit,* which pervades the nation, would proclaim the doctrine of prerogative and other peculiar properties of the royal character, as incompatible with the view of these states when they are settling the *form of a republican* government. Is it not therefore sufficient that every branch in the proposed system, be distinct and independent of each other—that no one branch might receive any accession of power (by taking part of another) which would tend to overturn the balance and thereby endanger the very *being* of the constitution? Whilst the king of England enjoys all the *regalia,* which are annexed to his crown—whilst he exercises a transcendent dominion over his subjects, the existence whereof is coeval with the first rudiments of their constitution—let the free citizens of America, consulting their true national happiness, wish for no innovation, but what is regulated according to the scale of equal liberty, or which may not destroy that liberty by too great a share of power being lodged in any particular hands;—let this collateral jurisdiction, which constitutes the *royal negative,* be held by kings alone, since with kings it first originated:—Let this remain in its native soil, as most congenial to it; there it will cumber-less, and be more productive,—here it will be an exotick, and may poison the *stock,* in which it may be engrafted.

It will be said, perhaps, that the power, granted the president, of *approving* or *disapproving* the proceedings, which have passed the senate and house of representatives, will not be so decisive in its nature as the king's *negative.* True it is, this power of rejecting does not extend so far as primarily to produce an entire ovehrtrow of any law, which has passed those *two houses:* but it may be expected that in many instances this *negative* will amount to a final and conclusive rejection. For as a law, which has been once disapproved by the president, cannot be re-passed without the agreement of *two-thirds* of *both houses*, there can be no doubt, it will frequently happen that this concurrence of *two thirds* cannot be obtained. The law must then fall: and thus the president, although he has not the power of *resolving* originally and *enacting* any laws, independent of those two houses, hath nevertheless in the legislative scale of government a weight almost equal to that of two thirds of the whole Congress. If the system proposed had been calculated to extend his authority a little farther, he would preponderate against all—he alone would possess the sovereignty of America. For if the whole executive authority and an absolute, entire *negative* on the legislature should become united in one person, these must, with regard to *that person*, destroy every idea of a subject. Thus circumstanced he cannot be the object of any laws; he will be above all law: as none can be enacted without his consent—he will be elevated to the height of supremacy.—

How near will the *president* approach to this consummate degree of power! The portion allotted him may, however, be amply sufficient to give him the ascendant in the constitution. He must continually acquire great accessions of weight in every scale of government, as *chief magistrate* and *generalissimo* of the United States—at the same time possessing so great a share in the legislature, as a revision of all *bills* and other proceedings which shall have passed the senate and house of representatives with a discretionary right of rejecting them—united with the senate in making treaties, appointing all public ministers, judges, and a train of other officers, who will be necessary for carrying on the business of government; thus dispensing honor and profit throughout America—whilst copious streams of influence must flow from him, as from a source. Can the different departments be duly balanced when all these high powers concenter in one branch? Is it not rather probable that this branch will destroy the balance, and eventually rise to the fulness of dominion?

When the *spirit* of America becomes such, as to ascribe to their president all those extraordinary qualities, which the subjects of kingly governments ascribe to their princes: then, it is presumed, and not till then, he may consistently be invested with a power similar to theirs.

It is remarkable how the president and senate mutually participate in the exercise of a two-fold jurisdiction. How, then, can it be surprising to any one, if some citizens, truly jealous of their liberties, are alarmed with the apprehensions of *aristocracy*? Those, who seriously reflect on the properties of human nature, and who possess republican principles, will suppose they conceive grounds for such apprehensions: those, who have different sentiments, will not care whether there are grounds for such apprehensions, or not.

Virginia Independent Chronicle

18 JUNE 1788

ESSAY V

The Impartial Examiner concludes with an examination of the question underlying any proposal for a new constitution: Are the defects in the current constitution specific and correctable, or are they so systemic and deep that a new system of government is required? He then argues that the Confederacy answers its practical purposes of securing equal justice between the states and maintaining peace and mutual intercourse among them. Relatively minor revisions would make the Confederacy adequate to America's needs, whereas the proposed Constitution, because it lacks a bill of rights, would be hostile to the people's liberties. Essays in The Federalist *of particular relevance: 21, 22, 83.*

WHEN a change, so momentous in it's nature, as that of new modelling a *plan* of government, becomes the object of any people's meditation, every citizen, whose mind is duly impressed with a regard for the welfare of his country, will consider himself under an indispensible obligation to make some such enquiries, as the following.—Whence flows the necessity of a change?—Does it proceed from certain *vicious properties*, which reside in the old system and form the essential parts of it?—Or will such a measure become eligible, because *evils* have arisen from the feeble texture of the plan, or a loose exercise of government, which could not well be avoided?—What are the *evils* complained of? and what will be their correspondent remedies?—Are the evils *radical*, and not to be removed but by a *general* reform throughout the constitution?—Or do they result from a defect in some particular branch only? and may an adequate remedy be effected by introducing a new regulation merely as to *that* branch?

If investigations like these are seriously and dispassionately pursued, and it should be found that the present confederation of the American states contains *vicious properties*, which are inherent, fundamental, and tending to produce a general corruption, the *necessity of a change* must then be manifest. This discovery will lead to another enquiry; and that is—Do such properties pervade the whole system and contaminate all the parts of it? If so—then a *thorough change* will appear to be expedient, and it may be necessary to new model the system.

If, on the other hand, *evils* are found existing, which proceed, not so much from any internal corrupt *qualities*, as from the *feeble texture* of any parts of the system, or a *laxity* in the exercise of it's powers, it should seem adviseable to make alterations so far as to add a due degree of strength to the *weak parts*, and thereby insure *efficacy* in the government.

Should it appear, after a proper enquiry into the nature of the evils, that they are *radical*, and strike at the *vital principles* of the constitution—then to apply a *correspondent remedy*, an institution, which would produce a *general reform*, might with great propriety be deemed requisite.

If the defects are of a trivial nature, and subsist merely in some particular department or branch of the system—then amendments in the *defective branch*, tending to give energy where it had hitherto been wanting, would be amply sufficient for removing the *evils* and forming a competent remedy.

In order to discover how far the present system is vicious, or inadequate to the purposes of *this* great confederated society, for which it was established, a retrospect of the *original design* of the confederacy *itself* may afford no small degree of assistance.—Let it be recollected, then, that the *primary* object was to *form a perfect union*. This is manifested by the very "stile of the confederacy."—That it was intended to promote *justice* equally between all the states cannot be doubted; because it is an institution, calculated to unite a number of *independent republics* under a *firm league* of amity, and to provide that contributions of every kind, which had been, or might be, necessary towards supporting their *general* government, should be furnished in due proportions— whilst it was stipulated that a *mutual intercourse* and *reciprocal privileges* and *immunities* should subsist between the citizens of *all* the several states. Again, to *ensure domestic tranquility* must have been another important object with the framers of this confederation: for union, harmony and justice cannot fail to promote tranquility; and whenever a contract is formed for the purpose of procuring the *three first*, it follows, as a regular consequence, that the *other* should partake of the intention.—This great association is expressly declared to be entered into between the states "for their common defence, the security of their liberties, and their mutual and general welfare, binding themselves to assist each other against all force offered to, or attacks made upon, them, or any of them, on account of religion, sovereignty, trade, or any other pretence whatever."

The objects herein recited do certainly form the chief design of the present confederation; and the same are declared to be the great *ends* of the *proposed* plan of government. So far then do they agree. A subject of much contention, however, and with which the minds of different citizens are variously agitated, has arose.

It has been said that some of *these advantages*, and of high import too, cannot be obtained under the present system. It is the opinion of some citizens that the constitution proposed to us will secure all *these objects* and form a complete remedy for every *evil* now subsisting; whilst it is asserted by others that amendments might be introduced in the former, which would be competent to every *good* purpose, and promote *some* of very great consequence, that might be endangered by an adoption of the latter. Thus it is inferred that *this* system extends too far—and, like many human institutions, flits by a rapid progress from *one* extreme to *another*.

Those, who cannot approve of this plan, have very strong objections to it, because they apprehend that no *security for their liberties* will remain after it's adoption: and although some of the *ends* proposed might be obtained thereby; yet they think the sacrifice will be too great for the benefit to be received. To enjoy a competent degree of *liberty* they consider as the greatest of human blessings—for the loss of which no acquisitions whatsoever can compensate. They esteem this (and deservedly too) as the *soul* of all political happiness.

It seems to be agreed on all sides that in the present system of union the Congress are not invested with sufficient powers for *regulating commerce*, and procuring the *requisite contributions* for all expences, that may be incurred for the *common defence* or *general welfare*. Hence arise the *principal* defects;—and it is presumed that the *evils* resulting from *these weak* branches in the fœderal government might be adequately remedied by making due amendments merely *therein*.

It is thought by some that the powers of making and enforcing the observance of treaties are not ample enough at present. If so— cannot these be enlarged so as to answer every desirable purpose of *that branch* in the fœderal institution? Thus, while many citizens cannot think that the confederation is *fundamentally vicious*, but that all the *evils* now complained of do rather proceed from a weakness in some of its parts, they apprehend no necessity for an innovation further than strengthening *those parts*. If such measures were effectually established, they conceive that all the great ends of the *general* government might be promoted.—No contention, therefore, subsists about supporting a *union*, but only concerning the *mode*; and as well those, who disapprove of the proposed plan, as those, who approve of it, consider the existence of a *union* as essential to their happiness.

Speeches of Patrick Henry
before the
Virginia Ratifying Convention

The speeches of Patrick Henry included here were delivered in the Virginia ratifying convention and published in the Debates and Other Proceedings of the Convention of Virginia. *They illustrate the great rhetorical skill of this Virginia statesman, as well as his determination to protect the rights of Virginia and his fellow Virginians. According to Henry, the Constitution, by establishing a central government that would rest directly on the people's consent, rather than the consent of the states, and that would act directly on the people rather than only through the states, would essentially destroy the states. The product of a desire for glory, the Constitution, in Henry's view, was unfit for a free people, because the Constitution's checks and balances were only paper barriers to rulers' self-interest. Essays in* The Federalist *of particular relevance: 1, 17, 51.*

<hr>

5 JUNE 1788

<hr>

Mr. *Henry.*—Mr. Chairman—I am much obliged to the very worthy Gentleman for his encomium. I wish I was possessed of talents, or possessed of any thing, that might enable me to elucidate this great subject. I am not free from suspicion: I am apt to entertain doubts: I rose yesterday to ask a question, which arose in my own mind. When I asked that question, I thought the meaning of my interrogation was obvious: The fate of this question and America may depend on this: Have they said, we the States? Have they made a proposal of a compact between States? If they had, this would be a confederation: It is otherwise most clearly a consolidated government. The question turns, Sir, on that poor little thing—the expression, *We, the people,* instead of the States of America. I need not take much pains to shew, that the principles of this system, are extremely pernicious, impolitic, and dangerous. Is this a Monarchy, like England—a compact between Prince and people; with checks on the former, to secure the liberty of the latter? Is this a Confederacy, like Holland—an association of a number of independent States, each of which retain its individual sovereignty? It is not a democracy, wherein the people retain all their rights securely. Had these principles been adhered to, we should not have been brought to this alarming transition, from a Confederacy to a consolidated Government. We have no detail of those great considerations which, in my opinion, ought to have abounded before we should recur to a government of this kind. Here is a revolution as radical as that which separated us from Great Britain. It is as radical, if in this transition, our rights and privileges are endangered, and the sovereignty of the States be relinquished: And cannot we plainly see, that this is actually the case? The rights of conscience, trial by jury, liberty of the press, all your immunities and franchises, all pretensions to human rights and privileges, are rendered insecure, if not lost, by this change so loudly talked of by some, and inconsiderately by others. Is this tame relinquishment of rights worthy of freemen? Is it worthy of that manly fortitude that ought to characterize republicans: It is said eight States have adopted this plan. I declare that if twelve States and an half had adopted it, I would with manly firmness, and in spite of an erring world, reject it. You are not to inquire how your trade may be increased, nor how you are to become a great and powerful people, but how your liberties can be secured; for liberty ought to be the direct end of your Government. Having premised these things, I shall, with the aid of my judgment and information, which I confess are not extensive, go into the discussion of this system more minutely. Is it necessary for your liberty; that you should abandon those great rights by the adoption of this system? Is the relinquishment of the trial by jury, and the liberty of the press, necessary for your liberty? Will the abandonment of your most sacred rights tend to the security of your liberty? Liberty the greatest of all earthly blessings—give us that precious jewel, and you may take every thing else: But I am fearful I have lived long enough to become an old fashioned fellow: Perhaps an invincible attachment to the dearest rights of man, may,

in these refined enlightened days, be deemed *old fashioned:* If so, I
am contented to be so: I say, the time has been, when every pore
of my heart beat for American liberty, and which, I believe, had a
counterpart in the breast of every true American: But suspicions
have gone forth—suspicions of my integrity—publicly reported
that my professions are not real—23 years ago was I supposed a
traitor to my country: I was then said to be a bane of sedition,
because I supported the rights of my country: I may be thought
suspicious when I say our privileges and rights are in danger: But,
Sir, a number of the people of this country are weak enough to think
these things are too true: I am happy to find that the Honorable
Gentleman on the other side, declares they are groundless: But, Sir,
suspicion is a virtue, as long as its object is the preservation of the
public good, and as long as it stays within proper bounds: Should it
fall on me, I am contented: Conscious rectitude is a powerful consolation: I trust, there are many who think my professions for the
public good to be real. Let your suspicion look to both sides: There
are many on the other side, who, possibly may have been persuaded
of the necessity of these measures, which I conceive to be dangerous to your liberty. Guard with jealous attention the public liberty.
Suspect every one who approaches that jewel. Unfortunately, nothing will preserve it, but downright force: Whenever you give up
that force, you are inevitably ruined. I am answered by Gentlemen, that though I might speak of terrors, yet the fact was, that
we were surrounded by none of the dangers I apprehended. I conceive this new Government to be one of those dangers: It has produced those horrors, which distress many of our best citizens. We
are come hither to preserve the poor Commonwealth of Virginia, if
it can be possibly done: Something must be done to preserve your
liberty and mine: The Confederation; this same despised Government, merits, in my opinion, the highest encomium: It carried us
through a long and dangerous war: It rendered us victorious in that
bloody conflict with a powerful nation: It has secured us a territory greater than any European Monarch possesses: And shall a
Government which has been thus strong and vigorous, be accused
of imbecility and abandoned for want of energy? Consider what you
are about to do before you part with this Government. Take longer

time in reckoning things: Revolutions like this have happened in almost every country in Europe: Similar examples are to be found in ancient Greece and ancient Rome: Instances of the people loosing their liberty by their own carelessness and the ambition of a few. We are cautioned by the Honorable Gentleman who presides, against faction and turbulence: I acknowledge that licentiousness is dangerous, and that it ought to be provided against: I acknowledge also the new form of Government may effectually prevent it: Yet, there is another thing it will as effectually do; it will oppress and ruin the people. There are sufficient guards placed against sedition and licentiousness: For when power is given to this Government to suppress these, or, for any other purpose, the language it assumes is clear, express, and unequivocal; but when this Constitution speaks of privileges, there is an ambiguity, Sir, a fatal ambiguity;—an ambiguity which is very astonishing: In the clause under consideration, there is the strangest that I can conceive. I mean, when it says, that there shall not be more Representatives, than one for every 30,000. Now, Sir, how easy is it to evade this privilege? "The number shall not exceed one for every 30,000." This may be satisfied by one Representative from each State. Let our numbers be ever so great, this immence continent, may, by this artful expression, be reduced to have but 13 Representatives: I confess this construction is not natural; but the ambiguity of the expression lays a good ground for a quarrel. Why was it not clearly and unequivocally expressed, that they *should* be entitled to have one for every 30,000? This would have obviated all disputes; and was this difficult to be done? What is the inference? When population increases, and a State shall send Representatives in this proportion, Congress *may* remand them, because the right of having one for every 30,000 is not clearly expressed: This possibility of reduceing the number to one for each State, approximates to probability by that other expression, "but each State shall at least have one Representative." Now is it not clear that from the first expression, the number might be reduced so much, that some States should have no Representative at all, were it not for the insertion of this last expression? And as this is the only restriction upon them, we may fairly conclude that they *may* restrain the number to one from each State: Perhaps the same horrors may hang over my mind again. I shall be told I am continually afraid: But, Sir, I have strong cause of apprehension: In some parts of the plan before you, the great rights of freemen are endangered, in other parts absolutely taken away. How does your trial by jury stand? In civil cases gone—not sufficiently secured in criminal—this best privilege is gone: But we are told that we need not fear, because those in power being our Representatives, will not abuse the powers we put in their hands: I am not well versed in history, but I will submit to your recollection, whether liberty has been destroyed most often by the licentiousness of the people, or by the tyranny of rulers? I imagine, Sir, you will find the balance on the side of tyranny: Happy will you be if you miss the fate of those nations, who, omitting to resist their oppressors, or negligently suffering their liberty to be wrested from them, have groaned under intolerable despotism. Most of the human race are now in this deplorable condition: And those nations who have gone in search of grandeur, power and splendor, have also fallen a sacrifice, and been the victims of their own folly: While they acquired those visionary blessings, they lost their freedom. My great objection to this Government is, that it does not leave us the means of defending our rights; or, of waging war against tyrants: It is urged by some Gentlemen, that this new plan will bring us an acquisition of strength, an army, and the militia of the States: This is an idea extremely ridiculous: Gentlemen cannot be in earnest. This acquisition will trample on your fallen liberty: Let my beloved Americans guard against that fatal lethargy that has pervaded the universe: Have we the means of resisting disciplined armies, when our only defence, the militia is put into the hands of Congress? The Honorable Gentleman said, that great danger would ensue if the Convention rose without adopting this system: I ask, where is that danger? I see none: Other Gentlemen have told us within these walls, that the Union is gone—or, that the Union will be gone: Is not this trifling with the judgment of their fellow-citizens? Till they tell us the ground of their fears, I will consider them as imaginary: I rose to make enquiry where those dangers were; they could make no answer: I believe I never shall have that answer: Is there a disposition in the people of this country to revolt against the dominion of laws? Has there been a single tumult in Virginia? Have not the people of Virginia, when labouring under the severest pressure of accumulated distresses, manifested the most cordial acquiescence in the execution of the laws? What could be more awful than their unanimous acquiescence under general distresses? Is there any revolution in Virginia? Whither is the spirit of America gone? Whither is the genius of America fled? It was but yesterday, when our enemies marched in triumph through our country: Yet the people of this country could not be appalled by their pompous armaments: They stopped their career, and victoriously captured them: Where is the peril now compared to that? Some minds are agitated by foreign alarms: Happily for us, there is no real danger from Europe; that country is engaged in more arduous business; from that quarter there is no cause of fear: You may sleep in safety forever for them. Where is the danger? If, Sir, there was any, I would recur to the American spirit to defend us;— that spirit which has enabled us to surmount the greatest difficulties: To that illustrious spirit I address my most fervent prayer, to prevent our adopting a system destructive to liberty. Let not Gentlemen be told, that it is not safe to reject this Government. Wherefore is it not safe? We are told there are dangers; but those dangers are ideal; they cannot be demonstrated: To encourage us to adopt it, they tell us, that there is a plain easy way of getting amendments: When I come to contemplate this part, I suppose that I am mad, or, that my countrymen are so: The way to amendment, is, in my conception, shut. Let us consider this plain easy way: "The Congress, whenever two-thirds of both Houses shall deem it necessary, shall propose amendments to this Constitution, or, on the application of the Legislatures of two-thirds of the several States, shall call a Convention for proposing amendments, which, in either case, shall be valid to all intents and purposes, as part of this Constitution, when ratified by the Legislatures of three-fourths of the several States, or by Conventions in three-fourths thereof, as the one or the other mode of ratification may be proposed by the Congress. Provided, that no amendment which may be made prior to the year 1808, shall in any manner affect the first and fourth clauses in the ninth section of the first article; and that no State, without its con-

sent, shall be deprived of its equal suffrage in the Senate." Hence
it appears that three-fourths of the States must ultimately agree
to any amendments that may be necessary. Let us consider the consequences of this: However uncharitable it may appear, yet I must
tell my opinion, that the most unworthy characters may get into
power and prevent the introduction of amendments: Let us suppose
(for the case is supposeable, possible, and probable) that you happen to deal these powers to unworthy hands; will they relinquish
powers already in their possession, or, agree to amendments? Two-
thirds of the Congress, or, of the State Legislatures, are necessary
even to propose amendments: If one-third of these be unworthy
men, they may prevent the application for amendments; but what is
destructive and mischievous is, that three-fourths of the State Legislatures, or of State Conventions, must concur in the amendments
when proposed: In such numerous bodies, there must necessarily
be some designing bad men: To suppose that so large a number as
three-fourths of the States will concur, is to suppose that they will
possess genius, intelligence, and integrity, approaching to miraculous. It would indeed be miraculous that they should concur in the
same amendments, or, even in such as would bear some likeness to
one another. For four of the smallest States, that do not collectively
contain one-tenth part of the population of the United States, may
obstruct the most salutary and necessary amendments: Nay, in
these four States, six tenths of the people may reject these amendments; and suppose, that amendments shall be opposed to amendments (which is highly probable) is it possible, that three-fourths
can ever agree to the same amendments? A bare majority in these
four small States may hinder the adoption of amendments; so that
we may fairly and justly conclude, that one-twentieth part of the
American people, may prevent the removal of the most grievous
inconveniencies and oppression, by refusing to accede to amendments. A trifling minority may reject the most salutary amendments. Is this an easy mode of securing the public liberty? It is,
Sir, a most fearful situation, when the most contemptible minority
can prevent the alteration of the most oppressive Government; for
it may in many respects prove to be such: Is this the spirit of republicanism? What, Sir, is the genius of democracy? Let me read that

clause of the Bill of Rights of Virginia, which relates to this: 3d cl. "That Government is or ought to be instituted for the common benefit, protection, and security of the people, nation, or community: Of all the various modes and forms of Government, that is best which is capable of producing the greatest degree of happiness and safety, and is most effectually secured against the danger of mal-administration, and *that whenever any Government shall be found inadequate, or contrary to these purposes, a majority of the community hath, an undubitable, unalienable and indefeasible right to reform, alter, or abolish it, in such manner as shall be judged most conducive to the public weal.*" This, Sir, is the language of democracy; that a majority of the community have a right to alter their Government when found to be oppressive: But how different is the genius of your new Constitution from this? How different from the sentiments of freemen, that a contemptible minority can prevent the good of the majority? If then Gentlemen standing on this ground, are come to that point, that they are willing to bind themselves and their posterity to be oppressed, I am amazed and inexpressibly astonished. If this be the opinion of the majority, I must submit; but to me, Sir, it appears perilous and destructive: I cannot help thinking so: Perhaps it may be the result of my age; these may be feelings natural to a man of my years, when the American spirit has left him, and his mental powers, like the members of the body, are decayed. If, Sir, amendments are left to the twentieth or the tenth part of the people of America, your liberty is gone forever. We have heard that there is a great deal of bribery practised in the House of Commons in England; and that many of the members raised themselves to preferments, by selling the rights of the people: But, Sir, the tenth part of that body cannot continue oppressions on the rest of the people. English liberty is in this case, on a firmer foundation than American liberty. It will be easily contrived to procure the opposition of one tenth of the people to any alteration, however judicious. The Honorable Gentleman who presides, told us, that to prevent abuses in our Government, we will assemble in Convention, recall our delegated powers, and punish our servants for abusing the trust reposed in them. Oh, Sir, we should have fine times indeed, if to punish tyrants, it were only sufficient to

assemble the people. Your arms wherewith you could defend yourselves, are gone; and have no longer a aristocratical; no longer
democratical spirit. Did you ever read of any revolution in any
nation, brought about by the punishment of those in power, inflicted
by those who had no power at all? You read of a riot act in a country which is called one of the freest in the world, where a few neighbours cannot assemble without the risk of being shot by a hired
soldiery, the engines of despotism. We may see such an act in America. A standing army we shall have also, to execute the execrable
commands of tyranny: And how are you to punish them? Will you
order them to be punished? Who shall obey these orders? Will your
Mace-bearer be a match for a disciplined regiment? In what situation are we to be? The clause before you gives a power of direct taxation, unbounded and unlimitted: Exclusive power of Legislation in
all cases whatsoever, for ten miles square; and over all places purchased for the erection of forts, magazines, arsenals, dock-yards,
&c. What resistance could be made? The attempt would be madness. You will find all the strength of this country in the hands of
your enemies: Those garrisons will naturally be the strongest
places in the country. Your militia is given up to Congress also in
another part of this plan: They will therefore act as they think
proper: All power will be in their own possession: You cannot force
them to receive their punishment: Of what service would militia
be to you, when most probably you will not have a single musket
in the State; for as arms are to be provided by Congress, they may
or may not furnish them. Let me here call your attention to that
part which gives the Congress power, "To provide for organizing,
arming, and disciplining the militia, and for governing such part of
them as may be employed in the service of the United States,
reserving to the States respectively, the appointment of the officers, and the authority of training the militia, according to the discipline prescribed by Congress." By this, Sir, you see that their
controul over our last and best defence, is unlimitted. If they
neglect or refuse to discipline or arm our militia, they will be useless: The States can do neither, this power being exclusively given
to Congress: The power of appointing officers over men not disciplined or armed, is ridiculous: So that this pretended little remains

of power left to the States, may, at the pleasure of Congress, be rendered nugatory. Our situation will be deplorable indeed: Nor can we ever expect to get this government amended, since I have already shewn, that a very small minority may prevent it; and that small minority interested in the continuance of the oppression: Will the oppressor let go the oppressed? Was there ever an instance? Can the annals of mankind exhibit one single example, where rulers overcharged with power, willingly let go the oppressed, though solicited and requested most earnestly? The application for amendments will therefore be fruitless. Sometimes the oppressed have got loose by one of those bloody struggles that desolate a country. A willing relinquishment of power is one of those things which human nature never was, nor ever will be capable of: The Honorable Gentleman's observations respecting the people's right of being the agents in the formation of this Government, are not accurate in my humble conception. The distinction between a National Government and a Confederacy is not sufficiently discerned. Had the delegates who were sent to Philadelphia a power to propose a Consolidated Government instead of a Confederacy? Were they not deputed by States, and not by the people? The assent of the people in their collective capacity is not necessary to the formation of a Federal Government. The people have no right to enter into leagues, alliances, or confederations: They are not the proper agents for this purpose: States and sovereign powers are the only proper agents for this kind of Government: Shew me an instance where the people have exercised this business: Has it not always gone through the Legislatures? I refer you to the treaties with France, Holland, and other nations: How were they made? Were they not made by the States? Are the people therefore in their aggregate capacity, the proper persons to form a Confederacy? This, therefore, ought to depend on the consent of the Legislatures; the people having never sent delegates to make any proposition of changing the Government. Yet I must say, at the same time, that it was made on grounds the most pure, and perhaps I might have been brought to consent to it so far as to the change of Government; but there is one thing in it which I never would acquiesce in. I mean the changing it into a Consolidated Government; which is so abhorent to my mind. The Honorable Gentleman then went on to the figure we make with foreign nations; the contemptible one we make in France and Holland; which, according to the system of my notes, he attributes to the present feeble Government. An opinion has gone forth, we find, that we are a contemptible people: The time has been when we were thought otherwise: Under this same despised Government, we commanded the respect of all Europe: Wherefore are we now reckoned otherwise? The American spirit has fled from hence: It has gone to regions, where it has never been expected: It has gone to the people of France in search of a splendid Government—a strong energetic Government. Shall we imitate the example of those nations who have gone from a simple to a splendid Government. Are those nations more worthy of our imitation? What can make an adequate satisfaction to them for the loss they suffered in attaining such a Government for the loss of their liberty? If we admit this Consolidated Government it will be because we like a great splendid one. Some way or other we must be a great and mighty empire; we must have an army, and a navy, and a number of things: When the American spirit was in its youth, the language of America was different: Liberty, Sir, was then the primary object. We are descended from a people whose Government was founded on liberty: Our glorious forefathers of Great-Britain, made liberty the foundation of every thing. That country is become a great, mighty, and splendid nation; not because their Government is strong and energetic; but, Sir, because liberty is its direct end and foundation: We drew the spirit of liberty from our British ancestors; by that spirit we have triumphed over every difficulty: But now, Sir, the American spirit, assisted by the ropes and chains of consolidation, is about to convert this country to a powerful and mighty empire: If you make the citizens of this country agree to become the subjects of one great consolidated empire of America, your Government will not have sufficient energy to keep them together: Such a Government is incompatible with the genius of republicanism: There will be no checks, no real balances, in this Government: What can avail your specious imaginary balances, your rope-dancing, chain-rattling, ridiculous ideal checks and contrivances? But, Sir, we are not feared by foreigners; we do not make nations tremble: Would this, Sir, constitute happiness, or secure liberty? I trust, Sir, our political hemisphere will ever direct their operations to the security of those objects. Consider our situation, Sir: Go to the poor man, ask him what he does; he will inform you, that he enjoys the fruits of his labour, under his own fig-tree with his wife and children around him, in peace and security. Go to every other member of the society, you will find the same tranquil ease and content; you will find no alarms or disturbances: Why then tell us of dangers to terrify us into an adoption of this new Government? and yet who knows the dangers that this new system may produce; they are out of the sight of the common people: They cannot foresee latent consequences: I dread the operation of it on the middling and lower class of people: It is for them I fear the adoption of this system. I fear I tire the patience of the Committee, but I beg to be indulged with a few more observations: When I thus profess myself an advocate for the liberty of the people, I shall be told, I am a designing man, that I am to be a great man, that I am to be a demagogue; and many similar illiberal insinuations will be thrown out; but, Sir, conscious rectitude, out-weighs these things with me: I see great jeopardy in this new Government. I see none from our present one: I hope some Gentleman or other will bring forth, in full array, those dangers, if there be any, that we may see and touch them: I have said that I thought this a Consolidated Government: I will now prove it. Will the great rights of the people be secured by this Government? Suppose it should prove oppressive, how can it be altered? Our Bill of Rights declares, "That a majority of the community hath an *undubitable, unalienable,* and *indefeasible right* to reform, alter, or abolish it, in such manner as shall be judged most conducive to the public weal." I have just proved that one-tenth, or less, of the people of America, a most despicable minority may prevent this reform or alteration. Suppose the people of Virginia should wish to alter their Government, can a majority of them do it? No, because they are connected with other men; or, in other words, consolidated with other States: When the people of Virginia at a future day shall wish to alter their Government, though they should be unanimous in this desire, yet they may be prevented therefrom by a despicable minority at the extremity of the United States:

The founders of your own Constitution made your Government changeable: But the power of changing it is gone from you! Whither is it gone? It is placed in the same hands that hold the rights of twelve other States; and those who hold those rights, have right and power to keep them: It is not the particular Government of Virginia: One of the leading features of that Government is, that a majority can alter it, when necessary for the public good. This Government is not a Virginian but an American Government. Is it not therefore a Consolidated Government? The sixth clause of your Bill of Rights tells you, "That elections of members to serve as Representatives of the people in Assembly, ought to be free, and that all men having sufficient evidence of permanent common interest with, and attachment to the community, have the right of suffrage, and *cannot* be *taxed* or *deprived* of *their property* for public uses, without their own consent, or that of their Representatives so elected, nor bound by any law to which they have not in like manner assented for the public good." But what does this Constitution say? The clause under consideration gives an unlimitted and unbounded power of taxation: Suppose every delegate from Virginia opposes a law laying a tax, what will it avail? They are opposed by a majority: Eleven members can destroy their efforts: Those feeble ten cannot prevent the passing the most oppressive tax law. So that in direct opposition to the spirit and express language of your Declaration of Rights, you are taxed, not by your own consent, but by people who have no connection with you. The next clause of the Bill of Rights tells you, "That all power of suspending law, or the execution of laws, by any authority without the consent of the Representatives of the people, is injurious to their rights, and ought not to be exercised." This tells us that there can be no suspension of Government, or laws without our own consent: Yet this Constitution can counteract and suspend any of our laws, that contravene its oppressive operation; for they have the power of direct taxation; which suspends our Bill of Rights; and it is expressly provided, that they can make all laws necessary for carrying their powers into execution; and it is declared paramount to the laws and constitutions of the States. Consider how the only remaining defence we have left is destroyed in this manner: Besides the expences of maintaining the Senate and other House in as much splendor as they please, there is to be a great and mighty President, with very extensive powers; the powers of a King: He is to be supported in extravagant magnificence: So that the whole of our property may be taken by this American Government, by laying what taxes they please, giving themselves what salaries they please, and suspending our laws at their pleasure: I might be thought too inquisitive, but I believe I should take up but very little of your time in enumerating the little power that is left to the Government of Virginia; for this power is reduced to little or nothing: Their garrisons, magazines, arsenals, and forts, which will be situated in the strongest places within the States: Their ten miles square, with all the fine ornaments of human life, added to their powers, and taken from the States, will reduce the power of the latter to nothing. The voice of tradition, I trust, will inform posterity of our struggles for freedom: If our descendants be worthy the name of Americans, they will preserve and hand down to their latest posterity, the transactions of the present times; and though, I confess, my exclamations are not worthy the hearing, they will see that I have done my utmost to preserve their liberty: For I never will give up the power of direct taxation, but for a scourge: I am willing to give it conditionally; that is, after non-compliance with requisitions: I will do more, Sir, and what I hope will convince the most sceptical man, that I am a lover of the American Union, that in case Virginia shall not make punctual payment, the controul of our custom houses, and the whole regulation of trade, shall be given to Congress, and that Virginia shall depend on Congress even for passports, till Virginia shall have paid the last farthing; and furnished the last soldier: Nay, Sir, there is another alternative to which I would consent: Even that they should strike us out of the Union, and take away from us all federal privileges till we comply with federal requisitions; but let it depend upon our own pleasure to pay our money in the most easy manner for our people. Were all the States, more terrible than the mother country, to join against us, I hope Virginia could defend herself; but, Sir, the dissolution of the Union is most abhorent to my mind: The first thing I have at heart is American *liberty;* the second thing is American Union; and I hope the people of Virginia will endeavor to preserve that Union: The increasing population of the southern States, is far greater than that of New-England: Consequently, in a short time, they will be far more numerous than the people of that country: Consider this, and you will find this State more particularly interested to support American liberty, and not bind our posterity by an improvident relinquishment of our rights. I would give the best security for a punctual compliance with requisitions; but I beseech Gentlemen, at all hazards, not to give up this unlimitted power of taxation: The Honorable Gentleman has told us these powers given to Congress, are accompanied by a Judiciary which will connect all: On examination you will find this very Judiciary oppressively constructed; your jury trial destroyed, and the Judges dependent on Congress. In this scheme of energetic Government, the people will find two sets of tax-gatherers—the State and the Federal Sheriffs. This it seems to me will produce such dreadful oppression, as the people cannot possibly bear: The Federal Sheriff may commit what oppression, make what distresses he pleases, and ruin you with impunity: For how are you to tie his hands? Have you any sufficient decided means of preventing him from sucking your blood by speculations, commissions and fees? Thus thousands of your people will be most shamefully robbed: Our State Sheriffs, those unfeeling blood-suckers, have, under the watchful eye of our Legislature, committed the most horrid and barbarous ravages on our people: It has required the most constant vigilance of the Legislature to keep them from totally ruining the people: A repeated succession of laws has been made to suppress their inequitous speculations and cruel extortions; and as often have their nefarious ingenuity devised methods of evading the force of those laws: In the struggle they have generally triumphed over the Legislature. It is a fact that lands have sold for five shillings, which were worth one hundred pounds: If Sheriffs thus immediately under the eye of our State Legislature and Judiciary, have dared to commit these outrages, what would they not have done if their masters had been at Philadelphia or New-York? If they perpetrate the most unwarrantable outrage on your persons or property, you cannot get redress on this side of Philadelphia or New-York: And how can you get it there? If your domestic avocations could permit you to go thither, there you must appeal to Judges sworn to support this Constitution, in opposition to that of any State, and who may also be inclined to favor their own officers: When these harpies are aided by excise men, who may search at any time your houses and most secret recesses, will the people bear it? If you think so you differ from me: Where I thought there was a possibility of such mischiefs, I would grant power with a niggardly hand; and here there is a strong probability that these oppressions shall actually happen. I may be told, that it is safe to err on that side; because such regulations *may* be made by Congress, as shall restrain these officers, and because laws are made by our Representatives, and judged by righteous Judges: But, Sir, as these regulations may be made, so they may not; and many reasons there are to induce a belief that they will not: I shall therefore be an infidel on that point till the day of my death.

This Constitution is said to have beautiful features; but when I come to examine these features, Sir, they appear to me horridly frightful: Among other deformities, it has an awful squinting; it squints towards monarchy: And does not this raise indignation in the breast of every American? Your President may easily become King: Your Senate is so imperfectly constructed that your dearest rights may be sacrificed by what may be a small minority; and a very small minority may continue forever unchangeably this Government, although horridly defective: Where are your checks in this Government? Your strong holds will be in the hands of your enemies: It is on a supposition that our American Governors shall be honest, that all the good qualities of this Government are founded: But its defective, and imperfect construction, puts it in their power to perpetrate the worst of mischiefs, should they be bad men: And, Sir, would not all the world, from the Eastern to the Western hemisphere, blame our distracted folly in resting our rights upon the contingency of our rulers being good or bad. Shew me that age and country where the rights and liberties of the people were placed on the sole chance of their rulers being good men, without a consequent loss of liberty? I say that the loss of that dearest privilege has ever followed with absolute certainty, every such mad attempt. If your American chief, be a man of ambition, and abilities, how easy is it for him to render himself absolute: The army is in his hands, and, if he be a man of address, it will be attached to him; and it will be the subject of long meditation with him to seize the first auspicious moment to accomplish his design; and, Sir, will the American spirit solely relieve you when this happens? I would rather infinitely, and I am sure most of this Convention are of the same opinion, have a King, Lords, and Commons, than a Government so replete with such insupportable evils. If we make a King, we may prescribe the rules by which he shall rule his people, and interpose such checks as shall prevent him from infringing them: But the President, in the field, at the head of his army, can prescribe the terms on which he shall reign master, so far that it will puzzle any American ever to get his neck from under the galling yoke. I cannot with patience, think of this idea. If ever he violates the laws, one of two things will happen: He shall come at the head of his army to carry every thing before him; or, he will give bail, or do what Mr. Chief Justice will order him. If he be guilty, will not the recollection of his crimes teach him to make one bold push for the American throne? Will not the immense difference between being master of every thing, and being ignominiously tried and punished, powerfully excite him to make this bold push? But, Sir, where is the existing force to punish him? Can he not at the head of his army beat down every opposition? Away with your President, we shall have a King: The army will salute him Monarch; your militia will leave you and assist in making him King, and fight against you: And what have you to oppose this force? What will then become of you and your rights? Will not absolute despotism ensue? {Here Mr. Henry strongly and pathetically expatiated on the probability of the President's enslaving America, and the horrible consequences that must result.} What can be more defective than the clause concerning the elections?—The controul given to Congress over the time, place, and manner of holding elections, will totally destroy the end of suffrage. The elections may be held at one place, and the most inconvenient in the State; or they may be at remote distances from those who have a right of suffrage: Hence nine out of ten must either not vote at all, or vote for strangers: For the most influential characters will be applied to, to know who are the most proper to be chosen. I repeat that the controul of Congress over the *manner*, &c., of electing, well warrants this idea. The natural consequence will be, that this democratic branch, will possess none of the public confidence: The people will be prejudiced against Representatives chosen in such an injudicious manner. The proceedings in the northern conclave will be hidden from the yeomanry of this country: We are told that the yeas and nays shall be taken and entered on the journals: This, Sir, will avail nothing: It may be locked up in their chests, and concealed forever from the people; for they are not to publish what parts they think require secrecy: They *may* think, and *will* think, the whole requires it. Another beautiful feature of this Constitution is, the publication from time to time of the receipts and expenditures of the public money. This expression, from time to time, is very indefinite and indeterminate: It may extend to a century. Grant that any of them are wicked, they may squander the public money so as to ruin you, and yet this expression will give you no redress. I say, they may ruin you;—for where, Sir, is the responsibility? The yeas and nays will shew you nothing, unless they be fools as well as knaves: For after having wickedly trampled on the rights of the people, they would act like fools indeed, were they to publish and devulge their iniquity, when they have it equally in their power to suppress and conceal it.—Where is the responsibility—that leading principle in the British government? In that government a punishment, certain and inevitable, is provided: But in this, there is no real actual punishment for the grossest maladministration. They may go without punishment, though they commit the most outrageous violation on our immunities. That paper may tell me they will be punished. I ask, by what law? They must make the law—for there is no existing law to do it. What—will they make a law to punish themselves? This, Sir, is my great objection to the Constitution, that there is no true responsibility—and that the preservation of our liberty depends on the single chance of men being virtuous enough to make laws to punish themselves. In the country from which we are descended, they have real, and not imaginary, responsibility—for there, maladministration has cost their heads, to some of the most saucy geniuses that ever were. The Senate, by making treaties may destroy your liberty and laws for want of responsibility. Two-thirds of those that shall happen to be present, can, with the President, make treaties, that shall be the supreme law of the land: They may make the most ruinous treaties; and yet there is no punishment for them. Whoever shews me a punishment provided for them, will oblige me. So, Sir, notwithstanding there are eight pillars, they want another. Where will they make another? I trust, Sir, the exclusion of the evils wherewith this system is replete, in its present form, will be made a condition, precedent to its adoption, by this or any other State. The transition from a general unqualified admission to offices, to a consolidation of government, seems easy; for though the American States are dissimilar in their structure, this will assimilate them: This, Sir, is itself a strong consolidating feature, and is not one of the least dangerous in that system. Nine States are sufficient to establish this government over those nine: Imagine that nine have come into it. Virginia has certain scruples. Suppose she will consequently, refuse to join with those States:—May not they still continue in friendship and union with her? If she sends her annual requisitions in dollars, do you think their stomachs will be so squeamish that they will refuse her dollars? Will they not accept her regiments? They would intimidate you into an inconsiderate adoption, and frighten you with ideal evils, and that the Union shall be dissolved. 'Tis a bugbear, Sir:—The fact is, Sir, that the eight adopting States can hardly stand on their own legs. Public same tells us, that the adopting States have already heart-burnings and animosity, and repent their precipitate hurry: This, Sir, may occasion exceeding great mischief. When I reflect on these and many other circumstances, I must think those States will be fond to be in confederacy with us. If we pay our quota of money annually, and furnish our rateable number of men, when necessary, I can see no danger from a rejection. The history of Switzerland clearly proves, we might be in amicable alliance with those States without adopting this Constitution. Switzerland is a Confederacy, consisting of dissimilar Governments. This is an example which proves that Governments of dissimilar structure may be Confederated; that Confederate Republic has stood upwards of 400 years; and although several of the individual republics are democratic, and the rest aristocratic, no evil has resulted from this dissimilarity, for they have braved all the power of France and Germany during that long period. The Swiss spirit, Sir, has kept them together: They have encountered and overcome immense difficulties with patience and fortitude. In this vicinity of powerful and ambitious monarchs, they have retained their independence, republican simplicity and valour. {Here he makes a comparison of the people of that country, and those of France, and makes a quotation from Addison, illustrating the subject.} Look at the peasants of that country and of France, and mark the difference. You will find the condition of the former far more desirable and comfortable. No matter whether a people be great, splendid, and powerful, if they enjoy freedom. The Turkish Grand Seignior, along-side of our President, would put us to disgrace: But we should be abundantly consoled for this disgrace, when our citizen should be put in contrast with the Turkish slave. The most valuable end of government, is the liberty of the inhabitants. No possible advantages can compensate for the loss of this privilege. Shew me the reason why the American Union is to be dissolved. Who are those eight adopting States? Are they averse to give us a little time to consider, before we conclude? Would such a disposition render a junction with them eligible; or is it the genius of that kind of government, to precipitate people hastily into measures of the utmost importance, and grant no indulgence? If it be, Sir, is it for us to accede to such a government? We have a right to have time to consider—We shall therefore insist upon it. Unless the government be amended, we can never accept it. The adopting States will doubtless accept our money and our regiments—And what is to be the consequence, if we are disunited? I believe that it is yet doubtful, whether it is not proper to stand by a while, and see the effect of its adoption in other States. In forming a government, the utmost care should be taken to prevent its becoming oppressive; and this government is of such an intricate and complicated nature, that no man on this earth can know its real operation. The other States have no reason to think, from the antecedent conduct of Virginia, that she has any intention of seceding from the Union, or of being less active to support the general welfare: Would they not therefore acquiesce in our taking time to deliberate? Deliberate whether the measure be not perilous, not only for us, but the adopting States. Permit me, Sir, to say, that a great majority of the people even in the adopting States, are averse to this government. I believe I would be right to say, that they have been egregiously misled. Pennsylvania has *perhaps* been tricked into it. If the other States who have adopted it, have not been tricked, still they were too much hurried into its adoption. There were very respectable minorities in several of them; and if reports be true, a clear majority of the people are averse to it. If we also accede, and it should prove grievous, the peace and prosperity of our country, which we all love, will be destroyed. This government has not the affection of the people, at present. Should it be oppressive, their affection will be totally estranged from it—and, Sir, you know that a Government without their affections can neither be durable nor happy. I speak as one poor individual—but when I speak, I speak the language of thousands. But, Sir, I mean not to breath the spirit nor utter the language of secession. I have trespassed so long on your patience, I am really concerned that I have something yet to say. The honorable member has said that we shall be properly represented: Remember, Sir, that the number of our Representatives is but ten, whereof six is a majority. Will these men be possessed of sufficient information? A particular knowledge of particular districts will not suffice. They must be well acquainted with agriculture, commerce, and a great variety of other matters throughout the Continent: They must know not only the actual state of nations in Europe, and America, the situation of their farmers, cottagers, and mechanics, but also the relative situation and intercourse of those nations. Virginia is as large as England. Our proportion of Representatives is but ten men. In England they have 530. The House of Commons in England, numerous as they are, we are told, is bribed, and have bartered away the rights of their constituents: What then shall become of us? Will these few protect our rights? Will they be incorruptible? You say they will be better men than the English Commoners. I say they will be infinitely worse men, because they are to be chosen blindfolded: Their election (the term, as applied to their appointment, is inaccurate) will be an involuntary nomination, and not a choice. I have, I fear, fatigued the Committee, yet I have not said the one hundred thousandeth part of what I have on my mind, and wish to impart. On this occasion I conceived myself bound to attend strictly to the interest of the State; and I thought her dearest rights at stake: Having lived so long—been so much honored—my efforts, though small, are due to my country. I have found my mind hurried on from subject to subject, on this very great occasion. We have been all out of order from the Gentleman who opened to-day, to myself. I did not come prepared to speak on so multifarious a subject, in so general a manner. I trust you will indulge me another time.—Before you abandon the present system, I hope you will consider not only its defects, most maturely, but likewise those of that which you are to substitute to it. May you be fully apprised of the dangers of the latter, not by fatal experience, but by some abler advocate than me.

7 JUNE 1788

Mr. *Henry*.—I have thought, and still think, that a full investigation of the actual situation of America, ought to precede any decision on this great and important question. That Government is no more than a choice among evils, is acknowledged by the most intelligent among mankind, and has been a standing maxim for ages. If it be demonstrated that the adoption of the new plan is a little or a trifling evil, then, Sir, I acknowledge that adoption ought to follow: But, Sir, if this be a truth that its adoption may entail misery on the free people of this country, I then insist, that rejection ought to follow. Gentlemen strongly urge its adoption will be a mighty benefit to us. But, Sir, I am made of such incredulous materials that assertions and declarations, do not satisfy me. I must be convinced, Sir. I shall retain my infidelity on that subject, till I see our liberties secured in a manner perfectly satisfactory to my understanding.

There are certain maxims by which every wise and enlightened people will regulate their conduct. There are certain political maxims, which no free people ought ever to abandon. Maxims of which the observance is essential to the security of happiness. It is impiously irritating the avenging hand of Heaven, when a people who are in the full enjoyment of freedom, launch out into the wide ocean of human affairs, and desert those maxims which alone can preserve liberty. Such maxims, humble as they are, are those only which can render a nation safe or formidable. Poor little humble republican maxims have attracted the admiration and engaged the attention of the virtuous and wise in all nations, and have stood the shock of ages. We do not now admit the validity of maxims, which we once delighted in. We have since adopted maxims of a different but more *refined nature:* New maxims which tend to the prostration of republicanism.

We have one, Sir, *That all men are by nature free and independent, and have certain inherent rights, of which, when they enter into society, they cannot by any compact deprive or divest their posterity.* We have a set of maxims of the same spirit, which must be beloved by every friend to liberty, to virtue, to mankind. Our Bill of Rights contains those admirable maxims.

Now, Sir, I say, let us consider, whether the picture given of American affairs ought to drive us from those beloved maxims.

The Honorable Gentleman (Governor *Randolph)* has said, that it is too late in the day for us to reject this new plan: That system which was once execrated by the Honorable member, must now be adopted, let its defects be ever so glaring. That Honorable member will not accuse me of want of candour, when I cast in my mind what he has given the public,* and compare it to what has happened since. It seems to me very strange and unaccountable, that that which was the object of his execration, should now receive his encomiums. Something extraordinary must have operated so great a change in his opinion. *It is too late in the day?* Gentlemen must excuse me, if they should declare again and again, that it was too late, and I should think differently. I never can believe, Sir, that it is too late to save all that is precious. If it be proper, and independently of every external consideration, wisely constructed, let us receive it: But, Sir, shall its adoption by eight States induce us to

Alluding to his Excellency's letter on that subject to the Speaker of the House of Delegates.

receive it, if it be replete with the most dangerous defects? They urge that subsequent amendments are safer than previous amendments, and that they will answer the same ends. At present we have our liberties and privileges in our own hands. Let us not relinquish them. Let us not adopt this system till we see them secured. There is some small possibility, that should we follow the conduct of Massachusetts, amendments might be obtained. There is a small possibility of amending any Government; but, Sir, shall we abandon our most inestimable rights, and rest their security on a mere possibility? The Gentleman fears the loss of the Union. If eight States have ratified it unamended, and we should rashly imitate their precipitate example, do we not thereby disunite with several other States? Shall those who have risked their lives for the sake of union, be at once thrown out of it? If it be amended, every State will accede to it; but by an imprudent adoption in its defective and dangerous state, a schism must inevitably be the consequence: I can never, therefore, consent to hazard our most unalienable rights on an absolute uncertainty. You are told there is no peace, although you fondly flatter yourselves that all is peace—No peace—a general cry and alarm in the country—Commerce, riches, and wealth vanished—Citizens going to seek comforts in other parts of the world—Laws insulted—Many instances of tyrannical legislation. These things, Sir, are new to me. He has made the discovery—As to the administration of justice, I believe that failures in commerce, &c. cannot be attributed to it. My age enables me to recollect its progress under the old Government. I can justify it by saying, that it continues in the same manner in this State, as it did under former Government. As to other parts of the Continent, I refer that to other Gentlemen. As to the ability of those who administer it, I believe they would not suffer by a comparison with those who administered it under the royal authority. Where is the cause of complaint if the wealthy go away? Is this added to the other circumstances, of such enormity, and does it bring such danger over this Commonwealth as to warrant so important, and so awful a change in so precipitate a manner? As to insults offered to the laws, I know of none. In this respect I believe this Commonwealth would not suffer by a comparison with the former Government. The laws are as well executed, and as patiently acquiesced in, as they were under the royal administration. Compare the situation of the country—Compare that of our citizens to what they were then, and divide whether persons and property are not as safe and secure as they were at that time. Is there a man in this Commonwealth, whose person can be insulted with impunity? Cannot redress be had here for personal insults or injuries, as well as in any part of the world—as well as in those countries where Aristocrats and Monarchs triumph and reign? Is not the protection of property in full operation here? The contrary cannot with truth be charged on this Commonwealth. Those severe charges which are exhibited against it, appear to me totally groundless. On a fair investigation, we shall be found to be surrounded by no real dangers. We have the animating fortitude and persevering alacrity of republican men, to carry us through misfortunes and calamities. 'Tis the fortune of a republic to be able to withstand the stormy ocean of human vicissitudes. I know of no danger awaiting us. Public and private security are to be found here in the highest degree. Sir, it is the fortune of a free people, not to be intimidated by imaginary dangers. Fear is the passion of slaves. Our political and natural hemisphere are now equally tranquil. Let us recollect the awful magnitude of the subject of our deliberation. Let us consider the latent consequences of an erroneous decision—and let not our minds be led away by unfair misrepresentations and uncandid suggestions. There have been many instances of uncommon lenity and temperance used in the exercise of power in this Commonwealth. I could call your recollection to many that happened during the war and since—But every Gentleman here must be apprized of them.

The Honorable member has given you an elaborate account of what he judges tyrannical legislation, and an *ex post facto law* (in the case of Josiah Philips.) He has misrepresented the facts. That man was not executed by a tyrannical stroke of power. He was a fugitive murderer and an out-law—a man who commanded an infamous banditti, at a time when the war was at the most perilous stage. He committed the most cruel and shocking barbarities. He was an enemy to the human name.—Those who declare war against the human race, may be struck out of existence as soon as they are apprehended. He was not executed according to those beautiful legal ceremonies which are pointed out by the laws, in criminal cases. The enormity of his crimes did not entitle him to it. I am truly a friend to legal forms and methods; but, Sir, the occasion warranted the measure. A pirate, an out-law, or a common enemy to all mankind, may be put to death at any time. It is justified by the laws of nature and nations. The Honorable member tells us then, that there are burnings and discontents in the hearts of our citizens in general, and that they are dissatisfied with their Government. I have no doubt the Honorable member believes this to be the case, because he says so. But I have the comfortable assurance, that it is a certain fact, *that it is not so.* The middle and lower ranks of people have not those illumined ideas, which the well-born are so happily possessed of—They cannot so readily perceive latent objects. The microscopic eyes of modern States-men can see abundance of defects in old systems; and their illumined imaginations discover the necessity of a change. They are captivated by the parade of the number ten—The charms of the ten miles square.—Sir, I fear this change will ultimately lead to our ruin. My fears are not the force of imagination—They are but too well founded. I tremble for my country: But, Sir, I trust, I rely, and I am confident, that this political speculation has not taken so strong a hold of men's minds, as some would make us believe.

The dangers which may arise from our geographical situation, will be more properly considered awhile hence. At present, what may be surmised on the subject, with respect to the adjacent States, is merely visionary. Strength, Sir, is a relative term. When I reflect on the natural force of those nations that might be induced to attack us, and consider the difficulty of the attempt and uncertainty of the success, and compare thereto the relative strength of our country, I say that we are strong. We have no cause to fear from that quarter—We have nothing to dread from our neighboring States. The superiority of our cause would give us an advantage over them, were they so unfriendly or rash as to attack us. As to that part of the community, which the Honorable Gentlemen spoke of as being in danger of being separated from us: What incitement or inducement could its inhabitants have to wish such an event? It

is a matter of doubt whether they would derive any advantage to
themselves, or be any loss to us by such a separation. Time has
been, and may yet come, when they will find it their advantage and
true interest to be united with us. There is no danger of a dismemberment of our country, unless a Constitution be adopted which will
enable the Government to plant enemies on our backs. By the Confederation, the rights of territory are secured. No treaty can be
made without the consent of nine States. While the consent of nine
States is necessary to the cession of territory you are safe. If it be
put in the power of a less number, you will most infallibly lose the
Mississippi. As long as we can preserve our unalienable rights, we
are in safety. This new Constitution will invole in its operation the
loss of the navigation of that valuable river. The Honorable Gentleman cannot be ignorant of the *Spanish transactions.*—A treaty
had been nearly entered into with Spain, to relinquish that navigation. That relinquishment would absolutely have taken place, had
the consent of seven States been sufficient. The Honorable Gentleman told us then, that eight States having adopted this system, we
cannot suppose they will recede on our account. I know not what
they may do; but this I know, that a people of infinitely less importance, than those of Virginia, stood the terror of war.—Vermont,
Sir, withstood the terror of thirteen States. Maryland did not
accede to the Confederation till the year, 1781. These two States,
feeble as they are comparatively to us, were not afraid of the whole
Union. Did either of these States perish? No, Sir, they were admitted freely into the Union. Will not Virginia then be admitted? I
flatter myself that those States who have ratified the new plan of
Government will open their arms and chearfully receive us,
although we should propose certain amendments as the conditions
on which we should ratify it. During the late war, all the States
were in pursuit of the same object. To obtain that object they made
the most strenuous exertions. They did not suffer trivial considerations to impede its acquisition. Give me leave to say, that if the
smallest States in the Union were admitted into it, after having
unseasonably procrastinated their accession; the greatest and most
mighty State in the Union, will be easily admitted, when her reluctance to an immediate accession to this system, is founded on the

most reasonable grounds. When I call this the most mighty State in the Union, do I not speak the truth? Does not Virginia surpass every State in the Union, in number of inhabitants, extent of territory, felicity of position, and affluence and wealth? Some infatuation hangs over men's minds, that they will inconsiderately precipitate into measures the most important, and give not a moment's deliberation to others, nor pay any respect to their opinions. Is this federalism? Are these the beloved effects of the federal spirit, that its votaries will never accede to the just propositions of others? Sir, were there nothing objectionable in it but that, I would vote against it. I desire to have nothing to do with such men as will obstinately refuse to change their opinion. Are our opinions not to be regarded? I hope that you will recollect, that you are going to join with men who will pay no respect even to this State.

Switzerland consists of thirteen cantons expressly confederated for national defence. They have stood the shock of 400 years: That country has enjoyed internal tranquillity most of that long period. Their dissentions have been comparatively, to those of other countries, very few. What has passed in the neighbouring countries? Wars, dissentions, and intrigues. Germany involved in the most deplorable civil war, thirty years successively—Continually convulsed with intestine divisions, and harrassed by foreign wars. France with her mighty monarchy perpetually at war. Compare the peasants of Switzerland with those of any other mighty nation: You will find them far more happy—for one civil war among them, there have been five or six among other nations—Their attachment to their country, and to freedom—their resolute intrepidity in their defence; the consequent security and happiness which they have enjoyed, and the respect and awe which these things produced in their bordering nations, have signalized these republicans. Their valor, Sir, has been active; every thing that sets in motion the springs of the human heart, engaged them to the protection of their inestimable privileges. They have not only secured their own liberty, but have been the arbiters of the fate of other people. Here, Sir, contemplate the triumph of republican Governments over the pride of monarchy. I acknowledge; Sir, that the necessity of national defence has prevailed in invigorating their councils and arms, and has been in a considerable degree the means of keeping these honest people together. But, Sir, they have had wisdom enough to keep together and render themselves formidable. Their heroism is proverbial. They would heroically fight for their Government, and their laws. One of the illumined sons of these times would not fight for those objects. Those virtuous and simple people have not a mighty and splendid President—nor enormously expensive navies and armies to support. No, Sir, those brave republicans have acquired their reputation no less by their undaunted intrepidity, than by the wisdom of their frugal and œconomical policy. Let us follow their example, and be equally happy. The Honorable member advises us to adopt a measure which will destroy our Bill of Rights. For, after hearing his picture of nations, and his reasons for abandoning all the powers retained to the States by the confederation, I am more firmly persuaded of the impropriety of adopting this new plan in its present shape.

I had doubts of the power of those who went to the Convention; but now we are possessed of it, let us examine it—When we trusted the great object of revising the Confederation to the greatest, the best, and most enlightened of our citizens, we thought their deliberations would have been solely confined to that revision. Instead of this, a new system, totally different in its nature and vesting the most extensive powers in Congress, is presented. Will the ten men you are to send to Congress, be more worthy than those seven were? If power grew so rapidly in their hands, what may it not do in the hands of others? If those who go from this State will find power accompanied with temptation, our situation must be truly critical. When about forming a Government, if we mistake the principles, or commit any other error, the very circumstance promises that power will be abused. The greatest caution and circumspection are therefore necessary—Nor does this proposed-system in its investigation here, deserve the least charity.

The Honorable member says, that the National Government is without energy. I perfectly agree with him;—and when he cried out, *Union*, I agreed with him: But I tell him not to mistake the end for the means. The end is Union. The most capital means, I suppose, are an army, and navy: On supposition I will acknowledge this;

still the bare act of agreeing to that paper, though it may have an amazing influence, will not pay our millions. There must be things to pay debts. What these things are, or how they are to be produced, must be determined by our political wisdom and œconomy.

The Honorable Gentleman alledges, that previous amendments will prevent the junction of our riches from producing great profits and emoluments which would enable us to pay our public debts, by excluding us from the Union. I believe, Sir, that a previous ratification of a system notoriously and confessedly defective, will endanger our riches—our liberty—our all.—Its defects are acknowledged—They cannot be denied. The reason offered by the Honorable Gentleman for adopting this defective system, is the adoption by eight States. I say, Sir, that if we present nothing but what is reasonable in the shape of amendments they will receive us. Union is as necessary for them as for us. Will they then be so unreasonable as not to join us? If such be their disposition, I am happy to know it in time.

The Honorable member then observed, that nations will expend millions for commercial advantages—That is, that they will deprive you of every advantage if they can. Apply this another way.—Their cheaper way—instead of laying out millions in making war upon you, will be to corrupt your Senators. I know that if they be not above all price, they may make a sacrifice of our commercial interests. They may advise your President to make a treaty that will not only sacrifice all your commercial interests, but throw prostrate your Bill of Rights. Does he fear their ships will out number ours on the ocean, or that nations whose interest comes in contrast with ours, in the progress of their guilt, will perpetrate the vilest expedients to exclude us from a participation in commercial advantages? Does he advise us, in order to avoid this evil, to adopt a Constitution, which will enable such nations to obtain their ends by the more easy mode of contaminating the principles of our Senators? Sir, if our Senators will not be corrupted it will be because they will be good men; and not because the Constitution provides against corruption, for there is no real check secured in it, and the most abandoned and profligate acts may with impunity be committed by them.

With respect to Maryland—What danger from thence? I know none. I have not heard of any hostility premeditated or committed. Nine-tenths of the people have not heard of it. Those who are so happy as to be illuminated, have not informed their fellow-citizens of it. I am so valiant as to say, that no danger can come from that source, sufficient to make me abandon my republican principles.— The Honorable Gentleman ought to have recollected, that there were no tyrants in America, as there are in Europe.—The citizens of republican borders are only terrible to tyrants—Instead of being dangerous to one another, they mutually support one another's liberties. We might be confederated with the adopting States, without ratifying this system. No form of Government renders a people more formidable.—A confederacy of States joined together becomes strong as the United Netherlands.—The Government of Holland (execrated as it is) proves that the present Confederation is adequate to every purpose of human association. There are seven Provinces confederated together for a long time, containing numerous opulent cities and many of the finest ports in the world.—The recollection of the situation of that country, would make me execrate monarchy. The singular felicity and success of that people are unparalleled—Freedom has done miracles there in reclaiming land from the ocean. It is the richest spot on the face of the globe. Have they no men or money? Have they no fleets or armies? Have they no arts or sciences among them? How did they repel the attacks of the greatest nations in the world? How have they acquired their amazing affluence and power? Did they consolidate Government, to effect these purposes as we do? No, Sir, they have triumphed over every obstacle and difficulty; and have arrived at the summit of political felicity, and of uncommon opulence, by means of a confederacy; that every Government which Gentlemen affect to despise. They have, Sir, avoided a consolidation as the greatest of evils. They have lately, it is true, made one advance to that fatal progression. This misfortune burst on them by inequity and artifice. *That Stadtholder, that Executive Magistrate,* contrived it in conjunction with other European nations. It was not the choice of the people. Was it owing to *his energy* that this happened? If two provinces have paid nothing, what have not the rest done? And have not these two provinces made other exertions? Ought they, to avoid this inconvenience, to have consolidated their different States, and have a ten miles square? Compare that little spot, nurtured by liberty, with the fairest country in the world. Does not Holland possess a powerful navy and army, and a full treasury? They did not acquire these by debasing the principles and trampling on the rights of their citizens. Sir, they acquired these by their industry, œconomy, and by the freedom of their Government. Their commerce is the most extensive in Europe: Their credit is unequalled: Their felicity will be an eternal monument of the blessings of liberty: Every nation in Europe is taught by them what they are, and what they ought to be. The contrast between those nations and this happy people, is the most splendid spectacle for republicans. The greatest cause of exultation and triumph to the sons of freedom. While other nations, precipitated by the rage of ambition or folly, have, in the pursuit of the most magnificent projects, rivetted the setters of bondage on themselves and descendants, these republicans secured their political happiness and freedom. Where is there a nation to be compared to them? Where is there now, or where was there ever a nation, of so small a territory, and so few in number, so powerful—so wealthy—so happy? What is the cause of this superiority? Liberty, Sir, the freedom of their Government. Though they are now unhappily in some degree consolidated, yet they have my acclamations, when put in contrast with those millions of their fellow-men who lived and died slaves. The dangers of a consolidation ought to be guarded against in this country. I shall exert my poor talents to ward them off. Dangers are to be apprehended in whatever manner we proceed; but those of a consolidation are the most destructive. Let us leave no expedient untried to secure happiness; but whatever be our decision, I am consoled, if American liberty will remain entire only for half a century—and I trust that mankind in general, and our posterity in particular, will be compensated for every anxiety we now feel.

Another Gentleman tells us, that no inconvenience will result from the exercise of the power of taxation by the General Government; that two shillings out of ten may be saved by the impost; and that four shillings may be paid to the federal collector, and four to the State collector. A change of Government will not pay money. If from the probable amount of the impost, you take the enormous and extravagant expences, which will certainly attend the support of this great Consolidated Government, I believe you will find no reduction of the public burthens by this new system. The splendid maintenance of the President and of the members of both Houses; and the salaries and fees of the swarm of officers and dependants on the Government will cost this Continent immense sums. Double sets of collectors will double the expence. To these are to be added oppressive excise-men and custom-house officers. Sir, the people have an hereditary hatred to custom-house officers. The experience of the mother country leads me to detest them. They have introduced their baneful influence into the administration and destroyed one of the most beautiful systems that ever the world saw. Our forefathers enjoyed liberty there while that system was in its purity—but it is now contaminated by influence of every kind.

The stile of the Government (we the people) was introduced perhaps to recommend it to the people at large, to those citizens who are to be levelled and degraded to the lowest degree; who are likened to a *herd**; and who by the operation of this *blessed* system are to be transformed from respectable independent citizens, to abject, dependent subjects or slaves. The Honorable Gentleman has anticipated what we are to be reduced to, by degradingly assimilating our citizens to a herd.—{Here Governor *Randolph* arose, and declared that he did not use that word to excite any odium, but merely to convey an idea of a multitude.}—Mr. *Henry* replied, that it made a deep impression on his mind, and that he verily believed, that system would operate as he had said,—He then continued. I will exchange that *abominable* word for requisitions—requisitions which Gentlemen affect to despise, have nothing degrading in them. On this depends our political prosperity. I never will give up that *darling* word requisitions—My country may give it up—A majority may wrest it from me, but I will never give it up till my grave. Requisitions are attended with one singular advantage. They are attended by deliberation.—They secure to the States the benefit

*Governor Randolph had cursorily mentioned the word herd in his second speech.

of correcting oppressive errors. If our Assembly thought requisitions erroneous—If they thought the demand was too great, they might at least supplicate Congress to reconsider,—that it was a little too much. The power of direct taxation was called by the Honorable Gentlemen the soul of the Government: Another Gentleman, called it the lungs of the Government. We all agree, that it is the most important part of the body politic. If the power of raising money be necessary for the General Government, it is no less so for the States. If money be the vitals of Congress, is it not precious for those individuals from whom it is to be taken? Must I give my soul—my lungs, to Congress? Congress must have our souls. The State must have our souls. This is dishonorable and disgraceful. These two co-ordinate, interferring unlimited powers of harrassing the community, is unexampled: It is unprecedented in history: They are the visionary projects of modern politicians: Tell me not of imaginary means, but of reality: This political solecism will never tend to the benefit of the community. It will be as oppressive in practice as it is absurd in theory. If you part with this which the Honorable Gentleman tells you is the soul of Congress, you will be inevitably ruined. I tell you, they shall not have the soul of Virginia. They tell us, that one collector may collect the Federal and State taxes. The General Government being paramount to the State Legislatures; if the Sheriff is to collect for both; his right hand for the Congress, his left for the State; his right hand being paramount over the left, his collections will go to Congress. We will have the rest. Defficiencies in collections will always operate against the States. Congress being the paramount supreme power, must not be disappointed. Thus Congress will have an unlimited, unbounded command over the soul of this Commonwealth. After satisfying their uncontrouled demands, what can be left for the States? Not a sufficiency even to defray the expence of their internal administration. They must therefore glide imperceptibly and gradually out of existence. This, Sir, must naturally terminate in a consolidation. If this will do for other people, it never will do for me.

If we are to have one Representative for every 30,000 souls it must be by implication. The Constitution does not positively secure it. Even say it is a natural implication, why not give us a right to that proportion in express terms, in language that could not admit of evasions or subterfuges? If they can use implication *for* us, they can also use implication *against* us. We are *giving* power, they are *getting* power, judge then, on which side the implication will be used. When we once put it in their option to assume constructive power, danger will follow. Trial by jury and liberty of the press, are also on this foundation of implication. If they encroach on these rights, and you give your implication for a plea, you are cast; for they will be justified by the last part of it, which gives them full power, "To make all laws which shall be necessary and proper to "carry their powers into execution." Implication is dangerous, because it is unbounded: If it be admitted at all, and no limits be prescribed, it admits of the utmost extension. They say that every thing that is not given is retained. The reverse of the proposition is true by implication. They do not carry their implication so far when they speak of the general welfare. No implication when the sweeping clause comes. Implication is only necessary when the existence of privileges is in dispute. The existence of powers is sufficient. If we trust our dearest rights to implication, we shall be in a very unhappy situation.

Implication in England has been a source of dissention. There has been a war of implication between the King and people. For 100 years did the mother country struggle under the uncertainty of implication. The people insisted their rights were implied: The Monarch denied the doctrine. Their Bill of Rights in some degree terminated the dispute. By a bold implication, they said they had a [right] to bind us in all cases whatsoever. This constructive power we opposed, and successfully. Thirteen or fourteen years ago, the most important thing that could be thought of, was to exclude the possibility of construction and implication. These, Sir, were then deemed perilous. The first thing that was thought of, was a Bill of Rights. We were not satisfied with your constructive argumentative rights.

Mr. *Henry* then declared, a Bill of Rights indispensably necessary; that a general positive provision should be inserted in the new system, securing to the States and the people, every right which was not conceded to the General Government; and that every implication should be done away. It being now late, he concluded by observing, that he would resume the subject another time.

9 JUNE 1788

Mr. *Henry.*—Mr. Chairman,—I find myself again constrained to trespass on the patience of this Committee. I wish there was a prospect of union in our sentiments—so much time would not then be taken up. But when I review the magnitude of the subject under consideration, and of the dangers which appear to me in this new plan of Government, and compare thereto, my poor abilities to secure our rights, it will take much more time, in my poor unconnected way, to traverse the objectionable parts of it.—There are friends here, who will be abler than myself to make good those objections which to us appear well founded. If we recollect, on last Saturday, I made some observations on some of those dangers, which these Gentlemen would fain persuade us hang over the citizens of this Commonwealth, to induce us to change the Government, and adopt the new plan. Unless there be great and awful dangers, the change is dangerous, and the experiment ought not to be made. In estimating the magnitude of these dangers, we are obliged to take a most serious view of them, [   ] them, and to be familiar with them. It is not sufficient to feign mere imaginary dangers: There must be a dreadful reality. The great question between us, is, does that reality exist? These dangers are partially attributed to bad laws, execrated by the community at large. It is said, the people wish to change the Government. I should be happy to meet on that ground. Should the people wish to change it, we should be innocent of the dangers. It is a fact, that the people do not wish to change their Government. How am I to prove it? It will rest on my bare assertion, unless supported by an internal conviction in mens' breasts. My poor say-so is a mere non-entity. But, Sir, I am persuaded that four-fifths of the people of Virginia must have amendments to the new plan, to reconcile them to a change of their

Government. It is a slippery foundation for the people to rest their political salvation on my or their assertions. No Government can flourish unless it be founded on the affection of the people. Unless Gentlemen can be sure, that this new system is founded on that ground, they ought to stop their career.

I will not repeat what the Gentlemen say—I will mention one thing. There is a dispute between us and the Spaniards about the right of navigating the Mississippi. This dispute has sprung from the Federal Government. I wish a great deal to be said on this subject. I wish to know the origin and progress of the business, as it would probably unfold great dangers. In my opinion the preservation of that river calls our most serious consideration. It has been agitated in Congress. Seven States have voted so as that it is known to the Spaniards, that under our existing system, the Mississippi shall be taken from them. Seven States wished to relinquish this river to them. The six southern States opposed it. Seven States not being sufficient to convey it away; it remains now ours. If I am wrong, there is a number on this floor, who can contradict the facts—I will readily retract. This new Government, I conceive, will enable those States who have already discovered their inclination that way, to give away this river. Will the Honorable Gentleman advise us to relinquish this inestimable navigation, and place formidable enemies on our backs? This weak, this poor Confederation cannot secure us. We are resolved to take shelter under the shield of Federal authority in America. The southern parts of America have been protected by that weakness so much execrated. I hope this will be explained. I was not in Congress when these transactions took place. I may not have charged every fact. I may have misrepresented matters. I hope to be fully acquainted with every thing relative to the subject. Let us hear how the great and important right of navigating that river has been attended to; and whether I am mistaken in my opinion, that federal measures will lose it to us forever. If a bare majority of Congress can make laws, the situation of our western citizens is dreadful.

We are threatened from danger for the non-payment of the debt due to France. We have information come from an illustrious citizen of Virginia, who is now in Paris, which disproves the suggestions of such danger. This citizen has not been in the airy regions of theoretic speculation. Our Ambassador is this worthy citizen. The Ambassador of the United States of America, is not so despised as the Honorable Gentleman would make us believe, A servant of a Republic is as much respected as that of a Monarch. The Honorable Gentleman tells us, that hostile fleets are to be sent to make reprisals upon us—Our Ambassador tells you, that the King of France has taken into consideration, to enter into commercial regulations on reciprocal terms with us, which will be of peculiar advantage to us. Does this look like hostility? I might go further—I might say, not from public authority, but good information, that his opinion is, that you reject this Government.—His character and abilities are in the highest estimation—He is well acquainted in every respect, with this country—Equally so with the policy of the European nations. This illustrious citizen advises you to reject this Government, till it be amended. His sentiments coincide entirely with ours. His attachment to, and services done for this country, are well known. At a great distance from us, he remembers and studies our happiness. Living in splendour and dissipation, he thinks yet of Bills of Rights—Thinks of those little despised things called maxims—Let us follow the sage advice of this common friend of our happiness. It is little usual for nations to send armies to collect debts. The House of Bourbon, that great friend of America, will never attack her for the unwilling delay of payment. Give me leave to say, that Europe is too much engaged about objects of greater importance to attend to us. On that great theatre of the world, the little American matters vanish. Do you believe, that the mighty Monarch of France, beholding the greatest scenes that ever engaged the attention of a Prince of that country, will divert himself from those important objects, and now call for a settlement of accounts with America? This proceeding is not warranted by good sense. The friendly disposition to us, and the actual situation of France, render the idea of danger from that quarter absurd.—Would this countryman of ours be fond of advising us to a measure which he knew to be dangerous? And can it be reasonably supposed, that he can be ignorant of any premeditated hostility against this country? The Honorable Gentleman may suspect the account, but I will do our friend the justice to say, that he would warn us of any danger from France.

Do you suppose the Spanish Monarch will risk a contest with the United States, when his feeble Colonies are exposed to them? Every advance the people here make to the westward, makes him tremble for Mexico and Peru.—Despised as we are among ourselves, under our present Government, we are terrible to that Monarchy. If this be not a fact, it is generally said so.

We are in the next place frightened by dangers from Holland. We must change our Government to escape the wrath of that Republic.—Holland groans under a Government like this new one. A Stadtholder, Sir, a Dutch President has brought on that country, miseries which will not permit them to collect debts with fleets or armies. The wife of a Dutch Stadtholder brought 100,000 men against that Republic, and prostrated all opposition. This President will bring miseries on us like those of Holland. Such is the condition of European affairs, that it would be *unsafe for them to send* fleets or armies to collect debts. But here, Sir, they make a transition to objects of another kind—We are presented with dangers of a very uncommon nature. I am not acquainted with the arts of painting. Some Gentleman have a peculiar talent for them. They are practised with great ingenuity on this occasion. As a counterpart to what we have already been intimidated with, we are told, that some lands have been sold, which cannot be found; and that this will bring war on this country. Here the picture will not stand examination. Can it be supposed, that if a few land speculators and jobbers have violated the principles of probity, that it will involve this country in war? Is there no redress to be otherwise obtained, even admitting the delinquents and sufferers to be numerous? When Gentlemen are thus driven to produce imaginary dangers, to induce this Convention to assent to this change, I am sure it will not be uncandid to say, that the change itself is really dangerous.—Then the Maryland compact is broken, and will produce perilous consequences. I see nothing very terrible in this. The adoption of the new system will not remove the evil. Will they forfeit good neighbourhood with us, because the compact is broken?—Then the disputes concerning the Carolina line are to involve us in dangers. A strip of land running from the westward of the Allegany to the Mississippi, is the subject of this pretended dispute. I do not know the length or breadth of this disputed spot. Have they not regularly confirmed our right to it, and relinquished all claims to it? I can venture to pledge, that the people of Carolina will never disturb us. The strength of this despised country has settled an immense tract of country to the westward.—Give me leave to remark, that the Honorable Gentleman's observations on our frontiers, North and South, East and West, are all inaccurate.

Will Maryland fight against this country for seeking amendments? Were there not 60 members in that State who went in quest of amendments? Sixty against 8 or 10 were in favor of pursuing amendments. Shall they fight us for doing what they themselves have done? They have sought amendments, but differently from the manner in which I wish amendments to be got. The Honorable Gentleman may plume himself on this difference. Will they fight us for this dissimilarity? Will they fight us for seeking the object they seek themselves? When they do, it will be time for me to hold my peace.—Then, Sir, comes Pennsylvania, in terrible array. Pennsylvania is to go in conflict with Virginia. Pennsylvania has been a good neighbour heretofore. She is federal—Something terrible—Virginia cannot look her in the face. If we sufficiently attend to the actual situation of things, we will conclude, that Pennsylvania will do what we do. A number of that country are strongly opposed to it. Many of them have lately been convinced of its fatal tendency. They are disgorged of their federalism. I beseech you to bring this matter home to yourselves. Was there a possibility for the people of that State to know the reasons of adopting that system, or understand its principles, in so very short a period after its formation? This is the middle of June. Those transactions happened last August. The matter was circulated by every effort of industry, and the most precipitate measures taken to hurry the people into adoption.—Yet now, after having had several months since to investigate it, a very large part of this community, a great majority of this community, do not understand it. I have heard Gentlemen of respectable abilities declare, they did not understand it. If after great pains, men of high learning, who have received the aids of a regular education, do not understand it; if the people of Pennsylvania understood it in so short a time, it must have been from intuitive understandings, and uncommon accuteness of perception. Place yourselves in their situation—Would you fight your neighbours for considering this great and awful matter? If you wish for real amendments, such as the security of the trial by jury, it will reach the hearts of the people of that State. Whatever may be the disposition of the aristocratical politicians of that country, I know there are friends of human nature in that State. If so, they will never make war on those who make professions of what they are attached to themselves.

As to the danger arising from borderers, it is mutual and reciprocal. If it be dangerous for Virginia, it is equally so for them. It will be their true interest to be united with this. The danger of our being their enemies, will be a prevailing argument in our favor. It will be as powerful to admit us into the Union, as a vote of adoption without previous amendments could possibly be.—Then the savage Indians are to destroy us. We cannot look them in the face. The danger is here divided; they are as terrible to the other States as to us: But, Sir, it is well known that we have nothing to fear from them. Our back settlers are considerably stronger than them. Their superiority increases daily. Suppose the States be confederated all round us, what we want in number, we shall make up otherwise. Our compact situation and natural strength will secure us. But to avoid all dangers, we must take shelter under the Federal Government. Nothing gives a decided importance but this Federal Government. You will *sip sorrow*, according to the vulgar phrase, if you want any other security than the laws of Virginia.

A number of characters of the greatest eminence in this country, object to this Government, for its consolidating tendency. This is not imaginary. It is a formidable reality. If consolidation proves to be as mischievous to this country, as it has been to other countries, what will the poor inhabitants of this country do? This Government will operate like an ambuscade. It will destroy the State Governments, and swallow the liberties of the people, without giving them previous notice. If Gentlemen are willing to run the hazard, let them run it; but I shall exculpate myself by my opposition, and monitory warnings within these walls. But, then comes paper money. We are at peace on this subject. Though this is a thing which that mighty Federal Convention had no business with, yet I acknowledge that paper money would be the bane of this country. I detest it. Nothing can justify a people in resorting to it, but extreme necessity. It is at rest however in this Commonwealth. It is no longer solicited or advocated. Sir, I ask you, and every other Gentleman who hears me, if he can retain his indignation, at a system, which takes from the State Legislatures the care and preservation of the interests of the people; 180 Representatives, the choice of the people of Virginia cannot be trusted with their interests. They are a mobbish suspected *herd*. This country has not virtue enough to manage its own internal interests. These must be referred to the chosen ten. If we cannot be trusted with the private contracts of the citizens, we must be depraved indeed. If he can prove, that by one uniform system of abandoned principles, the Legislature has betrayed the rights of the people, then let us seek another shelter. So degrading an indignity—so flagrant an outrage to the States—so vile a suspicion is humiliating to my mind, and many others.

Will the adoption of this new plan pay our debts? This, Sir, is a plain question. It is inferred, that our grievances are to be redressed, and the evils of the existing system to be removed by the new Constitution. Let me inform the Honorable Gentleman, that no nation ever paid its debts by a change of Government, without the aid of industry. You never will pay your debts but by a radical change of domestic œconomy. At present you buy too much, and make too little to pay. Will this new system promote manufactures, industry and frugality? If instead of this, your hopes and designs will be disappointed; you relinquish a great deal, and hazard infinitely more, for nothing. Will it enhance the value of your lands? Will it lessen your burthens? Will your looms and wheels go to work by the act of adoption? If it will in its consequence produce these things, it will consequently produce a reform, and enable you to pay your debts. Gentlemen must prove it. I am a sceptic—an infidel on this point. I cannot conceive that it will have these happy consequences. I cannot confide in assertions and allegations. The evils that attend us, lie in extravagance and want of industry, and can only be removed by assiduity and œconomy. Perhaps we shall be told by Gentlemen, that these things will happen, because the administration is to be taken from us, and placed in the hands of the luminous few, who will pay different attention, and be more studiously careful than we can be supposed to be. With respect to the œconomical operation of the new Government, I will only remark, that the national expences will be increased—if not doubled it will approach it very near. I might, without incurring the imputation of illiberality or extravagance, say, that the expence will be multiplied ten-fold. I might tell you of a numerous standing army—a great powerful navy—a long and rapacious train of officers and dependents, independent of the President, Senators and Representatives, whose compensations are without limitation. How are our debts to be discharged unless the taxes are increased, when the expences of Government are so greatly augmented? The defects of this system are so numerous and palpable, and so many States object to it, that no Union can be expected, unless it be amended. Let us take a review of the facts. New-Hampshire and Rhode-Island have rejected it. They have refused to become Federal. New-York and North-Carolina are reported to be strongly against it. From high authority, give me leave to tell, that New-York is in high opposition. Will any Gentleman say that North-Carolina is not against it? They may say so, but I say, that the adoption of it in those two States amounts to entire uncertainty. The system must be amended before these four States will accede to it—Besides, there are several other States who are dissatisfied, and wish alterations—Massachusetts has, in decided terms, proposed amendments; but by her previous ratification, has put the cart before the horse. Maryland instituted a committee to propose amendments. It then appears, that two States have actually refused to adopt— Two of those who have adopted, have a desire of amending. And there is a probability of its being rejected by New-York and North-Carolina. The other States have acceded without proposing amendments. With respect to them, local circumstances have, in my judgment, operated to produce its unconditional instantaneous adoption. The locality of the seat of Government, ten miles square,

and the seat of justice, with all their concomitant emoluments, operated so powerfully with the first adopting State, that it was adopted
without taking time to reflect.—We are told that numerous advantages will result from the concentration of the wealth and grandeur
of the United States in one happy spot; to those who will reside in
or near it. Prospects of profit and emoluments have a powerful
influence on the human mind. We, Sir, have no such projects, as that
of a grand seat of Government for thirteen States, and perhaps for
100 States hereafter. Connecticut and New-Jersey have their localities also. New-York lies between them. They have no ports, and
are not importing States. New-York is an importing State, and taking advantage of its situation, makes them pay duties for all the
articles of their consumption: Thus, these two States, being obliged
to import all they want, through the medium of New-York, pay the
particular taxes of that State.—I know the force and effect of reasoning of this sort, by experience. When the impost was proposed
some years ago, those States which were not importing States,
readily agreed to concede to Congress, the power of laying an
impost on all goods imported for the use of the Continental treasury. Connecticut and New-Jersey therefore, are influenced by
advantages of trade in their adoption. The amounts of all imposts
are to go into one common treasury. This favors adoption by the
non-importing States; as they participate in the profits which were
before exclusively enjoyed by the importing States. Notwithstanding this obvious advantage to Connecticut, there is a formidable
minority there against it. After taking this general review of American affairs, as respecting federalism, will the Honorable Gentleman
tell me, that he can expect Union in America? When so many States
are pointedly against it; when two adopting States have pointed
out, in express terms, their dissatisfaction as it stands; and when
there is so respectable a body of men discontented in every State,
can the Honorable Gentleman promise himself harmony, of which
he is so fond? If he can, I cannot. To me it appears unequivocally
clear, that we shall not have that harmony. If it appears to the other
States, that our aversion is founded on just grounds, will they not
be willing to indulge us? If disunion will really result from Virginia's
proposing amendments, will they not wish the re-establishment of

the Union, and admit us, if not on such terms as we prescribe, yet on advantageous terms? Is not Union as essential to their happiness, as to ours? Sir, without a radical alteration, the States will never be embraced in one federal pale. If you attempt to force it down men's throats, and call it Union, dreadful consequences must follow.

He has said a great deal of disunion and the dangers that are to arise from it—When we are on the subject of Union and dangers, let me ask, how will his present doctrine hold with what has happened? Is it consistent with that noble and disinterested conduct, which he displayed on a former occasion? Did he not tell us that he withheld his signature? Where then were the dangers which now appear to him so formidable? He saw all America eagerly confiding, that the result of their deliberations would remove their distresses. He saw all America acting under the impulses of hope, expectation and anxiety, arising from their situation, and their partiality for the members of that Convention: Yet his enlightened mind, knowing that system to be defective, magnanimously and nobly refused its approbation. He was not led by the illumined—the illustrious few. He was actuated by the dictates of his own judgment; and a better judgment than I can form. He did not stand out of the way of information. He must have been possessed of every intelligence. What alteration have a few months brought about? The internal difference between right and wrong does not fluctuate. It is immutable. I ask this question as a public man, and out of no particular view. I wish, as such, to consult every source of information, to form my judgment on so awful a question. I had the highest respect for the Honorable Gentleman's abilities. I considered his opinion as a great authority. He taught me, Sir, in despite of the approbation of that great Federal Convention, to doubt of the propriety of that system. When I found my Honorable friend in the number of those who doubted, I began to doubt also. I coincided with him in opinion. I shall be a staunch and faithful disciple of his. I applaud that magnanimity which led him to withhold his signature. If he thinks now differently, he is as free as I am. Such is my situation, that as a poor individual I look for information every where. This Government is so new it wants a name. I wish its other novelties were as harmless as this. He told us, we had an American Dictator in the year 1781—We never had an American President. In making a Dictator, we follow the example of the most glorious, magnanimous and skilful nations. In great dangers this power has been given.—Rome had furnished us with an illustrious example.—America found a person worthy of that trust: She looked to Virginia for him. We gave a dictatorial power to hands that used it gloriously; and which were rendered more glorious by surrendering it up. Where is there a breed of such Dictators? Shall we find a set of American Presidents of such a breed? Will the American President come and lay prostrate at the feet of Congress his laurels? I fear there are few men who can be trusted on that head. The glorious republic of Holland has erected monuments of her warlike intrepidity and valor: Yet she is now totally ruined by a Stadtholder—a Dutch President. The destructive wars into which that nation has been plunged, has since involved her in ambition. The glorious triumphs of Blenheim and Ramillies were not so conformable to the genius, nor so much to the true interest of the republic, as those numerous and useful canals and dykes, and other objects at which ambition spurns. That republic has, however, by the industry of its inhabitants, and policy of its magistrates, suppressed the ill effects of ambition.—Notwithstanding two of their provinces have paid nothing, yet I hope the example of Holland will tell us, that we can live happily without changing our present despised Government. Cannot people be as happy under a mild, as under an energetic Government? Cannot content and felicity be enjoyed in a republic, as well as in a monarchy, because there are whips, chains and scourges used in the latter? If I am not as rich as my neighbour, if I give my mite—my all—republican forbearance will say, that it is sufficient—So said the honest confederates of Holland.—*You are poor—We are rich.—We will go on and do better, far better, than be under an oppressive Government.*—For better will it be for us to continue as we are, than go under that tight energetic Government.—I am persuaded of what the Honorable Gentleman says, that separate confederacies will ruin us. In my judgment, they are evils never to be thought of till a people are driven by necessity.—When he asks my opinion of consolidation—of one power to

reign over America, with a strong hand; I will tell him, I am persuaded, of the rectitude of my honorable friend's opinion (Mr.
Mason) that one Government cannot reign over so extensive a
country as this is, without absolute despotism. Compared to such a
consolidation, small Confederacies are little evils; though they
ought to be recurred to, but in case of necessity.—Virginia and
North-Carolina are despised. They could exist separated from the
rest of America. Maryland and Vermont were not over-run when
out of the Confederacy. Though it is not a desirable object, yet I
trust, that on examination it will be found, that Virginia and North-
Carolina would not be swallowed up in case it was necessary for
them to be joined together.

When we come to the spirit of domestic peace—The humble
genius of Virginia has formed a Government, suitable to the genius
of her people. I believe the hands that formed the American Constitution triumph in the experiment. It proves, that the man who
formed it, and perhaps by accident, did what design could not do in
other parts of the world. After all your reforms in Government,
unless you consult the genius of the inhabitants, you will never succeed—your system can have no duration. Let me appeal to the candour of the Committee, if the want of money be not the source of
all our misfortunes. We cannot be blamed for not making dollars.
This want of money cannot be supplied by changes in Government.
The only possible remedy, as I *have before* asserted, is industry
aided by œconomy. Compare the genius of the people with the Government of this country. Let me remark, that it stood the severest
conflict, during the war, to which ever human virtue has been
called. I call upon every Gentleman here to declare, whether the
King of England had any subjects so attached to his family and
Government—so loyal as we were. But the genius of Virginia called
us for liberty.—Called us from those beloved endearments, which
from long habits we were taught to love and revere. We entertained
from our earliest infancy, the most sincere regard and reverence for
the mother country. Our partiality extended to a predilection for
her customs, habits, manners and laws. Thus inclined, when the
deprivation of our liberty was attempted, what did we do? What did
the genius of Virginia tell us? *Sell all and purchase liberty.* This

was a severe conflict. Republican maxims were then esteemed—
Those maxims, and the genius of Virginia, landed you safe on the
shore of freedom. On this awful occasion, did you want a Federal
Government? Did federal ideas possess your minds? Did federal
ideas lead you to the most splendid victories? I must again repeat
the favorite idea, that the genius of Virginia did, and will again lead
us to happiness. To obtain the most splendid prize, you did not consolidate. You accomplished the most glorious ends, by the assistance of the genius of your country. Men were then taught by that
genius, that they were fighting for what was most dear to them.
View the most affectionate father—the most tender mother—operated on by liberty, nobly stimulating their sons—their dearest
sons—sometimes their only son, to advance to the defence of his
country. We have seen sons of Cincinnatus, without splendid magnificence or parade, going, with the genius of their great progenitor
Cincinnatus, to the plough—Men who served their country without
ruining it—Men who had served it to the destruction of their private patrimonies—Their country owing them amazing amounts, for
the payment of which no adequate provision was then made. We
have seen such men, throw prostrate their arms at your feet. They
did not call for those emoluments, which ambition presents to some
imaginations. The soldiers, who were able to command every thing,
instead of trampling on those laws, which they were instituted to
defend, most strictly obeyed them. The hands of justice have not
been laid on a single American soldier. Bring them into contrast
with European veterans. You will see an astonishing superiority
over the latter. There has been a strict subordination to the laws.
The Honorable Gentleman's office gave him an opportunity of viewing if the laws were administered so as to prevent riots, routs, and
unlawful assemblies. From his then situation, he could have furnished us with the instances in which licentiousness trampled on
the laws.—Among all our troubles we have paid almost to the last
shilling, for the sake of justice: We have paid as well as any State:
I will not say better. To support the General Government, our own
Legislature, to pay the interest of the public debts, and defray contingencies, we have been heavily taxed. To add to these things, the
distresses produced by paper money, and by tobacco contracts,

were sufficient to render any people discontented. These, Sir, were
great temptations; but in the most severe conflict of misfortunes,
this code of laws—this genius of Virginia, call it what you will, triumphed over every thing.

Why did it please the Gentleman (Mr. *Corbin*) to bestow such epithets on our country? Have the worms taken possession of the
wood, that our strong vessel—our political vessel, has sprung a-
leak? He may know better than me, but I consider such epithets to
be the most illiberal and unwarrantable aspersions on our laws. The
system of laws under which we have lived, has been tried and found
to suit our genius. I trust we shall not change this happy system. I
cannot so easily take leave of an old friend. Till I see him following
after the pursuing other objects, which can pervert the great
objects of human legislation, pardon me if I withhold my assent.

Some here speak of the difficulty in forming a new code of laws.
Young as we were, it was not wonderful if there was a difficulty in
forming and assimilating one system of laws. I shall be obliged to
the Gentleman, if he would point out those glaring, those great
faults. The efforts of assimilating our laws to our genius has not
been found altogether vain.—I shall pass over some other circumstances which I intended to mention, and endeavor to come to the
capital objection, which my Honorable friend made. My worthy
friend said, that a republican form of Government would not suit a
very extensive country; but that if a Government were judiciously
organized and limits prescribed to it; an attention to these principles might render it possible for it to exist in an extensive territory.
Whoever will be bold to say, that a Continent can be governed by
that system, contradicts all the experience of the world. It is a work
too great for human wisdom. Let me call for an example. Experience has been called the best teacher. I call for an example of a
great extent of country, governed by one Government, or Congress,
call it what you will. I tell him, that a Government may be trimmed
up according to Gentlemen's fancy, but it never can operate—It will
be but very short-lived. However disagreeable it may be to
lengthen my objections, I cannot help taking notice of what the
Honorable Gentleman said. To me it appears that there is no check
in that Government. The President, Senators, and Representatives

all immediately, or mediately, are the choice of the people. Tell me not of checks on paper; but tell me of checks founded on self-love. The English Government is founded on self-love. This powerful irrisistible stimulous of self-love has saved that Government. It has interposed that hereditary nobility between the King and Commons. If the House of Lords assists or permits the King to overturn the liberties of the people, the same tyranny will destroy them; they will therefore keep the balance in the democratic branch. Suppose they see the Commons incroach upon the King; self-love, that great energetic check, will call upon them to interpose: For, if the King be destroyed, their destruction must speedily follow. Here is a consideration which prevails, in my mind, to pronounce the British Government, superior in this respect to any Government that ever was in any country. Compare this with your Congressional checks. I beseech Gentlemen to consider, whether they can say, when trusting power, that a mere patriotic profession will be equally operative and efficatious, as the check of self-love. In considering the experience of ages, is it not seen, that fair disinterested patriotism, and professed attachment to rectitude have never been solely trusted to by an enlightened free people?—If you depend on your President's and Senators patriotism, you are gone. Have you a resting place like the British Government? Where is the rock of your salvation? The real rock of political salvation is *self-love* perpetuated from age to age in every human breast, and manifested in every action. If they can stand the temptations of human nature, you are safe. If you have a good President, Senators and Representatives, there is no danger.—But can this be expected from human nature? Without real checks it will not suffice, that some of them are good. A good President, or Senator, or Representative, will have a natural weakness.—Virtue will slumber. The wicked will be continually watching: Consequently you will be undone. Where are your checks? You have no hereditary Nobility—An order of men, to whom human eyes can be cast up for relief: For, says the Constitution, there is no title of nobility to be granted; which, by the bye, would not have been so dangerous, as the perilous cession of powers contained in that paper: Because, as Montesquieu says, when you give titles of Nobility, you know what you give; but *when you give power, you know not what you give.*—If you say, that out of this depraved mass, you can collect luminous characters, it will not avail, unless this luminous breed will be propagated from generation to generation; and even then, if the number of vicious characters will preponderate, you are undone. And that this will certainly be the case, is, to my mind, perfectly clear.—In the British Government there are real balances and checks—In this system, there are only ideal balances. Till I am convinced that there are actual efficient checks, I will not give my assent to its establishment. The President and Senators have nothing to lose. They have not that interest in the preservation of the Government, that the King and Lords have in England. They will therefore be regardless of the interests of the people. The Constitution will be as safe with one body, as with two. It will answer every purpose of human legislation. How was the Constitution of England when only the Commons had the power? I need only remark, that it was the most unfortunate æra when that country returned to King, Lords and Commons, without sufficient responsibility in the King. When the Commons of England, in the manly language which became freemen, said to their King, *you are our servant*, then the temple of liberty was complete. From that noble source, have we derived our liberty:—That spirit of patriotic attachment to one's country:— That zeal for liberty, and that enmity to tyranny which signalized the then champions of liberty, we inherit from our British ancestors. And I am free to own, that if you cannot love a Republican Government, you may love the British Monarchy; for, although the King is not sufficiently responsible, the responsibility of his agents, and the efficient checks interposed by the British Constitution, render it less dangerous than other Monarchies, or oppressive tyrannical Aristocracies. What are their checks of exposing accounts?—Their checks upon paper are inefficient and nugatory.— Can you search your President's closet? Is this a real check? We ought to be exceeding cautious, in giving up this life—this soul—of money—this power of taxation to Congress. What powerful check is there here to prevent the most extravagant and profligate squandering of the public money? What security have we in money matters? Enquiry is precluded by this Constitution. I never wish to see Congress supplicate the States. But it is more abhorent to my mind to give them an unlimited and unbounded command over our souls—our lives—our purses, without any check or restraint. How are you to keep enquiry alive? How discover their conduct? We are told by that paper, that a regular statement and account of the receipts and expenditures of all public money, shall be published from time to time. Here is a beautiful check! What time? Here is the utmost latitude left. If those who are in Congress please to put that construction upon it, the words of the Constitution will be satisfied by publishing those accounts once in 100 years. They may publish or not as they please. Is this like the present despised system, whereby the accounts are to be published monthly?

I come now to speak something of requisitions, which the Honorable Gentleman thought so truly contemptible and disgraceful. That Honorable Gentleman being a child of the revolution, must recollect with gratitude the glorious effects of requisitions. It is an idea that must be grateful to every American. An English army was sent to compel us to pay money contrary to our consent. To force us by arbitrary and tyrannical coercion to satisfy their unbounded demands. We wished to pay with our own consent.— Rather than pay against our consent, we engaged in that bloody contest, which terminated so gloriously. By requisitions we pay with our own consent; by their means we have triumphed in the most arduous struggle, that ever tried the virtue of man. We fought then, for what we are contending now: To prevent an arbitrary deprivation of our property, contrary to our consent and inclination. I shall be told in this place, that those who are to tax us are our Representatives. To this I answer, that there is no real check to prevent their ruining us. There is no actual responsibility. The only semblance of a check is the negative power of not re-electing them. This, Sir, is but a feeble barrier when their personal interest, their ambition and avarice come to be put in contrast with the happiness of the people. All checks founded on any thing but self-love, will not avail. This Constitution reflects in the most degrading and mortifying manner on the virtue, integrity, and wisdom of the State Legislatures: It presupposes that the chosen few who go to Congress will have more upright hearts, and more enlightened minds, than those who are members of the individual Legislatures. To suppose that ten Gentlemen shall have more real substantial merit, than 170 is humiliating to the last degree. If, Sir, the diminution of numbers be an augmentation of merit, perfection must centre in one. If you have the faculty of discerning spirits, it is better to point out at once the man who has the most illumined qualities. If 10 men be better than 170, it follows of necessity, that one is better than 10—The choice is more refined.

Such is the danger of the abuse of implied power, that it would be safer at once to have seven Representatives, the number to which we are now entitled, than depend on the uncertain and ambiguous language of that paper. The number may be lessened instead of being increased; and yet by argumentative constructive implied power, the proportion of taxes may continue the same, or be increased.—Nothing is more perilous than constructive power, which Gentlemen are so willing to trust their happiness to.

If Sheriffs prove now an over-match for our Legislature: If their ingenuity has eluded the vigilance of our laws, how will the matter be amended when they come cloathed with federal authority? A strenuous argument offered by Gentlemen, is, that the same Sheriffs may collect for the Continental and State treasuries. I have before shewn, that this must have an inevitable tendency to give a decided preference to the federal treasury in the actual collections, and to throw all deficiencies on the State. This imaginary remedy for the evil of Congressional taxation will have another oppressive operation. The Sheriff comes to-day as a State collector—next day he is federal—How are you to fix him? How will it be possible to discriminate oppressions committed in one capacity, from those perpetrated in the other? Will not his ingenuity perplex the simple honest planter? This will at least involve in difficulties, those who are unacquainted with legal ingenuity. When you fix him, where are you to punish him? For, I suppose, they will not stay in our Courts: They must go to the Federal Court; for, if I understand that paper right, all controversies arising under that Constitution; or, under the laws made in pursuance thereof, are to be tried in that Court. When Gentlemen told us, that this part deserved the least exception, I was in hopes, they would prove that there was plausibility in their suggestions, and that oppression would probably not follow. Are we not told, that it shall be treason to levy war against the United States? Suppose an insult offered to the federal laws at an immense distance from Philadelphia, will this be deemed treason? And shall a man be dragged many hundred miles to be tried as a criminal, for having perhaps justifiably resisted an unwarrantable attack upon his person or property? I am not well acquainted with federal jurisprudence; but it appears to me that these oppressions must result from this part of the plan.—It is at least doubtful, and where there is even a possibility of such evils, they ought to be guarded against.

There are to be a number of places fitted out for arsenals and dock-yards in the different States. Unless you fell to Congress such places as are proper for these, within your State, you will not be consistent after adoption; it results therefore clearly that you are to give into their hands, all such places as are fit for strong holds. When you have these fortifications and garrisons within your State, your State Legislature will have no power over them, though they see the most dangerous insults offered to the people daily.—They are also to have magazines in each State: These depositaries for arms, though within the State, will be free from the controul of its Legislature. Are we at last brought to such a humiliating and debasing degradation, that we cannot be trusted with arms for our own defence? Where is the difference between having our arms in our own possession and under our own direction, and having them under the management of Congress? If our defence be the *real* object of having those arms; in whose hands can they be trusted with more propriety, or equal safety to us, as in our own hands? If our Legislature be unworthy of legislating for every foot in this State, they are unworthy of saying another word.

The clause which says, that Congress shall "provide for arming, organizing, and disciplining the militia, and for governing such part of them as may be employed in the service of the United States, reserving to the States respectively, the appointment of the officers," seemed to put the States in the power of Congress. I wished to be informed, if Congress neglected to discipline them, whether the States were not precluded from doing it. Not being favored with a particular answer, I am confirmed in my opinion, that the States have not the power of disciplining them, without recurring to the doctrine of constructive implied powers. If by implication the States may discipline them, by implication also, Congress may officer them; because, in a partition of power, each has a right to come in for part; and because implication is to operate in favor of Congress on all occasions, where there object is the extension of power, as well as in favor of the States. We have not one-fourth of the arms that would be sufficient to defend ourselves. The power of arming the militia, and the means of purchasing arms, are taken from the States by the paramount powers of Congress. If Congress will not arm them, they will not be armed at all.

There have been no instances shewn of a voluntary cession of power, sufficient to induce me to grant the most dangerous powers: A possibility of their future relinquishment will not persuade me to yeild such powers.

Congress by the power of taxation—by that of raising an army, and by their controul over the militia, have the sword in one hand, and the purse in the other. Shall we be safe without either? Congress have an unlimited power over both: They are entirely given up by us. Let him candidly tell me, where and when did freedom exist, when the sword and purse were given up from the people? Unless a miracle in human affairs interposed, no nation ever retained its liberty after the loss of the sword and purse. Can you prove by any argumentative deduction, that it is possible to be safe without retaining one of these? If you give them up you are gone. Give us at least a plausible apology why Congress should keep their proceedings in secret. They have the power of keeping them secrets as long as they please; for the provision for a periodical publication is too inexplicit and ambiguous to avail any thing. The expression *from time to time* as I have more than once observed, admits of any extension. They may carry on the most wicked and pernicious of schemes, under the dark veil of secrecy. The liberties of a people never were nor ever will be secure, when the transactions of their rulers may be concealed from them. The most iniquitous plots may be carried on against their liberty and happiness. I am not an advocate for divulging indiscriminately all the operations of Government, though the practice of our ancestors in some degree justifies it. Such transactions as relate to military operations, or affairs of great consequence, the immediate promulgation of which might defeat the interests of the community, I would not wish to be published, till the end which required their secrecy should have been effected. But to cover with the veil of secrecy, the common rotine of business, is an abomination in the eyes of every intelligent man, and every friend to his country.

{Mr. *Henry* then, in a very animated manner, expatiated on the evil and pernicious tendency of keeping secret the common proceedings of Government; and said that it was contrary to the practice of other free nations. The people of England, he asserted, had gained immortal honor by the manly boldness wherewith they divulged to all the world, their political disquisitions and operations; and that such a conduct inspired other nations with respect. He illustrated his argument by several quotations.}—He then continued,—I appeal to this Convention if it would not be better for America to take off the veil of secrecy. *Look at us—hear our transactions.* If this had been the language of the Federal Convention, what would have been the result? Such a Constitution would not have come out to your utter astonishment, conceding such dangerous powers, and recommending secrecy in the future transactions of Government. I believe it would have given more general satisfaction, if the proceedings of that Convention had not been concealed from the public eye. This Constitution authorizes the same conduct. There is not an English feature in it. The transactions of Congress may be concealed a century from the public, consistently with the Constitution. This, Sir, is a laudable imitation of the transactions of the Spanish treaty. We have not forgotten with what a thick veil of secrecy those transactions were covered.

We are told that this Government collectively taken, is without an example—That it is national in this part, and federal in that part, &c. We may be amused if we please, by a treatise of political anatomy. In the brain it is national: The stamina are federal—some limbs are federal—others national. The Senators are voted for by the State Legislatures, so far it is federal.—Individuals choose the members of the first branch; here it is national. It is federal in conferring general powers; but national in retaining them. It is not to be supported by the States—The pockets of individuals are to be searched for its maintenance. What signifies it to me, that you have the most curious anatomical description of it in its creation? To all the common purposes of Legislation it is a great consolidation of Government. You are not to have a right to legislate in any but trivial cases: You are not to touch private contracts. You are not to have the right of having arms in your own defence: You cannot be trusted with dealing out justice between man and man. What shall the States have to do? Take care of the poor—repair and make highways—erect bridges, and so on, and so on. Abolish the State Legislatures at once. What purposes should they be continued for? Our Legislature will indeed be a ludicrous spectacle—180 men marching in solemn farcical procession, exhibiting a mournful proof of the lost liberty of their country—without the power of restoring it. But, Sir, we have the consolation that it is a mixed Government: That is, it may work sorely on your neck; but you will have some comfort by saying, that it was a Federal Government in its origin.

I beg Gentlemen to consider—lay aside your prejudices—Is this a Federal Government? Is it not a Consolidated Government for every purpose almost? Is the Government of Virginia a State Government after this Government is adopted? I grant that it is a Republican Government—but for what purposes? For such trivial domestic considerations, as render it unworthy the name of a Legislature. I shall take leave of this political anatomy, by observing that it is the most extraordinary that ever entered into the imagination of man. If our political diseases demand a cure—this is an unheard of medicine. The Honorable member, I am convinced, wanted a name for it. Were your health in danger, would you take new medicine? I need not make use of these exclamations; for every member in this Committee must be alarmed at making new and unusual experiments in Government. Let us have national credit and a national treasury in case of war. You never can want national resources in time of war; if the war be a national one; if it be necessary, and this necessity obvious to the meanest capacity. The utmost exertions will be used by the people of America in that case. A republic has this advantage over a monarchy, that its wars are generally founded on more just grounds. A republic can never enter into a war, unless it be a national war—unless it be approved of, or desired by the whole community. Did ever a republic fail to use the utmost resources of the community when a war was necessary? I call for an example. I call also for an example, when a republic has been engaged in a war contrary to the wishes of its people. There are thousands of examples, where the ambition of its Prince precipitated a nation into the most destructive war. No nation ever withheld power when its object was just and right. I will hazard an observation; I find fault with the paper before you, because the same power that declares war, has the power to carry it on. Is it so in England? The King declares war: The House of Commons gives the means of carrying it on. This is a strong check on the King. He will enter into no war that is unnecessary; for the Commons having the power of withholding the means, will exercise that power, unless the object of the war be for the interest of the nation. How is it here? The Congress can both declare war, and carry it on; and levy your money, as long as you have a shilling to pay.

I shall now speak a little of the Colonial confederacy which was proposed at Albany. Massachusetts did not give her consent to the project at Albany, so as to consolidate with the other Colonies. Had there been a consolidation at Albany, where would have been their charter? Would that confederacy have preserved their charter from Britain? The strength and energy of the then designed Government would have crushed American opposition.

The American revolution took its origin from the comparative weakness of the British Government; not being concentred in one point. A concentration of the strength and interest of the British Government in one point, would have rendered opposition to its tyrannies fruitless.—For want of that consolidation do we now enjoy liberty, and the privilege of debating at this moment. I am pleased with the Colonial establishment. The example which the Honorable member has produced, to persuade us to depart from our present confederacy, rivets me to my former opinion, and convinces me that consolidation must end in the destruction of our liberties.

The Honorable Gentleman has told us of our ingratitude to France. She does not intend to take payment by force. Ingratitude shall not be laid to my charge. I wish to see the friendship between this country, and that magnanimous ally, perpetuated. Requisitions will enable us to pay the debt we owe France and other countries. She does not desire us to go from our beloved Republican Government. The change is inconsistent with our engagements with those nations. It is cried out that those in opposition wish disunion. This is not true. They are the most strenuous friends to it. This Government will clearly operate disunion.—If it be heard on the other side of the Atlantic, that you are going to disunite and dissolve the confederacy: what says France? Will she be indifferent to an event that will so radically affect her treaties with us? Our treaty with her is founded on the confederation—We are bound to her as 13 States confederated. What will become of the treaty? It is said that treaties will be on a better footing. How so? Will the President, Senate and House of Representatives be parties to them? I cannot conceive how the treaties can be as binding if the confederacy is dissolved, as they are now. Those nations will not continue their friendship then: They will become our enemies. I look on the treaties as the greatest pillars of safety. If the House of Bourbon keeps us, we are safe. Dissolve that confederacy—who has you? The British. Federalism will not protect you from the British. Is a connexion with that country more desirable? I was amazed when Gentlemen forgot the friends of America. I hope that this dangerous change will not be effected. It is safe for the French and Spaniards, that we should continue to be Thirteen States—But it is not so, that we should be consolidated into one Government. They have settlements in America—Will they like schemes of popular ambition? Will they not have some serious reflections? You may tell them you have not changed your situation; but they will not believe you. If there be a real check intended to be left on Congress, it must be left in the State Government. There will be some check, as long as the Judges are uncorrupt. As long as they are upright, you may preserve your liberty. But what will the Judges determine when the State and Federal authority come to be contrasted? Will your liberty then be secure, when the Congressional laws are declared paramount to the laws of your State, and the Judges are sworn to support them?

I am constrained to make a few remarks on the absurdity of adopting this system, and relying on the chance of getting it amended afterwards. When it is confessed to be replete with defects, is it not offering to insult your understandings, to attempt to reason you out of the propriety of rejecting it, till it be amended? Does it not insult your judgments to tell you—adopt first, and then amend? Is your rage for novelty so great, that you are first to sign and seal, and then to retract? Is it possible to conceive a greater solecism? I am at a loss what to say. You agree to bind yourselves hand and foot—For the sake of what?—Of being unbound. You go into a dungeon—For what? To get out. Is there no danger when you go in, that the bolts of federal authority shall shut you in? Human nature never will part with power. Look for an example of a voluntary relinquishment of power, from one end of the globe to another—You will find none. Nine-tenths of our fellow men have been, and are now depressed by the most intolerable slavery, in the different parts of the world; because the strong hand of power has bolted them in the dungeon of despotism. Review the present situation of the nations of Europe, which is pretended to be the freest quarter of the globe. Cast your eyes on the countries called free there. Look at the country from which we are descended, I beseech you; and although we are separated by everlasting insuperable partitions, yet there are some virtuous people there who are friends to human nature and liberty. Look at Britain—fee there, the bolts and bars of power—see bribery and corruption defiling the fairest fabrick that ever human nature reared. Can a Gentleman who is an Englishman, or who is acquainted with the English history, desire to prove these evils? See the efforts of a man descended from a friend of America—see the efforts of that man, assisted even by the King, to make reforms. But you find the faults too strong to be amended. Nothing but bloody war can alter them.—See Ireland—That country groaned from century to century, without getting their Government amended. Previous adoption was the fashion there. They sent for amendments *from time to time*, but never obtained them, though pressed by the severest oppression, till 80,000 volunteers demanded them sword in hand— Till the power of Britain was prostrate; when the American resistance was crowned with success. Shall we do so? If you judge by the experience of Ireland, you must obtain the amendments as easy as possible.—But, I ask you again, where is the example that a Government was amended by those who instituted it? Where is the instance of the errors of a Government rectified by those who adopted them.

I shall make a few observations to prove, that the power over elections, which is given to Congress, is contrived by the Federal Government, that the people may be deprived of their proper influence in the Government; by destroying the force and effect of their suffrages. Congress is to have a discretionary controul over the time, place and manner of elections. The Representatives are to be elected consequently, when and where they please. As to the time and place, Gentlemen have attempted to obviate the objection by saying, that the time is to happen once in two years, and that the place is to be within a particular district, or in the respective counties. But how will they obviate the danger of referring the *manner* of election to Congress? Those illumined Genii, may see that this may not endanger the rights of the people; but to my unenlightened understanding, it appears plain and clear, that it will impair the popular weight in the Government. Look at the Roman history. They had two ways of voting: The one by tribes, and the other by centuries. By the former, numbers prevailed: In the latter, riches preponderated. According to the mode prescribed, Congress may tell you, that they have a right to make the vote of one Gentleman go as far as the votes of 100 poor men. The power over the manner admits of the most dangerous latitude. They may modify it as they please. They may regulate the number of votes by the quantity of property, without involving any repugnancy to the Constitution. I should not have thought of this trick or contrivance had I not seen how the public liberty of Rome was trifled with by the mode of voting by centuries, whereby one rich man had as many votes as a multitude of poor men. The plebians were trampled on till they resisted. The patricians trampled on the liberties of the plebians, till the latter had spirit to assert their right to freedom and equality. The result of the American mode of election may be familiar.— Perhaps I shall be told, that I have gone through the regions of fancy—that I deal in noisy exclamations, and mighty professions of patriotism. Gentlemen may retain their opinions; but I look on that paper as the most fatal plan, that could possibly be conceived to enslave a free people.—If such be your rage for novelty, take it and welcome, but you never shall have my consent. My sentiments may appear extravagant, but I can tell you, that a number of my fellow-citizens have kindred sentiments—And I am anxious that if my country should come into the hands of tyranny, to exculpate myself from being in any degree the cause; and to exert my faculties to the utmost to extricate her. Whether I am gratified or not in my beloved form of Government, I consider that the more she is plunged into distress, the more it is my duty to relieve her. Whatever may be the result, I shall wait with patience till the day may come, when an opportunity shall offer to exert myself in her cause.

But I should be led to take that man to be a lunatic, who should tell me to run, into the adoption of a Government, avowedly defective, in hopes of having it amended afterwards. Were I about to give away the meanest particle of my own property, I should act with more prudence and discretion. My anxiety and fears are great, left America by the adoption of this system, should be cast into a fathomless bottom.—Mr. *Henry* then concluded, that as he had not gone through all he intended to say, he hoped he would be indulged another time.

Articles
of
Confederation

ACT OF CONFEDERATION OF THE UNITED STATES OF AMERICA

To all to whom these presents shall come, we the undersigned delegates of the states affixed to our names, send greetings.

Whereas the Delegates of the United States of America in Congress assembled did on the 15th day of November in the Year of our Lord One Thousand Seven Hundred and Seventy seven, and in the Second Year of the Independence of America agree to certain articles of Confederation and perpetual Union between the states of Newhampshire, Massachusetts-bay, Rhodeisland and Providence Plantations, Connecticut, New York, New Jersey, Pennsylvania, Delaware, Maryland, Virginia, North Carolina, South Carolina and Georgia in the Words following, viz.

ARTICLES OF CONFEDERATION AND PERPETUAL UNION BETWEEN THE STATES OF NEWHAMPSHIRE, MASSACHUSETTS-BAY, RHODEIS-LAND AND PROVIDENCE PLANTATIONS, CONNECTICUT, NEW YORK, NEW JERSEY, PENNSYLVANIA, DELAWARE, MARYLAND, VIRGINIA, NORTH CAROLINA, SOUTH CAROLINA AND GEORGIA

ARTICLE I. The Stile of this confederacy shall be "The United States of America."

ARTICLE II. Each State retains its Sovereignty, freedom and independence, and every Power, Jurisdiction and right, which is not by this confederation expressly delegated to the United States in Congress assembled.

ARTICLE III. The said states hereby severally enter into a firm league of friendship with each other, for their common defence, the security of their Liberties, and their mutual and general welfare, binding themselves to assist each other, against all force offered to, or attacks made upon them, or any of them, on account of religion, sovereignty, trade, or any other pretence whatever.

ARTICLE IV. The better to secure and perpetuate mutual friendship and intercourse among the people of the different states in this union, the free inhabitants of each of these states, paupers, vagabonds and fugitives from Justice excepted, shall be entitled to all privileges and immunities of free citizens in the several states, and the people of each state shall have free ingress and regress to and from any other state, and shall enjoy therein all the privileges of trade and commerce, subject to the same duties, impositions and restrictions as the inhabitants thereof respectively, provided that such restrictions shall not extend so far as to prevent the removal of property imported into any state, to any other state of which the Owner is an inhabitant, provided also that no imposition, duties or restriction shall be laid by any state, on the property of the united states, or either of them.

If any Person guilty of, or charged with treason, felony or other high misdemeanor in any state, shall flee from Justice, and be found in any of the united states, he shall upon demand of the Governor or executive power, of the state from which he fled, be delivered up and removed to the state having jurisdiction of his offence.

Full faith and credit shall be given in each of these states to the records, acts and judicial proceedings of the courts and magistrates of every other state.

ARTICLE V. For the more convenient management of the general interest of the united states, delegates shall be annually appointed in such manner as the legislature of each state shall direct, to meet in Congress on the first Monday in November, in every year, with a power reserved to each state, to recall its delegates, or any of them, at any time within the year, and to send others in their stead, for the remainder of the Year.

No state shall be represented in Congress by less than two, nor by more than seven Members; and no person shall be capable of being a delegate for more than three years in any term of six years; nor shall any person, being a delegate, be capable of holding any office under the united states, for which he, or another for his benefit receives any salary, fees or emolument of any kind.

Each state shall maintain its own delegates in a meeting of the states, and while they act as members of the committee of the states.

In determining questions in the united states, in Congress assembled, each state shall have one vote.

Freedom of speech and debate in Congress shall not be impeached or questioned in any Court, or place out of Congress, and the members of congress shall be protected in their persons from arrests and imprisonments, during the time of their going to and from, and attendance on congress, except for treason, felony, or breach of the peace.

ARTICLE VI. No state without the Consent of the united states in congress assembled, shall send any embassy to, or receive any embassy from, or enter into any conference, agreement, alliance or treaty with any King, prince or state; nor shall any person holding any office of profit or trust under the united states, or any of them, accept of any present, emolument, office or title of any kind whatever from any king, prince or foreign state; nor shall the united states in congress assembled, or any of them, grant any title of nobility.

No two or more states shall enter into any treaty, confederation or alliance whatever between them, without the consent of the united states in congress assembled, specifying accurately the purposes for which the same is to be entered into, and how long it shall continue.

No state shall lay any imposts of duties, which may interfere with any stipulations in treaties, entered into by the united states in congress assembled with any king, prince or state, in pursuance of any treaties already proposed by congress to the courts of France and Spain.

No vessels of war shall be kept up in time of peace by any state, except such number only, as shall be deemed necessary by the united states in congress assembled, for the defence of such state, or its trade; nor shall any body of forces be kept up by any state, in time of peace, except such number only, as in the judgment of the united states, in congress assembled, shall be deemed requisite to garrison the forts necessary for the defence of such state; but every state shall always keep up a well regulated and disciplined militia, sufficiently armed and accoutred, and shall provide and constantly have ready for use, in public stores, a due number of field-pieces and tents, and a proper quantity of arms, ammunition and camp equipage.

No state shall engage in any war without the consent of the united states in congress assembled, unless such state be actually invaded by enemies, or shall have received certain advice of a resolution being formed by some nation of Indians to invade such state, and the danger is so imminent as not to admit of a delay, till the united states in congress assembled can be consulted: nor shall any state grant commissions to any ships or vessels of war, nor letters of marque or reprisal, except it be after a declaration of war by the united states in Congress assembled, and then only against the kingdom or state and the subjects thereof, against which war has been so declared, and under such regulations as shall be established by the united states in congress assembled, unless such state be infested by pirates, in which case vessels of war may be fitted out for that occasion, and kept so long as the danger shall continue, or until the united states in congress assembled shall determine otherwise.

ARTICLE VII. When land-forces are raised by any state for the common defence, all officers of or under the rank of colonel, shall be appointed by the legislature of each state respectively by whom such forces shall be raised, or in such manner as such state shall direct, and all vacancies shall be filled up by the state which first made the appointment.

ARTICLE VIII. All charges of war, and all other expences that shall be incurred for the common defence or general welfare, and allowed by the united states in congress assembled, shall be defrayed out of a common treasury, which shall be supplied by the several states, in proportion to the value of all land within each state, granted to or surveyed for any Person, as such land and the buildings and improvements thereon shall be estimated according to such mode as the united states in congress assembled, shall from time to time direct and appoint.

The taxes for paying that proportion shall be laid and levied by the authority and direction of the legislatures of the several states within the time agreed upon by the united states in congress assembled.

ARTICLE IX. The united states in congress assembled, shall have the sole and exclusive right and power of determining on peace and war, except in the cases mentioned in the sixth article—of sending and receiving embassadors—entering into treaties and alliances, provided that no treaty of commerce shall be made whereby the legislative power of the respective states shall be restrained from imposing such imposts and duties on foreigners, as their own people are subjected to, or from prohibiting the exportation or importation of any species of goods or commodities whatsoever—of establishing rules for deciding in all cases, what captures on land or water shall be legal, and in what manner prizes taken by land or naval forces in the service of the united states shall be divided or appropriated—of granting letters of marque and reprisal in times of peace—appointing courts for the trial of piracies and felonies committed on the high seas and establishing courts for receiving and determining finally appeals in all cases of captures, provided that no member of congress shall be appointed a judge of any of the said courts.

The united states in congress assembled shall also be the last resort on appeal in all disputes and differences now subsisting or that hereafter may arise between two or more states concerning boundary, jurisdiction or any other cause whatever, which authority shall always be exercised in the manner following. Whenever the legislative or executive authority or lawful agent of any state in controversy with another shall present a petition to congress stating the matter in question and praying for a hearing, notice thereof shall be given by order of congress to the legislative or executive authority of the other state in controversy, and a day assigned for the appearance of the parties by their lawful agents, who shall then be directed to appoint by joint consent, commissioners or judges to constitute a court for hearing and determining the matter in question: but if they cannot agree, congress shall name three persons out of each of the united states, and from the list of such persons each party shall alternately strike out one, the petitioners beginning, until the number shall be reduced to thirteen; and from that number not less than seven, nor more than nine names as congress shall direct, shall in the presence of congress be drawn out by lot, and the persons whose names shall be so drawn or any five of them, shall be commissioners or judges, to hear and finally determine the controversy, so always as a major part of the judges who shall hear the cause shall agree in the determination: and if either party shall neglect to attend at the day appointed, without showing reasons, which congress shall judge sufficient, or being present shall refuse to strike, the congress shall proceed to nominate three persons out of each State, and the secretary of congress shall strike in behalf of such party absent or refusing; and the judgment and sentence of the court to be appointed, in the manner before prescribed, shall be final and conclusive; and if any of the parties shall refuse to submit to the authority of such court, or to appear or defend their claim or cause, the court shall nevertheless proceed to pronounce sentence, or judgment, which shall in like manner be final and decisive, the judgment or sentence and other proceedings being in either case transmitted to congress, and lodged among the acts of congress for the security of the parties concerned: provided that every commissioner, before he sits in judgment, shall take an oath to be administered by one of the judges of the supreme or superior court of the state, where the cause shall be tried, "well and truly to hear and determine the matter in question, according to the best of his judgment without favour, affection or hope of reward": provided also that no state shall be deprived of territory for the benefit of the united states.

All controversies concerning the private right of soil claimed under different grants of two or more states, whose jurisdiction as they may respect such lands, and the states which passed such grants are adjusted, the said grants or either of them being at the same time claimed to have originated antecedent to such settlement of jurisdiction, shall on the petition of either party to the congress of the united states, be finally determined as near as may be in the same manner as is before prescribed for deciding disputes respecting territorial jurisdiction between different states.

The united states in congress assembled shall also have the sole and exclusive right and power of regulating the alloy and value of coin struck by their own authority, or by that of the respective states—fixing the standard of weights and measures throughout the united states—regulating the trade and managing all affairs with the Indians, not members of any of the states, provided that the legislative right of any state within its own limits be not infringed or violated—establishing and regulating post-offices from one state to another, throughout all the united states, and exacting such postage on the papers passing thro' the same as may be requisite to defray the expences of the said office—appointing all officers of the land forces, in the service of the united states, excepting regimental officers—appointing all the officers of the naval forces, and commissioning all officers whatever in the service of the united states—making rules for the government and regulation of the said land and naval forces, and directing their operations.

The united states in congress assembled shall have authority to appoint a committee, to sit in the recess of congress, to be denominated "A Committee of the States," and to consist of one delegate from each state; and to appoint such other committees and civil officers as may be necessary for managing the general affairs of the united states under their direction—to appoint one of their number to preside, provided that no person be allowed to serve in the office of president more than one year in any term of three years; to ascertain the necessary sums of Money to be raised for the service of the united states, and to appropriate and apply the same for defraying the public expences—to borrow money, or emit bills on the credit of the united states, transmitting every half year to the respective states an account of the sums of moneys so borrowed or emitted—to build and equip a navy—to agree upon the number of land forces, and to make requisition from each state for its quota, in proportion to the number of white inhabitants in such state; which requisitions shall be binding, and thereupon the legislature of each state shall appoint the regimental officers, raise the men and cloath, arm and equip them in a soldier like manner, at the expence of the united states; and the officers and men so cloathed, armed and equipped shall march to the place appointed, and within the time agreed on by the united states in congress assembled: But if the united states in congress assembled shall, on consideration of circumstances judge proper that any state should not raise men, or should raise a smaller number than its quota, and that any other state should raise a greater number of men than the quota thereof, such extra number shall be raised, officered, cloathed, armed and equipped in the same manner as the quota of such state, unless the legislature of such state shall judge that such extra number cannot be safely spared out of the same, in which case they shall raise, officer, cloath, arm and equip as many of such extra number as they judge can be safely spared. And the officers and men so cloathed, armed and equipped, shall march to the place appointed, and within the time agreed on by the united states in congress assembled.

The united states in congress assembled shall never engage in a war, nor grant letters of marque and reprisal in time of peace, nor enter into any treaties or alliances, nor coin money, nor regulate the value thereof, nor ascertain the sums and expences necessary for the defence and welfare of the united states, or any of them, nor emit bills, nor borrow money on the credit of the united states, nor appropriate money, nor agree upon the number of vessels of war, to be built or purchased, or the number of land or sea forces to be raised, nor appoint a commander-in-chief of the army or navy, unless nine states assent to the same; nor shall a question on any other point, except for adjourning from day to day be determined, unless by the votes of a majority of the united states in congress assembled.

The Congress of the united states shall have power to adjourn to any time within the year, and to any place within the united states, so that no period of adjournment be for a longer duration than the space of six Months, and shall publish the Journal of their proceedings monthly, except such parts thereof relating to treaties, alliances or military operations as in their judgment require secrecy; and the yeas and nays of the delegates of each state on any question shall be entered on the Journal, when it is desired by any delegate; and the delegates of a state, or any of them, at his or their request shall be furnished with a transcript of the said Journal, except such parts as are above excepted, to lay before the legislatures of the several states.

ARTICLE X. The committee of the states, or any nine of them, shall be authorized to execute, in the recess of congress such of the powers of congress as the united states in congress assembled, by the consent of nine states, shall from time to time think expedient to vest them with; provided that no power be delegated to the said committee, for the exercise of which, by the articles of confederation, the voice of nine states in the congress of the united states assembled is requisite.

ARTICLE XI. Canada acceding to this confederation, and joining in the measures of the united states, shall be admitted into, and entitled to all the advantages of this union: but no other colony shall be admitted into the same, unless such admission be agreed to by nine states.

ARTICLE XII. All bills of credit emitted, monies borrowed and debts contracted by, or under the authority of congress, before the assembling of the united states, in pursuance of the present confederation, shall be deemed and considered as a charge against the united states, for payment and satisfaction whereof the said united states, and the public faith are hereby solemnly pledged.

ARTICLE XIII. Every state shall abide by the determinations of the united states in congress assembled, on all questions which by this confederation are submitted to them. And the Articles of this confederation shall be inviolably observed by every state, and the union shall be perpetual; nor shall any alteration at any time hereafter be made in any of them; unless such alteration be agreed to in a congress of the united states, and be afterward confirmed by the legislatures of every state.

AND WHEREAS it has pleased the Great Governor of the World to incline the hearts of the legislatures we respectively represent in congress, to approve of, and to authorize us to ratify the said articles of confederation and perpetual union. KNOW YE that we the undersigned delegates, by virtue of the power and authority to us given for that purpose, do by these presents, in the name and in behalf of our respective constituents, fully and entirely ratify and confirm each and every of the said articles of confederation and perpetual union, and all and singular the matters and things therein contained: And we do further solemnly plight and engage the faith of our respective constituents, that they shall abide by the determinations of the united states in congress assembled, on all questions, which by the said confederation are submitted to them. And that the articles thereof shall be inviolably observed by the states we respectively represent and that the union shall be perpetual.

IN WITNESS whereof we have hereunto set our hands in Congress. DONE at Philadelphia in the state of Pennsylvania the ninth Day of July in the Year of our Lord one Thousand seven Hundred and Seventy-eight, and in the third year of the independence of America.

On the part and behalf of the State of New Hampshire.

JOSIAH BARTLETT, JOHN WENTWORTH, JUNR. AUGUST 8, 1778.

On the part and behalf of the State of Massachusetts Bay.

JOHN HANCOCK,	FRANCIS DANA,
SAMUEL ADAMS,	JAMES LOVELL,
ELBRIDGE GERRY,	SAMUEL HOLTEN.

ON THE PART AND IN BEHALF OF THE STATE OF RHODE ISLAND AND PROVIDENCE PLANTATIONS.

WILLIAM ELLERY,	JOHN COLLINS.
HENRY MARCHANT,	

ON THE PART AND BEHALF OF THE STATE OF CONNECTICUT.

ROGER SHERMAN,	TITUS HOSMER,
SAMUEL HUNTINGTON,	ANDREW ADAMS.
OLIVER WOLCOTT,	

ON THE PART AND BEHALF OF THE STATE OF NEW YORK.

JAS DUANE,	WILLIAM DUER,
FRAS LEWIS,	GOUVR MORRIS.

ON THE PART AND IN BEHALF OF THE STATE OF NEW JERSEY.

JNO WITHERSPOON,	NATHL SCUDDER, NOV. 26, 1778.

748   THE ANTI-FEDERALISTS

On the part and behalf of the State of Pennsylvania.

ROBT. MORRIS,   WILLIAM CLINGAN,
DANIEL ROBERDEAU,   JOSEPH REED, JULY 22, 1778.
JONA BAYARD SMITH,

On the part and behalf of the State of Delaware.

JOHN DICKINSON, MAY 5, 1779,   THO. M'KEAN, FEB. 12, 1779.
NICHOLAS VAN DYKE,

On the part and behalf of the State of Maryland.

JOHN HANSON, MARCH 1, 1781,   DANIEL CARROL DO

On the part and behalf of the State of Virginia.

RICHARD HENRY LEE,   JNO HARVIE,
JOHN BANISTER,   FRANCIS LIGHTFOOT LEE.
THOMAS ADAMS,

On the part and behalf of the State of North Carolina.

JOHN PENN, JULY 21, 1778,   JNO WILLIAMS.
CORNS. HARNETT,

On the part and behalf of the State of South Carolina.

HENRY LAURENS,   RICHARD HUTSON,
WILLIAM HENRY DRAYTON, THOS. HEYWARD, JUNR.
JNO MATHEWS,

On the part and behalf of the State of Georgia.

JNO WALTON, 24TH JULY 1778,   EDWD. LANGWORTHY.
EDWD TELFAIR,

Constitution of the
United States of America

WE THE PEOPLE of the United States, in Order to form a more perfect Union, establish Justice, insure domestic Tranquility, provide
for the common defence, promote the general Welfare, and secure
the Blessings of Liberty to ourselves and our Posterity, do ordain
and establish this CONSTITUTION for the United States of
America.

ARTICLE I

SECTION 1. All legislative Powers herein granted shall be vested
in a Congress of the United States, which shall consist of a Senate
and House of Representatives.

SECTION 2. The House of Representatives shall be composed of
Members chosen every second Year by the People of the several
States, and the Electors in each State shall have the Qualifications
requisite for Electors of the most numerous Branch of the State
Legislature.

No Person shall be a Representative who shall not have attained
to the Age of twenty five Years, and been seven Years a Citizen of
the United States, and who shall not, when elected, be an Inhabitant of that State in which he shall be chosen.

Representatives and direct Taxes shall be apportioned among
the several States which may be included within this Union, according to their respective Numbers, which shall be determined by
adding to the whole Number of free Persons, including those bound
to Service for a Term of Years, and excluding Indians not taxed,
three fifths of all other Persons. The actual Enumeration shall be
made within three Years after the first Meeting of the Congress of
the United States, and within every subsequent Term of ten Years,
in such Manner as they shall by Law direct. The Number of Representatives shall not exceed one for every thirty Thousand, but

each State shall have at Least one Representative; and until such enumeration shall be made, the State of New Hampshire shall be entitled to chuse three, Massachusetts eight, Rhode-Island and Providence Plantations one, Connecticut five, New-York six, New Jersey four, Pennsylvania eight, Delaware one, Maryland six, Virginia ten, North Carolina five, South Carolina five, and Georgia three.

When vacancies happen in the Representation from any State, the Executive Authority thereof shall issue Writs of Election to fill such Vacancies.

The House of Representatives shall chuse their Speaker and other Officers; and shall have the sole Power of Impeachment.

SECTION 3. The Senate of the United States shall be composed of two Senators from each State, chosen by the Legislature thereof, for six Years; and each Senator shall have one Vote.

Immediately after they shall be assembled in Consequence of the first Election, they shall be divided as equally as may be into three Classes. The Seats of the Senators of the first Class shall be vacated at the Expiration of the Second Year, of the second Class at the Expiration of the fourth Year, and of the third Class at the Expiration of the sixth Year; so that one-third may be chosen every second Year; and if Vacancies happen by Resignation, or otherwise, during the Recess of the Legislature of any State, the Executive thereof may make temporary Appointments until the next Meeting of the Legislature, which shall then fill such Vacancies.

No Person shall be a Senator who shall not have attained to the Age of thirty Years, and been nine Years a Citizen of the United States, and who shall not, when elected, be an Inhabitant of that State for which he shall be chosen.

The Vice President of the United States shall be President of the Senate, but shall have no Vote, unless they be equally divided.

The Senate shall chuse their other Officers, and also a President pro tempore, in the absence of the Vice President, or when he shall exercise the Office of President of the United States.

The Senate shall have the sole Power to try all Impeachments. When sitting for that Purpose, they shall be on Oath or Affirmation. When the President of the United States is tried, the Chief Justice shall preside: And no Person shall be convicted without the Concurrence of two-thirds of the Members present.

Judgment in Cases of Impeachment shall not extend further than to removal from Office, and disqualification to hold and enjoy any Office of honor, Trust, or Profit under the United States: but the Party convicted shall nevertheless be liable and subject to Indictment, Trial, Judgment, and Punishment, according to Law.

SECTION 4. The Time, Places and Manner of holding Elections for Senators and Representatives, shall be prescribed in each State by the Legislature thereof; but the Congress may at any time by Law make or alter such Regulations, except as to the Places of chusing Senators.

The Congress shall assemble at least once in every Year, and such Meeting shall be on the first Monday in December, unless they shall by Law appoint a different Day.

SECTION 5. Each House shall be the Judge of the Elections, Returns, and Qualifications of its own Members, and a Majority of each shall constitute a Quorum to do Business; but a smaller Number may adjourn from day to day, and may be authorized to compel the Attendance of absent Members, in such Manner, and under such Penalties as each House may provide.

Each House may determine the Rules of its Proceedings, punish its Members for disorderly Behavior, and, with the Concurrence of two thirds, expel a Member.

Each House shall keep a Journal of its Proceedings, and from time to time publish the same, excepting such Parts as may in their Judgment require Secrecy; and the Yeas and Nays of the Members of either House on any question shall, at the Desire of one fifth of those Present be entered on the Journal.

Neither House, during the Session of Congress, shall, without the Consent of the other, adjourn for more than three days, nor to any other Place than that in which the two Houses shall be sitting.

SECTION 6. The Senators and Representatives shall receive a Compensation for their Services, to be ascertained by Law, and paid out of the Treasury of the United States. They shall in all Cases, except Treason, Felony and Breach of the Peace, be privileged from Arrest during their Attendance at the Session of their respective Houses, and in going to and returning from the same; and for any Speech or Debate in either House, they shall not be questioned in any other Place.

No Senator or Representative shall, during the Time for which he was elected, be appointed to any civil Office under the Authority of the United States, which shall have been created, or the Emoluments whereof shall have been encreased during such time; and no Person holding any Office under the United States, shall be a Member of either House during his Continuance in Office.

SECTION 7. All Bills for raising Revenue shall originate in the House of Representatives; but the Senate may propose or concur with Amendments as on other Bills.

Every Bill which shall have passed the House of Representatives and the Senate, shall, before it become a Law, be presented to the President of the United States; if he approve he shall sign it, but if not he shall return it, with his Objections to that House in which it shall have originated, who shall enter the Objections at large on their Journal, and proceed to reconsider it. If after such Reconsideration two thirds of that House shall agree to pass the Bill, it shall be sent, together with the Objections, to the other House, by which it shall likewise be reconsidered, and if approved by two thirds of that House, it shall become a Law. But in all such Cases the Votes of both Houses shall be determined by yeas and Nays, and the Names of the Persons voting for and against the Bill shall be entered on the Journal of each House respectively. If any Bill shall not be returned by the President within ten Days (Sundays excepted) after it shall have been presented to him, the Same shall be a Law, in like Manner as if he had signed it, unless the Congress by their Adjournment prevent its Return, in which Case it shall not be a Law.

Every Order, Resolution, or Vote to which the Concurrence of the Senate and House of Representatives may be necessary (except on a question of Adjournment) shall be presented to the President of the United States; and before the Same shall take Effect, shall be approved by him, or being disapproved by him, shall be repassed by two thirds of the Senate and House of Representatives, according to the Rules and Limitations prescribed in the Case of a Bill.

SECTION 8. The Congress shall have Power To lay and collect Taxes, Duties, Imposts and Excises, to pay the Debts and provide for the common Defense and general Welfare of the United States; but all Duties, Imposts and Excises shall be uniform throughout the United States;

To borrow money on the credit of the United States;

To regulate Commerce with foreign Nations, and among the several States, and with the Indian Tribes;

To establish an uniform Rule of Naturalization, and uniform Laws on the subject of Bankruptcies throughout the United States;

To coin Money, regulate the Value thereof, and of foreign Coin, and fix the Standard of Weights and Measures;

To provide for the Punishment of counterfeiting the Securities and current Coin of the United States;

To establish Post Offices and post Roads;

To promote the Progress of Science and useful Arts, by securing for limited Times to Authors and Inventors the exclusive Right to their respective Writings and Discoveries;

To constitute Tribunals inferior to the supreme Court;

To define and punish Piracies and Felonies committed on the high Seas, and Offenses against the Law of Nations;

To declare War, grant Letters of Marque and Reprisal and make Rules concerning Captures on Land and Water;

To raise and support Armies, but no Appropriation of Money to that Use shall be for a longer Term than two Years;

To provide and maintain a Navy;

To make Rules for the Government and Regulation of the land and naval Forces;

To provide for calling forth the Militia to execute the Laws of the Union, suppress Insurrections and repel Invasions;

To provide for organizing, arming, and disciplining the Militia, and for governing such Part of them as may be employed in the Service of the United States, reserving to the States respectively, the Appointment of the Officers, and the Authority of training the Militia according to the discipline prescribed by Congress;

To exercise exclusive Legislation in all Cases whatsoever, over such District (not exceeding ten Miles square) as may, by Cession of particular States, and the acceptance of Congress, become the Seat of the Government of the United States, and to exercise like Authority over all Places purchased by the Consent of the Legislature of the State in which the Same shall be, for the Erection of Forts, Magazines, Arsenals, dock-Yards, and other needful Buildings;—And

To make all Laws which shall be necessary and proper for carrying into Execution the foregoing Powers, and all other Powers vested by this Constitution in the Government of the United States, or in any Department or Officer thereof.

SECTION 9. The Migration or Importation of Such Persons as any of the States now existing shall think proper to admit, shall not be prohibited by the Congress prior to the Year one thousand eight hundred and eight, but a tax or duty may be imposed on such Importation, not exceeding ten dollars for each Person.

The privilege of the Writ of Habeas Corpus shall not be suspended, unless when in Cases of Rebellion or Invasion the public Safety may require it.

No Bill of Attainder or ex post facto Law shall be passed.

No capitation, or other direct, Tax shall be laid, unless in Proportion to the Census or Enumeration herein before directed to be taken.

No Tax or Duty shall be laid on Articles exported from any State.

No preference shall be given by any Regulation of Commerce or Revenue to the Ports of one State over those of another: nor shall Vessels bound to, or from, one State be obliged to enter, clear, or pay Duties in another.

No money shall be drawn from the Treasury, but in Consequence of Appropriations made by Law; and a regular Statement and Account of the Receipts and Expenditures of all public Money shall be published from time to time.

No Title of Nobility shall be granted by the United States: And no Person holding any Office of Profit or Trust under them, shall, without the Consent of the Congress, accept of any present, Emolument, Office, or Title, of any kind whatever, from any King, Prince, or foreign State.

Section 10. No State shall enter into any Treaty, Alliance, or Confederation; grant Letters of Marque and Reprisal; coin Money; emit Bills of Credit; make any Thing but gold and silver Coin a Tender in Payment of Debts; pass any Bill of Attainder, ex post facto Law, or Law impairing the Obligation of Contracts, or grant any Title of Nobility.

No State shall, without the Consent of the Congress, lay any Imposts or Duties on Imports or Exports, except what may be absolutely necessary for executing its inspection Laws: and the net Produce of all Duties and Imposts, laid by any State on Imports or Exports, shall be for the Use of the Treasury of the United States; and all such Laws shall be subject to the Revision and Control of the Congress.

No State shall, without the Consent of Congress, lay any duty of Tonnage, keep Troops, or Ships of War in time of Peace, enter into any Agreement or Compact with another State, or with a foreign Power, or engage in War, unless actually invaded, or in such imminent Danger as will not admit of delay.

ARTICLE II

Section 1. The executive Power shall be vested in a President of the United States of America. He shall hold his Office during the Term of four years, and, together with the Vice-President, chosen for the same Term, be elected, as follows:

Each State shall appoint, in such Manner as the Legislature thereof may direct, a Number of Electors, equal to the whole Number of Senators and Representatives to which the State may be entitled in the Congress: but no Senator or Representative, or Person holding an Office of Trust or Profit under the United States, shall be appointed an Elector.

The Electors shall meet in their respective States, and vote by Ballot for two persons, of whom one at least shall not be an Inhabitant of the same State with themselves. And they shall make a List of all the Persons voted for, and of the Number of Votes for each; which List they shall sign and certify, and transmit sealed to the Seat of the Government of the United States, directed to the President of the Senate. The President of the Senate shall, in the Presence of the Senate and House of Representatives, open all the Certificates, and the Votes shall then be counted. The Person having the greatest Number of Votes shall be the President, if such Number be a Majority of the whole Number of Electors appointed; and if there be more than one who have such Majority, and have an equal Number of Votes, then the House of Representatives shall immediately chuse by Ballot one of them for President; and if no Person have a Majority, then from the five highest on the List the said House shall in like Manner chuse the President. But in chusing the President, the Votes shall be taken by States, the Representation from each State having one Vote; A quorum for this Purpose shall consist of a Member or Members from two-thirds of the States, and a Majority of all the States shall be necessary to a Choice. In every Case, after the Choice of the President, the Person having the greatest Number of Votes of the Electors shall be the Vice-President. But if there should remain two or more who have equal Votes, the Senate shall chuse from them by Ballot the Vice-President.

The Congress may determine the Time of chusing the Electors, and the Day on which they shall give their Votes; which Day shall be the same throughout the United States.

No person except a natural born Citizen, or a Citizen of the United States, at the time of the Adoption of this Constitution, shall be eligible to the Office of President; neither shall any Person be eligible to that Office who shall not have attained to the Age of thirty-five Years, and been fourteen Years a Resident within the United States.

In case of the Removal of the President from Office, or of his Death, resignation, or Inability to discharge the Powers and Duties of the said Office, the same shall devolve on the Vice President, and the Congress may by Law provide for the Case of Removal, Death, Resignation or Inability, both of the President and Vice President, declaring what Officer shall then act as President, and such Officer shall act accordingly, until the Disability be removed, or a President shall be elected.

The President shall, at stated Times, receive for his Services, a Compensation, which shall neither be encreased nor diminished during the Period for which he shall have been elected, and he shall not receive within that Period any other Emolument from the United States, or any of them.

Before he enter on the Execution of his Office, he shall take the following Oath or Affirmation:—"I do solemnly swear (or affirm) that I will faithfully execute the Office of President of the United States, and will to the best of my Ability, preserve, protect and defend the Constitution of the United States."

SECTION 2. The President shall be Commander in Chief of the Army and Navy of the United States, and of the Militia of the several States, when called into the actual Service of the United States; he may require the Opinion, in writing, of the principal Officer in each of the executive Departments, upon any subject relating to the Duties of their respective Offices, and he shall have Power to grant Reprieves and Pardons for Offenses against the United States, except in Cases of Impeachment.

He shall have Power, by and with the Advice and Consent of the Senate, to make Treaties, provided two-thirds of the Senators present concur; and he shall nominate, and by and with the Advice and Consent of the Senate, shall appoint Ambassadors, other public Ministers and Consuls, Judges of the supreme Court, and all other Officers of the United States, whose Appointments are not herein otherwise provided for, and which shall be established by law; but the Congress may by Law vest the Appointment of such inferior Officers, as they think proper, in the President alone, in the Courts of Law, or in the Heads of Departments.

The President shall have Power to fill up all Vacancies that may happen during the Recess of the Senate, by granting Commissions which shall expire at the End of their next Session.

SECTION 3. He shall from time to time give to the Congress Information of the State of the Union, and recommend to their Consideration such Measures as he shall judge necessary and expedient; he may, on extraordinary Occasions, convene both Houses, or either of them, and in Case of Disagreement between them, with Respect to the Time of Adjournment, he may adjourn them to such Time as he shall think proper; he shall receive Ambassadors and other public Ministers; he shall take Care that the Laws be faithfully executed, and shall Commission all the Officers of the United States.

SECTION 4. The President, Vice President and all civil Officers of the United States, shall be removed from Office on Impeachment for, and Conviction of, Treason, Bribery, or other high Crimes and Misdemeanors.

ARTICLE III

SECTION 1. The judicial Power of the United States, shall be vested in one supreme Court, and in such inferior Courts as the Congress may from time to time ordain and establish. The Judges, both of the supreme and inferior Courts, shall hold their offices during good Behaviour, and shall, at stated Times, receive for their Services a Compensation which shall not be diminished during their Continuance in Office.

SECTION 2. The judicial Power shall extend to all Cases, in Law and Equity, arising under this Constitution, the Laws of the United States, and Treaties made, or which shall be made, under their Authority;—to all Cases affecting Ambassadors, other public Ministers and Consuls;—to all Cases of admiralty and maritime Jurisdiction;—to Controversies to which the United States shall be a Party;—to Controversies between two or more States;—between a State and Citizens of another State;—between Citizens of different States;—between Citizens of the same State claiming Lands under Grants of different States, and between a State, or the Citizens thereof, and foreign States, Citizens or Subjects.

In all Cases affecting Ambassadors, other public Ministers and Consuls, and those in which a State shall be Party, the supreme Court shall have original Jurisdiction. In all the other Cases before mentioned, the supreme Court shall have appellate Jurisdiction, both as to Law and Fact, with such Exceptions, and under such Regulations as the Congress shall make.

The trial of all Crimes, except in Cases of Impeachment, shall be by Jury; and such Trial shall be held in the State where the said Crimes shall have been committed; but when not committed within any State, the Trial shall be at such Place or Places as the Congress may by Law have directed.

SECTION 3. Treason against the United States, shall consist only in levying War against them, or in adhering to their Enemies, giving them Aid and Comfort. No Person shall be convicted of Treason unless on the Testimony of two Witnesses to the same overt Act, or on Confession in open Court.

The Congress shall have power to declare the Punishment of Treason, but no Attainder of Treason shall work Corruption of Blood, or Forfeiture except during the Life of the Person attainted.

ARTICLE IV

SECTION 1. Full Faith and Credit shall be given in each State to the public Acts, Records, and judicial Proceedings of every other State. And the Congress may by general Laws prescribe the Manner in which such Acts, Records and Proceedings shall be proved, and the Effect thereof.

SECTION 2. The Citizens of each State shall be entitled to all Privileges and Immunities of Citizens in the several States.

A Person charged in any State with Treason, Felony, or other Crime, who shall flee from Justice, and be found in another State, shall on demand of the executive Authority of the State from which he fled, be delivered up, to be removed to the State having Jurisdiction of the Crime.

No Person held to Service or Labour in one State, under the Laws thereof, escaping into another, shall, in Consequence of any Law or Regulation therein, be discharged from such Service or Labour, but shall be delivered up on Claim of the Party to whom such Service or Labour may be due.

SECTION 3. New States may be admitted by the Congress into this Union; but no new State shall be formed or erected within the Jurisdiction of any other State; nor any State be formed by the Junction of two or more States, or parts of States, without the Consent of the Legislatures of the States concerned as well as of the Congress.

The Congress shall have Power to dispose of and make all needful Rules and Regulations respecting the Territory of other

Property belonging to the United States; and nothing in this Constitution shall be so construed as to Prejudice any Claims of the United States, or of any particular State.

SECTION 4. The United States shall guarantee to every State in this Union a Republican Form of Government, and shall protect each of them against Invasion; and on Application of the Legislature, or of the Executive (when the Legislature cannot be convened) against domestic Violence.

ARTICLE V

The Congress, whenever two-thirds of both Houses shall deem it necessary, shall propose Amendments to this Constitution, or, on the Application of the Legislatures of two-thirds of the several States, shall call a Convention for proposing Amendments, which, in either Case, shall be valid to all Intents and Purposes, as part of this Constitution, when ratified by the Legislatures of three-fourths of the several States, or by Conventions in three-fourths thereof, as the one or the other Mode of Ratification may be proposed by the Congress; Provided that no Amendment which may be made prior to the Year One thousand eight hundred and eight shall in any Manner affect the first and fourth Clauses in the Ninth Section of the first Article, and that no State without its Consent, shall be deprived of its equal Suffrage in the Senate.

ARTICLE VI

All Debts contracted and Engagements entered into, before the Adoption of this Constitution shall be as valid against the United States under this Constitution, as under the Confederation.

This Constitution, and the Laws of the United States which shall be made in Pursuance thereof, and all Treaties made, or which shall be made, under Authority of the United States, shall be the supreme Law of the Land, and the Judges in every State shall be bound thereby, any Thing in the Constitution or Laws of any State to the Contrary notwithstanding.

The Senators and Representatives before mentioned, and the Members of the several State Legislatures, and all executive and judicial Officers, both of the United States and of the several States, shall be bound by Oath or Affirmation, to support this constitution; but no religious Test shall ever be required as a Qualification to any Office or public Trust under the United States.

ARTICLE VII

The Ratification of the Conventions of nine States shall be sufficient for the Establishment of this Constitution between the States so ratifying the Same. Done in Convention by the Unanimous Consent of the States present the Seventeenth Day of September in the Year of our Lord one thousand seven hundred and Eighty seven and of the Independence of the United States of America the Twelfth. In witness whereof We have here unto subscribed our Names,

Go WASHINGTON—
Presidt. and deputy from Virginia.

New Hampshire
JOHN LANGDON,   NICHOLAS GILMAN.

Massachusetts
NATHANIEL GORHAM,   RUFUS KING.

Connecticut
WM. SAML. JOHNSON,   ROGER SHERMAN.

New York
ALEXANDER HAMILTON.

New Jersey
WIL: LIVINGSTON,   WM. PATERSON,
DAVID BREARLEY,   JONA. DAYTON.

Pennsylvania
B. FRANKLIN,   THOMAS MIFFLIN,
ROBT. MORRIS,   GEO: CLYMER,
THO: FITZSIMONS,   JARED INGERSOLL,
JAMES WILSON,   GOUV: MORRIS.

Delaware
GEO: READ,   GUNNING BEDFORD, JUN'R,
JOHN DICKINSON,   RICHARD BASSETT.
JACO: BROOM,

Maryland
JAMES M'HENRY,   DAN: OF ST. THOS. JENIFER.
DANL CARROLL,

Virginia
JOHN BLAIR,   JAMES MADISON, JR.
NORTH CAROLINA
WM. BLOUNT,   RICH'D DOBBS SPAIGHT.
HU. WILLIAMSON,

South Carolina
J. RUTLEDGE,   CHARLES COTESWORTH PINCKNEY,
CHARLES PINCKNEY,   PIERCE BUTLER.

Georgia
WILLIAM FEW,   WILLIAM JACKSON, SECRETARY.

    ATTEST:
ABR. BALDWIN.

ARTICLES IN ADDITION TO, AND AMENDMENT OF, THE CONSTITU-
TION OF THE UNITED STATES OF AMERICA, PROPOSED BY CON-
GRESS, AND RATIFIED BY THE LEGISLATURES OF THE SEVERAL
STATES, PURSUANT TO THE FIFTH ARTICLE OF THE ORIGINAL CON-
STITUTION

AMENDMENT I

Congress shall make no law respecting an establishment of religion, or prohibiting the free exercise thereof; or abridging the freedom of speech, or of the press; or the right of the people peaceably
to assemble, and to petition the Government for a redress of grievances.

AMENDMENT II

A well regulated Militia, being necessary to the security of a free
State, the right of the people to keep and bear Arms, shall not be
infringed.

AMENDMENT III

No Soldier shall, in time of peace be quartered in any house, without the consent of the Owner, nor in time of war, but in a manner to be prescribed by law.

AMENDMENT IV

The right of the people to be secure in their persons, houses, papers, and effects, against unreasonable searches and seizures, shall not be violated, and no Warrants shall issue, but upon probable cause, supported by Oath or affirmation, and particularly describing the place to be searched, and the persons or things to be seized.

AMENDMENT V

No person shall be held to answer for a capital, or other wise infamous crime, unless on a presentment or indictment of a Grand Jury, except in cases arising in the land or naval forces, or in the Militia, when in actual service in time of War or public danger; nor shall any person be subject for the same offenses to be twice put in jeopardy of life or limb; nor shall be compelled in any criminal case to be a witness against himself, nor be deprived of life, liberty, or property, without due process of law; nor shall private property be taken for public use, without just compensation.

AMENDMENT VI

In all criminal prosecutions, the accused shall enjoy the right to a speedy and public trial, by an impartial jury of the State and district wherein the crime shall have been committed, which district shall have been previously ascertained by law, and to be informed of the nature and cause of the accusation; to be confronted with the witnesses against him; to have compulsory process for obtaining witnesses in his favor, and to have the Assistance of Counsel for his defence.

AMENDMENT VII

In suits at common law, where the value in controversy shall exceed twenty dollars, the right of trial by jury shall be preserved, and no fact tried by a jury, shall be otherwise reexamined in any

Court of the United States, than according to the rules of the common law.

AMENDMENT VIII

Excessive bail shall not be required, nor excessive fines imposed, nor cruel and unusual punishments inflicted.

AMENDMENT IX

The enumeration in the Constitution, of certain rights, shall not be construed to deny or disparage others retained by the people.

AMENDMENT X

The powers not delegated to the United States by the Constitution, nor prohibited by it to the States, are reserved to the States respectively, or to the people.

AMENDMENT XI

The Judicial power of the United States shall not be construed to extend to any suit in law or equity, commenced or prosecuted against one of the United States by Citizens of another State, or by Citizens or Subjects of any Foreign State.

AMENDMENT XII

The electors shall meet in their respective states, and vote by ballot for President and Vice-President, one of whom, at least, shall not be an inhabitant of the same state with themselves; they shall name in their ballots the person voted for, as President, and in distinct ballots the person voted for as Vice-President, and they shall make distinct lists of all persons voted for as President, and of all persons voted for as Vice-President, and of the number of votes for each, which lists they shall sign and certify, and transmit sealed to the seat of the government of the United States, directed to the President of the Senate;—The President of the Senate shall, in the presence of the Senate and House of Representatives, open all the certificates and the votes shall then be counted;—The person having the greatest number of votes for President, shall be the President, if such number be a majority of the whole number of

Electors appointed; and if no person have such majority, then from the persons having the highest numbers not exceeding three on the list of those voted for as President, the House of Representatives shall choose immediately, by ballot, the President. But in choosing the President, the votes shall be taken by states the representation from each state having one vote; a quorum for this purpose shall consist of a member or members from two-thirds of the states, and a majority of all the states shall be necessary to a choice.5 And if the House of Representatives shall not choose a President whenever the right of choice shall devolve upon them, before the fourth day of March next following, then the Vice-President shall act as President, as in the case of the death or other constitutional disability of the President.—The person having the greatest number of votes as Vice-President, shall be the Vice-President, if such number be a majority of the whole number of Electors appointed, and if no person have a majority, then from the two highest numbers on the list, the Senate shall choose the Vice-President; a quorum for the purpose shall consist of two-thirds of the whole number of Senators, and a majority of the whole number shall be necessary to a choice. But no person constitutionally ineligible to the office of President shall be eligible to that of Vice-President of the United States.

AMENDMENT XIII

SECTION 1. Neither slavery nor involuntary servitude, except as a punishment for crime whereof the party shall have been duly convicted, shall exist within the United States, or any place subject to their jurisdiction.

SECTION 2. Congress shall have power to enforce this article by appropriate legislation.

AMENDMENT XIV

SECTION 1. All persons born or naturalized in the United States, and subject to the jurisdiction thereof, are citizens of the United States and of the State wherein they reside. No State shall make or enforce any law which shall abridge the privileges or immunities of citizens of the United States; nor shall any State deprive any person of life, liberty, or property without due process of law, nor deny to any person within its jurisdiction the equal protection of the laws.

SECTION 2. Representatives shall be apportioned among the several States according to their respective numbers, counting the whole number of persons in each State, excluding Indians not taxed. But when the right to vote at any election for the choice of electors for President and Vice-President of the United States, Representatives in Congress, the Executive and Judicial officers of a State, or the members of the Legislature thereof, is denied to any of the male inhabitants of such State, being twenty-one years of age, and citizens of the United States, or in any way abridged, except for participation in rebellion, or other crime, the basis of representation therein shall be reduced in the proportion which the number of such male citizens shall bear to the whole number of male citizens twenty-one years of age in such State.

SECTION 3. No person shall be a Senator or Representative in Congress, or elector of President and Vice-President, or hold any office, civil or military, under the United States, or under any State, who, having previously taken an oath, as a member of Congress, or as an officer of the United States, or as a member of any State legislature, or as an executive or judicial officer of any State, to support the Constitution of the United States, shall have engaged in insurrection or rebellion against the same, or given aid or comfort to the enemies thereof. But Congress may by a vote of two-thirds of each House, remove such disability.

SECTION 4. The validity of the public debt of the United States, authorized by law, including debts incurred for payment of pensions and bounties for services in suppressing insurrection or rebellion, shall not be questioned. But neither the United States nor any State shall assume or pay any debt or obligation incurred in aid of insurrection or rebellion against the United States, or any claim for the loss or emancipation of any slave; but all such debts, obligations and claims shall be held illegal and void.

SECTION 5. The Congress shall have power to enforce, by appropriate legislation, the provisions of this article.

AMENDMENT XV

SECTION 1. The right of citizens of the United States to vote shall not be denied or abridged by the United States or by any State on account of race, color, or previous condition of servitude.

SECTION 2. The Congress shall have power to enforce this article by appropriate legislation.

AMENDMENT XVI

The Congress shall have power to lay and collect taxes on incomes, from whatever source derived, without apportionment among the several States, and without regard to any census or enumeration.

AMENDMENT XVII

The Senate of the United States shall be composed of two Senators from each State, elected by the people thereof, for six years; and each Senator shall have one vote. The electors in each State shall have the qualifications requisite for electors of the most numerous branch of the State legislatures.

When vacancies happen in the representation of any State in the Senate, the executive authority of such State shall issue writs of election to fill such vacancies: Provided, That the legislature of any State may empower the executive thereof to make temporary appointments until the people fill the vacancies by election as the legislature may direct.

This amendment shall not be so construed as to affect the election or term of any Senator chosen before it becomes valid as part of the Constitution.

AMENDMENT XVIII

SECTION 1. After one year from the ratification of this article the manufacture, sale, or transportation of intoxicating liquors within, the importation thereof into, or the exportation thereof from the United States and all territory subject to the jurisdiction thereof for beverage purposes is hereby prohibited.

SECTION 2. The Congress and the several States shall have concurrent power to enforce this article by appropriate legislation.

SECTION 3. This article shall be inoperative unless it shall have been ratified as an amendment to the Constitution by the legislatures of the several States, as provided in the Constitution, within seven years from the date of the submission hereof to the States by the Congress.

AMENDMENT XIX

The right of citizens of the United States to vote shall not be denied or abridged by the United States or by any State on account of sex.

Congress shall have power to enforce this article by appropriate legislation.

AMENDMENT XX

SECTION 1. The terms of the President and Vice-President shall end at noon on the 20th day of January, and the terms of Senators and Representatives at noon on the 3d day of January, of the years in which such terms would have ended if this article had not been ratified; and the terms of their successors shall then begin.

SECTION 2. The Congress shall assemble at least once in every year, and such meeting shall begin at noon on the 3d day of January, unless they shall by law appoint a different day.

SECTION 3. If, at the time fixed for the beginning of the term of the President, the President elect shall have died, the Vice-President elect shall become President. If a President shall not have been chosen before the time fixed for the beginning of his term, or if the President elect shall have failed to qualify, then the Vice-President elect shall act as President until a President shall have qualified; and the Congress may by law provide for the case wherein neither a President elect nor a Vice-President elect shall have qualified, declaring who shall then act as President, or the manner in which one who is to act shall be selected, and such person shall act accordingly until a President or Vice-President shall have qualified.

SECTION 4. The Congress may by law provide for the case of the death of any of the persons from whom the House of Representatives may choose a President whenever the right of choice shall have devolved upon them, and for the case of the death of any of the persons from whom the Senate may choose a Vice-President whenever the right of choice shall have devolved upon them.

SECTION 5. Sections 1 and 2 shall take effect on the 15th day of October following the ratification of this article.

SECTION 6. This article shall be inoperative unless it shall have been ratified as an amendment to the Constitution by the legislatures of three-fourths of the several States within seven years from the date of its submission.

AMENDMENT XXI

SECTION 1. The eighteenth article of amendment to the Constitution of the United States is hereby repealed.

SECTION 2. The transportation or importation into any State, Territory, or possession of the United States for delivery or use therein of intoxicating liquors, in violation of the laws thereof, is hereby prohibited.

SECTION 3. This article shall be inoperative unless it shall have been ratified as an amendment to the Constitution by conventions in the several States, as provided in the Constitution, within seven years from the date of the submission hereof to the States by the Congress.

AMENDMENT XXII

SECTION 1. No person shall be elected to the office of the President more than twice, and no person who has held the office of President, or acted as President, for more than two years of a term to which some other person was elected President shall be elected to the office of the President more than once. But this Article shall not apply to any person holding the office of President when this Article was proposed by the Congress, and shall not prevent any person who may be holding the office of President, or acting as President, during the term within which this Article becomes operative, from holding the office of President or acting as President during the remainder of such term.

SECTION 2. This article shall be inoperative unless it shall have been ratified as an amendment to the Constitution by the legisla-

tures of three-fourths of the several States within seven years from
the date of its submission to the States by the Congress.

AMENDMENT XXIII

SECTION 1. The District constituting the seat of Government of
the United States shall appoint in such manner as the Congress
may direct:

A number of electors of President and Vice President equal to
the whole number of Senators and Representatives in Congress to
which the District would be entitled if it were a State, but in no
event more than the least populous State; they shall be in addition
to those appointed by the States, but they shall be considered, for
the purposes of the election of President and Vice President, to be
electors appointed by a State; and they shall meet in the District
and perform such duties as provided by the twelfth article of
amendment.

SECTION 2. The Congress shall have power to enforce this article by appropriate legislation.

AMENDMENT XXIV

SECTION 1. The right of citizens of the United States to vote in
any primary or other election for President or Vice President, for
electors for President or Vice President, or for Senator or Representative in Congress, shall not be denied or abridged by the
United States or any State by reason of failure to pay any poll tax
or other tax.

SECTION 2. The Congress shall have power to enforce this article by appropriate legislation.

AMENDMENT XXV

SECTION 1. In case of the removal of the President from office or
of his death or resignation, the Vice President shall become
President.

SECTION 2. Whenever there is a vacancy in the office of the Vice
President, the President shall nominate a Vice President who shall
take office upon confirmation by a majority vote of both Houses of
Congress.

SECTION 3. Whenever the President transmits to the President pro tempore of the Senate and the Speaker of the House of Representatives his written declaration that he is unable to discharge the powers and duties of his office, and until he transmits to them a written declaration to the contrary, such powers and duties shall be discharged by the Vice President as Acting President.

SECTION 4. Whenever the Vice President and a majority of either the principal officers of the executive departments or of such other body as Congress may by law provide, transmit to the President pro tempore of the Senate and the Speaker of the House of Representatives their written declaration that the President is unable to discharge the powers and duties of his office, the Vice President shall immediately assume the powers and duties of the office as Acting President.

Thereafter, when the President transmits to the President pro tempore of the Senate and the Speaker of the House of Representatives his written declaration that no inability exists, he shall resume the powers and duties of his office unless the Vice President and a majority of either the principal officers of the executive department or of such other body as Congress may by law provide, transmit within four days to the President pro tempore of the Senate and the Speaker of the House of Representatives their written declaration that the President is unable to discharge the powers and duties of his office. Thereupon Congress shall decide the issue, assembling within forty-eight hours for that purpose if not in session. If the Congress, within twenty-one days after receipt of the latter written declaration, or, if Congress is not in session, within twenty-one days after Congress is required to assemble, determines by two-thirds vote of both Houses that the President is unable to discharge the powers and duties of his office, the Vice President shall continue to discharge the same as Acting President; otherwise, the President shall resume the powers and duties of his office.

AMENDMENT XXVI

SECTION 1. The right of citizens of the United States, who are eighteen years of age or older, to vote shall not be denied or abridged by the United States or by any State on account of age.

Section 2. The Congress shall have power to enforce this article by appropriate legislation.

AMENDMENT XXVII

No law, varying the compensation for the services of the Senators and Representatives, shall take effect, until an election of Representatives shall have intervened.

Note on the Editors

Bruce Frohnen holds a Ph.D. in government from Cornell University and a J.D. from Emory University's School of Law. A frequent contributor to academic journals, magazines, and newspapers, Frohnen is the author of *Virtue and the Promise of Conservatism: The Legacy of Burke and Tocqueville* and *The New Communitarians and the Crisis of Modern Liberalism.* He is also the editor, with George Carey, of *Community and Tradition: Conservative Perspectives on American Experience.*

Conservative Leadership Series editor Christopher B. Briggs is Senior Book Editor at the Intercollegiate Studies Institute and is also assistant editor of *Humanitas,* a journal of the humanities published in Washington, D.C. Briggs holds degrees from Bowdoin College and The Catholic University of America.